# ARCADIAN AMERICA

NEW DIRECTIONS IN NARRATIVE HISTORY

John Demos and Aaron Sachs, Series Editors

The New Directions in Narrative History series includes original works of creative nonfiction across the many fields of history and related disciplines. Based on new research, the books in this series offer significant scholarly contributions while also embracing stylistic innovation as well as the classic techniques of storytelling. The works of the New Directions in Narrative History series, intended for the broadest general readership, speak to deeply human concerns about the past, present, and future of our world and its people.

# ARCADIAN AMERICA

*The Death and Life of an Environmental Tradition*

Aaron Sachs

Yale

UNIVERSITY
PRESS

*New Haven & London*

Yale University Press books may be purchased in quantity for educational, business,
or promotional use. For information, please e-mail sales.press@yale.edu (U.S. office)
or sales@yaleup.co.uk (U.K. office).

Set in Electra and Trajan types by Westchester Book Group.
Printed in the United States of America.

Library of Congress Cataloging-in-Publication Data

Sachs, Aaron (Aaron Jacob)
Arcadian America : the death and life of an environmental tradition / Aaron Sachs.
p. cm. — (New directions in narrative history)
Includes bibliographical references and index.
ISBN: 978-0-300-17640-7 (hardback)
1. Cemeteries—United States—History—19th century.   2. Cemeteries—Social aspects—
United States.   3. Cemeteries—Environmental aspects—United States. 4. Arcadia in
literature.   5. Arcadia in art.   6. Environmentalism—Social aspects—United States.
7. Environmental responsibility—United States.   I. Title.
GT3203.S34 2013
393'.10973—dc23
2012035284

A catalogue record for this book is available from the British Library.

This paper meets the requirements of ANSI/NISO Z39.48–1992 (Permanence of Paper).

10 9 8 7 6 5 4 3 2 1

*For Christine*

When the leaves fall, the whole earth is a cemetery pleasant to walk in.

—Henry David Thoreau

# CONTENTS

# ILLUSTRATIONS

———————◆———————

# WATERFALLS AND CEMETERIES

Earth, that nourished thee, shall claim
Thy growth, to be resolved to earth again,
And, lost each human trace, surrendering up
Thy individual being, shalt thou go
To mix forever with the elements,
To be a brother to the insensible rock
And to the sluggish clod, which the rude swain
Turns with his share, and treads upon. The oak
Shall send his roots abroad, and pierce thy mould.
—William Cullen Bryant, "Thanatopsis," 1817

I have one of the best commutes in the world: I walk to work through a gorge. Around each twist of the trail is another waterfall. On hot days, the gorge feels about ten degrees cooler than the rest of town. In winter, the blooms of shape-shifting snow and ice provocatively defy the distinction between solid and liquid. When we Ithacans are lucky enough to see the sun, it slants through the trees and makes the crystals, or the currents, or the spray, come alive.

Ithaca is justifiably notorious for its progressive politics and hippie culture, but its waterfalls are also town-defining features. You might have seen the famous Kelly-green T-shirts: "Ithaca Is Gorges." (Variations have included "Ithaca Is Cold" and, during the 2004 presidential campaign, "Ithaca Is Not George's.") Since the 1830s, tourists and potential residents have sought out this area specifically for its arresting natural scenery.[1]

Waterfalls and gorges, for many landscape aficionados, embody American sublimity. Their thrusting rock and surging water appear again and again in our art and literature, from nineteenth-century paintings of Niagara, to Ansel Adams's mountain photographs, to John Muir's jaunts in misty Sierra valleys, to James Dickey's nightmare river novel, *Deliverance*. We are drawn to waterfalls and gorges and yet also a bit afraid of them, which means that their spiritual power rarely comes to seem stale or sugary. Few would claim not to be impressed by the waterfalls of Ithaca's Cascadilla Gorge. It is not uncommon, during one of our not-uncommon rainy periods, to witness vast tree trunks being hurled past boulders. And it's striking that all this sublimity is in fact integrated into the town: walking over to a viewing point in the midst of a thunderstorm takes no great effort. The gorge has a path carved along its edge and several bridges spanning its cascades; tales of the gorge are woven into town lore and Cornell tours. Its creek bed is often marked by the sculptural efforts of a mysterious local artist, who gathers slabs of shale at off hours and arranges them into mini-megaliths, evoking a Stonehenge-like resonance with natural forces and patterns.[2] Yet for most Ithacans and most Cornellians, it somehow remains a place apart. Such landscapes remind us of nature's awe-inspiring forcefulness—and also its indifference. Many locals associate Ithaca's sublime scenery, most immediately, with stories of suicide.[3] In the end, waterfalls and gorges tend to be humbling.

Humility can be a useful feeling, especially in the context of the environmental movement. Many environmentalists, myself included, have consistently invoked humility as an ideal attitude to take toward nature, one that should encourage us to make certain concessions to its unpredictability and sheer destructive power. We need to plan for nature's capacity to overwhelm us. Yet this kind of humility leaves many feeling overly vulnerable, even helpless. And it often adds to a sense of separation from nature.

American environmentalism has traditionally reinforced that separateness by emphasizing the preservation of particular, awe-inspiring landscapes—like waterfalls and gorges.[4] For a certain segment of the population—many of those who come to environmentalism "naturally"—the experience of such places, with their relative profusion of animal and plant life, can in fact lead to a sense of full communion with the natural world. Many people are willing to go out of their way to save these places specifically because sublime nature provides so much inspiration that even one weekend of exposure to it can make the rest of the week, or even month, significantly more bearable, even if that week or month is passed in a crowded, polluted, work-obsessed, paved-over environment.

As many before me have noted, though, this kind of approach to environmentalism implicitly endorses the status quo in the city and suburbs. It invites greenwashing. Any number of car companies would be happy to sell you an SUV that will take you into the wilderness in style, for a sublime weekend of gazing at birds and trees and waterfalls. On Monday, though, you're back in the rat race, and your warren has gotten more toxic while you were gone. Environmentalism as wilderness escapism might help save certain key ecosystems, and it might soothe your soul temporarily, but it has done little to halt our steady, corporate-driven onslaught against ourselves and the planet.[5]

So, over the last several years, sometimes in desperation, I've wondered if it might be worth reconnoitering some less sublime landscapes and some alternative versions of humility. Gorges are spectacular, but it is hard to feel immersed in them, hard to feel part and parcel of them, hard to feel that harming the gorge means harming yourself. Certainly, immersed in a waterscape like Cascadilla Gorge, you might find yourself thinking ecologically, wondering about where the water comes from, how it connects you to other ecosystems; you might come to ponder the paradox of water's life-giving force and its potential destructiveness. But you can never really get lost in a gorge. There's just one straight trajectory: you follow the water upstream or down. A gorge makes for a perfectly reasonable commute.

Other landscapes might actually throw you off the track to your office—but, interestingly, they are the kinds of landscapes that many environmentalists, and environmental historians, have until recently tended either to denigrate or ignore. I mean landscapes that are powerfully, indubitably, overtly, shaped by human artifice—and shaped specifically so as to inspire an experience of blending. I mean both real and imagined places that contain palpable reminders of how, like it or not, we are inextricably intertwined with our environment. I mean landscapes whose fundamental hybridity suggests permeable borders and impure categories.[6] I mean cemeteries, most importantly; but also city parks; and public gardens; and farmers' markets; and utopias—or, more appropriately, Arcadias—like Atlantis. I mean landscapes that conjure a humility more like gratitude and empathy than fear. I mean landscapes whose greatest potential could be to spur a constant, radical consideration of how we do business every day—of how we consume resources and spew pollutants, of how we get from the planet only what we put in, of how we owe our lives to the earth's cycles of death and regrowth.

———————

I've come to believe that we Americans have a long tradition of creating and celebrating such landscapes.[7] It is not nearly so well known as the one that venerates the majestic waterfalls at Niagara and Yosemite, but it deserves to be, for at times it was even more central in American culture than the wilderness mythos—and it may well be more relevant today. The nature lovers of the nineteenth century, in particular, embroiled in their society's desperate struggles over the transition from agrarianism to urban-industrial capitalism, bequeathed to us a cornucopia of productive environmental ideas, as well as actual environments.[8] They held harvest festivals, gave drunken toasts to fermented fruits, planted experimental gardens and garden-like cemeteries.[9] Their aesthetic tended less toward the grand, timeless sublimity of waterfalls than toward what they thought of as the picturesque—scenes that were distinctive enough to become imprinted on a viewer's mind but also calm enough that the senses would not be overwhelmed. Today, we are so conditioned to respond positively to sublimity that the very word "picturesque" seems sentimental, but in the nineteenth century it came to represent the complex flowering of American Romanticism, capturing nature's rough borders and irregularities, where earth, air, rock, and water came together; where humanity struggled to erect solid structures that inevitably became weathered, blending back into the environment; where hard physical reality balanced spiritual fantasy, and viewers were shocked into a sudden apprehension of the sunlight and shadows, the exhilaration and melancholy, that mark every life.[10]

Historians have tended to argue that environmental awareness in the United States simply increased over time, as people used up more natural resources and as access increased to the sublime wilderness of the west.[11] But I think the edginess of environmental thought may actually have faded—as the layered understanding of picturesqueness faded, and the cultural fortitude to confront mortality faded—over the course of the nineteenth century. The land—not just the Land—was ravaged by the Civil War. Blood had stained the soil, and America was left with too many one-armed farmers. As markets expanded and the Gilded Age came into full swing, as the North's pattern of industrialization became not just an economic but a spatial and cultural model, many middle-class Americans, understandably exhausted, began to abandon long traditions of growing their own food, making their own clothing, and shaping their local environments.[12] They also, not coincidentally, abandoned communitarian traditions of dealing with death in favor of new professional practices associated with private hospitals and funeral parlors.[13] American modernity came to be characterized by a desperate retreat indoors, toward consumerism and specialization.

By 1900, people pushing ecological agendas often framed them in purely negative terms: we are marching heedlessly into a desert, squandering our most precious resources. And the modern environmental movement has inherited that lack of a program, that puritanical rhetoric of hopeless lamentation. During the previous century, though, many nature-conscious Americans had actually outlined positive social visions meant to generate more fruitful relationships between people and their environments. Our forebears were obsessed with the possibilities of Arcadia—that ancient society of solid rural values, of pastoralists who wandered free over a broad country-side of mountain meadows and forest glens, yet who also, somehow, established the kinds of stable civic institutions that ennobled Aristotle's Athens.[14] Arcadia seemed within reach to Americans who paused in the quieter corners of particular land-scapes, on the back acres of farms, in parks and gardens, where the atmosphere was restful, where nature and culture seemed at peace with each other. Of course, it is quite likely that no true Arcadia has ever come into being; in any case, it would de-mand a huge amount of hard labor. So, predictably—but distressingly—scholars have tended to dismiss nineteenth-century Arcadians—like Thoreau, or the pioneering landscape architect Andrew Jackson Downing, or Populists like Ignatius Donnelly and Henry George and Hamlin Garland—as dreamers or elitists who were ultimately complicit in the mainstream embrace of Manifest Destiny.[15] I think of them as both men of their time and, in some respects, environmental prophets.

In the twenty-first century, the idea of Arcadia seems remote; it may not even be an appropriate model any longer. On the other hand, though, it could be precisely what's needed in the age of global warming. In any case, I'd like to linger with America's nineteenth-century Arcadians for a little while, get to know them in their home envi-ronments, try to understand why their visions became bleaker and narrower as the nineteenth century advanced—and why they ultimately became marginalized. To see what these writers and painters and city planners and travelers and gardeners and poli-ticians meant to their culture—and could mean to ours—is to explore the most pro-found kinds of interactions with nature. For true Arcadians, landscapes are matters of life and death. And in the twenty-first century, approaching our environmental per-ceptions and practices with precisely that kind of earnestness may be a prerequisite for our survival—though that does not preclude also rediscovering the radical sense of playfulness and pleasure with which so many Americans once immersed themselves in local landscapes.

There, back in the 1840s and 50s, is Thoreau, sounding the depths of Walden Pond, bounding through swamps, floating with the currents and eddies of New En-gland rivers, wandering among the blowing dunes of Cape Cod, haunting elemental borderlands in both his physical and his intellectual life, wondering whether estab-lishing a home meant sheltering oneself from nature's forces or exposing oneself to them. There, too, is Andrew Jackson Downing, insisting that streets be lined with trees, establishing new kinds of gardens and orchards, developing designs for afford-able houses in the rural gothic style that would dominate the "middle landscape" of the first American suburbs. "Plant spacious parks in your cities," Downing said, in

1848, "and unloose their gates as wide as the gates of morning to the whole people."[16] There is the nature poet William Cullen Bryant, constantly writing eulogies and elegies that managed to convey both acute grief and a stubborn persistence. There is Ignatius Donnelly in the 1870s, studying the ruins of Indian civilizations, pondering climatological history and new strands of mythical and mystical religion, writing one of the best-selling nonfiction books of the century, about the Arcadia of Atlantis and its destruction in a natural catastrophe. There is his contemporary Henry George, arguing that "progress" has benefited the few at the expense of the many, that American society will prove unsustainable unless its government forces a radical redistribution of land. There is Hamlin Garland a decade later, exploring what he called the "middle border" of the prairies, asking what it means to be a homesteader in a society that still celebrates agrarian ideals and yet has directed every possible economic incentive toward urbanization and the development of industrial capitalism. And there, back in the 1820s and 30s, is the loosely organized (and often inebriated) group of Boston horticulturists, who founded the world's first garden-style cemetery, Mount Auburn, taking burial out of grim church graveyards and incorporating human bodies into the cycles of nature, creating the winding, lush, picturesque strolling grounds, solemn yet uplifting, morbid yet undeniably lovely, that would become the precursors to landscapes like New York's Central Park. (Figure 1.)

Figure 1. W. H. Bartlett, *Cemetery of Mount Auburn*, 1839,
hand-colored engraving.

Through their shaping of landscapes, these Arcadians conscientiously wove both mortality and regeneration, nature's primal realities, into everyday life. Their sensibility was not that of the naïve extoller of rural society, which, after all, can be marked by grueling drudgery; nor did they embrace some nonexistent golden mean of perfect balance between the purely wild and the purely artificial. Rather, nineteenth-century Arcadians seemed to embody the layered meanings of the famous seventeenth-century painting by Nicolas Poussin, *Et in Arcadia Ego*, which depicts a group of shepherds coming upon a tomb and recognizing that death holds sway even in the seeming paradise of their utterly natural society. (Figure 2.)

Figure 2. Nicolas Poussin, *The Shepherds of Arcadia (Et in Arcadia Ego)*, 1640, oil on canvas. "Et in Arcadia Ego" is the inscription on the tomb; we're meant to imagine the embodiment of Death speaking those words: "I am present even in Arcadia."

Look closely at the innocent Arcadian reading the tomb's inscription, and the shadow cast by the curve of his arm takes on the appearance of the Grim Reaper's scythe. Death, suddenly, seems the most natural of all forces, and nature, therefore, as human beings understand it, seems to begin not in the waterfall or the tree or even the blade of grass but in the human body itself.[17] This acknowledgment of mortality does not negate the shepherds' pastoral idyll, but rather makes it richer, shoves it from the realm of the purely imaginary to a tangled borderground between realism and idealism. A perfect Arcadia may not ultimately be realizable, but the presence of death gives Arcadian life new meaning. Without death paradise is static, lacking the possibility of creative transformation: if it is perpetually spring, then spring is no longer a blissful riot of awakening life but rather a kind of permanent . . . death. With death in mind, though, Arcadians are freed to work for change, to blend the contours of culture and nature, and to pause occasionally and immerse themselves, as many nineteenth-century Americans did, in the hundreds of different flavors one might experience on a trip through an apple orchard, or in the delightfully eerie silence of a walk through a snow-covered cemetery.

---

Some of the Arcadian spaces carved into our culture are almost as sublime as the gorges carved into our lithosphere, but others are much simpler—more humble. As it turned out, I moved to Ithaca just months before a perfect example of this kind of picturesque landscape got ripped from the fabric of the local environment by backhoes, bulldozers, and administrative blindness. Of course, it is a matter of some dispute whether anything as aesthetically oriented as a landscape—no matter how sublime or straightforward—can actually make a difference in our environmental struggles. Maybe the most important thing is the impact of corporate behaviors and government policies on the soundness of the global environment; after all, plenty of individual "nature lovers" and appreciators of scenic landscapes knowingly contribute to all kinds of ecological degradation. But we experience landscapes every day, and one need not be an environmental determinist to suggest that those landscapes have an impact on our thoughts and emotions, our belief systems and our psyches.[18] Nature may not be inherently good or healthful—having more parks will not cure all our ills or fundamentally readjust society's most important power imbalances—but landscapes that feature natural elements at least give people opportunities to connect to the world, to appreciate and even celebrate their environmental contexts, their interdependence, perhaps even their mortality. Creating an ecologically sustainable society is going to demand sacrifices, and liminal Arcadian landscapes, sites of pleasure and illumination as well as dark realism, have the potential both to explain the necessity of those sacrifices and to inspire them.[19]

That is why I joined the struggle to save Cornell's Redbud Woods—a tiny slice of borderland that has now been replaced by a parking lot.[20] It was definitely a struggle.

Students and other activists set up platforms in the trees and chained themselves to pipes buried deep in the ground. Faculty members put their bodies in the way of hulking machines. Community groups provided food and music and materials for posters. Yet, throughout this stand-off, Cornell administrators came across as strangely befuddled. They were going to build their parking lot no matter what, but meanwhile they genuinely seemed to have difficulty understanding what motivated this opposition to their eminently reasonable expansion plan. Why, they repeatedly asked, do you people care so much about this weedy, overgrown patch of tangled shrubbery? What's so special about these trees?

Those questions have continued to haunt me—in part because they were reiterated by a number of my colleagues and friends, who truly wanted to understand. Their first assumption was sound: obviously, we need to use natural resources in order to survive and thrive. We can't simply choose preservation and stasis over development and change. What shook me was their second assumption—that the decision about which trees were eligible to be sacrificed in the name of progress should be based on a simple hierarchy. If the trees were striking and unusual, or part of a sublime landscape—if they were clinging to the cliffs of Cascadilla Gorge, for instance—then they merited protection. Otherwise, shouldn't market forces or administrative priorities govern our environmental practices? Of course, this line of thinking makes perfect sense in American culture, given an environmental history dominated, on the one hand, by aggressive expansion, and, on the other, by the celebration of certain wilderness jewels, most commonly preserved as "scenic wonderlands" in national parks, the first of which was established in 1872. The national park system, sometimes referred to as "America's Best Idea," is colored by its origins in an era when industrialization seemed to touch almost every aspect of American life: it explicitly protects *only* those landscapes that have always been places apart, "natural curiosities" and "wonders" that meet exceedingly high standards of beauty and "interest."[21] And since many Americans understand wilderness preservation to be at the heart of environmentalism, they approach most environmental debates as straightforward problems of prioritizing the best landscapes: all you have to do is establish specialness.

In our day, specialness has, fortunately, taken on a broader meaning: a landscape can now be worthy of preservation on scientific grounds as well as scenic grounds—if, for instance, it provides some crucial ecological service to its bio-region. So I can certainly agree that national park–style preservation is a good idea. But it also has serious limitations. Indeed, the ethos and assumptions of the national park ideal gave the developers of Redbud Woods a huge advantage, because the onus in the negotiations was on the environmental activists to demonstrate that this shabby piece of land was worth enshrining. The fetishization of specialness effectively takes the basic question of development off the table: we start with the assumption that we will always need more parking lots, and then we simply figure out where to put them. But maybe the questions raised by Redbud Woods should have been less about what made it a sacred place for some people (and not for others) and more about why the university was interested in using its precious land to accommodate and encourage car use.

The ecological angle is crucial as well, of course, but in this case it turned out to be particularly fraught—because redbuds are classified as an invasive species. Words have power: that simple label was enough to convince many people of the rightness of the parking lot. Redbuds are invasive; Redbud Woods must therefore be a low-diversity ecosystem, from which better, native species have been crowded out. Send in the bulldozers. But ask ten different ecologists or horticulturists what "invasive" means, and you'll get at least three or four different definitions. In the last twenty years, the new ecology of "discordant harmonies" has thrown into question the basic concepts of biodiversity and ecosystem stability. Some environments, especially in temperate-to-cold climates, seem to be most stable when they are dominated by just a few species. And not all invasives are always, as it were, pestiferous. Much depends on context. Indeed, the well-intentioned people who run the Cornell Plantations have even been known to ornament our campus with invasive species, including redbuds.[22]

I favored the preservation of Redbud Woods, in part, because it's on a hillside, where pavement would create more runoff and speed up its flow. For more than a century, these trees had been absorbing water and stabilizing the soil of East Hill. I favored preservation because the neighbors who lived just downhill considered the woods an important ecological *and* social buffer zone between the university and the city of Ithaca. The city itself took Cornell to court twice to try to block the parking lot. I favored preservation because, to the community, the woods symbolized not a wilderness retreat but an incorporation of nature into normal, everyday life. And I favored preservation because I could not see the advantage of facilitating automobile use, which contributes both to local pollution and to the global trend toward destabilizing climate change. A thick, mysterious stand of trees, thanks to long cultural traditions, spurs many of us to explore, to set off on foot; a new parking lot, as any city planner will tell you, generally spurs us to drive.

Even these arguments sounded dubious to many of my colleagues, though. It was not that they wanted to defend cars; it was that they wanted me to express more sympathy for the people who had to drive them, for the Cornell staff who had to commute every day, even for the Cornell students who wanted cars with them so that they could explore the surrounding countryside or escape to New York City for the weekend. What they were saying is that they suspected environmentalists of being anti-automobile in an utterly knee-jerk fashion, as if all drivers were just pawns of the capitalist-industrial complex. They were reminding me that American environmentalism has always been tinged not only with a puritanical moralism but also with a simple elitism. Walkers are made to seem better, higher, more righteous, and more sophisticated than drivers. My colleagues were not unsympathetic to environmental concerns; they just wanted, ultimately, to be sure that there was some measure of fairness here, that the needs of the nature lovers were being weighed against the needs of other legitimate human beings who could see using this space for different purposes. The overall health of the global environment is crucial to our survival, but that doesn't make every single bit of parkland inviolable. Environmentalists like to trumpet the inherent good of places like Redbud Woods, but my colleagues reminded me that parks, for the realists who have to make planning decisions, can sometimes be sites of violence and crime, and that higher densities of people and traffic can actually be conducive to social health. And suddenly I realized that I needed to learn more about how the history of environmental thought intersected with the history of city planning—that, in particular, I needed to reread Jane Jacobs's classic book, *The Death and Life of Great American Cities.*

I had first read the book about a decade earlier, as a researcher and writer for the Worldwatch Institute, where I was trying to think through and connect different aspects of the modern environmental crisis. At the time, I considered Jacobs a founding mother of environmentalism, because her book, published in 1961, a year before *Silent Spring*, made such a strong case against car culture and, by implication, suburban sprawl. Yet her acerbic prose also betrays a powerful distrust of all green spaces and anyone who might want to impose them on city dwellers. At Worldwatch, I simply passed over this seeming inconsistency; my colleague Marcia Lowe seemed to have it exactly right when she cited Jacobs's vision of "compact development" as a key to fostering "humane cities."[23]

I found myself in an entirely different intellectual context, though, as I stood on the edge of Redbud Woods in 2005 and tried to get my twenty-month-old son to stop ogling the construction trucks and start hugging the trees. What would Jane Jacobs do? Obviously, Ithaca is not a "Great City," and Jacobs was adamant about not confusing a town with a metropolis.[24] Yet Ithaca *is* just large enough to earn official urban status from the federal government, and it has identifiable neighborhoods, none of which Jacobs would want to see overrun with cars. I felt I could easily make the case to my colleagues in the City and Regional Planning Department, most of whom surely taught Jacobs's works in their courses, that this parking lot had to be defeated. But as I read through *Death and Life* with new eyes, I also began to see more clearly how those same colleagues, even after forty-five more years of environmental thinking, could argue that green spaces were often just salves on a society's conscience, used by the few and resented by the many—as weedy, overgrown patches of tangled shrubbery, where people might well get mugged.

I now paused—not necessarily with sympathy, but with deeper deliberation—when I came upon Jacobs's dismissal of "the science-fiction nonsense that parks are 'the lungs of the city,'" and her assault on the Garden City and City Beautiful movements as hopelessly "paternalistic," and her snide mockery of urban plans showing space for nothing but "grass, grass, grass."[25] Even later in her life, after environmentalism had established itself, Jacobs carefully distinguished between ecological and social health in certain tough cases, and when she had to choose she came down on what she perceived to be the side of human civilization. And so I began to see more clearly how it was not just the wilderness tradition that had made environmentalists sometimes seem uninterested in social issues. What we needed to do at Redbud Woods was present a vision of grass and trees and ecological systems as ultimate social goods. Fortunately, my own diggings in nineteenth-century history have led me to believe that such a vision is actually part of America's democratic tradition. Jacobs was mostly right about neighborhoods, I think, but mostly wrong about ecology and environmental history. A deeper historical perspective than the one she brought to bear on her work might help us defend some form of Arcadia against both the Right and the Left. In the antebellum period, when many Americans confronted mortality openly, publicly, continually, as human beings' defining limit, they consequently believed that the highest expression of human civilization might entail accepting nature rather than subduing it.

———————

I learned of the conflict over Redbud Woods during my first semester at Cornell, in the fall of 2004, from a student who was taking my seminar on travel in American history and culture. As we talked, in that course, about how mobility was a key characteristic of modernity, about how Americans have tended to emphasize space over place, and as I began to revise my dissertation, which dealt with nineteenth-century travelers and explorers, I found myself worrying that I was not sufficiently balancing my embrace of cosmopolitanism with a sense of rootedness in any locality, and that I was perhaps giving so much attention to wilder, frontier environments that I was overlooking some highly suggestive in-between landscapes. So, as the weather got colder, and the trail up Cascadilla Gorge got icier, I adjusted my commute. I tried to give myself more time to explore. It took only a couple of days to find Redbud Woods—though there were no signs next to the trails or marks on any map. But then it took a solid week for me actually to learn my way around those interlocking pathways, despite the fact that in absolute terms the wooded area was quite small—not even three acres. There was nothing immediately or inherently special about the trees and dirt and animals I encountered in that tiny plot of land—though I did take a certain amount of pleasure in plowing through the dead leaves on the trails, and in learning to recognize the hackberries and yellow oaks, and in imagining that, from above, the woods might look like a giant pink triangle when the redbuds bloomed in the spring. Ultimately, what made the place seem almost magical was the simple experience of getting lost there for a couple of minutes, trapped in a pocket of time and space between home and work, between city and campus. And because there were so many trails, and so many points of egress, walking through Redbud Woods seemed to suggest endless possibilities and opportunities for further discovery—until, one day, a random turn set me on a new trajectory and pointed me down a path into the Ithaca Cemetery. (Figure 3.)

I have been walking through the cemetery for a few years now, and I still sometimes discover new patches of turf and stone folded into its contours. In the mid-1840s, when Ithaca's Board of Trustees expanded the site and started shaping it into its current form, the nameless village burying ground became Mount Repose, and those who took an interest in the new civic institution clearly relished its evocative topography.[26] But the earliest surveyors and "keepers" of the cemetery also saw fit to create massive earthworks, shaping the steep hill into terraces, mounds, and ridges, adding steps and retaining walls, creating small depressions and enclaves, artificial dells where Ithacans could feel completely immersed in this landscape of mourning that was nevertheless so full of exuberant life. Needless to say, it is difficult to tell which banks of sod are "natural" and which "artificial." In other sections of the cemetery, meanwhile, are obvious lookout points, opportunities to engage with the world at large, the business of the town, the surrounding fields and forests. Sometimes I reach a ridgeline, in my walks, or come around a long, sweeping curve, and can suddenly see the sunset through a break in the trees, or the slate blue of Cayuga Lake fingering its way northward toward the Erie Canal, which was completed in 1825. It almost feels as though I am following a path laid out for me by some ancient druid or geomancer, who studied the position of the sun at certain times of day on the solstices and equinoxes and then threaded his trails through the woods in search of just the right cosmological convergences. Or maybe it was all the work of John W. Pickering, who became keeper of Mount Repose in 1848 and held the position on

Figure 3. J. M. Wilgus, *Map of the City of Ithaca, N.Y.*, 1896. The site of Redbud Woods is just to the northeast of the cemetery, where University Avenue curves.

and off for the following thirty years.[27] Pickering's topographical legacy speaks eloquently of a moment in American history when the art of picturesque landscaping was at the very heart of our culture.[28] There is something alluring about the light in cemeteries designed during the middle of the nineteenth century; Pickering seemed to know just how many trees to have, and how far apart they should be, so that, on cloudless days, the protean pattern of sun and shadow would create a flickering effect, balancing openness and separation, clarity and mystery. Unfortunately, he left almost no written records that might explain his rationale or inspiration—though we do know that, at a time when most Ithacans were farmers, craftsmen, merchants, or mill or factory workers, Pickering listed his previous occupation as "gardner."[29]

The garden-style cemetery designed for a metropolitan center was an American innovation (most of Britain's were based on those of the United States), and Ithaca's retains its astonishing power to embrace both wildness and serenity, freshness and tradition, the local and the cosmic.[30] Mount Repose has of course evolved in the past century and a half, but it was common in Pickering's day to take a very long view in landscape plans, so the overall feel of Ithaca's cemetery has been less transformed by time than one might think. Its ancient trees, its vaults built into the hillside, its curious woodchucks, its sturdy stone bridge over a tiny stream, its simple monument to nineteenth-century firefighters, which has taken on new meaning in the twenty-first century—this landscape still calls to all kinds of people. Perhaps it is just as quintessentially American as, say, the Empire State Building or the Grand Canyon. The latter two icons represent America as modernity, America at its moment of international dominance in the twentieth century, America as the imperial, industrial city balanced by America as the ultimate in majestic wilderness. Many of our social, economic, and environmental histories lead us to believe that the impetus toward empire and grandiosity was all-encompassing and unstoppable. Americans simply spread out to embrace the opportunities presented by new resources and new markets. But I find myself stuck on the question of why, with the onset of modernity, places like Mount Auburn Cemetery were obliterated as national icons. Historians of the nineteenth century have not fully grappled with the question of how Americans thought about space and how their thinking changed over time. Why did the core textbook I assigned in my first U.S. environmental history course not even mention Central Park? In a country whose early nineteenth-century leaders insisted on a pastoral culture, why have we been reduced to choosing between the City and the Wilderness?[31]

———————————

Twice each day, I choose between walking through the gorge or the cemetery. Both landscapes, of course, have been intensively shaped, have clear paths carved into them for me to follow. Both also happen to be significantly wilder than the routes taken by the vast majority of American commuters wending their way between suburb and metropolis. Neither one of my routes constitutes a working landscape: though they potentially could produce food or drinking water—and another nearby gorge actually does generate some electricity—they currently serve only as spaces for recreation and reflection. And the scope of that reflection is severely limited: both the gorge and the cemetery trails effectively erase the trails walked by Cayuga Indians and the violence done to numerous local Natives by white settlers and soldiers in the late eighteenth century.[32] Neither waterfalls nor cemeteries can explain all of U.S. history nor solve the world's most serious social and environmental problems. Yet I still find it useful to start thinking through the differences between these two places and to try to understand the roles they have played in the constant formation and re-formation of our culture. My commute, as my soles come into contact with rock and asphalt and water and grass and dirt, sometimes spurs basic questions about how we live—and die—in this country.[33] We need to be able to wander through these kinds of history-laden landscapes. Sometimes, in the cemetery, I find myself thinking of one of my adopted ancestors, the peripatetic Jewish critic Walter Benjamin, and his vision, in his fragmentary magnum opus, *The Arcades Project*, of the ideal walker in the tree-lined streets of Paris. And I start imagining this book as a tribute to Benjamin, as an Arcadia Project, and I enter a reverie like that of his pedestrian, for whom "far-off times and places interpenetrate the landscape and the present moment," as "his steps awaken a surprising resonance," as his path leads him "into a vanished . . . past that can be all the more spellbinding because it is not his own, not private."[34] In dark times, when the waters seem to be rising, certain kinds of public spaces might foster solidarity, and a haunted, backward-looking melancholy might foster hope.

When friends and family members have come to visit Ithaca, I've generally made Cascadilla Gorge one of our first stops on the city tour. Everyone likes a good waterfall. Not everyone likes a good cemetery. I've always assumed that visitors would prefer the gorge because it seemed like a choice between uplifting and morbid, wild and tame, sublime and subdued. But my walks have helped me reconsider my assumptions—and confront my mortality. The cemetery initially drew me in with its shade and its curves and its sparkling greenery, but now I appreciate it most for the way it slows me down on my way to the office: it gives me the space I need to remember not to get caught up in my work, to remember that I should take some time today to call my parents, who are in their eighties, who will probably not be reachable in another few years. I will never reject or scorn Ithaca's gorges; I don't mean to dismiss this country's compelling tradition of celebrating wilderness. The politics of wild waterscapes, in particular, will become increasingly relevant as we experience more widespread shortages of life's basic element. I don't intend to stop soaking my head in local waterfalls. Meanwhile, though, I have started to explore the different kind of humility offered by the cemetery—a humility that is more of earth than of rock, more humic, perhaps more human. I don't feel less solidarity with environmentalists, but

I do feel more solidarity with urbanists and agrarians and families who go on vacation to Gettysburg rather than Yellowstone. The gorge sometimes seems too stark, too ethereal, too limiting in its trajectory. The cemetery, with its inscriptions, its animals scratching in the dirt, its nut casings and ephemeral blossoms and newly laid bouquets, now makes me think about how we house both the dead and the living, how we nourish our bodies and souls, how beings die so that others can grow, how culture and nature can regenerate themselves.[35] It has, perhaps, helped me come to grips both with my habits of resource consumption and with middle age; it has helped me accept limits. It makes dying a fact of life. Some may take offense at such admonishment; or at the distinctions between grand and humble monuments, seeming to reflect the pernicious divisions of a capitalist culture; or at the ways in which the aesthetic emphasis of this landscape hides other social problems.[36] But these are precisely the kinds of concerns that ought to be raised as we conscientiously reevaluate our relationship to the environment. Besides, many people immediately recognize the power of old cemeteries as soon as they walk through the gates, immediately sense the paradoxical capacity of such places both to comfort and to chasten. So, from now on, my Ithaca tours will begin on the Arcadian pathways of Mount Repose.

------◆-◆------

# 1

# COMMON SHADE:
# CULTIVATING A PLACE FOR DEATH

The neighborhood was well calculated to foster the reveries of a mind like mine. . . .
I would throw myself, during the panting heats of a summer noon, under the shade
of some wide-spreading tree, and muse and dream away the hours, in a state of mental
intoxication. . . . There is a repose in our mighty forests, that gives full scope to
the imagination.
—Washington Irving, "Mountjoy," 1839

Repose: it conjures ambivalence. In the twenty-first century, we spend our time in
motion. Mostly we work. And when we pause, we note the dip in our average produc-
tivity. Those of us with antimodern tendencies might speak wistfully of peace and
restfulness. We might try to read more slowly, eat more slowly, have longer conversations; we might even walk to work, through a gorge or cemetery—but only if we can
still get to the office on time.[1] Repose sounds lovely as long as we are keeping busy.
Perhaps in our golden years we'll finally stop climbing, having attained some sort of
acceptable plateau, and then we'll proceed down the other side of the mountain,
gradually slowing, until we reach the angle at which rest becomes inevitable.[2] We go
to Mount Repose to die.

Many nineteenth-century Americans, though, went to Mount Repose to live. A
city's cemetery was often its center of vitality; it served the living every day, offering
gifts not only of fresh air, but of continuity through time, and the promise of regrowth.
"Repose" was associated with death, but death was integrated into life. Mortality and
mourning suffused antebellum culture: children attended funerals and burials; manuals and pamphlets, printed by the thousands on new, steam-powered presses, laid

out examples of gruesome deaths handled with nobility and grace, of unlucky citizens going gently, philosophically, into that good night.[3] Cholera and yellow fever epidemics, which regularly ravaged the cities of the eastern seaboard, could have inspired a culture of denial, but instead Americans attempted both to embrace and to transcend death, to confront its urgency, acknowledge its power, and then smile and nod to it. They were well practiced in the navigation of the borderland between living and dying, convinced of the links between past, present, and future.

Notwithstanding the efforts of some religious leaders, who tended to minimize the immediate and wide-ranging pain of earthly departures in their emphasis on ethereal glories to come, the prevailing attitude, I think, was marked not by a naïve, gleeful welcoming of mortality but by a deep engagement with it.[4] The ideal seemed to be a repose that did not deny restlessness. In literary circles, "repose" became almost an obsession, representing a reconciliation of individual desire and social necessity, an acceptance of sacrifice, a recognition that young nations would have growing pains.[5] Emerson, Thoreau, Fuller, Irving, Cooper, Longfellow, Hawthorne, Whitman, all asserted their faith in America's ability to adjust to unnerving new technologies, to tensions with Indians, to the sudden expansion of commerce and industry and settlement. The adjustment period might cast a long shadow over American history, but even as the exalted Revolutionary generation passed on, the nation would persist.

Many of these early writers found repose in nature, and none more so than the foremost literary celebrity of his day, William Cullen Bryant.[6] If Bryant is even noticed in the twenty-first century—he carries with him that damning epithet, "minor poet"—he is generally portrayed as a sentimentalist, a simple extoller of nature's sacred beauty.[7] Despite the easy accessibility and popularity of his verses, though, I think of him as a subtle social critic; he never ceased exploring the impact of massive social changes on America's relationship to death and the natural world. A poem he wrote in 1827, for instance, called "A Scene on the Banks of the Hudson," suffers from hackneyed images of landscaped peace—water that is "clear" and "unrippled," "Sabbath bells," a circle of trees, blooming roses—but ends with a surprising sense of unease:[8]

> River! in this still hour thou hast
> Too much of heaven on earth to last;
> Nor long may thy still waters lie,
> An image of the glorious sky.
> Thy fate and mine are not repose,
> And ere another evening close,
> Thou to thy tides shall turn again,
> And I to seek the crowd of men.

Bryant takes so much delight from his Sunday stroll to the paradisal river that he can't be happy about having to go back to work and society—and The City—on Monday. Yet he naturalizes that return by invoking the turning of the tides: the Sabbath is but one day, a pause, a respite from motion and change, which are both laws of history and defining features of the modernizing Western world. Repose is glorious but temporary, serene but deathlike, and meanwhile on we go, until in fact repose does become our fate, at which point we can possibly take comfort both in the repose itself and in the continuity of life around us. In the tumult of living, though, comfort is fleeting: though neither the still countryside nor the insistent city seems oppressive, the obvious tension between them leaves us somewhat unsettled.

Such shadowy renderings of rest and motion, calmness and striving, are at the center of countless poems, paintings, stories, and even speeches in this period. "I know where the young May violet grows," says an Indian in another of Bryant's moody works from the 1820s, "In its lone and lowly nook,/On the mossy bank, where the larch-tree throws/Its broad dark bough, in solemn repose, /Far over the silent brook." Though in some ways a stereotypical "noble savage," this hero seems unusually meditative, reflecting on the inner strength necessary to acknowledge the darkness of the world and still maintain some kind of balance—a balance he will need when his "dark-haired maid" is stolen away by a rival, and he must restore order and honor by pursuing his foe not with reckless passion but with steadfast deliberation.[9] Bryant and his contemporaries placed reposeful metaphors in many different contexts, referring sometimes to a restorative, even generative sleep; sometimes to the balanced containment of emotion; sometimes to a brooding, gloomy stillness; sometimes to a dreamy laziness; sometimes even to a sense of humor. But probably the most common context was the simple phrase "place of repose"—used to describe American cemeteries.

Repose was the guiding principle from the time America's first true cemetery, Mount Auburn, was consecrated—as a secular institution—on September 24, 1831, in Cambridge, about six miles from the center of Boston.[10] The opening ceremony, according to one of the founders, was marked by an "impressive solemnity": "A temporary amphitheatre was fitted up with seats, in one of the deep vallies of the wood, having a platform for the speakers erected at the bottom. An audience of nearly two thousand persons were seated among the trees." Another witness, writing for the *Boston Courier,* insisted that it would be impossible "to furnish any adequate description of the effect produced by the music of the thousand voices which joined in the hymn, as it swelled in chastened melody from the bottom of the glen." The highlight, though, was the dedication address by Joseph Story, of the United States Supreme Court; his words were met by "the perfect silence of the multitude."[11] Story wanted his listeners, pillars of what was still a puritanical city, despite the growing influence of Unitarians and Universalists, to understand that the idea of the cemetery was grounded in tradition, rooted in the fertile soil of ancient Greece. Though Mount Auburn would serve to draw burial away from the authority of the Church, the cemetery's radicalism was balanced by its classical resonances, which carried a lot of weight at a time when towns were being given names like Ithaca.[12] The Greeks, Story explained, "consigned their reliques to shady groves, in the neighborhood of murmuring streams and mossy fountains, close by the favorite resorts of those, who were engaged in the study of philosophy and nature, and called them, with the elegant expressiveness of their own beautiful language, CEMETERIES, or 'Places of Repose.'"[13]

The word "cemetery" did not actually come into common usage in American culture until after Story's speech. For two centuries, people had been interred in village graveyards or the burying grounds adjacent to churches. Those were the terms: graveyards and burying grounds. They suggest that early Americans treated the disposal of dead bodies with a grim disinterest.[14] Corpses had no business atop Mount Repose; it was only spirits that could rise and come to rest. Urban churchyards and charnel houses became places of dark neglect, as religious leaders, predictably, privileged the immortal soul over the merely physical or material: the Church retained its control over the meaning of death by swallowing the bodies of its parishioners. Unfortunately, though, when the population of the northeastern United States exploded at the beginning of the nineteenth century, corpses quickly started spilling out of official enclosures; the simple grave markers dating back to Puritan settlement were upended and jumbled together; and odors of putrescence competed with the sour stink of sewage and factory fumes in the region's raw industrial centers. The concept of removing American corpses to a cemetery, then, was part of the broad antebellum spirit of liberal reform—the spirit of the Second Great Awakening, which saw the founding of several new religions and the opening of the spiritual realm to a much wider diversity of seekers. This was also the spirit of Transcendentalism, and abolitionism, and the women's movement—a spirit that, as many scholars have argued, was in many ways elitist and aligned with notions of regularity and progress held by leaders of the commercial classes, the Whigs who so often seemed to oppose the spread of Jacksonian democracy. Yet much Whig-supported reform, especially in New England, was also surprisingly radical.[15] The shift from graveyards and burying grounds to cemeteries signaled an entirely new sense of place and a transformed ecology of death.[16] Of course, living amidst moldering bones that rest on picturesque hillsides is not guaranteed to have a chastening effect. But at the precise moment when Western society seemed to focus itself most powerfully on the death-denying conquest and harnessing of nature, some members of that society were using landscapes of death to preach a humble acknowledgment of natural limitations.

By enshrining their kin in sacred groves, antebellum Americans established kinship with the land.[17] The double meaning of the phrase "place of repose," in other words, was entirely deliberate: the dead would have plenty of room to stretch out, at Mount Auburn, in a posture of peaceful sleep, surrounded by the wonders of nature—which would make cemeteries reposeful for the living as well. Indeed, Story suggested that cemetery sites must always be "selected with the same tender regard to the living and the dead; that the magnificence of nature might administer comfort to human sorrow, and incite human sympathy."[18] The material realm now mattered. Americans were making a commitment to see the continuity between bodies and environments, and to approach both with a heightened sense of appreciation and caring—to raise them to a higher level.

From the perspective of many Bostonians, nature had not been faring well in recent years.[19] Its fate seemed to mirror that of the crowded urban burial grounds: "the noisy press of business," as Story put it, had rendered churchyards "loathsome" and "narrow," though previously they might have served as welcoming green spaces.[20] With the rise of the factory system in the 1820s, most notoriously in Lowell, New England life had become significantly less bucolic. Many in Story's circle worried that the very survival of the American republic would be threatened if its citizens lived out their days amidst smokestacks and machinery rather than sunshine, clean air, teeming rivers, and ancient trees. In 1824, when the newly incorporated city of Boston was considering a plan to develop its beloved Common, at the center of town, one enraged citizen, signing himself "A Boston Boy," wrote a series of sarcastic letters attacking his community's new definition of "progress":

> Mark the spirit of *improvement.*—This spot, which should never have been infringed upon, which should remain henceforth and forever open, and form an integral part of the most beautiful park in the world, is to be converted into streets, lanes, and squares! . . . The pure westerly breezes which we now respire through the only ventilator left us are to be sur-charged with the dense vapor of sea-coal smoke from the new suburb, and the manufactories which will naturally accumulate there, intermingled with the effluvia of vaults and common sewers, dirt, and dust. In place of the retirement for which our Common is remarkable, we shall have the bustle and confusion of a new Market Place, with all its concomitant evils.[21]

Scholars sometimes still assert that virtually everyone in antebellum America supported the same kind of "improvement,"[22] but environmentally important places like the Common tended to complicate the issue, bringing out deep divisions both between and within classes. Another letter printed in an 1824 newspaper pointed out that "the advocates for the sale of the Common, or any part thereof, must undoubtedly be the advocates of the rich." And a third notice insisted that "the Common is emphatically called the poor man's inheritance; and so it is, for all may enjoy it. It is ours, and it is our duty to transmit it to posterity inviolate as we received it."[23]

The founders of Mount Auburn, who cared a great deal about cultural inheritance, hoped that their cemetery would be a bigger, better, wilder version of Boston Common.[24] Though it was far from downtown crowds, it was still accessible, a public space open to all classes of people. And while it is certainly true, as scholars have been quick to point out, that some of the elites who supported the idea of Mount Auburn were also busily contributing to urban development and industrialization,[25] they nevertheless saw the cemetery as a spatial argument in favor of balance and limitation. Ambitious Americans, everywhere conquering nature and driving it out of their lives as if it were irrelevant, as if the Revolution had rendered them independent of the land itself, needed to be reminded of the moral and reposeful value of all things natural, of the services provided by the environment: Mount Auburn was meant to have shade as well as shades. Indeed, one of the most striking aspects of Story's speech was the way he luxuriated in nature's gifts. "There are around us all the varied features of her beauty and grandeur—" he said—"the forest-crowned height; the abrupt acclivity; the sheltered valley; the deep glen; the grassy glade; and the silent grove. Here are the lofty oak . . . , and the drooping willow;—the tree, that sheds its pale leaves with every autumn, a fit emblem of our own transitory bloom; . . . and there is the wild-flower creeping along the narrow path, and planting its seeds in the upturned earth. All around us there breathes a solemn calm, as if we were in the bosom of a wilderness."[26]

Was Mount Auburn a wilderness—or even *like* a wilderness? As a teenager growing up in the Boston area and visiting Mount Auburn periodically in the 1980s, I would have considered that a nonsensical question. I took strolls in the cemetery; it was a gentle, innocent, pastoral landscape. "Wilderness" required hiking boots and a means of Going West. But of course the concept of wilderness has changed drastically over the years; in 1831, seemingly, it was something you could experience within a city. Might it not be worth recapturing that kind of experience, even while recognizing the value of preserving larger tracts of wilder land? Are the environmental qualities of Mount Auburn necessarily inferior to those of, say, Yosemite?

I love Yosemite; when I first arrived in the Sierran backcountry, I felt I had finally grown up, had finally become myself. I've relished several week-long camping trips in western wildernesses, relished the distance from settled life and from the most obvious kinds of pollution, relished the long, challenging climbs into thinning air, relished the magical sightings of large animals that require broad tracts of undeveloped land if they are to thrive. But those were vacations—rare privileges. Ultimately, they didn't feel sustainable. I don't imagine that my attachment to classic wilderness areas will ever fade, but in recent years I have been able to see the wilder side of tamer landscapes. Mount Auburn is small: I don't mean to exaggerate the scope of its ecological significance. But its cultural significance—at its founding and 180 years later—has been vastly underestimated, because its complexity, its diversity, its intensity, all foster a lasting awareness of the inextricability of human society and wild nature.

In 1831, wilderness was one element of a reposeful Arcadia. Justice Story asked his listeners to imagine climbing up to Mount Auburn's highest point, from which they might see the Charles River, "with its rippling current, like the stream of time hastening to the ocean of eternity," and downtown Boston, too, with its "proud eminences . . . , its crowded haunts of business and pleasure, which speak to the eye, and yet leave a noiseless loneliness on the ear." Here is death, and nature's humbling power, and the alienation of society; but "melancholy meditations" can actually serve to "solace our hearts," provide catharsis, reinspire us to embrace "the sparkling lake, the rich valley, and the distant hills," as well as "the fresh and varied labors of man." Atop Mount Auburn, Story reminds us, we can see "within our reach, every variety of natural and artificial scenery, which is fitted to awaken emotions of the highest and most affecting character. We stand, as it were, upon the borders of two worlds." It is this compelling sense of betweenness and balance, this agitated repose, that Story meant to evoke when, in his concluding remarks, he insisted that Mount Auburn be called a *Rural* Cemetery."[27]

Rural: one of the most egregiously oversimplified concepts in our language. We have no grounded way of understanding it. Does "rural" connote good, wholesome values, or a dull, narrow provincialism? A sensitive, appreciative attachment to the land, or an embittered awareness of the necessity of hard, repetitive labor, despite always-uncertain yields? A radical protest against industrial capitalism, or a retreat from politics?[28] Is it merely a spatial term—the opposite of urban? Some scholars of American cemeteries have interpreted it that way, assuming that Mount Auburn's primary purpose was nothing more than to take corpses out of the miasmic city center and into peripheral areas. But I think the dozens of rural cemeteries created between 1831 and the Civil War, all easily reached from downtown neighborhoods, were both intended and experienced as true "middle landscapes"—not stylized spaces that aestheticized death, not therapeutic escapes from cities, but material attempts at confronting and coming to grips with the way of the world.[29]

In 1838, another angry Bostonian published *The Boston Common, or Rural Walks in Cities,* and his goal was not to prettify the downtown area with elite, country-style estates, but to inject it with a wildness that would serve to bring local capitalists back down to earth. The Boston Common, threatened again by developers, would have to become a leveling landscape, a downtown version of the cemetery it had helped to inspire—as the anonymous author signaled on the second page of his text, through his approving citation of "the Hon. H. A. S. Dearborn," who was president of the Massachusetts Horticultural Society when it was founded in 1829 and a driving force behind Mount Auburn when it, in turn, was established by the Horticultural Society two years later.[30] Up until this point, the capitalists had been doing the leveling, literally flattening out the rolling topography of their coastal city, but more and more people were now willing to speak on behalf of the environment: "That spirit which has torn our green hills from their bases, and sold them for gain, may never invade this abode of peace." The position was not just defensive, though. While the "Boston Boy" had mocked the very idea of improving anything back in 1824, the author of *The Boston Common* actually called himself "A Friend of Improvement," trying to redefine the idea by proposing that his home town be redesigned according to wilder principles. "As we are ourselves children of nature," he wrote, "let us here learn from her the pleasures and the advantages of yielding to her dictates. . . . Man . . . must gaze upon green trees, and breathe the breath of fresh flowers; his brow must be fanned by gales that have sped over green forests and fields—or his spirit will be faint within him. Ay, he must bring away garden and grove, and plant them in the very midst of the marts of trade."[31]

Rural. Improvement. One thinks of refined gentlemen claiming to tame the wild frontier, to soften its rough edges by calling upon human art and ingenuity. But here we have an activist trying to import "the sublime solitude of the wilderness," so as "to remind us that the world in which we live is not, like the little world of the city, one of our own contriving." Though culture can be fantastically impressive, its power depends not on our genius but on our submission. "Art is naked . . . ," he insists. "Proud as she may be, she must needs be a borrower of beauty; and her grandest designs must be sculptured with imagery of Nature's more perfect workmanship." Boston will have to be re-greened, in the image of the Common, which he calls "the gift of our ancestors," a "sacred inheritance," "consecrated ground"—phrases immediately evocative of Mount Auburn. And he enhances this connection by dwelling on how the oldest trees on the Common glow most impressively in autumn, when "these temples of nature are curtained with the same gorgeous colors of decay which meet the eye of the wanderer in the still and solitary forest temples. . . . One who has never witnessed it can hardly imagine the varying harmonies of shade and light which here melt into each other—the grandeur which these autumnal hues impart to the picture, combining, in one view, the beauty of art and nature."[32] The blending of seeming opposites, the sensory experience of the land, the stunningly lovely images of death and decay, the preservation of the past in sacred soil and thickening trees as well as in sturdily elegant human constructions—these are the qualities that made a landscape truly "rural" in the antebellum period.

---

Just as important, though, as the author of *The Boston Common* insisted, was the availability of these environmental qualities to all kinds of people. Americans, in the midst of abandoning the countryside, had pursued development for too long without any "consideration of the circumstances of the poor, on whom all the evils produced by the accumulation of human dwellings in cities fall with a double weight." An older moral economy had linked parcels of common land with a commitment to common wealth, but the new capitalist economy drove marginal people into marginal environments: "Let us have no mean, or disagreeable, or unwholesome places in our cities. . . . Who will venture, in these days, to bring into comparison the moral and physical degradation which ensue from heaping together human beings by thousands in confined and unhealthy localities, with the pecuniary interests of a few, which may seem to require that every inch of ground be converted into gold?"[33]

Similar concerns—about the perniciousness of capitalism and the need for public, accessible green spaces—were raised by the founders of Mount Auburn. In 1831, General Henry A. S. Dearborn, the authority cited in *The Boston Common,* issued a Horticultural Society report about the newly opened cemetery that emphasized its broad appeal and democratic openness: "Such is the exalted estimation in which it is held by the public, so universal is the approbation, so intense the interest, that, beside the constant requests for permission to become subscribers, by the more affluent, numerous applications have been made for cemetery lots, by farmers, mechanics, and dealers in building materials, on condition, that they may be paid for in labor, or such articles as shall be required in the prosecution of the proposed improvements. . . . And as it was the intention and is the anxious desire of the Society, that every citizen should have an opportunity of participating in the advantages of the establishment, the committee has availed itself of the services thus tendered."[34] Though horticulture did tend to be a fairly elite undertaking in early America, the Horticultural Society, according to Dearborn, had a populist mission: he hoped to "increase the enjoyment of all classes of citizens."[35]

The working classes, then, were not only expected to have plots at Mount Auburn, but also to take walks there, to use the cemetery as a park and "pleasure ground." Some scholars, understandably, have treated this expectation as a classic example of reformist condescension and social control,[36] but it can also be seen as a genuine attempt to grant universal access to the kinds of environmental "amenities" that were clearly being threatened by industrialization and urbanization. All Americans, exclaimed Justice Story, should have the opportunity to "dwell in the bosom of their mother earth! The rich and the poor, the gay and the wretched, the favorites of thousands, and the forsaken of the world."[37] While, as many have noted, the design of Mount Auburn was clearly influenced by the elitist English landscape tradition of the eighteenth century, the radicalism of American horticulture was that it threw open what in the old country had been exclusive garden estates, aristocratic enclosures, to the entire public.

In England, as in America, the trend was toward privatization of land: wealthy men, abetted by the government, were buying up large tracts, either to use themselves or to resell at a profit. Starting in the middle of the eighteenth century, England's Enclosure Acts helped politically dominant lords capture about a quarter of the country's cultivated land, almost all of which had previously been considered part of the common domain, at least by custom.[38] Farms, homes, even entire towns had been planted on these common lands—which explains the title of Oliver Goldsmith's famous 1770 poetic lamentation, "The Deserted Village." Goldsmith wished both to recapture what he thought of as an idyllic pastoral life and to condemn the injustices of modernity: "Sweet smiling village, loveliest of the lawn,/Thy sports are fled, and all thy charms withdrawn;/Amidst thy bowers the tyrant's hand is seen,/And desolation saddens all thy green:/One only master grasps the whole domain,/And half a tillage stints thy smiling plain." The dream of many of these "tyrants" was actually to shape their new properties into extensive gardens and hunting grounds, and though their aesthetic success would eventually be admired internationally, Goldsmith would not let them forget that peasants working for their own sustenance did a much better job of cultivation than any aristocrat ever could, even with the help of the cleverest gardeners. Under the new capitalist regime, the greenery has become desolate, the fields and yields stinted. "Ill fares the land, to hastening ills a prey,/Where wealth accumulates, and men decay." Even decay, the most natural of all processes, has now become ominously artificial, though previously both people and land had thrived in their interconnection and mutual dependence, and growing old had been a pleasure: "How often have I paused on every charm,/The sheltered cot, the cultivated farm,/The never-failing brook, the busy mill,/The decent church that topped the neighbouring hill,/The hawthorn bush, with seats beneath the shade,/For talking age and whispering lovers made."[39] Goldsmith's nostalgic—and bitterly angry—narrator is dreaming of his childhood home and protesting that political and economic leaders have deprived him of the opportunity to complete his life's circle, to return and live in a place layered with memories, and thus to die in peace. This theme, touching on the timeless and universal but grounded in the realities of industrialization and rural-urban migration, became especially resonant in antebellum America; Goldsmith's were among the most cited verses within New England's literary culture, and everyone knew the name of his Deserted Village—"Sweet Auburn."

---

The political economy of the United States was of course somewhat different: the land was stolen from Indians, not peasants. And when Americans living in the countryside in the nineteenth century started expanding their operations beyond the subsistence level, or even moved to the city to take manufacturing jobs—when they joined the "market revolution"—many did so quite enthusiastically. It is crucial to consider the eloquent warning issued by the literary scholar Raymond Williams that, while Goldsmith and his admirers may have been right to honor the possibilities of the old rural balance, they were too prone "to exclude from the so-called organic society the penury, the petty tyranny, the disease and mortality, the ignorance and frustrated intelligence which were also among its ingredients."[40] In any case, many American writers, responding directly to Goldsmith with poems called "The Flourishing Village" or "The Populous Village," were keen to show that in the New World capitalism's impact on both society and nature might ultimately be benign.[41] Certainly, the name Mount Auburn starts to seem strangely ironic when one considers that the cemetery's landscape had much more in common with an English lord's hunting grounds—containing, in Goldsmith's acerbic rhyme, "Space for his lake, his park's extended bounds,/Space for his horses, equipage, and hounds"[42]—than with a rural community where people actually lived and worked.

Yet the Massachusetts Horticultural Society did consider Mount Auburn to be something of a working landscape—most immediately, because each proprietor was expected to shape and maintain his family's plot. You couldn't invest in this piece of land and still think of nature merely as scenery; establishing your place in the environment took steady labor. Moreover, at its founding, the cemetery shared space with a large experimental garden, which, in Henry A. S. Dearborn's words, was designed to "present all possible varieties of soil, common in the vicinity of Boston," and was "diversified by hills, valleys, plains, brooks, and low meadows, and bogs, so as to afford proper localities for every kind of tree and plant that will flourish in this climate." Dearborn's plan, which quickly came to fruition, also stipulated that "the ornamental grounds of the GARDEN should be apparently blended with those of the Cemetery, and the walks of each so intercommunicate, as to afford an uninterrupted range over both, as one common domain." And the whole scheme was justified as having "great public advantages."[43]

Indeed, General Dearborn's associate, Dr. Jacob Bigelow, who was responsible for procuring the original seventy-two acres that became Mount Auburn, just north of the Charles River, emphasized that the previous owner, George Brimmer—"a gentleman whose just appreciation of the beautiful in nature had prompted him to preserve from destruction the trees and other natural features of that attractive spot"—could have offered the land "to private purchasers, at no distant period, for a large advance," but instead sold it at a loss to the Horticultural Society, as "an object of public benefit."[44] Dearborn, Bigelow, Story, and the other horticulturists were clearly worried that the majority of Boston capitalists, not so enlightened as their friend Brimmer, would continue planting factories along the Charles and driving out the rural way of life. Just upriver, after all, were the rapidly expanding industrial operations of Watertown and Waltham, communities that had been utterly reshaped in the previous two decades, after the Boston Manufacturing Company and other capitalistic establishments had opened their first textile and paper mills there.[45]

Though Brimmer's land had been dubbed "Sweet Auburn" many years before, by a couple of poetry-loving Harvard students who enjoyed exploring its knolls and rolling forests,[46] it was Jacob Bigelow who settled on the cemetery's final name in 1831, during the most rapid phase of New England's industrialization.[47] Bigelow was the original visionary behind Mount Auburn, having called a meeting back in 1825 specifically to discuss the medical, aesthetic, historical, and environmental reasons for creating a new burial tradition.[48] In history books, however, he is more often noted as the first popularizer of the word "technology," and therefore as a principal purveyor of American triumphalism and a general celebrator of human progress.[49] But even Bigelow's classic work, *Elements of Technology*, published to great acclaim in 1829, turns out to reflect a much more ambivalent perspective on humanity's manipulations of nature. "The economy of the ancients," Bigelow noted, "consisted in diminishing their personal wants; ours, in devising cheap means to gratify them. . . . Their stateliest edifices were destitute of chimnies and glass windows, yet when left to themselves, they have stood for thousands of years. Ours abound in the means of making their present tenants comfortable, but are often built too cheaply to be durable."[50] True "improvement," to Bigelow, might under certain circumstances be achieved through powerful, industrial-style technologies, but he tended to emphasize the greater possibilities of simply attending more closely to the directives of the natural world.

In his medical writings, Bigelow expressed skepticism about most of the technological interventions being pushed by his colleagues and instead embraced the idea "that Nature was the great healer."[51] He gave lectures on "Self-Limited Diseases," and, in his practice, he encouraged patients to take fewer drugs and to recognize the contributions they could make to their own recovery, instead of passively relying on experts. "With all his science and experience," explained his first biographer, writing just a year after his death, "he comes with empty hands to his patient, and standing calmly and thoughtfully by the bedside, witnesses and tries to interpret the action of a power higher than his own art,—Nature." Much of his life's work seemed to focus on the process of coming to grips with limitation. Though he took a great interest in the founding of the Massachusetts Institute of Technology in 1861, he delivered a lecture there four years later, right at the end of the Civil War, called "The Limits of Education." Long before America's great tragedy, though, he seemed to accept that there would always be outrages and frustrations and disappointments and difficulties, that human beings would always struggle to thrive, that diseases would come and go and come again. Besides, as he put it, "the progress of all organized beings is toward decay."[52]

How, then, do we cope most fruitfully with our gradual demise, with our limitedness? Bigelow found solace and redemption in a proto-ecological worldview, which he hoped would be woven into the design of Mount Auburn. In "A Discourse on the Burial of the Dead," which he delivered in 1831 before the Boston Society for the Promotion of Useful Knowledge, Bigelow noted that "the plant which springs from the earth, after attaining its growth and perpetuating its species, falls to the ground, undergoes decomposition, and contributes its remains to the nourishment of plants around it. The myriads of animals which range the woods or inhabit the air, at length die upon the surface of the earth, and if not devoured by other animals, prepare for vegetation the place which receives their remains. Were it not for this law of nature, the soil would be soon exhausted, the earth's surface would become a barren waste, and the whole race of organized beings, for want of sustenance, would become extinct."[53] No doubt the earth would get along just fine without the organic contributions of human bodies, but Bigelow nonetheless effected a stunning secularization of the afterlife, which allowed him simultaneously to celebrate the most terrifying of natural forces. One of the great advantages of a rural cemetery, he explained, is that, far from "the tumultuous and harassing din of cities," it permits mourners to spend time "where the harmonious and ever-changing face of nature reminds us, by its resuscitating influences, that to die is but to live again." Bigelow, whose second child died at six months, recognized the horror of mortality, but hoped that a place like Mount Auburn, "by the joint influence of nature and art," could transcend it. "When nature is permitted to take her course—" he explained, "when the dead are committed to the earth under the open sky, to become early and peacefully blended with their original dust," then mourners, too, might become enfolded "in the surrounding harmonies of the creation."[54]

———————————

For all his humility in the face of natural limitations, Bigelow conceived of Mount Auburn as an ambitious project, with national significance. Culture and cultivation could be strong forces balancing out the abuses and excesses of modernity. Rural refinement might counter the coarseness of the urban-industrial complex; a personal attitude of repose might quiet the bustle of social striving. A key question confronting people like Bigelow, though—and his literary counterparts, especially William Cullen Bryant and Washington Irving—was how to import the sophistication of Europe without giving up on establishing a distinct American culture. The scholarly consensus has long held that Irving's generation (he was the oldest of his cohort, born in 1783) "all followed English literary models that were conservative in their reflection of English society," that the children of the Revolutionary generation were condemned to nostalgia and "nervous emulation."[55] It was not until the emergence of Emerson, Thoreau, Hawthorne, and Melville, in the 1840s, that America found its true, original voice. But a reconsideration of Mount Auburn might cast shadows on these assumptions. Bigelow and Dearborn, like all American horticulturists, looked to England for advice and inspiration (and even seeds and cuttings) but made it their highest goal to *adapt* English ideas and models to the particular ecological circumstances of the New World. In a speech commemorating the first anniversary of the Massachusetts Horticultural Society in 1830, one of its vice presidents, Zebedee Cook, Jr., explained that "the opinions of foreign writers, however applicable they may be in practice to the mode of cultivation pursued in those regions of which they treat, are not always suited to the climate and soil of that which adopts them."[56] Dearborn, a devoted Anglophile, derided the American "fashion . . . of congregating in large towns and cities" and hoped his compatriots would adopt the high-class English taste for living "under the blue vault of the firmament, amidst the sublime and glorious works of the creation"—but the point was to appreciate the specific natural works native to America, the "lofty mountains, from whose rugged flanks gush forth perennial springs," the "broad estuaries," the "superb forest trees," and the "profusion of shrubs, and wild flowers, which are so unrivalled in variety and splendor, that they constitute some of the most choice collections in the conservatories, sumptuous gardens, and rural plantations of Europe."[57] Mount Auburn Cemetery, like many literary works of the period, too often dismissed as derivative, was actually a complicated hybrid, designed both to honor and to shatter Old World cultural forms by molding them to New World landforms.

The founders of Mount Auburn admitted to being deeply influenced by the Père Lachaise cemetery, for instance, which removed burial beyond the walls of Paris in 1804.[58] But ultimately they wanted something less monumental, designed not "for the poor purpose of gratifying our vanity or pride," in Justice Story's words, but for the teaching of nature's lessons, which would spur "thoughts full of admonition, of instruction, and slowly but surely, of consolation also."[59] Senator Charles Sumner took a stroll through the new cemetery in Cambridge and announced that "nature had done as much for Mount Auburn as man has done for Père-la-Chaise."[60] As it turned out, Mount Auburn would gain its fair share of bombastic funerary sculpture by mid-century, but in the early days Bostonians took great pains to distinguish their thickly forested city of the dead from what the author of Mount Auburn's first guidebook called "the great show-place of the gay and vain French capital." Père Lachaise had history, but in its dense classical grandeur it seemed too stupendous, too glib on the subject of death, too approving of human "progress" and dominance over the material world. What mattered, in America, was the chance to be humbled, to be immersed in "the depths of nature," to experience "this uncrowded quietude and primitive simplicity—this glistening turf,—these cool, sweet-winding avenues and paths—this green, fresh beauty of the woods."[61]

The most significant aspect of those curvaceous avenues and pathways was that they were "adapted to the natural inequalities of the surface."[62] (Figure 4.) Both the designers and the users of the cemetery repeated this observation again and again, emphasizing the way in which horticulture as a form of high art was meant not to mark the wild land with a new vision but to enhance the land's self-expression. Nature, as Bigelow might put it, was encouraged to take its course. And nature's inclination, through all its variety of forms, was toward "beautiful repose"—an attitude to which we might aspire. Just as the cemetery was adapted to Sweet Auburn's local topography, so should our works, our buildings, our culture, take account of our native ecology, so should American ambition be checked by American conditions: "we may well gain a lesson from nature amid such scenes of tranquil beauty,

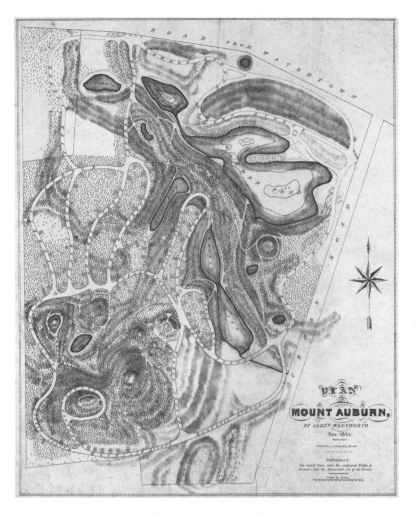

Figure 4. Alexander Wadsworth, *Plan of Mount Auburn*, 1831.

and learn to conform our lives to the order of her works, in view both of the present and the future."[63]

Nature can always be interpreted in multifarious ways, but in the specific context of Mount Auburn, following nature's laws meant, in part, not thinking of lives as narratives of linear progress. There would be detours, and the detours might be worth savoring. There were cycles to consider. Cycles and circles remind us of our common humanity, our common mortality: we are all subject to the revolutions of the spheres, the alternation of day and night, the turning of the seasons.[64] But too many

Americans had moved to the city and started living in straight lines, at right angles to each other; collisions were becoming more common and more inflammatory. In the previous two decades, since the institution of New York's infamous Commissioners Plan of 1811, the grid had become the defining spatial feature of American life.[65] It was designed explicitly to enshrine commerce as the nation's core cultural value, and it quickly became the template not only for urban growth in the east but for the laying out of towns along the frontier. The grid was both the symbol and the instrument of expansion, speculation, efficiency, economy, uniformity, convenience, rationality, progress. Twice reduced to ashes by the British, New York would now rise up again to map the American dream of individual success.[66] Cities would be conceived as places where traffic could flow freely and properties could be exchanged easily, rather than as living spaces for groups of human beings. The commissioners made no provision for public health or recreation—or topography. Already, since the 1780s, federal surveyors in the west (meaning Ohio) had been treating landforms as abstractions, running their lines indiscriminately over forests, fields, rivers, mountains, swamps.[67] But it was only with the development of the urban grid that this denial of nature came home to Americans in their everyday lives (especially as they took their wagons up and down hills without the benefit of switchbacks).

Mount Auburn's design, then, posed a series of challenges not only to the direction of America's development but to the nation's very sense of directedness. Anticipating the kind of social and environmental critique honed by Thoreau in the 1840s and 50s, the cemetery's founders seemed worried about their compatriots' self-condemnation to lives of unquestioned haste and accumulation. Where was everybody going in such a rush? Did they expect to outrun death? Why not pause—slow down—turn back to nature's cyclical rhythms? By 1843, as one of the most popular guidebooks noted, Mount Auburn had expanded to 110 acres, with 30 miles of trails, "so curved and winding in their course, as to make it difficult for a stranger to keep the even tenor of his way and thread the mazy labyrinth with a mind serene. . . . The grounds are mostly overshadowed by foliage of large forest trees, the whole combining to affiliate the spot, as a suitable place for the living to visit and there ponder on the ever changing state of man's mortality."[68] Mount Auburn's repose was decidedly unsettling, with a wildness valued both for its humane resonance and peacefulness and for its uncanny, beyond-human potency. The cemetery's founders, rather than attempting to commodify and incorporate the natural world, hoped to get lost in it.

William Cullen Bryant, who in the 1840s would be the first to propose a Central Park for New York City, one big enough to get lost in,[69] grew up in Massachusetts and by the 1820s had become a great inspiration to the horticulturists of Boston. He published his first nature poem in 1817 and called it "Thanatopsis"—a meditation on death. It is not an easy poem. Nor is "An Indian at the Burial-Place of His Fathers" (1824), nor "The Murdered Traveler" (1825), nor "Hymn to Death" (1825), nor "The Two Graves" (1826).[70] Again and again, Bryant went to nature seeking solace; sometimes he found it, and waxed romantic on the nourishing power of the earth, and the "still voice" of the "venerable woods," and his sense of solidarity with the departed. At other times, he found only a darker repose, marked by the senselessness of mortality, the wastage of the land that accompanied the conquest of the Indians, the loss of sacred traditions in the rush to seize opportunities: "Their kindred were far, and their children dead,/When the funeral-prayer was coldly said." Bryant was profoundly moved by the poetry of Wordsworth at an early age, but in his own works he dwelt not on Romantic ruins, but on the ambivalent scenes of New World settlement. He wrote poems addressed to forest springs that had witnessed "the Indian warrior . . . smitten with his death-wound," to deep fountains "whose sweet waters run/Crimson with blood," whose "cool murmur" is drowned out by "the crash of trees" and the "shouts of men who fired/The brushwood, or who tore the earth with plows"—the pioneers and entrepreneurs who continuously "Seek out strange arts to wither and deform/The pleasant landscape which thou makest green."[71]

Washington Irving, too, was influenced by the Old Country in his embrace of "rural repose"[72] and his many writings on death and nature. In his extremely popular *Sketch Book* (1819–20), he tarried in the country churchyards of England, attended rural funerals, admired the "touching and ennobling graces" of burial grounds dominated by natural features, and generally raved about the "rich vein of melancholy" that ran through British culture. But it is too simple to say that he was merely nostalgic for some eighteenth-century rural ideal that he hoped would be sustained in the United States. It seems to me he was after something wilder, more complicated, when, for instance, he quoted the seventeenth-century diarist John Evelyn to suggest the urgency of placing American burial in the context of a naturalistic horticulture, celebrating plants as "natural hieroglyphics of our fugitive, umbratile, anxious, and transitory life." And the critique of American culture implied in Irving's embrace of unsettling landscapes often had a sharp edge to it. His hope for every rural cemetery in his home country, once he saw that the Mount Auburn model had caught on, was that it might become "a beautiful and umbrageous neighborhood sacred from the anti-poetical and all-leveling axe." Again, capitalists leveled nature, ignored topography, but Irving hoped we would inhabit spaces whose very shape would keep us mindful of the ultimate leveler: "the equality of the grave . . . brings down the oppressor to a level with the oppressed."[73] Of course, a consciousness of death could go only so far in any real struggle against economic or social oppression, but Irving did see the tradition of rural melancholy in England as something that could be creatively combined with the wilder landforms of America, with the "grandeur and solemnity in our spacious forests," to construct both a spatial and a cultural check against the excesses of speculators and developers.[74] Ultimately, he drew on European experiences to help him understand the impact of industrialization and urbanization on society and nature in America—which perhaps explains why, in 1825, he published a seventy-eight-page introduction to the collected works of Oliver Goldsmith.[75]

———————

I have been to Mount Auburn on many occasions, and each time I have gotten lost. Admittedly, I don't try very hard to stay oriented. When I'm with my kids, the one important thing is eventually to find the tower, with its spiral staircase and panoramic view. But even with antsy toddlers, the experience of getting lost in Mount Auburn is almost magically pleasant, simultaneously relaxing and stimulating. Well before I knew any of the cemetery's history, I found its chastening effect somehow uplifting. Various friends have frowned on my habit of taking my children to play in cemeteries, but our family has spent long, enchanted hours observing turtles and frogs, strolling in and out of light and shadow, considering the cycles of death and birth, deciphering engraved tributes, pondering both biological and cultural diversity. Are there Jews buried at Mount Auburn? And African Americans? Yes: from the start, the cemetery has been open to everyone.[76]

I have always balked at religion's exclusionary tendencies, but if Mount Auburn is a decidedly sacred and spiritual place, its Christian overtones do not strike a sectarian note. It was founded, after all, at precisely the moment when Massachusetts was, at last, officially disestablishing the Congregational Church. Unitarians, in particular, having gained a foothold at Harvard's Divinity School as early as 1816, now carried considerable cultural weight in New England, and their vision of death and nature was almost pantheistic. The liberal thinkers who established Mount Auburn (mostly Unitarians) hoped that detaching burial from any specific church would actually make death rituals more spiritual, more broadly meaningful, and to this day any reverent person is welcome to blend with the cemetery landscape; both the terrain and the rhetoric of the memorials suggest not a rigid divide between the sacred and profane but an invitation to worship the continuity of life and death, nature and the human body, earth and the heavens. Some form of religion was almost universally embraced in 1830s America precisely because there was so much space for individualistic expressions of religiosity.[77]

My own relationship to religion is continually evolving, and I'm certain that my conversations with my kids will get much more complicated in future years, as they come to a deeper understanding of mortality and start to ask harder questions, and as I try to play father and historian and rabbi all at once. Though my wife Christine grew up as a Mormon, she left the Church during college, and we've decided to raise our three children, Sam, Abe, and Oscar, as Jews, in line with my background. I want them to know the truth about American anti-Semitism, not to mention racism and sexism and violence and environmental destruction. I also want them to develop some sense of hope, and the fortitude to struggle for social change. For now, though, we just wend our way along the paths, over the cemetery's hills, pausing at the ponds and lawns, never encountering a straight line. The landscape feels well maintained, but not manicured: we are not at Versailles. As one extoller of Mount Auburn's charms put it in 1861, the design of the cemetery has always emphasized "the spontaneous wildings of nature, rather than the careful products of art and cultivation."[78] Yet some kind of design has always been evident, unifying the landscape, even while the individual styles of all the different plots multiply and diversify the impressions one receives while walking the grounds. Rural cemeteries make space for both solidarity and self-expression.

Each visit to Mount Auburn spawns new connections; the kids keep raising different issues. They might touch the spiky needles on Spruce Knoll, or sit down under the cascading leaves of a weeping willow, or notice that lilac bushes can be many different shades of purple or pink. They might wonder how thick the ice is on Halcyon Lake, and how the lake got made in the first place, and why the robins seem to have gone away for the season. They might ask if my parents, who still live nearby, will be buried here. They might try to pry open one of the gothic doors of Bigelow Chapel, or have a staring contest with the Sphinx, or point at the broken chains sculpted into the base of a monument to a former slave. The historian David Schuyler has justly called rural cemeteries "didactic landscapes"; certainly, at Mount Auburn, I find myself wanting to teach and preach.[79] But a carefully designed cemetery speaks in a whisper, not a shout. It's easy to drop the lessons and just play for a while, lose oneself in immediate experience. When the kids are older, maybe I'll explain to them how Jacob Bigelow designed the African Sphinx as a Civil War memorial, to signify the destruction of African American slavery and celebrate the nation's ultimate "repose, strength, beauty, and duration" after its greatest trial—and that the twin emblems on the sculpture are the Egyptian lotus and the American water-lily, plants native to different continents but both in the genus *Nymphaea*.[80] Meanwhile, we wander around, and climb trees, and spy canoes on the Charles River, and sometimes roll down hills until we come to our angle of repose.

Mount Auburn's shape has changed continuously. You can still tramp along most of the original paths and avenues, but now dozens more fill the cemetery's 175 acres, almost all named for flowers and trees, both native and exotic. When the landscape seemed to get too overgrown in the late nineteenth century, the trustees cleared space and planted lawns. In the 1840s and 50s a craze developed for elaborately sculpted monuments and cast-iron fencing, and then came a craze to simplify, to combat the growing sense of enclosure, privatization, division, and distinction. Dutch elm disease devastated the cemetery's central canopy in the twentieth century, but a reforestation campaign in the 1990s brought back some of the feel that Mount Auburn seems to have had in its very first decade.[81]

Sadly, the Horticultural Society's experimental garden, despite producing some beautiful Rose Demi Long radishes, exhibited triumphantly in June of 1833 as the first food grown at a cemetery, lasted only a few years.[82] The horticulturists wanted to see which plant varieties and hybrids would thrive in the New England soil and climate, and hoped that Mount Auburn might ultimately become "an Institution for the education of scientific and practical gardeners."[83] But very few of the people who bought plots in the new cemetery shared those goals. In 1835, wishing to fold their funds into the creation of a picturesque landscape rather than the cultivation of radishes, several of the proprietors banded together to negotiate a separation from the Horticultural Society, establish sole ownership of the property, and found their own private nonprofit organization to run the cemetery. For the next 140 years, the trustees of Mount Auburn had to pay the Horticultural Society a substantial annuity, but the cemetery's consistent success in attracting customers (people were dying to get in, as the old saying goes) kept both organizations flush with cash. Indeed, the proceeds from the cemetery helped the Horticultural Society to build three new headquarters between 1845 and 1901.[84]

Today, Mount Auburn boasts a number of ornamental gardens and greenhouses: it is clearly still a working landscape. But, as much as I love the old cemetery, I can't help but find it somehow impoverished for its lack of radishes. Dearborn had collected vegetable seeds from London and Bombay, apple and plum scions from Montreal;[85] the zeal he felt for his nurseries translated into a powerful, primordial evocation of the connection between death and food. The dead are perpetually hungry, according to countless cultural traditions; they must be propitiated with the offerings of living horticulturists, fruits, the juicier the better, preferably heart-shaped, and the color of blood—apples and plums, to be sure; also cherries and pomegranates.[86] Modern Americans, though, just as they have shied away from death, have also shied away from the hard labor of growing food. At best, even when we're immersed in a landscape like Mount Auburn, our sense of place consists not in any kind of cultivation of the ground but in fairly superficial aesthetic impressions; few Americans can claim a deep *cultural* investment in any locality. "For the first time in millennia," as Robert Pogue Harrison has put it, "most of us don't know where we will be buried." I certainly don't—though I have begun to ponder the question more regularly. Mount Auburn? Mount Repose? Meanwhile, "this indeterminacy . . . goes hand in hand with another indeterminacy that until recently would have been equally unthinkable for the majority. Most of us have no idea where the food we eat comes from."[87]

Imagine kids in New England picking apples in their local cemetery, lit up with fall colors. Imagine them in the 1830s, when they knew not just the six varieties available at twenty-first-century supermarkets, but hundreds of varieties—apples that tasted like pears, or oranges, or bananas, or strawberries. The Massachusetts horticulturists kept sumptuous lists of the fruit they produced, to be relished at their annual harvest festival: in 1832, if you were looking for apples, you might have tasted a Ribstone Pippin, or a Porter, Moody, Pomme Reine, Early Greening, Spitzenberg, Bell Flower, Doctor, Borroseau, Red Calville, Summer Pearmain, Blue Pearmain, Summer Gilliflower, Winter Gilliflower, or Hubbardston Nonsuch—among many others. (Some of these, now referred to as rare and antique varieties, can be found on October Saturdays at the Ithaca Farmers Market.) Or, back in the day, you could have sampled the grape varieties: Horatio, Hamburg, Black Hamburg, St. Peter's, White Sweet-Water, Shurtleff's Seedling, Red Chasselas, White Chasselas, Grisly Tokay, Black Cape, Miller's Burgundy, Frontignac, or Isabella. Or maybe you'd have sought out one of the famous pears grown by Enoch Bartlett.[88] (Figure 5.)

My own sympathies, admittedly, used to tend toward the crabby Thoreau, who generally thought of horticulturists as commodifiers and capitalists, and who shunned grid-like orchards in favor of the "irregularly planted" trees he encountered on his long walks, trees that might produce apples with "more racy and wild American flavors," strong enough to *"pierce* and *sting* and *permeate* us with their spirit."[89] I have always loved wilderness and wild apples. But the cultivated apple, too, like the cultivated landscape, can be a potent, compelling force. As Michael Pollan has been suggesting for the last couple of decades, in eloquent, meditative essays growing ever more urgent, Americans could start coming to grips with environmental crises by visiting fewer National Parks and supermarket chains and spending more time tending trees and plants in their local communities. In the same way that we deny mortality, we deny global warming, and drive over to the strip mall. Planting a garden is not going to halt climate change, but it might, in Pollan's words, "reduce your sense of dependence and dividedness."[90] As the founders of the Massachusetts Horticultural

Figure 5. *Yellow Belle-Fleur*, 1850,
lithograph.

Society seemed to realize, one of the great dangers of modernity was that urban wage workers could easily begin to feel confused and ineffectual, tangled in a vast web of commodities and machines and expertise. We benefit greatly from the industrial networks that place food on our table at the click of a button; we can also sense the costs of those networks, even without extensive knowledge of ecology. Growing food is one small way not only to lessen one's environmental impact and remind oneself of the gifts of nature but also to regain a basic sense of agency. And: home-grown tomatoes can permeate you with their flavor.

I will never have Pollan's conviction or credibility on these issues, though, because I am not actually a gardener. I've tried to be. Certainly, it would not be unreasonable to expect my decidedly green spirit to be accompanied by a green thumb. But I always find myself itching to stretch my limbs, to join Thoreau on his rambles, to taste "The Saunterer's Apple": I have "a walker's appetite and imagination."[91] When my kids grew fond of "The Garden Song" ("Inch by inch, row by row, gonna make this garden grow"), I insisted on teaching them the alternative verse ("Sunburned face, skinned-up knees, my garden's choked with zuc-chi-nis").[92] I hate zucchinis; they never fail to give me a stomachache. Though I like the idea of digging in the dirt, I don't like bending to the task. I even have chronic back pain.

In graduate school, bending my will to the gods of academic research, I thought my sense of discipline might benefit from some horticultural training, and Christine was enthusiastic about the experiment, so we secured a plot in a nearby community garden and set to work. And then summer came. We went to see my family. We went to see her family. We went to the beach. We went camping. Our plot started to look thirsty, scraggly, bedraggled—deathly. So the garden coordinators, petty dictators that they were, eventually planted the tall, glowing Stake of Shame in our weedy patch. The stake's tip—believe it or not—was painted a bright scarlet. Christine, in characteristic fashion, laughed off our failure and now grows vegetables, herbs, and sunflowers; I have never gardened again.

Reading the records of the Massachusetts Horticultural Society over the past few years, though, I've started to get reinspired. I am too much of a suburban Jew, too much of a happily coddled intellectual, to claim that the drudgery of working the land will confer a sense of uplift, unless you are already inclined toward field labor. But I find myself wondering, these days, if we could handle a pear tree in our yard. We've settled down; we travel much less frequently. Often, in summer, my wife's family members come to Ithaca to visit us, and our only trip is to see my relatives in Massachusetts, to swim in the ocean and wander through Mount Auburn. I'm jealous of the horticulturists' joy, the clear satisfaction they took in their work, the way they engaged so deeply with the forces of nature and then paused at length to savor the seasoning imparted by the New England seasons.[93] Though I realize that I may be romanticizing these "cultivating gentlemen," as one historian has called them, and though I am aware of the Boston Brahmins' great privilege, conferred by their sex, their race, and their class, and though I know that horticulturists held a diverse range of beliefs about nature and that some focused primarily on "improving" and "enriching" their nation's inadequate wild plants—still, I remain convinced that many of them were, in a sense, social ecologists and cultural critics.[94] They understood how crucial it was, in a capitalist society, to maintain land in a public trust, and to form associations "whose pursuits are pleasant, and lead to results, not, like many others, founded on *selfishness*, but conferring *essential benefits* on the whole human race."[95] They made a point of making toasts, and puns, of drinking and laughing late into the night: they realized the importance of simple pleasures in cultivating a sense of continuity in the face of death. The taste of an apple can make you feel as though you have truly lived: perhaps you can taste the timelessness of sunshine, the steadfastness of nature's cycles. Perhaps that simple taste is something humans will treasure until the end of their days. Perhaps that simple taste is all we need to experience paradise on earth.[96] One early Massachusetts horticulturist, toasting "the Fruits of this day's Exhibition," suggested that "if the forbidden Fruit was equal to this, Madam Eve would scarcely need an

apology for yielding to the temptation which it presented."[97] Another member of
the Horticultural Society, similarly drawn to the theme of the ideal garden, toasted
"Eden—The first abode of the living," and "Mount Auburn, the last resting place
of the dead."[98]

––––––––––––––

One of my favorite walks in Mount Auburn is along Indian Ridge Path, which follows
an esker running through the northeast section of the cemetery and provides both a
sense of immersion in the woods and several sweeping views. Thanks to the geological
work of the Harvard scientist Louis Agassiz, who proposed his theory of the ice age a
few years after Mount Auburn was established, a modern observer can envision Indian
Ridge as the gravelly deposit of a glacier retreating through a valley.[99] But it was the
deliberations of Mount Auburn's founders that have allowed us to understand more of
this landscape's human history. In October of 1831, Dearborn and Bigelow were collaborating with the surveyor Alexander Wadsworth—who in a few years would get the
commission to expand Boston Common into the Boston Public Garden—in laying
out and naming the first avenues and pathways in the cemetery. Given their shared
desire to make all the trails "conform to the natural face of the ground,"[100] it was inevitable that the two horticulturists would direct walkers to the top of the esker. But
the name "Indian Ridge Path" seems to have been a compromise: while Bigelow
expressed his preference for "Indian Ridge," Dearborn insisted, in a letter back to Bigelow, that *"Indian Path* is more emphatic than Ridge. They peculiarly appropriate that
name to their lines of inter-communication; they actually have no other routes than
*paths*. It is a term known all over the U.S, as expressed by *Indian*, and I have no doubt
that there was a real *Indian Path* on the ridge. They sought out all such places for passing across the country."[101]

Maybe Bigelow and Dearborn were just getting tired of collaborating; maybe each
was looking for ways to show the other up. But it is striking, first, that they both wanted
to use the term "Indian" when virtually every other trail was named for flora,[102] and
then that Dearborn wanted so adamantly to preserve the integrity of the phrase "Indian
Path." What was at stake? It's only one walkway, but it leads definitively away from
Europe, away from Père Lachaise and English gardens, and into American woodlands.

When the famous Salem horticulturist (and cousin to Nathaniel Hawthorne) Robert Manning, Jr., set out in the late 1870s to write the first history of the Massachusetts
Horticultural Society, he started not with Henry A. S. Dearborn in 1829 but with
seventeenth-century Indians. "The agriculture of the aborigines," he noted, with
reference to various primary sources, ". . . would appear to be more careful than has

generally been supposed."[103] Indeed! When I first picked up Manning's book, I had no suspicion that Indians would even make an appearance in it. If you'd told me in advance that Manning discussed them, my assumption would have been that, as an American writing at the height of the Indian Wars out west, he probably would have depicted Native Americans as wandering hunter-gatherers, savage foils to the highly civilized planters and growers who were surely the heroes of his narrative. Well, my assumption—though based on a familiarity with some relevant works of scholarship—would have been wrong. Manning did sometimes call them "savages"—but they were savages who used burning as a technique of landscape gardening, so that "the trees grew here and there, as in parks." They were savages who taught the Pilgrims how to use manure and other natural fertilizers; who "possessed varieties [of corn] adapted to the warmer or colder parts of the country," so that they had success with vast grain fields even in the remote corners of Maine; who were so knowledgeable about nature's cycles, and so expert at interpreting natural signals, that their "practice of planting corn when the leaves of the white oak were as large as a mouse's ear has come down to our own time."[104]

One of the most remarkable passages in Manning's book is actually a lamentation, expressing nostalgic amazement at the extensive plantings of the Six Nations of the Iroquois Confederacy, especially in the Finger Lakes region just above Ithaca, New York—plantings ruthlessly set to flame during the post-Revolutionary campaign of General John Sullivan, who did not have landscape gardening in mind when he ordered the land to be burned. He and the other generals deployed to the region by George Washington were intent on clearing space where the soldiers of the Revolutionary army could settle down: this would become the famous grid of the Military Tract, subdivided into parcels of soil that served as pensions. Mustered near what has become the city of Elmira, the American battalion of several thousand enthusiastic men routed about 750 Iroquois and Loyalists in the late summer—near harvest time—of 1779. Some passed through Ithaca, but the main body of the army marched straight up the eastern shore of Seneca Lake, toward Kanadesaga (now Geneva), where the British had built a fort under the auspices of the Seneca Indians (even though two of the other Iroquois tribes had joined the Americans).[105] According to Manning, the Iroquois living near the lake grew "fine gardens of beans, pease, turnips, cabbages, melons, carrots, parsnips, and potatoes. At one village of the Indians the corn fields comprised two hundred acres. The apple and peach orchards were very extensive: at one village an orchard of fifteen hundred fruit trees was destroyed, and, at another, fifteen hundred peach trees alone."[106]

Some of the best evidence we have of these horticultural accomplishments is the writings of Sullivan's soldiers, one of whom surveyed the gardens surrounding him and decided that the whole region was "a veritable Eden."[107] Another of Sullivan's chosen men was the future father of the Massachusetts horticulturist Henry A. S. Dearborn—also a general named Henry. Again and again, the senior Dearborn described coming upon land that was "exceeding fine" and then methodically destroying its productions. At one settlement "on an excellent Intervale near a small lake," he and his men "found a large quantity of corn, beans, squashes, potatoes, water Mellons, cucumbers &c &c." On the fifth of September, he arrived at "an old Indian town Call'd Candaia or apple Town—where there is a very old orchard of 60 trees, & many other fruit trees.—the Town consists of 15 or 20 houses very beautifully situated near the Lake. In the Town are 3 Sepulchers which are very Indian fine, where I suppose some of their chief[s] are deposited."[108]

General Henry Dearborn the elder seems to have felt perfectly justified in burning the Indians' fields and gardens and trampling their graves. It was a military strategy used by the Indians themselves, and in the Revolutionary era Americans were desperate to establish spaces in their brand-new nation where they could be free from the threat of attack. It was too risky to live near the natives, no matter how unsavage their habits. Indians had to be pushed northward and westward.

By the time the younger Dearborn's generation had come into adulthood, though, Americans could afford to think of Indians more romantically, nostalgically, sentimentally. The country had more space now, and a stronger sense of security. Certainly, many people of European descent still regarded Natives with a great deal of viciousness and racism. And, as many scholars have emphasized, even those who identified themselves as "friends" of the "noble savages" mostly talked about them in wistful terms and thus just reinforced the cultural understanding that Indians would gradually, inevitably, fade from view. Yet Natives did not simply vanish, and, as the revisionist scholar Laura Mielke has recently argued, some white Americans in the antebellum period made genuine gestures toward mediation, tried to establish "the promise (however fleeting) of a sustained relationship between Natives and non-Natives."[109] Ironically, given the terrible fact of Indian dispossession, I think some of the most important common ground between the two groups had to do, literally, with common ground—with the sacralization of land, with the establishment of kinship with the earth in specific, garden-like places. "I have seen memorable monuments to Crassus and to Caesar," wrote Chateaubriand, his words quoted in a popular 1843 book called *Rural Cemeteries of America*, "but I prefer the airy tombs of the Indians, those mausoleums of flowers and verdure refreshed by the morning dew, embalmed and fanned by the breeze, and over which waves the same branch where the blackbird builds his nest, and utters forth his plaintive melody."[110]

Mount Auburn was never going to be a sanctuary for Native Americans: it could not block Andrew Jackson's new Removal policy, which was confirmed just a few months before the establishment of the cemetery.[111] But the rural cemeteries sprouting up all over the nation did have significant symbolic value in the context of the Removal era, because they were explicitly modeled—in part—on the burial practices of Indians. Seemingly convinced that Boston Brahmins like Dearborn and Bigelow must have been focused exclusively on European precedents, scholars have offered exhaustive explanations of Mount Auburn's debt to the elite English landscape tradition without considering its echoing of the kinds of Native "sepulchers" that Dearborn the elder found in upstate New York in 1779. It is certainly true that Europe held a great deal of cultural sway in antebellum America, but we seem to have forgotten, as the historian Steven Conn recently commented, that "for citizens of the United States in the late eighteenth and early nineteenth centuries, Indians were everywhere."[112] The Seneca were routed from the Finger Lakes by Sullivan's men—but they didn't go far, and every year until the middle of the nineteenth century a band of them came back to their old capital at Kanadesaga specifically to visit a sacred burial mound.[113] The local farmers and villagers consistently kept their promise to the Indians to protect and maintain the site, and the elegant, unassuming mound was just one of many such places to attract widespread admiration, though some of them, of course, had not been as carefully guarded as the Senecas'. (Figure 6.)

In 1840, at the founding of Harmony Grove Cemetery in Salem, Massachusetts, one of the speakers noted that the "pilgrim fathers of Plymouth" had referred to a now long-forgotten "rural cemetery of the Indians, which might well be imitated by many of their civilized successors."[114] And Joseph Story himself, consecrating Mount Auburn, insisted that his audience acknowledge the grief of Natives and the compelling grace of their traditions:[115]

> To many, nay, to most of the heathen, the burying-place was the end of all things. They indulged no hope, at least, no solid hope, of any future intercourse or re-union with their friends. . . . Yet, when the first tumults of anguish were passed, they visited the spot, and strewed flowers, and garlands, and crowns around it, to assuage their grief, and nourish their piety. They delighted to make it the abode of the varying beauties of Nature; to give it attractions, which should invite the busy and the thoughtful; and yet, at the same time, afford ample scope for the secret indulgence of sorrow.
>
> Why should not Christians imitate such examples?

Figure 6. The Kanadesaga monument, Geneva, NY, 2010.

It is easy to see Story's condescension here, and perhaps even his racism, and to note his use of the past tense—as if all the "heathen" were already gone—and to wonder if his relationship to Indians was merely appropriative.[116] But it is also easy to look up Justice Story's documented opinions of Indian Removal. Story was on the Supreme Court, after all, and so he had to rule in the infamous case of *Cherokee Nation v. Georgia*, decided on March 18, 1831. His was one of the two dissenting voices. The majority opinion, which favored President Jackson's Removal policy, left Story despairing for the Cherokee "and all their race. . . . I feel, as an American, disgraced by our gross violation of the public faith towards them." A year later, his resentment of Jackson deepening, he expressed his sense that the nation had undermined its claim to democratic republicanism, had forever blackened its reputation, had put itself in the same category as such greedy, ruthless empires as Spain: "I blush for my country, when I perceive that such legislation, destructive of all faith and honor towards the Indians, is suffered to pass with the silent approbation of the present Government of the United States."[117]

Story's commitment to follow Indian practices at Mount Auburn, then, was couched in a hope that the cemetery's landscape would be chastening on a number of different levels. It was designed not to expiate cultural guilt but to spur more humane attitudes. And, as it turned out, many of the most thoughtful visitors to the cemetery found in it reminders of both Native American honor and Euro-American dishonor. In 1843, the poet Isaac McLellan, already the author of an epic called *The Fall of the Indian*, published his tribute to Mount Auburn and emphasized that the new cemetery derived its power from its adherence to the Native tradition of bringing mourners closer to God, a tradition all the more poignant now that Natives were often living at a remove from their most sacred burial sites:[118]

> E'en the rude Indians build the cairn,
> The swelling mound and barrow heap;
> And love, poor exiles of the land,
> By their ancestral graves to weep. . . .
>
> Sweet Auburn! 'mid thy soothing shades
> And verdurous lanes, how dear to walk. . . .
> How dear to climb thy breezy height,
> And view the lovely landscape o'er. . . .
>
> To the rapt soul that sacred gloom
> Sheds mystic influence on the heart;
> And turfy mound and marble tomb
> The tenderest teachings may impart.

————————

Two years later, in 1845, the newspaperman John L. O'Sullivan, arguing in favor of the annexation of Texas, famously coined the phrase "Manifest Destiny," and many Americans quickly embraced a national identity based on spatial expansion, with or without honor.[119] But the cemeterians of this period, most of whom resisted expansionism, tried to keep people's attention focused on time rather than space—on history, contingency, and commemoration.[120] Picking up on the tendency of the Romantic poets in Europe to dwell on images of mist-enshrouded ruins, which symbolized a solid cultural antiquity but also warned against the hubris of imperial ambition, supporters of the rural cemetery movement took a keen interest in the excavation of America's own ruined structures—massive earthworks, often called Indian Mounds, just being discovered on the Midwestern frontier.[121] These ancient monuments were often presumed to be grave markers, and, as one excavator put it, "their origin must be sought for among the Antideluvians."[122] Whether or not Justice Story's colleagues shared his belief in the worthiness and sovereignty of Indian nations, they clearly wanted to define America less as a nascent empire being carved out of the wilderness and more as a land with its own ancestry and ancient cultural traditions. And Henry A. S. Dearborn, as it happened, was not the only Boston horticulturist with a father who had direct experience of indigenous burial mounds.

In the fall of 1832, the main speaker at the Massachusetts Horticultural Society's annual harvest festival, which in this case also marked Mount Auburn's first anniversary, was a doctor and entomologist named Thaddeus William Harris. Recently appointed as the head librarian of Harvard College, a job that had been held briefly by his father—also called Thaddeus Harris (though his middle name was Mason)—he offered a discourse informed by a wealth of knowledge, especially in his academic specialty. But what really came through was his appreciation—something else he shared with his father—for all aspects of the plant and animal kingdoms and for expressions of culture that reflected humanity's attachment to nature. "To insects," he explained, "we are indebted for many valuable drugs employed in medicine and the arts, and to them also for materials for clothing, unrivalled in richness and durability."[123]

The elder Thaddeus Harris, a Unitarian minister still alive at the time of his son's oration, was well known in New England as the author of a book published in 1805 called *The Journal of a Tour into the Territory Northwest of the Alleghany Mountains.*[124] It is unsurprising that Harris, seeking relief from a long "wasting sickness," decided to travel to the old Northwest for a "change of climate": the Ohio River valley had been celebrated as a fertile, welcoming land ever since 1786, when a group of New Englanders, in Harris's immediate circle of acquaintances, had established a speculative real estate venture called the Ohio Company. What is remarkable about Harris's book is that, while it does occasionally pause to admire "rising settlements" and "the industry and art of man" and "the buzz of employment," it most often wallows in the sublimity of wilderness. Harris's dedication of his journal to his friend Rufus Putnam, surveyor general of the United States and founder of the Ohio Company, would seem to indicate a commitment to expansionist progress.[125] But instead of emphasizing Putnam's success at cutting up the wild, wooded land into cleared, marketable rectangles, Harris pointedly "remarked, with regret and indignation, the wanton destruction of these noble forests."[126]

Harris was not a mere Romantic, though; he did not imagine that settlement would simply stop, nor did he discount the possibility of settling on the land in a more respectful, adaptive mode, one attuned to aesthetic as well as pragmatic concerns. He was especially impressed by the Indians' adaptations to nature's contours and by their deep knowledge of their surroundings. With what we might think of now as an inclination toward ethnobotany, Harris suggested what white settlers might learn from the Natives: "We garnished our bouquet to day with the beautiful white flowers of the Blood root, (Sanguinaria Canadensis) called by the Indians 'Puccoon.' . . . The root yields a bright red tincture, with which the Indians used to paint themselves, and to color some of their manufactures, particularly their cane baskets.—The root possesses emetic qualities.—Transplanted into our gardens, this would be admired as an ornamental flower, while the roots would furnish artists with a brilliant paint or dye, and perhaps be adopted into the Materia Medica as a valuable drug."[127] And, ultimately, Harris sought to uphold a compromise between pastoral and sublime landscapes, a capturing of nature's "varied prospect," a hybridization of bright, thriving orchards and the "sequestered glooms" of "umbrageous forests." His ideal seemed to express itself one day in "the contrast, between the verdant meads and fertile arable ground of this secluded spot, and the rugged mountains and frowning precipices by which it is environed," yielding "a mixture of romantic wildness and cultivated beauty which is really delightful."[128]

The climax of Harris's narrative, though, is not achieved until he starts to come upon the famous antiquities of the Ohio valley: "The vast mounds and walls of earth, discovered in various parts of this western region, have excited the astonishment of all who have seen or heard of them." Having devoted dozens of passages to a valuation of nature's wondrous features over and above the creations of his fellow Americans, who sometimes seemed to chart a path of desolation across the wilderness, Harris now pointed out that even the most admirable accomplishments of the modern era seemed like paltry scratchings in the dirt compared to, say, "the antient monuments about Grave Creek," in what is now Moundsville, West Virginia. Pondering "the multitude of workmen, the length of time, and the expense, requisite to form such a stupendous mound," not to mention "the spirit of ambition which suggested the idea of this monument, of great but simple magnificence," Harris felt that the only proper response for the pioneers of his day was a deep sense of humility. On a smaller scale, he was also struck by the constant "proofs of art and design" that he saw in the earthworks, by the sophistication with which these ancient peoples had conformed their structures to natural patterns and rhythms: "The places called GRAVES, are small mounds of earth, from some of which human bones have been taken. In one were found the bones, in their natural position, of a man buried nearly east and west, with a quantity of isinglass [mica] on his breast."[129] Whatever his readers might have thought of present-day Indians, and whether or not tribes like the Miami were descended from the Mound Builders, Harris made a point of demonstrating that America had once been inhabited by people who, through close, extended observation of the shifting seasons, had built sacred burial structures aligned to the path of the sun.[130]

———————

By the time Thaddeus Mason Harris's son participated in the founding of Mount Auburn, the mystery of the Mound Builders had captivated men of learning all along the eastern seaboard. Numerous works had been published about the gigantic tumuli, the conical and pyramidal mounds, the vast earthworks in the shape of circles, squares, and octagons, the effigy mounds seeming to represent birds, snakes, and bears—including several books and pamphlets by Benjamin Smith Barton, the Philadelphia doctor and natural historian who had served as Jacob Bigelow's mentor.[131] In 1812, another group of enterprising Bostonians had formed the American Antiquarian Society, specifically in order to study the earthworks on the Ohio frontier. Eight years later, the society published a long essay by Caleb Atwater confirming and expanding Harris's observations, expressing awe at the "many hundreds of mounds in this country . . . situated on the highest hills, surrounded by the most fertile soils." (Figure 7.)

Figure 7. Charles Sullivan, *Great Mound at Marietta, Ohio*, 1848, lithograph.

Atwater also cited another authority, approvingly, who argued that these kinds of mounds "present the simplest and sublimest monuments, which any generation could raise over the bodies of their progenitors."[132] The founders of Mount Auburn, in creating a lofty place of repose that was aligned with wild nature and designed to honor the very idea of ancestry, also seem to have been honoring their fathers' and teachers' profound respect for the most ancient Americans to have left traces of a culture. As one writer put it in 1831, responding to Dearborn's first published report about the new cemetery, "the moss-grown stone outlasts the most durable habitations of our fathers." The hope was that Mount Auburn, a sacred enclave protected from the onrush of progress and development, would, like the Mounds of Ohio, "resist the waste of time."[133]

Of course, not all of the Mounds were burial sites, and debates raged over who the Mound Builders might have been—Asians? Welshmen? Toltecs? The lost tribe of Israel? Atlanteans?—and what relationship they might have had to present-day Indians. For several decades, the majority opinion was that they were a separate race that had been completely wiped out, perhaps in a flood, because they were clearly so much more sophisticated than nineteenth-century tribes. It suited most white Americans to imagine an ancient, indigenous group whose civilized accomplishments added a sheen of monumentality to the New World but who did not force a reconsideration of Indians—those savages who needed to be swept aside to accommodate the far superior settlers from Europe.[134] Yet it also occurred to some observers that the mighty Mound Builders could have "degenerated" into nineteenth-century Indians, and this theory appealed especially to social critics like the cemeterians who emphasized the ultimate decay of all things and worried that white American civilization, given its imperial ambitions, might be destined for a particularly precipitous fall. In the same volume that contained Caleb Atwater's study of the Ohio earthworks, the founders of the American Antiquarian Society observed that "the decline as well as the rise of nations is in the course of nature" and that, at some point, "a decline may be the state of our country."[135] Many writers and artists in the 1820s and 30s actually compared the United States to Rome in quite explicit and ominous terms, citing the slippery slope from republicanism to imperialism: Thomas Cole's famous series of paintings, completed in 1836 and titled *The Course of Empire*, concluded with an image of *Desolation*.[136] (Figure 8.)

Probably the most important thing about the Mounds, though, was that they could be invoked in the creation of a new national culture, as embodied by Mount Auburn Cemetery. Americans did not simply have to imitate Europe any longer, nor rely solely on the distinctive features of the "virgin" American wilderness. "Foreign travelers com-

Figure 8. Thomas Cole, *The Course of Empire: Desolation*, 1836, oil on canvas.

plain," wrote the antiquarian Josiah Priest in 1833, "that America presents nothing like *ruins* within her boundaries. . . . But what are mouldering castles, falling turrets, or crumbling abbeys, in comparison with those ancient and artificial aboriginal hills, which have outlived generations, and even all tradition?"[137] One of the essays in a book called *Mount Auburn: Its Scenes, Its Beauties, and Its Lessons* drew a line directly from the ancient tumuli to the new cemetery, suggesting that Mount Auburn's key contribution lay in its humility, which, like that of the Mounds, derived from its paradoxical status as an enduring testament to impermanence: "America is rich in its stores of antique knowledge; and he who would feel most deeply the vanity of human ambition and human greatness, needs only to dwell here upon the lessons which it teaches. . . . The vast territory stretching from Maine to Florida, from the Atlantic to the Rocky Mountains, contains in itself wonders of nature and wonders of art which no other country possesses; and while we learn to admire what is worthy of admiration in other lands, let us also study and venerate the wonders of our own country."[138]

Even if the nation was headed down the path of greed, mechanization, decadence, inequality, and resentment, even if these were the Last Days, New Englanders felt sure that Mount Auburn would persist. One admirer, who climbed to the highest point in the cemetery just before the consecration ceremony, admitted to envisioning a punishing deluge that might sweep over all of Boston at any moment, a "gale of desolation" that would leave nothing in its wake—save Mount Auburn. "No city shall be eternal but the City of the Dead."[139] Just over a decade later, Nathaniel Hawthorne wrote a story called "The New Adam and Eve," about what might have happened if William Miller, founder of the Adventist religion, had been right that the world was scheduled to come to an end in 1843. Hawthorne imagined that "The Day of Doom has burst upon the globe, and swept away the whole race of men," but that humanity's "abodes" have been preserved, as the setting in which two newly created people, "with no knowledge of their predecessors, nor of the diseased circumstances that had become encrusted around them," could ponder the relationship between human beings and their environment. Ultimately, the story seems intended as a commentary on America's gradual abandonment of nature: "Art has become a second and stronger Nature; she is a step-mother, whose crafty tenderness has taught us to despise the bountiful and wholesome ministrations of our true parent." The new Adam and Eve, their "instincts and intuitions" leading them toward "the wisdom and simplicity" of nature, wander with disgust through the deserted streets of Boston, rejecting the "squareness and ugliness" of the banks, the courts, the churches, the stores, the hospitals, the prisons. They are hard pressed to find anything edible—the smell of the Parisian pasties and bowls of turtle soup that they find in a mansion on Beacon Street make them want to retch—until—of course—they stumble upon "a red-cheeked apple." And then they finally wend their way to "the cemetery of Mount Auburn," where, as "they tread along the winding paths," admiring both the wild vegetation and the elegantly carved monuments, they at last feel at home, and at peace. They seem strangely happy as they suddenly understand "that Time and the elements have an indefeasible claim upon their bodies."[140] At the end of the story, they settle themselves on the grass, calmly, in a posture of deep repose.

———————————

Many Americans came to see Mount Auburn as a new paradise. Their experiences of the cemetery, though, suggest a garden not of carelessness but of caring—not of gratification but of gratitude. It was a grounded, earthly Eden.[141] Within just a few years, Mount Auburn became perhaps the leading tourist attraction of the young republic, often mentioned in the same breath as Niagara Falls and George Washington's estate at Mount Vernon. It must have inspired a wide range of responses, the majority of which were never recorded. But what leaps out from the guidebooks—and the magazine articles, and poems, and speeches, and traveler's accounts—is an earnest engagement with Mount Auburn as a place, and an intense awareness of the way it wove together seemingly opposing elements: "It was surely fitting," said Alexander Everett, celebrating the cemetery's first anniversary, "that Art and Nature should combine their beauties, to grace a scene devoted to purposes so high and holy."[142] Rather than a naïve prelapsarian landscape, where labor was unnecessary and technology irrelevant, the cemetery provided its visitors with a space where wildness could be conscientiously cultivated.

Mount Auburn's spatial and moral juxtapositions made a powerful impact. The cemetery offered serenity but also excitement—a sense of seclusion in sheltered dells, but also the confusion of labyrinthine trails and the stimulation of broad views. It was a product of the new New England's liberal inclusiveness and the old New England's somber seriousness. It embodied the Whig party's critique of Andrew Jackson's arrogant bluster—about slavery, and expansion, and Indian Removal—but it also critiqued the mainstream Whig conception of commercial "improvement." It taught the ravishing beauty of autumnal decay, the Romantic pleasure of melancholy. It suggested that the fullness of life could be tasted only through a constant awareness of death. It offered the consolation of regeneration even as it reinforced the pain and anxiety of limitation. It was an asylum, a sanctuary, but not necessarily an evasion.

Visitors sometimes came to the cemetery not just to recuperate from modernity, but to rethink their role in it. "The rivalries of the world will here from the heart," said Justice Story; "the spirit of forgiveness will gather new impulses; the selfishness of avarice will be checked; the restlessness of ambition will be rebuked."[143] Lovers sauntered along the trails, and laborers visited from factories to soak up the cemetery's "deep and quiet beauty," as one working girl put it, and to "go back in imagination to our own homes"—the sweet rural villages they had deserted in order to join the city's labor force.[144] Both men and women spent their leisure time at Mount Auburn, seeing in the landscape a stereotypically male restraint balanced by a stereotypically female emotiveness. Mourners at family plots, meanwhile, wept over the graves of lost brothers and sisters, parents and children. The cemetery clearly cultivated a spectrum of emotions, and it was large enough to accommodate expressions of both joy and grief, but most people at Mount Auburn seem to have experienced a reverent, satisfying mixture of the two.[145]

People came by the tens of thousands, not just locals but also travelers from Europe and from all over the United States. Even in the cemetery's first two years, its trails were so frequently used that the trustees felt obliged "to prohibit the entrance of *persons on horseback altogether*"; apparently, those on foot felt that the hordes of riders were upsetting "the quiet and good order which ought to prevail in a place of burial."[146] Sundays were soon reserved for proprietors, the initial investors in Mount Auburn, to ensure their peaceful communion with nature and the dead. From the beginning, though, these restrictions, sparked by the cemetery's popularity, were balanced by the trustees' commitment to bolster that popularity, by promoting Mount Auburn's reputation as "in the truest and noblest sense a public institution" and by ensuring easy, open access, six days a week, from daybreak to dusk.[147] In 1834, a traveler from England noted that "parties of pleasure come hither from the city in great numbers every day. No less than six hundred visitors had been there on one day the preceding week."[148]

It was no coincidence that, in that same year, the first local omnibus service had started making regular runs to Mount Auburn from Harvard College, where Bostonians could get dropped off every hour by the Cambridge Stage Company.[149] By the end of the decade, the main road leading from Cambridge to Watertown had been renamed Mount Auburn Street, and the cemetery's first lavishly illustrated guidebook had been published: *The Picturesque Pocket Companion, and Visitor's Guide, through Mount Auburn.* Dozens of competing publications came out in the following years, some devoted exclusively to the cemetery, others covering all of Cambridge and Boston but claiming Mount Auburn as the number one attraction of the region, whether you were traveling by foot, carriage, bus, or railroad.[150] In 1849, Andrew Jackson Downing, the man who seems to have coined the term "landscape architecture," insisted that the rural cemetery concept "took the public mind by storm. Travelers made pilgrimages to the Athens of New England solely to see the realization of their long cherished dream of a resting place for the dead, at once sacred from profanation, dear to the memory, and captivating to the imagination." Downing claimed that "the road to Mount Auburn is now lined with coaches, continually carrying the inhabitants of Boston by thousands and tens of thousands." They came from mansions on Beacon Hill but also from apartments in Lowell, and from the new mills of Watertown and Waltham.[151]

Even by the late 1830s, it had become clear that Mount Auburn had started a movement. The editor of the *Picturesque Pocket Companion* told the public what the trustees already knew to be true: "Our Cemetery has become, within the few years of its existence, a model for all similar institutions in the United States. . . . At this moment, associations in several of our principal cities and towns are engaged in such undertakings. . . . Applications are continually made from these parties, for information relating to Mount Auburn."[152] The idea of a rural cemetery, though developed within a particular, local culture, hit a taproot of anxiety that was driving emotions across the entire nation. "We are a hard, practical people," asserted the same editor, "intensely absorbed in business . . . , educated and impelled in every way to undervalue and lose sight of what we might call the graces of civilization." America had been following the example of Manchester and Liverpool; the country could be saved only if it recaptured the spirit of Sweet Auburn. While most guidebook authors pander to their potential audience, the person who wrote the *Picturesque Pocket Companion* took pains to shake up his readers' assumptions, insisting that a truly civilized culture valued a kind of republican wildness: "Give me the grave-yards of the common people, and the poor; the expressions of a nature which deems itself unobserved; the . . . stones and sods, and trees, and chequered turf."[153]

---

This embrace of social unity, of a public spirit manifested in environmental terms, of wild nature as a tonic and a countervailing force against a hubristic Progress, was expressed by civic leaders again and again, in Philadelphia, Baltimore, Brooklyn, Rochester, Albany, Pittsburgh, Cincinnati, Providence, Louisville, Savannah, Charleston, Richmond, Buffalo, Detroit, St. Louis, Milwaukee, Atlanta, New Orleans, Memphis, and Cleveland—each of which consecrated a nonprofit rural cemetery between 1836 and 1853.[154] Of course, every city had its own locally significant motivating factors, and few shared the truly liberal spirit infused into Mount Auburn by its Unitarian founders. You would not have seen any African Americans, for instance, at the opening ceremony for Magnolia Cemetery in Charleston in November 1850. But you would have heard an extraordinary poem read by William Gilmore Simms called "The City of the Silent," in which Simms explained the importance of creating new landscapes in a rapidly urbanizing country—the importance of visiting the dead under sheltering trees, atop hills that afforded broad prospects: "When in the twilight hour and pensive mood,/Thought seeks repose . . . ,/To sacred shadows of the wood repair,/Far from the crowded mart, the world whose strife/Still mocks at death, and seldom honors life."[155] At the same dedication service, Simms's colleague Charles Fraser made a speech explicitly expressing his hope that Magnolia would prove to be "as happily suited to [its] object as Mount Auburn, near Boston."[156]

In Baltimore, in 1835, the preacher Stephen Duncan Walker, punning on his own surname, published a book called *Rural Cemetery and Public Walk*, in which he proposed following "a plan corresponding to that of Mount Auburn" designed both to honor the dead and to convert his fellow citizens into promenading pilgrims. "A public walk," he explained, "is a commonwealth, a kind of democracy, where the poor, the rich, the mechanic, the merchant and the man of letters, mingle on a footing of perfect equality." The ultimate goal was to create a society of engaged, public-minded pedestrians who would inhabit a middle landscape that balanced death and life. Having recently visited Mount Auburn, Walker felt justified in asserting that a cemetery in the woods, "properly exhibited and set before us . . . , breathes with 'miraculous organs' over the mystic chords of sensibility, to the heart and to the judgment. So-journing in the 'pale cities of the dead,' elevates humility and humbles pride; it sub-dues the arrogance of wealth, and the insolence of office—within their sacred and solemn purlieus, the crest of the noble bows, and the spirit of the slave grows to the level of his master."[157] Two years later, the gates of Green Mount Cemetery opened in Baltimore, and ten years after that, the author of *Rural Cemeteries of America* agreed with Walker that "the holiness of nature is ever a lofty contemplation; and it is well amidst the quiet wildwood and beneath the forest-shades, to be reminded some-times of death."[158]

When Green-Wood, the rural cemetery in Brooklyn, was established in 1838, on the rolling heights overlooking New York harbor, one of its founders explained that the place had to be understood as "a Public Institution, unconnected with any purposes of profit or gain to any individual whatever," and that this identity was woven into its de-sign, which emphasized "*verdure, shade, ruralness, natural beauty*; every thing, in short, in contrast with the *glare, set form, fixed rule, and fashion* of the city."[159] (Figure 9.)

Figure 9. John Bachmann, *Bird's Eye View of Greenwood Cemetery, near New York*, 1852, lithograph.

It was just the kind of place that would appeal to nature-oriented New Yorkers who escaped to the Hudson valley whenever they could—people like the solidly supportive William Cullen Bryant.[160] And one of its most popular attractions, by the end of its first decade, was the "Indian Mound: Monument to Do-hum-me," commemorating the daughter of a Sac chief who died in New York at age eighteen in March of 1843.[161]

Green-Wood was technically a private nonprofit enterprise, like Mount Auburn, but a few new cemeteries were owned and operated by municipalities—most prominently, Mount Hope, in Rochester, founded in 1838.[162] Over in Albany, meanwhile, the local cemeterians decided to follow the Green-Wood model and form an incorporated trust; predictably, though, their chosen dedication speaker, the prominent Whig politician D. D. Barnard, struck all the familiar chords of public-spiritedness when the cemetery opened in 1844: "Yonder city, where . . . the harmonies of society are apt to be broken by petty feuds, by ungentle rivalries, by disturbing jealousies, by party animosities, by religious dissensions, shall . . . send up her multitudinous population to these grounds, and here they shall take their respective places, in amiable proximity to each other, peaceful, harmonious, undisturbed and undisturbing."[163]

The cultural contexts in which all these places were established have passed on with the cemeteries' founders, and we will never fully understand their deepest meanings. To what extent were rural cemeteries conservative, moralistic spaces? To what extent did they actually ease urban tensions? To what extent were they religious, perhaps evoking the conversionary camp meetings of the Second Great Awakening? To what extent were the white cemeterians simply fleeing blacks, and immigrants, and laborers, and their own guilt about Indian Removal? I've been able to puzzle over these questions in movingly beautiful surroundings, because the cemeteries themselves have persisted—have even, in most cases, grown larger. Many of them are surrounded by the most threatening urban spaces of industrial capitalism: I was warned away by friends, in fairly vigorous terms, before I visited Bellefontaine in St. Louis and Laurel Hill in Philadelphia. The pressures of the twentieth century made every piece of land in the United States vulnerable to development, but it seems that burying people on hillsides is a good way of preserving hillsides. What has struck me most during my visits to the rural cemeteries founded in the middle of the nineteenth century is the way they have all remained enclaves of nature, the way they still manage to swallow up the living as well as the dead. "Nature, in all her luxuriance," said the consecration speaker at Spring Grove Cemetery in Cincinnati, in 1845, "should be here preserved and so cultivated as to expand her wildest beauties."[164] My mother grew up near the gates of Spring Grove, as I grew up near the gates of Mount Auburn,

and I am convinced that both of us owe part of our concern for nature to the conviction of many nineteenth-century Americans—people who seem to us, in the twenty-
first century, decidedly morbid—that our habits and our built environment should
keep us ever mindful of the cycles of death and life. Almost every nineteenth-century
cemetery has at least a couple of perfectly circular ponds, offering stillness, reflection,
the chance to come back around to what's most important. Most also have promonto-
ries that look down on a meandering river, whose curves lead the eye outward, put
us back in motion, remind us of distant connections: from Bellefontaine, you can
see the Mississippi; from Laurel Hill, the Schuylkill; from Green-Wood, the mouth
of the Hudson. Perhaps Thoreau launched his twinned writing projects—which became *Walden* and *A Week on the Concord and Merrimack Rivers*—after pondering
the ponds at Mount Auburn and tracing the flow of the sinuous Charles from the
factories of Watertown all the way down to Boston Harbor.[165]

---

"There is scarcely a city of note in the whole country," exclaimed Andrew Jackson
Downing in 1849, "that has not its rural cemetery." So why were those same cities
also becoming more and more dreary, polluted, gridlocked? Downing decided that
people like himself, who had spent most of their professional energy helping private
citizens beautify their property, would have to take a cue from the cemeterians and
transfer their work to the public sphere. A new class of designers could perhaps counteract the forces of commerce when it came to the spatial manifestation of Progress.
And he felt sure that he would have the people's support. To demonstrate "the influence which these beautiful cemeteries constantly exercise on the public mind," and
"how largely they arouse public curiosity, we may mention that at Laurel Hill . . . ,
an account was kept of the number of visitors during last season; and the sum total,
as we were told by one of the directors, was nearly 30,000 persons, who entered the
gates between April and December 1848. Judging only from occasional observations,
we should imagine that double that number visit Greenwood, and certainly an equal
number, Mount Auburn, in a season."[166] It had become obvious "how much our
citizens, of all classes, would enjoy public parks on a similar scale."[167] The logical,
liberal implication of the startling, across-the-board success of the rural cemetery
movement was that all of society's living spaces should be redesigned.

That was the difficult path. Less committed elites simply gave up on the public
sphere and fled to the countryside. So many of them, in fact, chose this escape route,
that a number of scholars have seen the American embrace of nature during the
mid-nineteenth century as little more than an effete longing for a life of privilege on

an aristocratic country estate. There was nothing wild or radical about it.[168] But some of the horticulturists, and cemeterians, and walkers, and poets, and landscape architects, undeniably tried to keep back the rising tide of modernity. They knew their fellow citizens had to be humbled. They also knew that rural seclusion was self-defeating: the screech of the train whistle could be heard at Walden Pond, could penetrate even to the wooded neighborhood in Concord known as Sleepy Hollow, where a new cemetery would be consecrated by Ralph Waldo Emerson in 1855.[169] Besides, death held sway even on country estates. Both mortality and modernity had to be confronted head-on.

In 1839, the editor of the first guide to Mount Auburn, the *Picturesque Pocket Companion*, decided to include a brand-new story by Nathaniel Hawthorne, a strange, haunting fable called "The Lily's Quest." The two main characters are the fairy-like Eve figure, Lilias Fay, and her suggestively named lover, Adam Forrester. And their entire purpose, in this "twice-told tale," is to "ramble over the wide estate which they were to possess together" in search of the perfect spot for their private Eden, their "little summer-house," a monument to their love. Alas, everywhere they wander, they are followed by one of Lily's disenchanted family members, Walter Gascoigne, the pure embodiment of sorrow, of "Earth's gloomiest shade." "For every spot that looked lovely in their eyes, he had some legend of human wrong or suffering, so miserably sad, that his auditors could never afterwards connect the idea of joy with the place where it had happened." At last, though, Lily and Adam are able to throw off Walter's shadow, and they defiantly build themselves their "Temple of Happiness," amidst a grove of trees that lets in just enough of the sunshine's "softened glory" to nurture "a pale lily . . . growing at their feet." The marble structure goes up easily. But on the "day appointed for a simple rite of dedication," Adam finds Lily lying dead just within the temple's threshold. The temple becomes a tomb—as Walter seemed to know that it would. Adam can do nothing but dig below the marble floor, where his spade almost immediately clinks against bone. Here was "no virgin earth, such as was meet to receive the maiden's dust, but an ancient sepulchre, in which were treasured up the bones of generations that had died long ago."[170] *Et in arcadia ego.*

# 2

# THE MIDDLE LANDSCAPES OF
# NEW ENGLAND CULTURE

"Would it not be well, even before we have absolute need of it, to fix upon a spot for a cemetery? Let us choose the rudest, roughest, most uncultivable spot, for Death's garden-ground; and Death shall teach us to beautify it, grave by grave. By our sweet, calm way of dying, and the airy elegance out of which we will shape our funeral rites, and the cheerful allegories which we will model into tombstones, the final scene shall lose its terrors. . . ."

"That is to say," muttered Hollingsworth, "you will die like a Heathen, as you certainly live like one!"
—Nathaniel Hawthorne, *The Blithedale Romance* (1852)

Arcadia has always managed to be an ideal that defies abstraction. Death brings it back down to earth, keeps it close to home.

In August 2008, while I was immersed in my work on Mount Auburn, there was a death in my extended family: Stuart, a still-active seventy-year-old psychologist, my mother's cousin's husband. He had lived in the Boston area for decades, so I'd known him my entire life, and he had become a trusted, avuncular advisor. When I told him where I was going to graduate school, and what I planned to study, he suggested that I look up an acquaintance of his in my department, even though this person worked on a different time period and in a different subfield. Stuart's acquaintance became my most important mentor. I sought Stuart out at Thanksgiving dinners, Passover seders, weddings, bar and bat mitzvahs, funerals, and he made a point of getting to know Christine, even Christine's brother, who lived in Cambridge for a few years. He had survived a heart attack, and he seemed to be outmaneuvering his cancer. The focus of his work, appropriately enough, was on human resilience.[1]

Shortly before he died, he sent me a note referring to his illness as a sabbatical: between chemotherapy treatments, relieved of his usual responsibilities, he'd been getting a lot of writing done. It was a sudden hospital infection that claimed him. I couldn't fathom that I would never hear his voice again, never see him smiling through his orange-gray beard, squinting, thinking. In his optimism, Stuart had declined to make any arrangements for his possible death, and so it fell to his wife, Bobbie, to figure out where he should be buried. She chose Mount Auburn. Driving to the interment, I wondered how my kids would react if they saw me crying. They got excited when they recognized the cemetery, but as they sprinkled fresh sod on Stuart's coffin, as they noted my tears, they seemed to realize that this familiar landscape had changed forever. Pond, frogs, turtles, tower, sphinx, Stuart. In the face of constant change, exhilaration and grief, commingling.

As I tried to turn back to this book project, while still grieving for Stuart, I found myself stuck on the archetypal still life at the end of "The Lily's Quest," with its bones and dirt, its seeming fatalism.[2] Maybe, as Hawthorne suggested, Arcadia was merely a doomed aesthetic. Darker visions of the world often seem more compelling; hopeful perspectives come across as naïve. Yet Hawthorne himself shook me out of my despair. In the spring of 1841, two years after publishing "The Lily's Quest," he embarked on a quest of his own, joining the famous communitarian experiment at Brook Farm, just southwest of Boston, where a few hard-working New Englanders sought to live with greater repose. Though these kinds of communities, sprouting up every few months across the nation, are known best for their religious beliefs, or their varieties of socialism, many of them also sought to establish better environmental connections—through the food they grew and consumed, through their critique of private landownership, and through their architecture and general design principles. The Shakers, for instance, in more than twenty different locations, constructed hilltop sanctuaries that were meant to facilitate a kind of earth-worship. At Brook Farm, as one supporter explained, the main goal of the communitarians was to make "agriculture the basis of their life, it being the most direct and simple in relation to nature. A true life, although it aims beyond the highest star, is redolent of the healthy earth. The perfume of clover lingers about it."[3]

The experiment did not end well for Hawthorne: he went back to living in town after just half a year, and he would later refer to Brook Farm as a "counterfeit Arcadia."[4] But that very phrase suggests his belief in the possibility of a more real Arcadian society. Thanks to the tenor of much of his fiction, he persists in our imagination as the Walter Gascoigne of the American Renaissance, the gloomy critic reminding ambitious schemers that they were predestined for failure. For Hawthorne himself, though, the recognition of limits did not preclude idealism. Indeed, his embrace of Brook Farm makes him seem almost as politically engaged as his acquaintance Margaret Fuller, the great feminist who at this time was well known for organizing a series of public "Conversations" in Boston on culturally important topics, and who felt intrigued by the utopian experiment down in West Roxbury, but not enough to relinquish her individualistic ideal of remaining "entirely unpledged, unbound."[5] Hawthorne, during his first few weeks at Brook Farm, actually celebrated the community's sense of "fraternity"—which quite deliberately included both men and women, on an equal footing, doing the same work—and he thrilled to the task of reshaping humanity's relationship to nature. One cold April day, when he was buzzing with spring fever and good humor, he wrote to Sophia Peabody—his wife to be, his own Lilias Fay, whom he planned to bring to the community as soon as it had stabilized—and assured her that he would "make an excellent husbandman. I feel the original Adam reviving within me."[6]

Places like Mount Auburn Cemetery and Brook Farm, both of which were established alongside the Charles River, Boston's primary waterway, embodied critiques of the mainstream—of industrialism, of the market revolution, of competition, of the antagonism between city and country and between male and female spheres— that were not purely negative. They provided space for new visions of progress, improvement, society as a whole. During what was often characterized as an age of "American go-aheadism," when ambition first became a positive value,[7] American Arcadians came together to propose a slowing down, a more reposeful development, an individualism tempered by ecology. But they were not calling a halt, not drawing a line past which the nation could not expand; rather, they were offering alternative approaches to expansion. They opposed urban capitalism not simply with sentimental nostalgia for life on the farm, nor with the rationality of Jeffersonian agrarianism, but with a new vision of nature that celebrated the margins, the semiwild periphery, the picturesque in-between, as the very core of the nation's identity.

While there is no escaping the familiar story of how the spatial dynamics of the New England factory system spread westward through the country—in the form not just of urban grids but also of penitentiaries and hospitals and asylums, structures of regularization and separation—one can also trace the elaboration and diffusion of the cemetery model, in real and imagined landscapes of subtle, integrative power, from the first suburbs, to the first urban park systems, to frontier communities, to the paintings of the Hudson River School, and to other works of art and literature and landscape architecture that expressed the interdependence of limitation and possibility. Because the rural cemeteries of antebellum America were so popular, because they so profoundly shaped the assumptions and sensibilities of people like Nathaniel Hawthorne, the landscape ideal of this period had a noticeably shady quality to it, and many people seem to have associated nature with death and to have cultivated an environmental awareness marked by humility. But American Arcadians also saw the value of continuing to grow, improve, make progress—so long as their culture embraced a mode of blending rather than displacement.

For Hawthorne, the dominant mode in America was embodied by the custom houses of its port cities. In the late 1830s, he had labored at the one in Boston as a measurer of coal and salt; then, a few years later, desperate for steady income, he moved back to his native Salem to work at the custom house that he would eventually satirize in the opening section of *The Scarlet Letter* (1850). These were places of almost pure abstraction, Hawthorne felt, where government bureaucracy met commercial excess, where men often got buried alive "under a bulk of incommodities" and displayed "that lack of energy that distinguishes . . . human beings who depend for subsistence on charity, on monopolized labor, or anything else but their own independent exertions." When Hawthorne worked at the Salem Custom House, inspecting, surveying, overseeing, he was possessed by a "wretched numbness" stemming from his awareness that "the very nature of his business" did not allow him to "share in the united effort of mankind." The structures of trade left him alienated, displaced from true work and fellow workers, from his gifts of imagination, from the land. Try as he might to go on "sea-shore walks and rambles into the country . . . to seek that invigorating charm of Nature, which used to give me such freshness and activity of thought," he always found that it was "hidden from me; and all the imaginative delight, wherewith it had been spiritualized, passed away out of my mind." The expanding spaces of industrial capitalism crowded out inspiration and creativity; people all around were crushed by "the mighty flood of commerce."[8]

Hawthorne discovered few ways of holding back the flood. Much of his writing seems deeply cynical, and his worldview, judging from the way he lived, seems rooted in a middle-class embrace of privacy, a writerly withdrawal. In this sense, as many scholars have remarked, his sojourn at Brook Farm seems highly "uncharacteristic," and what really resonates with the rest of his life and work is his departure from the community, not to mention his critique of its impracticality in his satirical novel *The Blithedale Romance* (1852).[9] Hawthorne left because the utopians handled their finances so poorly that their farm work became more and more frantic, leaving them with no time or energy for intellectual labor, and it became increasingly clear to the aspiring husband and author that the community would not provide him with the kind of home he had hoped to establish for himself and Sophia. "A man's

soul," Hawthorne found, "may be buried and perish under a dungheap or in a fur-
row of a field, just as well as under a pile of money."[10] But even if he never could have
believed fully in socialist agriculture, and even if, on the surface, he seems less environmentally inclined than writers like Thoreau, Emerson, and Whitman, he actually
felt a powerful communion with nature at Brook Farm, and I think his initial commitment to the community was consistent with a lifelong attempt to develop an ecological
version of The Good Life.[11]

   Hawthorne's ideal was actually a social vision in that it depended on retaining
access to nature, on living amidst middle landscapes and cultivating environmental
relationships. He sought out precisely the kind of world denied and threatened by
the stark Custom House, with its "atmosphere" that was "so little adapted . . . to the
delicate harvest of fancy and sensibility." Again and again, in his writing, Hawthorne
insisted that he was looking for "an available foothold between fiction and reality," a
setting for his work that could serve as a sort of "Faery Land"—a place "where the
Actual and the Imaginary may meet, and each imbue itself with the nature of the
other."[12] These were spatial requirements that could not be fulfilled just anywhere:
Hawthorne needed protected borderlands, needed a house on the edge of a wood,
with a "deserted parlour, lighted only by the glimmering coal-fire and the moon,"
and he needed a "desolate extent of country-road" such as the one leading to Brook
Farm, where "there was better air to breathe. . . . Air, that had not been spoken into
words of falsehood, formality, and error, like all the air of the dusky city!"[13] He found
his practical Arcadia in the interstices—not necessarily in the rigid logic of Brook
Farm itself, but on the experiment's edges.

———————

I knew it was possible to visit the site of Brook Farm, knew its marginal land had
survived the rush of Boston-area development, but what I hadn't realized was that
technically it was no longer in West Roxbury but rather fell just within the borders of
the town I'd grown up in, Newton, which is nicknamed the "Garden City." As I
scanned maps and websites, planning a family walk on a sunny February Saturday,
while we were visiting my octogenarian parents—we don't observe the Jewish Sabbath
rigorously, but we do try to make Saturdays into long pauses from our workweek
routines—it occurred to me that, as a kid, I had taken places like Brook Farm, pockets
of greenery and history, for granted. Now, at forty, I was having constant flashbacks,
and this time I suddenly remembered being eleven, in the summer after sixth grade,
in 1981, remembered trekking all over town as part of the Environmental Science
Program (or ESP, as we called it). We had visited Norumbega Park and Lost Pond

and Hammond Woods, wandered along all the city's waterways, tested pH and dissolved oxygen levels, discovered animal populations—deer, beaver, muskrat, fox—that seemed impossible in a suburb of 100,000 people. But we had never made it to that far southeastern corner of the city, never discussed Newton's idealistic agrarian heritage. We walked and walked, got to know our home town intimately, and I think it was that summer that I got addicted to walking, that I began to haunt local greenways wherever I went, began to appreciate the magic of half-wild enclaves. Yet whenever I asked people—the ESP leaders, park rangers, trail crews—about such places, the stories they told almost always had to do with conservation easements in the twentieth century. I didn't learn about Brook Farm until my college mentor told me to read *The Blithedale Romance.*

The maps that showed Brook Farm as part of Newton also revealed it to be surrounded, of course, by cemeteries. Their names were standard, Christian-sounding—Gethsemane, Mount Lebanon, Mount Benedict, St. Joseph's—so I was a bit puzzled when we arrived in the vicinity of the historic site and a prominent Star of David came into view on the first cemetery gate. I wanted to pull over, but one of my kids was desperate for a bathroom, so I pressed on toward the farm, where, thankfully, a Gethsemane gatekeeper opened up some facilities for us.

We had a lovely walk. The buildings of Brook Farm had long since burned, but we read the engaging historical marker (Hawthorne! Fuller! Transcendental Utopianism!) and investigated the sagging remains of a print shop dating from the 1870s. Especially with the snow and ice melting in the late morning sun, the land seemed waterlogged, marshy, and for a while we strolled alongside the reedy Saw Mill Brook, which ultimately leads to the Charles River but which first brought us to some old fields and a red maple swamp. The kids ran ahead and found an unlocked iron gate leading into a chamber that had been carved out of the hillside—a winter storage room where bodies were stowed until the ground thawed enough for proper burial. Next came a plaque commemorating Camp Andrew, where the 2nd Massachusetts Infantry had done a few brief training drills before heading south at the start of summer 1861. And then the kids clambered up Pulpit Rock, about twenty feet high, a pile of overgrown granite boulders and chunks of Roxbury puddingstone where, the narrator of *The Blithedale Romance* imagined, John Eliot, "the holy Apostle of the Indians," might have preached to the Massachusett people in their own language back in the seventeenth century. We also explored Gethsemane, sharing the gardens and graves with a flock of Canada geese and a few mourners being led through a service by a Russian Orthodox priest. "We wandered off," as Hawthorne put it, "in various directions, to enjoy our interval of repose."[14]

Driving back to my parents' house, I again noted the gate with the Jewish star, and this time there was something uncanny about how it looked, as if I had stared at it from exactly this angle sometime in the distant past. Again I wanted to stop, but didn't. Then, just a few seconds later, when I saw the sign showing that Baker Street was turning into Dedham Street, I gasped with recognition. I told Christine: I think that's where Benjamin is buried. Once, maybe thirty years before, my mother and I had been caught in a traffic jam on the VFW Parkway, and she had taken an unusual route home, approaching Newton from West Roxbury, and had pointed out this cemetery. The iron gate, the stone wall, the Dedham Street sign—all were engraved in my memory, but for three decades I had thought the cemetery was actually in the town of Dedham, rather than right here in Newton.

Benjamin Tevya Sachs was born in November 1967, and died nine months later. I expect those were the most difficult months of my parents' lives, though they have never said as much. They almost never mention Benjamin. They don't visit his grave. What I know of him comes almost entirely from a three-page memoir my mother wrote a few years ago, when she reached her late seventies. I was startled when she showed it to me, grateful, eager to try to understand. It spurred flashbacks: once, during my first semester of college, when my mother was dropping me off at my dorm after I'd spent a weekend at home, she told me that it was the day Benjamin would have turned twenty. I had just turned eighteen. Fifteen years later, when Christine and I were disconsolate over a miscarriage, my father reminded me that there are worse losses.

Benjamin suffered from a rare chromosomal abnormality; his vital organs barely functioned, and the autopsy showed that most of his brain was missing. My parents knew he was going to die, but they didn't know when. How did they get through their days and nights, feeding him with a sterile syringe every couple of hours, desperate to make sure the formula didn't run up into his nose through his cleft palate? "As his parents," my mother wrote, "we insisted we could see hopeful aspects, and he also had an appealing presence. We were probably just fooling ourselves, we knew."[15] As a parent of three blessedly healthy children, I cannot read those sentences without starting to cry. Both my mother and father are quiet, reserved—deeply emotional, but usually matter-of-fact in their speech and writing. My older sister, Debbie, has inherited those qualities; for whatever reason, I tend a bit more toward sentimental expressiveness. It turns out that Debbie also inherited the unusual chromosomal pattern—shared by our mother and grandmother, but not me—that, the doctors thought, had caused Benjamin's difficulties.

Debbie was four and a half when Benjamin was born and must have felt utterly forgotten. After he died, it must have been a leap of faith when my parents decided to try to have another child (having thought hard about adoption). How did they summon the fortitude? How did I come to exist? I must have been horribly spoiled when I was a baby. And I fear that Debbie resented all three of us for a long time, understandably, perhaps unavoidably. I admired her, listened to her Beatles albums, read her favorite authors, but she kept herself at a careful distance. Then she got married, and, after multiple miscarriages, probably caused by the family chromosomes (my mother and grandmother went through the same thing), she had twins, and both were healthy. Then, three and a half years later, came another thriving child. We all get along well now, but we rarely speak about any of this. Almost everything about Benjamin and his impact on our family was buried, deep, for decades. Perhaps nothing affected my childhood so much as his life and death. Yet my closest friends don't know he existed; I am astounded to be writing about him. It took the experience of sturdy, stable markers, of historical landscapes—it took the cultivation of spatial memory—for me to draw this out of myself. I don't blame my parents for avoiding memories of the greatest pain they have ever felt. But I felt grateful, after that trip to Brook Farm, for history's invitations, for long Sabbath mornings, for moments of connection and rediscovery.

———————————

Hawthorne, from the beginning of his time at Brook Farm, despite his sometimes morbid misgivings about the entire venture, referred to the surrounding area as "one of the most beautiful places I ever saw in my life," emphasizing both the rural improvements and the "woods, in which we can ramble all day, without meeting anybody." Such a setting made for "a delectable way of life." Once fall came around, he told Sophia that he was making time—especially on the Sabbath—to take long walks through the meadows, where he "found white and purple grapes, in great abundance, ripe, and gushing with rich juice when the hand pressed their clusters. . . . If we dwell here, we will make our own wine."[16] Hawthorne's notebooks from September and October overflow with a harvest of autumnal impressions, with a writer's experiences of perfect middle landscapes, in which nature and culture gently bleed into each other. Wandering down dirt paths and along fields, he noted a sleigh leaning against the side of a house, "with weeds sprouting up through the crevices of its bottom," and "large trees, almost a wood, principally of pine, with the green pasture glades intermixed, and cattle feeding." Less solitary scenes take shape as well: Hawthorne helped to dig potatoes and gather apples and squash, and joined in a great "picnic party in the woods."[17]

Fall, the season of dying, having "made rapid progress in the work of decay," created color schemes that balanced diversity and unity, so "that every tree in the wood, and every bush among the shrubbery, seems to have a separate existence, since, confusedly intermingled, each wears its peculiar hue, instead of being lost in the universal verdure of the summer. And yet there is a oneness of effect, likewise, when we choose to look at a whole sweep of woodland, or swamp shrubbery." Perhaps it might be possible, after all, to combine individualism and communalism. Look carefully, and you might "see a spiral wreath of scarlet leaves twining up to the tip-top of a green tree, intermingling its bright hues with the verdure, as if all were of one piece." Listen, and you'll hear "the cawing of the crow" from "the blasted tip-top of a pine tree," and then the sound of wings "flapping darkly," carrying dozens of black birds along the border they haunt between forest and field. Walk softly past the local cemetery, catch the sound of iron spade against sod, and notice how death and burial bring the community together: "one inhabitant after another turned aside from the street to look into the grave, and talk with the digger. I heard him laugh."[18]

In one of the most remarkable passages in all of Hawthorne's private writings, he described a late September evening of surreal, Dionysian encounters, on the margins of Brook Farm, that "left a fantastic impression on my memory," despite his congenital malaise and increasing frustration with his utopian companions. Life, for a few hours, seemed to become the romance he had always envisioned. The festivities began with a child's birthday party, but soon, as Hawthorne and a friend wandered slightly deeper into the woods, the rites grew more mystical: "we went onward, and came to a company of fantastic figures, arranged in a ring for a dance or game." Some of these "denizens of the wild wood" were recognizable to Hawthorne as associates of Brook Farm—the two teenaged girls, for instance, who had dressed up as Diana, goddess of the hunt, and "a young gipsey fortune teller." But others were strangers: "an Indian chief, dressed in appropriate costume of blanket, feathers, and paint, and armed with a musket," not to mention "a Swiss girl, an Indian squaw, a negro of the Jim Crow order, one or two foresters," and several plainly dressed people who seemed to have ambled over from the nearby village. When Hawthorne turned this material into a scene in *The Blithedale Romance*, he threw in a couple of "shepherds of Arcadia." Even at the time, though, he felt he was witnessing an "intermingling of wild and fabulous characters with real and homely ones. . . . I remember them with the sunlight breaking through overshadowing branches, and they appearing and disappearing confusedly—perhaps starting out of the earth; as if every day laws of Nature were suspended for this particular occasion." Apparently Hawthorne could not write a page, during this season of the year, without developing some sort of image of "interwreathing" or "strange tangled confusion."[19]

Had the young idealist been drinking? Had he eaten one of the mushrooms or toad-stools he delighted in discovering, those fungal "mysteries, and objects of interest, to me, springing, as they do, so suddenly from no root or seed, and growing nobody can tell why"? No: Hawthorne was just making himself at home in the enchantment of the forest's edge, on the border between nature and culture. And his delight was further enhanced when, out of the blue, two acquaintances from town, "Mr. Emerson and Miss Fuller, who had arrived an hour or two before, came forth into the little glade where we were assembled. Here followed much talk."[20]

Hawthorne lived for such enchantments and chance meetings. How, then, to cultivate them?

About a year later, in the summer of 1842, having given up on Brook Farm, Hawthorne finally married Sophia Peabody, and the joyous couple moved to Concord, where Emerson leased them a family property that Hawthorne called "the Old Manse." Here, perhaps, was a new Arcadia. Hawthorne befriended Thoreau, hiked around Walden Pond, swam every day in the muddy Concord River, which flowed next to his orchard, and made use of some of the gardening techniques he had prob-ably learned in childhood from his uncle Robert Manning, who helped raise him, and who was another of the founders of the Massachusetts Horticultural Society (and father to Robert Manning, Jr., the society's first historian).[21] "The natural taste of man for the original Adam's occupation," Hawthorne wrote, positing that Eden required at least some care, "is fast developing itself in me. I find that I am a good deal interested in our garden." The experience of growing food even seemed to lead him toward a more ecological frame of mind: "I love, also, to see my own works contributing to the life and well-being of animate nature—it is pleasant to have the bees come and suck honey out of my squash-blossoms." At first, he despaired to see the orchard's "fruits decaying on the ground," but he quickly realized that he could count upon swarms of insects to "hold a festival upon them; so that they will not be thrown away, in the great scheme of nature."[22]

It is perhaps unsurprising that someone so obsessed with sin would take a particu-lar interest in the Manse's apple trees, especially since they had been nurtured for the previous seven decades by a parson, Ezra Ripley, Emerson's step-grandfather. But it was precisely during this era in New England that fruit went from being a temptation to being a reminder of our interdependent bond with the natural world:

> It pleases me to think of the good minister, walking in the shadow of these old, fan-tastically shaped apple-trees. . . . And the same trees offer their fruit to me, as freely as they did to him—their old branches, like withered hands and arms, holding out

apples of the same flavor as they held out to Dr. Ripley, in his life-time. Thus the trees, as living existences, form a peculiar link between the dead and the living. . . . They have become a part of the family. . . . And when they have stood around a house for many years, and held converse with successive dynasties of occupants, and gladdened their hearts so often in the fruitful autumn, then it would seem almost sacrilege to cut them down.

Hawthorne was clearly most comfortable in the private, domestic sphere, but his sense of kinship with the land represented a developing environmental ethic that also allowed him to sympathize with less tame sensibilities—as suggested by his close connection to Thoreau, whom he admired explicitly because the infamous Concord misfit had so much "of wild original nature still remaining in him." After all, even if apple trees eventually become "humanized, by receiving the care of man, and by contributing to his wants," they nevertheless retain a certain feral quality, "into such strange postures do they put themselves, and thrust their contorted branches so grotesquely in all directions."[23]

During his time at the Old Manse, Hawthorne experienced a wonderful sense of possibility, yet, even in midsummer, he sometimes felt that "in every breath of wind, and in every beam of sunshine, there is an autumnal influence," a "faint, doubtful, yet real perception, or rather prophecy, of the year's decay—so deliciously sweet and sad in the same breath." On one particular Sunday in late August 1842, at the start of the "quiet, sunny, warm, yet autumnal afternoon," Hawthorne, comfortable in his ambivalence, had just set out on a long walk through his favorite stretch of Concord woods, Sleepy Hollow, when he suddenly "perceived a lady reclining near the path which bends along its verge." It was Margaret Fuller: "We talked about Autumn— and about the pleasures of getting lost in the woods—and about the crows, whose voices Margaret had heard—and about the experiences of early childhood, whose influence remains upon the character after the collection of them has passed away." And then, within minutes, they were joined by "Mr. Emerson, who in spite of his clerical consecration, had found no better way of spending the Sabbath than to ramble among the woods."

Hawthorne had an agitated soul, but his Arcadian wandering offered hints of peace and communion. That night, "there was the most beautiful moonlight that ever hallowed this earthly world; and when I went to bathe in the river, which was as calm as death, it seemed like plunging down into the sky."[24]

Thirteen years later, in 1855, the woods of Sleepy Hollow were consecrated as Concord's new rural cemetery, where Hawthorne would be buried another nine years after that, in 1864, while the Civil War raged. He hated the war, and wrote constantly in his final years about what he considered to be the pointless, needless fatalities that were ravaging the nation's families.[25] "Life, which seems such a priceless blessing, is made a jest, emptiness, delusion, a flout, a farce, by this inopportune Death."[26] Some of his intimates, frustrated at the mysteriousness of his final, wasting illness, considered Hawthorne yet another casualty of the Civil War. "There is no remoteness of life and thought," he had written in 1862, "no hermetically sealed seclusion, except, possibly, that of the grave, into which the disturbing influences of this war do not penetrate."[27] Perhaps, then, death was something of a relief; perhaps he took some solace in knowing that his body would lie on a favorite knoll in Sleepy Hollow. "Yes," he said, laughing, to a friend whom he had taken to see the cemetery, "we New Englanders begin to enjoy ourselves—when we are dead."[28] But, of course, his enjoyment of the cemetery derived from many years of walking through Concord's woods.

Sleepy Hollow Cemetery was carefully designed, following the contours of the land, by Robert Morris Copeland and H. W. S. Cleveland, both of whom would go on to become prominent landscape architects and public intellectuals. In the late 1860s, Cleveland, who had grown up in close contact with the Peabody family and had known Sophia intimately as a child, took his New England experiences and lit out for the urban frontier, to work on the park systems in Chicago and Minneapolis and to publish *Landscape Architecture as Applied to the Wants of the West* (1873), in which he argued that cemeteries, parks, and tree-lined boulevards ought to be conceived as "integral portions of the city, instead of being merely ornamental appendages."[29] It is almost as if Cleveland, haunting the same embowered pathways, had spent his early adulthood in conversation with Hawthorne, Fuller, and Emerson.

———

Even back in the 1840s, westward was the crucial direction of travel if you were passionate about new models of improvement, new possibilities for wildly human landscapes. Hawthorne had made a point of taking passage on a packet boat plying the Erie Canal just a few years after it was completed, and he saw some promise in this new, calm waterway, which had turned New York into the Empire State. Every few miles he came across a fresh, "thriving village, built of wood or small gray stones, a church-spire rising in the midst," as he noted a decade later, in the book he wrote while living in Concord, *Mosses from an Old Manse* (1846).[30] Certainly, Hawthorne preferred the canal boat, which traveled at the speed of nature, to the train, which he referred to as a "steam-fiend."[31] But even the Erie Canal sometimes seemed to signify little more than "the encroachments of civilized man" on "the wild Nature of America": too often, he passed ruined wetlands, "decayed and death-struck, by the partial draining of the swamp into the great ditch of the canal."[32] It was an unpardonable sin, Hawthorne insisted, echoing Oliver Goldsmith, for technology and progress to speed up the process of decay, to bump it from the natural realm to the artificial.

Hawthorne's friend Margaret Fuller, both intrigued and appalled by what she heard of such developments on the frontier, decided, in characteristic fashion, that she must see for herself, and that she must go much farther west—that, in fact, Niagara Falls, the ultimate goal of so many New England tourists on the canal, would be her jumping-off point, as it were, for a much longer journey. Fuller was concerned not only about the displacement of wilderness but also about the displacement of Indians, whose main communities had now been pushed to the plains; she saw in their unjust treatment by white society a parallel to the treatment of women by men. And she took it all very personally. On the margins of the Great Lakes, she hoped she might find clarity for herself and redemption for her society—perhaps in the form of a small town, showing "the harmonious effect of a slow growth, which assimilates, naturally, with objects round it." Indeed, when she arrived at the main settlement on Mackinaw Island, in the summer of 1843, she found that "the people in its streets, Indian, French, half-breeds, and others, walked with leisure step, as of those who live a life of taste and inclination, rather than of the hard press of business, as in American towns elsewhere."[33]

During the previous summer, when Fuller visited with Emerson and Hawthorne in Concord, she had been in the midst of her life's deepest crisis. At a time when many prominent figures, male and female, were arguing for a rigid circumscription of women's social roles within the dominion of sentiment and domesticity, Fuller was pressing her body, soul, and mind to the task of exploding boundaries and categories. She wanted a life both private and public, a life of mystical spirituality and keen intellection, of love and work, of individualistic fulfillment and communal sympathy. She was, in short, a Romantic, and while Romantics tended to be miserable in general, Fuller was an unmarried Romantic in her early thirties having what today seems like one of the first modern, feminist midlife crises.[34]

She spent time at Brook Farm regularly—indeed, she was more supportive of the utopians' full range of political goals than Hawthorne—yet she could not commit herself to communal life. Though indebted to Emerson for his mentorship and encouragement, nevertheless, in the spring of 1842, approaching her thirty-second birthday, she felt she had to resign the editorship of *The Dial*, Emerson's Transcendentalist literary journal. Deeply committed to the Emersonian ideal of self-culture, and, equally, to Goethe's aesthetic drive and the personal morality of Christianity and classical philosophy, Fuller also desperately wanted to correct power imbalances in society, to address the structures of domination that corrupted every relationship, that resulted in so many different forms of slavery. She had an admirable but impossible agenda. And though her diligence and engagement put her at the center of every important cultural debate—over abolitionism, women's rights, western settlement, commercial expansion, millennialist mysticism—she somehow always remained isolated, alienated.

Again and again Fuller fell in love with men and women who were, in various ways, unavailable, and she was devastated at the changes in her friendships with women as they married and started families. "I feel that the darkest hue on my own lot," she wrote, in December 1842, "is that I have neither children, nor yet am the parent of beautiful works by which the thought of my life might be represented to another generation." Living in Cambridge at the time, she tried to draw some comfort from an old, familiar "view"—of "the river so slow and mild, the gentle hills, the sunset over Mt. Auburn."[35] But she remained haunted by unfinished writing projects and broken relationships and, consistently, by nightmares of being overwhelmed by water. One of the worst dreams had come two months earlier, when she was sharing a bed with her old friend Anna Ward, whose husband Sam was out of town. Fuller had harbored very intense feelings for both Anna and Sam, so in a sense their marriage had left her doubly rejected. Now, though she at first "took pleasure" in the effort to reclaim intimacy with Anna, she wound up having "a frightful dream of being imprisoned in a ship at sea, the waves all dashing round, and knowing that the crew had resolved to throw me in. While in horrible suspense, many persons that I knew came on board. At first they seemed delighted to see me & wished to talk, but when I let them know my danger," this group of friends and loved ones "with cold courtliness glided way. Oh it was horrible these averted faces and well dressed figures turning from me . . . , with the cold wave rushing up into which I was to be thrown."[36]

That winter was one of gloom and illness, but Fuller emerged in the spring of 1843 with a fierce desire to attempt a new kind of writing and then, possibly, to break her bonds with New England. The immediate result was her most trenchantly radical essay, "The Great Lawsuit. Man *versus* Men. Woman *versus* Women." It is a diatribe, predictably, against definitiveness, but also against a kind of Emersonian abstraction. Though Fuller shared her mentor's politics, generally speaking, she worried that Emerson's Transcendental inclination toward ideation—his perennial search for the thought lying behind the thing itself—could wind up justifying the worst kinds of discrimination. What did Emerson mean when he insisted that "every natural fact is a symbol of some spiritual fact," that "every appearance in nature corresponds to some state of the mind"?[37] Wasn't this logic, at its base, the same as the logic that categorized

Africans as black-hearted and Indians as bloodthirsty and women as the weaker sex? In the case of Emerson's own assumptions, this problem manifested itself in his casual sexism, which made Fuller impatient. "Though no son, yet a sacred event," he wrote to her in a letter of April 1843, describing the birth of a friend's daughter. Fuller was just then working on "The Great Lawsuit," but she cleared her desk to offer a quick retort: "Why is not the advent of a daughter as 'sacred' a fact as that of a son? I do believe, O Waldo, most unteachable of men, that you are at heart a sinner on this point."[38]

In her essay, Fuller decried "what has been done towards the red man, the black man," in the name of white ideas about redness and blackness, as well as all the crimes against women that were based on men's narrow definitions of womanhood. All judgments, she insisted, should be of "individual minds, which live and aspire, as flowers bloom and birds sing, in the midst of morasses." To make it clear, though, that she was not just defending the best and brightest within any given category of people, she extended her metaphor to argue that, while nature provided many different kinds of habitat for the growth of different species, still, each organism could benefit from some cultivation: "Plants of great vigor will almost always struggle into blossom, despite impediments. But there should be encouragement, and a free, genial atmosphere for those of more timid sort, fair play for each in its own kind. Some are like the little, delicate flowers, which love to hide in the dripping mosses by the sides of mountain torrents, or in the shade of tall trees. But others require an open field, a rich and loosened soil, or they never show their proper hues." There is no ideal person, just as there is no ideal plant; the trick is to work with nature, blend with its forces, hold open-ended Conversations with it, so as to foster the most liberal forms of personal development. Perhaps women do have a certain "especial genius"; perhaps there is some kernel that could be "spoken of as Femality. But," as Fuller argued, at the climax of her essay,

> it is no more the order of nature that it should be incarnated pure in any form, than that the masculine energy should exist unmingled with it in any form.
>
> Male and female represent the two sides of the great radical dualism. But, in fact, they are perpetually passing into one another. Fluid hardens to solid, solid rushes to fluid. There is no wholly masculine man, no purely feminine woman.
>
> History jeers at the attempts of physiologists to bind great original laws by the forms which flow from them. They make a rule; they say from observation, what can and cannot be. In vain! Nature provides exceptions to every rule.[39]

Culture, too, provides exceptions. For all of the rapid currents of progress, modernity, delineation, separation, there were backwaters of blending, places of true fluidity that Arcadians sought to map even while immersed in them. Fuller herself, having embraced New England social reform, ultimately decided, immediately after finishing "The Great Lawsuit," that she could no longer stand "the petty intellectualities, cant, and bloodless theory" of her circle, and would have to seek new kinds of exceptions, new minglings of nature and society, of facts and truth, in America's northwestern borderlands.[40] At the end of May 1843, having just turned thirty-three, she left Boston with a few friends, ready to read "bolder lines in the manuscript of nature," dismissing "merely gentle and winning scenes," dreaming of "the sources of the streams, where the voice of the hidden torrent is heard by night, where the eagle soars, and the thunder resounds in long peals from side to side, where the grasp of a more powerful emotion has rent asunder the rocks."[41] Even more than the primitive wilderness, though, Fuller looked forward to finding, somewhere, a perfect "mixture of culture and rudeness" that might offer "a feeling of freedom," an exemplary "habitation of man" that she might compare to "a nest in the grass," where "the buildings and all the objects of human care harmonized with what was natural."[42]

---

Within a year, her "summer's wanderings" had become a meandering, eclectic manuscript, published as *Summer on the Lakes, in 1843*.[43] Much scholarship on Fuller passes right over this book to get to her magisterial work of 1845, *Woman in the Nineteenth Century*, but it is in her travel writing, I think, that the real breadth and depth of her radicalism become clearest. In composing *Summer on the Lakes*, Fuller seems quickly to have realized that her wide-ranging observation could provide her with the empirical means to unsettle even the deepest assumptions and strictest definitions of her society. Though the valuing of middle landscapes, stereotypically, is associated with a conservative provincialism, Fuller's Arcadian ideal was explicitly cosmopolitan, combining deep experiences of particular places with open-minded journeying. So when Fuller celebrated all the earthly Edens she found during her travels—the settled places "on which 'improvement' yet has made no blot, / But Nature all-astonished stands, to find / Her plan protected by the human mind"—she was, simultaneously, arguing that, with the right, fluid attitude, in the right environment, any kind of individual could change the generally imperial trajectory of American history.[44] Nothing, besides the dates of one's birth and death, was carved in stone.

Frontier women, for instance, Fuller sometimes found to be victims, having been dragged along to lives of toilsome drudgery by their husbands, who focused narrowly on the prospect of "larger accumulation" and better hunting;[45] yet, at other times, female pioneers seemed heroic in their warm hospitality and their adaptation to certain kinds of labor, their embrace of a more "instinctive life, so healthy and so near the ground."[46] Fuller also insisted on pointing out all the ways in which the Indians were victims—sinned against, dispossessed, beaten down by the American government and its people. Still, though, they could be kind, courageous, knowledgeable, and eloquent. "Why will people look only on one side?" she asks. "They either exalt the Red man into a Demigod or degrade him into a beast."[47] Fuller attempted to meet natives as human beings—the same way she opened herself to encounters with the white settlers who were spilling into the spaces that the Indians had formerly inhabited, before being scattered by armies and legislators and surveying crews. Some of the emigrants were clearly opportunists, "whose bivouac fires blacken the sweetest forest glades": they marked the land with "the rudeness of conquest," with a spirit "scarce less wanton than that of warlike invasion." Others, though, forsaking the places "where 'go ahead' is the only motto" and instead idealizing "the firm fibre of a slow and knotty growth," built log cabins so well blended into their environments that they "disturbed the scene no more than a stray lock on the fair cheek"; Fuller saw one cottage standing "beneath trees which stooped as if they yet felt brotherhood with its roof tree." Indeed, she found many an American settler figuring out ways "to carry out his own plans without obliterating those of nature."[48]

But what plans could be considered purely natural? Fuller cannily refused to give nature any singular meaning, granting it the same diversity she recognized in humanity. Indeed, her understanding of nature and culture as mutually constitutive seems almost postmodern. At the very start of her trip, as she gazed at Niagara Falls and prayed for some unscripted reaction to this most famous of natural sights, Fuller found some solace at the edges of the view, in the "bordering mosses" and blossoms and mists, where "all the lineaments become fluent, and we mould the scene in congenial thought with its genius."[49] All landscapes are constructed, but, with the right kind of dissolving effort, one can construct them from the inside rather than simply imposing readymade understandings.

Farther west, confronted with the flat prairie for the first time, Fuller found in it "the very desolation of dullness." But almost immediately she realized that it was merely her "accustomed eye" that had made her feel a lack of scenic mountains and sheltering valleys and glorious waterfalls. Once she had actually experienced the prairie, had learned "to look at it by its own standard," had noticed the flowers and the "island groves" amidst the grasses, had considered its fertile soil, she came to think of it as yet another Eden. Indeed, the path to her Edenic ideal explicitly involved an effort to see the human in the natural and the natural in the human. If God's role was to create temptation in the form of forbidden fruit, the role of the Arcadian was to partake eagerly of both the cultivated apple and "the wild crab," and give "both room to grow in the garden."[50]

Fuller's ideal of human settlement, displaying the "beauty of soft, luxuriant wildness" and reflecting an "intelligent appreciation of the spirit of the scene," could easily be mistaken for a nostalgic celebration of the motherland, a yearning for Americans to take up the English tradition of landscape gardening.[51] And Fuller acknowledged a clear debt to her pastoralist forebears, who taught her to open herself to nature, to see the poignancy of "the uprooted flower in the ploughed field" and to "lie under a green tree and let the wind blow on me": "nothing is truer than the Wordsworthian creed . . . , that we need only look on the miracle of every day, to sate ourselves with thought and admiration."[52]

Fuller's true exemplars, though, in keeping with her interest in forming a new, native culture, were Indians. "Seeing the traces of the Indians, who chose the most beautiful sites for their dwellings, and whose habits do not break in on that aspect of nature under which they were born, we feel as if they were the rightful lords of a beauty they forbore to deform." It was not that the Sacs and Foxes who lived on the Illinois prairie never used resources or never modified their environment; rather, they shaped their traditions, and their living spaces, their "regularly arranged mounds," so that their children would grow up attuned to astronomical and climatological cycles, would relate "familiarly with the deer and the birds." Indeed, the Indians seemed always to recognize their dependence on animals and to see their fate as intertwined with that of other living things, to look on beavers and bears and snakes "with a mixture of sympathy and veneration, as on their fellow settlers in these realms. There is something that appeals powerfully to the imagination in the ceremonies they observe, even in case of destroying one of these animals."[53] And though sometimes Fuller did see this kind of potential in white settlers, for the most part she was realistic about expansion as a mass movement that could not be tightly controlled and whose basic structures precluded Indian-style development: "I have no hope of liberalizing the missionary, of humanizing the sharks of trade, of infusing the conscientious drop into the flinty bosom of policy." She imagined that the pioneers' "mode of cultivation will, in the course of twenty, perhaps ten, years, obliterate the natural expression of the country."[54] She never gave up her faith in alternative settlement patterns, but she saw that the strongest trends were toward displacement.

An elegiac mood, then, often creeps into *Summer on the Lakes*, as in so much Arcadian writing. But what's remarkable about Fuller's modulation of her tone is the way she carefully distinguishes between the tragedy of American cultural politics and the tragedy of more universal limitations—between, as it were, artificial and natural decay.

She mourns the disappearing Indians and forests, but she never paints their retreat as inevitable. Those tragedies have perpetrators, who could conceivably act differently. Indians could be treated with integrity, in a mode of fair exchange and open mingling; the land could be shaped with sensitivity and care. The problem was that western migrants so often "brought with them their habits of calculation," and were forever thinking "not of what they should do, but of what they should get in the new scene"; they approached expansion with the "barbarous selfishness" that Andrew Jackson had endorsed with his Indian Removal policy. If, instead, the pioneers built settlements in the grateful spirit of a springtime maple-sugaring festival, learning techniques from the locals, tasting the sweetness of labor "done in the open air," reaping a harvest from the trees without cutting too many of them down—then they might find a path toward "a more equal, more thorough, more harmonious development."[55]

Yet trees must sometimes fall: here is an inescapable truth, one worthy of elegy. Everywhere we go, we also reap decay and death. At the very center of *Summer on the Lakes* is a sadly hopeful portrait of a frontier couple who had all the necessary virtues to thrive on the margins of civilization. Fuller could tell immediately, approaching their cabin, that they had come to the upper Mississippi valley not for material gain but for a "better and more intimate communion with one another and with beauty: the wild road led through wide beautiful woods, to the wilder and more beautiful shores of the finest lake we saw." But, as it turned out, "sickness had been with them, death, care, and labor." The husband was crippled; the wife could "feel the weight of each moment as it passed." Their "hope and joy had given place to resolution." The frontier was exhilarating and liberating but also lonely and difficult; it provided, in sum, a life of "tormented independence." So: perhaps that bittersweet paradox, that sense of balance between potential and limitation, could be the key contribution of pioneer life to a new national identity. Instead of fostering a sense of abundance and entitlement, Americans might "bring up children so as to be fit for vicissitudes; that is the meaning of our star."[56]

As Fuller left the Illinois prairie and made her way back to Chicago, she learned in a letter from Emerson that a friend had died—Washington Allston, the well-known landscape painter, and mentor to Fuller's traveling companion, Sarah Clarke, whose seven engravings would illustrate Fuller's book. The bad news forced Fuller to pause, reminded her that wandering shepherds will always come across tombs: "Farewell, ye soft and sumptuous solitudes!/Ye fairy distances, ye lordly woods,/Haunted by paths like those that Poussin knew." But, as in Poussin's version of Arcadia, the tombs might harmonize with the landscape, their stones echoing the weathered rock and humble dirt of their surroundings, their cracks filled with stubborn mosses and lichens. Fuller's picture of frontier life is unsettling but still welcoming, offering a chance at regeneration: "A tender blessing lingers o'er the scene, / Like some young mother's thought, fond, yet serene, / And through its life new-born our lives have been."[57] The entire book, in fact, owes much to Poussin's landscapes, as filtered through more recent theories of the Romantic picturesque, which taught Fuller to keep the edges of her prose rough and unpredictable and energetic—to break suddenly into poetry, to insert long, allegorical fictions into her travel narrative, to juxtapose moments of grimness and hope.

For all that Fuller learned from Poussin and Wordsworth, though, she learned even more from Native Americans—especially about living with death. In the passage of *Summer on the Lakes* just preceding her poetic tribute to Poussin, she had been expounding on the significance of Indian burial sites, both ancient and recent— the "many grassy mounds" filled with "the bones of the valiant." Fuller made a point of speaking with Indians whenever she could (sometimes resorting to sign language), and one lesson from those conversations stood out: every individual, she thought, should have the right to affirm his continuity with his ancestors and the land, by revisiting "that fair hill, which contained for the exile the bones of his dead, the ashes of his hopes." That continuity, that acknowledgment of death and descent, cast a new light on life—as Fuller perhaps understood most fully at the very end of her trip, while observing some cheerful Indian women going about their chores and rituals, near the rapids of Sault Ste. Marie, in the shade of a nearby hill, atop which sat "the old Chippeway burying ground."[58] They could feel at home in nature because nature housed their dead fathers and mothers, whose repose, so far, remained undisturbed.

Fuller, having returned home to Massachusetts, finished her manuscript on the morning of May 23, 1844—her thirty-fourth birthday. Then, as she would note in her journal late that evening, she passed a few hours in a favorite spot: "Spent the afternoon at Mt. Auburn. It was of heavenly beauty, but Oh, I am very, very sad. . . . The state of my mind is so deep, I think this must be an important era in my life. . . . I should go to bed. The young moon is sinking in her beauty."[59] Fuller was still trying to feel at home in New England, but gradually recognizing that she had to leave again—perhaps, this time, for good. "I am deeply homesick," she had noted the year before, while passing through Chicago, "yet where is that home?"[60] Fortunately, *Summer on the Lakes* was printed right away and received a great deal of admiring attention, which opened up new possibilities. Of course, within Transcendentalist circles, the publication of Margaret Fuller's first book was a major event, and even Thoreau, who, as Emerson put it, "will never like anything," seems to have appreciated its formal experimentation and its radical combination of inward searching and social critique: it became an important model for his own elegiac work of avant-garde travel literature, *A Week on the Concord and Merrimack Rivers*.[61] But what ultimately mattered most to Fuller was that the book sold well across the country, proving that a female author could make a splash writing in an unsentimental style, and landing her a job in the exclusively male world of New York journalism. That fall, she became a correspondent for Horace Greeley's *Tribune*, and over the next few years she would file first-hand reports not only from New York's opera houses but also from Sing Sing prison, from England, and from Italy—where, at last, she fell in love with a man capable of reciprocating, Giovanni Ossoli. Their son, Angelo, was born on September 5, 1848.

Still, Fuller did not feel settled. In the spring of 1850, she acknowledged an overwhelming urge to go back home. Most of her friends, including Emerson, thought she should stay in Italy, where she seemed to have found more happiness in her private life than she had previously thought possible. Clearly, it had been important for her to wander. But now it seemed equally important to circle back to New England with her husband and son, to have her new identity confirmed. Her ship, the merchantman *Elizabeth*, made the crossing easily, despite the captain's death from smallpox at Gibraltar (Fuller's son was infected as well, but recovered after a nine-day ordeal). The real trouble came only at the end of the voyage, in coastal waters, when the replacement captain allowed the ship to build up too much speed in the midst of an unusually bad storm. The storm turned out to be a hurricane, and the ship turned out to be much closer to land than the captain had thought. Everyone on board awoke at about four in the morning, on July 19, when a sandbar just south of Fire Island smashed open the ship's side.

It took twelve hours for the *Elizabeth* to come apart completely and sink into its permanent home. Meanwhile, daylight showed that the wreck was just three hundred yards from shore. Amidst the wind and waves, the vessel stayed relatively stable during the morning hours, so that, after the initial terror wore off, the seventeen crewmen and six passengers were able to brace themselves against piles of furniture and cast about for ways of saving themselves. One passenger made it to land on a plank guided by a skilled and experienced officer. But no one could come up with a scheme that would ensure the safety of Fuller's twenty-two-month-old son, and Fuller was unwilling to part with him. At about noon, a lifeboat appeared on the beach, giving everyone a sudden burst of hope. By this time, though, the gusts had picked up, throwing water and debris in every direction, and the people who had gathered onshore—mostly scavengers and scoundrels, by all accounts—were unwilling to launch the boat. At last, as the foremast toppled over, Fuller and Ossoli agreed to let the ship's steward try for land with Angelo in his arms. Then, according to another crewman, Fuller sat down, leaned her back against the ruined mast, and waited for death.[62]

She should have been buried at Mount Auburn, in her family's plot. You can find a monument to her there, honoring her life and career and attachment to her husband and son. But her body was never recovered.[63]

Henry Thoreau, at Emerson's request, traveled to the scene of the shipwreck and spent several days walking the beaches and talking to witnesses, searching for both Fuller's remains and her manuscripts, and piecing together a narrative of what had happened. It seems that Angelo—whom Fuller usually called Angelino, or just Nino—had almost made it. His body was still warm when it washed ashore. Fuller and Ossoli were carried out to the open ocean on the tides. In all, five of the six passengers had died, along with three members of the crew. Thoreau, in his wanderings over the dunes, did come across part of one unidentifiable corpse, and it left him shaken. His journal from this time reflects his struggle to confront physical ruin by upholding the power of thoughts and spirits: "we are ever dying to one world & being born into another." Meanwhile, though, he would seek to live and labor in the world he knew best, would continue with his writing, and his walking, even under a "blood stained sky," for as long as he could. With death in the air, life sometimes seemed more purposeful. "Do a little more of that work," he told himself, "which you have sometime confessed to be good—which you feel that society & your justest judge rightly demands of you. . . . Cultivate the tree which you have found to bear fruit in your soil."[64]

———————————

Thoreau knew death—it was an undercurrent in all of his work—and he knew environmental borderlands—coasts, shorelines, riverbanks, swamps. Less than a year before he searched for Margaret Fuller's body, he had been roving the dunes of Cape Cod just after a passenger ship, full of immigrants to the United States, had wrecked against an infamous rock called the Grampus. Here, where liquid met solid, was a portal, a launching point for further journeying and mingling, a place where one could grasp, suddenly, the solidarity of bodies, souls, and nature. The corpses Thoreau found now belonged, he felt, to "the worms or fishes." But what of the "owners" of these bodies? "I saw their empty hulks that came to land; but they themselves, meanwhile, were cast upon some shore yet further west, toward which we are all tending, and which we shall reach at last, it may be through storm and darkness, as they did." It was not that Thoreau dismissed these deaths as transcendent; indeed, he made a point of envisioning the pain of the people who "would watch there many days and nights for the sea to give up its dead," and the grief of the "mourners far away, who as yet knew not of the wreck."[65] The people who had actually died, though, had merely arrived at the place where all of us will eventually gather—a place that no one ever gets to know but that, considered rightly, from the perspective of life, could unite us with each other and with the world. For Thoreau, the key was to recognize the direction in which everyone was moving—he always imagined it as westward—and then to embrace that tendency, and to find heaven on earth by merging with the sun and following its daily path.

Thoreau actually traveled west just once, a month after the Civil War broke out, in search of a drier climate to ease the pulmonary difficulties from which he was already dying. The trip seems to have made hardly any impression on him: he covered much of the same ground Fuller had eighteen years before, but instead of comparative notes on settlement and Indians and the possibilities of middle landscapes, he just jotted down a few botanical observations.[66] Still, he generally agreed with Fuller that the west held considerably more promise than the east. New England was dominated by the "petty triumphs" of technology and industry, Fuller had thought—by custom houses and all their kin, "dock, railroad, and canal, / Fort, market, bridge, college, and arsenal, / Asylum, hospital, and cotton mill, / The theatre, the lighthouse, and the jail." But in the less stony soil of the Lakes region a gentler culture could surely be planted and sustained. "I admire these bluffs of red, crumbling earth," she explained, as she reached the Northwest. "Here land and water meet under very different auspices from those of the rock-bound coast to which I have been accustomed. . . . Here they meet to mingle, are always rushing together, and changing places; a new creation takes place beneath the eye."[67] Just so could right-minded settlers join with the western soil and rivers and trees. Thoreau suggested that "it would be some advantage to live a primitive and frontier life," which to him meant remaining "but a sojourner in nature."[68] The east was too settled, its people too hardened in their ways; in the west, perhaps, was true fluidity, was the river of his imagination, into whose current he longed "to launch myself . . . and float whither it would bear me."[69]

Thoreau's most extended musings about the west, though, came almost immediately after Fuller's death in 1850, in the lecture notes that eventually became his essay "Walking." It's an essay I have read more times than I can remember, and I don't expect it will ever leave me in peace. Today, its most famous line is surely the one that has become the motto of the Sierra Club: "In Wildness is the preservation of the World." Yet "Walking" also has a long, excursive section devoted to the glorious spread of civilization, even empire, throughout the American west. Despite Thoreau's undeniable radicalism, despite his almost vicious criticisms of mainstream progress— "nowadays almost all man's improvements, so called, as the building of houses, and the cutting down of the forest and of all large trees, simply deform the landscape"—this particular essay nevertheless has several passages that, even to the most sensitive and sympathetic readers, suggest "a patriotic ode to manifest destiny."[70] Such sentiments are, at the very least, puzzling. Yes, the west had more space, bigger skies, wilder forests, wider rivers. But why did Thoreau start daydreaming about building castles in those forests and conquering the rivers by throwing inconceivably long bridges across them? What does it mean for a testy antebellum individualist to embrace "the prevailing tendency of my countrymen" and "go westward as into the future, with a spirit of enterprise and adventure"? Why did he suddenly seem so grateful that "from this western impulse . . . sprang the commerce and enterprise of modern times"? Could he really have experienced pleasure when he went to a triumphalist exhibit about development along the Mississippi River, when he saw the panoramic display gradually unrolling before him, "saw the steamboats wooding up, counted the rising cities"? Having spent so much of his life trying to learn how to exist peacefully in nature by following the example of Native Americans, did he really feel patriotic as he pondered Removal, as he "beheld the Indians moving west across the stream"? Did he really believe "that *this was the heroic age itself*"?[71]

I'm still not sure. Was he possibly just trying to win the sympathy of his jingoistic audience? Doubtful: those who invited Thoreau to speak generally knew what they were getting, and what they got was often enough a barrage of insults. "I wish to speak a word for Nature," Thoreau said, right at the start of "Walking," "for absolute freedom and wildness, as contrasted with a freedom and culture merely civil. . . . There are enough champions of civilization: the minister and the school-committee and every one of you will take care of that."[72]

A more typical scholarly explanation is that even the most radical member of a society is still deeply influenced by that society's fundamental structures and discourses: abolitionists and Indian advocates were nevertheless racists; even those who endorsed rural values probably still believed in the conquest of nature.[73] Yet, in Thoreau's case, the evidence doesn't hold together. He was never shy about condemning the American hunger for land; in 1846, to make the point that he should not have to pay taxes to finance an expansionist war with Mexico that he did not support, he was willing to go to jail.[74] Moreover, as the country pressed westward, the most pressing question back east always seemed to be whether or not new states would allow slavery, and the tensions surrounding this issue repeatedly forced the North into unsavory compromises with the South. For Thoreau, 1850 was a breaking point: California, newly won from Mexico, and newly overrun with gold miners and speculators, would be admitted to the Union as a free state, but as compensation there would be a new, harsher Fugitive

Slave Law, which, in effect, from Thoreau's perspective, brought slavery back to Massachusetts. In April 1851, when Thoreau first delivered "Walking" as a lecture, his thoughts were on the well-publicized plight of Thomas Sims, a black man who just days earlier had been arrested in Boston and remanded to his former master in Georgia; in fact, Thoreau's first scrawled line offered an "apology" to his audience, since he felt guilty "for speaking to them tonight on any other subject than the Fugitive Slave Law."[75] Usually, when Thoreau thought about American expansionism, he thought about profligacy, and slavery, and speculation, and thoughtless desperation, and displacement, and he grew disgusted: "The whole enterprise of this nation . . . towards Oregon, California, Japan, etc.," he wrote, in an 1853 letter, "is totally devoid of interest to me, whether performed on foot or by a Pacific railroad. . . . No, they may go their way to their manifest destiny which I trust is not mine."[76]

In "Walking," then, when western "enterprise" somehow becomes an admirable ambition, Thoreau's meaning must be at least partially metaphorical. After all, as he explained, "the West of which I speak is but another name for the Wild." Perhaps he dreamed of western pioneers who would have more "commerce" with nature and Indians. "I believe," he said, "that the forest which I see in the western horizon stretches uninterruptedly toward the setting sun," so perhaps he could imagine that it would continue to flourish, despite the inroads made by frontiersmen and the wood collectors feeding the steamboats. Perhaps, like Fuller, he envisioned not the immediate replanting of eastern culture but the slow development of a brand-new kind of civilization, marked by wilder cities, bearing the imprint of western climes. Maybe, given a kind of environmental determinism, life on the frontier—undertaken properly, in a reflective rather than a conquering mode—could be the very thing to save the country from itself? "I trust that we shall be more imaginative," he wrote, "that our thoughts will be clearer, fresher, and more ethereal as our sky,—our understanding more comprehensive and broader, like our plains,—our intellect generally on a grander scale, like our thunder and lightning, our rivers and mountains and forests." If New England, with its notoriously difficult soil and unpredictable weather, had bred men who worked themselves to death and were always angling for a slightly higher profit margin, then perhaps the expanse of the west, "so fertile and so rich and varied in its productions," would allow for the development of a quieter, more humble society, a society in which people could be satisfied with their log cabins and small villages and not feel the need to clear land for commercial farms and factories.[77]

Still, shouldn't Thoreau have been able to predict the number of factories and corporations that would rise in the West? In the era of manifest destiny and the Gold Rush, of steam power and coal power and the railroad, couldn't he see where the nation was headed? But there's the rub: no particular kind of progress was inevitable. In early 1862, when Thoreau prepared the final version of "Walking" for publication, he suspected that he was on the verge of dying, but he could not have known the ultimate significance of something like the 1859 discovery of oil in Pennsylvania. The Industrial Revolution was far from complete, and there was actually a long tradition of assuming that its fingers would never really stretch beyond the Appalachians. In the last decade of Thoreau's life, the west was nothing if not contested terrain. Though, retrospectively, the course of empire seems clear, no one could have prophesied the massive frontier migration following the Civil War, or the campaigns against the bison and the plains Indians in the 1870s, or the towering impact of petroleum and steel on the shape of western development.[78]

Like many environmentalists and academics, I was educated in a tradition of protest and criticism, so I am most comfortable with Thoreau when he is exposing society's wrongs and excoriating those who seem responsible, whether politicians or captains of industry or his narrow-minded, greedy neighbors. "I cannot believe," he wrote, at his most persuasive, "that our factory system is the best mode by which men may get clothing. The condition of the operatives is becoming every day more like that of the English; and it cannot be wondered at, since, as far as I have heard or observed, the principal object is, not that mankind may be well and honestly clad, but, unquestionably, that the corporations may be enriched."[79] But, these days, I am coming to see that the most remarkable thing about Thoreau may be his insistence on not remaining merely a snide critic; his determined hopefulness, his faith that everything could be different in the west, make him that much more of an Arcadian. He wound up being mostly wrong, but at least he had a vision—at least he was engaged in a positive struggle over how to define the land and our relationship to it. Locating wildness in the open West, though it might seem like a cop-out from some perspectives, actually allowed him to refine both "wildness" and "the west" as ingredients in an ideal society that would be based on middle landscapes, on a culture "in sympathy with surrounding Nature."[80]

For all his vagueness, in "Walking," for all his disgust with the vile villains who inhabit villages, for all his mucking about in marshes and his celebration of "instinct" and his embrace of "this vast, savage, howling mother of ours, Nature," Thoreau was ultimately talking about new forms of Progress and the founding of a new Civilization. He still wanted and needed villages, just as he had when he lived on Walden Pond; it served him well to accept the polarity of culture and nature, because that opened up the spaces between. "I feel that with regard to Nature I live a sort of border life," he explained in "Walking," a life built on long, daily strolls, through the same landscapes that Hawthorne so enjoyed, on pathways that linked town and farm and wood and meadow and river. Concord itself, in some lights, was still Thoreau's ideal, which, adapted to the spacious west, could produce just the right kind of American: "I would not have every man nor every part of a man cultivated, any more than I would have every acre of earth cultivated: part will be tillage, but the greater part will be meadow and forest, not only serving an immediate use, but preparing a mould against a distant future, by the annual decay of the vegetation which it supports."[81] A paradisal civilization would nourish itself, in part, by lying fallow on its edges, and the American Adam would be a gentle-footed sojourner.

Paradise, Eden, Utopia, Arcadia, the Elysian Fields, the Fortunate Isles: the Good Life has often been pictured as an environmental fantasy. "The island of Atlantis," Thoreau noted, in "Walking," "and the islands and gardens of the Hesperides, a sort of terrestrial paradise, appear to have been the Great West of the ancients, enveloped in mystery and poetry."[82] Today, in the industrial world, after a century of mass production and mass consumption, such myths and fantasies seem almost pernicious: they sound hubristic, like gated communities or elite estates or manicured golf courses, places of denial, where necessaries are provided via some sort of automated delivery system, and the inhabitants, preserved in a solution of timeless carelessness, never confront the truths of labor, waste, disagreement, death. Environmental idealism surely makes little sense in the age of chemical pollution and global warming. Yet to relinquish the mythical ecology of the Good Life is to let it be co-opted by the proponents of gated communities—or, in Thoreau's day, by the purveyors of manifest destiny.[83] "Eden" does not always have to mean entitlement, or an endorsement of luxury and escapism; indeed, the apples are sometimes poisoned, and expulsion is usually quite likely. Thoreau, in staking his claim to an American paradise, wove into it an awareness of decay and dependence.

Though no one could have foreseen the industrial-style development of the West— America was still predominantly agricultural in 1860—Thoreau at least recognized that the region was going to be developed in some fashion, and soon. That, at least, seemed as inevitable as his own imminent death. Like Fuller, he saw frontier migration as a democratic instinct, almost a force of nature, a process that had to be accepted. The question was whether it would be a journey into darkness or into light.

Thoreau refused to give up his vision of a brighter future. Throughout "Walking," he ambles toward death, toward heaven, toward the holy land—all of which, in the essay's final image, turn out to be a meadow just outside Concord, during a November sunset: "it was such a light as we could not have imagined a moment before, and the air also was so warm and serene that nothing was wanting to make a paradise of that meadow." There were long shadows, and long grasses, and some birds, and a brook, "just beginning to meander, winding slowly round a decaying stump. . . . The west side of every wood and rising ground gleamed like the boundary of Elysium, and the sun on our backs seemed like a gentle herdsman driving us home at evening." We are all headed westward, toward our season of dying; our duty is to transfigure that migration, to arrive at a more intense kind of living, now, here, on the edge of the clearing, by the river: "So we saunter toward the Holy Land, till one day the sun shall shine more brightly than ever he has done, shall perchance shine into our minds and hearts, and light up our whole lives with a great awakening light, as warm and serene and golden as on a bankside in autumn."[84]

---

About twenty years ago, when I was about twenty, I dropped out of college for a while and moved to the woods, because people I knew were starting to die. It did not feel like escapism, and, in fact, the deaths continued for another two and a half years. Actually, it was regular life that seemed escapist: modern culture, with its impetus toward constant production, doesn't offer anyone the time and space to acknowledge loss. In withdrawing for a while, I thought of myself as following Thoreau's lead. Thoreau had established himself on the shore of Walden Pond, he said, because he "wished to live deliberately."[85] I wished to face what I was feeling—or, at least, to test my feelings against the cycles of nature instead of the cycles of academic striving. For the scholar Robert Harrison, the whole point of Thoreau's experiment was "to reduce life to the essentiality of its facts, in other words to the fact of death."[86] To dwell truly in nature is perhaps to dwell on mortality. The land, ideally, reminds us of death's darkness and also its afterglow.

Thoreau went to Walden in 1845, in part, to cope with the death of his brother John. It had already been three years, but John was the closest friend Thoreau would ever have, a person he could communicate with silently; certainly, one of his main goals at the pond was to write about the river trip they had taken together in 1839. After John died of lockjaw, Thoreau was bedridden for a month and even experienced, sympathetically, some of John's same symptoms for a couple of days. "Neither will nature manifest any sorrow at his death," he wrote in a letter, "but soon the note of the lark will be heard down in the meadow, and fresh dandelions will spring from the old stocks where he plucked them last summer." Even if the world at first seemed unsympathetic, he ultimately found it comforting to acknowledge that death was "a law and not an accident—It is as common as life. . . . When we look over the fields we are not saddened because the particular flowers or grasses will wither—for the law of their death is the law of new life. Will not the land be in good heart *because* the crops die down from year to year . . . ? So it is with the human plant."[87] One of his life's projects was to recognize and understand loss, and to find a new energy in grief; when he insisted that "all intelligences awake with the morning," he was also thinking of his times of mourning. Why is it, he wondered, that "every one believes practically that health is the rule and disease the exception," when "disease is, in fact, the rule of our terrestrial life"? He appreciated what he perceived as a Native American tendency to have more realistic expectations: "the Indian," he thought, ". . . measures his life by winters," and by moons, and by nights, which made the long days of healthy summer sun that much more joyous.[88] Indeed, though Thoreau is still sometimes misconstrued as a dour misanthrope, and though he spent many months of his life stricken with illness and grief, the genius of his writing, it seems to me, lies in its articulation of exuberance amidst pain. "The first sparrow of spring!" he exclaims near the end of *Walden*. "The year beginning with younger hope than ever! . . . Walden was dead and is alive again."[89] This was a man who held melon parties for his friends and neighbors during the summer, as his lush melon patch, famous for its many varieties, produced far more fruit than he could eat by himself.

I went to the woods of Minnesota after my sophomore year, in part, to cope with the death of my friend Ian. We were not nearly so close as the Thoreau brothers; in fact, we hadn't even met until the beginning of college. But I had a powerful feeling, as a freshman, that I was in the wrong place, that I would never re-create my community of friends from high school, and my connection with Ian had at least given me some hope. We were both quiet, both alienated yet idealistic, both attached equally to books and the outdoors. We agonized together over which courses to sign up for, lit Chanukah candles together—"a Jew from Oklahoma?" my parents asked— and often looked at his pictures from a long canoe trip he had taken the previous summer, in the Boundary Waters, the protected wilderness area on the Minnesota-Canada border. On Valentine's Day, in our freshman year, while I was trying to save my relationship with my girlfriend, Ian was diagnosed with lymphoma, and he died on August 29. I was so scared and pained, during the last six months of his life, and perhaps so self-centered, that I found it virtually impossible to communicate with him: I had not been able to integrate his dying into my life. And I had never felt worse about myself. More than anything else, I wanted to learn how to live with mortality, how to experience it as a connective rather than an isolating force. Eventually, I realized that I couldn't learn that in college.

It was in the following spring that I decided to apply for the internship at Wolf Ridge Environmental Learning Center, hours from any city, on the shore of Lake Superior. Ian's photographs were full of rich blues and greens, with moose, sometimes, and loons, and he said you could hear wolves, and he said you could dip your water bottle straight into the lakes, and just drink.

I thought I was following Thoreau's lead, but I also felt I could never live up to his example. He had figured out how to build his own house, after all; he had grown his own beans, in a patch of ground that he thought of as "the connecting link between wild and cultivated fields."[90] It was obvious to me that I could never be quite so self-sufficient, or skilled, or disciplined. In Minnesota, I lived in a dormitory and ate most of my meals in a dining hall.

Twenty years later, I think of Thoreau's work less as a call to arms or independence and more as a guide for the perplexed, a series of suggestions about how to think and live, reminding us that a person who is truly at home both "wanders and reposes at the same time."[91] Even when I was teaching at Wolf Ridge, I started to appreciate the more hesitant, experimental undertone in his writing, started understanding that there was no single path to follow. If Thoreau was sometimes dauntingly industrious, he was also conscientiously lazy: "I love a broad margin to my life. Sometimes, in a summer morning, having taken my accustomed bath, I sat in my sunny doorway from sunrise till noon, rapt in a revery, amidst the pines and hickories and sumachs, in undisturbed solitude and stillness, while the birds sang around or flitted noiseless through the house. . . . It was morning, and lo, now it is evening, and nothing memorable is accomplished."[92] Idleness: could there have been anything more radical for a New Englander at the dawn of industrial capitalism?[93] I learned, in Minnesota, to open my door to the birds, to walk out of my house with no route in mind, to savor the sunshine, and to remember its warmth even on black winter afternoons. I learned, from this interval in my life, the importance of pausing.

--------

The frigid weather was just another Minnesota fact: we added a layer of clothing and went about our business. Every class I taught was three hours long, and the house rules said that at least two of those hours had to be passed out of doors. I will never forget how electric it felt when, in late March, the thermometer finally nosed above freezing; we all wore shorts.

Mostly, I remember walking, at every different hour of day and night, through liminal landscapes, spaces for which I will always remain grateful. We say that images are "frozen" in our minds, and I was certainly cold a lot in Minnesota, but these pictures seem to have remained limber, liquid: the local black bear sidling by the dorm, or chomping the bright red berries of a mountain ash; the leaves of the ghostly, green-gray aspens quaking in a breeze on the edge of Wolf Lake; the unreal pinks and greens, the insane flashing, the long, bold streaks of the Northern Lights. The longest walks were in September, with Cree, the wolf we had adopted. Two of us always took him out, on a leash, for hours at a time, and he seemed to take to me as if I were a brother. If I handed over the leash and stopped for a quick snack or a photograph, Cree would sit down and refuse to budge until I was ready. He could pull on that leash, hard, especially when he smelled a deer or an owl, but we had an understanding—until early October. I had spent the weekend in the Twin Cities to observe Yom Kippur, and when I got back to Wolf Ridge, just after dinner, I went for a hike and ran into two of my co-workers and Cree. Excitedly, I squatted down and reached out for his fur, and he tensed his whole body, showed me his teeth, growled deeply, and sprang at my throat.

Fortunately, the person holding the leash that night was strong enough to yank him back just in time. My body quivered all night long. Had I picked up some strange smell in the city? Even the local experts were unsure of what was going on. But, a few days later, when Cree had exactly the same reaction to the one other male intern who was approximately my age, we realized that our wolf was reaching maturity and asserting his dominance in the pack. He was, after all, a wolf. I never walked him again: whenever I got within a few feet, I heard the slow rumble of his growl—a sound that traveled directly from his belly to mine. It terrified me—but there was also a sense in which that growl confirmed our kinship. "We are both inside and outside of nature," writes Robert Harrison: "this is our dismay, that we come up against its insurmountable limit. We gain our freedom not by overcoming but by recognizing that limit. Just as freedom is not a question of rights, so too it is not a question of emancipation. Its essence lies in acknowledgment. . . . Acknowledgment does not save us from ourselves; at most it spares us the indignity of leaving the world kicking and screaming like the infants who came into it."[94]

Ever since Wolf Ridge, I have felt called to teach, to experience that full engagement with a group of students—not so much to impart knowledge as to share a sense of wonder at the world's beckoning mysteries. And I have looked for habitations close to trailheads. I used to dream of backpacking trips in high mountain ranges, and I still do sometimes, but now I am more likely to ponder, gratefully, the prospect of wandering out my front door with my kids on a weekend afternoon and being lost in either the gorge or the cemetery five minutes later. Thoreau was quick to remind his readers that "the wilderness is near as well as dear to every man. Even the oldest villages are indebted to the border of wild wood which surrounds them. . . . There is something indescribably inspiriting and beautiful in the aspect of the forest skirting and occasionally jutting into the midst of new towns." Preserving or creating such wild edges, everywhere people live, would perhaps go far in establishing the potential for a more ecological way of life. But what seems even more important to take from Thoreau is his understanding of how to relate to that wild borderland—how to see both its inviting porousness and its hard and fast limits. "The constant abrasion and decay of our lives makes the soil of . . . our second growth," he wrote, in *A Week on the Concord and Merrimack Rivers*—the first book he produced at Walden, the book that served as his elegy to his brother. "Every man casts a shadow; not his body only, but his imperfectly mingled spirit. This is his grief. . . . But . . . light is diffused almost entirely around us. . . . At any rate, our darkest grief has that bronze color of the moon eclipsed."[95] Other of my friends have died since Ian, and grief will always be overwhelming. But, in sending me to Minnesota, Ian gave me the gift of a second growth, a determination, in the midst of mourning, to renew ties of kinship and community.

The longest tangent in *A Week* deals with friendship, whose "drama . . . is always a tragedy," and which ultimately stands in for kinship, since, for Thoreau, "my Friend is not of some other race or family of men, but flesh of my flesh, bone of my bone. He is my real brother." Thoreau was talking about John, certainly, but also about the broad ideal of a brotherly (or sisterly) relationship, which posits a blood tie uniting all people—which, in turn, means that we might feel a twinge whenever anyone dies. Again and again, Thoreau referred to the decimation of Native Americans as the worst tragedy in American history, but at the center of his meditation on friendship stands the fraternal bond of the fur trader Alexander Henry and the Ojibwa chief Wawatam, a "stern, imperturbable warrior," who "comes to the white man's lodge, and affirms that he is the white brother whom he saw in his dream," after which the two strangers "hunt and feast and make maple-sugar together." If these two nominal enemies can join their spirits in celebrating and appreciating the bounty of nature, then perhaps, Thoreau suggests, we can all also recognize our kinship with the entire world, can simultaneously acknowledge nature's unsettling differentness and confirming sameness: "As surely as the last strain of music which falls on my decaying ear shall make age to be forgotten, or, in short, the manifold influences of nature survive during the term of our natural life, so surely my Friend shall forever be my Friend. . . . As I love nature, as I love singing birds, and gleaming stubble, and flowing rivers, and morning and evening, and summer and winter, I love thee, my Friend."[96] Nature will outlast you, but, in the interim, if you accept it as your kin, loving even its flaws and what you perceive as its outrages toward you—siblings always have their battles—it will at least provide you with a home.[97]

A *Week*'s narrative arc begins on a Saturday, with Henry and John shoving off from Concord and rowing with the current on what Emerson called "our Indian rivulet"; Thoreau, also thinking of the region's former inhabitants, usually referred to it as "the Musketaquid, or Grass-ground River." On Sunday, the brothers reached the Merrimack and turned inland, now struggling against the water's rough energy. For the next few days, they rowed hard, and then they grounded their skiff and paused to climb some mountains. In the book, their backpacking trip lasts only one day, taking the form of the chapter called "Thursday," though in 1839 they had actually rambled on foot for a full week. Then, in the book's final chapter, "Friday," Henry and John hoist a sheet to capture the cool wind, which signals to them "a change in the weather. . . . We had gone to bed in summer, and we awoke in autumn." And then they fly back down the Merrimack until they reach the gentle Concord again, where, newly energized, they take out their oars and row all the way home, to sleep that night in their own beds. It was of course comforting to be back, but Thoreau was careful, in his last chapter, to emphasize that what mattered most was being alive to the possibilities of the journey, to the experience of passing through the in-between places: "How fortunate were we who did not own an acre of these shores, who had not renounced our title to the whole. . . . The poor rich man! all he has is what he has bought. What I see is mine. I am a large owner in the Merrimack intervals." He could not imagine passing on to some "better" paradise: "Here or nowhere is our heaven."[98]

When he finally knew that his own life was ending, on the morning of May 6, 1862, he had his sister Sophia read to him from his "Thursday" chapter, and when she finished, he immediately thought ahead to "Friday." "Now comes good sailing," he whispered.[99]

Thoreau had surveyed a part of Sleepy Hollow Cemetery back in 1855, making sure that the ground was level at the spot where H. W. S. Cleveland and Robert Morris Copeland wanted to put in an ornamental pond. His bones now rest on one of Sleepy Hollow's ridges, though he was first buried in a family plot near the North Primary School House. To his family and friends, he seemed to have achieved full repose long before he actually passed away. "Never saw a man dying with so much pleasure and peace," said Sam Staples, the man who had put Thoreau in jail for a day in 1846. Sophia remarked that "his perfect contentment was truly wonderful. None of his friends seemed to realize how very ill he was, so full of life and good cheer did he seem." As Thoreau suggested in his essay "Autumnal Tints," if we spent more time observing the "fresh, crisp" leaves of the fall, bright and vivid in their withering, more colorful in America than anywhere else in the world, they might "teach us how to die." Had he made his peace with the Lord? his Aunt Louisa wondered—well, he said, "I did not know we had ever quarreled." His room was full of spring flowers, and he was often visited by many of the children of Concord, with whom he had a special bond. They, perhaps more than anyone, having encountered him in huckleberry patches and on riverbanks, knew his warmth and playfulness and easy generosity. Indoors, he told them stories of his childhood and his travels and read to them from *The Canterbury Tales*. For a child, there is perhaps nothing more daunting than going to visit someone on his deathbed. But, as one Concord neighbor attested, "we went often, and he always made us so welcome that we liked to go. I remember our last meetings with as much pleasure as the old play-days." By the very end, though, his voice had faded enough to become almost unintelligible. Sophia was there to hear his final sentence, as his breathing slowed, but the only two words she could make out were "moose" and "Indian."[100]

# 3

# SLEEPY HOLLOW:
# A YOUNG NATION IN REPOSE

There is no such "right of property" possible in a republic. . . . To fence out a genial eye from any corner of the earth which Nature has lovingly touched with that pencil which never repeats itself—to shut up a glen or a waterfall for one man's exclusive knowing and enjoying—to lock up trees and glades, shady paths and haunts along rivulets—it would be an embezzlement by one man of God's gift to all. A capitalist might as well curtain off a star, or have the monopoly of an hour. Doors may lock, but out-doors is a freehold to feet and eyes.
—Nathaniel P. Willis, *Out-Doors at Idlewild* (1855)

Before Thoreau and Hawthorne were buried at Sleepy Hollow Cemetery in Concord, there was another Sleepy Hollow, on the Hudson River, named by Washington Irving in 1820—a wild, wooded area haunted not only by moose and Indians but also by the ghosts of Dutch settlers and former slaves, by all the spirits of the local borderlands. It was an imaginary place, but it was based on Irving's impressions of towns along the Hudson River valley, and "The Legend of Sleepy Hollow" took on such force in American culture during the antebellum years that Irving's imagined community got mapped onto the actual landscape of upstate New York. In 1849, Irving's townsmen incorporated the new Tarrytown Cemetery beside the Pocantico River, but within a few years its name was changed to Sleepy Hollow.[1]

If Thoreau, Fuller, and Hawthorne best expressed the different aspects of a new Arcadian spirit in New England intellectual culture, it was Irving and his New York compatriots who developed it most fully on a national scale, in ways that allowed it to seep into many layers of society. With Thomas Cole's paintings of the Hudson valley ushering in a new landscape craze in the visual arts; with Andrew Jackson Downing editing the *Horticulturist* in Newburgh and turning landscape architecture into a legitimate profession; with new religions and utopian communities sprouting up in the Burned-Over District; with urban-edge towns starting to become known as suburbs; with the construction of the elaborate Croton Aqueduct and its system of protected reservoirs; with dozens of thriving cemeteries; and with a regional literature dominated by the pastoral sensibility not only of Irving but also of William Cullen Bryant and Susan Fenimore Cooper and the country gentleman Nathaniel P. Willis, and many others—well, much of the state seemed to be a shady borderground, an almost continuous middle landscape.[2] By the 1840s and 50s, then, the immense hinterland of New York City, extending up the Hudson and then along the Erie Canal into the Finger Lakes, formed the heart of Arcadian America.[3] (Figure 10.)

Figure 10. Mount Repose Cemetery, Haverstraw, NY, 2010.

"There was an air of repose and comfort along the road," wrote the morbidly named Nathaniel Coffin, in his book *The Forest Arcadia of Northern New York* (1864); ". . . the fields were well cleared for half a mile on either side, and . . . beyond the clearings, and flanking them for miles, were dense groves of sugar maples,—called in this country sugar bushes,—their luxuriant plumes nodding to each other in the evening breeze as we rode by." Alas, any careful observer could see that American society was becoming more and more destructive and imperial, and that "the waste of the forest has been, beyond all power of computation, disproportionate to the necessary uses of the people." But there was still just enough left of "these vast contiguous shades, these shoreless seas of emerald bloom, this incalculable wealth of vegetable life," that Coffin could cling to the hope of resuscitating "the rude but hearty civilization which flourished among our people when the forest was an institution." Development, after all, could take many different forms. Coffin came from a thoroughly deforested section of New England—but wouldn't it have been possible, he asked, for the woods of America to "have been thinned and husbanded, instead of being utterly destroyed, with great gain to all? Might not our cold northern soil have been made to double its present production under their grateful warmth and shelter? Might not our population have retained that braced and healthful vigor and tone, both of mind and body, which characterized our ancestors of two or three generations back?"[4]

So: was this the age of go-aheadism or the age of repose? I think it was both. Urban industrialism and Arcadianism grew up together, in an interdependent relationship. But because industrialism eventually became so dominant, it often gets portrayed as always having been the overweening brother, the alpha male. As with the rise of Mount Auburn as a cultural icon in the 1830s, historians are too quick to dismiss the strong expressions of Arcadian commitment from the 40s, 50s, and 60s—claiming, for instance, that such expressions never go beyond the realm of the aesthetic, as if aesthetics were somehow not important to human experience, or as if pleasing, carefully tended, healthful surroundings mattered only to the wealthy. Alternatively, scholars have sometimes taken isolated criticisms offered by people like Coffin—"all true ideas of the value of the tree to the soil, all appreciation of the instructive spirit of the woods, seem to have become merged and lost in a mad cupidity"—as evidence that environmentalist perspectives have always been merely reactive or nostalgic rather than constructive. Or, just as misleadingly, they have taken comments about development out of context—"the mineral resources of the plateau," Coffin noted, "are of great value, and will hereafter make a large item in the productive wealth of the Empire State"—in order to posit that even environmental critics ultimately embraced imperialist, capitalist, accommodationist notions of progress, welcoming the machine into the garden as if it posed no threat.[5] Even worse, antebellum Arcadians, in spinning out visions of picturesque rural retreats, might be accused of covering up certain realities of the development that was actually occurring—the rank smell of tanneries on the edge of the Catskills, for instance, or the pollution created by mines and forges, or the plight of tenant farmers barely scraping by as they struggled to feed mushrooming urban populations, or the labor strife at clay quarries and brick factories, or the drudgery that went into maintaining ornamental gardens and lush lawns.[6]

These objections to Arcadianism, most of which are in tension with one another, suggest just how confusing the rise of modernity must have been. Certainly, it seems probable that some of the wealthy industrialists who commissioned lovely landscapes from antebellum artists may have been seeking an escape or even a kind of absolution, and certainly, 180 years later, one might look on such borderland scenes and not realize that modernity had arrived in upstate New York in the 1830s. But for many mid–nineteenth-century Americans, such images seem much more likely to have been interpreted as alternatives, or arguments, than as simple denials. After all, there were pictures of tanneries, too.[7] (Figure 11.)

Figure 11. B. G. Stone, *View of Samsonville Tannery, Olive Township, Ulster County, New York*, c. 1855, lithograph.

Industry was well established in the northeast by mid-century, and certainly some capitalists were pushing for perpetual expansion. But, despite the obvious benefits of a growing economy, many Americans remained deeply ambivalent about this kind of development, especially in areas like this one—the Catskills—with a generally agreed-upon scenic value.[8] Remarkably, the three picnicking children in this picture do not seem particularly happy about their outdoor experience. The girl's red dress provides the only real splash of rich color, which serves to highlight the drab gray-brown atmosphere of the entire scene—a scene that all three figures have conspicuously turned away from. The eldest child, standing upright, is linked visually by his posture and his black coat and hat to the powerfully obtrusive smokestack, which, though relatively thin, is spewing enough pollution to have contaminated the atmosphere around the town, causing a thick, dark haze to hover just under the already low-hanging horizontal line of lighter clouds, whose configuration slices the mountain in half and echoes the horizontal slicing of the factory complex through the main body of the picture. One could say that the scene is dominated by images of cutting and a sense of erosion, as the eye wanders along the scrubby foreground, to the stacks of wood and bark sitting next to bare stretches of dirt, to the bleak, clear-cut fields on the sides of the mountains.

Tanneries, increasingly specializing in the production not just of shoes and saddles but also of the leather drive belts used to run more and more complicated machines, imported skins from all over the world, but extracted an especially heavy toll on their local environments, since their chemical processes required the tannin-rich bark of freshly cut hemlock trees. So, in addition to the smoke in the air and the acid and grease in nearby rivers, these kinds of factory towns always produced broad scars in formerly dense forests: many hills, lamented the *Catskill Messenger* in 1848, were now "stripped of their timber so as to present their huge rocky projections." Successful tannery owners might have found sublimity in those protruding rocks, and one, Zadock Pratt, had a sculptor carve images of himself and his accomplishments into some outcroppings above his company town, Prattsville. (Figure 12.) But other people felt that, once "the border of the living forest retreated up the mountain sides, . . . the beauty of the mountains had departed forever." Indeed, as another observer lamented, tanning "discolors the once pure waters—and, what is worse than all, drives the fish from the streams! Think of the sacrilege!"[9]

At the most basic level, this kind of capitalistic progress would have seemed objectionable to many people in a democratic republic not just because it spoiled everyone's view—and fresh air and fresh water and timber supply—but also because it so blatantly exploited large swaths of land for the benefit of very few people. And in this

Figure 12. W. Endicott, *Prattsville, Greene Co., N.Y., 1850,* lithograph.

era of energetic idealism, there were plenty of activists ready to counter this modern tendency with different social models of land use. George Henry Evans, for instance, ran a radical newspaper in the 1840s called *The Workingman's Advocate* that supported the rent strikes of tenant farmers in upstate New York, insisted that large chunks of land be given back to Native Americans, and condemned all real estate profiteering.[10] Up at the Oneida Association, meanwhile, which would become one of the most successful free-love communities in history, a central tenet was "the renunciation of exclusive claim to private property" and of the whole "grab-game," in which goods and lands and other resources "are not distributed by any rules of wisdom and justice, but are seized by the strongest and craftiest."[11] Founded in 1847, this upstate utopia, just south of Syracuse, shared a number of beliefs with Horace Greeley's National Reform Association (NRA), which in the mid-1840s was focused on the free distribution of small parcels of public land to individuals and families rather than to speculators and industrialists. "Probably the discovery will soon be made," said the NRA's secretary, Alvan Bovay, in 1845, "that if a man has a right to life, he has, by inevitable consequence, the right to the elements of life, to the earth, the air, and the water."[12] Holding land in common and engaging in a more conscientious sharing of resources, the members of the Oneida community also found that they were rethinking many traditional agricultural and consumption patterns, which they now deemed inefficient. "The largest part of the labor of the world," wrote John Humphrey Noyes, the driving force behind Oneida, "is now spent on the growth of annual plants and animals. Cattle occupy more of the soil at present than men." Noyes thought that horticulture was the key to a more compassionate, egalitarian, and sustainable future: "As society becomes vital and refined, drawing its best nourishment from love, the grosser kinds of food, and especially animal food, will go out of use. The fruits of *trees* will become the staple eatables."[13]

The spiritual practice of the Oneidans was called Perfectionism, and in the early 1850s a fellow practitioner, Llewellyn Haskell, founded one of the nation's first planned, picturesque suburbs—Llewellyn Park, in West Orange, New Jersey. Sitting just a dozen miles outside New York City, it was beautifully integrated into the hilly terrain that rolls southward from the Hudson River's Palisades. "To stand upon the crest of it," said one enraptured observer, "looking down into the great, green depths below, and then looking up into the illimitable blue above, is to be at the midway point between heaven and earth, between life and death." Another enthusiast for the view, experiencing a similarly soulful shiver, claimed that he could see as far as Greenwood Cemetery, in Brooklyn. Unlike Oneida, Llewellyn Park required residents to own private property, and while its first investors included a number of middle-class radicals and bohemians—"long-haired men and short-haired women," as one observer put it—it eventually started attracting a wealthier clientele, who cultivated exclusivity. Today, it is a gated community. In the 1850s and 60s, though, Haskell and his designer, Alexander Jackson Davis, a friend and associate of Andrew Jackson Downing, made sure that their suburb's plan was thoroughly communitarian— "every estate was designed to be an adjunct of every other," with no fences or "middle walls of partition between neighbors"—in both its generous allotment of common areas and its facilitation of residents' desire to blend and commune with all kinds of landscapes, from a central waterfall to groves of ancient elms and oaks, from "half-cultivated" farms to cliff walks providing river and harbor views, from a rough ravine to a pond ringed by weeping willows. In 1857, Haskell donated fifty acres of parkland right at the heart of the community, a "central common of original wilderness," a public space to be owned and enjoyed by all. (Figure 13.)

With alternating woods and meadows, and a brook running its length, and with rustic bridges, benches, gazebos, and a "wigwam" as ornaments, this common area immediately came to be known as the "Ramble"—the same name that would be used for the wildest portion of New York's Central Park, whose construction was launched the following year by two more of Downing's associates, Calvert Vaux

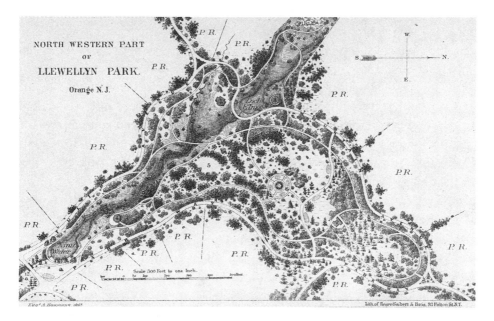

Figure 13. E. Baumann, *North Western Part of Llewellyn Park*, 1853, lithograph.

and Frederick Law Olmsted. One frequenter of Llewellyn Park, where you could buy in for the price of just two acres, emphasized how communal and public the whole place felt, asserting that each resident was in "a happy partnership with every other, possessing the whole park in common, so that the fortunate purchaser of two or three acres becomes a virtual owner of the whole five hundred: a plan by which a poor man . . . may buy a country-seat that challenges comparison with the Duke of Devonshire's."[14]

These kinds of developments, offering alternatives not only to bleak cities but also to company towns and the gridded suburbs laid out by speculators, were bolstered by countless democratic-minded artists and writers who thought of an engagement with landscape as being at the very center of a thriving public culture. William Cullen Bryant, in particular, labored to make sure that his compatriots in New York and throughout the nation would cultivate not only an aesthetic sense and a taste for scenery but also a healthy respect for the "venerable art" of agriculture: even if people continued to move away from the farm, it was imperative "that the plough should be restored to its ancient reverence—that all classes and professions of men should pay homage to that primitive and honourable occupation upon which all are dependent—that they should gratefully conspire to cherish and water that root of all wealth."[15] Just as with rural cemeteries, then, the point of the broader Arcadian movement was not to revert to any particular form of country living but to integrate certain environmental values into all the different modes of modern existence. The soil, the trees, the shade, should be everywhere with us, in our physical reality and in our thoughts: there should be room within our communities for the nests of birds and the hives of bees, so that such creatures might skirt our pathways, flit in and out of our consciousness, remind us of the cycles of pollination and incubation and regeneration.

By 1844, Bryant was ready to start insisting that such wildness be both preserved and newly cultivated in the heart of Manhattan itself. "If the public authorities," he wrote, in an *Evening Post* editorial, "who expend so much of our money in laying out the city, would do what is in their power, they might give our vast population an extensive pleasure ground for shade and recreation in these sultry afternoons, which we might reach without going out of town." He had in mind a specific tract of land whose "surface is varied in a very striking and picturesque manner, with craggy eminences, and hollows, and a little stream. . . . There never was a finer situation for the public garden of a great city. Nothing is wanting but to cut winding paths through it, leaving the woods as they are now, and introducing here and there a jet from the Croton aqueduct, the streams from which would make their own waterfalls over the rocks, and keep the brooks running through the place always fresh and full." And in 1845 Bryant extended his proposal to encompass a whole "range of parks and public gardens along the central part of the island," to try to compensate for "the corrupt atmosphere generated in hot and crowded streets."[16] If "progress" continued the way it had been going, then the corruption would become pervasive—live human bodies working at a frenetic pace could produce just as rank a miasma as rotting corpses—but there was still time to reengineer the city, to improve improvement, to change the way people thought about their mode of life.

Throughout the antebellum period, Bryant and his various collaborators in literature and the visual arts, taking advantage of new printing technologies, produced an outpouring of appealing books in the vein of his park system proposal for New York. They were meant to establish the young American republic as nature's nation—a country whose inhabitants had studied the landscape tradition of England and adapted it to new, wilder, more expansive conditions, in which cultivation would add refinement without allowing artifice to dominate. In *The American Landscape* (1830), one of Bryant's key points was that his countrymen ought to arrange their communities to be more like those of Native Americans, who "had the most exquisite taste for rural scenery: their villages and small settlements all prove the truth of this remark; and the names they gave to favourite lakes, rivers, and shores, were expressive, delicate, and appropriate."[17] A decade later, Bryant's friend Nathaniel P. Willis, in his *American Scenery* (1840), chose illustrations that explicitly demonstrated how certain parts of his country—including the "Cemetery of Mount Auburn" and "Fairmount Gardens, Philadelphia" and "Hudson City," at the base of the Catskills—could avoid the fate of the most congested, corrupted metropolitan areas and instead become urban or suburban Arcadias.[18] (Figure 14.)

Figure 14. W. H. Bartlett, *View of Hudson City, and the Catskill Mountains*, 1840, engraving.

Washington Irving was particularly optimistic, determinedly emphasizing the transporting, magical properties of liminal landscapes, "hallowed ground for fancy and the muses," where it was easy to perceive that "there is an affinity between all nature, animate and inanimate." In many writings of the 1850s, his last decade, he evoked the "Indian legends and grotesque stories" about all the "hobgoblin places" of upstate New York—places governed, for instance, by "an old squaw spirit," who "made new moons every month, and hung them up in the sky, cutting up the old ones into stars," but who could also "brew up black thunder-storms, and send down drenching rains."[19] Even after Irving retired to his own picturesque home along the Hudson, an estate first called Wolfert's Roost and then Sunnyside, he wrote enchantingly of the hauntedness that added so much to his vision of Arcadia. Apparently, in olden days, his neighborhood had been ruled by an old "wizard sachem," who defeated his local enemies by somehow causing them to fall "asleep, among the rocks and recesses of the valley, where they remain asleep to the present day, with their bows and war-clubs beside them. This was the origin of that potent and drowsy spell, which still prevails over the valley of the Pocantico, and which has gained it the well-merited appellation of Sleepy Hollow. Often, in secluded and quiet parts of that valley, where the stream is overhung by dark woods and rocks, the ploughman, on some calm and sunny day, as he shouts to his oxen, is surprised at hearing faint shouts from the hill sides in reply; being, it is said, the spell-bound warriors, who half start from their rocky couches and grasp their weapons, but sink to sleep again." Upstaters, of course, still encountered living Indians in the mid-nineteenth century: "This ground lies within the former bounds of the Six Nations," Susan Fenimore Cooper wrote in 1850, "and a remnant of the great tribes of the Iroquois still linger about their old haunts, and occasionally cross our path." That Irving made them into ghosts suggests his deep ambivalence, his mixture of nostalgia and guilt, and though we might blame him for contributing to the myth of the vanished Indian, he at least understood that Natives would persist in white American consciousness. In the quiet calm of a rural retreat, even when immersed in the daily round of hard labor, an American farmer, no less than any European, had to acknowledge complex histories and pastoral traditions, nature's shadows, the shallowly buried ghosts of the borderland.[20]

Perhaps Irving somehow knew that these regions would remain haunted by his own ghost for centuries to come. After all, though he ascribed the appellation "Sleepy Hollow" to the notoriety of a local sachem, it was Irving himself who had manufactured that notoriety: "Sleepy Hollow" would forevermore be associated with his authorial genius. Moreover, as William Cullen Bryant noted in his 1860 eulogy for Irving, admirers flocked to Sunnyside constantly during the 1850s, as the most famous resident of the Hudson valley became "more than ever the object of public veneration"; "Rip Van Winkle" and the "Legend of Sleepy Hollow" had been read in the United States "by nearly everybody who can read at all."[21] Irving was especially pleased when visitors to his neighborhood reported having seen, on nighttime strolls through the woods, the occasional monster or ghoul, which, often enough, appeared headless. On his final evening, though he was yearning for a greater repose—"I must arrange my pillows," he said, "for another weary night"—he nevertheless savored the wine he took with dinner, and seemed to see its deep red reflected in the clouds as he gazed out across the Hudson at sunset. Death came quickly, quietly, as a slight pain in his left side, while his niece was helping him get ready for bed.[22]

Even as Irving was being laid to rest in Sleepy Hollow on December 1, 1859, Charles H. Lyon was finishing the job of laying out the grounds for his new suburban development at Tarrytown, called Irving Park. Another picturesque community within commuting distance of New York City and boasting fifty acres of green space "to be used in common by all the occupants," Irving Park offered lots ranging from one to eight acres and took advantage not only of striking river views but also of the neighborhood's contiguity with some land protected within the Croton Aqueduct system, which since 1842 had been providing New York City with some of the nation's healthiest water. In January 1860, a writer for *Harper's Weekly* who had visited the new development suggested that "the contrast between the thickly-shaded groves of the lower section, and the wide-spread lawns and terraces of the higher ground, the wild scenery explored by labyrinthine walks in the western quarter, and the picturesque effect of the bold declivities of the east park looking down through the vista of Sleepy Hollow, make up a most agreeable variety of rural scenes." Rather than "strife and tumult," rather than the "dust and din and uproar of a large city," the park offered an "air of quiet repose."[23] Rural cemeteries, the new cities of the dead, had become models for new living spaces.[24]

———————

A haze of gentility hangs over the careers of those who argued for good country living in antebellum America. But perhaps their seeming withdrawal to private estates helped them express, in environmental terms, a novel combination of community-oriented republicanism and modern, democratic individualism. As American culture came to seem more dominated by striving, by perpetual uprootings in search of land and gold, and as Barnum-style capitalism seemed to take over the public sphere, rural-oriented artists and activists celebrated the virtues of settling down and the opportunities available in the borderlands to pioneer a more fulfilling and sustainable way of life.

In the 1840s, many Americans anticipated the dawning of some new golden age, and the cultural debates about what the new era ought to look like were fought openly and often bitterly. But the environmental aspect of those debates has not yet been fully captured in our histories. Every conflict over the expansion of settlement, slavery, industry, commerce, and technology was accompanied by conflicts over how people interacted with nature. In Nathaniel Hawthorne's famous 1843 story "The Celestial Rail-road," for instance, when it turns out that the narrator, styled after Christian in *The Pilgrim's Progress*, has ridden a train to hell instead of heaven, we immediately grasp the critique of Americans' easy faith in their nation's inevitable advancement. Yet railroads must travel through actual physical spaces, and as Hawthorne's train approaches each of Bunyan's famous allegorical landscapes, we quickly learn the environmental cost of taking Progress so literally: the Slough of Despond, "a disgrace to all the neighborhood," already has a bridge over it and is slated to be drained and "converted into firm ground"; the Hill Difficulty has a tunnel through it, and the "materials" carved out of its "heart" have been "employed in filling up the Valley of Humiliation, thus obviating the necessity of descending into that disagreeable and unwholesome hollow"; and of course the Valley of the Shadow of Death (a volcano, it turns out) is now aglow with red gaslamps and traversed by the most modern of causeways.[25] For Hawthorne, who spent so much time haunting the dark swamps and hollows of Concord in the early 1840s, the railroad represented a bargain with the devil: true American pilgrims would have to go back to walking, would have to get bogged down, would have to learn the difficulties and dangers of uneven terrain.

*The Pilgrim's Progress* was one of the most widely known books in antebellum America, and anyone who could read at all knew that Christian's arduous journey and eventual arrival at the Celestial City signaled an ascent from the realm of striving to the realm of repose. Back in 1840, when Bryant put together a volume in the Harper's Family Library called *Selections from American Poets*, he had included some verses by Richard Henry Dana with a famous epigraph from Bunyan: "The Pilgrim they laid in a large upper chamber, whose window opened towards the sun rising: the name of the chamber was Peace; where he slept till break of day, and then he awoke and sang." The narrator of Dana's poem, which is called "Daybreak," yearns to embrace the morning and arise in joyous song, but he finds the American scene too demoralizing:[26]

> With thousand scatter'd beauties nature's rife;
> And airs, and woods, and streams breathe harmonies:
> Man weds not these, but taketh art to wife;
> Nor binds his heart with soft and kindly ties:
> He, feverish, blinded, lives, and feverish, sated, dies.

Dana's compatriots seemed suddenly to be leading lives of consuming desperation, specifically because they had broken their long-standing bonds with nature and were instead joining themselves to technology. Cities, with their modern transportation systems, provided speed and anonymity, severed connections in the name of liberation and limitlessness.

It is no coincidence that in 1849 Nathaniel P. Willis published a book called *Rural Letters*; and, a year later, Susan Fenimore Cooper came out with *Rural Hours*; and, three years after that, Andrew Jackson Downing's *Horticulturist* articles and editorials were collected into a volume of *Rural Essays*. For environmental critics in antebellum America, the new symbol of Progress was the country home, the chamber of peace, the rural retreat. The logic sounded almost antisocial, but it was intended to reorient public debates, and it was echoed by more and more social commentators.[27]

Writing at a time when cities seemed to have the most obvious claim to the liveliest kinds of public culture—urban politics, and even events like Margaret Fuller's Conversations, could get quite rowdy—Willis argued that public space was actually more continuous in the countryside. Once, he explained, a neighbor's daughter had fallen sick with a brain fever, a fact he learned after greeting the local physician on his way out of the neighbor's house. Wherever the doctor's horse appeared, tied to a tree or a gatepost, there followed a stream of visitors and supporters. In this case, alas, the girl died, but long before her passing the whole community had expressed its concern and provided help and solace. It would have been different in the city, Willis thought, where "houses are closer. . . . We pass daily along the street, under the windows of sick chambers, and close to thresholds that lead in where hearts are breaking, and beloved forms coffined, and waiting to be borne away. Nothing comes to our knowledge. The brick wall shuts in their sorrow and its lesson." The open space of rural villages, then, turns out to matter in fairly subtle ways: perhaps we all breathe "better air . . . where the fibres of neighborly recognition and sympathy have life and room. . . . Nature has her sad but needed lessons, which she gives us thus incidentally and unsought, in a life not too crowded and artificial. You hear them in the country, always—in the city, almost never."[28] Though small-town life can also be stiflingly invasive, nevertheless, certain kinds of roomy, rural settlements, like well-designed cemeteries, create spaces where, as Robert Harrison has put it, we might feel "alive in our estrangement," might "speak our death to one another," might ultimately discover that "loss is the rock bottom foundation of the communal. . . . To live loss as a matter of fact means to live poetically, knowing that we are not the possessors of the world we inhabit."[29]

Susan Fenimore Cooper, too, in her rather Thoreauvian *Rural Hours*, a naturalist's chronicle of a year spent at her home in the Otsego Lake region, where her grandfather had founded Cooperstown, made time to dwell on loss and grief, and to suggest how helpful a rustic life might be in developing a healthier relationship to death. One day in mid-May, forced to recognize that "there is sorrow on earth amid the joys of spring," and exasperated by the "tedious" and "insipid" bromides being offered to her by various wise townsmen, she decided to walk through some "quiet fields by the river, where sloping meadows and a border of wood shut one out from the world." Only there did she begin to feel she could cope with life's vicissitudes: "the ear, wearied with the din of folly and falsehood, will gladly open to sounds of gentle harmony from the gay birds, the patient cattle, the flowing waters, the rustling leaves. . . . When the spirit is harassed by the evils of life, it is then the works of God offer to us most fully the strengthening repose of a noble contemplation." Yet she also believed in the importance of shaping the works of humanity so that they, too, could express and inspire a sense of connectedness. The goal was not mere comfort, but an open-eyed engagement and loving acknowledgment.

*Rural Hours* has four sections, named for the seasons, and in "Autumn" it is only a matter of a few pages before Cooper comes to the question of cemeteries. "The character of a place of burial," she insisted, "the consideration or neglect it receives, the nature of the attention bestowed upon it, are all intimately connected with the state of the public mind on many important subjects." And she wanted a more reverent mentality in America when it came to public space and death and nature. "In this utilitarian age," which she characterized elsewhere as one of "selfish avarice, or wastefulness, as when a country is stripped of its wood to fill the pockets or feed the fires of one generation," she wanted some compatriots who would seek not just to use land but to meld with it, to live as if they were already "mouldering remains" turning back into dust and soil. Perhaps a person's highest duty, wherever she sojourned, was the public act of caring for her ancestors' graves and their surroundings: "Just so long, therefore, as each significant mound bears a trace of its solemn character, just so long should it be held sacred by the living. Shall we, in a Christian land, claim to have less of justice, less of decency and natural feeling, than the rude heathen whose place on earth we have taken; a race who carefully watched over the burial-places of their fathers with unwavering fidelity?"[30]

---

I often wince at the righteousness of nineteenth-century reformers. Scholars and critics are trained to maintain distance from their subjects, and so our writings, understandably, and sometimes quite productively, tend to chip away at reputations, expose assumptions and prejudices, excoriate what we perceive today as narrowness or viciousness. But what about our own assumptions and prejudices? And what about the *built-in* distance between ourselves and people who lived in different centuries? It's relatively easy to sound smarter than historical figures. More and more, though, as I find myself at odds with my own destructive society, I see the struggles of nineteenth-century Arcadians as worthy of admiration. How do you change the social structures that cause something like global warming? Technological solutions are absolutely essential, but they often remain unimplemented unless mindsets also change. And what makes mindsets change? Is there any way to work actively for shifts in social psychology? Clearly, there's no tried and true technique, but history suggests that some critiques, even when they are sustained for decades at a time by just a few elites in a few obscure books, can return to have a hauntingly broad impact. And I am convinced, now, that the work of people like Thoreau, Fuller, and Hawthorne, people like Irving, Cooper, Willis, and Bryant, adds up to a rare combination of art, criticism, and activism. It's not that they were heroic, or that they overcame all of their own narrow assumptions: Christianity, for someone like Cooper, was always inherently superior to the religion of heathen.[31] But these writers did see the need for human beings to think differently about their environment and their social relations, and instead of simply attacking people's stupidity and selfishness—a temptation then, at the dawn of the industrial age, as it is now, in the age of climate change—they actu-ally proposed other ways of dwelling on and with the earth, other ways of housing the living and the dead, other ways of broadening and strengthening the ties of kinship.

Who can say exactly how and where to live and die? What is the right combina-tion of urban and rural, public and private, mobility and settledness? All we can ever do is keep looking for the best blend. I felt a little trapped when I first moved to Ithaca, yearned to be back in a larger city. The greenery was wonderful, and this com-munity is much quirkier and more progressive than most, but sometimes it seemed small, provincial, isolated, homogeneous. As often as we could, Christine and I took our kids to more urban settings, lingering in public parks and markets where we might see different kinds of people and hear different languages and sense the excite-ment of diversity, the buzz and friction of difference. In Boston, New York, New Haven, Washington, Chicago, Houston, and Los Angeles, where many of our relatives and friends have settled down, life sometimes feels more exciting and broad; looking out from a North American metropolis, I can't help but see much of the countryside as rather white, Protestant, private, and conservative. Which raises the question: did the elite rural reformers of the mid-nineteenth century help produce what we now think of, stereotypically, as the dominant Red State mentality?

Of all the Hudson valley writer-activists, Andrew Jackson Downing was clearly the most influential, the greatest "taste-maker," sometimes compared by scholars to Martha Stewart.[32] And so, predictably, he tends to get blamed for driving middle-class American families into the private sphere of the suburbs, where, within a few years, they supposedly cared only for their lawns and their level of consumption.[33] Downing, according to his critics, tried to cover up any hint of the labor necessary to maintain grounds and gardens; aligned himself with "the most paternalistic and narrowly didactic dimensions to nineteenth-century social reform," imagining the landscapes and houses he designed as contributing to a "forcible education of the masses," who were often drunk, and often Irish, and, in any case, needed to be disciplined and refined; upheld capitalistic acquisitiveness and property ownership and "evoked a sense of mastery over the environment"; and, ultimately, thought of horticulture and landscape architecture as most suitably and effectively pursued by retiring gentlemen in the privacy of their homes.[34] One can certainly find isolated passages in Downing's writings to support these portrayals of his career, and the antebellum period did see the rise of a particular kind of reactionary suburbanism. But, especially when you factor in his deep environmental commitments, I think it makes more sense to see Downing as an Arcadian balancer of individualism and communalism, urging Americans to cultivate a mode of life in conversation with "the rich and varied charms" of wild nature, with "the groves and gardens, which . . . creep beyond the nominal boundaries of the estate, and re-appear in the pot of flowers in the window, or the luxuriant, blossoming vines which clamber over the porch of the humblest cottage by the wayside."[35]

Downing hoped that he could convince every American to plant and cultivate a fruit tree, and that it would seem evident to each cultivator "how much both himself and the public will be, in every sense, the gainers." In a climate of intense speculation, with private land becoming the defining American commodity, Downing saw an engagement with nature as a countervailing public act, since nature put each individual human being in touch with a vast world characterized by interdependence. His own epicurean delight in horticulture—in nurturing "trees full of soft foliage; blossoms fresh with spring beauty; and, finally,—fruit, rich, bloom-dusted, melting, and luscious"—was partially a means of encouraging both an ethic of care and a constant sense of gratitude.[36] And he was convincing: his manual, *The Fruits and Fruit Trees of America*, first published in 1845, was reprinted annually for the next seven years, until his death in 1852. (Figure 15.)

Though Downing didn't think in technical, ecological terms, he was responsible, more than any other American, for conveying to the public a deep appreciation for all the gifts trees provide: sweetness, shade, shelter, beauty, fresh air, the retention of

Figure 15. *Dearborn's Seedling,* 1850,
lithograph. Downing noted that this pear
was "raised in 1818 by the Hon. H. A. S.
Dearborn, of Boston," who of course went
on to help found the Massachusetts
Horticultural Society and Mount Auburn.

water, habitat for birds. As the utopians at Oneida understood, trees are easier on the
soil than other crops, and better at inspiring a kind of communal attachment. "No
one," Downing wrote, "who has sense enough rightly to understand the wonderful
system of life, order, and harmony, that is involved in one of our grand and majestic
forest-trees, could ever destroy it."[37]

Just as Cooper emphasized the tending of graves, whether on private or public
property, as one of the most crucial of all human actions; just as the author of a guidebook to Mount Auburn suggested that, "in the place of marble, our departed friends
might be commemorated by a noble tree, that should, every year when it put forth its
leaves . . . , be regarded as the medium of constant messages from the dead to the
living"[38]—so did Downing celebrate the purposeful shaping of one's home environment as an expression of connection and continuity through time and space. A stretch
of land is not a home until it is haunted, in the best possible sense, by mourned ancestors, and by things like trees, "to which," Downing noted, "old Time himself grants

longer leases than he does to ourselves; so that he who plants them wisely, is more *certain* of receiving the thanks of posterity, than the most persuasive orator, or the most prolific writer of his day and generation."[39]

Though Downing's insistence on settling down—through his horticultural handbooks, his collections of designs and patterns for cottages and farms and gardens, his advice columns on aesthetics—could certainly seem moralistic, conservative, and exclusive, it took its deepest meaning from the context of land rushes and the general "SPIRIT OF UNREST," which, in the era of Manifest Destiny, Downing thought of as perhaps "the most striking of our national traits." The average American was taking independence too far, repeatedly pulling up stakes, allowing ambition and greed to make of him "a feverish being, in whose Tantalus' cup *repose* is the unattainable drop."[40] Like Thoreau, Downing preached civic engagement through personal "simplicity—an honest resting on the earth":[41] it wasn't that you necessarily had to be rooted in one spot, but you did have to feel some sense of responsibility to the public sphere, to the human and natural community through which you wandered. And he dared to hope that, if "the joint culture of the earth and the heart" actually caught on, his compatriots might embrace new settlement patterns, and he might live to "see the great valleys of the West the garden of the world."[42]

The book that made Downing's reputation was not his pomological manual but his wildly popular *Treatise on the Theory and Practice of Landscape Gardening, Adapted to North America* (1841), and his genius lay in his local and timely adaptations. His Arcadia looked a bit like Oliver Goldsmith's village of Sweet Auburn, but it incorporated the brilliant autumnal hues of New England and New York; and the building style sometimes known as rural (or American) gothic; and a climate perfect for apples and pears; and a naturalistic, picturesque mode of design that emphasized "a certain spirited irregularity, surfaces comparatively abrupt and broken, and growth of a somewhat wild and bold character."[43] It suited Americans in the 1840s and 50s to invoke a Jeffersonian attachment to land and a sense of British cultivation but then to be able to plant a simple tree or small, republican garden in town instead of managing an entire farm—to be able to substitute horticulture for agriculture.[44] Downing accepted many modern trends but asked his fellow citizens to stay in touch with nature, to integrate the environment into modernity instead of shutting it out. A habitation could be thought of as an opening to the wider world instead of a shelter from the elements.[45] Ultimately, his design ethic was based on a close "study of *nature* . . . in a state of free and graceful development" and then an effort "to work in her own spirit."[46] And though Downing's many books did in a sense package and commodify a version of middle-class culture, they also grounded an often untethered society, offering a common commitment to the more thoughtful shaping of space, as well as a common language of landscape, which Americans embraced with the same considerable enthusiasm that they showed for the prints and lithographs that popularized the paintings of the Hudson River School.

---

Even though Downing's financial situation was never particularly stable—in 1846 he had to close his nursery, which had previously produced 150 varieties of apples and 200 varieties of pears—his fame offered him more and more opportunities to reinforce what he believed to be the public-minded element of his teachings. Landscape architecture, in other words—or landscape gardening, as it was still most often called—was finally being incorporated into urban and suburban planning: all the Llewellyn Parks and Irving Parks and Central Parks of the 1850s can be traced directly to Downing's writings and activities of the preceding fifteen years. Downing focused less on the shadow of mortality than some other Arcadians, but he was enamored of rural cemeteries, which stirred "the feeling of human sympathy and the love of natural beauty, implanted in every heart," and whose popularity, he thought, proved "that public gardens, established in a liberal and suitable manner, near our large cities, would be equally successful."[47] Though he often passed architectural commissions to his friend and collaborator Alexander Jackson Davis, who took the Llewellyn Park job just a year after Downing's death, Downing eagerly joined in the process of designing a chapel, front gate, and grounds for the new Cemetery of the Evergreens, chartered in 1849 in Brooklyn.[48] He also had very close ties with the Massachusetts Horticultural Society, which led to his participation in the initial planning of the Boston Public Garden; his design wasn't ultimately used, and his drawings have not survived, but a letter he wrote suggests that he envisioned the land adjacent to the Boston Common as an arboretum, for which he had "prepared a list of trees and indicated the precise places where they were to be planted."[49]

Downing was especially quick to see the possibilities inherent in a new kind of suburban life—so long as it was arranged according to the principles of landscape gardening instead of the principles of speculation. He did not actually design any picturesque suburbs himself, but he laid down guidelines for them, in response to some troubling developments in his home territory. By the late 1840s, a number of speculators were seeking to capitalize on improved railroad and steamboat service in the Hudson valley: they bought up land, subdivided it into small lots according to a simple grid, and advertised their wares. In at least one documented case, these entrepreneurs also attempted to capitalize on Downing's reputation by printing their ads with illustrations from one of his books—despite the fact that their "design" contradicted every element of Downing's style and philosophy.[50] The development in question, located next to Tarrytown and eventually to be known as Irvington (as opposed to Irving Park, established a decade later), could easily have been adapted to the local picturesque topography, instead of offering, in Downing's words, "mere rows of houses upon streets crossing each other at right angles." But legal codes and precedents, ever since the Land Ordinance of 1785, had explicitly encouraged this kind of efficient, gridded "Progress," and though Downing insisted that "the plan and arrangement of new towns ought to be a matter of national importance," it seemed to him that no one was paying attention except the most ruthless capitalists.[51]

He articulated his own approach most cogently in an angry *Horticulturist* essay of June 1850, called "Our Country Villages," offering Americans "a neighborhood where, without losing society, they can see the horizon, breathe the fresh air, and walk upon elastic greensward." For Downing, the one "indispensable" feature of an ideal town would always be "a large open space, common, or park, situated in the middle of the village—not less than twenty acres; and better if fifty or more in extent . . . , held as joint property, and for the common use of the whole village." It is true that Downing's perspective was not radically democratic, since he had a pretty specific idea about what constituted appropriate behavior for public spaces, but he did express a kind of egalitarianism in arguing for unrestricted access to environmental amenities and public culture: "Those who had neither the means, time, nor inclination, to devote to the culture of private pleasure-grounds, could thus enjoy those which belonged to all." Of course, not wanting to be thought a "communist," Downing noted that he still believed firmly "in the power and virtue of the *individual home*"; for the United States to become truly *"republican,"* though, its citizens would have to dwell, also, in "public parks, public gardens, public galleries, and tasteful villages."[52] Especially given the power of Downing's influence, it was not out of the question for American society to develop precisely along these lines. Though urban planning did not become a widely established profession until half a century later, the rural cemetery movement and various Arcadian thinkers had made landscape a crucial issue in American development by the 1840s. As Downing's biographer, David Schuyler, has pointed out, Llewellyn Haskell, who happened to be one of Downing's former clients, was by no means alone in his effort to counter modern trends with his own vision of picturesque development: "Dozens, perhaps hundreds" of such "planned communities" came into being in the 1850s, but the long impact of the Civil War severely "retarded the realization of the suburban ideal."[53]

Meanwhile, Downing's thoughts were turning toward a reconceptualization of the city as well as the countryside, and perhaps the most ambitious public project of the second half of his too-brief career was his design for the land surrounding the Capitol in Washington. The goal, as he explained to Joseph Henry, head of the newly formed Smithsonian Institution, was to create the first "*real* park in the United States," which might then encourage every other metropolitan area in the nation to establish its own parks. Downing's plan called for an "extended landscape garden" balancing dense woodland and open fields, with examples of "all the varieties of trees and shrubs which will flourish in this climate," and of course shaded drives, and curvilinear pathways. "A national park like this," he insisted, "laid out and planted in a thorough manner, would *exercise as much influence on public taste* as Mount Auburn Cemetery."[54] (Figure 16.)

Figure 16. B. F. Smith, *Washington, D.C., with Projected Improvements*, 1852 lithograph. This rendering was based directly on Downing's plan.

Downing oversaw only about a year's worth of work in Washington before dying at age thirty-six, and once he was out of the picture the environmental improvements stalled, eventually passing into others' hands and taking on a much less naturalistic feel. Indeed, his career was so short, and the last century and a half has seen so much destruction, that virtually none of his own projects—not even his estate, in Newburgh, overlooking the Hudson—can be visited today by curious historians or landscape enthusiasts. Yet his vision in many ways came to fruition in one of America's most famous places, at the heart of our biggest city.

In the summer of 1851, when Downing was focused mostly on Washington, he paused to publish a passionate article arguing for a "New-York Park." The city had just acquired a 160-acre tract of land, known as Jones Wood, along the East River, and the possibility of establishing some kind of public park was being actively discussed by the mayor, the aldermen, some state senators, leading businessmen, and public intellectuals like Horace Greeley and of course William Cullen Bryant. Downing wanted to push the conversation: he lauded "public opinion" for having "fairly settled that a park is necessary," but he objected to Jones Wood as being simply "*too small*"— "It is only a child's playground." New York needed at least five hundred acres, to provide "a real feeling of the breadth and beauty . . . , the perfume and freshness of nature," and the park had to be centrally located, so that it could be easily "enjoyed in common by . . . all classes without distinction," and especially by those who could not afford "to escape for a couple of months, into the country, to find repose for body and soul." Perhaps it was "needful in civilized life for men to live in cities," Downing conceded, but that did not mean people had to be "utterly divorced from all pleasant and healthful intercourse with gardens, and green fields." How could Americans, inhabiting such a continent, with such a climate, find themselves "voluntarily and ignorantly living in a state of complete forgetfulness of nature"? Downing saw it as his duty to remind New Yorkers "that cool umbrageous groves have not forsworn themselves within town limits, and that half a million of people have a *right* to ask for the 'greatest happiness' of parks and pleasure-grounds, as well as for paving stones and gas-lights." Ideally, if the new space were arranged carefully enough, if it were truly adapted to local circumstances, then "the thoughtful denizen of the town would go out there in the morning, to hold converse with the whispering trees, and the weary tradesmen in the evening, to enjoy an hour of happiness by mingling in the open space with 'all the world.'" In short, a central park, if it were big enough and bold enough, might make of New York, in its entirety, a new "Arcadia."[55]

It was just one year later, on July 28, 1852, that Downing boarded the steamboat *Henry Clay* in Newburgh, bound for New York, and then drowned in the cold Hudson River a few miles north of the metropolis, while trying to save some of his fellow passengers from a fire that had broken out on board. At first, the predicament did not seem quite so threatening as the one Margaret Fuller had faced near Fire Island, and Downing's wife Caroline in fact survived the wreck, along with close to a hundred other passengers. Ultimately, though, because there were so many people clinging to each other in the waves in an effort to stay afloat, conditions became chaotic and desperate: there were eighty-one documented casualties, including Nathaniel Hawthorne's sister Maria Louisa, whose identity was confirmed by her cousin, the Salem horticulturist Robert Manning, Jr. Apparently, Downing first attended to his wife, then tossed chairs into the water for people to hold onto if they couldn't swim, and then proceeded to bring as many people as he could to shore. According to an eyewitness writing for the *Knickerbocker*, Downing, "after having rescued several from the deep, and returning again on his errand of mercy, was himself swallowed up by the waters, as if in revenge for the victims, of which he had deprived them."[56]

His body washed ashore the next morning. It was identified by his architectural partner, Calvert Vaux, a young Englishman who had come to the United States specifically to work with him. Later that afternoon, according to another friend, George William Curtis, Downing's body was brought back to his library in Newburgh, as "a terrific storm burst over the river and crashed among the hills, and the wild sympathy of nature surrounded that blasted home." One of his eulogists, Marshall P. Wilder, who was both president of the Massachusetts Horticultural Society and also a personal friend, and to whom Downing had dedicated *The Fruit and Fruit Trees of America*, judged that Downing's legacy was evident not just in countless cottages and gardens and grounds but also "in the forests which he has preserved from the merciless axe." Four years later, Vaux erected a monument to him on the grounds of the Smithsonian; on its south face he engraved a quotation from Downing's essay, "The New-York Park." It surely makes sense that Downing is buried on the cliffs above the Hudson, near his home, but Central Park might also have made an appropriate place for his final repose.[57]

If Downing had lived until 1857, he probably would have gotten the commission to design New York's park, the land for which had finally been secured the previous year. Certainly, he would have been delighted by the site's size—843 acres—and location. As it happened, though, the park's newly created Board of Commissioners held a competition to determine who would get the job; thirty-three plans came in, almost all of them covered with Downing's thoughtprints. Among the most prominent professionals who submitted a design were Robert Morris Copeland and H. W. S. Cleveland, fresh from their success with Sleepy Hollow Cemetery in Concord. Within a couple of years, Copeland would go on to publish *Country Life: A Handbook of Agriculture, Horticulture, and Landscape Gardening*, modeled directly on Downing's *Treatise* (and perhaps also, given its seasonal structure, on Susan Cooper's *Rural Hours* and Thoreau's *Walden*). Cleveland, having acted as the corresponding secretary of the New Jersey Horticultural Society in the 1840s, had published a number of articles in the *Horticulturist*; in 1855, he paid tribute to Downing directly by writing a review of the new fifth edition of the *Treatise*, in which he lambasted the "speculators, who lay out rectangular villages . . . and offer rural felicity for sale in lots of thirty by fifty feet," and concluded, in defiance of his conservative childhood, part of which he had spent in Salem, Massachusetts, that "we must learn to open our hearts to Nature's witchery." The two partners said publicly, in *A Few Words on the Central Park*, that their design would eschew "artificial embellishment" and instead make the most of the site's "rude cliffs" and "moss covered rocks" by leaving them essentially as they were.[58]

Of course, the winners of the competition were ultimately Calvert Vaux, Downing's old partner, and Frederick Law Olmsted, who, like Cleveland, had corresponded with Downing and published articles in the *Horticulturist*. Far from leaving the earth and rock untouched, Olmsted and Vaux reshaped or ripped out many landforms and neighborhoods, including a lively African American and Irish community with the resonant name of Seneca Village. Still, their plan, like that of Copeland and Cleveland, was extremely naturalistic, with, as Olmsted put it, "very rugged ground, abrupt eminences, and what is technically called picturesque in distinction from merely beautiful or simply pleasing scenery." I think the new development represented a kind of improvement, despite the unjust displacements and despite the park's tendency to mask its own hauntedness. In the end, it was meant to provide "something more than a mere exemption from urban conditions"; the space itself was the "antithesis" of the capitalist grid.[59] It was not an escape from modernity but an attempt to shift modernity's contours. And when the lower part of the park was opened to the public in 1860, Vaux and Olmsted, ever aware of the long shadow cast by their mentor's death, lobbied to create a memorial that would serve as an "appropriate acknowledgment of the public indebtedness to the labors of the late A. J. Downing, of which we feel the Park itself is one of the direct results."[60] Like many of their best ideas for Central Park, that part of the plan fell through, but in the end the park as a whole, and all of their subsequent landscaping work, and all the public spaces designed by Copeland and Cleveland, all the living, breathing trees they planted and protected, in groves and gardens and forests, from Boston to San Francisco, from Minneapolis to Birmingham, might constitute as much of a monument as Downing could ever have desired.

––––––––––––

For all the naturalism of his design style, Downing also cherished the human culture of public spaces, and his vision for New York was perhaps not truly fulfilled until the founding, decades after his death, of places like the New York Public Library (adjacent to a small park named for William Cullen Bryant), and the Metropolitan Museum of Art (on the eastern edge of Central Park). "Open wide, therefore, the doors of your libraries and picture galleries, all ye true republicans!" shouted Downing, in "The New-York Park." "Build halls where knowledge shall be freely diffused among men, and not shut up within the narrow walls of narrower institutions."[61] Books and pictures, after all, had for centuries performed the same kind of memorializing services as statues and graves—and trees, for that matter—and could therefore contribute to a deeper cultural memory and a publicly shared sense of home. And Downing, as a successful writer, was keenly aware of the recent shifts in printing technologies that had suddenly made books and pictures available to a much larger portion of the population. The wider circulation of artifacts was creating the first real popular culture of the industrial age, a culture that was dominated by the dazzling visual effects of prints produced inexpensively by steam presses from engravings on wood, steel, and stone. And those prints were predominantly of picturesque landscapes. Three of the most successful books of the 1840s, thanks largely to their illustrations, were Downing's own *Treatise*, Willis's *American Scenery*, and Cornelia Walter's *Rural Cemeteries of America*. When customers "subscribed" to such publications, they were able to detach individual prints, and it quickly became customary to display these images in parlors as markers of middle-class status and taste. The entire Arcadian tradition of the antebellum period, from its literary expressions to its horticultural societies, from its vision of cities to its vision of the frontier, was undergirded by the public's fascination with a new visual culture of American landscapes, which was embodied by the Hudson River School of painting, which, in turn, was led by yet another upstate aesthete, Thomas Cole.[62]

Cole, the best-known American artist throughout the 1830s and 40s (his friendship with Bryant, a born promoter, didn't hurt), painted almost exclusively landscapes. Even when he pursued a more allegorical mode, as in his two most popular serial works, *The Course of Empire* (1836) and *The Voyage of Life* (1840), it was the human relationship to different aspects of nature that seemed to be at the center of his art. Thanks to new developments in natural science, and the liberalization of religion, and a patriotic curiosity about landforms that might lend the nation more of a place-based identity, American culture was ready for a kind of painting that transcended traditional subjects, that brought history and the realm of the sacred into a more grounded, local context.[63] So people crowded together at New York and Boston galleries to see Cole's interpretations of pioneer life, and the different forms of settlement, and autumn foliage, and the legacy of Native Americans, and the power of the wilderness—to consider, in short, his vision of Arcadia.

Cole's paintings are in almost every sense middle landscapes. Even the sharpest, starkest scenes seem to dissolve into ambiguity and ambivalence. It is easy, at first, to follow the trajectory in the five stages of *The Course of Empire:* we travel from the dark wilderness of *The Savage State* to the early, gentle glow of civilization in *The Pastoral or Arcadian State;* to the glaring decadence of *The Consummation of Empire;* to the fire and smoke of civilization's *Destruction;* and finally to the calm reassertion of nature's ways in *Desolation.* But was the progression inevitable? Or could America avoid the course of empire simply by putting an end to Jacksonian expansion and reverting to its republican roots? Is there an ideal discernible in the second painting, a paradise we could recapture? (Figure 17.)

Figure 17. Thomas Cole, *The Course of Empire: The Arcadian or Pastoral State,* 1836, oil on canvas.

Cole's Arcadia is framed, in the immediate foreground, by one of his characteristic "blasted trees" on the left, a reminder of nature's destructive force, and by a massive stump on the right, which on the one hand suggests a parallel human power but which also, with its jagged, jutting spikes of heartwood, remains unsubdued. Human culture has carved out a relatively calm existence here, with sheltering groves and open pastures, but the terrain seems slightly disorienting in its cracked, rocky unevenness, and in two places the structures of civilization are sending up plumes of ugly black smoke into the atmosphere. The past, present, and future mingle in a solution of uncertainty. How to shape the land, make a home, without starting down the path of violent confrontation or hubristic erasure?[64]

Even in a much brighter canvas like *Dream of Arcadia* (1838), Cole seemed to question the very idea of an ideal. Yes, he wished to live in rural surroundings that preserved some elements of wildness: that's why, since the late 1820s, he had been mostly planted in the Hudson River town of Catskill. But he also recognized that every earthly paradise had a dark side and that the best-intentioned human plans had ways of subverting themselves. In *Dream of Arcadia*, the upper hillside has been shaped into a sunny pasture for sheep and is topped by the solidly republican image of a white, Doric temple, a symbol of Apollonian reason and order, while the adjacent land survives in all its bold, rocky grandeur, with an untamed waterfall spilling down the right side of the scene. (Figure 18.)

Figure 18. Thomas Cole, *Dream of Arcadia*, c. 1838, oil on canvas.

The shady, lower woodland, though, is the realm of Dionysus: the mild sheep have been replaced by dogs and goats, and revelers of all ages are playing music and dancing and throwing garlands of flowers around the statue of their horned, Pan-like god, who looks down on them with an air of impish dominion. "I took a trip to Arcadia in a dream," Cole wrote, with his own sense of impishness, to his friend and fellow artist Asher B. Durand.[65]

> At the first start the atmosphere was clear, and the traveling delightful: but just as I got into the midst of that famous land, there came on a classic fog, and I got lost and bewildered. I scraped my shins in scrambling up a high mountain—rubbed my nose against a marble temple—got half suffocated by the smoke of an altar, where the priests were burning offal by way of sacrifice (queer taste the gods had, that's certain)—knocked my head against the arch of a stone bridge—was tossed and tumbled in a cataract—just escaped—fell flat on my back among high grass, and was near getting hung on some tall trees: but the worst of all are the inhabitants of that country. . . . There is one thing, dream or reality, that is pleasant—that is, the river is open, and spring is come.

If there was a prescription in *Dream of Arcadia*, it was less about the precise definition of Arcadia and more about the pleasant confusion of dreaming, about the beguiling search for the realms that so enchanted Hawthorne, the border territories between fantasy and reality, the spaces where one could wander forever and feel both lost and at home.

A few years later, when Cole painted *Evening in Arcady* (1843), the twilight tone of his idealism became even more pronounced. (Figure 19.) Though it is possible to see in this image "a quintessentially arcadian moment . . . , made still more calm and more tender by the serenade of the shepherd boy and the little dance of his female companion, the pair of gliding swans, and the trio of deer who carefully cross the stream underneath the natural arch," there is no escaping the picture's ominous strangeness. If the lyre player is a shepherd, then where are his sheep—and, indeed, where is the classic green pasture that would make this scene pastoral in the first place? The whole composition, and especially the dominant rock archway, in all its darkness, recalls Cole's much earlier work, *Expulsion from the Garden of Eden* (1828): we are in a land marked as much by barrenness as by fertility. And what is that snake doing on the sand? Is this, as one scholar has suggested, a representation of the myth of Orpheus and Eurydice, in the moment just before Eurydice gets bitten by the snake and dies?[66] In any case, Cole's Arcadia clearly parallels that of Poussin, whose works Cole saw in Paris and whom he admired as "one of the greatest mas-

Figure 19. Thomas Cole, *Evening in Arcady*, 1843, oil on canvas.

ters": "you are always transported" by his landscapes, Cole wrote; they absorb you, and "you live in a world—in a time, far removed from this."[67] In Arcadia, life takes on more richness and depth specifically because you become more aware of your own progress toward death.

Like so many other antebellum Arcadians, Cole turned to nature for repose, but repose turned out to be an impossibly complex quality. Back in early October 1828, after what Cole perceived as the failure of his *Expulsion*, he decided to take some time off and soak up the colorful New England autumn by going climbing in the White Mountains. Coming through Franconia Notch and stumbling upon two preternaturally calm lakes, he found that "the perfect repose of these waters and the unbroken silence reigning through the whole region, made the scene peculiarly impressive and sublime; indeed, there was an awfulness in the deep solitude, pent up within the great precipices, that was painful." A couple of days earlier, he had set out to ascend Chocorua Peak (now called Mount Chocorua), and he did ultimately get to the summit, but there were so many downed trees along the path that he felt as though he were tracking a tornado, and he paused a long while at "a lonely and deserted clearing, just at the foot of the mountain. The cause of this abandonment is, they say, the poisonous effects of the water upon the cattle, the result, according to tradition, of the curse of Chocorua, an Indian, from whom the peak, upon which he was killed by the whites, takes its name." The view from the top of the mountain, Cole initially thought, was "too extended and map-like for the canvas," but in the end he decided to paint a summit picture that would show the mortally wounded Chocorua confronting his murderer, a local settler, and the dramatic painting inspired the Indian advocate Lydia Maria Child to write up the legend as a short story.[68] "A curse upon ye, white men!" shouts the Indian prophet, as "the blood bubbled from his neck. . . . Chocorua had a son—and ye killed him while his eye still loved to look on the bright sun, and the green earth! The Evil Spirit breathe death upon your cattle . . . ! Chocorua goes to the Great Spirit—his curse stays with the white men!" And from then on, not only did the cattle start to die, but the whole community, having taken a typically arrogant and antagonistic stance toward both Natives and nature, now felt their enemies' full wrath: "the tomahawk and scalping knife were busy among them, the winds tore up trees and hurled them at their dwellings, their crops were blasted."[69]

Cole, drawing on his own experience as a young man in Ohio, actually painted many pioneer settlers, most of them much less violent than the killer of Chocorua; in general, the middle landscapes in which they participate seem equally promising and foreboding. Dark skies sometimes loom in the upper left of these scenes, and since we tend to read paintings from left to right, the future feels uncertain for these lonely outposts and homesteads; have they, too, been cursed? In another New Hampshire nook, known as Crawford Notch, which Nathaniel Hawthorne also visited, referring to it as "majestic, and even awful,"[70] Cole created an almost painfully complicated scene, showing a rider racing homeward, and directly toward the storm, on a black mount, passing dead trees and blasted trees, coming through a long, bumpy field of stumps. (Figure 20.)

And yet the autumn colors are lovely, glowing in a patch of mellow, golden sunshine, and the house nestled in the trees is of a fine construction and seems to blend in perfectly with its surroundings, as if living up to Margaret Fuller's ideal of frontier settlement. What will happen next in this scene, and on America's far frontiers? Well, when Cole visited Crawford Notch in 1828, he called it a "desolate and savage spot," noting that "the wind blew violently down the pass as we approached, and the gray, heavy clouds were rushing round the overhanging crags." All the bridges on the wild Saco River had been "washed away by late floods," and there was no dwelling place at all save the infamous, deserted house built by Samuel Willey, which "naturally recalled to mind the horrors of the night when the whole family perished beneath an avalanche of rocks and earth."[71] Did Cole's scene, painted 11 years after

Figure 20. Thomas Cole, A *View of the Mountain Pass Called the Notch of the White Mountains (Crawford Notch)*, 1839, oil on canvas.

his first visit to this area, intend to re-inscribe the well-known Willey tragedy of 1826, or to transcend it, to show Americans confidently starting over and keeping the faith?

The same question lingers over his earlier picture of *Daniel Boone at His Cabin at Great Osage Lake.* (Figure 21.) Is this the archetypal American hero, determined and courageous, attractive both to expansionists and to Arcadians, leading a life in close touch with nature, building his log cabin right into the hillside, soaking up the energizing sun as it shines down from the approving heavens? Is he Thoreau's backwoodsman in paradise? Or is he a tired old man, isolated from any communal spirit, dwarfed by bold, rocky outcroppings, grim-faced, and wearing a rough brown garment that identifies him with dead leaves and the twisted, shattered tree leaning just over his head?

In part because Cole focused more on individual homesteaders than on villages or towns, the scholarly consensus still holds that most of his paintings are overly romanticized: as Angela Miller has put it in her canonical book, *The Empire of the Eye*, "the fundamentally destructive character of settlement is disguised by the pastoral aesthetics of the middle landscape, which smooths over the contest between nature and

Figure 21. Thomas Cole, *Daniel Boone at His Cabin at Great Osage Lake*, c. 1826, oil on canvas.

culture."[72] Indeed, according to the geographer M. K. Heiman, Cole must be seen as "veiling the disagreeable facts of production," as constructing an "ideal" instead of documenting "the reality," since "the Hudson Valley was certainly not the rural semi-wilderness depicted" in so many of his paintings.[73] But surely a region as large as the Hudson valley does not have one simply defined "reality," and surely Cole's ravaged stumps and trees suggest both historical and transhistorical conflicts between humanity and nature.

Cole, in both his public and private writings, including one poem, "The Lament of the Forest," in which he speaks for and through the trees, decried the industrial scale of environmental destruction: "Our doom is near: behold from east and west/The skies are darkened by ascending smoke;/Each hill and every valley is become/An altar unto Mammon. . . . We feed ten thousand fires: in our short day/The woodland growth of centuries is consumed."[74] On walks through the countryside surrounding his own village, Cole could see the swaths of woodland being removed for the railroad and the tanneries, and by the mid-1830s he was sometimes overcome with "gloom," and with a desire to cast "maledictions on all dollar-godded utilitarians."[75] "The wayside," he wrote, "is becoming shadeless, and another generation will behold spots, now rife with beauty, desecrated by what is called improvement; which, as yet, generally destroys Nature's beauty without substituting that of Art."[76] But perhaps improvement could become more artful, and, besides, nature was not simply going to succumb to the capitalists. Cole could still find inspiring environments as he wandered around his home valley; the Hudson region, he insisted, was "still lovely: man cannot remove its craggy hills, nor well destroy all its rock-rooted trees: the rapid stream will also have its course."[77] And he continued to paint magical borderlands hovering between fantasy and reality, continued to include in his pictures both a confrontation with the environmental damage that human beings always caused—not to mention the violence inherent in nature's own systems—and a hopefulness about the possibility of minimizing the damage, and surviving the violence, and constructing some new kind of society in the wilderness.[78]

Cole became more religious in the 1840s, the final decade of his life, and for a long time I thought that his later works suggested a move toward abstraction, almost a spiritual retreat from nature, especially in comparison with the paintings that his only student, Frederic Church, would eventually complete—paintings that show more of a commitment to scientific detail than to the assumed truths of religion.[79] In recent years, though, I have come to see Cole's overtly religious scenes as conscientious attempts to integrate death and life, to acknowledge nature's unsettling ability both to terrify and to console. A painting like *The Voyage of Life: Manhood* (1840) used to look to me like a banal sermon on the necessity of faith in God and heaven, but now I can see in Cole's composition a more earthly message about the recognition of light in darkness and darkness in light: so we saunter toward the Holy Land, and honor nature's unimaginable breadth as we go, and honor our own pleasure and pain. (Figure 22.)

And then came *The Cross in the Wilderness* (1845), which was painted without a commission, and which seems to be an expression of true kinship, of Cole's desire to overcome his nation's hubris in this particular historical moment by emphasizing the possibility of a timeless, universal human engagement with nature and mortality.[80] (Figure 23.) The autumnal scene, set in a clearing poised between wildness and civilization, and based on a poem by Felicia Hemans, a well-loved British sentimentalist, suggests the deepest empathy between humanity and the environment, and between the white, Christian viewers of the painting and the Native American viewer of the tomb, who may or may not be Christianized himself, but who is dressed in the traditional clothing of his tribe, and whose own outline, given his

Figure 22. Thomas Cole, *The Voyage of Life: Manhood*, 1840, oil on canvas.

Figure 23. Thomas Cole, *The Cross in the Wilderness*,
after a poem by Felicia Hemans, 1845, oil on canvas.

posture, clearly echoes the shape of both the hill in the distance and the raised mound below the cross.[81] We are different, the picture seems to say, but related. And the earth, by accepting our wandering bodies when we die, gives all of us a potentially permanent home, which every person has an equal right to inhabit, and an equal reason to protect.

---

It makes as much sense to think of ourselves as separate from the environment as it does to think of ourselves as part of the environment. Binaries like nature and culture, death and life, night and day, male and female, public and private, help us understand the world. I still prefer the interstices, the twilight zone, still find it valuable to question every pairing and to look for the full spectrum of grays between what we perceive as the extremes of black and white—but black and white, as long as we don't define them too rigidly, are what make the grays possible.[82] Kinship is a much more powerful concept when it crosses a gulf of difference than when it simply unifies things that are thought to be virtually the same; true middle landscapes preserve the tension of polarity but also open up liminal spaces where the poles bleed into each other, revealing their interdependence and complementarity. And nineteenth-century Americans, steeped in a culture of engagement with death and nature, conceived of middle landscapes in uniquely creative terms, dreaming of new Arcadias until such places no longer seemed possible.

The last picture Cole finished, the last Arcadia he imagined, was called *The Good Shepherd* (1848), and when he was asked to comment on it, he simply quoted the opening of the Twenty-third Psalm: "The Lord is my Shepherd, I shall not want. / He maketh me to lie down in green pastures."[83] (Figure 24.)

Immediately, when I read that, in the catalogue for the memorial exhibition held in Cole's honor shortly after he died, I thought of my grandmother, who was a poet, and whose best-known work was a reinterpretation of those same lines. "The Lord is my Shepherd, /" her poem begins, "I shall not bleat. / But I shall want, / because the world is want— / is stones instead of pasture. / I will be stubborn, stand into the wind."[84] My grandfather, her husband, was a biblical scholar and a rabbi, but I have never been able to figure out whether the two of them would have called themselves religious. The last time I saw my grandmother was when I visited from Minnesota, at the end of my year at Wolf Ridge Environmental Learning Center, in spring, the season of Passover, when the whole extended family used to gather at my grandparents' house. Grandma was a bird lover, and she became suddenly alert as I told her about the thrill of seeing my first pileated woodpecker in Minnesota. I stayed in the extra bedroom,

Figure 24. Thomas Cole's grave, Catskill, NY, 2010.

which used to be my mother's, and which had only one memorable decoration: a small picture frame on the dresser, with the quotation about the Chamber of Peace from the end of *The Pilgrim's Progress*. That frame now sits atop one of my bookcases. I also told Grandma that I had gone canoeing in the Boundary Waters and had seen a bald eagle, and that I had just been looking through the house and had discovered Grandaddy's old paddle—which, today, leans against another of my bookcases. "Your mother hated it when we took her canoeing," Grandma said. "Too many bugs." The bugs have never really bothered me.

At my grandmother's funeral, and at virtually every family gathering since then, one of her grandchildren has stood before the rest of us and read her psalmic poem. It feels like my life's central text, with its invocations of pain and persistence, death and nature. I still read it regularly, often right after I visit my parents.

Benjamin would have turned twenty on November 19, 1987; Ian was diagnosed on Valentine's Day, 1988, and died on August 29; Grandaddy died on Valentine's Day, 1989, Grandma on September 17, 1990—Grandaddy's birthday. Jewish culture takes careful note of death dates, and I have always marked the anniversaries of my grandparents' passing, their *yahrzeits*. Exactly seventeen years after Grandaddy died, my second son was born, on Valentine's Day.

In the autumn of 1989, as I paddled along borders and pondered death and learned to live with a wolf, my mother visited Grandma as often as she could and prepared for the passing of a generation. My grandparents had been towering figures in our family's life, at the center of every gathering—the only grandparents I ever knew, scholars, writers, teachers, canoeists, birdwatchers, gentlest of elders. Their greatest bequest, the gift they tried to pass on through the generations, was their sense of repose. "I am afraid, /" says Grandma's poem. "Oh! let me not deceive myself. . . . /And yet . . . and yet. . . . /" Given the bounties of nature, the possibilities of culture and cultivation, it would be just as deceptive to dwell only on darkness and want, wind and stones, the shrieking fear we all sometimes feel, the depths of our winters. A sense of limitation can be strangely liberating, can offer groundedness, guidelines. And so the poem ends with the expectation of ripeness and morning and continuity:

> My cup runneth over
> 　with vintage of the ripened vine.
> 　There is, despite,
> 　a spring of birds in me.
>
> Goodness and mercy
> 　and hope before the sun
> 　follow into the night.
>
> And I shall dwell
> 　whether by quiet waters
> 　or on shifting sands—
> 　still in his house.

I have often found quiet waters in the valleys of the nineteenth century; it can be consoling to care for pockets of history, and I am grateful for that vocation. Still, I think constantly about my parents' age and mortality, and about the vulnerability of my children, and about the limits on my own life and capabilities. I am afraid. And yet—and yet. . . .

Thomas Cole's last words, apparently, were "I want to be quiet." At his funeral, in the spring of 1848, it was, of course, William Cullen Bryant who delivered the most cogent eulogy. "With what reverence he copied the forms of nature," Bryant said, "and how he blended with them the profoundest human sympathies."[85] Bryant wanted his audience to know that his friend had died quietly: "The close of his life was like the rest of it, serene and peaceful, and he passed into that next stage of existence, from which we are separated by such slight and frail barriers, with unfaltering confidence in the divine goodness, like a docile child guided by the kindly hand of a parent, suffering itself to be led without fear into the darkest places."[86]

When Asher B. Durand, the organizer of the memorial exhibition, painted his own tribute to Cole, he honored the friendship between Cole and Bryant, and called his picture *Kindred Spirits* (1849). (Figure 25.)

Figure 25. Asher Brown Durand, *Kindred Spirits*,
1849, oil on canvas.

The title comes from Keats's "Seventh Sonnet," in which the poet dreams of stealing away to "Nature's observatory" with a dear friend, where they might "dwell" together and hold "converse" with each other and with the world.[87] Durand's scene bursts with pairings: there are two men, one from the country and one from the city, representing the sister arts of painting and poetry, with both their names carved into a paper birch tree; and there are two birds, two waterfalls, two rocky outcroppings, two pairs of seemingly joined mountains, two clouds, two blasted trees. Cole and

Bryant stand on a ledge, an edge of the natural world, and the rock seems just slightly precarious, and they are by no means unaware of nature's dark power, which snaps trees and raises granite cliffs and carves valleys and strews boulders—yet they seem balanced, calm in the glow of the sun, bridging the chasm with their imaginative vision, absorbed in kinship. They've wandered off into the wilderness of the Catskills, but it's familiar to them; they are clearly not far from home. The dead man's memory remains alive in his old haunts. Today, if you hike the short trail to the twinned Kaaterskill Falls from County Road 23A, especially in the spring, when you are likely to find trees felled by wind and flood, you might feel as though you are walking into Durand's picture.

Cole's student, Church, also painted an elegiac memorial. (Figure 26.)

Figure 26. Frederic Edwin Church, *To the Memory of Cole*, 1848, oil on canvas.

*To the Memory of Cole* (1848) shows an idealized gravesite near Cole's home on the Hudson, in Catskill. The actual burial place had no such marker, so Church's perfectly centered, garlanded cross seems like a clear echo of his mentor's attempt to combine symbolism with the realistic depiction of nature in *The Cross in the Wilderness*. There are significant differences, though, which point, perhaps, to imminent shifts in both American painting and American society. Most notably, Church did not include any human figures. The viewer's witnessing of Cole's death and his close relationship to nature is implied, but the image itself, rather than touching any communal chords, seems to strike a note of serene solitude, as if preserving some sort of purity that would almost inevitably be marred by the presence of a living person. And the scene is much broader than Cole's, with a more distant horizon; it feels expansive. We are not under the shady canopy of Mount Auburn. While the prominent deciduous trees in both *The Cross in the Wilderness* and *Kindred Spirits* seem to reach out their sheltering branches toward the center of the frame, the evergreens in Church's painting are much more vertical, almost erect, in their stretching toward heaven. Cole, back in 1836, observing the deforestation around Catskill, had taken some cold comfort in the news that the "tree-destroyers" were at least going to spare a few patches of woodland. "Thank them for that," he wrote, mischievously, to his wealthy patron. "If I live to be old enough, I may sit down under some bush, the last left in the utilitarian world, and feel thankful that intellect in its march has spared one vestige of the ancient forest for me to die by."[88] In Church's picture, though, the land seems thoroughly opened, and Cole reposes not under a tree but next to a rough, ragged stump.

# 4

## STUMPS

What husky huzzahs in the hazy groves—
What flying encounters fell;
Pursuer and pursued like ghosts disappear
In gloomed shade—their end who shall tell?
The crippled, a ragged-barked stick for a crutch,
Limp to some elfin dell—
Hobble from the sight of dead faces—white
As pebbles in a well.

*Few burial rites shall be;*
*No priest with book and band*
*Shall come to the secret place*
*Of the corpse in the foeman's land. . . .*

None can narrate that strife in the pines,
A seal is on it—Sabaean lore!
Obscure as the wood, the entangled rhyme
But hints at the maze of war—
Vivid glimpses or livid through peopled gloom,
And fires which creep and char—
A riddle of death, of which the slain
Sole solvers are.
—Herman Melville, "The Armies of the Wilderness," 1866

Stumps haunted the American landscape in the 1850s, the decade after Thomas Cole's death. (Figure 27.)

Figure 27. John Quidor, *The Headless Horseman Pursuing Ichabod Crane*, 1858, oil on canvas.

In the 1860s, the phantoms multiplied unimaginably.[1] (Figure 28.)

Many Americans noted the grim parallel, the linguistic echo, the bond of kinship between wounded veterans and devastated trees, the limbs and trunks cut down in their prime. Amputees, formerly a tiny minority, now became the limping symbols of the entire nation: they lined city streets, begging, singing melancholy ballads, demanding attention, sympathy, prosthetics. They embodied the lingering of war's horror.[2] And out in the countryside, rough patches of woodland from Maine to Georgia, from Virginia to California, ravaged by rapid expansion and military necessity, cast thin shadows on the blood-soaked fields, and reeked of ruination and wastage. (Figure 29.)

Figure 28. Civil War amputee
Lieutenant Burritt Stiles, Co. A,
14th Connecticut Volunteers,
1867, photograph.

Figure 29. "Ft. Sanders, Knoxville, Tenn.," 1863, stereoscopic photograph.

The collection of poems Herman Melville published in 1866, his first book in nine years, was called *Battle-Pieces and Aspects of the War*. His nation had been reunified; his world was in pieces. Between 1846 and 1857 he had produced a constant flow of prose, a book every year, novels and stories. Then he had hit middle age and sequestered himself on his rock-strewn farm in Massachusetts, which he called Arrowhead, since the plow often turned up suggestions that New England might be better suited to Indian-style hunting than to European-style agriculture. Melville was already haunted, and the war just amplified his alienation and isolation, his paralysis, his guilt, his sense of being out of joint. In Pittsfield, the town nearest to his estate, he watched as returned soldiers paraded through the streets on horseback, with crutches dangling from saddles. In April 1864, he visited a cousin at the front and toured several of Virginia's battlefields. Then, a few days later, a few miles away, came that notorious inferno, the Battle of the Wilderness. At war's end, in a burst of emotion, Melville began to write elegies, eulogies, lamentations, canticles, pleas, inscriptions, memorials, meditations, epitaphs, requiems. At least he was writing. But the images that dominate these fragments are of blank monuments and unmarked mounds. Too often, the verses seem clipped. In poems like "The Armies of the Wilderness," Melville tried to invoke the rich American tradition of enlisting nature in the act of commemoration. What happens, though, when the armies and the wilderness suffer a parallel erasure, akin to Indian displacement? Imagining postwar Virginia, he saw "stumps of forests for dreary leagues / Like a massacre."[3]

Walt Whitman, born in the same year as Melville, was more in tune with his times, more capable of direct involvement, more fluid in his work and his sympathies. But even his flow was stanched by the war. He did continue writing, but the results, he thought, were mere echoes, "drum-taps," "stray glimpses," "scraps and distortions." Aspiring to head-on confrontation, he found his poems drifting toward aversion: "From the stump of the arm, the amputated hand, / I undo the clotted lint, remove the slough, wash off the matter and blood, / Back on his pillow the soldier bends with curv'd neck and side falling head, / His eyes are closed, his face is pale, he dares not look on the bloody stump, / And has not yet look'd on it."

In December of 1862, hearing that his brother had been wounded, Whitman had rushed to Virginia, and commenced making rounds at all the medical camps there and in Washington. George was fine, it turned out, and quickly returned to the lines of battle. Walt stayed in the capital, became "The Wound-Dresser," ministering to the prostrated, the fevered, the delirious, the dying, offering consolation, conversation, pencils, stamped envelopes, rice pudding, whiskey, kisses. For two and a half years he wandered the nearby woods and haunted the hospitals, and "kept little note-books . . . , forming a special history of those years, for myself alone, full of associations, never to be possibly said or sung." When he finally published his *Memoranda During the War*—eleven years after war's end—he claimed that many of the prose fragments were copied verbatim from those "soil'd and creased livraisons, each composed of a sheet or two of paper, folded small to carry in the pocket, and fasten'd with a pin . . . , blotched here and there with more than one blood-stain, hurriedly written, sometimes at the clinique, not seldom amid the excitement of uncertainty, or defeat, or of action, or getting ready for it, or a march."[4]

Who better, as a guide to the war years, than one so full of both horror and love, so eager to embrace all of humanity and nature as a brother, so committed to memorializing, despite a sinking conviction that the countless unknown soldiers were inherently unknowable, that the everyday facts of such a war were inherently unnameable: "Of scenes like these, I say, who writes—who e'er can write the story?" A consummate Arcadian, Whitman had always looked to nature for his narratives of death and regeneration, and had always been comforted by the intermingling of animals and plants: "And as to you corpse I think you are good manure, but that does not offend me, / I smell the white roses sweetscented and growing." After the war, though, the new growth would be different, for the earth had absorbed not just the decaying flesh of beloved elders, but "the red life-blood oozing out from heads or trunks or limbs" of anonymous young soldiers, "soaking roots, grass, and soil," leaving "the land entire saturated." Whitman tried obsessively—"convulsively," he said—to transfigure the war, to imagine it as a great thunderstorm or earthquake that might one day be understood as clarifying and renewing. But he feared, I think, that the memory of the conflict would instead linger on like the phantom pain felt by an amputee, or like the jolt experienced by a plowman who had temporarily forgotten about the overgrown stump in the middle of his field.[5]

---

Often, of course, American fields were so cluttered with stumps that there was no question of forgetting about them for any length of time. (Figures 30 and 31.)

Stumps before the war; stumps after the war. Much had changed—though stumps remained in the foreground.

We've traveled from a fertile valley, bathed in early sunlight, to a denuded mountain and its darkening, red meadows. We've traded neat, clean, industrial development for a rough-and-tumble rural homestead. Inness's gently curving train seems to blend smoothly with its environment; its smoke, like the smoke of the village factories, echoes the morning mist, becoming a natural feature of the scene. As the critic

Figure 30. George Inness, *The Lackawanna Valley*, c. 1856, oil on canvas.

Figure 31. Sanford Robinson Gifford, *Hunter Mountain, Twilight*, 1866, oil on canvas.

Leo Marx would later write, the painting "is a striking representation of the idea that machine technology is a proper part of the landscape." The classic pastoral observer seems perfectly calm, at peace, accepting all the changes surrounding him, proud of American Progress. Inness must have pleased his patron—the president of the Delaware, Lackawanna and Western Railroad.[6] But then twilight came to America. A stump field, one year after the end of the Civil War, could not represent progress and development: the destiny manifest here was tragic. The war had costs, just as frontier settlement did. Americans finally began to realize, in the 1860s, that they had to confront limits, that logging caused ugly, long-lasting scars, that the renewal of timber resources would take a mighty effort. Perhaps Gifford's ravaged scene directly inspired a movement to protect trees in the United States: the artist sold his painting to a dear friend, James Pinchot, who one year earlier had named his first son Gifford; the canvas hung on the wall throughout the boy's childhood; Gifford Pinchot went on to become Theodore Roosevelt's chief forester and the author of *The Fight for Conservation*.[7]

Historical transitions, though, are never quite so neat. Americans did see stumps differently in the aftermath of the war; they did become more broadly aware of forest destruction than ever before.[8] But they had already been worrying about the killing of trees, to some extent, for decades, and both settlement and industrial development, rather than getting reined in, entered a period of massive, devastating expansion as soon as the war ended.

If the president of the Delaware, Lackawanna and Western approved of Inness's painting, he missed the work's clear debt to Thomas Cole's ambivalence. Does the classical pose of the observer imply that he is truly satisfied with his view, that his repose will be undisturbed by the crash and clank of the straining locomotive? Has he willingly traded the curve of a river for the curve of track and fence, the shelter of a wood for a field of dead stumps? We can't be sure: we see only his hat, worn for shade, and his back, whose bright orange tint causes him to stick out of the foreground like another amputated tree. And then there are the layers of haze hovering over the valley, seeming to throw the town's future into doubt: the mountain mist, at least, will burn off as the day progresses, but the smoke of the train and factories will cause a permanent veil of pollution. This is Scranton we're looking at, during the iron and coal boom in eastern Pennsylvania, which had already left deep scars on the landscape; anyone who was paying attention had already noticed how double-edged the axe of Progress could be.[9]

Ten years later, Gifford chose to confront industrial development in a much less direct way, despite the massive technological changes that had been occurring. His painting hints at the power of American capitalism: Hunter Mountain is at the heart of the Catskills—at the heart of tanning country. But the local tanning industry had already peaked: Gifford's grandfather was the last one in his family to be engaged in the trade. The story here was a romantic, nostalgic, rose-colored one, focused on a classic American family attempting to carve out a life in a beautiful bit of wilderness. But these settlers found themselves worrying that maybe the wilderness was not what it once had been. Just like *The Lackawanna Valley*, this scene pays clear homage to Cole, celebrating the mythic beauty of America's gently sloping valleys, but also asking whether we could ever dwell in such places without obliterating all of their sheltering qualities, without carving up the land and starving our cattle: the thinness of the animals in this pasture perhaps echoes the thinning of the surrounding forest. There is a desperate yearning here for the possibilities of the past. Immediately after the Civil War, Americans were convinced that they had to go back to the land, in order to heal themselves—but they were also convinced that the land had been tainted.[10]

In 1855, a foreground littered with tree stumps would have forced Americans to confront the killing of trees and the onset of industrialism, would have pointed to the sacrifices required by Progress, would have reminded everyone of the distinction between a good, necessary death and a potentially unnatural death. In 1866, Americans desperately wanted to understand every death as good and necessary, but suspected that almost all the killing of the war years had been utterly unnatural. In 1866, then, a foreground littered with tree stumps could no longer stand for itself. In a way, *Hunter Mountain, Twilight*, seems the perfect Arcadian picture, capturing a full awareness of mortality and a heightened sense of connection between people and trees. But there's a strange slippage here, a denial, a failure to acknowledge that Civil War mortality had to be understood on an industrial rather than a pastoral scale. Rather than spurring the conservation movement in America, perhaps this painting marked the twilight of America's Arcadian landscape tradition.[11]

---

WW (1876):

*There they lie, in the largest, in an open space in the woods, from 500 to 600 poor fellows—the groans and screams—the odor of blood, mixed with the fresh scent of the night, the grass, the trees—that Slaughter-house!—O well is it their mothers, their sisters cannot see them—cannot conceive, and never conceiv'd, these things . . . One man is shot by a shell, both in the arm and leg—both are amputated—there lie the rejected members. Some have their legs blown off. . . . Such is the camp of the wounded—such*

*a fragment, a reflection afar off of the bloody scene—while over all the clear, large
moon comes out at times softly, quietly shining.*

*Such, amid the woods, that scene of flitting souls—amid the crack and crash and
yelling sounds—the impalpable perfume of the woods—and yet the pungent, stifling
smoke—shed with the radiance of the moon, the round, maternal queen, looking from
heaven at intervals so placid—the sky so heavenly—the clear-obscure up there, those
buoyant upper oceans—a few large placid stars beyond, coming out and then
disappearing—the melancholy, draperied night above, around . . . And there, upon the
roads, the fields, and in those woods, that contest, never one more desperate in any age
or land—both parties now in force—masses—no fancy battle, no semi-play, but fierce
and savage demons fighting there.*[12]

---

It's hard to understand how even the most robust cultural tradition could have survived the Civil War. Wouldn't every aspect of life—and every assumption about
death—have been thrown into doubt?[13]

I'm convinced by Whitman when he insists that the war's "interior history will not
only never be written, its practicality, minutia of deeds and passions, will never be
even suggested."[14] What went on in these men's souls? Scholars have unearthed vast
stores of evidence suggesting the diversity of reasons men had for fighting: to preserve slavery; to end slavery; to preserve the Union; to preserve the economy; to
achieve honor; to achieve a good death; to be considered a good comrade; to be
considered a true man.[15] Each causal explanation—like most causal explanations, I
suppose—seems partially convincing, but hopelessly reductive. I have never been
able to empathize with Civil War soldiers, despite my sense that I have a more
grounded understanding of the mid-nineteenth century than of the late twentieth
and early twenty-first. I started trying in college, started clearing away the assumptions I'd grown up with in my liberal Massachusetts environment in the 1970s. It
didn't work. The best I could do was to imagine myself as an antebellum Bostonian,
listening to the speeches of William Lloyd Garrison, eager to wage a cultural war for
abolition. But would I kill to end slavery? Would I risk being killed myself? I thought
not. What I did start to understand, though, at least to some limited extent, was the
harrowing impact of the war, owing to the many people around me, during my college years, who suddenly died.

It started with Ian. Then: my only grandfather, my only grandmother, two of my
three aunts (cancer), another friend (lupus), a beloved high school teacher (rare
nervous system disorder), and a beloved college professor (heart attack). Only my

grandparents reached a ripe old age; the others departed much too early. And all this happened in a short span of years—the amount of time it takes to earn a college degree, or fight a Civil War.

They were not victims of direct human violence. But the scale changed my worldview: I went from virtually no familiarity with death to the sense that mortality was the defining force in my life. Whenever someone asked me how I was doing, my mind flashed to the most recent funeral I'd attended. I generally tried to dodge the question. Eventually, though, the passing of so many friends and family members shoved me into some form of grim adulthood, just as, in a sense, the Civil War shoved America into modernity. How to brace for such transitions? For postbellum Americans, the future looked to be fast, violent, ironclad, overwhelming, each helpless individual but a speck, a statistic, a cog, pulled lurchingly back and forth by elaborate machines, by systems far beyond anyone's ken. Escapist denial must have seemed a reasonable choice.

In my sophomore year of college I encountered the photographs of Timothy H. O'Sullivan for the first time. I was most drawn to his geological survey pictures, his western landscapes—I dreamed constantly of living in nature, doing months of "fieldwork," exploring distant hillsides—but I paused for a few days on his Civil War deathscapes. *A Harvest of Death*: in college it was merely stark, but now it strikes me as utterly wrenching, for it marks the devastation of the horticultural and agrarian traditions, the bodies rotting in the field suggesting crops that will rot in other fields, and on vines, and trees, for lack of any harvesters. O'Sullivan worked with Alexander Gardner, who, along with Matthew Brady, captivated the American public throughout the war with their true-to-life images from the front lines. But when Gardner published his *Photographic Sketch Book of the War* in 1866, including several of O'Sullivan's best pictures, nobody bought it. Who wanted to look at corpses in 1866?[16] (Figure 32.)

I talk about my sophomore year of college about as often as I talk about my brother Benjamin. I've done my best to bury all my memories of how immobilized I was by grief, self-pity, self-disgust. Ian died a couple of weeks before school started, and I should have dropped out right then, but instead I pressed on, until the pressing on came to seem more like farce than fortitude. Thanks to denial, I was generally able to function. All too often, though, despair would seize me, and I would freeze, or explode. The week after my grandfather's funeral, in February, I burst out sobbing in my sophomore "tutorial," an intensive introduction to the history and literature of France and America. History? Literature? They seemed like the worst kinds of abstractions, and the discussion felt phony to me, bloodless, drained of all emotion. There were five other students and two teachers sitting in a cozy circle, books open on their

Figure 32. Timothy H. O'Sullivan, *A Harvest of Death*, 1863, photograph.

laps, and no one knew what to do or say when I lost control. It was the kind of thing that just never, ever happened. At the time, I hated them and their silence, and hated myself, hated my shame, hated our privilege, hated the plush, crimson fabric of the chairs, the dark wood of the walls, the Victorian décor. Eventually I stopped crying and just sat there with my mouth closed, looking down, while they continued the conversation. By the next week, I was once again able to go through the motions. I've told so few people about what happened that I've almost begun to distrust the memory. But that moment in sophomore tutorial captured the turmoil I felt all that year after Ian passed away, as I tried to confront my failure of friendship, my inability to reach out to him as he lay dying.

Some of what I went through that year clearly stemmed from my own immaturity. Another aspect of my experience, though, was the confusion I felt about my culture's seeming inability—or unwillingness—to confront mortality. When my grandfather died—my grandfather the rabbi, famous for leaving everyone in tears at weddings and bar mitzvahs, so gentle, so generous, so humble and calm, so open-minded, so dedicated to the pursuit of understanding, so willing to reach out, so skilled at making private emotion something that could be shared publicly—I wanted the world to stop for him. But life in the modern world doesn't ever slow down, let alone pause. At least I could tell myself that he had lived nine long decades and that he passed away knowing how important he had been to his community. When Ian started to die, though, I'd had no well to draw on. I still berate myself for not being strong enough, creative enough, to figure out what to do on my own. At nineteen, though, I could have used some support. There can never be a simple formula for such situations, but couldn't there be some guidelines? What do you say to someone who has terminal cancer? What do you say to his parents? Do you ask for details about his treatment? Do you mention the banalities of your own life? Do you try to distract him, cheer him up? Today, in middle age, I immediately think: it probably doesn't matter what you say, as long as you say something. Twenty years ago, though, I was paralyzed, and then Ian was suddenly gone, and suddenly everyone was saying: "Move on—you need to move on." And it sounded to me like: "Embrace denial." Our rites of acknowledgment, in recent years, seem to have withered on the vine. We move on too quickly, without first living our grief: "Don't dwell on it."

Many friends and family members suggested that I focus my energy on my studies, and that seemed reasonable enough, given my long-standing inclinations. But suddenly the value of learning was no longer implicit to me; I no longer thrilled to the task of trying to understand, or of trying to piece words together to express my understanding. A tradition of intellectual engagement that had buoyed me my entire life now started to seem empty, arid, academic. My sophomore tutorial should have been an educational haven: it provided just the kind of intimate, engaged learning environment that I had always craved. But during most of that year, for the first and only time in my life, I simply could not connect to books. Ask me about any other year of college, and I can rattle off titles that I first encountered in particular classes and that have remained important to me for the last two decades. But virtually all I remember about sophomore year—beyond the scorn I felt for myself—is looking at Timothy O'Sullivan's photographs. For the first and only time in my life, I felt as though I was losing the capacity to care.

It was Minnesota that saved me. I needed both to start over and to dwell with my pain. And I needed an Arcadian wilderness.

––––––––

WILDERNESS: Before the war, there was a full spectrum of meanings. It could be a dark, howling place, full of wild beasts and "savage" Indians. It could be a place of sublime refreshment, dominated by natural elements, perhaps a waterfall, far from the madding crowd, offering a small minority a reprieve from the majority. It could be a wasteland, a desert not suitable for human dwelling, or a place already ruined by human misuse. Or it could be a rural region, a swath of middle landscapes, deriving its meaning from its lack of urbanity—a frontier, a margin, the forested edge of settlement, where human art blended with the forces of nature.

After May 1864, though, "the wilderness" meant a bloody, ragged patch of central Virginia, meant the stench of scorched wood blending with scorched flesh. (Figure 33.)

Figure 33. Alfred Waud, "Wounded Escaping from the Burning Woods of the Wilderness," 1864, pencil and "Chinese white" on brown paper.

Timothy O'Sullivan was there, but, in one of the most significant lapses of his photographic career, he failed to take a single shot at the Battle of the Wilderness.

For many years, not yet having dug into the documentary history of the Civil War, and not having found any photographs of the landscape, I assumed that this particular "wilderness" was largely symbolic. All battles are chaotic (and all named retrospectively), but this one was particularly gruesome and confused. In a series of desperate flanking maneuvers, many men, including the Confederate General James Longstreet, endured not only flames but friendly fire, and the casualty rate made the Wilderness almost as infamous as Gettysburg and Antietam. Over the course of just two days, some twenty thousand soldiers either died, received wounds, went missing, or became prisoners. "More desperate fighting has not been witnessed on this continent than that of the 5th and 6th of May," claimed General Grant, newly promoted to general in chief of the Armies of the United States. On the sixth, Grant supposedly smoked twenty cigars and spent part of the night in tears in his tent; "if the nervous strain under which he labored is to be measured by the number of cigars consumed," remarked an acquaintance, "it must have been greater on the 6th of May than at any period of his life, for he is said never to have equaled that record."[17]

It was at the Wilderness that Grant would truly earn his reputation as an indomitable commander—and a butcher. Since the Confederates had established Richmond as their capital, most Americans, North and South, considered Virginia—George Washington's Virginia, Thomas Jefferson's Virginia—to be the war's crucial battleground. For three years, engagements in this contested borderland tended to be stand-offs: the Army of the Potomac had more men and more firepower, but Lee's Army of Northern Virginia knew the terrain better and had entrenched itself in the strongest positions. The typical pattern had been for the Union forces to surge southward, suffer terrible casualties, and then back off, chastened, though having at least thinned Lee's troops and learned a bit more about his tendencies. Grant, pressed by his president, decided that this year's spring campaign would have to be different. It was an election year; Northern civilians were tiring of the carnage and the stalemates; Lincoln felt sure he would be unseated by the Democrats, who were preaching peace, who seemed willing to offer independence to the Confederacy. The new leader of the U.S. military had only a few months in which to march on Richmond. And so it was on the night of May 5, after sustaining devastating losses, that he revealed the North's new strategy, the strategy that would lead to Appomattox one year later: absorb the casualties, bring in reinforcements, and press on. General George Meade, who had commanded the Army of the Potomac for the previous year and was known for being cautious with his men's lives, wanted to retreat back across the Rapidan River, which the Union forces had crossed on the fourth. But Grant gave the order to prepare another assault. His faith would waver the following day, but in the dark of that night, when he met with a correspondent for the *New York Tribune* who was about to leave for Washington, he apparently offered a clear statement of his resolve, one that would spur Lincoln to kiss the newspaperman on the forehead upon delivery of the message in the White House: "Whatever happens, there will be no turning back."[18] To reach the Promised Land, Grant decided, he had to go through the Wilderness.

Yet Virginia's Wilderness was also an actual piece of physical and cultural geography, whose name had been in use for decades before it saw the ruination of war, before it became Grant's desert. And while my superficial reading of Civil War history at first made me think of the Battle of the Wilderness mostly in metaphorical and biblical terms, its reputation in postbellum America, I now realize, hinged not just on its casualty rate and its strategic importance, but also on its notorious terrain. This was a phantom struggle, for, unlike most other Civil War battles, it was waged not in open fields but in a dense, tangled wood. One soldier called it "a battle of invisibles with invisibles,"[19] and almost every commentator mentioned the seeming impenetrability of the understory, the briery maze, thick with dead leaves, that led sometimes to dark groves of oak and pine, sometimes to bright swaths of pink lady's slippers, sometimes to crackling conflagrations, sometimes to smoking muskets. The Battle of the Wilderness brought out the significance of land, made Americans consider the collision of humanity, technology, and nature. Henry Elson, an early historian of the war, discovered an uncredited photograph showing the battle's impact on the region, which he published under the title, "Trees in the Track of the Iron Storm": "Over ground like this," he wrote, "where men had seldom trod before, ebbed and flowed the tide of trampling thousands on May 5 and 6, 1864. Artillery, of which Grant had a superabundance, was well-nigh useless, wreaking its impotent fury upon the defenseless trees."[20]

What Elson seems to have gotten wrong was the frequency with which the ground had been trodden. This was a human-made Wilderness. As early as the 1720s, the region's old-growth forest had started to fall, under the orders of Lieutenant Governor Alexander Spotswood, who had secured permission from England to mine and smelt the local iron ore and so needed a vast supply of wood (and labor) to fuel his blast furnaces. Depending on how densely packed the trees were on a given patch of ground, a single furnace could consume more than two acres of woodland in a day. Six smelters were in operation by 1750. With his slaves and a supply of indentured servants from Germany, Spotswood could be said to have launched the Industrial Revolution in the colonies, sending cheap pots, kettles, andirons, firebacks, and possibly even cannon over to the mother country, and leaving much of Orange and Spotsylvania Counties littered with stumps. The sylvan character of the region started coming back later in the century, though, as iron supplies dwindled, because Virginians found the local soil to be too acidic and too poorly drained for extensive farming. Gradually, in the age of American independence, a second-growth "Wilderness" developed, dominated by thickets of scrub and brush amidst undersized trees that struggled to soak up enough nutrients from the ground.[21] By the 1850s, when Frederick Law Olmsted took a trip through the area, the Wilderness came across as somewhat ominous, "sadly worn and misused . . . , all-shadowing, all-embracing," though Olmsted also noted occasional small farms with a mixture of black and white tenants, who used the copses and brakes as a commons for running their hogs—those "long, lank, bony, snake-headed, hairy, wild beasts," so foreign to an urbane northerner.[22]

In May of 1864, both northerners and southerners tended to feel threatened and puzzled by the nature of the Wilderness. Unable to get comfortable, despite the reassurance of his comrades, a soldier from Texas found the battle site to be strangely chilling; he referred to it as a "peculiar tangled forest of stunted oak."[23] Union General A. A. Humphreys, getting the lay of the land, saw to his dismay that he would be sending his front lines to be slaughtered, "for an enemy remaining on the defensive awaiting attack where this undergrowth existed, would be unseen, while the troops advancing to attack would make their presence known, and thus the tangled growth would serve in some measure as an intrenchment, at least for the first and most destructive fire."[24]

Many people tripped on the region's name: "I have been much in the North Woods," wrote Corporal Norton C. Shepard, from upstate New York, "and find a great contrast in the meaning of 'wilderness' there and in the South. In the North a wilderness is a wood in a state of nature with great trees that have stood for ages. . . . In the South, however, most especially in Virginia, [much] of the land has been cleared off . . . and abandoned as useless. Then it grows up to pine and scrub oak to become a wilderness."[25] Of course, even within New York, "wilderness" could refer to different kinds of landscapes. Corporal Shepard had grown up near the Adirondacks; further south, Andrew Jackson Downing explored a part of the Hudson valley called "The Wilderness" in 1847 and insisted that it was far from pristine, and "by no means savage in the aspect of its beauty. . . . The whole of this richly wooded valley is threaded with walks, ingeniously and naturally conducted so as to penetrate to all the most interesting points; while a great variety of rustic seats, formed beneath the trees, in deep secluded thickets, by the side of the swift rushing stream, or on some inviting eminence, enables one fully to enjoy them."[26] What Corporal Shepard effectively highlighted, though, was that when Americans tried to come to grips with the Battle of the Wilderness, they were struggling not just with the sickening brutality of the Civil War, but also with their evolving relationship to nature—with the creeping anxiety that they might no longer be able to look to certain landscapes for solace, renewal, confirmation, kinship.

In one of the most emotive of all Civil War memoirs, the Union officer Morris Schaff openly expressed his determination to recast his experience of guerilla warfare in the Wilderness. It certainly seemed as though the snarled scrubland had aided the Confederates in the same way that the forests of New England had aided Indians when they needed to fend off seventeenth-century colonists: the nature of the Wilderness, its thickness and combustibility, fostered deadly violence. But Schaff reminded his countrymen that it was precisely the terrain's tangles that had caused the Southerners to injure their own General Longstreet, and it was in the ensuing confusion that the righteous Unionists had finally made their way into clearer country. There was an independent "Spirit of the Wilderness," Schaff thought, that recognized slavery as utterly unnatural and that aligned itself with those who fought for unity, harmony, equality: "Reader, if the Spirit of the Wilderness be unreal to you, not so is it to me. Bear in mind that the native realm of the spirit of man is nature's kingdom, that there he has made all of his discoveries . . . , each proclaiming that nature's heart beats with our own."

Yes, there was death in the Wilderness: scattered all around were "human legs and arms, resembling piles of stove wood," and trees that "in falling have been caught in the arms of their living competitors and rest there with their limbs bleaching, and now and then is one standing upright, alone, with lightning-scored trunk and bare, pronged limbs, dead, dead among the living green." Yes, the cultural memory of Civil War brutality was almost too painful to bear; Schaff probably understood that most Americans just wanted to move on, rather than revisit the "half-open graves, displaying arms and legs with bits of paling and mildewed clothing still clinging to them," surrounded by "barked and splintered trees, dead, or half-dead, dangling limbs, and groves of saplings, with which the woods abound, topped by volleys as if sheared by a blast." But perhaps the trees of the Wilderness, in witnessing and absorbing that brutality, and in offering "sweet shade to the dying soldier" on both sides of the battle, had become comrades in arms. Looking back on the war as an old man, Schaff insisted on memorializing the Wilderness as a sacred space, insisted on imagining and inscribing it as a kind of cemetery, a place of kinship between humanity and nature. His writing, clearly intended as a gift of peace to his fellow citizens, sometimes seems sentimental and naïve. But if his memoir edges into nostalgia, it's a nostalgia not of escapism but of repose: "The bark-scored and bullet-pitted trees . . . are wreathed in smoke, and, like sheaves of wheat, bodies are lying on the leaf-strewn ground, unconscious now of the deafening crashes with which the gloomy Wilderness jars far and wide, and roars to the over-arching, listening sky."[27]

---

WW (1865):

*As toilsome I wander'd Virginia's woods,*
*To the music of rustling leaves kick'd by my feet, (for 'twas autumn,)*
*I mark'd at the foot of a tree the grave of a soldier;*
*Mortally wounded he and buried on the retreat, (easily all could I understand,)*

*The halt of a mid-day hour, when up! no time to lose—yet this sign left,*
*On a tablet scrawl'd and nail'd on the tree by the grave,*
Bold, cautious, true, and my loving comrade.[28]

---

Winslow Homer was there, or at least imagined he was, at a crucial turning point in his career, as he gave up commercial illustration in favor of oil painting; the battle inspired him to make a portrait of a tree. (Figure 34.)

Figure 34. Winslow Homer, *Skirmish in the Wilderness*, 1864, oil on canvas mounted on masonite.

Homer had passed much of the first half of the war on the front lines, making drawings for the wood engravers at *Harper's Weekly*. His movements in 1864 are harder to track with any certainty, though it's clear that he spent time in a studio in New York City and at his home in Belmont, just outside of Boston; several of his drawings and paintings from this year, meanwhile, seem to claim immediate, first-hand knowledge of Virginia. In any case, he didn't complete any of his Civil War oils on the spot: they lean more toward reflection than photographic realism. The Battle of the Wilderness, with its close, cramped confrontations, in a forested landscape somewhat reminiscent of New England, seems to have given him much to ponder. His tendency was to depict the spatial and emotional margins of battle: the boredom of encampment, the tension of waiting in a trench or a tree, balancing a gun. But where were the margins in the Wilderness? And where was the enemy?[29]

The Confederates are mere specters in this picture, hidden by the Wilderness, producing just a faint puff of gunsmoke on the far left edge of the frame. The Union soldiers do their best to attack, but at the same time they need to flee the flames licking the vegetation to the right. Their lines are jumbled, and as the reinforcements stumble into the uneven terrain of the clearing they seem to be entering the line of fire, and the fallen among them blend with the dark undergrowth, the brush and brown leaves and downed branches, the shadows of death: men become stumps. Amidst all the impressionistic brushstrokes, amidst the confusion of firing and advancing and fleeing and crawling and reconnoitering, amidst the tender spring foliage, the central tree stands firm, sharp, distinct, provides at least a bit of cover for the Federals, catches the picture's only direct sunlight and thus draws our gaze—and we see at once that its branches are cracked and leafless, that it is dead or dying, that its wood is rotten. In the swirling chaos, this solitary tree anchors the picture, becomes a beacon for the nation, but ultimately it, too, will probably be sacrificed without ritual, its individuality forgotten.

Homer painted another tree in 1864, this one in Belmont, and though the picture's mood is similarly somber—there is no direct sunlight at all—its message seems more hopeful. (Figure 35.) In the North, at least, the trees will survive to serve as memorials. "If we have neither old castles nor old associations," Andrew Jackson Downing had said, in 1847, "we have at least, here and there, old trees that can teach us lessons of antiquity, not less instructive and poetical than the ruins of a past age."[30] A well-off woman in a sky-blue dress has come to these woods in a spirit of mourning and determination: thanks to this sanctified place, preserved through the wisdom of Yankee restraint, she will be able to remember her loved one; she will make her mark (or perhaps she already has) and will always return to it. We can't tell exactly what she's carving or looking at in the tree's living flesh, but we can see, on our side of the trunk, the shape of a heart, and perhaps two letters, and perhaps a date, and, without question, two cavalry swords crossed near their hilts.[31]

The war seems both to have intensified Americans' close relationship to trees and to have endangered it. Of course, throughout the nineteenth century, in all regions of the country, men and women cleared vast forests, sometimes with a vengeance,

Figure 35. Winslow Homer, *The Initials*, 1864,
oil on canvas.

often for fuel, but also for agriculture, for industries like tanning, for houses, for ships, for railroad ties, for fences, for plank roads, even for water pipes. But, at least since the 1820s and 30s, they had also started to set aside sacred groves, to celebrate woodlands as sheltering and resonant, and to identify individual trees—like the staunch Great Elm on the Boston Common or the Balmville Tree, an ancient cottonwood in Newburgh, New York, linked in local lore to General Washington, who had his headquarters nearby—as representative of their civilization's core values. Children's books sought explicitly to "cultivate a fondness for trees," and cemetery guides touted the perfect "funereal characters" of certain varieties, like yews, weeping willows, and junipers, which expressed melancholy and inspired humility but also invigorated mourners with their "floating, graceful spray" of branches and foliage.[32] Andrew Jackson Downing, in particular—who lived in the Balmville district of Newburgh—had tried to ensure that an arboreal tradition lay at the heart of Arcadian America, along with the horticultural and agrarian traditions. It was perhaps only natural, then, for

Americans to turn to trees to help them make sense of the Civil War, and, as Whitman noted in the woods of Virginia, even soldiers were sometimes able to pause long enough to appreciate the memorial capacity of individual trees. At the same time, though, especially given the war's massive affront to nature, Americans were becoming more powerfully aware of how thin their forests were getting as spiritual resources, even if there seemed to be plenty more timber out west.

In an 1850s picture book called *The Trees of America*, R. U. Piper insisted that the taste for woodland scenery now had an "almost universal prevalence" among his fellow citizens, and he quoted Downing's joyful—perhaps wishful—conclusion that the schools must have been teaching courses on landscape aesthetics, with "especial professorships" devoted just to "the beauty of shade trees."[33] Some observers even suggested that the old surveying technique of cutting blazes onto so-called witness trees—a practice familiar to many landowners and westward migrants, including George Washington, who actually spent three years as a surveyor in Virginia—had fostered a symbiotic relationship between a number of Americans and at least certain parcels of their woodlands: the trees served as crucial reminders of the land's bounds and contours and so required stewards to preserve them. When Nathaniel Coffin published *The Forest Arcadia of Northern New York* in 1864, he devoted a section of his book to "Communion with Trees" and made a point of relating his encounter with a local "squire," who told of making marks with an axe not just on his own property but throughout the wilderness for miles around, as he got to know his home region. "I never see a blaze of my own making," the old man claimed, "though it may have been years ago, and altered by the healing process, without recalling the circumstances under which it was made—perhaps the train of thought which occupied me at the time." Coffin was charmed: "Thus you have been for years writing your history upon these old trees!—symbolizing your joys and griefs, and the secret aspirations of your soul." Of course, Coffin also admitted that he was "one of those who believe in the sensibility, if not consciousness of vegetable life," and so suspected that no one could "cut a tree in that manner without hurting it."[34]

Such concern for trees may seem unusual and sentimental and maybe even meaningless in a country so bent on deforestation, but many kinds of citizens in the United States—not just Romantic writers and landscape painters—started decrying the destruction of their woodlands only a few decades after the new, highly efficient American axe was developed, in the late eighteenth century.[35] Sometimes even seemingly triumphal narratives of swift-marching Progress paused for a moment of lamentation: the pioneering settler, explained Zachariah Allen in 1832, "applies his axe with persevering strokes, and every hour witnesses the fall and crash of sturdy

trees which have been . . . rooted in the spot for centuries." After a few days of cutting, and then some burning, "naught remains of a noble tract of forest but scattered
heaps of white ashes."[36] By 1846, George B. Emerson was upset enough to insist, in
his state-commissioned *Report on the Trees and Shrubs Growing Naturally in the
Forests of Massachusetts*, that "the axe has made, and is making, wanton and terrible
havoc. The cunning foresight of the Yankee seems to desert him when he takes the
axe in hand." Emerson was writing not for politicians, nor for scientists, nor for businessmen, but, he said, "for the common, unlearned citizens, who live on farms, in
the country, and have few books and little leisure." And his goal was, by enumerat-
ing the many social and biological services performed by trees, and by exposing the
"wasteful destruction of the forests," to attack any "false views of immediate economy," and then to give his fellow citizens "a deeper sense of the value of some of the
blessings by which they are surrounded, and lead them, or any of them, to resolve to
preserve the old forests and plant new."[37] Picking up on Emerson's arguments about
the way that trees not only provide beauty but also stabilize the soil, protect lakes
and rivers, and moderate the climate, Piper often interrupted his pleasant musings
about American trees to express his anxiety that the United States might well become a desert of blowing sands if his readers failed to act on their supposed affection
for the woods. Citing everyone from the great scientist Alexander von Humboldt to
the poet William Cullen Bryant, and explaining his own experiments and annual
observations, Piper offered hard evidence that, owing to deforestation, "the seasons
are becoming subject to greater extremes of heat and cold—of dryness and mois-
ture."[38] With his nation reeling, with his countrymen shedding each other's blood in
Kansas, with manufactures and markets and railroads expanding faster than anyone
could have predicted, Piper perhaps hoped that at least natural cycles might be relied on for some stability and reassurance.[39]

Images and reports of Civil War confrontations exposed the vulnerability of America's trees to an even broader swath of the public. Some of Homer's pictures of Virginia
were dominated by rows of stumps. And some of O'Sullivan's pictures of Virginia,
showing the fortifications made after an area had been clear-cut, looked as barren as
the Badlands of the West. (Figure 36.)

Toward the end of the war, the Reverend Frederick Starr, Jr., wrote a report for the
Department of Agriculture called *American Forests; Their Destruction and Preservation*, in which he emphasized that "the destruction of forests and timber during the
war of rebellion has been immense." Soldiers on both sides, Starr explained, had
cleared trees for fuel (for cooking, heating, and especially trains); for construction of
camps, railroads, and bridges; and for various strategic purposes, such as improving

Figure 36. Timothy H. O'Sullivan, *Quarters of Men in Fort Sedgwick*, 1865, photograph.

sight lines, or facilitating (or hindering) the movement of troops, or erecting elaborate defensive fortifications like abatis, arrangements of felled trunks and branches with sharpened points sticking out toward the enemy. "We are told that native Virginians," Starr wrote, "in some sections of that State, are removing, because the war has swept away the timber; and, for the same reason, emigrants decline to go into some of the finest parts of the State as regards the soil."[40] Starr emphasized that the fate of the American forests and soils ought to matter keenly to everyone, and if the politicians in Washington truly cared about Union, they would think about attending to wounded trees in the same terms as wounded veterans: "Let us then inquire, why government should aid such efforts? *The work is national.* Every part of the land suffers together."[41]

Perhaps by coincidence, or perhaps not, it was in 1864 that George Perkins Marsh published his magnum opus, *Man and Nature; or, Physical Geography as Modified by Human Action*, which has often been called the book that launched environmental conservation in the Western world, and which argued, in essence, that all the great failed civilizations had fallen because they had felled their forests. The war was not the impetus for Marsh's book—he had been working on it for close to two decades—and he said very little, explicitly, about the military context of its publication. But he did mention that, "since the commencement of the present rebellion," he had been looking forward to the time when swords would be shaped back into plowshares and gunpowder would once again be used for construction projects, when the arts of war would be "so modified as to be eminently promotive of the blessings of peace, thereby in some measure compensating the wrongs and sufferings they have inflicted on humanity." In a sense, then, perhaps *Man and Nature* could be read, in places, as a guide for Americans who were ready to turn away from violent conflict and start repairing their relationship to the natural world.[42]

First, Marsh argued, in his Introductory note, the nation would have to forswear the greed-driven development promoted by corporate capitalism: he railed against "the unscrupulousness of the private associations that now control the monetary affairs, and regulate the transit of persons and property" throughout the United States; he lobbied for a surge of public-minded activism to counteract the "influence of joint-stock banks and manufacturing and railway companies." Then, perhaps most importantly, Americans would have to start settling down and reinvigorating the forest, immediately developing "means for maintaining the permanence of its relations to the fields, the meadows, and the pastures, to the rain and the dews of heaven, to the springs and rivulets with which it waters the earth." Sounding a lot like Andrew Jackson Downing, Marsh lamented how infrequently "a middle-aged American dies in the house where he was born," and he prayed "for some abatement in the restless love of change which characterizes us, and makes us almost a nomade rather than a sedentary people." I imagine that Marsh knew it would be tricky to argue for a settled, rural way of life in 1864, since that mode of existence was associated with the South, and since industrial "progress" seemed to be providing the North with its most important advantage in the war; clearly, he was taking a grave risk with his word choice when he advocated for the reforestation of farms and suggested that "the very fact of having begun a plantation would attach the proprietor more strongly to the soil for which he had made such a sacrifice."[43] But he felt that Americans had no choice. Even if his general approach was more scientific and utilitarian than Romantic, Marsh was an Arcadian, in that his environmental vision arose from a sense of commonwealth and connection passed down through generations.

Frederick Starr cited Marsh extensively, as did an official 1867 *Report on the Disastrous Effects of the Destruction of Forest Trees Now Going on so Rapidly in the State of Wisconsin.*[44] And so did William Cullen Bryant, updating his old-style Arcadian perspective with Marsh's more modern, pragmatic rhetoric, in an 1865 essay called "The Utility of Trees" (Marsh himself had actually quoted Bryant, as well as R. U. Piper and a number of other like-minded antebellum authors). "While Congress is occupied with the disposition of the public lands," Bryant noted, "it has been suggested, by persons who can think of something else besides railroads, that it will be an act of provident wisdom to reserve considerable tracts of forest in different parts of the country, as the public domain, with . . . a body of foresters to watch it and keep out trespassers." Bryant was getting old; his most important Arcadian work was behind him. As soon as the war ended, though, he saw an opportunity to help renew the ties of kinship Americans felt with their national and local landscapes, to remind them of the historical and cultural importance of sustaining a public commons that would be protected from the pressures of industrial capitalism. Building to the climax of his short essay, Bryant saw fit to quote some lines (without attribution) from one of his own poems, written back in 1824, lines that, on the one hand, emphasized the devastating effect that deforestation was thought to have on climate and water supplies, but that also created an atmosphere thick with grief, mourning, and, most importantly, attachment, for the words are spoken by one of the nation's "aboriginal inhabitants" and come from the poem called "An Indian at the Burial Place of His Fathers":[45]

> Before these fields were shorn and tilled,
> Full to the brim our rivers flowed;
> The melody of waters filled
> The fresh and boundless wood. . . .
>
> Those grateful sounds are heard no more. . . .
> The realm our tribes are crushed to get
> May be a barren desert yet.

As the Civil War came to an end, certain soldiers, grieving for their fallen brethren, might have felt something akin to what Bryant's Indian felt, as they returned to old familiar battlegrounds in search of corpses, ghosts, memories, legacies. (Figure 37.)

The crossed sabers on this soldier's cap are the same ones carved into the tree in Belmont in *The Initials*, but these trees are in the South, probably Virginia, as we can tell from the scattered, makeshift grave markers. The cross formed on the cap is echoed by the cross that the trooper is contemplating, which in turn is echoed by the trees, with all their clipped horizontal branches. In shadow, one side of the soldier's blue jacket becomes the precise brown of the forest in the background. And, if we are clearly meant to identify him with a tree, then the opening in his jacket comes to seem like a black, bloody wound to his heartwood. He will survive,

Figure 37. Winslow Homer,
*Trooper Meditating beside a
Grave*, c. 1865, oil on canvas.

though. His posture is somber but sturdy; he seems absorbed in elegy, rooted, fully connected, through active remembering, to a person and a place. This is a sacred wilderness.[46]

"And so good-bye to the war," Whitman wrote, with his uncanny rhythm, with his defiant sadness, with his sure knowledge that he would never be able to say goodbye to the war.[47] Homer's most powerful parting gesture came in another 1865 painting, this one set back up North. (Figure 38.) A Union soldier has thrown off his jacket and canteen to attend to the harvesting of his winter wheat, which is thick and tall and welcoming, lit warmly by the sun. There is a lithe resilience in the posture of both man and grain. The red trefoil on the veteran's canteen identifies him as an officer of General Barlow's First Division of the Second Corps; it is perhaps the same splash of red that can be seen on the cap of the officer leading his troops into the *Skirmish in the Wilderness*. But this soldier has traded the wild forest for a landscape of rural

Figure 38. Winslow Homer, *The Veteran in a New Field*, 1865, oil on canvas.

repose. For four years, "field" had meant only one thing: a site of battle. Homer's "new field" was really an old one, allowing his veteran to travel back in time to the antebellum world. At first Homer had painted him with a modern grain cradle, whose several blades are now visible as a pentimento, but then he simplified the tool to a traditional scythe, which seems to be cutting the sheaves smoothly and easily. With the sun on his back, his weapons traded in for agricultural equipment, the soldier becomes Cincinnatus, the Roman general who famously served his country in time of need and then retired back to his farm. In 1865, most Americans seemed to interpret this image—it was also produced as a wood engraving in *Frank Leslie's Illustrated Newspaper*—as hopeful and affirming, symbolic of the nation's return to the rhythms of peace, the responsibilities of life. This man is married to the land: the nation will endure because nature, once again properly husbanded, will provide.

Yet the soldier's homecoming is a remarkably quiet and lonely one: traditionally, harvests were communal, or at least familial. His physical isolation could suggest the emotional gulf between veterans and the homebound people who had no access to the incommunicable experiences of the front: perhaps this image represents the rise of the unapproachable male patriarch in modern America, the husband and father with his back turned, consumed by work and a complex sense of loss—loss of gentleness and innocence, and other traditionally female virtues; loss of friendship and community; loss of wonderment at the wide world. Indeed, the picture creates a sense of enclosure in nature, or even of premature burial, especially now that the cut sheaves are starting to pile up around the legs of the straining figure. Is the atmosphere truly serene—or solemn? Is the wheat representative of future sustenance, or of fallen comrades? Grain and bread, the staff of life, have long been linked with the natural cycle of death and regeneration; sheaves of wheat adorn many gravestones.[48] The noble soldier, it seems, has returned home to Arcadia, where, even at high noon, he will always cast the shadow of the Grim Reaper.

---

WW (1871):

*In the future of these States must arise poets immenser far, and make great poems of death. . . . America needs, and the world needs, a class of bards who will, now and ever, so link and tally the rational physical being of man, with the ensembles of time and space, and with this vast and multiform show, Nature, surrounding him, ever tantalizing him, equally a part, and yet not a part of him, as to essentially harmonize, satisfy, and put at rest. . . . Surely this universal ennui, this coward fear, this shuddering at death, these low, degrading views, are not always to rule the spirit pervading future society.*[49]

---

Walt Whitman was there, a witness, at All Souls' Unitarian Church, in Manhattan, on June 14, 1878, for William Cullen Bryant's funeral. Later that day, Bryant would be buried in a small country cemetery on Long Island, next to his wife, but first his life and death had to be marked in the heart of the city. Who would eulogize the greatest eulogist of the century? Whitman did not feel up to the task, which fell ultimately to Bryant's pastor, Henry Bellows, who in turn fell back on the words of Bryant himself. He had the choir sing Bryant's hymn, "Blessed Are They That Mourn," and, given the timing of Bryant's death, Bellows decided to close his address with the poem "June," which Bryant had written in a wistful mood in 1825, just before leaving his home in the Berkshires to make a career in New York City:[50]

> I gazed upon the glorious sky,
> And the green mountains round,

> And thought that when I came to lie
> At rest within the ground,
> 'Twere pleasant that in flowery June,
> When brooks send up a cheerful tune,
> And groves a cheerful sound,
> The sexton's hand, my grave to make,
> The rich, green mountain-turf should break.

Spring, season of rebirth and weddings, could also be, as at the Wilderness, a time of dying. Whitman noted in his book *Specimen Days* that All Souls' was "dim even now at approaching noon, in its light from the mellow-stain'd windows"—but the atmosphere seemed appropriate: it was "a solemn, impressive, simple scene, to spirit and senses." In early adulthood, when all writers need the enthusiasm of their elders, Whitman had cherished the sense of kinship he felt with Bryant, this friend to Thomas Cole and Washington Irving, this "bard of the river and the wood, ever conveying a taste of open air, with scents as from hayfield, grapes, birch-borders—always lurkingly fond of threnodies, beginning and ending his long career with chants of death"—this original American Arcadian. "I had known Mr. Bryant over thirty years ago," Whitman wrote, "and he had been markedly kind to me. . . . We were both walkers, and when I work'd in Brooklyn he several times came over, middle of afternoons, and we took rambles miles long, till dark, out towards Bedford or Flatbush, in company."[51] They probably passed some twilights together in Greenwood Cemetery.

*Specimen Days*, a species of autobiography, published in 1882, the year Whitman turned sixty-three, is one of the strangest books I have ever read. Whitman himself, with a winking exaggeration, called it "the most wayward, spontaneous, fragmentary book ever printed."[52] I first encountered it in college, when my mentor told me to read the parts about the Civil War—my mentor, Lou Masur, the advisor who had been assigned to me when I came back after my year in Minnesota, assigned not randomly, but by the professor, now an administrator, with whom I'd studied the writing of poetry in my freshman year, Jan Thaddeus. Lou—and Jan, too, who in my senior year told me I was never going to be a poet but that I might be getting somewhere with my experiments in memoir—gave me the encouragement and understanding I needed to finish college. I think Lou suggested that I read *Specimen Days* mostly because he was amazed at Whitman's ability to draw readers back into the abyss of the war, but also, possibly, because he realized that I was obsessed with death and trauma and denial, that I needed a writer who would dwell, constructively, on loss and grief. I still have the edition he told me to buy twenty years ago, though the pages, the browned leaves, are starting to fall out. In 1990, I devoured Whitman's stories of death and caring with gratitude but also a desperate jealousy, since he had clearly transcended the self-consciousness that I found so debilitating in my halting efforts to reach out to dying and grieving friends and family members. Today, I am just as immersed in the battle and hospital scenes, the moments of dread and connection, but I am even more struck by the framing of these years, which Whitman saw as constituting the central, defining period of his life, and which left him both inspired and crippled.

The book begins with a brief section, just eighteen pages, of childhood reminiscences, portraits of Long Island, spurred by recent visits to family graveyards full of warped apple trees, "depress'd mounds, crumbled and broken stones"—begins with memories of "wandering through those solitary cross-roads, inhaling the peculiar and wild aroma . . . , absorbing fields, shores, marine incidents, characters, the bay-men, farmers, pilots," and meeting "strange, unkempt, half-barbarous herdsmen" and "the few remaining Indians," and haunting the coastlines, becoming a witness to the area's "long history of wrecks," including "the destruction of the brig 'Elizabeth,' a fearful affair, in one of the worst winter gales, where Margaret Fuller went down, with her husband and child." And then we jump ahead, past his rise as a poet, past the publication of *Leaves of Grass*, to Washington and Virginia, to eighty pages of fragmented immediacy, a slightly revised version of *Memoranda During the War*, a litany of explosions and amputations and wound-dressing.

Then: a pause. A quick breath. "Several years now elapse before I resume my diary." Beyond that, we get almost no transition or explanation. Once the war was over, finding himself unable to leave Washington, Whitman had worked for the attorney general for a few years, but that hardly seemed worth mentioning. All we need to understand is that he was shell-shocked. "Some time after the war ended," he had explained, with deliberate vagueness, in a prefatory note, "I had a paralytic stroke, which prostrated me for several years." After 1865, the balance of the book—it goes on for another 150 pages—sketches a protracted, partial convalescence, an attempt to rediscover, mostly in a "charmingly recluse and rural spot" in New Jersey, a way to embrace life. The "trick," Whitman decided, was to accept limitation—to "tone your wants and tastes low down enough, and make much of negatives, and of mere daylight and the skies." So, at rest in the woods, "seated on logs or stumps," obeying his urge to scribble some notes, that "ruling passion strong in age and disablement," he began to make journal entries describing his local "affinities," his connections to a restorative Nature, to "the open air, the trees, fields, the changes of seasons—the sun by day and the stars of heaven by night," in the humble hope that his literary fragments might ultimately serve as "breaths of common air, or draughts of water to drink," simple tastes of freshness offered "to denizen of heated city house, or tired workman or workwoman," or to anyone with "fever'd mouth or latent pulse" languishing "in sickroom or prison."[53] Like *Leaves of Grass*, *Specimen Days* was meant to preserve organic relationships in its pages, creating a specific, alternative environment, a space that could act as a counterforce against the violent, overweening, homogenizing trends of the modern, gridded, institutional, industrial world.

Recent critics and scholars have expressed considerable skepticism about Whitman's project, about his bizarrely sudden shift in tone and theme, about his seeming effort to counter modernity by hiding from it. After all, in comparison to someone like Thoreau, who sustained his scorn for certain social tendencies over hundreds of pages, and who developed his own political economy, Whitman can come across as something of an accommodationist patriot, with a merely therapeutic relationship to nature. Perhaps he was so desperate for any sense of unification and harmony, so desperate for "sanity" and a "buoyant equilibrium," that he turned to the pastoral mode in an attempt to deny the insane lack of balance that led to the violence of war. Contemplating placid ponds and perfumed woods and singing birds and buzzing insects, he could assume that there had been a point to the fighting, that it was part of a plan, that people must be good because they are one with nature, and nature's trend is always toward recovery. Whitman's Arcadia, instead of confronting mortality and morality, naturalizes history, elides politics, invokes the inevitable turning of the seasons, the washing of tides, the winds of change, the natural cycles that transcend any human ethics or agency.[54]

There can be little doubt but that the Civil War dealt a traumatic blow to the complex Arcadianism that Whitman had long embraced, to the border-wandering, the joyous sense of tragedy, the organic burgeoning of the antebellum versions of *Leaves of Grass*, in which the compost of stinking feces and fevered corpses and rotting carcasses incomprehensibly, terrifyingly, produced bright, bold foliage and healthful food. The second half of *Specimen Days*, like many of Whitman's postbellum writings, tends to emphasize universality rather than attempting to blend unity and diversity, tends to find common ground between nature's inclinations and American Progress, tends toward the resolution of binaries rather than a flowing acceptance of their contradictions. Too often, Whitman sees his escapes into the woods as "restoration-hours," as if not only his antebellum health but all of antebellum America could be restored. The new version of the nation would be even stronger, though: he posits a "real geographic, democratic, indissoluble American Union," as embodied by the prairie states, with their "busy towns" and their close relationship to "the mighty father of waters" and their new commitment to the transcontinental railroad, that "conqueror of crude nature, which it turns to man's use," stitching to-gether the nation and its resources in a magical bond of mutual development. Yet I think this shift signals not an abandonment of the Arcadian tradition but rather an impossible, anguished desire to apply it to the clearly insoluble conundrum of the Civil War's aftermath.

Even when *Specimen Days* immerses both writer and reader in the supposedly curative depths of the natural world, we all remain haunted by the memory of those pages about war, by that truncated narrative—by a phantom pain. Anyway, it seems unfair, even cruel, to blame Whitman for choosing a version of denial, for actively seeking solace, for pursuing some kind of escape from a thoroughly debilitating con-dition: "I am a half-paralytic, and likely to be so, long as I live." For much of the 1870s, his life felt reduced; it was a good day if he could find a reason to pull his un-responsive body out of bed. So, given his "physical shatter and troubled spirit," if the pastoral mode could be temporarily soothing, if his "soul is calm'd and expanded beyond description" by the smell of "autumn leaves, the cool dry air," by the simple blue sky above "a broad grassy upland field," do we really want to begrudge him the connective inspiration? One February day, he spent twilight out in a grove of young trees by a pond, "exercising arms, chest, my whole body, by a tough oak sapling thick as my wrist, twelve feet high—pulling and pushing," bending it, tussling with it, and ultimately he was able to "feel its young sap and virtue welling up out of the ground and tingling through me from crown to toe, like health's wine." Health is always a relative term, and some landscapes are liable to make you sick, but it seems reason-able that Nature, approached with openness and energy, is at least as likely to bolster as to undermine. When Whitman calls to the "disconsolate" of his country to "come get the sure virtues of creek-shore, and wood and field," I find myself less sure than he of any inherent virtues in the natural world, but I admire his fluid sense of kinship— "I merge myself in the scene"—and I believe him when he says that "peace and nutri-ment from heaven subtly filter into me as I slowly hobble down these country lanes and across fields, in the good air—as I sit here in solitude with Nature—open, voice-less, mystic, far removed, yet palpable, eloquent Nature."[55] I appreciate both the celebration of outdoor freshness and the acknowledgment of its mystery and foreign-ness: perhaps the crippled poet and his chastened compatriots still had access to some kind of Arcadia.

Then, a couple of pages later, Whitman actually becomes a tree—and grass, and sunshine: "Somehow I seem'd to get identity with each and every thing around me, in its condition. Nature was naked, and I was also." But he is especially fixated on his oakenness: he flexes his "trunk-muscles," feels not just sap but an arboreal "sinew rising through me, like mercury to heat." And here I suddenly find myself stumbling on his presumption, wondering at his metaphorical projection, which is precisely the kind of thing that—as far as we know—trees are not capable of. And I hope we, in turn, are not capable of a tree's (seeming) indifference, its lack of interest in distinguishing between the provision of shade for a poet and the provision of sturdy branches for a lynch mob. A fantasy of identity strikes me as significantly different from a fantasy of kinship; while I don't mind pondering the possibility of an arboreal consciousness—"may-be we interchange—may-be the trees are more aware of it all than I ever thought"—I worry that asserting sameness could lead to biological determinism on the one hand (ignoring the power of our metaphors, our culture) or to narcissism on the other. If we see a lining of bark in our souls, or if we see our souls mirrored back to us by the bark of a tree, then we never experience the struggle, the bridging work, necessitated by real difference: unity feels like a given rather than a gift. Whitman, in his own and his nation's time of weakness, yearned for "the resistless silent strength" of a tree, and thus sometimes failed to acknowledge the painful difficulty of forging and maintaining responsible kinship relations both among different groups of human beings and between humans and trees.[56]

Yet, in the flow of *Specimen Days*, Whitman's oaken reverie ends abruptly, after just another couple of pages, interrupted—of course—by thoughts of death, and by potent memories of—what else?—the Civil War. It's as if he realized he had gone too far in the direction of escape and easy confirmation. We seem to be more inclined toward violence than trees are; no sense of kinship with nature will endure without an acute awareness of that difference. Our habit of divisive aggression demands a human response. So Whitman turned back to memorialization, determined to stop averting his eyes: "I got to thinking to-day of young men's deaths—not at all sadly or sentimentally, but gravely, realistically. . . . Let me give the following three cases from budgets of personal memoranda, which I have been turning over, alone in my room, and resuming and dwelling on, this rainy afternoon. . . . As reminiscences, I find them soothing, bracing, tonic." Nature's solace is short-lived, but when immersion in the landscape is accompanied by a consciousness of immersion's impossibility—when autumn leaves also smell of hacked corpses, when upland fields appear as cemeteries, when country lanes echo with the faltering footsteps of wounded soldiers—then blood and sap can truly flow together.

The final hundred pages of *Specimen Days* are marked by undulation: though Whitman often indulged in fantasies of recovery and progress, he also offered a chastened commitment to the hard work of sustaining an Arcadian America. As his body gradually grew sturdier and more flexible, he made trips out west, into the future; he also frequented Central Park and made a point of visiting old New England, strolling through the Boston Common, seeking out Ralph Waldo Emerson in Concord. The prairies, he thought, were "America's Characteristic Landscape," already becoming "the inexhaustible land of wheat, maize, wool, flax, coal, iron, beef and pork, butter and cheese, apples and grapes"—yet he also worried that, in the middle of the country, with all that open land, "the tree question will soon become a grave one. . . . The matter of the cultivation and spread of forests may well be press'd upon thinkers who look to the coming generations of the prairie States." So it was with a certain amount of relief that Whitman turned back to the roots of the Arcadian tradition in America, finding himself, for instance, relaxing "under the shade of some old hickories and elms, just after 4 P.M., on the porch, within a stone's throw of the Concord river." His tone was sometimes elegiac, when he discussed the literary, cultural, and environmental milieus in which he came of age, but he seemed to know that elegy must be tough-minded or risk sounding pat, nostalgic, sentimental, even misleading. Lamenting the passing of Longfellow while hiding "deep in the shade of pines and cedars and a tangle of old laurel-trees and vines," Whitman dreamed of good country living and veered dangerously close to romanticizing the older poet's birdlike genius for melody; his final evaluation of his forebear's significance, though, emphasized the substantive qualities that made him just the kind of "counteractant most needed for our materialistic, self-assertive, money-worshipping, Anglo-Saxon races." In parallel fashion, at the very end of the book, Whitman seemed to hope that American society might revert to the "sunny and hardy and sane" relationship with Nature that it enjoyed in the antebellum years, but he quickly added that he had no desire to abolish the "factories, work-shops, stores, offices," held no resentment against "the dense streets and houses of cities, and all their manifold sophisticated life." Rather, he simply insisted that American Democracy, in its new urban industrial form, "must either be fibred, vitalized, by regular contact with out-door light and air and growths, farm-scenes, animals, fields, trees, birds, sun-warmth and free skies, or it will certainly dwindle and pale."[57]

For me, though, the most moving passages in the last section of *Specimen Days* take place in Massachusetts, which Whitman felt compelled to visit in the spring and fall of 1881 and again in the spring of '82. I'm fully aware that I could be projecting my own attachments onto my guide. Yet Whitman wrote about Boston and Concord as if they had become his spiritual and intellectual homes, despite the affectionate indebtedness he felt to Long Island, New York City, New Jersey, and Washington. He went to see Emerson in October 1881, just a few months, as it turned out, before the old sage passed away. Whitman and the other guests discussed Thoreau and Fuller, looked through old notes and manuscripts, harked back to days of hope, while

Emerson the fatherly patron looked on, silent, serene, beaming—Emerson, another of Whitman's early supporters, who wrote a letter to the young poet upon reading the first edition of *Leaves of Grass*, in 1855, to express the "joy" he felt at "your free and brave thought. . . . I greet you at the beginning of a great career."[58] And then Whitman, wandering through Concord, followed an itinerary that my eldest child, Sam, would immediately recognize. First, he explored "the old Manse, walk'd through the ancient garden, enter'd the rooms, noted the quaintness, the unkempt grass and bushes, the little panes in the windows, the low ceilings, the spicy smell, the creepers embowering the light"—all of which spurred him toward Sleepy Hollow Cemetery, where he spent "a half hour at Hawthorne's and Thoreau's graves," noting mournfully that "by Henry's side lies his brother John," who, like a soldier, had "died young." My family recently spent a half hour there, too, eating a picnic lunch, sandwiches and apples, while sitting under a tree in a misty drizzle. From Sleepy Hollow it was a pleasant stroll for Whitman over to Walden Pond and "the spot in the woods where Thoreau had his solitary house"—a clearing at which my family has paused on several occasions. I was delighted to learn, from Whitman, that by 1881 Thoreau's patch of the Walden woods had already become a pilgrimage site, with "quite a cairn of stones, to mark the place; I too carried one and deposited on the heap." That is also—as all my children know—the traditional way of paying respects at Jewish gravesites. To honor someone by building a cairn, like the ones you encounter on wilderness trails to help you find your way, is perhaps to acknowledge one's forebear as a guide.

Whitman then spent the better part of a week in Boston, visiting the Common every day at noon and twilight, where he got to "know all the big trees, especially the old elms along Tremont and Beacon streets, and have come to a sociable-silent understanding with most of them, in the sunlit air, (yet crispy-cool enough,) as I saunter along the wide unpaved walks." Of course, most of the curvilinear pathways are paved now, including those of the adjacent Boston Public Garden, laid out by Alexander Wadsworth, who had also been the primary surveyor at Mount Auburn. Though a few of the trees are large enough to make an impression, the shady elms are long gone, mostly victims of Dutch elm disease, and my kids tend to focus on the swan boats and the sculpture that captures a scene from one of their favorite books, *Make Way for Ducklings*, by Robert McCloskey—which was also one of my favorite books when I was a child, and which captures the Boston of an even earlier era. So our visits to the Common and the Public Garden also serve to propel me back into the past, offer me a visceral, experiential reminder of how books and trees and family and walking and time-traveling have always been intertwined for me, ever since I was five years old and begging for a ride on the swan boats myself. When Whitman perambulated these open spaces in October 1881, he couldn't help but recall an afternoon twenty-one years earlier, a "bright sharp February mid-day" just before the war, when he had spent two hours here with Emerson, listening to his elder dispense the best kind of advice about the writing of poetry, advice that was all the more eloquent and compelling because it allowed Whitman the space to disagree completely: "it afforded me, ever after, this strange and paradoxical lesson; each point of E.'s statement was unanswerable, no judge's charge ever more complete or convincing, I could never hear the points better put—and then I felt down in my soul the clear and unmistakable conviction to disobey all, and pursue my own way"—a conviction that Whitman freely and openly articulated, "whereupon we went and had a good dinner at the American House."

In May of the following year Whitman was back at Sleepy Hollow, standing before Emerson's "new-made grave" and feeling not grief but "a solemn joy and faith." The old Concord poet, having loved and encouraged so many younger men and women of letters, had departed this world at last with a kind of "ripen'd grandeur," Whitman thought, with a "play of calm and fitness, like evening light on the sea." Here was no soldier-sapling cut down prematurely, but a stately patriarch ready to accept the pull of gravity. Yet even while pondering this good death, even while celebrating Emerson's many rich legacies, Whitman found himself needing to acknowledge that all dying in America would forever be inflected by our collective memory of the Civil War: "We can say, as Abraham Lincoln at Gettysburg, It is not we who come to consecrate the dead—we reverently come to receive, if so it may be, some consecration to ourselves."[59] Our lives would be impossible without the sacrifices of our ancestors; we must work incessantly to try to repay our debt to them, and that reverent labor, in a way, constitutes the very foundation of culture. But surely some generations sacrifice more than others; surely some deaths, as Whitman knew far too intimately, are never adequately honored, and surely we survivors are sometimes unworthy of consecration.

———————

I was there—at King David Memorial Gardens, in Falls Church, Virginia, just outside of Washington, for the unveiling of Ian's grave—though it was only recently that I remembered, after visiting the Wilderness, an hour to the south. Ian grew up in Oklahoma—went canoeing in the North Woods of Minnesota—attended a semester of college in Cambridge, about two miles from Mount Auburn—died back in his home state—but was buried in a Jewish cemetery in Virginia. I remembered the memorial service in a flash—while walking to work through the Ithaca City Cemetery—partly because of a pileated woodpecker.

When the memory first flooded my consciousness, I couldn't figure out the Virginia connection. So I dug out the journals I kept in the late 80s, which I hadn't looked at since I finished scrawling in them. They had an answer: when Ian died, at the end of August 1988, his parents were getting ready to relocate to the Washington area. His father, a prominent doctor and geneticist in Oklahoma City, had gotten some kind of job offer. What I don't know is whether the move was already in the works when Ian got sick or whether his parents had decided in the midst of their ordeal that they might need to reformulate their lives in a new place. In any case, they buried Ian in the northern Virginia suburbs, where they could easily visit his grave in the coming years. And they held the memorial service, the unveiling, in the following June, at the end of my sophomore year, as I was preparing to leave for Minnesota. I took a train down to D.C., stayed with my aunt and uncle in the Maryland suburbs, and took the Metro out to Falls Church—though I have a vague memory of being lost, of rushing to make it to the service in time. King David is adjacent to a cemetery called the National Memorial Park, which I think I mistook for Arlington National Cemetery, only a few miles away but on a different Metro line. In any case, I eventually got there and found my way across the rolling green fields to the grave. I stood there for the fifteen-minute service, praying that I was in some way atoning for how poorly I had handled my relationship to Ian during his illness. And then, amazingly, Ian's father and mother, and his two older sisters, who had both interrupted their graduate programs to spend the year with their parents, invited me and a couple of other of Ian's friends back to their new house—drove us there, fed us, showed us pictures, shared memories with us, asked us questions, talked with us for hours.

Now, straining to recapture that afternoon, I find myself empathizing more easily with Ian's parents than with the nineteen-year-old version of myself, and I think of the historian and journalist John Gunther struggling to write about the loss of his seventeen-year-old son to a brain tumor, struggling to express what it means to have known and loved someone, his child, his kin, struggling to articulate "what goes into a brain—the goodness, the wit, the sum total of enchantment in a personality, the very will, indeed the ego itself— . . . everything that makes a human being what he is, the inordinately subtle and exquisite combination of memory, desire, impulse, reflective capacity, power of association, even consciousness."[60] I suppose, on that June afternoon in that house in suburban Maryland, we were all trying to share our understanding and appreciation of Ian's uniqueness. What a potent, anxious, cathartic day of witnessing. Yet it was unavailable to my active memory for more than two decades.

Why did I block that experience? Why is it that, during the three and a half years I spent in Washington in the mid-90s, I didn't once think to revisit Ian's grave? How could I have forgotten the simple fact that his body was buried right there—how could I have buried the memory? I have no choice but to conclude that I was simply unable to confront my own weakness, to acknowledge the violence I felt I had done to Ian and his family by having withdrawn during their greatest time of pain.

So I'm grateful to the woodpecker I saw that day in Ithaca, bringer of multiple, layered memories. I'm grateful to the dead and dying trees on the edge of the cemetery, breeding ground for the juiciest of insects, where the woodpecker likes to browse, digging in the trees' hard, fibrous flesh. It is thanks to those trees, I suppose, that I am beginning to face my failings, my limitations, the finitude of my capacities.

I saw my first pileated woodpecker in Minnesota, so I will always associate the species with Ian. But there's more to it than that. It's a gigantic bird, usually about eighteen inches tall—the size of a crow—with a stark scarlet crest, a wild cackle, and a hammering peck capable of splitting a small tree in half. I was terrified by the first one I saw, because it seemed primeval: I remember freezing, scanning the woods for other anomalies, feeling as though I had passed through some sort of portal to the distant past. But then I got to know that woodpecker. A pileated, either on its own or with a mate, will stay in the same home area for months at a time, and this one seemed utterly unconcerned by my repeat visits, sometimes with color film, to capture the red of its crest, sometimes with black and white, in direct homage to Timothy O'Sullivan. And I knew, as I took my pictures, that they were meant for my dying grandmother, the poet, the person who had introduced me to birdwatching during walks in Maine and in her own backyard in Cincinnati. She and my grandfather were particularly fond of loons and owls, and at first I had adopted those birds as my guides to the lakes and trees of the North Woods. Cree, the wolf, also offered me an immediate sense of kinship for that first short month of my time in Minnesota. By the winter, though, the pileated woodpecker, symbol (for me) of both persistence and mortality, had become my totem animal. (Figure 39.)

I shipped off a framed photograph of the woodpecker to my grandmother and prayed it would mean something to her—prayed she would survive at least until my planned visit in April—prayed that she was still reading and writing poetry and was sometimes able to watch the birds outside her window, though I knew she was mostly confined to her bed, pining for her husband of sixty years, who had just died the previous Valentine's Day.

Still reeling from sophomore year, I didn't do much reading and writing myself in those months, but, on a weekend trip down to the Twin Cities, guided by my new girlfriend, I visited an irresistible bookstore, and picked up a new paperback that I found myself digging into again and again, a relatively thin volume with a humble,

Figure 39. Pileated woodpecker, near Finland, MN, 1989.

muted cover, written by Robert Coles, who happened to be a professor at the stuffy university I had recently abandoned: *The Call of Stories: Teaching and the Moral Imagination.* It turned out to be about death, and empathy. That autumn had been somewhat difficult—there are so many different ways in which I could characterize my time in Minnesota—but *The Call of Stories* helped me cope with a case of mononucleosis that lasted several weeks, and with my indecision about whether to try to transfer to a different college, and with the pain my girlfriend and I both experienced and inflicted as we haltingly got together with each other and broke up with old flames. My internship contract at Wolf Ridge lasted only through December, but eventually I asked for three more months and then wrote an agonizing letter to my old poetry teacher, Jan Thaddeus, telling her that I thought I would eventually come back to Harvard, but asking her, meanwhile, in her administrative capacity, to extend my leave of absence at least through the spring semester. I ultimately decided not to transfer, in part because of Robert Coles. His book pivots on an "Interlude" called "Bringing Poems to Medical School Teaching," in which he offers future doctors the discretion and indirection of good literature, the careful, subtle invitation to imagination and empathy, the suggestion that his students might do their work most effectively not by distancing themselves from their terminal patients but by trying—in the words of one of his own patient-poets—to see through the dying person's "invisible new veil / Of finity," by pausing to recall the way that poems can capture "those high moments of consciousness that philosophers say make us what we are, creatures of language who find phrases that display the I clinging to itself and who know that our turn, too, will come."[61]

At the start of the new year, which was also the start of a new decade, for the calendar and for me (I had turned twenty in November 1989), I was spending hours every day on skis and snowshoes in the silent woods, and gradually finding my way back to books—I was renewing connections—I was trying to get used to finitude. I thought often of my father, the most bookish person I knew at the time, a professor of French literature who had been on the older side when I was born and so was already eligible for retirement as I entered my twenties. He had always struck me as being at ease with his limitations, perhaps because he agreed with Flaubert, his favorite writer, that the most appropriate way to live was to embrace a "religion of despair. One must be equal to one's destiny, that's to say, impassive like it. By dint of saying 'That is so! That is so!' and of gazing down into the black pit at one's feet, one remains calm."[62] My father's embrace of despair sometimes did leave him downcast, and I have rarely known him to be silly or spontaneous, but he has almost always seemed to be at peace with the world.

I had been relatively calm myself in early January 1990; then, about three weeks into the new decade, on consecutive days, I learned of two more deaths, both unexpected—a new friend, and my favorite history professor. Chrisi was my age, but she'd suffered from lupus for about five years already, and finally she came down with an infection that she just couldn't withstand. John Clive was sixty-five, exactly my father's age; he had a heart attack in a car after what seems to have been a lovely dinner party with friends and colleagues. Suddenly, again, I was swimming in guilt and fear. It can be dizzying to stare into the pit. The previous summer, when I met Chrisi, through one of my closest friends, she had trusted me with the most intimate details of her life, and I had given virtually nothing in return. At a time when I was a committed letter-writer, I had intended to bring her address with me to Minnesota—but I hadn't. And I had never told John Clive that he had gotten me through my sophomore year. A week before my grandfather died, during an informal talk at my dorm with about fifteen undergraduates, Professor Clive had explained his job as a true vocation: he had become a historian not to answer some abstract scholarly question but simply to indulge his burning curiosity about the human character. His comfortable roundness, his gentle humility, the pleasure he took in a well-turned phrase or a carefully spun story, his tendency toward irony and the observation of shared human weaknesses, his cherished personal connections with particular writers and scholars, his wryly smiling eyebrows—all, indubitably, had reminded me of my father, and reminded me of why I loved the humanities. For months, I'd wanted to thank him, wanted to give something back.

In the depth of winter, I went again and again to look for the woodpecker, and seemed to find it less and less often. I turned back to Robert Coles, hoped I could eventually take a course with him, tried to find in his book a combination of self-forgetting—through a caring focus on other people's problems—and a committed, critical self-scrutiny that was never proud of itself and never complete. Mostly I failed, and just railed against myself and the heavens in my journal.

The denial of death sometimes seems necessary for human beings to persist in their lives and work.[63] If we constantly pondered our mortality, then we might be all the more susceptible to the dark stillness of depression, in an age when life itself frequently feels overwhelming. Yet the cultural sanctioning of death-avoidance might mean that many of us will never have the opportunity to learn how to accept our mortality. When does it become tolerable to talk openly about dying and attempt to come to grips with it? When the oncologist gives you a month to live? But even more troubling to me is the seeming correlation, in the modern era, between the approved denial of death and the approved denial of all the violence we do every day in the industrial world—the damage we inflict by hoarding our money, eating the flesh of factory-farmed animals, flipping on light switches, driving cars, withholding love. Just as it has become taboo, over the last 150 years or so, to admit into our lives "the disturbance and the overly strong and unbearable emotion caused by the ugliness of dying," as the historian Philippe Ariès has argued, so too must we exclude absolutely anything that might contradict our modern assumption that society is functioning smoothly, "that life is always happy."[64] Of course, no individual can bear the responsibility for global systems of oppression; too much conscientiousness can be immobilizing and alienating, and it often leads to self-righteousness. Moreover, most of us are unwilling to follow Thoreau and go off the grid. We sometimes have to buy gas from the local Shell station, which means we somehow have to come to grips with the people dying as a direct result of Shell's oil production in the Niger Delta.[65] The key step, I think, is admitting to ourselves that purchasing gas is at least partially an evil—that in purchasing gas we may be participating in destruction.

What I started to understand in Minnesota was that I might have been able to reach out to Ian if I had simply admitted that he was dying—and, for that matter, that I was dying, too, since we never know how much time we're going to have to grow up and get over our anxiety and self-consciousness and self-centeredness. I also started to understand how stories could help with that kind of acknowledgment. Coles taught me that the reaching out did not have to take any particular form, that there was no such thing as perfect closure. With a good, complex tale of death worming its way through our minds, we may be more likely to remember that the moral life consists not in a search for "'solutions' or 'resolutions' but [in] a broadening and even a heightening of our struggles."[66]

I tried my best, despite the shock of hearing about Chrisi and John Clive, to let my grandmother know how important she was to me, how much I treasured her poetry and her tea parties and her birds—even though, in truth, I still felt stung by the comment she had made when, at the end of my freshman year, I showed her a couple of the poems I'd written in my seminar with Jan Thaddeus: "They're clever, but they're not from the gut."

My mother and I had a good visit to Cincinnati in April. I sat on Grandma's bed and talked with her about canoeing in Minnesota and about the pileated woodpecker—the framed photo I'd sent was right there on her bedside table, sometimes propped up, sometimes serving as a coaster for a cup of tea—and about my plans to travel to Europe and perhaps visit one of her oldest friends, who still lived in London. When I said goodbye to her, she gathered herself together, smiled, told me she was glad that I would inherit Grandaddy's canoe paddle, thanked me for visiting, and said, "I felt I got to know you this time." Then, as I shuffled out, my mother came in to say her temporary goodbye (she visited about once a month). I heard Grandma's screeching hearing aid, and then her creaky voice. "I enjoyed yesterday," she told my mother; "I had a very nice talk with that boy."

I went to Europe, studied in France, had high tea with Grandma's friend Dorothy, and then came back to Harvard in September to start my junior year. Grandma died on the seventeenth, Grandaddy's birthday, in the first week of classes. I talked it over with my parents and decided to skip the funeral, go to my lectures and seminars, and then come out to Cincinnati for the weekend, to help dismantle the house. It was a bad decision. What I really wanted to do was *preserve* the house: I wanted to quit school again and move to Cincinnati for good, wanted to try to absorb the meaning of my grandparents' lives, wanted to understand how they had brought all of us together so easily, so powerfully, for all those Passover seders and bar and bat mitzvahs and weddings, year after year.

As soon as I arrived at the house, I sat down in the living room and read through the eulogies with some of my cousins. My father's, in particular, left me anguished, and suddenly I was crying—suddenly all my grief and guilt and anger came pouring back out. I understood why he had taken my mother's place, understood my mother's shyness, understood the churning emotion that would not let her stand calmly before the family to deliver a charming, wistful talk. It made perfect sense: my father was a sharp and sensitive observer who understood the family as well as anyone, and he was a professor—he knew how to speak. His eulogy was eloquent, wise, comforting, and learned, with numerous quotations from Montaigne, which ran along these lines: "to philosophize is to learn to die"; "let us rid [death] of its strangeness, come to know it, get used to it. Let us have nothing on our minds as often as death"; "Nature forces us to it. Go out of this world, she says, as you entered it. The same passage that you made from death to life, without feeling or fright, make it again from life to death. Your death is a part of the order of the universe; it is part of the life of the world."[67] I couldn't help but agree. But all of my father's emotion remained under the surface, repressed, and, for my taste, the talk put too much emphasis on the generic acceptance of mortality and not enough on the specifics of Grandma's irretrievable life and character. I guess I wanted something wrenching, to match what I felt—in my gut. My father seemed to be rationalizing death, intellectualizing pain; I wanted to be done with intellection and books.

The pain did not dissipate, but I did go back to Cambridge on Monday, when my grandparents' house went up for sale, and fortunately I was also returning to Lou Masur, my new advisor, who listened to my story and told me to read Whitman. He also gave me one of the most meaningful gifts I have ever received: John Clive's last book, *Not by Fact Alone: Essays on the Writing and Reading of History.* I dove into it right away, but stopped short when I got to a section about the French historian Jules Michelet, on page 32, suddenly feeling as if I could hear Clive's voice speaking aloud:[68]

Michelet would have shaken his head in wonderment at our current discussions as to whether the past is or is not "usable." As far as he was concerned, the whole point of writing history was to re-create a past that not only could, but must, be used— eventually by the historian's readers, but in the first place by the historian himself—to satisfy his own psychic and spiritual needs, and to inspire him both to bear witness to past virtues and to do his share in the rooting out of present evils. For Michelet, writing history is tantamount to self-expression, to total commitment at the most personal level.

So in the fall of 1990, Lou helped me rediscover reading and writing as a way of broadening my struggles, as did Larry Buell, a new professor who had just arrived from Oberlin College and was teaching a course called "American Literature and the

American Environment," which spurred me to realize that I could take my experiences with environmental education in Minnesota and turn them into a focus for my academic work. Larry had told the class that he was eager to introduce us to some Ohio poetry, so when I returned from Cincinnati I showed him a book I had taken from Grandma's collection called *Contemporary Ohio Poetry,* published in the late 1950s. He borrowed it for a few days, and when he returned it he mentioned that he had been familiar with the work of only three or four of the featured poets—but one of those, it so happened, was Amy Blank.[69]

Unfortunately, one of Amy Blank's two daughters, my mother's only sibling, my beloved Aunt Bitsy, was going through chemotherapy all that year—was dying—as was my father's younger sister, Auntie Grace. And even after all I had gone through with Ian and Grandma, I still didn't know how to express the love and caring I felt for these two members of my family during their time of pain. I remember one solitary moment with Bitsy, in a car, as she was dropping me off at the Silver Spring Metro station—it might even have been when I was on my way to Ian's memorial service the year before—when I haltingly tried to tell her how much she was in my thoughts, how hard I was trying to struggle *with* her. She smiled kindly, as she always did, but I knew I had fumbled the words.

It was not until the winter of my senior year, when I turned back to Jan Thaddeus, when she agreed to do an independent study with me on the writing of personal essays, that I finally felt something start to shift in myself at the deepest level, that I finally felt I might someday be able to muster the capacity for acknowledgment. Week after week, she kept after me to remember more honestly, to look at myself unflinchingly. She had me read my essays out loud to her, because it was important how they sounded, but also because my voice and posture would tip us both off when my sentences veered toward aversion. We read Tolstoy, Nabokov, Mary McCarthy, Grace Paley, Paul Zweig. Jan, whose main field was British literature, taught me the periodic sentence, as practiced by writers like Milton and Gibbon and Churchill, the sentence that withholds its full meaning and punch until it releases its final breath. She also corrected my pronunciation of "pileated."[70] And she always brought me back to my grandparents, and to death, and to Minnesota, and to my attachments to animals and trees, and to my faltering efforts to become an adult—so that the final, long paper I wrote for her, the last thing I completed in college, turned into a humbling, meandering memorial and testimonial to the gifts of nurturing that my family of nature-lovers had bestowed upon me. It was also meant as a gift both to Ian and to Jan.

About six months after I graduated, in December 1992, my friend Josh, someone I'd been close to since sixth grade, was in a car accident with his family on Cape Cod;

his father, the driver, was killed instantly, and Josh landed in the hospital, with severe internal bleeding and intestinal damage. Given my own sense of shock, I couldn't imagine what Josh was feeling. But I desperately wanted to offer some kind of support, desperately wanted to set aside my grief and sense of inadequacy. I remember being grateful to another friend, Ari, who was in the same situation, who agreed that there was no way to know what to say, but who put it to me explicitly as a writing challenge: it's just another case where you have to find the words, any words. We went to the hospital together, and kissed our friend on the forehead, and told him we were sorry, and told him we were there, and told him that the doctors had assured us he would be passing gas again in no time. Eventually, with all sorts of disclaimers and trepidation, I also gave Josh that last essay I'd written for Jan. It was mostly about the death of my grandparents, I told him, which was not at all parallel to the death of his father—but maybe he would find something there, about mortality in general, that would resonate. I did not have a great deal of confidence in my words, but I think I had finally come back around to the idea that words are virtually all we have, and that the important thing is to offer them.

Two years later, having moved to Washington to work for an environmental organization, I was riding my bicycle to my office through Rock Creek Park, one of the most wondrous urban spaces in the world, on a preternaturally mild December morning (even in 1994, my co-workers and I were thinking: global warming), when I saw my second pileated woodpecker. I got off my bike and just stood there, breathing, taking in the bird's size. My mind jumped to Minnesota—to Ian—to my grandmother—and then to Jan. Jan, who was still alive, who could be contacted. I wrote to her. I told her about the woodpecker; I thanked her for all the time she had given me, for all she had taught me. I also remember telling her that, though I found my job stimulating and rewarding, and though I loved living in D.C., loved being surrounded by other young idealists, I was still struggling with my relationship to death and friendship and books and writing.

Two more friends had lost parents in those two years, to cancer; I felt I had not done enough to reach out to them. I still agonized over some of the same old questions: Did they want to talk about mortality, or be distracted from it? Was humor inappropriate or helpful? (At my grandfather's funeral, I had no idea how to react when my cousins started joking about being pall bearers: "Is this the right body? I thought Grandaddy's name was Sheldon, not Paul!") And, meanwhile, my twelfth-grade English teacher had passed away, four years after I had last been in touch with him, three years after I had set aside a card I had bought for him, with a photo of Louis Armstrong, because once, when we were reading Ralph Ellison's *Invisible*

*Man*, he had played an old scratchy record for us, of "What Did I Do to Be So Black and Blue," and because once, when my school orchestra played an event with a community orchestra, of which, it turned out, he was a member, I had bumped into him in one of the warm-up rooms at the concert hall, and he was carrying a trumpet. I explained to Jan that, right after my parents called to tell me about Mr. Harris's death, I had immediately dug out that Louis Armstrong card, and just sat there staring at it, crying, hating myself. Mr. Harris's growly voice was one of those that lurked in my head, and I kept remembering the way he had talked about finally, thankfully, mustering the nerve to have an honest, full conversation with his father, just before his father's death. The lesson seemed wasted on me, I wrote to Jan. But Jan, bless her, sent back a letter right away, and I carried it around with me for the next several years, because she seemed so full of pleasure at my woodpecker sighting, and because she managed to press me, in the gentlest, most supportive way, to keep up the struggle, to be both easier and harder on myself. She said she knew how complicated and busy my life would get in the immediate future, but she hoped I might take the time to write to her again on occasion, maybe every four or five years, just to check in. I never wrote back. And then, in the middle of graduate school, in December 2001, there was Lou Masur's voice on the phone, telling me that Jan had just died of a stroke.

So when I saw my third pileated woodpecker, on the edge of the Ithaca City Cemetery, its pecks making an impossibly loud, resounding echo, I thought first of Jan—before my memory jumped back to Washington—and Minnesota—and Ian—and then, shockingly, Virginia. It is still wrenching to confront my failures of connection, but I try to remind myself that at least I managed, if only once, to convey to Jan how much she had meant to me. In the last few years, I have also offered independent studies on creative writing to a few of my students, have listened to them read their work out loud to me in my office, and those have been incredibly resonant experiences. And I'm glad I made the effort to go to Jan's memorial service at Harvard, in May of 2002. The program from that event—it was another vivid, intensely quiet afternoon—still nests inside my copy of Jan's book of poems, *Lot's Wife*, which I bought at the Grolier Poetry Book Shop in Cambridge while I was taking Jan's seminar on the writing of poetry. At the service, I stood up and read the poem on page 46, called "A Thought of Marigolds".[71]

> When I opened your letter,
> I was thinking of marigolds.
> He is alive, you said,
> but in a week, please God, he will be dead.

Trusting your silence in November,
I had believed the antiseptic hands
would chisel out the cancered cells.
But now, in California's warm December,
your letter heaved with unadmitted pain,
while in Vermont,
as ice skates glinted on frozen lakes,
and snowballs caked in children's gloves,
you caressed his hollow face
and watched the weather on the sill—
icicles fingering toward the grave.

In a different sun,
one leaf withers on its stalk,
a single petal folds.
How can I face his death in the East?
I send a thought of marigolds.

While I was living in Washington, though I never remembered Ian's grave, I thought often of cancer, as I watched my friends Randy and Midori say goodbye to their dying mothers. I told Jan, in my woodpecker letter, that I wished I had done more to show my caring for my friends, but that at least, as with Josh, I had been able to give them the essay she had helped me write—at least I had regained some amount of hope that words could matter viscerally, could carry a spark of kinship. Spending my days with global development reports and policy analyses, I found myself turning to fiction in the evening, diving into stories, imagining characters and worlds, empathizing; I remember taking a grim pleasure in telling my environmentalist colleagues that I was trying to compensate for the bleak picture of global deforestation by reading uplifting novels like *Jude the Obscure*. So, as it turned out, I also felt moved to give Randy and Midori a couple of books: *The Call of Stories*, and a brand new hardcover I found while browsing in a shop near my office, a short memoir by the poet Donald Hall called *Life Work*.

It was *Life Work*, I think, that brought me back to a full and faithful engagement with reading and writing, and maybe even history. It was *Life Work* that helped me go back to my father's bookish eulogy for Grandma with empathy and appreciation, with an understanding of writing as ritual. I plowed through the entire book on the floor of the store where I first encountered it (note to the store owner: I then bought two copies). If a reader of *Specimen Days* might be forgiven for wondering occasionally how Whitman ever managed to support himself, given the amount of time he spent communing with trees, a reader of *Life Work* will more likely question, given Hall's writerly discipline, whether he ever left his house. We get painstaking lists of his endless scribbling chores, and, in keeping with the fact that he and his wife live in the New Hampshire farmhouse purchased by his great-grandparents in 1865, he explains that "it is the family farm—which historians of work's structure derive from utter antiquity—that provides a model for my own work; one task after another, all day all year, and every task different. Of course: It was precisely the Connecticut family business of the Brock-Hall Dairy—milk pasteurizing and bottling and delivering; every-day-the-same, temporarily efficient subdivision of the industrial world; my father's curse—that I grew up determined to avoid or evade. And did." Hall's endlessly varying jobs, then—his poems, his essays, his children's books, his memoirs, his book reviews, his baseball journalism, his short stories, his textbooks, his letters (five thousand a year, he says)—all serve to root him in a preindustrial cycle of work, despite his inevitable participation in the modern cash economy. And though he rarely seems to go outside except to walk his dog, his work routine makes him feel as close to nature as a farmer, or maybe an "ox-cart man," the central figure in one of Hall's children's stories, a tale he originally heard from his cousin Paul, who "said an old man had told him the story when he was a boy; and Paul said that the old man said that when *he* was a boy, an *old* man had told it to him." The ox-cart man was an old New Englander who every year would fill his cart with whatever his family had produced but didn't need to use themselves—"maple sugar, I suppose, wool and woolens, maybe linen or flaxseed, shingles, birch brooms, potatoes"—and then walk to Portsmouth Market, where he would sell it all, including the ox and cart. It is a story, Hall explains, "of human life compared to a perennial plant that dies to rise again."[72]

From the beginning of *Life Work*, it becomes clear that Hall is fully engaged with death. By page five, we are shivering with him and his wife at an outdoor memorial service for a friend, tossing tuberoses with them onto a bench; by page 19, we know that his mother is eighty-nine and dying; we quickly learn that as Hall scratches out this memoir, a couple of pages a day, he is also reworking a poem which has been gnawing at him for ten years, which has already been through more than five hundred drafts, and which is called "Another Elegy"; and soon we begin to understand that his commitment to work offers him a contented "absorbedness," a pure break from self-consciousness, a "total loss of identity," which sounds a lot like the merging-with-the-world that Freud, drawing on Indian mysticism, understood as one aim of the "death instinct."[73] So it comes as no surprise when, mid-way through the book, at the very end of Part One, Hall explains his realization that, throughout his life, work has always served as both an escape from mortality and a frank acknowledgment of it. The prose feels confident here, calm, clear-eyed, secure in the author's understanding that there are good days and bad days, warm days and cold days, days of joy and days of grief. And then we flip the page to start Part Two, and suddenly everything changes: his cancer has come back, he needs surgery, he's going to die within the next couple of years. The writing challenge is explicit: What to say, how to say anything, now that he is perpetually distracted, now that he "cannot stop speculating"? His only option, of course, is to try to restore old rhythms of work, to become engrossed again, and, remarkably, he manages to persist by turning to the past, by interrogating his family history.

As a child, Hall often spent his summers on this same New Hampshire farm, working alongside his grandparents, and now, as an adult, it strikes him that his grandparents' passing must have marked a new kind of modernity in America. He knows, given his stake in the subject, that he will be tempted to romanticize the life his grandparents led, but his observations of their working rhythms are careful and compelling. Citing Freud's awareness in the early twentieth century of the "wretchedness, torture, and misery fundamental to civilized human life," at least some of which stemmed directly from industrialism, Hall insists that when Freud refers to work as, potentially, a "major palliative," he means an older form of work, which was both physical and intellectual, and varied, and productive of things that the worker him- or herself could use, like carrot soup, or socks, or the warmth of a fire. One of the greatest pleasures of his grandparents' work life, he figures, was that they were equal partners in significant accomplishments, and their equality "carried weight, import, and impact." When Hall's own parents set up their household, they were so committed to the cash economy that his mother's work, no matter how extensive, simply couldn't matter as much as his father's. But his grandmother Kate, with her mitten-knitting, her wood-splitting, her bread-baking, her clothes-washing, her quilt-whacking, had provided just as many sustaining services as his grandfather Wesley, with his chopping, haying, milking, planting, harvesting. Together, Kate and Wesley, though poor, seemed to take "mild continual pleasure in completing tasks," in doing the work of the household, where each had a domain of competence, control, and special satisfactions. Hall, in his childhood, spent many days outdoors with Wesley, and he is especially keen to recall the ways in which the farm's economy was explicitly uneconomic. His grandfather, for instance, used his scythe to trim the edges of fields, where the mowing machine couldn't go (because of rocks and bits of wire and, of course, hidden stumps), despite the fact that a full hour of hand-cutting might yield only a few pennies' worth of hay. But Wesley never did what he did "for economic reasons. Things were done because it was the way to do them, an aesthetic of work, old habits bespeaking clarity and right angles, resolution and conclusiveness." Eventually Hall's grandfather taught him scythe mowing, "which is a rhythmic motion like dancing or lovemaking," a motion Hall will never forget: "finding a meter, one abandons oneself to the swing of it; one surrenders oneself to the guidance of object and task, where worker and work are one: There is something ecstatic about mowing with a scythe." So it was outside in the field with his grandfather that Hall learned the work rhythm he would follow for the rest of his days.

At the same time, though, Hall recognizes and remembers the difficulty of his grandparents' work life, the marginalization they experienced in an age of industrialism, even the gulf they felt in their own relationship, despite their equality, because so many of their tasks were solitary and performed in separate realms of the household. Relatively late in the book, Hall has to go in for an operation to remove part of his liver, and he ponders the possibility of posthumous publication. The last line he writes (before, happily, taking up the memoir again two and a half weeks later) is one that just hangs on the page: "In the winter Wesley chopped cordwood on the mountain." The white space after that sentence makes me think of New Hampshire birches, reminds me that these pages, too, are made of wood. I feel I can see a solitary figure striding uphill, either a lumberman or a writer, and he is firm in his step, though perhaps unsure of his next job. The air feels crisp and bracing; the trees are welcoming and sturdy, the vista rolling and expansive; but the journey, the work of making the passage, is lonely.

*Life Work*, over the last two decades, has offered me its own sustenance, its own rhythms of consolation and guidance. But until recently I had never owned a copy myself: all through the 90s and early 2000s I kept buying it and giving it away to friends. Then, after I saw the pileated woodpecker in the Ithaca Cemetery, I knew I had to reread it, cover to cover, and place it permanently on my shelf. As I looked into making the purchase, I found, through an online bookseller, that Hall had actually survived to put out a tenth-anniversary edition in 2003. Back in 1993, at the end of the book, he had admitted that "if I begin a thought about 1995 I do not finish the thought." In 2003, in the new preface, he reveals, shockingly, that, "in 1995, it was my wife Jane Kenyon who died, at forty-seven."[74] Cancer. But the most profound surprise I experienced upon finally picking up the new edition came when I suddenly noticed the art on the cover: it was a reproduction of a painting completed in 1865, the same year Hall's grandparents bought their New Hampshire farmhouse—it was Winslow Homer's *Veteran in a New Field*.

In 1865, the genuinely new field for American development lay in the territory beyond the Mississippi. "Go West, young man": this was the sentiment of the day, especially as popularized by Horace Greeley's *New York Tribune*, which used an editorial in July 1865 to urge migration on any able-bodied soldiers who had survived the war—"go West," people were saying, "and grow up with the country"—go west and forget about the recent unpleasantness in the east.[75]

From the beginning of Abraham Lincoln's political career, part of his agenda had been to transfigure the frontier, to build it into a new geography of hope. Lincoln understood that the Civil War was about the nation's future as it would be played out on the plains and the Pacific coast, that Americans were fighting and bleeding over Kansas, not Maine or Alabama. Would western spaces be filled with yeoman farmers raising golden rows of grain, or with slaves working on cotton and tobacco plantations? Perhaps the end of the war signaled an opportunity to plant a new democratic utopia out on the high prairie and in the mountain meadows. The *Tribune*, in 1865, invoked the Homestead Act of May 1862 as a kind of rededication of the republic: thanks to Lincoln and the Civil War Congress, the government was offering so-called quarter sections, 160 acres instead of 640, for the token fee of ten dollars, in a throwback spirit of agrarian individualism that was meant to discourage both plantation owners and speculators.[76] Now, the patriotic thing to do was to set aside rumors of the west's aridity and haul your family out to the empty, wide-open spaces, where the scenery was grand and the mood expansive.

Of course, the land wasn't actually empty, but Americans commonly assumed that the Indians would simply step aside—there was plenty of room out there, in the wilderness—and, anyway, after the white men of the North and South had fought each other over the fate of the black men, they were perhaps all too eager to join forces in taking on the "red men," in identifying and attacking a new common enemy, who, after all, were actually an old common enemy. The cultural discourse of the west in this era seems marked by denial: in the face of death and violent maiming and deep trauma, politicians, businessmen, writers, and artists all came together to make pronouncements notable for their glib triumphalism, their too-easy confidence, their blind certainty about a smooth future.[77] It was also Lincoln and the Civil War Congress who spurred the construction of the transcontinental railroad, through massive land grants and financial incentives and the promise of perfectly healed wounds: "Hail, then, all hail, this auspicious hour!" said one booster, delighting in the implications of the July 1862 Pacific Railroad Act. "Hail this bond of brotherhood and union . . . , the symbol, the harbinger, the pledge of a higher civilization and an ultimate and world-wide peace!"[78] And it was late in the fall of 1862 that Emmanuel Leutze completed his famous mural in the U.S. Capitol, entitled *Across the Continent: Westward the Course of Empire Takes Its Way*.

Indeed, just glance at the most popular landscape art of the 1860s, and it becomes clear how far Americans had traveled from the Hudson River School. The dazzling, glorious sunshine in Albert Bierstadt's western paintings, the open skies, the sublime mountains, the lush vegetation, the ample water, combined to make him the leading painter of the decade, and distracted viewers from the difficulty and conflict of settlement, turning the land into a scenic backdrop against which the drama of American Progress played out with an air of calm inevitability.[79] This was the true era of Manifest Destiny, because it was the era of American desperation: people *needed* new frontiers, a new sense of opportunity and possibility, so the mythic romance of the Wild West—all the new images of cowboys and scouts and miners and pioneers— took on an intense cultural power, a power that has persisted through many subsequent eras.

Buffalo Bill, who first appeared in a dime novel in 1869, should have been a flash-in-the-pan sensation, as it were: gold and silver mines boomed for just a few years and then left ghost towns in their wake, and the famous cattle drives on the plains lasted only about two decades, from 1865 to 1885, after which the Wild West essentially went bust. Yet Americans so fell in love with Buffalo Bill's model of confident strength that he remains one of our most prominent heroes almost 150 years later. He was brave, persevering, ambitious, independent-minded, skilled, in touch with nature but not awed by it, ready to compete with anyone, ready to find solutions even when confronted with difficult terrain or other rugged circumstances—ready to save the day when innocent American settlers were threatened by bloodthirsty outlaws, or Mexicans, or Indians.[80]

At the famous art show and fundraiser put on in New York in April 1864, by the U.S. Sanitary Commission, which coordinated medical relief efforts for federal troops, Bierstadt's monumental painting of *The Rocky Mountains* was clearly the central attraction.[81] (Figure 40.) About six feet high and ten feet wide, the painting draws its viewers easily into a picturesque Indian encampment by the edge of a clear lake, fed by a rushing waterfall and presided over by lofty, ethereal, snow-capped peaks. According to one prominent critic, Bierstadt had perfectly captured the crucial "quality of American light, clear, transparent, and sharp in outlines," and another reviewer claimed that the artist had led the public "into the very vestibule of virgin Nature."[82] While the aging disciples of Thomas Cole—painters like Sanford

Figure 40. Albert Bierstadt, *The Rocky Mountains, Lander's Peak*, 1863, oil on canvas.

Gifford and Frederic Church—continued to struggle with the stubborn question of how white Americans might settle the continent honorably, Bierstadt tended to avoid cultural politics and focus on the genuine inspiration he felt in the mountain air, and that approach won him countless fans and prizes. His work spoke to the growing interest in environmental sublimity as embodied by certain unusual wilderness formations, which, some advocates suggested, might even be worthy of official protection. But there is no hint in *The Rocky Mountains* of Whitman's hope that the west could support a new garden-style development blending agriculture and commerce, with "bustling, half-rural, handsome cities."[83] Nor is there any indication that the number of federal troops in the west had risen dramatically during the Civil War or that the Homestead Act had spurred not just a new flow of settlers but a new rash of Indian massacres, which, as it turned out, would continue unabated for the following two and a half decades. Though the frontier soldiers knew perfectly well how much violence went into protecting recently arrived pioneers—Henry Sibley famously swept the Sioux westward in the late summer of 1862, in defense of St. Paul, and in the Southwest Kit Carson conducted bloody raids and massive relocation campaigns that affected thousands of Navajos and Apaches throughout 1863—the American public was not always fully informed, and in any case Bierstadt can perhaps be forgiven for not wanting to emphasize such confrontations.[84] Still, though, it is notable that his Indians have already retreated peacefully into the bosom of the Rockies, to become elements of nature themselves, scenic decorations, confirming the depicted region as a place meant to be viewed, to provide uplift, rather than to be fully incorporated into white society.[85]

Bierstadt's picture of the Rockies was based on a trip he had taken to Colorado and Wyoming back in 1859, but in the summer of 1863 he had made it all the way to California, and by the end of 1864, back in New York, he had shown his first painting of Yosemite Valley. (Figure 41.)

Figure 41. Albert Bierstadt, *Valley of the Yosemite*, 1864, oil on paperboard.

This new work made such a splash, in part, because at the end of June Congress had granted Yosemite to the state of California as a new kind of park, "for public use, resort, and recreation."[86] The nation had suddenly launched a system of wilderness preservation that would forever reshape worldwide environmental debates—less than two months after the Battle of the Wilderness. When, a year later, after much study and debate, a board of commissioners issued a report about how they thought Yosemite should be managed as a public trust, the author was none other than Frederick Law Olmsted, and he was quick to point out just how important art, wilderness, and the west had been during the war, praising Bierstadt, in particular, for having "given to the people on the Atlantic some idea of the sublimity" of frontier scenery. Indeed, Olmsted wrote, "it was during one of the darkest hours, before Sherman had begun the march upon Atlanta or Grant his terrible movement through the Wilderness . . . , that consideration was first given to the danger that such scenes might become private property and through the false taste, the caprice or requirements of some industrial speculation of their holders; their value to posterity be injured."[87] In the crucible of a humiliating war, Americans could at least take pride in their newfound appreciation of certain kinds of land.

Olmsted was not in Manhattan to observe Bierstadt's success at the Metropolitan Fair of April 1864, but he heard a great deal about it, because he had a deep investment in the Sanitary Commission: fresh from his own New York triumph—the building of Central Park—he had actually overseen all of the commission's operations from its inception in the summer of 1861 until the fall of 1863, when, exhausted and despairing, he had left the east coast to become the superintendent of a famous gold-mining estate in California. "The war makes us all old . . . ," he wrote to a friend; "I feel toward death as an old man myself."[88] His experiences during the Union's bold but doomed Peninsular Campaign in eastern Virginia, in the summer of 1862, when he had arranged for the commission to provide special hospital transport services, had been particularly difficult. Despite his best planning efforts, conditions in the field repeatedly thwarted the efforts of his staff, as they negotiated the region's interlocking creeks and swamps, trying to ferry the wounded to secure medical camps. Once, having witnessed the "process of embarkation," Olmsted admitted to finding it "rude, shiftless, and painful, the poor wretches being made to climb a plank set at an angle of forty-five degrees, which they could only do by the aid of a rope thrown to them from the deck." And then there were "those who had suffered amputation" and needed help from a group of guards to get aboard the transport boats: "you can imagine, perhaps, what a cruel process it was."[89] His earlier travels in the south had made him a keen abolitionist, so he did not waver in his support of the war until he just couldn't take it anymore—at which point he seems simply to have dropped everything and embraced escapism, following the sun and entering the private sector.[90]

It was not long after Olmsted arrived in California that he got involved in the protection of Yosemite, and at the same time he also received a commission to design a rural cemetery in Oakland. Yet these new western projects, no matter how public-minded, no matter how consistent they seemed with his antebellum activities, turned out to have more in common with Bierstadt's paintings than with Central Park—turned out to reflect the profundity of the shift that was occurring in American environmental culture as the men and trees continued to fall back east. Though Olmsted had strong Arcadian inclinations, he also craved an all-encompassing order, especially amidst the chaos of war, and his work on western landscapes emphasized a unified grandeur that marks a break with northeastern traditions and that speaks more of an unreserved optimism than of an engagement with mortal limitation. When I visited Oakland's Mountain View Cemetery, I was struck by how open and airy and uncomplicated it was, how different from all the dense, dark, Mount Auburn–inspired cemeteries that I had seen in so many American cities—in Albany, Rochester, Philadelphia, Cincinnati, Chicago, St. Louis. I knew it had changed since Olmsted designed it in 1865, and I knew that not all of his design elements had been realized, and I knew that part of the difference stemmed simply from his desire to adapt the idea of a rural cemetery to an arid, less arboreal climate—but, still, I could not shake the strange effect of his decision to frame visitors' experiences by forcing them to enter via a long, broad, rigidly straight central boulevard, a valley turnpike from which one can see all the rest of the cemetery rising up gently on three sides. Indeed, Olmsted acknowledged that he was abandoning curvilinear confusion in favor of "a character of simplicity and of unity, and an orderly co-relation of parts."[91] This is the only nineteenth-century American cemetery of any considerable size that I have wandered in without ever feeling lost. And a few days after my visit it suddenly hit me: the experience of driving into Mountain View Cemetery is not unlike the experience of driving into Yosemite Village.

Olmsted did not actually design the landscape of what would eventually become Yosemite National Park—the roads and trails and viewing points—but he did influence the way in which it was conceived, and almost all of his recommendations were ultimately implemented. It is a stunningly beautiful place, full of towering trees and waterfalls. As Olmsted put it, "it is in no scene or scenes [that] the charm consists, but in the miles of scenery where cliffs of awful height and rocks of vast magnitude and of varied and exquisite coloring, are banked and fringed and draped and shadowed by the tender foliage of noble and lovely trees and bushes, reflected from the most placid pools, and associated with the most tranquil meadows, the most playful streams, and every variety of soft and peaceful pastoral beauty." Perhaps most of all, Yosemite is a place apart. You enter through a cleft in the valley, and you're in a new world, surrounded by splendor, inspired to gaze upward, having left your earthly concerns behind. "The occasional contemplation of natural scenes of an impressive character," Olmsted wrote, in the August 1865 report of the Yosemite Commission, "particularly if this contemplation occurs in connection with relief from ordinary cares, change of air and change of habits, is favorable to the health and vigor of men. . . . The want of such occasional recreation where men and women are habitually pressed by their business or household cares often results in a class of disorders the characteristic quality of which is mental disability . . . , incapacitating the subject for the proper exercise of the intellectual and moral forces."[92] Of course, he was writing at a time when a new class of people had been created who would always be incapacitated by their cares, who were haunted by phantoms of pain and grief that were impossible to leave behind, and in a sense Olmsted's new conception of a pure separation between awe-inspiring, escapist wilderness areas and the spaces of everyday life just mirrored the growing divide in America between veterans and all the other citizens who mostly wanted to forget about the war and move on.

There are certain obvious continuities between an old-style antebellum landscape like Mount Auburn and a new wilderness park like Yosemite, but the three decades separating them, culminating in the most traumatic event of the nation's history, make the discontinuities more potent. Yosemite is exceptional, not ordinary; removed, not integrated; sublime, not picturesque; gem-like, polished, pure, rather than messy, mixed, contingent, liminal. Its repose is wild but not bewildering. Perhaps most importantly, though, instead of inspiring a sense of kinship between human history and natural history, Yosemite was framed so as to sever the two: the deep time of geology and the shadows cast by some of the most ancient trees in the world served to erase the recent past, which involved the violent conquest of the valley's Native inhabitants. There were no resonant Mounds here; Olmsted's plan for the area did not mention any Indian Path; there were no monuments to Indian Removal or resistance or persistence. Plenty of Natives did still roam the Yosemite region, but they kept a low profile, since technically they had been banished to a distant reservation after a series of sweeps by the U.S. Army in the 1850s. On the rare occasions when Olmsted referred to Indians, it was usually to dismiss them as a nuisance: "Indians and others have set fire to the forests and herbage and numbers of trees have been killed by these fires." This was like saying that free blacks and radical Reconstructionists were disturbing the postwar peace. The clear emphasis, for Olmsted, was on protecting the forest, for he found Yosemite's giant sequoias to be of perfect "beauty and stateliness," and he was enamored of the "reverent mood to which they so strongly incite the mind." He felt sure that absolutely any visitor to the park would be inspired by the singular sequoia "known through numerous paintings and photographs as the Grizzly Giant, which probably is the noblest tree in the world."[93] His Bierstadt-like

overstatement was meant to dazzle and distract. Though Olmsted insisted, admira-
bly, that free, democratic access for all kinds of citizens was as important in Yosemite
Valley as it was in Central Park, he wanted visitors to see only apolitical landscapes,
unifying scenery, natural uplift.

Why concern yourself with all the stumps back east, when there were trees like
these in the Garden of the West?

---

Some Americans refused to forget—though, of course, there are many different ways
of remembering. Both individuals and nations can use memory to "recover" from a
trauma—to cover it up—or to live with it, dwell with it. Nations, by their very nature,
tend to prefer recovery, since traumatized citizens generally don't make good patri-
ots.[94] It seems clear that, ultimately, the majority of Americans succumbed to the
desire to get back to their business, and as the resurgent South flexed its cultural and
political muscle to put African Americans in their place, as vigilante Klansmen
blended their image with that of Buffalo Bill, as northern businessmen fixed their
eyes on the bountiful resources of the west, the nation chose reconciliation and
Progress over reflection and repose. But individual Americans contested the memory of the Civil War almost as passionately as they fought the war itself.

Robert Morris Copeland, partner of H. W. S. Cleveland in the design of Concord's
Sleepy Hollow Cemetery, never recovered from his wartime experiences, having
endured a dishonorable discharge, apparently because he dared to criticize a commanding officer in public, and perhaps also because he dared to promote the idea
of African American troops a few months before the idea became popular. (Had he
been slightly less outspoken, it might have been Copeland rather than his friend
Robert Gould Shaw who wound up leading the black soldiers of the 54th Massachusetts.) Having filed petitions signed by such Massachusetts luminaries as Emerson and Longfellow and James Russell Lowell, Copeland did receive a full pardon
in 1870, but all his postwar writings are limned with bitterness.[95] In 1872, when he
published *The Most Beautiful City in America: Essay and Plan for the Improvement
of the City of Boston*—which, after his death, would serve as a partial blueprint for
Frederick Law Olmsted's design of Boston's famous "Emerald Necklace" of parks
and greenways[96]—Copeland made it clear that he saw a connection between Americans' refusal to acknowledge the violence of the war and their refusal to acknowledge
the violence of industrial capitalism, which was guided by the "stupidity of men who
deny that beauty is of any consequence compared with utility." One of the most

powerful sections of the book is called "MURDERED TREES," whose climax arrives when Copeland imagines a parade of arboreal phantoms coming back to haunt the axe-wielders of the city:[97]

> As the ghastly column glides by, let us ask those who rely on Boston's natural attractions for its future park effects what may be expected. Only a tedious horse car ride will carry a poor person now where they can see any of the rural beauty of former days; it passes away and disappears before the spectator as the Indian before the white man. . . . Parker's hill still exists as a hill top, thanks to the prolonged life of Mrs. Parker, but its flanks and sides are cut and gashed; huge, ugly gravel banks stare at us in place of grassy hill sides, banks which are as unimprovable and hideous as the stump of an amputated leg.

Everywhere he looked, Copeland saw open wounds, and in the years after the war many Americans joined him in interrogating all the different kinds of damage that their society had inflicted on itself. The flood of public mourning and memorialization ceremonies that swept the nation in the late 1860s, for instance, did not express any unified set of sentiments but rather suggested a deep sense of confusion or ambivalence. How to account for all of the war's death and suffering? How even to count the bodies that were rotting in fields and forests and possibly getting consumed by hogs (and were the hogs safe to butcher and eat)? Were all the bodies—white and black, northern and southern—of equal value? How to grieve, especially when tens of thousands of men were listed simply as "missing," when tens of thousands of corpses were unidentified and unidentifiable?[98]

For a time, the rural cemeteries that had been built in the three previous decades took on even more cultural significance, as Americans lined up to honor their lost soldiers with memorial speeches and elaborate floral decorations. In the spring of 1868, John A. Logan, commander of the Grand Army of the Republic (GAR), the most prominent organization for Union veterans, issued general orders proclaiming an official Decoration Day across the nation. By the following year, this sacred pause for remembrance, which would later become Memorial Day, was observed in more than three hundred towns and cities throughout both North and South. In Boston, the GAR published a broadside announcing that their local members would be conducting "the touching ceremony of crowning with flowers the graves of their brother soldiers and sailors who gave their lives that their country might not perish. . . . We earnestly invite the community to join, that it may be the more clearly seen to be, what it truly represents, the outpouring of a nation's gratitude for the devotion to a holy cause, that hesitated not even before the sacrifice of life." The plan was for the crowd to parade through Mount Auburn, which already housed dozens of Civil War soldiers.[99] But why, exactly, had these men died? In a city like Boston, which had been home to the most radical of abolitionists, Decoration Day speakers frequently celebrated the emancipation of the slaves and the granting of full citizenship to African Americans: the war, said Thomas Wentworth Higginson in 1870, "has given union, freedom, equal rights."[100] Yet there was also pressure on a national scale to welcome the South into the new body politic and to respect Southern perspectives. As President Johnson pardoned elite Southerners by the hundreds, as free blacks were beaten back in their efforts to secure social status and economic opportunity and political power—the government quickly rescinded its promise that all freedpeople could have "40 acres and a mule" with which to create their own Arcadias—many Bostonians wondered to themselves whether the sacrifices of Northern soldiers had really meant anything at all.[101]

Moreover, it was unclear that the martyrs of Massachusetts *belonged* in places like Mount Auburn, because, in February 1867, Congress had passed a bill establishing several official, national cemeteries for Civil War soldiers, launching what was perhaps the biggest and most complicated program the federal government had ever undertaken, to identify and inter—in appropriately symbolic places—every single man who had fought and died for the Union.[102] Often, the directives of the program required that corpses be dug up, transported northward, and reburied. What, then, of the individual soldiers who had already been interred with their elders in cemeteries like Mount Auburn or Greenwood or Laurel Hill or Spring Grove? And what of the Confederate dead? Who exactly should be buried in the national cemeteries? What did comradeship and kinship mean in the reborn republic? Most families of dead Union soldiers requested that their bodies be brought home, if possible, so the majority of those buried in the national cemeteries were unidentified. In any case, the new graveyards marked a clear break from recent burial traditions: they were laid out in massive, democratic grids, with their simple, white, identical markers lined up in rows and columns that covered sprawling expanses of land—lined up in rigid military formation, with little topographical relief, to create an overwhelming effect of flatness and infinite extension, representing common, collective sacrifice, emphasizing unity over diversity, the group over the individual, statistics over human singularity. I find them deeply moving, humbling—yet also impersonal and abstract. To postbellum Americans, who had so recently embraced the rural cemetery movement, such places must have seemed strange and sobering. In these national burying grounds, the survivors of the war beheld the industrialization of death.[103] (Figure 42.)

Figure 42. Dayton National Cemetery, 2011.

Simply by virtue of its scale, the Civil War wrought broad, trenchant changes in the way Americans dealt with both the dead and the dying, ushering in the era of professional undertakers and embalmers and specialized surgeons, and displacing medical treatment from the home and the community to the hospital. Before the war, families had invited doctors into their houses or apartments to care for the ill, and treatment was based in part on individual character traits and family dynamics, and when someone passed away, it was usually in a setting marked by intimacy, and loved ones took care of every aspect of the burial. But a whole new set of industries arose during the war, and even though the demand for things like coffins, for instance, had slowed considerably by the 1870s, many of the new practices and institutions caught on, and people could subsequently make a living in the dying business, and medical training became much less personal and idiosyncratic as the profession expanded and ramified.[104] Veterans, in particular, who had witnessed humankind's latest ballistic power, and who often had first-hand experience of mammoth hospitals, understood that industrialism had now penetrated into the most personal and private areas of death and life. And amputees knew this best of all, since many of them had replaced one of their body parts with a simple machine. (Figure 43.)

Figure 43. Civil War amputee
Lieutenant Burritt Stiles, Co. A,
14th Connecticut Volunteers,
1867, photograph.

The U.S. Patent Office issued ninety-nine new licenses for prosthetic devices between 1861 and 1873, and the hospital that sprang up in New York's Central Park in 1862—embodying Frederick Law Olmsted's dual identity as landscape architect and Sanitary Commissioner—became well known as a place where convalescing veterans could try out different models of artificial limbs. These prosthetics were perhaps the most prominent cultural symbols of the nation's attempt to recover from the trauma of war. Army doctors performed some sixty-thousand amputations between 1861 and 1865, and about three-quarters of their patients survived.[105] In 1863, Oliver Wendell Holmes wrote that, two years earlier, "the sight of a person who had lost one of his lower limbs was an infrequent occurrence. Now, alas! there are few among us who have not a cripple among our friends, if not in our own families." Moreover, despite the honor bestowed on veterans, they inevitably served as reminders of violence and suffering, and amputees often felt that they, in particular, made people wonder whether the entire nation had been permanently disabled, even unmanned. Sporting a new arm or leg, though, they could much more easily pass for productive citizens, and in many cases the new technologies could actually help them contribute to society in ways they hadn't thought possible back when they had been given chloroform and had attempted to brace their bodies for the bone saw. If a veteran found an artificial limb that he could use comfortably, he would typically brandish it whenever possible, hoping to serve as living proof that America was still on the path to Progress, that industrial development could fix anything. To Holmes, artificial legs, in particular, signaled the genius of American manufacturing: his countrymen were already producing first-class sewing machines and steamboats and telescopes and "implements of husbandry which out-mow and out-reap the world," but if they could also make disabled veterans walk again, that would be a true accomplishment "for a nation which has hardly pulled up the stumps out of its city market-places."[106]

Some amputees, though, had little interest in industrial progress, had little desire to maximize agricultural yields and compete on the open market: they focused, instead, on trying to recapture the humble life of the antebellum farm. A backward-looking stance can entail just as much denial as an embrace of Progress, of course, but in this case I think the disabled soldiers who were drawn to America's Arcadian tradition were also intent on acknowledging the perennial pain and strife of living. Sometimes the best way of coping with fate is not to try to outpace it but to adapt oneself to its turnings, to limp along with its jarring rhythms. In May 1865, when Frederick Knapp of the Sanitary Commission announced the establishment of "Sanitaria, or Homes for Discharged, Disabled Soldiers," he emphasized that these places would offer Union veterans "the use of workshops, farm lands, gardens, and the like,"[107] and the first three National Homes, in Maine, Ohio, and Wisconsin, became extremely popular with amputees (other homes followed in Virginia, Kansas, and elsewhere over the next few decades).[108] (Figure 44.)

In a sense, the veterans at these homes were getting put out to pasture. At the same time, though, they were receiving care, and acknowledgment of their sacrifices, and opportunities to provide productive labor at their own tempo. And they worked together, gradually, to shape their habitation into a dynamic memorial of the war, a "living monument," which could be visited by civilians, especially on occasions like Decoration Day, when large crowds might witness "a detail of one-armed soldiers" marching with baskets through a home's carefully designed garden-style cemetery,

Figure 44. Louis Kurz, *National Soldiers' Home near Milwaukee, Wis.,*
*North-Western Branch*, between 1872 and 1878, lithograph.

strewing garlands, "to hold communion with unseen comrades through the unseen fragrance of flowers." While some veterans lamented their inability to take on
a full patriarchal role and provide for a family, others clearly enjoyed the all-male
environment of the Soldiers' Homes and even gleefully took on traditionally female
responsibilities, embracing not just floral decoration but also nursing, teaching, and
even mending: "Our fair readers, we trust," wrote one resident of the Ohio Home,
"will no longer doubt the ability of the masculine gender to repair the loss of the
impressible button, and to demonstrate that 'a stitch in time saves nine.' A jolly batch
of menders and patchers are industriously engaged all hours of the day in repairing
socks, shirts, drawers, pants, etc."[109]

These "sanitaria," then, took on a complex symbolism as the nation tried to recover
its sense of health and wholeness. Certainly, people like Knapp tended to harp on
the government's desire to send disabled veterans back into the community to live
independently, so they touted these facilities' fostering of "self-help, and consequent
self-reliance, followed by self-respect."[110] The residents of the homes, though, wanted

civilians to remember the convulsions of the war, and they worked diligently with landscape architects to create unique alternative spaces, so that visitors would stroll through magnificent flower gardens; and orchards and fields stocked with apples, pears, peaches, grapes, gooseberries, currants, blackberries, and strawberries; and "SHADY GROVES" marked by "drooping willows"; and aviaries full of "God's little songsters"—birds of both the North and South, "canaries, mocking-birds, robins, woodpeckers"—only to round a bend and stumble upon "a heavy gun mounted upon a pile of rough stones in the center of the lake," or "a small pond containing alligators." Certainly, any civilian walking through the grounds of the Ohio Home would note that there were many inmates "stumping along with an artificial leg, and many an empty sleeve flies idly in the breeze—doubtless the largest number of one-legged and one-armed men in any one institution in the world. A large number move only by the aid of crutches. Others there are with all their fair proportions; but a single glance will show the sign of the campaign, and that the hardships of the tented field have broken down their strong constitution, leaving only the wreck behind. All, however, have a comparatively cheerful expression." The cheer, of course, was forced, an afterthought, since the Arcadian tradition in the United States had never before dealt with such extreme violence and damage. Still, the Ohio resident-writer was especially eager to let the public know to what extent his home reflected the staunch labor and vision of his fellow veterans: "Much of the furniture in the buildings was made by disabled soldiers; and a considerable portion of the lighter work, such as smoothing and ornamenting the grounds, was done by them. They perform nearly all the work in the garden, orchards, and farm, and in improving and beautifying the place."[111] These were places of bright light and deep shadow, constructed by people who would never lose sight of human aggression and vulnerability—borderlands combining nature and art to inspire reflection and capture a fundamental ambivalence, an ambivalence derived from age-old landscape traditions but inflected in new ways in the context of a particular postwar mindset. The Soldiers' Homes, in their desperate invocation of antebellum lifeways, suggested that Arcadian America had been badly crippled.

---

WW (1882):

*A Discovery of Old Age*

*Perhaps the best is always cumulative. One's eating and drinking one wants fresh, and for the nonce, right off, and have done with it—but I would not give a straw for that person or poem, or friend, or city, or work of art, that was not more grateful the second time than the first—and more still the third. Nay, I do not believe any grandest eligibility*

*ever comes forth at first. In my own experience, (persons, poems, places, characters,) I*
*discover the best hardly ever at first, (no absolute rule about it, however,) sometimes sud-*
*denly bursting forth, or stealthily opening to me, perhaps after years of unwitting famil-*
*iarity, unappreciation, usage.*[112]

---

I have been to the Wilderness twice: first at the end of December 2009, when my
family was in northern Virginia anyway, seeing Christine's parents and siblings for
Christmas; and then exactly a year later, after I had already written most of this chapter. American battlefields had never attracted me before: as sites for the performance
of history, they always seemed too likely to glorify and sanctify violence. "Nations
rarely commemorate their disasters and tragedies," the historian David Blight has
noted, except in ways that erase the disastrous and the tragic.[113] Even after I started
this project and got drawn into the story of the Wilderness, my initial impulse was to
focus on the national cemeteries and a couple of the Homes for Disabled Volunteer
Soldiers, since they seemed like more complicated, contested places, and since they
were established immediately after the war, whereas the federal government did not
start preserving battlefields until the 1890s, when the nation's deepest psychic wounds
had started to heal, and the sites of actual fighting could be celebrated as memorials
to the heroism of everyone involved, could become straightforward symbols of reconciliation.[114] But then, in the summer of 2009, a friend told me that he had heard a
radio story about Walmart's efforts (abandoned in January 2011) to build a "super-
store" on part of the Wilderness battlefield, much of which is now managed by the
National Park Service.[115] And suddenly I knew I had to go down to the Wilderness.
What exactly was enshrined on this kind of battlefield? What would it feel like to
walk through the thickets? What kind of wilderness had it become a century and a
half later? Would it seem more like Yosemite or more like Mount Auburn? Would
the interpretive framework stretch beyond military strategy to suggest a broader cultural significance? In the coming lawsuit, would the Wilderness Battlefield Coalition call on environmentalists or historians or both?

James McPherson, an eminent scholar of the Civil War, in the foreword to a book
called *Paving Over the Past*, put out by the environmental publisher Island Press,
argued for the protection of battlefields on the grounds that geography is the best
spur to a full understanding of the past: "Standing on the battlefields, we can experience an emotional empathy with the men who fought there. With a little imagination
we can hear the first rebel yell at Manassas, commune with the ghosts that haunt
Shiloh, watch with horror as brush fires consume the wounded at the Wilderness."[116]

Empathy? I'm still not sure it's a real possibility. But I do believe in cultivating a sense of kinship, across time, and across the gulf between different human beings, and across the gulf between species. And I agree that if we want to revisit the past, we need places we can revisit—places dominated by Nature and removed from capitalist development, places where time slows down, where death and life mingle, where we come up against a solid, physical reality that forces us to reconsider, that forces us to examine the narrowness, even the selfishness, of our perspective.

Truth be told, I had initially wanted to go the Wilderness by myself, because, in addition to walking over parts of the battleground, I'd hoped to talk with some of the people who worked at the local interpretive centers and historical societies, hoped to make some connections and explore as many potential sources as possible. My research trip turned into a family outing, though, and ultimately I can't say I was disappointed to learn that Christine, our kids, and my in-laws were all intrigued by one of my work-related obsessions. I got directions, chose a central, flat, two-mile loop trail that seemed manageable for all ages, and prayed that the twelve people staying at my brother-in-law's smallish house, about to step into a couple of minivans for an hour-long drive southward, would all have a good time. My solo expedition could come later.

Perhaps it helped to be there in winter, with a gray, crusty snow on the ground, but we were all struck by how little glory was invoked at the Wilderness, and yet how strong an impression the battlefield made. The signs at the lonely exhibit shelter, where the trail started and ended, did proclaim Grant's heroic determination to press on despite enormous losses, but they also emphasized those losses, and the thick, difficult terrain, and the general brutality of the fighting. As we walked the trail, straining to see through the tangle of trees, wondering how the woods had changed over time, grateful for the occasional splinter of sunlight, my eyes kept turning downward, drawn to one particular feature of the landscape: the trenches. One hundred and forty-five years later, these scars remained, reminding us of the way men blended with the land as they struggled to kill and survive, as they sought to surprise each other and hide from each other, as they dug in, committed to all-out slaughter. Why hadn't these holes been filled in with dirt and leaves and branches and roots and decayed plants and animals? Wasn't a century and a half enough time for nature to heal itself, to recover? By the end of our hike, the image of those pervasive ditches was scorched into my memory.

Maybe, a few weeks later, in February, when I took my family to Brook Farm, that image helped me, with all its echoes of fraternity—brothers in arms, brothers nursing each other, brothers killing each other—to recognize the Baker Street

Cemetery, in the southeast corner of Newton, as the place where my brother was buried.

It took me until August to organize a trip to Baker Street, and, as my mother and father climbed into our minivan, with Christine and me and all three of our kids, I felt I was entering some new sort of wilderness. I couldn't find the words to speak to my parents about the central trauma of their lives. My mother was eighty, and relatively spry, but my father was eighty-six, and for the previous year and a half had been living in the shadow of an Alzheimer's diagnosis, though on some occasions he was still perfectly cogent and coherent. It had not been difficult to tell my parents that I wanted to see Benjamin's grave, or to ask them if they would like to come along. But once they said yes, once they both dropped their eyes to the floor, I didn't know how to continue the conversation. I worried that they thought of my interest in Benjamin as some sort of accusation. I worried that I was reopening old wounds. I worried that my father might become confused and distressed. I worried that new secrets might come flooding out.

I guess, in a sense, it actually was an accusation: you never brought me here. You never acknowledged this. You sheltered me so thoroughly that I grew up with too great a sense of entitlement and expectation. The tribulations of life have sometimes immobilized me, crippled me, because you didn't prepare me for them. But I would never say these things out loud, because ultimately I didn't blame my parents for anything, and when I did try to talk to them about Benjamin, I hoped my tone and body language would convey to them that I knew how much grief they had endured, that I understood their impulse to protect me, that I did not resent them for it, that I felt it was my own responsibility to acknowledge and address my failings, that I needed to see Benjamin's grave for my own reasons and that I hoped desperately that it would be cathartic for them, as well. All I actually said out loud to them was, "I'm glad you want to come."

It was raining—pouring, really—but I didn't want to postpone the cemetery visit, because Christine and the kids and I had to drive back to Ithaca that afternoon. Though my emotions choked most of my thoughts, I did manage to ask my parents, as we drove through Newton, where they thought the grave was in the cemetery. Did we need to stop at the office? And then suddenly they started volunteering information and opinions. They agreed: it was at the far back end, near the right corner, in a section maintained by an Orthodox congregation, even though we had never been anything but Reform Jews. That was just what was available at the time. The babies were always in the back row. The stones were always flat. It might be overgrown. You never know. These places aren't always tended very carefully. It might be desecrated. Jewish graves get desecrated more and more these days. It's been years since we've been here. Decades. Since the 70s. My father said he stopped coming in the 60s. My mother said she continued for a few more years. "I brought your sister. I never brought you."

We couldn't find the grave. We walked along all the back rows, beside the fence, holding umbrellas, kicking away grass and dirt, trying to explain the situation to the kids. Our second son, Abe, who was four, looked up at me and said, "I wish Benjamin was still alive." That was the one time that day I didn't manage to stanch my tears. The baby of the family, Oscar, toddled off among the upright stones, enjoying the rain and puddles, while our oldest, Sam, chased him, and said, "Where *is* that gravestone?" My father was angry, embarrassed. He sometimes realized that he couldn't trust his memory, but he was sure of the grave's location, if he was sure of anything. My mother just seemed tired. I went to the office, and though there was no attendant, I managed to find several boxes of alphabetized index cards nestled below a giant wall map of the cemetery, and there was even a card for Benjamin—but the coordinates listed on it did not match anything on the map, nor did they seem to correspond to any of the section signs we had seen while driving along the cemetery's entire length. We had to give up.

The drive back to my parents' house was silent. A couple of hours later, with the car packed, we said goodbye in the kitchen, and my father shook his head. "I hope that trip to the cemetery was worthwhile for your research," he said, perhaps trying to connect with me as a fellow scholar. I said it was; and I would call the people who managed the cemetery, and figure out exactly where to go next time, and we would find the grave in December, and I was sorry for how it had played out. "That's OK," he said, "as long as it was helpful to you. For us, it just brought back a lot of painful memories." Dementia, in my father's case, had broken down inhibitions, and I found the shift to be wrenching, agonizing: it undermined my basic understanding of his identity. Strangely, though, just a few seconds after this latest pronouncement, I felt a sense of relief wash over me: my genteel, considerate, mild-mannered father had voiced a difficult emotion that previously he would have kept to himself. It had taken me more than a year to get used to what my father might say under the influence of Alzheimer's, but in that moment I knew clearly that he didn't mean to blame me for his pain. I hugged him, kissed him on the cheek, felt that rough stubble I had known all my life, managed not to cry, told him, again, how sorry I was, and we left.

Instead of driving straight back to Ithaca, we decided to stop for dinner in Amherst, at my sister's house, and I told her all about the morning. Immediately, she said she knew where the grave was. I told her where we'd looked, and she said: "Yes. They were right. It's probably just overgrown. I visited it in the 90s." I smiled. I always know the least in our family, and Debbie always knows the most. I'm the historian;

she's the keeper of memory. Of course: I should have consulted her in advance. But maybe it was better this way. We made plans to go back in December, when we would all be together in Newton for the annual Chanukah party.

We revisited Baker Street on a crisp Sunday morning. This time, there was some sunshine, and we brought a rake. We had about ten more minutes of frustration, in the exact same part of the cemetery, as we stirred up dust and leaves. And then Debbie uncovered the corner of a stone, underneath an impossibly thick layer of organic matter. I ran over with the rake. We were right next to the fence, and I saw that the tree on the other side of it had pushed one of its thick roots across the gravestone, and I would have to do some hacking just to bend it out of the way. It took a couple of minutes to uncover enough letters to be sure, but I'd known it was Benjamin's grave as soon as Debbie had called out. Our brother's grave. I wanted to say it out loud: I had a brother. Once we had finally cleared it off, we all just stood around it in wonder and relief. My father seemed to be smiling. "Well, there it is," he said, taking off his glasses—a gesture I suddenly recognized as one of my earliest memories. Then my kids placed their pebbles on the gravestone, and Debbie's daughter added a flower she had brought with her from my parents' house, and Debbie's son spread out some pine cones. I noted that there was an "h" at the end of Benjamin's middle name that I hadn't expected: "Tevyah." "The engraver must have made a mistake," my mother said. (Figure 45.)

Three weeks later, we were in Virginia again for Christmas, and I told my kids we had another cemetery to visit. Christmas fell on a Saturday, so, the next day, when all my in-laws went to church, Christine, Sam, Abe, Oscar, and I went in search of Ian's grave, and as a light snow began to come down, we found it: I had made it back. This stone was flat in the ground, too, a detail I hadn't recalled, but my legs seemed to remember having stood in that exact spot more than two decades before, half my life ago. I had been hoping that Ian's parents would be able to meet us there, but that hadn't worked out. I could at least feel their presence: Ian's father had told me that they visited the grave often, and he referred to its inscription as "our message to Ian." The stone was large, maybe four times the size of Benjamin's, and the message was long and loving, capturing Ian's sense of calm and caring, and ending with his parents' summation of his character: "A good man to canoe with."

I wanted to get a sense of the cemetery as a place, so we strolled around a bit, shivering in the snow. It seemed almost perfectly flat, strangely treeless, with a wide-open, modern aesthetic, and there was clearly a prohibition against vertical gravestones. As we walked, we started to notice some vaguely circular patterns in the driveways and the bushes, and gradually some gentle, round rises took shape, subtle mounds

Figure 45.

of earth. It was starkly elegant, Christine and I thought, a 1950s version of a rural cemetery. But the kids were cold, and confused that there were no steep hills or ponds or towers or mazy paths. We got back in the minivan and found some soup for lunch.

After we arrived back at Christine's brother's house, after all the in-laws returned from church, after everyone started settling in for a quiet afternoon, with the younger children napping and the older ones cradling new toys, I asked Christine if this might be an opportune moment for me to head down to the Wilderness on my own. She smiled and nodded. Sam had overheard the question and said he might want to come along: he remembered it vividly from the previous year. But his cousin Emmet had just gotten the holy grail of Lego sets—the Portal of Atlantis—and that, somehow, proved more tempting to his seven-year-old sensibility than a long drive and a hike in the snow.

Revisiting places is a way of marking time: here I am, one year later, one year older, and this battlefield has probably changed as much, or as little, as I have. I felt, in some ways, like a new person, newly attuned to the ghosts of both my past and my future, to my failings and my finitude, to my parents' need for connection in their final years. And I felt I could see the Wilderness with fresh eyes, because I had read, and even written, so much about it in the interim, had become acquainted with Grant's pained stubbornness and Homer's elegiac questioning and Morris Schaff's sense that this place had a guiding "Spirit": by cultivating my imagination, by opening myself to open-ended stories of grief and faith, I hoped I had enhanced my chance at empathy. Yet I also still felt, keenly, the remoteness of the past, my isolation, my ignorance, the slant of my perspective.

I had chosen a section of the Federal Line Trail, just off Hill-Ewell Drive, not far from our first hike, but supposedly covering more varied terrain, with clearings, ravines, a stream. I had no grand goals, no more desire to find the local archives: I just wanted to walk around again for a couple of hours, soak up as much as I could before darkness fell. So I stepped out of the minivan and into the sprinkling snow, carrying my thirty-year-old camera and a granola bar, my eyes tilted slightly downward, scanning for trenches.

Not ten minutes later, I heard the calling and pecking of what I immediately recognized as a pileated woodpecker—and I was utterly paralyzed for a second. Then I took off in the direction of the sound, desperate, manic, unbelieving. And there it was: the fourth one of my life. For the next several minutes—I have no idea how long, to be honest—I just followed it through the woods, drunk on memories, not on any path, completely lost, stumbling on deadfall, sliding down hillsides, tripping over trenches, not caring about anything except watching this bird, until finally it outdistanced me, and I had to get my bearings and retreat to the road. The historian in me, the documentarian, had yearned for photographic evidence. Who would believe my story?[117] But the woodpecker hadn't been comfortable with my presence, and I hadn't brought my zoom lens. It seemed to lead me in an ever-widening spiral; occasionally it would disappear for a full minute or two before I saw it again. I never got close enough for a good shot. But, in the end, I found myself taking pleasure in its elusiveness.

I have lost my faith in this book project countless times over the last few years. Friends, colleagues, and publishers have all questioned my wisdom in combining history and memoir: do you really want to wreak such havoc on your readers' expectations? The book's own message has often driven me away from my computer and back to my wife, my kids, my parents, back to parks and cemeteries and woodlands. Again and again, my plans and perspectives have shifted: I had no idea, when I started, that I would wind up dwelling on Benjamin and pileated woodpeckers. Shouldn't I be more careful to wall off my life from my work? Shouldn't I stick to environmental and cultural history and keep my musings about mortality to myself? But for a moment, on December 26, 2010, everything seemed to connect, and there I was, quivering in my minivan, presented with this incredible gift, sensing what I had to do, fumbling for a felt-tip pen, and then scribbling, scribbling, frantic to make some kind of memorial, to capture this experience, whose emotional depth, I knew, I would never be able to convey to anyone—yet I also knew I had to try.

As I sat there in that scarred landscape, I found myself writing about a lull in the chase, when I thought the woodpecker had vanished for good, and I paused to stare at a tree that seemed like it could have been the bird's home base. It was a venerable specimen, tall and sturdy, though dying—with a gaping black hole at its center, where a pileated could surely stay warm. If I were ever to come back to the Wilderness again, I thought, this is where I would start: this is where I would bring my family. I wondered how old the tree was. Perhaps, as a sapling, it had witnessed a few skirmishes. It seemed stable enough to stay upright for many more years; its bark was starting to falter, but its roots were strong. As I looked harder, though, in the dim light, I couldn't help but see its fragility, its heaviness, maybe even its weariness. Soon enough, it would fall back to earth; for now, it was poised on a border.

# 5

# Three Men of the Middle Border (Part One): Twilight

All coming generations are to inhabit the cities and towns, and go to their daily labors in the streets, and seek recreation in the parks and pleasure grounds, and be laid to rest in the cemeteries, the foundations of which we are laying or preparing to lay, and whose essential features of arrangement are immutable from the time they are first occupied.
—H. W. S. Cleveland, *Landscape Architecture as Applied to the Wants of the West* (1873)

The official borders of the continental United States were at least roughly established as of the Civil War, thanks to topographical surveys conducted in the north and south during the 1850s. But the wavering western frontier, the zigzagging line of settlement, was still a place of violent uncertainty in the postbellum decades, a liminal space, a transitional zone, an area of constant contestation. As veterans looked across the Mississippi for new beginnings, some dreamed of planting Arcadian communities, but few were able to leave behind their belligerence, or their scars. The United States, on its way to some kind of modernity, had to pass through yet another bloody borderground. In the west, it was almost as if the humbled nation, having barely survived its mid-life crisis, now found itself confronting the prospect of a long, slow decline.

People like Albert Bierstadt and Frederick Law Olmsted, hoping for a national rebirth of sorts, had tried to transfigure the frontier's dangers and difficulties before the war had even ended, had tried to imagine the sun rising rather than setting in the west. Other environmentally inclined artists and thinkers, though, sank deeper roots in the region, took in long drafts of its atmosphere, bathed themselves in its changeable light, invested in its very flux and ambiguity—perhaps none more intriguingly than Hamlin Garland, who made a career writing about what he always referred to as the "middle border," which usually meant the prairie states but which could also extend to the Rockies and even California. Two somewhat older compatriots, Henry George and H. W. S. Cleveland, the west's leading political economist and landscape architect, had a greater impact than Garland on the immediate postbellum landscape of Arcadian reform. But it was Garland, looking back at the Gilded Age from the perspective of the early twentieth century, who most evocatively captured the simultaneous fading and persistence of Arcadian America, who understood that the tumult of the postwar west had fostered both an old-fashioned attachment to land and an escapist restlessness.

Born on a Wisconsin homestead in 1860, Garland spent his first four decades in transition, pulling up stakes, flitting between country and town, farmhouse and apartment, heading farther west and then retreating back east, seemingly trying to choose between Nature and Culture, art and politics, individualism and communalism, free-wheeling independence and family ties.[1] Meanwhile, hundreds of thousands of his countrymen traveled westward in search of farms and, in a third of a century, occupied more American land than had been opened in the previous 250 years[2]—though, at the same time, other multitudes were packing themselves into cities and securing the nation's new reputation as definitively urban.[3] As Garland entered middle age, then—where Whitman and Melville were at the start of the Civil War, where I am as I write this book—he was perfectly positioned to write Arcadia's epitaph. (I have to admit, I've been transfixed by Garland's anxious fence-sitting since my junior year of college: he is another tortured writer to whom I was guided by my advisor, Lou.)

Garland's first and most famous memoir, *A Son of the Middle Border* (1917), covers his life through his mid-thirties, and serves as a history of American turmoil in the final third of the nineteenth century. It begins, pointedly, with Garland's earliest memory: the scene of his father's homecoming from the Civil War, a scene Garland also put at the center of a short story called "The Return of a Private" (1890). In both tellings, though they were published twenty-seven years apart, the broad framing stirs an expectation of joyous reunion, but the mood turns out to be somber, pained. A ghost reappears—but why had Richard Garland gone to fight in the first place, abandoning a wife and three small children? And what had he accomplished on the battle lines? Hamlin's mother would always think of Richard's departure in 1863 as "one of the darkest moments of her life," and her lonely anxiety left Hamlin with a powerful awareness of men's tendency to make women suffer, whether simply by deserting them, or by forcing them to desert their community in pursuit of the next best chance. Would Isabelle ever be able to trust her husband again? Would the children, unable to recognize their father, find a way to accept him into their lives?[4]

In the fictional version, the soldier is an Everyman named Smith, a farmer deep in debt, "gaunt and pale, with signs of fever and ague upon him," traveling back north with three companions: "One had a great scar down his temple, one limped, and they all had unnaturally large, bright eyes, showing emaciation. There were no hands greeting them at the station, no banks of gaily dressed ladies waving handkerchiefs and shouting 'Bravo!'" Since their freight train winds up arriving in the middle of the night, they decide to camp at the La Crosse station, which feels a bit like Hell's ante-chamber, an eerie purgatory that echoes with the experience of limbo that their wives endured while the men were off chasing Confederates: "Lit by the oil lamps that flared a dull red light over the dingy benches, the waiting room was not an inviting place." Unable to sleep, Private Smith finds himself overcome by "a sickness at heart almost deadly," as he imagines himself utterly "worn out, taking up the work on his half-cleared farm, the inevitable mortgage standing ready with open jaw to swallow half his earnings." When the four compatriots part ways in the morning, each with many miles separating him from his homestead, Smith says, with a slight quaver in his throat, as he contemplates their shared hardships, that he hopes they'll get together occasionally to reminisce. "'Of course,' said Saunders, whose voice trembled a little, too. 'It ain't *exactly* like dyin'.'" But when Smith reaches the hill overlooking his family's farm, despite his sense of the valley's beauty and his gratitude for the bounty it was producing during this harvest season, "his head drooped forward on his palm, his shoulders took on a tired stoop, his cheek-bones showed painfully. An observer might have said, 'He is looking down upon his own grave.'" Having become "a blue-coated cog in a vast machine for killing men," could he ever learn to live again?[5]

Richard Garland was known for his rugged New England character, though, and he quickly set about enlisting his family in the struggle to win a living from the land. "Thus it happened that my first impressions of life were martial," Hamlin wrote, "and my training military, for my father brought back from his two years' campaigning under Sherman and Thomas the temper and the habit of a soldier." A few relatives had perished in the war—"Luke and Walter and Hugh were sleeping in The Wilderness"—but the wild land of Wisconsin seemed full of promise, and Richard drew on his army experience to project an air of energy and discipline, "although he walked a little bent and with a peculiar measured swinging stride—the stride of Sherman's veterans." By the age of seven, Hamlin was driving cows to pasture, splitting and hauling wood, and feeding the calves and chickens. At the same time, he began attending school and gradually broadened his view of the world, sharing meals with local Indians, gathering "clusters of beautiful strawberries" turned up by the men's scythes during haying season, and sometimes pausing as he passed the cemetery of the local town: "there was to me something vaguely awesome in that silent bivouac of the dead." Within three short years after the return of the private, despite Richard's painful memories and relentless task-mastering, despite "the haze of the passing war-cloud . . . , this mingled air of romance and sorrow, history and song, and . . . a deep-laid consciousness of maternal pain," the Garlands, in the company of a large extended family and a close-knit network of friends and neighbors, had shaped a homesteading life containing many elements of the Arcadia that Margaret Fuller and Henry Thoreau had envisioned for the frontier back in the 1840s.[6]

And then Richard decided to follow the sun. To Hamlin, it perhaps seemed that his father was perpetually reenacting Sherman's march, that he was driven by some unarticulated need to prove his mastery over a larger and larger swath of land, and as the family moved from Wisconsin to eastern Iowa to central Iowa and finally to Dakota over the next several years, the American frontier ethos appeared more and more like a disease spawned by the war, like a "pioneering madness." Regardless of the reason behind it, Garland eventually came to believe that this restlessness, this continual, manic displacement, was a defining force in his life and perhaps a defining fact of American history in the late nineteenth century. After the war, Garland thought, "every one looked forward to a pot of gold waiting for him at the rainbow's end just ahead. But my father never found his pot of gold; nor did most of his contemporaries. Again and again they moved with their families into ever increasing hardships, only to pull up stakes again and start afresh, always further west. With the years and repeated disappointment and failure a new note crept into the spirit of the pioneers. Hope dwindled. Buoyancy dwindled. Depression set in." While the historian Frederick Jackson Turner would famously declare in 1893 that everything virtuous and robust about American democracy was due to the westward press of settlement, Garland saw his family history as evidence that American democracy was characterized mostly by instability, isolation, capitalist exploitation, violent dispossession of Indians, despoilment of nature, and unending toil. He knew the appeal of the middle border, its romance, its hopeful exuberance, but he also "perceived the mournful side of American 'enterprise.'"[7]

*A Son of the Middle Border*, through all its meanderings, continually settles on a sense of ambivalence and confusion, as Garland bounces between a personal probing of his father's character and a broader exploration of historical changes and trends, in an effort to explain his own unsettled and unsettling childhood. While antebellum pioneers certainly covered great distances in some cases (on the Oregon Trail, especially), they rarely moved as many times as Dick Garland and some of the other war-weary patriarchs of his era. Over and over again, Hamlin asked himself what his father was looking for, why he kept feeling the need to break his ties with people and pieces of land, why he couldn't accept any sense of limitation: "the wood and prairie land of Winnishiek County [in northeastern Iowa] did not satisfy him, although it seemed to me then, as it does now, the fulfillment of his vision." Maybe the repeated moves were just a means of confirming for himself both that he was called by a higher purpose (patriotism, agrarianism, Manifest Destiny) and that his own will mattered in the world. Richard had felt the desire to strike out westward on his own even before the war, to make his fortune as a tiller of less rocky soil than that which had nearly broken his own father. But his experience as a soldier hardened the mold. When Hamlin was in his mid-twenties and periodically went back to see his parents on the plains, after he had already spent a few years in the east, he always found his father dreaming of larger holdings and excited to put his son to work in a spirit of insistent progress, of determined pressing-on.[8]

Gradually, though, Hamlin also came to understand his father in the context of a generalized land rush: there were new economic and environmental circumstances that militated against the old eastern pattern of diversified smallholdings. Starting out from Maine, and not wanting to go all the way to Oregon, Richard's father had heard about the fertile soil of the old northwest back in the 1850s, but he discovered, once his family was already on the trail, that he had to go all the way to the Wisconsin-Minnesota border to find open land. And what most Wisconsin pioneers eventually learned, through hard experience, in an era of limited environmental data, was that their soil was not as easily worked or as productive as the soil in Ohio, or Indiana, or Illinois, or western Kentucky. Rumors spread wildly about belts of fertility and moist microclimates—Richard left his Wisconsin "coolly" (the local word for a well-wooded river valley), with its "stumps and ridges which interrupted his plow," because he became convinced that "the glorious prairies" of southern Minnesota and northern Iowa would make for better farming—but average rainfall starts to decrease significantly once you cross the Mississippi. And conditions just got worse for Richard as he went further west, until he and his family reached central Iowa, the region of ravenous chinch bugs, which destroyed entire wheat harvests in the late 1870s and early 1880s, and which ultimately sent the Garlands scurrying to the even more arid plains of the Dakotas, where "the winds were hot and dry, and the grass, baked on the stem, had become as inflammable as hay. The birds were silent. The sky, absolutely cloudless, began to scare us with its light . . . , and many of the women began to complain bitterly of the loneliness, and lack of shade. . . . Timid souls began to inquire, 'Are all Dakota summers like this?' "[9]

The fantastic success of the pioneer communities that had taken root in places like southern Illinois in the 1830s and 40s had set up later pioneers for abject failure.[10] Just to subsist in the new wheat belt, farmers found that they needed to work far more land, and since speculators, including the railroad companies, had snatched up so many of the good parcels that were anywhere near established settlements, postwar pioneers got pushed further and further out onto the frontier, no matter what their personal inclinations. And, meanwhile, in the areas that were already settled, a new labor supply—ex-soldiers and European immigrants—working with better transportation systems and the latest mechanized threshers and reapers, drove production higher and prices lower, which put the yeomen on the far frontier in an even less competitive position. The Garlands prided themselves on "never taking the back trail," but by the time Hamlin graduated from Cedar Valley Seminary, an Iowa high school that also offered some college-level courses, he was dreaming of New England—not because he endorsed eastern industrialism and wanted to work in a factory, but because life on a far-western homestead seemed so bleak, and the east at least offered the benefits of settled society.[11]

*A Son of the Middle Border* takes a grimly honest look at both the triumphs of frontier development—which were always fleeting, and always fraught—and the clear difficulties of pioneering, the disadvantages of coming of age under a regime of oppressive agricultural labor, far removed from centers of urban culture and intellectual diversity. Garland's feeling for nature was genuinely powerful. He appreciated both the new landscape being shaped by settlers—the maples, poplars, and larches planted to block wind and provide shade; the kitchen gardens; the long stretches of waving wheat; the corn silks floating on the breeze—and, in equal measure, all the old prairie grasses and brightly colored flowers and wild animals, "all the swarming lives which had been native here for untold centuries," some of which might soon be "utterly destroyed"—the wolves, the badgers, the foxes, the "pinks, sweet-williams, tiger-lilies and lady-slippers," "the flash and ripple and glimmer of the tall sunflowers, the myriad voices of gleeful bobolinks, the chirp and gurgle of red-winged blackbirds swaying on the willows": in short, Garland celebrated an old-fashioned, complicated "spirit of the wilderness." Yet this prairie world could also appear utterly desolate to him, especially on those frequent occasions when the skies darkened and "the bitter wind blew from the north," or when (starting at age ten) he was forced by his father "to plow all day like a hired hand," or when "the dust arose from under the teeth of the harrow and flew so thickly that my face was not only coated with it but tears of rebellious rage stained my cheeks."

At least there were "certain ameliorations to child-labor on a farm," such as a good supply of "air and sunshine"—"Nature was our compensation"—but Garland noted that there was virtually no relief for women like his mother, who did not go "out into the fields or meadows long enough to enjoy the birds and the breezes," who were typically "too tired and too worried to react to the beauties of the landscape," whose "duties must have been as relentless as a tread-mill," who were never sure how lasting their friendships might be.[12] The founding of the Grange, or the Order of Patrons of Husbandry, in 1867, just after the war, did improve social conditions to some extent, especially because it admitted wives as well as husbands. Though the Grangers would eventually become better known for their cooperative efforts on the economic front—in June 1875, Richard became the Grange's official grain buyer for his county—the organization originally emphasized the simple need for farm families to come together in communities with tighter connections and better communication: typical events in Iowa, as Hamlin noted, were grand picnics, which were "almost as well attended as the circus," and "'oyster suppers,' with debates, songs, and essays."[13] As frontier farmers faced more isolation and drudgery, and as the national culture placed less value on turning the soil and more on turning profits, those who supported the agrarian tradition had to find ways of involving women and children in a broadly stimulating program of development. But Garland grew up feeling that his inner life was just as blighted as the wheat fields; he had to fight with his father for time to attend school, and when he did get to study for a few consecutive months, he grieved over the extra labor absorbed by his mother and siblings. Often, as a teenager, he found escape in whatever books he could lay his hands on, and he thought of their authors—Hawthorne was a particular favorite—as "demigods." "Writers," the young Hamlin thought, "were singular, exalted beings found only in the East—in splendid cities. They were not . . . toiling common creatures like us."[14]

One of the first books Garland mentions in *A Son of the Middle Border* is Hawthorne's novel about Brook Farm, *The Blithedale Romance*, perhaps because it deals so directly with the reality of agricultural toil: "The clods of earth," says Hawthorne's narrator, "which we so constantly belabored and turned over and over, were never etherealized into thought. Our thoughts, on the contrary, were fast becoming cloddish. Our labor symbolized nothing, and left us mentally sluggish in the dusk of the evening."[15] Garland's true passion, though, was for Hawthorne's mist-filled tales of the suburbs, especially the ones in *Mosses from an Old Manse*, which allowed Garland to enter a dream-world of "magic spells" and "half-lights," to abandon the middle border in favor of "the borderlands of the human soul." ("This book," he would later note, in an interview, "made such an impression on me that I decided I would be a writer, come what would.") As Garland lived through an era of massive transition on the frontier, he kept hoping to see new western communities as potential Arcadias, kept trying to imagine that his neighbors shared his poignant awareness of the ambiguous tragedies occurring on their farms even as they struggled to humanize the landscape. He invoked the memory of the Sioux hunters who had previously ruled the plains, referred to Bryant's poem "Thanatopsis," pointed out the bleached skeletons and antlers of bison and elk, noted the breaking of "the primeval sward," lamented the passing of all the wild and untamed things that "died or hurried away" as the plow ripped through the roots of "tender plants and shining flowers." Approached in a spirit of reverence and limitation, development on the border, no matter how dulling, could sometimes evoke the enchantments of New England. In the early 70s, in Iowa, Garland's "father was counted a good and successful farmer. Our neighbors all lived in the same restricted fashion as ourselves, in barren little houses of wood or stone." It was a hard but rewarding life: "worn and grimed as we were, we still could fall a-dream before the marvel of a golden earth beneath a crimson sky." The problem was that, in practice, bordermen seldom paused or even slowed down, so that dreaming was rare, and attachments dissolved as families perpetually uprooted themselves: pursuing the sun, they could not waste time watching the sunset. Even when "all nature . . . seemed to invite to repose rather than to labor," typical frontier circumstances forced every farmer to "strain his tired muscles and bend his aching back to the harvest."[16]

Meanwhile, parents died alone, unacknowledged, their descendants having abandoned them and their small plots of land for supposedly better conditions: "I wondered why it was," Garland wrote, thinking of the uncles and aunts and grandparents he had known in Wisconsin, "[that] we must be so widely separated from those we loved the best." When mortality did come to the homesteads of the farthest frontier, it was often young people who perished, removed from adequate medical care. Indeed, Garland's most important childhood encounter with death came when his sister Harriet, or Hattie, a perfectly healthy but overworked teenager, caught a "wasting fever"—"typhoid pneumonia" in official records—and simply declined, untreated, over the course of a few weeks. "Human life suddenly seemed fleeting and of a part with the impermanency and change of the westward moving Border Line," Garland noted, incisively. "Like the wild flowers she had gathered, Harriet was now a fragrant memory. Her dust mingled with the soil of the little burial ground just beyond the village bounds." Hamlin had few opportunities to visit his sister's grave, though, since his family would soon be on the move again. "From this spot we had seen the wild prairies disappear. . . . Here Hattie had died. . . . Each of our lives was knit into these hedges and rooted in these fields and yet, notwithstanding all this, in response to some powerful yearning call, my father was about to set out for the fifth time into the still more remote and untrodden west."[17]

At the age of twenty, as his parents prepared to leave Iowa for Dakota, Garland decided he was going to be a teacher rather than a farmer. Helping to harvest some of his family's barley crop, he said to himself, "This is the last time I shall ever lift a bundle of this accursed stuff." And soon enough, he and his younger brother Franklin had taken the back trail to the east, having identified the Boston Common as "the goal of our long pilgrimage." They eagerly absorbed the Massachusetts landscape, and were especially entranced by "the graceful, irregular, elm-shaded roads," which, they thought, "curved like Indian trails following bright streams, and the stone walls which bordered them were festooned with vines as in a garden"—in stark contrast to western thoroughfares, which "ran on section lines and were defined by wire fences." The very space of the west was characterized by the grid, by ownership and efficiency, by speculative land claims, by hard angles and exclusion; the space of the east "made *pictures* all the time." Roaming through the city and the countryside, sleeping where they could, starting to get desperate for a little work—Hamlin had failed to find a teaching position, though he had searched in Iowa, Minnesota, and Wisconsin—the Garland brothers knew they would soon risk getting labeled as worthless tramps, but before they cut off their travels they at least needed to see Concord. It was the summer of 1882, the year Whitman published *Specimen Days*, and Hamlin and Franklin seemed to be following the poet's itinerary: they went to "the gray old Manse where Hawthorne lived, the cemetery of Sleepy Hollow, the grave of Emerson. . . . All day we loitered along beautiful wood roads, passing wonderful old homesteads gray and mossy, sheltered by trees that were almost human in the clasp of their protecting arms."[18]

Garland had discovered that, though he might always be a Son of the Middle Border, he was nevertheless "also a Grandson of New England." Of course, he was still uncertain about life back east: there seemed to be no decent way of earning money; New York, though inspiring as a spectacle, often came across as "a storm, a cyclone, an abnormal unholy congestion of human souls"; and even Boston was bewildering, "roaring and turbulent." Unable to afford a house in the suburbs, Garland had a hard time imagining a place for himself in the industrializing regions of his nation. Moreover, despite his yearning for a sense of settledness, he was too much of a frontiersman himself to be able to understand why so many easterners were not even curious about the possibilities of western society: "This static condition of the population was a constant source of wonder to us. How could people stay all their lives in one place? Must be something the matter with them." By spring of 1883, then, he had to admit that he was just as susceptible as his father to "the call of 'the sunset regions,'" and though he still held to his goal of becoming a teacher, he decided that he would first go back to visit his family on their new acreage in Dakota—and maybe even invest in some land of his own. The west was what he knew: a simple existence, in the open air. There followed a few months of hopeful pioneering, during which Garland, as a yeoman and a land speculator, felt he was swimming with the true current of development and progress. The heat of the summer, though, brought a new sense of "bitterness," "defeat," "mockery," "futility": "a vague yet deep-seated longing to go east rendered me restless, sour and difficult." So, once and for all, he reoriented himself "toward settlement, eager to escape the terror and the loneliness" of the sprawling flatlands. It meant defying his father, who found Hamlin's equivocation deeply frustrating and felt sure that his son's plan to return to Boston would fail spectacularly and ultimately force him back to the frontier, anyway: "Why, it's against the drift of things. You can't make a living back east. Hang onto your land and you'll come out all right. The place for a young man is in the west." And it meant abandoning his mother to "all the drudgery of a pioneer house-wife. . . . It must have seemed to her as if she were never again to find rest except beneath the sod." Garland was tortured by guilt, "bitter and rebellious of mood, uneasy and uncertain of purpose." He worried that this separation might be permanent, that he might actually be repeating his father's mistake, might be on the verge of forsaking connection and kinship forever. But he also felt certain, as he gazed at his fellow soldiers in "the army of settlement," that his only chance to inhabit a borderland Arcadia lay in deserting the middle border.[19]

––––––––––

Garland was twenty-four when he abandoned the west; I was twenty-six when I abandoned the east. My decision to quit my job in Washington and then move to California—to live with Christine, who was starting a master's degree in San Jose—took me further from my parents than I'd ever been before. It's true that I'd spent several weeks, over the years, exploring France and Israel and India and Argentina—but this time I was planning to settle down for a while; and I didn't have a new job to go to; and I had known this woman for only a few months; and she had been raised as a Mormon—in California. Since Christine and I were married three years later, with the blessing of both sets of parents, I don't tend to remember my long drive into the sunset, in the early autumn of 1996, as being particularly fraught. But it was. My journal from that year reminds me that my father, in particular, was concerned about where I was going, and, in turn, that I was torn about whether I even wanted to explain myself to him. He had just retired that spring from Brandeis University, at the age of seventy-two, and he seemed depressed, withdrawn. Though he has never been the kind of parent to lash out at his children (or anyone else), and though he never passes harsh judgments (except on conservative politicians), and though he was self-aware enough to realize that his mood was due mostly to his change in professional identity (and to arthritis, and to headaches caused by a strange neurological virus), he did let me know, gradually, subtly, over the course of several months, in person and in letters, that my life decisions were adding to his burden of anxiety. I felt I should probably initiate a frank conversation with him about how I saw my future, but my strange sense of deference, combined with a slow-burning resentment, left me unable or unwilling to approach him.

I could understand why he might think I was being irresponsible, why he might be tempted, for the first time, to lump me with the rest of the supposed slackers of Generation X. I was actually desperate for a slackening of sorts: I wanted time to unwind, to write for no audience but myself, to explore a new place, to focus on being in love. Wasn't it better to be a slacker than a corporate drone? Besides, didn't it count for something that I had worked so hard in college, and then had landed a good, challenging job in the midst of the post–Gulf War recession of 1992, as an environmental researcher and writer, publishing magazine articles and book chapters and research reports and even managing to save a little money? I had clearly strayed from some sort of path, though, and had declared my allegiance to someone whose background seemed as different from mine as it could possibly be: I was eastern, Jewish, quiet, tortured; she was western, Mormon (though an apostate, by this time), gregarious, generally carefree. Was she serious enough, my father wondered, to follow me to a Ph.D. program after she finished her master's degree? Was I going to earn any money at all while I lived in San Jose? Had I put together an earthquake survival kit?

I was terrified of earthquakes, but to Christine they were just facts of life, and it seemed worthwhile, despite my father's disapproval, to see if, in her company, I could learn a new way of accepting the world—without sacrificing my idealism, without becoming fatalistic. In Washington, I had kept up a frantic pace; our stated goal at the Worldwatch Institute, after all, was to save the planet. In California, I wanted to pause, to give up that sense of urgency, not just in order to relax, but in order to remember that I couldn't do everything, that I didn't have to be perfect, that it was not about being a savior but just about reaching out and connecting, and that the best way of maintaining connections was to acknowledge that there would always be disconnection, that the ground would sometimes shake and gulfs would open up around each of us. I was still learning how to confront limitation and loss, and I felt like taking stock, felt I needed another sabbatical of sorts, like the "year off" from college that I'd spent in Minnesota.

In late November, when I went home to Boston for a few days, I was struck by my father's isolation. He sat silent and grim-faced through dinners, while my mother and I tried, half-heartedly, to chat. I felt sorry for him; I felt responsible, to some extent; but I was not going to prod unless he showed some sign of wanting to open up. On Thanksgiving night, he and my beloved great-uncle Irv, who was ninety-four, cast parallel shadows over the meal, though their disengagement had different valences: Irv occasionally smiled, if only to himself, while my father, even after a few glasses of wine, retained his sobriety. The rest of us stuttered and stammered our way through the evening, mostly avoiding their stares. I felt sure that Christine would have found a way to include both of them, but of course I just floundered in my discomfort. I couldn't wait to get back to California.

Still, I knew I would always be a son of New England. In December I spent time rereading the last talk my father had given at Brandeis, that spring, to a group of graduating seniors in his department, Romance and Comparative Literature, about his understanding of a liberal arts education. Without denying the tension in my relationship with my father, I firmly believed that, if I ever managed to explain myself to him, he would see that my California life actually conformed to his vision of how a thoughtful citizen ought to move through the world. I agreed with him that a careful study of history and literature and art should prepare a person to see deeper layers of meaning wherever he or she looked; to balance skepticism and faith; to build and appreciate community; to explore new ways of caring and understanding; to grasp the inspiring richness and complexity of consciousness in the face of alienation, angst, grief. Though I had relished my role as an environmental thinker and activist, and though I had every expectation of eventually pursuing a doctorate in history or some related field, I wanted to try out some alternative niches in San Jose, and I felt exhilarated by that effort, which involved sustained reflection, in libraries, on long hikes and bike rides, and during intense conversations with Christine and with a series of old friends who happened to be living in Palo Alto, Berkeley, and San Francisco. Within a few days of my arrival, at the beginning of October, I had mapped out a number of writing projects, one of which kept me occupied for the following two years, about the environmental and cultural history of the South Bay, the transformation of the Santa Clara Valley, the "fruit bowl" of the west, into Silicon Valley.[20] And by January I had started a volunteer job working with developmentally disabled children and a part-time paid job teaching clerical skills to developmentally disabled adults.

I could give a series of reasons for why I pursued those positions, but perhaps the fundamental one is that I wanted to offer help and care, in the most simple, direct way possible, to people who seemed in need, despite circumstances that might make me feel deeply uncomfortable and self-conscious. Bertha and Mitch, Kathryn and Patrick—whose faces I can see with perfect clarity, whose verbal tics and intonations echo in my memory—were, I suppose, stand-ins for my dying friends and relatives. But they were also themselves, endearing and frustrating, loving and bitter, demanding endless patience but also offering unconditional acceptance. I rarely worried about the root causes of their situations, rarely agonized over what public policies might best address their needs, because my job was simply to reach out to them and teach them a few things—and, in the case of a five-year-old boy named Ryan, who had memorized several children's books and liked to repeat parts of them to me over and over again, always concluding with the phrase, "And *that's* the end of today's story," I just had to be there to catch him when he dove off the top of the play structure. The warmth and understanding of those workplaces, despite occasional seizures and screaming fits and moans and the spilling of bodily and other fluids, were more than enough, in my mind, to justify my having slowed down any potential "progress" toward a long-term career. And though my father still had his doubts, my mother took a strong interest in my new line of work, since I think she realized I had inherited my visceral empathy from her. Certainly, we shared a basic shyness, which was debilitating to me at times, especially before college, but which, in its isolating power, paradoxically helped me to connect with anyone else whom I perceived as a fellow misfit. I remember several instances, in my earliest years, when a boy with a severe speech impediment, or a girl with Down's or some other Syndrome, wound up clinging to my mother and me as if we were family members, just because we seemed to understand them. Working with all those California misfits, I felt more at home than I generally had at college or at my Washington think tank.

By late April, in what was perhaps a bow to my father's concerns, I had added yet another job, teaching two evening courses, one on writing and one on environmental science, at a community college. Right before I started, though, Christine and I went east to Washington, where my uncle was living, for a family Passover gathering, at which, during a walk through the National Zoo (my sister and cousins had small children), my father made a point of pulling me aside for a serious talk. The topic was a total surprise: for the first time in my life, he wanted to tell me about the woman he had been married to before my mother—because, it turned out, she had just died.

I'd learned of her existence the summer I was eighteen, when I was in Toronto for a wedding. Toronto was my father's home town, and it was full of our relatives, because, as far as I knew, my father was the only member of his entire extended family who had moved away. (His decision to pursue a Ph.D. at Columbia had marked a clear severing of familial connections.) On the day before the wedding, I went for a jog with two of my older cousins, one of whom, Garry, asked, chattily, in between breaths, "Do you know what ever happened to Auntie Jeanette?"

"Who's Auntie Jeanette?" I asked.

"Whoops," he said.

I stopped running. Garry and Bryan explained, briefly, and assured me that there hadn't been any kids, but said I should get the full story from my father. Right, I thought. I should just go into his study one day, the way I used to as a child, but this time, instead of asking for a book recommendation or seeing if he wanted to watch the Red Sox game, I would casually inquire about a painful episode from his past that he had always conscientiously hidden from me. He had never wanted to talk about Benjamin; he clearly didn't want to talk about Jeanette. I'm sure many other children, in my situation, would have confronted their father immediately, but I told myself that, despite my feeling of betrayal, this bit of history didn't ultimately matter very much, and, besides, it would be disrespectful to dredge it up. So I stewed. I did ask my sister about Jeanette, and of course she already knew: "I found out because Cousin Ethel asked Dad about her once at a restaurant, when we were on vacation in the Berkshires. I was twelve, so you were five. You don't remember?" I didn't remember. And she had never followed up: she agreed that Dad would not take kindly to being pressed. That was nine years before the zoo conversation; I never followed up, either.

My father did apologize, but the explanation he gave for his sin of omission wound up sparking my indignation—which perhaps helped make the conversation more productive than it otherwise would have been. I had assumed that he'd kept this secret out of embarrassment, a sense of failure: he didn't want his children to think of him as tainted. But what he actually said was that he never thought we would find his experience relevant. I was eager to disabuse him, though I proceeded carefully, in the rational register that he seemed to favor. Of course it was relevant, I said: I had an inherent interest in understanding how he had become my father. I was also interested in relationships, and in marriage as an institution—after all, I might want to get married myself one day. Moreover, as he himself had taught me, an honest narration of one's most difficult experiences can do important work in the world, since it opens up the possibility of commiseration. What I did not say was, "How could you have failed to trust me with this story?" Still, I did ask more direct questions than

I might have if he had started off by expressing more emotion, rather than just saying he wanted to inform me of something, now that a chapter of his life had come to a close. I felt I had a right to know: how did this marriage come to be? How long did it last? What was wrong with it? Who ended it?

His answers were halting. I could hear his pain, his shame, as he spoke, and I did my best to sympathize. But my mind quickly clouded over as I started to realize how aloof he had been all my life. I had always spoken of him, thought of him, as the professor-dad whose study door was never closed, who seemed delighted to be interrupted when I wanted to play catch in the backyard, who came to all of my baseball games and concerts, who comforted me late at night when I felt friendless. I'll always be grateful for that aspect of our relationship. But I didn't know my father the way I knew my mother, because he had never talked about his family, had rarely taken us to see them, had avoided questions about his dead parents, working-class immigrants from Poland and Lithuania who clearly had little in common with his admired father-in-law the rabbi and mother-in-law the poet. Suddenly he was telling me about marrying Jeanette because his parents thought he ought to get married— and then about realizing, during their four years together, that she could never understand or support his commitment to a life of the mind. I tried to ask follow-up questions, tried to nail down the chronology. Was he already married when he left Toronto to go to graduate school at Columbia? No. So was he with Jeanette during his first teaching job, at Williams College, right before he moved to Brandeis and met Mom? No: Williams wasn't his first job. Wait, how many jobs had he held? Four. Four? Before Brandeis and Williams he had been at a Catholic college in Detroit and at Berkeley. Wait, Berkeley? Yes. He had lived in California? Yes. WHAT?

I guess the conversation didn't last nearly as long as it should have. His answers got shorter and shorter; I grew more and more flustered. We were at the zoo; there were kids to look after; it was cold. I felt genuinely thankful that he had opened up to me a little, but I also had a dawning awareness that I might have grown up in something like a fog of aversion. I craved openness. His desire to tell me about Jeanette could have signaled a new willingness to let me in, but after a few minutes I realized that my understanding of my father's emotional life would always be confined to occasional glimpses, clipped confessions. In the abstract, I could grant his right to privacy; what hurt was the experience of bumping against the limits of our relationship, acknowledging that we were not as close as I had thought.

Up until that Passover, I had assumed I would go back east for graduate school. But as Christine and I talked more about the future—I would be filling out applications that fall—and as we grew more attached to our immediate surroundings—the redwoods of the Santa Cruz mountains, the Bay Area's culture of bicycles and bookstores—I started trying to envision myself in the history department at Berkeley.

---

When Hamlin Garland decided to move back east, seemingly for good, in the autumn of 1884, his reasons were many, and muddled, both personal and political, but among the starkest was a new set of perspectives he had gotten from a book: *Progress and Poverty* (1879), by "the prophet of San Francisco," Henry George. During the winter, "brooding darkly" over the suspicion that he and all the other frontier speculators were "nothing but squatters," huddling by the fire as his "frail shanty" tried and failed to block blizzard after blizzard, Garland had picked up George's already-infamous book, "which was at that time engaging the attention of the political economists of the world." In retrospect, he felt that this volume "effected a profound change in my outlook on the world and led to far-reaching complications in my life." Yes, "complications": what if his family's land hunger had been not just wrong-headed but, quite simply, wrong? Could he sustain even a grudging respect for his father, the committed borderman? Even his self-respect was now in doubt. Until that winter, Garland "had never read any book or essay in which our land system had been questioned. I had been raised in the belief that this was the best of all nations in the best of all possible worlds, in the happiest of all ages." But George levied a direct, explicit attack against the frenzied enclosure of land in the United States over the previous several decades, against the American fetishization of private real estate, against the mythicization of speculative, winner-take-all capitalism in the name of nation-building—all of which had squeezed out the possibility of his utopia, a republic of usufruct. "Now," Garland explained, "as I read this book, my mind following step by step the author's advance upon the citadel of privilege, I was forced to admit that his main thesis was right. Unrestricted individual ownership of the earth I acknowledged to be wrong and I caught some glimpse of the radiant plenty of George's ideal Commonwealth."[21]

In our histories of this time period, George's utopian vision is often reduced to his advocacy for the "Single Tax on Land" as a solution to all the socio-economic problems of modernization, especially to the grinding, pervasive poverty that, paradoxically, had arrived hand in hand with fabulous wealth and "with all our railroads, and steamships, and power looms, and sewing machines"[22]—with, in short, the age's ballyhooed industrial Progress, all the developments that were supposed to make life easier, smoother, more pleasant, for everyone. Indeed, George could be single-minded in his promotion of the Single Tax. The basic idea was to subvert speculation and monopoly. First, George sought simply to establish the injustice of profiting from land, a God-given resource, through the strategy of locking it up and waiting for population pressure to increase its value. Once you accept that theoretical premise, the practice follows logically: why not impose an onerous levy precisely on the unearned increment, on the artificial inflation of the price of unimproved land? George hoped that such a tax would go far in redistributing wealth, and that, in combination with a parallel abolition of any tax on labor, or on the direct products of labor, it would succeed in eliminating poverty in his society, at least in all cases where people were willing and able to work. If you were using your land for a dwelling place or small business, or for crops or a garden—that is, for subsistence, or for social provision—then you could escape taxation altogether. You were living as a productive citizen. But if you were, say, a speculator on the Dakota frontier, or, worse, the owner-executive of a railroad line who had been granted huge parcels of land surrounding his track and stations, and you were merely holding those parcels in the expectation of selling them to the highest bidders once prices went up, then you would be considered a parasite, and your tax burden would drive you in the direction of bankruptcy, or at least toward liquidating your land assets in what would rapidly become a buyer's market. Then, after a short adjustment period, during which the Single Tax would have filled public coffers, land, the basic means of life, would finally become available to every citizen of the republic, either as a small, affordable private holding or as a town commons—fields, pastures, and woodlands that were held collectively, as a public trust. George conceived of the Single Tax as the most constructive possible response to the root cause of inequality.

It was clearly the straightforward idea of the Single Tax that propelled George to the forefront of a powerful political coalition in the 1880s and 90s, which, amazingly, not only united voters in both the country and the city but also brought together struggling workers with more comfortable members of the middle class, especially small-scale proprietors and entrepreneurs. All around the country, following the publication of *Progress and Poverty*, Single Tax leagues formed to protest the concentration of wealth—Hamlin Garland would join one in Boston, lecturing widely on its behalf—and, as less fortunate Americans continued to suffer from the jolts of the postbellum economy, George became the Gilded Age's leading social critic.[23] Yet the popularity of the Single Tax as a direct instrument of reform was based on a much broader, more complicated vision of how American society ought to evolve. Analyzed in isolation, the Single Tax platform has sometimes been understood by scholars as a nostalgic, retrogressive program designed to direct the nation back toward a full embrace of Jeffersonian agrarianism; or it has been understood exclusively in an urban context, as a celebration of self-employment and worker control, couched in an attack against corruption and what George often referred to as "industrial slavery," especially during his nearly successful campaign for mayor of New York, orchestrated in 1886 by the city's Central Labor Union.[24] George himself could emphasize either of these angles, depending on the situation, but, especially in his published writings, he frequently tried to lay out a more sweeping agenda that highlighted the interdependence of rural and urban lifeways and the intricacy of the links between them.

The final full-length chapter of George's 1884 study, *Social Problems*, is called "City and Country," and it describes a tendency, in late nineteenth-century America, for the country-based producers of food, spread out on huge, isolated, monoculture farms, and the city-based consumers, who "never, from year's end to year's end, press foot upon mother earth," to become "utterly divorced" from one another. And this divide, George thought, created in part by an "unnatural distribution of population," was organically connected to the "unnatural distribution of wealth which gives one man hundreds of millions and makes other men tramps."

George, echoing radical suburban theorists like Andrew Jackson Downing, but adapting their ideas for a new age, envisioned a spatial pattern that balanced smaller, greener cities with larger, more social towns, a pattern that would offer everyone both "breathing-space and neighborhood." Every resident of a tenement, he thought, should have windows and ventilation and some room to spread out, and should also be near parks and a kitchen garden (best of all would be to raze the tenements and rebuild with designs dedicated more to livability than profit). Every farmer's wife, meanwhile, utterly alone out on the middle border, condemned to a "steady drag of cares and toils," should be connected to a community and "supplied with light and heat, and power if needed," and should have access to "libraries, and lectures, and scientific apparatus, and instruction," not to mention concerts and plays. Under current conditions, perhaps the most dangerous problem was that neither city nor country dweller had a fully developed relationship to nature: for both producers and consumers, natural resources had become commodities rather than gifts. "In our mad scramble to get on top of one another," George lamented, in conclusion, "how little do we take of the good things that bountiful nature offers us! Consider this fact: To the majority of people in such countries as England, and even largely in the United States, fruit is a luxury. Yet mother earth is not niggard of her fruit. If we chose to have it so, every road might be lined with fruit-trees."[25] No matter where one lives, with however much in the way of resources, it is always possible to challenge systems and assumptions, and it is always possible to cultivate an appreciation for the offerings of the natural world.

Because *Progress and Poverty* was published in 1879, it has become commonplace to posit that the core of George's critique must have formed during the socioeconomic turmoil of the 70s[26]—the terrible depression of 1873–8, in which dozens of railroad companies went bankrupt; the massive, persistent unemployment; the violent labor conflicts, culminating in the railroad strikes of 1877, during which police opened fire on demonstrators in multiple cities. And certainly George's sympathetic perspective on those bleak years, when so many ex-soldiers became "tramps," when strikers were shot down like soldiers, was crucial to the framing of *Progress and Poverty*: from all across the nation, he observed, in his opening chapter, "come complaints of industrial depression; of labor condemned to involuntary idleness; . . . of want and suffering and anxiety among the working classes."[27] Yet it is also true that George had articulated many of the key elements of his worldview back in 1871, when he published his first significant study, *Our Land and Land Policy*. Even if the 70s hardened him in his radicalism, it seems that his childhood on a tree-lined street in antebellum Philadelphia, and his experience of California as a young man in the 60s, and his awareness of the massive industrial and agricultural expansion of the immediate postwar period, were enough to make him a latter-day Arcadian.

It was in the spring of 1858, when George was eighteen, that he arrived in San Francisco as a steward aboard the steamer *Shubrick*, a decade late for the Gold Rush but nevertheless dreaming of making his fortune. Fleeing the infamous Panic of 1857, when economic conditions were difficult and "getting worse and worse every day, factory after factory suspending and discharging its hands," George had been unsure of what he would do on the Pacific coast.[28] Once he arrived, though, he found that he was drawn to the gold regions, by an almost frenzied greed. Eventually, he would settle into the printing trade—he had served an apprenticeship as a typesetter back home, while also attending scientific lectures at the Franklin Institute—but first he had to try his hand at prospecting and investing, much like Hamlin Garland on the Dakota frontier fifteen years later. Needless to say, it didn't pan out, and though George would always claim to prefer the rough-and-tumble climate of the diggings, where lucky, hard-working individuals did occasionally make their bundle, to the oppressive structures of industrial manufacturing, he was ready to condemn his "lust for gold" by mid-September 1861 (even if he didn't completely abandon his mining ventures until a couple of years later). Writing to his favorite sister, Jennie, he explained that "sometimes I feel sick of the fierce struggle of our high civilised life, and think I would like to get away from cities and business, with their jostlings and strainings and cares altogether, and find some place on one of the hillsides, which look so dim and blue in the distance, where I could gather those I love, and live content with what Nature and our own resources would furnish."[29]

Meanwhile, he was falling in love with a young woman, Annie Fox, though he didn't tell anyone except Jennie, since he was so poor and his printing work so sparse that he knew the rest of his family would disapprove of his desire to get married. Fortunately, Jennie gave him his blessing—"marry her if you love her, for love is too precious a thing to be thrown away"—despite feeling "a sudden choking, a sudden loneliness and jealousy, when I first read your letter," and despite her misgivings about Annie's Catholicism. The wedding happened quickly (they eloped); the couple found their union genuinely blissful, a feeling they seem to have sustained for the following thirty-six years, until Henry's death; their economic fortunes swung upward; and Henry and Jennie quickly renewed their close bond, as Jennie came to realize that "there can be two places in your heart—one for Annie and one for me." Jennie at times expressed gratitude that Henry had stayed in California, since that kept him out of the Civil War, but she desperately wanted him to bring his wife home for a visit, and she tried to lure him with memories of their old haunts: "We had pretty nice times when we were children, didn't we? . . . Hen, in the Spring we used to have such a time planting seed in our garden. What a handsome garden!" In turn, Henry assured his sister that "I love you as much as ever, and I believe, long to see you more," but insisted that she give up her pestering and instead come to visit him in Sacramento, where he and Annie were delighted to be "living in one of the pleasantest parts of the town—a square from the State Capitol—and surrounded by trees of all kinds and the largest growth, and roses in greater profusion than I ever saw before."[30] These were the two most important relationships of his life, both of which he connected to his relationship with elements of the landscape, with the cultivated outdoors: as he went on long walks with Annie in the fresh evening air of California, he remembered long walks with Jennie along the greenways of Philadelphia.

And then, without warning, in July 1862, barely half a year after Henry and Annie were married, Jennie died. It was one of those brief, inexplicable illnesses, like the one that killed Hamlin Garland's sister. Disconsolate, Henry leaned harder into his work, and he leaned on Annie, and together they welcomed their first child into the world in November. But, just before the birth, he had written to his surviving siblings of his commitment to dwell forever with the bittersweet memory of his closest confidante: "One token is all I have—the little lock of hair that fell into my hand, shaken from your letter, on that Sabbath afternoon that is burned into my memory, and which to my dying day I never can forget. . . . I have a box full of Jennie's letters—all she has ever written to me, and you know what a treasure they are now. To look over them is like hearing her speak. They are the best mementos I could have. I can hardly bear to look at them now, but all through life there will be a sad, solemn pleasure in re-reading these letters and in recalling the old times when we were so happy."[31]

The next few years were grim ones. The November baby, once he grew up to be his father's biographer, referred to this period as one of "extreme privation," when his parents were "at dead low ebb." It was to Jennie that Henry had confided his initial anguish over the Civil War—"the storm howls around us with a strength and fury that almost unnerves one. Our country is being torn to pieces, and ourselves, our homes, filled with distress"[32]—and, later, he had insisted that she understand his frustration that the western regiments were being raised "merely to garrison posts and fight Indians," a mission he could not support, and that he could not pay his passage back east. "I cannot help feeling regret," he wrote, "that the contest will be over and the victories won without my having taken the slightest part in it. If I am East after the war is ended I will feel abashed among its heroes."[33] And so he stayed in the west, missing his sister, scrabbling to support his new family, with his vision darkened, but with a growing commitment to explore the ways in which his society structured itself—as he wondered about the extent to which he was responsible for his own poverty, as he observed the ebbs and flows of the war, not to mention the literal floodwaters that swept through Sacramento, followed by the stifling drought that crippled the California economy for two full years.

Looking around, getting his bearings, George began to understand that the agricultural and industrial sectors in California operated on parallel tracks, depended on a parallel pattern of exploitation. He had never tried to pursue his dream of moving to the countryside, but now he realized that yeoman farmers, as a class, were almost unheard-of in his adopted home. California agriculture was dominated by a few millionaires who held gargantuan estates: most had accumulated their land through somewhat shady deals in the late 1840s and early 50s, when the Mexicans were leaving and buyers were scarce, and though they had started out as cattle barons, they were now planting as many acres as possible with wheat, and relying on an itinerant labor force, whom they treated like disposable commodities. "Over our ill-kept, shadeless, dusty roads," George would write a few years later, in *Our Land and Land Policy*, "where a house is an unwonted landmark, and which run frequently for miles through the same man's land, plod the tramps, with blankets on back—the labourers of the California farmer—looking for work, in its seasons, or toiling back to the city when the ploughing is ended or the wheat crop gathered." If a prospective smallholder came along and dared to covet some obscure corner of an unsurveyed land claim, he could either pay a huge sum to any number of local swindlers and speculators who purported to represent the owner, or he could simply build a house without making inquiries and hope for the best—though in that case he would almost certainly be evicted within a few years, with all of his improvements just serving to enrich the owner even further. Those poor war veterans who came to California to start a new life, who had heard all about "the advantages with which nature has so lavishly endowed this Empire State of ours," who passed over the Sierras in the spring and then traveled through lush forests "of evergreen giants, past laughing rills and banks of wild flowers," to come upon "the vast fertile valleys stretching out to the dark blue of the Coast Range in the distance," would almost inevitably end up as migrant laborers, whether in the country or the city.[34]

Industrial development in California, of course, was dominated by the railroads. George had been living in Sacramento in 1863 when Leland Stanford, president of the Central Pacific (and governor of California), had broken ground on his new line, at the corner of Front and K Streets, and pointed eastward in anticipation of an eventual meeting with the Union Pacific, to make the transcontinental connection that was supposed to knit the nation together once and for all in a triumphant embrace of resource extraction and commerce. Stanford's power, George noted, was precisely that of the large agricultural landowners: whatever tracts had not been monopolized by ranchers and wheat farmers were now being granted to the Central Pacific (or the Western Pacific, or the Southern Pacific), so that Stanford and his colleagues could just sit on their holdings while they busily took advantage of their state's vast oversupply of low-priced laborers, including Chinese "coolies" who had originally come to California during the Gold Rush. While George always condemned racial violence, he ultimately failed to include Chinese immigrants in his sympathies, painting them not as additional exploited laborers being deprived of their fair share of the wealth of nature but rather as members of the exploiting classes themselves, as interlopers seeking to draw out American resources and send them back to China. Eventually, George became quite prominent as a proponent of Chinese Exclusion, and, immediately after the Civil War, his juxtaposition of the simple yeoman ideal with the California system, based on large landholdings and racial divisions, certainly packed a punch: his Arcadia was meant for white folks, and the racial stereotypes in which he trafficked, deeply offensive to twenty-first-century sensibilities, clearly reflected the general postbellum backlash against all people of color.[35] The true villains, though, to George, were never the Chinese themselves but the land barons, whether they dealt in wheat or trains, who seemed so eager to hire any degraded minorities, who used their considerable political power to make sure they always had access to the cheapest possible labor—who, in short, were not interested in any common good but only in their own competitive advantage.[36] In an 1868 article called "What the Railroad Will Bring Us," published in the *Overland Monthly*, George reminded Californians that the completion of the transcontinental line would "not be a benefit to all of us, but only to a portion. . . . Those who have lands, mines, established businesses, special abilities of certain kinds, will become richer for it and find increased opportunities; those who have only their own labour will become poorer, and find it harder to get ahead—first because it will take more capital to buy land or to get into business; and second, because as competition reduces the wages of labour, this capital will be harder for them to obtain."[37]

As George became more intently focused on the widening gap between rich and poor as an almost inevitable consequence of America's modernization, he was gradually managing to lift his own family out of poverty, having solidified his reputation not only as a printer and editor but also as a writer of essays, on themes ranging from the assassination of Lincoln to the historical significance of Constantinople. By December of 1868, he was finally able to take a trip back east, and in Philadelphia, at the age of twenty-nine, he was reunited with his parents for the first time in about eleven years. It was in New York, though, that he had what he would later refer to as his life's central epiphany—at first just "a thought," but then "a vision, a call," when "every nerve quivered"—when suddenly he recognized the struggle that lay ahead of him. In this most impressive of American cities, as he walked the streets, he felt revolted by the social forces that shoved some people into shanties while others, a few blocks away, lived in airy brownstones—felt compelled, as he explained in 1886, during his campaign for mayor, to confront the "monstrous injustice . . . that turns human beings into machines, robs childhood of joy, manhood of dignity, and old age of repose. . . . Years ago I came to this city from the West, unknown, knowing nobody, and I saw and recognized for the first time the shocking contrast between monstrous wealth and debasing want. And here I made a vow, from which I have never faltered, to seek out and remedy, if I could, the cause that condemned little children to lead such a life as you know them to lead in the squalid districts."[38]

All retrospective epiphanies come across as romantic, even suspect—perhaps none more so than those of politicians. But they can also reveal things about how a given person understands himself. In George's case, what might matter most of all is that he didn't let his New York story stand alone: it was complemented by a California story, a western story, a story of the countryside. To understand what "Progress" had wrought on the streets of the city, you had to go back to the land. George himself had led a thoroughly urban life in the 60s, and between 1863 and 1869 his letters and diaries almost never mentioned any personal attachment to the landscape. But after he returned to California in the summer of 1869—much to the dismay of his parents, who had hoped to keep him on the east coast—he took up horseback riding. As his son put it, "at any hour that he was free and had the inclination he would hire a horse and find mental change in a lope into the open country of the foothills." At this point, George was living in Oakland, not far from Olmsted's recently established Mountain View Cemetery, and working for a Democratic newspaper called the *Transcript*. Though a loyal Lincoln Republican who had voted for Grant in 1868, he now found himself "rapidly becoming disgusted" with the ruling party's clear inclination to cater to the ruling classes: the Republicans seemed to be in thrall to special interests like the railroads and giant manufacturing firms. So George wrote scathing articles about the perniciousness of railroad subsidies, and rode out into the hinterland, where speculators were eagerly buying up large plots in the hope that Leland Stanford would soon build a new spur connecting Oakland to the transcontinental line at Sacramento. One day, "absorbed in my own thoughts, I had driven the horse into the hills until he panted. Stopping for breath, I asked a passing teamster, for want of something better to say, what land was worth there. He pointed to some cows grazing off so far they looked like mice and said: 'I don't know exactly, but there is a man over there who will sell some land for a thousand dollars an acre.' Like a flash it came upon me that there was the reason of advancing poverty with advancing wealth. With the growth of population, land grows in value, and the men who work it must pay more for the privilege. I turned back, amidst quiet thought, to the perception that then came to me and has been with me ever since."[39] So the key was not the fall in wages caused by a growing labor supply; the real problem was that, in America, where there was supposed to be plenty of space for everyone to have his homestead, the wealthy had earned their money by tying up the land—by closing off the masses from their basic means of subsistence and thereby forcing them to become tenants or to fall back into the slums of the city. Instead of breeding democracy, America's land system had fostered a new kind of feudalism.[40]

In 1871, George received the Democratic nomination for a seat in the state legislature, on an explicitly antirailroad platform (he ultimately lost to the Republican candidate), and spent the months of April, May, June, and July writing *Our Land and Land Policy*, which he printed himself, attaching a folding map of California with the railroad land grants marked in red: "Observe the proportion which these reservations bear to the total area of the State, and observe at the same time the topography of California—how the railroad reservations cover nearly all the great central valleys, and leave but the mountains, and you may get an idea of how these reservations are cursing the State."[41] George's long pamphlet (reprinted as a book, it ran to 131 pages) was a spatially sophisticated critique of American modernity, a scathing account of the link between social and environmental exploitation—and a plea for an Arcadian mode of settlement, though with a greater emphasis on the limits of political economy than on the limit of mortality. Of course, I find George's racial views abhorrent, and I can't help but feel deeply skeptical of his reductionist perspective, his attempt to find one single root cause for all the multilayered problems of his complex society. Even the utter abolition of land monopolization and speculation could go only so far in eliminating poverty and human suffering, not to mention environmental damage. Yet George's particular style of protest mattered immensely at this precise moment in American history, because it shook the foundations of the nascent belief system being trumpeted by leading industrial capitalists.

In 1871, many Americans, as they acknowledged the gradual decline of agrarianism and moved to the city, were just beginning to lose consciousness of their basic, shared dependence on the fresh air, clean water, and fertile soil that are required for food production. Many of them were just beginning to buy into the idea that everything had its price, that the fruits of nature were best understood as commodities. Many of them were becoming convinced that the development of better industrial processes was the key to better living for all. So George made an impression when he reminded them that the convenience of buying food at a store, and the magic of "the ten thousand great labour-saving appliances which modern invention has brought forth," depended directly on access to money, and such access was by no means guaranteed, even to those who worked the hardest. Indeed, "concentration is the law of the time," and though "our millionaires are more numerous, and their wealth is more enormous," there was not much money left over for "the operatives of New England, the farmers of Ohio, the mechanics of San Francisco"—and "to say . . . that the people of a country shall consist of the very rich and the very poor, is to say that republicanism is impossible." How could an unemployed printer delude himself into believing that his vote was worth as much as Leland Stanford's? Democratic citizenship depended on something resembling a level playing field, and access to parcels of land in a particular climate might provide such a baseline for a just society, but the urban industrial economy clearly did not. "We are not called upon to guarantee to all men equal conditions," George conceded, "and could not if we would, any more than we could guarantee to them equal intelligence, equal industry or equal prudence; but we *are* called upon to give to all men an equal chance. If we do not, our republicanism is a snare and a delusion, our clatter about the rights of man the veriest buncombe in which a people ever indulged."[42]

Perhaps most remarkably, George insisted that, in the system of American republicanism, citizens were entitled not only to civil rights but to environmental rights. He believed, for instance, that all Americans had the right to quench their thirst, and so he decried the privatization of lakes and rivers: "It is not only the land and the timber, but even the water of California that is threatened with monopoly, as by virtue of laws designed to encourage the construction of mining and irrigation ditches, the mountain streams and natural reservoirs are being made private property, and already we are told that all the water of a large section of the State is the property of a corporation of San Francisco capitalists." He also believed that his children, and all future generations, had a right to witness the awe-inspiring bison herds on the plains: "What have the buffaloes done to us that we should sacrifice the heritage of our children to see the last of them extirpated before we die?" Broadly speaking, he believed that every person had the explicit right, "declared by the fact of his existence . . . , to the use of so much of the free gifts of nature as may be necessary to supply all the wants of that existence. . . . To deny this is to deny the right of man to himself, to assert the atrocious doctrine that the Almighty has created some men to be the slaves of others."[43] Hadn't his countrymen just fought a war to abolish that doctrine once and for all?

Of course, with environmental rights came environmental responsibilities. No one was entitled to *more* of nature's gifts than he or she actually *needed*, so the onus was on the individual citizen both to limit desire and to make sure that nothing was wasted: everyone had to cultivate an ethic of care. But, alas, George worried that a new version of the callous Southern system—a system of land commodification and cash cropping, which made for exhausted soil and degraded workers—had already been transferred to the west: "California is not a country of farms, but a country of plantations and estates. Agriculture is a speculation. The farm-houses, as a class, are unpainted frame shanties, without garden or flower or tree. The farmer raises wheat. . . . His interest is but to get for this season the greatest crop that can be made to grow with the least labour. He hires labour for his planting and his reaping, and his hands shift for themselves at other seasons of the year." A new land policy, then, should insist on small-scale subsistence, should aim "to give every one an opportunity of employing his own labour, and to give no opportunity to any one to appropriate the labour of others"—should provide free land directly to settlers, but only "*in limited quantities.*" ("Eighty acres," George thought, "is quite enough for any one, and I am inclined to think forty acres still nearer the proper amount.") Such a policy would foster deep investments, would encourage a landscape of groves and gardens and diversified crops, would slow down the whole process of development to a pace compatible with caution and nurturing:[44]

> Population would not in the same time spread over as much ground as under the present policy; but what it did spread over would be well settled and well cultivated. There would be no necessity for building costly railroads to connect settlers with a market. The market would accompany settlement. No one would go out into the wilderness, to brave all the hardships and discomforts of the solitary frontier life; but with the foremost line of settlement would go church and schoolhouse and lecture-room. The ill-paid, overworked mechanic of the city could find a home on the soil, where he would not have to abandon all the comforts of civilisation, but where there would be society enough to make life attractive, and where the wants of his neighbours would give a market for his surplus labour until his land began to produce; and to tell those who complain of want of employment and low wages to make for themselves homes on the public domain would then be no idle taunt.
>
> Consider, too, the general gain from this mode of settlement. How much of our labour is now given to transportation, and wasted in various ways, because of the scattering of our population which land grabbing has caused?

One could easily fault George for assuming too quickly that the urban poor would always want to go back to the hard labor of the farm—that they would willingly forgo commerce in favor of subsistence, that they would embrace his genteel code of responsibility, that they would in fact construct the attractive, half-urban, half-rural communities that he envisioned. And it is likely that he vastly exaggerated the impact that the Single Tax would have on the distribution of wealth.[45] Still, his critique of the heedless rush into modernity, and his advocacy for an environmentally inflected program of economic justice, make him perhaps the most radical Arcadian of the postwar era. He knew the sun was setting on his ideal society, but he clung to the possibility of breaking up the railroad reservations and opening the in-between spaces of the frontier to an alternative model of development.

------

By the time I moved to California, there was no remnant of the cultural expectation that each American deserved a piece of land to work. I would be hard pressed to say exactly when that expectation disappeared for good, but it seems relatively certain that it started to fade in the late nineteenth century, in concert with the dramatic shift in the ratio of city-dwellers to country-dwellers. On the eve of the Civil War, the United States was still clearly an agrarian nation: only 20 percent of its population lived in urban areas. By 1900, the percentage was up to 40 (66 in the northeast), and a majority of Americans were dependent on wages for their survival. The basic link between environment and subsistence had been broken: Americans now defined themselves primarily as consumers rather than producers, and generally felt disconnected from the basic concept of "land."[46]

I did assume, though, in the fall of 1996, that San Jose would have some parks or gardens where I could take long walks—where I might even be able to get lost. San Francisco, after all, was famous for its green spaces (Golden Gate Park and the Presidio, in particular), and in Washington I had gotten used to daily contact with the groves of Rock Creek Park, which somehow seemed to bleed into the city streets, at least in all the neighborhoods I tended to frequent. San Jose has a couple of gems, it turns out, if you're able to drive to the edge of the city—I loved Alum Rock Park, in the eastern foothills—but nature-craving pedestrians who live downtown are generally out of luck: "office parks" and the "campuses" of electronics firms don't count, except as possible markers of Superfund sites.[47]

At first, based on what I saw all around me and what I already knew about western history, I figured that San Jose, and the whole Santa Clara Valley, had started down the path to industrialism back in the postbellum era, and, indeed, the arrival of the railroad in the mid-1860s coincided with the rise of mercury mining in the area, which meant jobs, real estate sales, and a general boom.[48] But that period of growth tapered off rapidly. While other western cities exploded, San Jose, perhaps because of its gushing artesian wells and its topsoil of fine loam that ran forty feet deep in places, developed into a fairly sleepy rural suburb, offering a stark contrast to San Francisco and Oakland, its megalopolitan neighbors fifty miles up the Bay. No major landlords had stepped into the Santa Clara Valley, so there was room to spread out, and people found that they could live easily off the land on relatively small claims. In 1870, San Francisco was the largest city in the west (by a factor of eight), with Oakland and San Jose placing eighth and eleventh. Two decades later, San Francisco was holding steady as the leading western metropolis (though Omaha and Denver had made great strides), and Oakland had moved into the sixth position, but San Jose did not even make the top twenty. Local farmers had invested heavily in wheat, and they were just beginning to shift over to fruit; by the early twentieth century, the region's graceful pear, apricot, and cherry blossoms had transformed San Jose and vicinity into "The Valley of Heart's Delight." In the course of these decades, the dominant class of growers had not dealt kindly with the local Ohlone Indians, or the Californios and Mexicanos, or the Chinese and Japanese immigrants (San Jose's Chinatown was attacked by arsonists in 1870 and 1887), but in environmental and economic terms, for white settlers, including large numbers of Italian and Portuguese proprietors, the Santa Clara Valley looked like a version of paradise-according-to-Henry George.[49] At the peak of agricultural activity, just before World War II, there were about six thousand farms in the Valley, almost all of which covered less than fifty acres and were operated as family businesses: smallholder dominance had kept out the monopolists, who by this time ruled virtually every other California valley, making the state famous for its "factories in the fields." Together, the region's exceptionally modest plantings used 80 percent of the land in the county, and about half of that area comprised perhaps the largest near-continuous orchard in the world: some eight million flowering trees spread over 132,000 acres.[50] The flavor and variety of the fruit could not match what one might have found, for instance, in Andrew Jackson Downing's nurseries, since the pressures of commodification had narrowed the scope of all horticultural practices and put a priority on appearance and transportability. But if you had taken a stroll through San Jose during the first half of the twentieth century, you undoubtedly would have found the air pleasant to breathe.

The San Jose whose acrid atmosphere I experienced in the mid-90s was a direct product of the growth of the electronics industry between 1950 and 1970, when "The Valley of Heart's Delight" was transformed into "Silicon Valley." "They say San Jose is going to become another Los Angeles," said City Manager "Dutch" Hamann, a former oil executive, in 1965. "Believe me, I'm going to do everything in my power to make that come true." Hamann's main strategies were to annex land, rezone to favor industrial development over housing (since businesses like Westinghouse, IBM, Lockheed, Sylvania, and General Electric were clearly going to contribute more to the city's tax base than even the most luxurious apartment buildings), and close his eyes to the increasing smog, the seeping of the hydrocarbon solvents used to clean semiconductors into the local groundwater, and the dumping of the heavy-metal sludge that rendered the entire oyster population of the Bay inedible. Meanwhile, scholarly and business leaders focused on creating a clean, white, white-collar image for the entire high-tech industry, emphasizing its connection to the nation's best engineering departments, its high-class, often bespectacled workforce, and its commitment to research and development, conducted in manicured office parks nestled beside the pastoral campus of Stanford University (nicknamed "The Farm"), where it was hard to tell that the majority of the employees were printing circuits destined for Pentagon missile systems. Corporate facilities were designed under strict building codes that often mandated "complete concealment" of generators, transformers, ducts, air conditioners, storage tanks, and smokestacks—not to mention parking garages for huge fleets of production workers, most of whom were Mexican-American or

Filipino-American women who could not afford to live anywhere near where they worked, because so much of the local land had been dedicated to industry rather than housing. While the rest of the country actually was shifting over to a service-dominated economy, the proportion of employees working in manufacturing in Santa Clara County increased from 15 percent in 1940 to 35 percent in 1980. And though these workers never breathed in any dust in the "clean rooms" where they etched silicon wafers, they were regularly exposed to known carcinogens like dichloroethylene. Laboring under such conditions, you might want to take your lunch break in a local park, where the trees regularly produced fresh oxygen, but by 1970, despite the fact that Hamann had increased San Jose's official size from 17 to 135 square miles in the previous two decades, the city had only 8 acres of open space per 1,000 residents, half of which consisted in school playgrounds—compared to 35 acres per 1,000 people in San Francisco, and 71 per 1,000 in Washington, D.C.[51] When I showed some vintage footage of the Valley's horticultural glory days to my environmental science class, the students, some of whom worked in clean rooms, could barely believe that trees had been such dominant features of the landscape in their own home town: most of them had never seen an orchard.

As I learned more about the region's history, it became clearer that the Internet's implicit embrace of placelessness was not a straightforward technological phenomenon but rather a philosophy, which had its roots in the spatial and cultural dynamics of the electronics industry. When, in 1997, my Web browser asked me where I wanted to go today, implying the irrelevance of the space I was actually inhabiting, it reflected, in a sense, the realization of Dutch Hamann's vision, the reality that we all now live in a version of Los Angeles—a vast, polluted, high-traffic wasteland whose escapist, fantasy-oriented infrastructure is so well developed as to allow us not to care about pollution, traffic, or waste. The Internet, in environmental terms, had become our new National Park System: our obsession with it represented a logical extension of our obsession with sublime, far-off wilderness areas, which, as of the late nineteenth century, had provided Americans with a glorious, cleansing means of not thinking about what they were doing to their immediate environments.[52] In the Santa Clara Valley, not even a broad, communal commitment to earning a livelihood through rural pursuits, on some of the most fertile land in the world, could withstand the rush of place-obliterating industrial development, in part because high-tech firms made it seem as though true Progress in the modern world could occur only in offices and labs. The outdoor context of daily life—our use of natural resources, our soiling of our nests, the specific characteristics of the places, with all their animals, plants, and microclimates, in which we embed ourselves—just didn't seem to matter anymore.

By 1997, I found myself ranting in my journal about a new, pervasive ad campaign (called "Television Is Good") being run by one of the main networks and featuring billboards saturated with a laser-lemon yellow: "It's a beautiful day, what are you doing outside?" I felt trapped in my alienation. Though it was undeniably exhilarating to be mobile, to have a fluid identity, to explore a new coast, to try out new jobs, I could not get through a single day without needing to ask myself where I really was and what I was doing there. Silicon Valley? Honestly? Where everyone is a "software engineer," where all is abstraction, where the overarching metaphysical question is, "what's the coolest thing we can get our machines to do?"

I thought of my father the French literature professor, and I reread a Samuel Beckett novel, which my friend Ruth, whom I had known since nursery school, had given to me in 1988, and which I had once discussed with Lou, my college advisor: "you must go on, I can't go on, you must go on, I'll go on."[53] I set myself some solid, simple tasks: go to the farmer's market and buy some fruits and vegetables; come home and prepare them; sit down with Christine and eat what you've prepared. That could make for a good day.

My old friend Stephen Heywood was much less alienated than I, especially in 1997, when he was living just up the peninsula in Palo Alto, building a house. I would often spend late afternoons playing basketball on a Stanford court with Stephen and his brother, or, on lazier days, I would just bring him and his crew a six-pack of beer and watch them work. Stephen and I hadn't been particularly close in high school—I'd had much more in common with his quiet, serious girlfriend—but I found, in my twenties, three thousand miles from home, that the simple fact of long-standing acquaintance could mean a lot. And though I was sickened by the inflated housing market and the ridiculously conspicuous consumption of most Palo Alto residents, I found it amazingly satisfying to see that house going up under Stephen's hands. I even started to enjoy Stephen's taunting attempts to get me to loosen up, to live less in my head and more in the rest of my body. He had been a tall but somewhat scrawny kid in high school (and uninterested in basketball), but lately, besides doing physical labor every day, he had started lifting weights and running up into the foothills behind the Stanford campus (and was now becoming an immovable force on the basketball court). He said half the Stanford students went up into the hills every day for exercise, and the other half went to have sex, and he was getting to know both contingents. And that gave me an idea. I wasn't a runner, and I wasn't interested in any additional liaisons, but I was planning to apply to graduate school that fall, and I thought it would be nice to live in a place where I could walk out my door and be on a hiking trail a few minutes later. For about a day, I toyed with the idea of applying to Stanford. And then I remembered East Rock, in New Haven. I had a couple of friends who went to Yale, and they had always raved about being able to head out to the Orange Street neighborhood and hike up to the top of East Rock, which offered views of the harbor. I didn't know if I could get into Yale for grad school. But I'd visited my friends a couple of times, and I thought I could remember a bunch of old Victorian houses on Orange Street that were divided into rental units, and I imagined that New Haven rentals would probably cost about half as much as San Jose rentals.

In July 1997, I placed a letter to the editor in the *San Jose Mercury News*, under the headline "Valley goes boom; should we cheer?"[54] It is surely the most sarcastic thing I've ever published. One of my supervisors at the job where I worked with developmentally disabled adults thought the letter was somewhat intemperate, maybe immature. But it provided me with a huge sense of relief. I had finally been willing and able to articulate my feeling that the knee-jerk celebration of the economic boom in Silicon Valley was based on little more than greed and that, once again, the winner-take-all mentality was proving to be the most enduring American fundamentalism, leaving the poorer classes (often minorities) squeezed onto the fringes, forced to cope with a health-endangering, compromised environment. Besides, didn't everyone know that bust always follows boom? I was planning to stay in Silicon Valley at least until the end of the year—it wasn't clear if Christine would need one more semester or two to finish her degree—and I would make the best of it, but I no longer felt the need to excuse the hubris of my neighbors. San Jose was unique among large western cities in that it had been a haven for horticultural smallholders for half a century, and then, once it finally got paved over, it was dominated by a single industry. In the end, though, this development history seemed to have made little difference. As of 1997, San Jose bore a close resemblance to Denver and Dallas: it was just another speculative sprawl.

---

The cities that exploded in the west immediately after the Civil War, with no pause for rural pursuits—the Dallases and Denvers of the region—typically followed the growth patterns that Henry George would have predicted for them. And the results were unfortunate, in terms of both political economy and the local landscape. They were almost always laid out before any planners or architects had arrived, by promoters, who cared for little beyond the efficient sale of lots.[55]

Back east, though the war had curtailed the rural cemetery movement and the picturesque suburb movement, an ascendant group of landscape architects was at least striving to sustain the urban park movement that had been launched by Olmsted and Vaux in New York.[56] Olmsted himself had retreated from California in 1865, having stayed only a couple of years, and for the next three decades he would carve out green spaces in urban areas from Montreal to Atlanta.[57] But even he consistently acknowledged that such piece work was never going to make eastern cities as livable as they should have been: they were already too old, too rigidly gridded. The true opportunity to design a new kind of garden city lay in the west, but virtually no reformers were willing to wrangle with the speculators and monopolists—save the somewhat desperate H. W. S. (Horace William Shaler) Cleveland, the Massachusetts-based co-designer of Sleepy Hollow Cemetery, who moved to the mushrooming metropolis of Chicago in 1869 in search of whatever commissions might become available on the middle border.[58] The following summer, struggling to find work, Cleveland wrote to Olmsted, with whom he had collaborated on Brooklyn's Prospect Park in 1868, to say that he was now thinking about writing a book: "My recent trip on the Kansas Pacific Rail Road served to strengthen my conviction of the urgent importance of making a vigorous protest on the subject of the arrangement of towns. It is appalling to think of the evils which threaten and which might be averted, and yet when one talks with these western people it seems a hopeless task to try to move their rectangular ideas. . . . Your examples of the impossibility of making radical changes in an old city are very valuable as arguments in favor of doing it right in the first place."[59] Cleveland's treatise, *Landscape Architecture as Applied to the Wants of the West; with an Essay on Forest Planting on the Great Plains* (1873), turned out to be one of the most radical and enduring works of the late nineteenth century—even if Cleveland himself only rarely got to put his ideas into practice.

Cleveland was in many ways the consummate nineteenth-century Arcadian, having been born a year before Andrew Jackson Downing, in 1814, but living almost fifty years longer, until 1900, by which time he had put his subtle stamp on public spaces throughout New England and far out on the frontier, in Illinois, Indiana, Michigan, Wisconsin, Minnesota, Iowa, Nebraska, Kansas, Dakota Territory, and Colorado. Yet he was an unlikely advocate—soulful, humble, retiring, likely to offer poignant tinges of emotion in his letters, at a time when much correspondence was becoming increasingly professional and businesslike. I think of him as having constructed a cemetery in his mind, to which he often retreated, feeling that it was his duty to confront loss, limits, the passage of time, modernization, and that such a duty, in its rightness, could provide the thrill of a mingled pleasure and pain. He mourned the fading of his own religious sentiments, but knew it was right for him to embrace the secular; he mourned the speed at which his fellow citizens were living, but noted the opportunities that were created by such frenzied activity; he mourned his society's mobility, its rootlessness, the fraying of ties to family and to particular places, but he saw that by unsettling himself he could more effectively challenge assumptions and consider alternatives. Cleveland never seemed sure about anything, yet he somehow found a sense of repose in his wavering, his haunting of mental borderlands. "Unfortunately," he wrote to Olmsted, at the age of seventy-six, when he was living in Minneapolis and serving as an advisor to new Parks Commissioners in Duluth and Omaha, "my confidence in my ability . . . does not increase with increasing experience, but on the contrary, I do but realize more fully how much there is that I *don't* know—but luckily those I deal with don't see it in that light. I get very tired at times and wish I was in Boston, but doubt if I ever shall be again, and suppose it is better for me to be here."[60]

Back in 1842, Cleveland had established a ninety-acre farm that he called Oatlands (echoing "Fruitlands," the Transcendental utopian experiment of the same era) on the Delaware River in New Jersey, where, as he put it, he "successfully engaged in fruit culture, and took an active part in the promotion of horticultural interest and knowledge." Indeed, he helped launch the National Pomological Congress and became a close correspondent of Downing's.[61] By 1854, though, despite more than a decade of excellent results on his farm, where the soil and climate were significantly better than in Massachusetts, he and his wife Maryann decided that they were homesick and that they wanted their two young sons to grow up further north: "the debilitating effect of the long continued heat of summer in New Jersey upon my wife and myself, was the cause of my leaving our pleasant home on the Delaware and returning to New England, and we soon experienced the benefit of the change in the renewed vigor and strength we derived from our native air."

At age thirty-nine, living in and around Salem, Cleveland joined with Robert Morris Copeland to follow in Downing's footsteps and make the transition from horticulturist to landscape gardener. And the friends' practice thrived, especially after the resounding success of Sleepy Hollow Cemetery in 1855: Cleveland had "attained a strong love of the art [of landscape design] and studied its principles as an amateur, for many years," and now, in middle age, he was gratified to have become a paid practitioner. For the rest of his life, he would concern himself with planning and planting, with forest trees and family trees, looking deep into the past for inspiration and always pondering his responsibilities to the far future. Pausing in 1882 to collect his mother's genealogical research and add some of his own notes and recollections, he used a horticultural metaphor to explain that he considered himself merely a "temporary representative of a line" whose many "honorable" generations had spurred his "effort to prove himself a worthy scion of the parent stock."[62] Ultimately, that effort took the form of the long-range landscape work he was doing on the cemeteries and park systems out west, though it was sometimes hard to maintain his faith in these projects, especially since "hardly one man in a hundred knows who designed such work ten years after it is done. But I *do* find a keen satisfaction in the thought of the value of the work to countless generations who will neither know or care who was the author."[63] Just as today's environmentalists strive to consider the impact of their actions on the resources and ecosystems that future people will depend upon, Cleveland insisted on planning the development of cities so that the children of the next century—"and above all the children of the poorer classes"—would have access to clean air and breathing space and "the occasional relief of the quiet seclusion of rural scenes," would pass their lives in "the presence of trees and shrubs, and flowers and grass," would experience the "wonder and delight" of close interactions with animals, would, in short, inherit a fundamental "love of nature"—which, in turn, would have an inestimable "value to the health and happiness of countless generations."[64]

Cleveland remained focused on children even in his old age, in part because he and his wife had taken responsibility for their two young granddaughters after their son, Henry, an engineer working in remote regions of South America, had died of dysentery in 1880, at age thirty-three. When Cleveland set out to revise his mother's genealogical notes, he was still in mourning for his son, and though he never questioned the rightness of his family obligations, he often acknowledged how sad and weighty they could be. Enclosing a couple of photographs of his granddaughters with a letter to a friend, he noted that "the beautiful *spiritual* expression which looks out so plainly from their faces impresses me with such a sense of responsibility at the thought that their training is committed to my charge, that it is at times almost painful. But the thought of my dear son's dying expression of confidence that I would care for them inspires me with the conviction that no holier duty remains to me in life."[65] Meanwhile, for the handwritten book that he called "Ancestry and Descendants of H. W. S. Cleveland, in line from Moses Cleveland of Woburn, Massachusetts, 1635," he chose an epigraph from an essay written by his friend George William Curtis: "Beyond the river of time that flows between, walk the brave men and the beautiful women of our ancestry, grouped in twilight upon the shore. . . . We acknowledge our inheritance; we accept our birthright; we own that their careers have pledged us to noble action." One could say that Cleveland may have been overly proud of his long Puritan heritage, but the tone of his notes remains modest and melancholy;

perhaps thinking of what Montaigne had said of his essays, he explained that he was writing all this down "without other object than the benefit of my children and their descendants."[66]

My sense is that Cleveland had always been serious about his family and his obligations both to the past and the future—but that, before Henry's death, he also had a well-developed lighter side. His partner, Copeland, first introduced him to Olmsted by emphasizing his lively warmth, which tended to produce strong affection: "let me say if you are fond of humor that he is an exceedingly good storyteller."[67] In Cleveland's 1855 essay, "Landscape Gardening," a tribute to Downing, his playful dismissal of faddish techniques for communicating with the dead served to redirect his readers to the small, mysterious marvels that might be discovered on the communicative pathways of rural cemeteries. "He who sets himself seriously to study the natural history of the simplest plant," Cleveland began, preparing to set tongue to cheek, "will find the subject quite as wonderful and incomprehensible as that of table-turning and spirit-rapping, and productive of much more satisfactory results." Cleveland also shared Downing's epicurean delight in horticulture, and, from the start of his career, he understood it as a stay against the alienation of industrialism and commodification, a link to old-fashioned gift economies: "Of the pleasures incidentally connected with the garden, the power of making presents of the fruits of one's own labors is certainly one of the highest. A rare bouquet to one who can appreciate its loveliness, a dish of blushing fruit, or a basket of choice vegetables, contributed on some special occasion to a friend's bill of fare—or a rich cluster of grapes to bless the fading sight of some poor consumptive, to whose parched lips they seem almost a foretaste of heaven,—affords a degree of satisfaction to the giver from being the result of his own skillful labor, which can be but faintly realized by him whose gifts involve only a demand upon his purse."[68]

The success and enthusiasm of the firm Cleveland and Copeland put them on par with Olmsted and Vaux—until the coming of the war. Copeland, barely thirty, enlisted, and went on to the disaster of his dishonorable discharge, but Cleveland was already in his mid-forties, and though he "deliberated on the propriety of entering the service of my country," he ultimately "decided that I could render more efficient help at home than in the field." With work scarce, however, and no Sanitary Commission to direct, he had plenty of time to feel guilty, and soon noted, with concern, "that multitudes of men were enlisting from the factories and shops of New England who had never fired a gun in their lives."[69] Since he had been raised as a hunter, and since it was well known that the soldiers of the less industrial South were far more skilled in the outdoors than their Northern counterparts, and since he worried that his urban compatriots might have become "enervated by the prosperity and luxury which we have enjoyed," Cleveland took it upon himself to write several articles offering tips about the use of guns in nature, which he eventually collected in a book called *Hints to Riflemen*, published in 1864, with an ominous frontispiece showing a lone man and his dog confronting a wild scene in Virginia.[70] Thus did he ease his conscience, somewhat; meanwhile, though, "the fact that during the war there was no call whatever for my professional services as a landscape gardener . . . left me penniless."[71] By 1865, he was so desperate to try to refill his purse that he took a job as a traveling salesman with the Massachusetts Arms Company, translating his expertise with guns into a convincing pitch on behalf of a repeating rifle called the Maynard. Eventually he did get some private landscape work in Tarrytown, New York—the original Sleepy Hollow!—and then did some plantings with Olmsted in Prospect Park, and then spent some time helping a friend whose eyesight had failed in Baltimore—but he didn't really get his career back until he made the decision to move west and become not just a horticulturist and landscape architect but also a city planner.

*Landscape Architecture as Applied to the Wants of the West* was, in some senses, the first urban planning textbook. Cleveland's approach was not so "comprehensive" as that of the professional planners who would come to prominence in the early twentieth century,[72] but his book did go far beyond aesthetics, to consider labor conditions, housing patterns, ecology, economics, sanitation, recreation, transportation, and the troubling rise of a distinctly American consumerist capitalism, which seemed likely to have a massive impact on spatial dynamics. Like Henry George, Cleveland blamed the government—especially the corporation-infatuated Republicans (Horace was a distant relative of Grover Cleveland, the only Democratic president of the late nineteenth century)—for entrusting frontier development to the railroads, which had perfected the "mechanical process of manufacturing and selling towns," and for allowing free rein to "the selfish greed of real estate proprietors," who focused exclusively on procuring "the largest immediate returns from the sale of lots, with the least possible outlay in preparing them for market," and who were clearly "callous to the sufferings they inflict upon the future inhabitants."[73] At the same time, though, Cleveland fully accepted that the United States was going to be an urban nation, so he focused on improving the conditions in which the mass of people were likely to be living, rather than on sending workers back out to the countryside.

From Cleveland's perspective, most of his countrymen already seemed to have accepted a kind of modern passivity: it no longer fell to them to shape the landscape but merely to adapt to the shaping performed by more powerful members of their society. But even if the average American, in the wake of the Civil War, understood the clear advantages of industrialization and commodification, understood the comforts of a more mechanistic mentality, understood the compulsion to keep his eye on his own best chance and abandon old-fashioned commitments to commonality, would he really want to depend on the profit motive and the rectangular plat to supply his children with access to sunlight and clean air and water, not to mention a patch of dirt where his body might one day repose? Wouldn't it behoove settlers on the middle border to elect local officials who might take an interest in countering the power that had already been ceded to the land dealers? Was it truly liberating to be so dependent on the elaborate supply chains that provided consumer goods, many of which were quickly coming to be seen as "necessities"? Yes, the railroads stitched together a broken nation, offered the comforts of rationalization, salved the wounds of war with carloads of cigarettes, shirts, nails, mechanical reapers, artificial limbs. But, Cleveland asked, citing George Perkins Marsh and echoing all the other environmental critics of the 1860s, wasn't it significant that track construction involved an "enormous draft . . . upon the natural supplies of timber," that many parts of the arid west were already "utterly destitute" of trees, that the balm of consumerism was just widening the gap between people and the natural resources on which they relied?[74]

If you want to understand the impact of the railroad on urban (and moral) development in the west, Cleveland proposed, just "take the common case of a town on a river bank . . . , intersected by one or more ravines." Where Henry George emphasized the broad injustice of land monopolization, Cleveland emphasized the problem of design. The classic town grid, imposed on even the most jagged topography, ringingly echoed the straight lines of the train tracks; the right angles suggested square dealing; the reassuring regularity confirmed that human ingenuity could conquer any of the inconvenient, chasmal challenges that nature might pose. Unfortunately, "the invariable custom . . . is to place the roads at such a distance from the ravine as to admit one tier of lots, the houses on which, fronting on the street, will have their back yards running to the bottom or across the ravine, the object being simply that the proprietors may get paid for the land comprised in the ravine, which is unavailable for any useful purpose." Instead of becoming a public commons, then, a cherished space between two rows of houses whose fronts looked out onto its "fine growth of forest trees," the ravine would inevitably get turned into a badly eroded dump, "the dirt hole in which every family deposits its accumulating store of old barrels, boxes and battered tinware."[75]

If it had been up to Cleveland, as he explained in an 1871 letter to Olmsted, describing the extension of a rail line through Nebraska, he would always have started with "the selection and arrangement of nursery sites, which in every instance would be the nucleus of a town."[76] Plant the trees first—not only at the town's center, but in an ever-widening spiral—and then gradually fold in the roads and buildings and people. The keys were balance, fairness, and integration: in the newer settlements of the west, all the green spaces ought to be arranged so that "the inhabitants of every part of the city would find in these small parks and boulevards attractive pleasure grounds immediately accessible to their homes, to which they could resort when the toils of the day were over." Indeed, "the elements of beauty should be everywhere present, pervading all portions of the city as an essential ingredient, instead of being confined to a point which is set apart expressly for the purpose."[77]

The older, larger cities, meanwhile, would have to be reengineered to whatever extent was possible, and it was crucial that they not simply follow the faddish Central Park model: "every city has a character of its own, resulting from the nature of its situation, and the topography of its surroundings, as well as from its history and growth," and in the creation of any new "public grounds," Cleveland thought, "the aim should always be, if possible, to give them a character of individuality which shall harmonize with that of the city itself."[78] In almost all cities, though, he believed that a system of several smaller green spaces linked by modest "parkways" would be preferable to an investment in any single, more sizable park, no matter how grandiose or alluring.[79] In the case of Chicago, Cleveland's new home, the city fathers desperately wanted a couple of new, gigantic, flagship parks, but acknowledged that they would have to be "very distant from the thickly peopled districts of the city, because land in those districts is too valuable to be secured in sufficient quantities for such a purpose." Cleveland condemned their proposal, because he figured that such places would serve only the upper classes, who probably took frequent trips to the country anyway, and who would ultimately want to snatch up the surrounding land.[80]

As Cleveland explained to his readers, Chicago deserved a park system more along the lines of his former partner's new design for Boston: Copeland's *Essay and Plan for the Improvement of the City of Boston* explicitly catered to underprivileged workers, "providing for those classes who are least able to provide for themselves, the refreshment of pleasure gardens within easy access of their homes." Yet, since Chicago was in fact much newer than Boston, and it benefited from a layout that was less cramped and confined, Cleveland thought the most important intervention he could make, on the shore of Lake Michigan, might consist in a grand boulevard stretching up to fourteen miles, with thickly planted borders and islands—a greenway that would bring every element of rural culture into the midst of the city, allowing a Chicagoan to spend all day walking through town without ever feeling overwhelmed by the "din and turmoil of the streets."[81] "First," he wrote to Olmsted, a part of it would be "used as a nursery, in which the whole system of arboriculture could be displayed and yet managed in a way as to make the grounds ornamental and interesting; then a portion devoted to Agricultural experiments of all possible descriptions and the testing of all kinds of agricultural products; then fish ponds in which could be shown the whole process of fish culture. . . . Throughout the whole length, the plantations would constitute an arboretum, and on an area of such extent the different varieties of trees instead of being confined to specimens, could be planted in forests, and so arranged as to secure tasteful effects while exhibiting their natural habits."[82]

Cleveland's emphasis on the practical demonstration of arboriculture, agriculture, and aquaculture, as well as his nod to forest ecology, suggest an awareness of just how much the United States had changed in recent years, as more Americans simultaneously broke their connections with the land and started to realize the costs of that untethering. Changed circumstances demanded new, adaptive strategies: habitat mattered. But the valorization of adaptation per se, in the realm of landscape design—as Cleveland well knew—dated back to Mount Auburn Cemetery.

Some of Cleveland's specific approaches seemed newer than others, of course. One could point out, for instance, that his characterization of park systems and boulevards as serving public health was based, in part, on the need to adjust to the explosive urban growth of the immediate postbellum period, to a kind of crowding that had not been imagined back in 1831. The founders of Mount Auburn had not been concerned with what Cleveland referred to in 1873 as "the nervous debility which so generally prevails" in urban areas, especially among women, who lived a predominantly "indoor life," and were therefore deprived of the "health giving power" of sunlight. From Cleveland's perspective, this state of affairs could be traced not just to the cultural shift that often confined women to the private sphere but also to the spatial shift that forced houses closer together on a grid that had been arranged according to the cardinal directions: "every house on the south side of a street running east and west must have its front rooms, which are generally its living rooms, entirely secluded from the sun during the Winter, and for most of the day during the Summer."[83] (Alas, that is a perfect description of my house in Ithaca.)

Indeed, a general embrace of new sanitation regimes marked the early 1870s,[84] owing not just to urbanization rates but also to the prominence and success of Olmsted's Sanitary Commission during the Civil War, and to the terrible cholera epidemic of 1866–7, and to the writings of people like Cleveland's fellow Chicagoan John Rauch, the city's Sanitation Superintendent, who in 1869 published *Public Parks: Their Effects upon the Moral, Physical and Sanitary Condition of the Inhabitants of Large Cities.* Yet while Rauch's argument, like that of his 1866 treatise, *Intramural Interments in Populous Cities, and Their Influence upon Health and Epidemics,* drew deeply on the experience of "the late war of rebellion"—"ventilation and removal of effluvia" seemed in many cases more important than "the most approved disinfectants" in combating the spread of disease among "the wounded affected with erysipelas, sloughing stumps, or hospital gangrene"—it nevertheless circled back to the same basic point that the cemeterians had made four decades before in Boston: the human body, both alive and dead, emits various forms of waste that can compromise the health of other bodies, and is therefore best adapted to rural conditions, where trees, plants, soil, water, and air serve as filters.[85] By the late 1870s, the diffusion and acceptance of the germ theory of disease would force a full rethinking of landscape-related sanitation measures, but when Cleveland published *Landscape Architecture as Applied to the Wants of the West,* he was insisting, in a classically Arcadian way, that public health would be best served by an acknowledgment of humanity's interpenetration with nature.

Moreover, just like the founders of Mount Auburn, Cleveland asserted that all landscape design, whether you're talking about a kitchen garden or an entire city, should be thoughtfully "adapted to the natural shape of the ground."[86] The word "adapt," in this specific sense, implying not a Darwinian fatalism but an active responsibility, is among the most common in Cleveland's book, since it lies at the heart of his critique of the grid. Some earth-moving would always be necessary, but the point was to be open and sensitive to certain cues, and to bear in mind long-term stability and aesthetics. Again, Cleveland suggested, consider "the river towns of the West": you will immediately "recall innumerable instances of enormously expensive works in cutting down hillsides and building up embankments . . . , while all the naturally beautiful or picturesque features of the place have been destroyed or rendered hideous in the effort to make them conform to a rectangular system, as if the human intellect were as powerless to adapt itself to changing circumstances as the instinct of insects, whose cells are constructed on an unvarying pattern."[87] Like the railroad itself, the leading cultural symbol of mechanization, American towns simply cut through space, directly, automatically, imposing the rigid will of the land dealers on the chaotic land, squeezing it dry in the name of urgent profit and immediate conquest and the corralling power of an orthogonal orderliness. "No regard is paid to the topography of the ground," Cleveland noted; "no reference is had to future interests or necessities of business or pleasure. . . . Even the certainty that where there is life there must also be death, is never recognized by such previous provision of a properly arranged place of burial as would seem simply consistent with a decent sense of propriety."[88] Town planning in the west had gone awry because the rural cemetery movement had ultimately failed: in the aftermath of the Civil War, the unwillingness of Americans to adapt to nature's contours ran rigidly parallel to their unwillingness to confront mortality.

---

# 6

# THREE MEN OF THE MIDDLE BORDER
# (PART TWO): AMERICAN HOMELESSNESS

They cut us off from our game. They ordered us to farm, and this without knowing the character of our reservation. The soil of this country is very hard and dry and the climate severe. . . . For the most part the crops burn up under the fierce sun and the still more savage wind. In winter it is a terrible place to live unless one is sheltered by the cottonwood and willow groves on the river. It was given us originally because they thought it useless to the plowmen. . . . We all saw that as the years went on and the old joys slipped away no new ones came to take their places. . . . We have given our freedom, our world, our traditions, for a dark cabin, cruel boots, the settler's contempt, and the soldier's diseases. . . . If we cannot persist as Sioux, why persist at all? There are enough white beggars in the world, why add ourselves to the army of the poor?
—Hamlin Garland, "The Silent Eaters" (composed 1901)

I knew that I had started to confront mortality in my college years—when Ian died, and then my grandparents, and Aunt Bitsy, and Auntie Grace. But it felt different when I started to think about the imminent death of my parents—which happened right after I had submitted my graduate school applications, in January 1998, when my mother called me in California to tell me she had just been diagnosed with breast cancer. A few weeks later, my father crumpled at the dinner table: his heart had stopped. Both of them survived, thanks to a couple of surgeries, and, in my mother's case, radiation treatment. It could have been much worse. This obvious dip in their physical health, though—my father was seventy-three and my mother sixty-eight at the time—was enough to shake up a number of my assumptions. I was suddenly shoved from the casual contemplation of expansive potentialities to a sharp awareness of strict limits. By the end of April, I had decided to move back to New England—I did get into Yale, as it turned out—and Christine and I had gotten engaged.

At the beginning of the previous October, as I was getting my applications together and starting to compose the necessary essays and compile the necessary writing samples, I flew home to observe Yom Kippur with my parents, and had another strange, memorable conversation with my father. I'd wanted to consult him about academia, discuss my options, get his advice, so I'd sent him some of my recent pieces of writing, including my sarcastic letter to the editor. He didn't appreciate the humor; he didn't register the painfulness of the alienation I felt in San Jose. While he was clearly pleased that I wanted to follow his own chosen path and become a humanities professor, he seemed concerned that I might stumble in the application process, that I might come across as too certain of my own beliefs, as pretentious, even arrogant or snide, and certainly, as he put it, "prolix." A decade and a half later, that word makes me smile: here I am, drafting yet another chapter that will probably come out about 50 percent longer than I expected. At the time, though, my father's judgment was devastating. He found it especially interesting, he said, to consider the contrast between my self-indulgent wordiness and my older sister's terse precision. How did we wind up with such different writing styles? he wondered. I will never know what he really meant, what he was driving at, but it felt as though he were accusing me of betraying the family's commitment to modesty and moderation. Did I really want to be so accusatory in my environmental writings? Did I really want to be a polemicist? Well, I told him, I want to be politically engaged; I want to question authority and work for change and justice; I am not content merely to accept the way things are and withhold criticism. I was probably terrified that he might be right about me, and I'm sure I yearned for his approval, but my immediate reaction was to embrace distance: yes, I would enter the academy, but in my own field, with my own style, far from my home town and the influence of my parents. Maybe I could never adjust to San Jose, but Berkeley was different—radical, even—and you could walk directly from campus into the hills of a park.

Throughout that fall, Christine and I talked about how pleasant it would be to move to the northeast side of the Bay, and the back-up plan involved the upper midwest: I raved about my time in Minnesota and claimed that the whole region was full of down-to-earth intellectuals and accessible public greenways. My old college advisor, Lou, assured me that I was hitting just the right notes in the draft of my application essay. I never felt like dismissing my father's opinion, but clearly I needed a new sense of home, a new kind of grounding.

The cancer diagnosis, resulting from a routine annual mammogram, spurred a literal reorientation: it immediately pointed me back east. In retrospect, it would be easy to say that I decided right then that I would go to Yale if I got in. After all, time seemed short. I felt I should be close to the people I loved, the people to whom I owed my life, while I still could. Again, though, the relevant documents serve as something of a corrective: my journal entries from that time, as sparse and inadequate as they might be, reinscribe the complexity of emotion and family dynamics, remind me of the fallibility of memory. I did want to race home, did want to take up the challenge I had been anticipating, in a sense, ever since Ian got sick. I wanted to support my parents fully, unwaveringly, in the most trying time of their lives since Benjamin's death. Yet I also felt the need to maintain some separation, to keep striking out in different directions, to let them know I had my own life now and my own way of handling trials.

I was surprised, the day after the phone call from my mother, to find myself bound for San Jose's main library. (The library—embodiment of indoor public space—modern town commons.) I had already taken a long walk and had a long bout of crying, and now, I guess, my instincts were telling me to go back to reading, to dwell with someone else's thoughts about the world. I checked out two very thick books: a guide to breast cancer treatment by Dr. Susan Love, and a volume of Montaigne's complete essays. In my mother's hour of illness, I was trying to become reconciled with my father. I still wasn't sure about his stoicism, his seeming tendency to offer intellectual pursuits as an answer to emotional distress; I still thought that if I had spoken at Grandma's funeral, my eulogy would have been less about accepting death and more about Grandma. Yet, in the intervening years, having shared books with grieving friends, I had rediscovered the emotional charge of reading, and now I was desperate for that potential shock of connection, recognition, empathy. Somehow I knew I would find it in Montaigne, knew that his wisdom would provide a resonant solace, knew how much I ultimately had in common with my father.

The sense of kinship came almost immediately, when I turned to the opening essay of Book 2, "On the Inconsistency of Our Actions" (though I also found it in many others, like "Of Sadness," and "Of the Power of the Imagination," and "Of the Uncertainty of Our Judgment," and "Of the Vanity of Words," and "Of the Resemblance of Children to Fathers"): "All contradictions may be found in me by some twist and in some fashion. Bashful, insolent; chaste, lascivious; talkative, taciturn; tough, delicate; clever, stupid; surly, affable; lying, truthful; learned, ignorant; liberal, miserly, and prodigal: all this I see in myself to some extent according to how I turn; and whoever studies himself really attentively finds in himself, yes, even in his judgment, this gyration and discord. I have nothing to say about myself absolutely, simply, and solidly, without confusion and without mixture, or in one word."[1] I wanted to go home and show my caring for my parents, but I also wanted to stay in California, survive some earthquakes, overturn assumptions. "Gyration and discord"—the widening gyre—the winding pathways of prose—the pleasure and discomfort of losing one's way—the humbling confusion, preferable, at least, to the presumption of certainty: how did this Renaissance nobleman worm his way into my consciousness, my family, the postmodern age?

Montaigne, as I well knew, has had this effect on many readers over the centuries.[2] I had actually taken a course on sixteenth-century France in my first year of college, at the suggestion of my father, who knew the professor. At age eighteen, I found that I enjoyed Montaigne, though perhaps he did not stir my passions; at twenty-eight, I was comforted by him, though perhaps he did not fulfill my desire for radicalism; but by thirty-eight (a couple of years ago), I relied on him, consistently, for intensification and release, for companionship and solitude, for a flooding illumination and the deliciousness of obfuscation—for his ability to "live according to nature" while simultaneously acknowledging that "Nature . . . has utterly unknown ways of her own."[3] Montaigne was thirty-eight when he retired (temporarily) from public life and began to write his essays; perhaps it is easier in middle age to accept that light becomes more meaningful when you know darkness, that distance is necessary to an appreciation of closeness.[4]

I still sometimes bristle when Montaigne reminds us of his studied rejection of political engagement: "I doubt if I can decently admit at what little cost to the repose and tranquility of my life I have passed more than half of it amid the ruin of my country."[5] In words like those, I hear my father's emphasis on acceptance: people will always kill each other over religion; the powerful will always exploit the weak; stay calm; use reason to check your emotion. Yet don't we need our emotions in the struggle for justice and social change? Aren't the exploiters counting precisely on our fatalism, our assumption that each of us is too insignificant to stand up to societal forces? I suppose I'm expressing my own guilt: as the twenty-first-century global economy careens toward collapse in a warming world with shrinking resources, as political leaders continue to send soldiers out to sow and reap death, I am not marching the streets in protest, but entrenched in what Montaigne would call my "arrière-boutique," my back office—reading Montaigne.[6] It helps me to remember that Montaigne himself did keep a foot in the public sphere, did work actively to foster tolerance between Catholics and Protestants at a time of religious massacres, did speak out regularly against cruelty and abuses of power. He even defended nature: "there is a certain respect, and a general duty of humanity, that attaches us not only to animals, who have life and feeling, but even to trees and plants. We owe justice to men, and mercy and kindness to other creatures that may be capable of receiving it. There is some relationship between them and us, and some mutual obligation." His reposeful posturing, then, may have indicated not complacency but a realistic assessment of just how much external, political agitation he could absorb before becoming overwhelmed and losing any hope of helping anyone. Retreating to one's study for part of a day, or part of a year, or for a large chunk of one's life, may be the best way to enlarge one's sympathies and cultivate one's resilience in the face of constant tumult, the eternal assault on our sense and sensibility.[7] In part, Montaigne's significance may lie in his determination to retain a focus on the ordinary and the internal, no matter what— the implication being that less alienated people would probably do less damage to each other and the world: "the corruption of the age is produced by the individual contribution of each one of us." The sense of "mutual obligation," Montaigne seems to argue, often derives from the kind of close examination of one's everyday thoughts and actions that leads to an acute awareness of one's contradictions, and instability, and fallibility, and limitations, all of which suggest the appropriateness of giving everyone else the benefit of the doubt, suspending judgment, treading lightly. Montaigne's brand of self-analysis breeds not narcissism but solidarity.

Reading Montaigne in 1998, I came to understand much better how my father could have interpreted my political engagement as arrogance. I had chosen to live in San Jose; what right did I have to scorn everyone around me? Or—maybe I was just humbled by my father's heart problems, and my mother's breast cancer. Maybe I was just frightened. It used to be that my parents called me every couple of weeks to see how I was getting along; now I called them, every few days, to check on their health. *Health?* Montaigne sometimes reminds me of Thoreau: "Our structure . . . is full of imperfection," he insists. And "our being is cemented with sickly qualities." What I am sure of is that Montaigne helped me develop a style of unflinching self-criticism that had much less in it of self-disgust. I understood the objection to my letter to the editor, but I did not regret having written it: it captured how I felt, who I was at the time, and if I became someone different immediately afterward, that was merely to be expected. "I cannot keep my subject still," says Montaigne, explaining his attempt to catch himself in a viewfinder. "It goes along befuddled and staggering, with a natural drunkenness. . . . If my mind could gain a firm footing, I would not make essays, I would make decisions; but it is always in apprenticeship and on trial." My decisions of that spring, I think, were firm enough: it felt right to be with Christine and to take the back trail to New England. What remained disorienting about my reorientation, as it were, was the question of how to adjust my relationship to my parents, given my new consciousness of the limitedness of their lives. If I could accept my father's criticism, at least partially, could I also accept his refusal to talk openly about his past? And what to make of my parents' absolute insistence that they did not want to be a factor in my decision about where to go to graduate school, that they would not allow me, under any circumstances, to interrupt my studies in order to take care of them? If they both "recovered"—whatever that might mean—would Christine and I resent having moved to starchy New Haven rather than sunny, exhilarating, unpredictable Berkeley?

It was an incredible privilege to be granted the choice, but, even with an unlimited number of pages, I could never fully explain why I wound up at Yale. Sometimes I try, when current or former students of mine are making up their own minds about where to go to graduate school: I appreciated the intellectual flexibility and openness of the American Studies program; I found the people I met there to be friendly, engaged, and happy; it was close enough to Boston to feel like home, but far enough away that Christine and I could establish some sense of independence. But imagine all the factors I never mention. For one thing, it wasn't only my decision: Christine and I chose to move together, just as we had chosen to get married together; for her, it was not a homecoming but an adventure. As for me, maybe I needed to perform some sort of filial duty. Maybe I was hoping that both of my parents would open up to me in their old age, make themselves vulnerable, share their emotional histories, divulge their secrets. Maybe I missed the deep green of the temperate broadleaf and mixed forest; maybe I missed the glacial ponds, the stone walls, the old farms, the giant boulders. Maybe I was planning to hike up to the top of East Rock every day, and form a writing group with my friends in New York City, and periodically take the train to Boston to catch a Red Sox game and observe holidays and sabbaths with the only spiritual leader I have ever felt connected to (outside of my family), Al Axelrad, author of *Meditations of a Maverick Rabbi*. Maybe I thought that my parents might teach me how to die. Acceptance has its place: "nor do I complain," Montaigne says, in his final essay, "of the natural decay that has hold of me . . . any more than I regret that my term of life is not as long and sound as that of an oak."[8]

———————————

H. W. S. Cleveland never moved back to New England. Over the final thirty years of his life, he did seek commissions in the east, working on Swan Point Cemetery and Roger Williams Park in Providence, Rhode Island, and even designing a cemetery in his home town of Lancaster, Massachusetts, in 1874, the year after he published

*Landscape Architecture as Applied to the Wants of the West.* He was clearly homesick again, as he had been in New Jersey in the 1850s. In 1881, when he heard about a "scheme" being proposed to set aside four thousand acres of green space, "to be preserved *in its natural condition,*" just north of Boston, about the same distance from the Common as Mount Auburn Cemetery, he immediately let it be known that, if he could be sure of steady employment, he would be delighted to relocate his family: "I should be very glad to be connected with the work, for several reasons. In the first place, the development of natural beauty by simply putting it in the best light, is a specialty for which I have more confidence in my own powers than anything else, and the whole of that region is so familiar to me that it would be a labor of love with me to take charge of it and enter (with reverent hands) upon the work of opening up its charms." Moreover, it would "enable me to pass the evening of my life among the best friends who are yet left to me." But ultimately that job fell through, and Cleveland felt compelled to remain a stranger on the middle border, upholding "the value of the work I am doing in the new cities of the West."[9]

More than anything else, Cleveland was a cemeterian—perhaps because Sleepy Hollow had been such a success and quickly became connected, in the public mind, with so many eminent Massachusetts literati;[10] perhaps because his character was sometimes dominated by soulfulness; or perhaps simply because he saw the rural cemetery movement as providing the lifeblood of the Arcadian tradition in America. It took a profound effort to hawk his services in Chicago, to lobby for their importance: "the trial of my life here, is the necessity of flaunting my own merits in the eyes of the world as a means of getting business. . . . I have been doing it with all my might, but am all the while trampling upon my own feelings."[11] The work came more easily, though, when it involved cemeteries. In 1871, when Cleveland published a brochure called *A Few Hints on Landscape Gardening in the West*, he devoted an entire section to the topic, reminding American pioneers that planning for the location of a cemetery was just as urgent as carving out space for a school or church: "wherever a community is established, it should be considered a primary duty to provide for the interment of the dead . . . , and with so many beautiful examples as our country affords, it cannot be other than a stigma upon the character of any place to find that so sacred a duty has been neglected."[12]

Ten years later, Cleveland wrote to his friend William Watts Folwell, the first president of the University of Minnesota, to note that he had "a pamphlet ready to publish on 'rural cemeteries,' which I think will serve a good purpose as an advertisement," and in which Cleveland again emphasized the dangers of not having burial grounds laid out by trained landscape architects, who knew how to read the land: "One of the most beautiful cemeteries in the country—in the neighborhood of an Eastern city—owes its origin to the fact that a citizen who was about to commit to the earth the body of a beloved and beautiful child, was horror-struck at discovering several inches of water in the grave which had been prepared for its reception. He at once forbade the interment, and rested not till he had induced others to join him" in hiring professionals to help with the choosing and laying out of a new site.[13] Throughout Cleveland's western career, as he bounced between Illinois and Minnesota, in particular, he would often tell his correspondents that he was "occupied with cemetery work."[14] And, ultimately, he contributed full or partial cemetery designs to a number of just-founded towns in the midwest, ranging from Cedar Rapids, Iowa, to Junction City, Kansas, as well as to the region's metropolises, Chicago, Minneapolis, and St. Paul.

What is even more remarkable about Cleveland's work, though, is the way in which he transferred his cemeterian's sensibility to his broader urban design projects—something I did not fully appreciate until I spent a few mornings exploring the greenways of the Minneapolis–St. Paul park system, perhaps his most remarkable and enduring achievement. Certainly, that sensibility is clear from the documentary record—for instance, in a letter he wrote to President Folwell about his plans for expanding the campus of the University of Minnesota, in which he highlighted "repose" as being the foremost quality among all the "essential elements in the composition of such an institution as I know you are aiming to create."[15] (Repose: what better word for the atmosphere of an ideal college campus, where scholars and students might gain access to quiet seclusion as well as lively public exchange, both of which are necessary to foster the posing and re-posing of crucial questions?) There are spatial patterns, though, that don't show up so clearly in the archives—hints, subtle slopes and shapes, curved pathways highlighting the contours of nature and culture, suggesting the intermingling of death and life. Fortunately, in this case, the relevant archive (at the Minnesota Historical Society) usually didn't open until noon, which left lots of time for field trips.

Cleveland's vision is impossible to capture, for it was meant to be incorporated into countless branching boulevards and parkways: it flows through the Twin Cities like sap. But, one morning, in October of 2010, as I walked along the baseball field at Farview Park, in northern Minneapolis, I felt the sticky shock of recognition: staring at the park's central hill, with its gentle undulations, its benches, its faint tracks, and knowing that it represented what was left of Cleveland's vision of this particular green space, I could almost hear an old-fashioned slide projector clicking in my mind, as it superimposed, first, the image of Oakland Cemetery, in St. Paul, also designed by

Cleveland; and then the image of St. Paul's Indian Mounds Park, alongside the Mississippi River; and then the image of Mount Auburn—not the whole cemetery, but the actual topographical feature from which the cemetery takes its name, the rounded fold of earth that rises up to offer views of the still-mixed urban-rural landscape stretching for miles around, west along the Charles River, east to Boston Harbor, north to Fresh Pond, South to Jamaica Pond and the rest of Olmsted's Emerald Necklace. We are drawn to these rises—we see them from far off—we forget whether they were created by natural forces or human industry—we wonder at them—we gather at them—they become centers. Climbing their heights, we often feel surprisingly grounded, provided with a means of understanding our surroundings. Their roundness connects us to the sun and moon and the turning of the round earth, to cycles, to loss and renewal, to pregnancy and nourishment and dependence and gratitude. They often carry the exhilarating and devastating weight of history. (Figures 46 and 47.)

Figure 46. Farview Park, designed by H. W. S. Cleveland, Minneapolis, 2010.

Figure 47. Indian Mounds Park, St. Paul, MN, c. 1900, photograph.

In what other major metropolitan area can you visit an Indian Mounds Park? Many American cities were built on sites favored by Native Americans, where they left numerous traces, but almost all such traces have long been erased (the nineteenth-century development of St. Louis, home to many ancient burial sites, was particularly egregious).[16] The Mounds in St. Paul are about two miles from the Capitol. You just walk along the Mississippi, on the edge of its ravine, and then cross the railroad tracks, and there you are, reading a plaque, facing the past: "Between 1500 and 2000 years ago, Indian people chose this high bluff above the Mississippi River as the resting place for their dead. The impressive burial mounds built over a period of many years remind us of the diverse peoples and cultures that flourished here long before the first European explorers arrived in the late 1600's." If I were rewriting the caption, I would bring the story up to the 1800s and mention the settlers and soldiers, the invaders, who ultimately displaced most of the local Indians. But, in a sense, H. W. S. Cleveland tried to inscribe that story in the city's landscape.

Commemoration is inevitably imprecise: time changes everything. One could certainly make the argument that Cleveland's echoing of the Indian Mounds might have distracted his fellow citizens from their status as invaders, by encouraging them to focus on the far distant past, when the Mound Builders roamed the continent. Yet that seems unlikely, given the notoriousness of the Indian fighting that had occurred around St. Paul in the 1860s, not to mention Custer's humiliation at the Battle of the Greasy Grass in 1876, the nation's centennial year. Indians were very much alive in the thoughts of late nineteenth-century dwellers along the middle border. The more serious question might be whether or not Minnesotans even registered the echoing: did they see Indian Mounds in Cleveland's parks and cemeteries?

I don't know: the sources are scarce, and it's always hard to get at perceptions, anyway.[17] I can't even tell you, for sure, what I saw on that fall day at Farview Park. Maybe I see Indian Mounds everywhere I look. (Figure 48.)

Figure 48. Gold Medal Park, adjacent to the new Guthrie Theater, on the shore of the Mississippi River, Minneapolis, MN, 2010.

All I knew, when I photographed Gold Medal Park, was that it looked familiar, and that I could see it only through the lenses of my own identity and experience—through my sense of kinship with Cleveland—through my self-awareness and research as a historian—through the nostalgic excitement I felt at being back in Minnesota twenty years after my internship at Wolf Ridge Environmental Learning Center. I think I can make a solid historical case for focusing on H. W. S. Cleveland's shaping of the unique park system of the Twin Cities, rather than on, say, Olmsted's designs in Buffalo, or the work of any other of the prominent landscape architects from this period, such as George Waring, Jr., or Frank Scott, or Nathaniel Southgate Shaler, or Jacob Weidenmann. (Until the early twentieth century, Olmsted was the only city planner besides Cleveland who consistently attempted to construct *systems* of parks in urban areas, and the scope of Olmsted's work had to be smaller because he was dealing with the more fully developed cities of the east.)[18] But I also know that I wound up writing about Cleveland, in part, because I am an ex–New Englander with emotional ties to the green spaces of Minnesota. In other words, it was through both rational analysis and coincidence that I stumbled onto the truth that the landscape architects who built Gold Medal Park in 2007 were in fact "inspired by the Dakota Indians' burial mounds found throughout Minnesota," and did in fact want to create a "public place" that would recall "the intentions of the city founders and planners—those who had the foresight to set aside open space for the Chain of Lakes and the Grand Rounds—and as a result, created some of the most revered and enjoyable places in Minneapolis and the metropolitan region."[19]

I can tell you, based on the archival record, that Cleveland started lecturing in the Twin Cities as early as 1872, invited first by the Common Council of St. Paul, to offer tips about how the metropolitan area ought to develop, about which areas ought to be preserved at any cost, about how a complete park system might be constructed through "adaptation to the natural topography."[20] The process moved slowly, but Cleveland stayed in close touch with many municipal leaders, constantly contributing ideas and opinions (and some designs for St. Paul's Oakland Cemetery), and in the early spring of 1883 he received an official appointment to supervise the work of Minneapolis's newly created Committee on Parks and Public Grounds (which soon became the Board of Park Commissioners). Five years later, he also became the official landscape architect of St. Paul.[21] He was able to get involved, in other words, while the cities were still young: "When I was first invited to devise a system of parks for [Minneapolis], the fact that such a scheme had been attempted at so early a stage of the city's growth was so unprecedented in my own experience that it inspired a feeling of profound respect."[22] No other American cities, to my knowledge, had the benefit of oversight by a landscape architect so near the beginning of their development.[23] Predictably, Cleveland made use of his opportunity to implement the theories he had proposed in *Landscape Architecture as Applied to the Wants of the West*, integrating public green space as thoroughly as possible into the cityscape through a series of parks, gardens, cemeteries, and boulevards, connected to each other wherever possible, accessible to all classes of citizens, paying appropriate tribute to the most prominent elements of the local environment, and affording everyone some "relief and refreshment" from the "monotony" of the grid and the "din and turmoil" of industrial life, "the sense of jarring friction, which grinds the nerves and constitutes the wear and tear of body and soul."[24] Moreover, though the bulk of his work was in Minneapolis, and though the two cities collaborated much less than he desired (he thought they should merge, for the sake of better-coordinated planning), Cleveland took special care to insist that St. Paul protect the bluffs on its side of the river, just as Minneapolis was planning to do on its side—partly for the sake of parallelism, but mostly for the sake of "the promontory on which are situated the picturesque mounds, which should be religiously preserved for their historical interest."[25] Fortunately, St. Paul's Board of Park Commissioners took his advice: that promontory was one of the first pieces of land the board secured.

Today, if you want to explore Minneapolis's debt to Cleveland, you can start down at Fort Snelling State Park,[26] at the sacred confluence of the Minnesota and Mississippi Rivers, and then spend an entire day making your way along a grand greenway—past the grounds of the Soldiers' Home intended for Civil War veterans (and designed by Cleveland in 1888), through Hidden Falls Regional Park, and then on to Minnehaha Falls (the city's gem, Cleveland thought)[27]—and then along Minnehaha Parkway to Lake Hiawatha and Lake Nokomis, to Pearl Park and Diamond Lake, to Lynnhurst Park and Lake Harriet and Lyndale Park and Lakewood Cemetery and Lake Calhoun and Lake of the Isles and Kenwood Park and Cedar Lake and Theodore Wirth Park.[28]

The scope is astounding, even leaving aside Riverside Park and Mississippi Park and Powderhorn Park and many others: Cleveland's system clearly grew *with* the city, resulting in an organic (though not "natural") scattering of green spaces capable of accommodating the population density even of our current century (so Cleveland, in effect, succeeded in "pleading the cause of future generations, who . . . might justly charge me with neglecting their rights if I failed to call attention to matters which so vitally affect them").[29] Just as important, though, is the common culture that developed in Minneapolis: all of these parks are well used, even in the middle of winter, when the lakes become rinks for skaters and hockey players—in large part, I think, because Cleveland's design so carefully emphasized public over private space. In my home town of Newton, Massachusetts, one of the central attractions is called Crystal Lake, but its waters are available to the public only via a tiny slice of shoreline managed by the city parks department; otherwise, you have to own one of the expensive lakefront properties. In Minneapolis, though, by Cleveland's order, houses were permitted only on the far side of the roads that had been built around most of the lakes: the city was careful to "reserve for public use every foot of land between the avenue and the water," making it clear that the entire lake and shoreline were intended as a commons, to be enjoyed freely by anyone visiting the neighborhood.[30]

In its emphasis on public-mindedness, Cleveland's park system clearly harkened back to the Arcadianism of the antebellum period and simultaneously looked ahead to the demands of the future, but it also enacted a critique of the present, of the expansive, rapid-fire, materialistic dynamics of the Gilded Age. Again and again, when he addressed the citizens of the Twin Cities in the 1870s and 80s, he decried the mansions, and "hotels, and places of amusement, and temples of mammon" that had come to dominate the urban landscape back east, and he expressed sympathy for the industrial workers who had traded "the silent influence of field and forest" for "the wear and tear of life in the crowded marts of commerce."[31]

Of course, when Cleveland tried to explain that he didn't want St. Paul or Minneapolis to become "a mere monotonous hive of workshops and operatives' dwellings," he was sometimes understood as an anti-labor elitist—and, especially given the way park construction had proceeded in other cities, workers had reason to be suspicious of landscape architects.[32] Park boards, after all, did not typically draw their membership from the laboring classes, and when they seized private property "for the public good" (as in New York), the condemned habitations were much more likely to belong to the impoverished than the middle classes or the wealthy. Cleveland himself occasionally fell back on financial arguments to sell his greenway schemes, pointing out that parks almost always raised nearby property values and that a good reputation for green spaces (as in Paris) could attract a steady stream of tourist dollars.[33] So, especially early in the process, before he'd had the chance to accomplish much, he faced entrenched opposition from groups like the Knights of Labor, who objected to Minneapolis's very first park bill, in 1883, on the grounds that "the door is left open to rob the working classes of their homes and make driveways for the rich at the expense of the poor." That bill, though, put up to a referendum, passed by a vote of 5,327 to 3,922, and, for the most part, Cleveland and the Board of Park Commissioners enjoyed wider and wider support as time went on.[34]

Cleveland tried to harp on the issue of access, reminding local citizens that if the speculators and real estate dealers were left to their own devices, the greatest "gifts of nature" would become country clubs and private estates (as in England): there had to be as much public land as possible, but also as much public control as possible over the broader cityscape—which meant, really, that the robber barons and captains of industry had to be reined in, "to prevent every infringement of private interest upon public rights." Like Henry George, he criticized tenements not because he scorned their inhabitants but because he felt that their inhabitants deserved a better quality of life. The factory owners who employed these workers had thrown around enough cash, in a culture that was beginning to endorse the accumulation of wealth as the highest good, to get permission for any kind of development they saw fit to propose and pay for. Meanwhile, "little attention is paid to the municipal regulation of many of the daily necessities, on which the health and comfort of the people are largely dependent, but which . . . are so often regarded as matters which must be left to regulate themselves." The most crucial such matter, of course, was the fate of undeveloped land, which, to Cleveland, had an intrinsic value that "no money can purchase," and therefore deserved respect, nurturing, cultivation: "I would have the city itself such a work of art as may be the fitting abode of a race of men and women whose lives are devoted to a nobler end than money-getting, and whose efforts shall be inspired and sustained by the grandeur and beauty of the scenes in which their lives are passed." Aesthetics could be the answer to greed and exploitation—but only if the public claimed for itself the seemingly tyrannical power to check the American tendency toward individualism, absolute liberty, fetishization of "personal rights": "no single member of the community, has the right to do that which is hurtful or offensive to all, and therefore . . . all persons should be prevented from doing so by the exercise of despotic authority." American industrialists had been allowed to bring into the city "manufactures of everything deleterious to health"; they had devastated local landscapes and workers. The only solution was to adopt the French policy: apparently, one of the reasons that Paris maintained its reputation for parks, gardens, and public squares that were the delight of both visitors and residents, was that any citizen had the power to step in if he felt that his access to clean air and green space was being threatened by industry. In Paris, Cleveland asserted, "any machinery or manufactory, however safe, however innocuous, and whatever may have been its cost, may be closed by a simple order of police, if from noise, from smell, or any other cause, it prove offensive or inconvenient to the neighborhood."[35]

The broader point was always about the significance of public culture, and the way in which the concept of a "commonwealth" was under constant siege in the Gilded Age. It was in the postbellum period, after the nation's elected officials had plunged the people who elected them into violent conflict, that many Americans began to lose their faith in the public sphere. Even wealthy capitalists had always supported parks, to some extent (especially on land not deemed fit for profitable development), but now they took pains to paint the common domain as a place of stifling regulation and limitation, while claiming the private realm, governed by the market, as the hub of creative, constructive activity. The laissez-faire ideology of capitalism had started to infect culture and politics: the government's main job was now to get out of the way and allow the supposedly pure American meritocracy to function.[36] "Public space" and the "public sphere" are of course not one and the same, but Cleveland seemed to recognize that clearly demarcated, well cared-for public areas could serve as invitations to participate in the debates that are crucial to any common culture, whereas political apathy went hand in hand with a retreat from the plaza and the schoolyard to the fenced-in estate. Cleveland had come of age at a time when true manhood depended on a sense of self-restraint and sacrifice for the communal good: you used only so much land as you needed and preserved the rest for common pasturing or timber. Now, in his old age, it seemed that "the common good" was defined as the clear opportunity for each private citizen to get as much as he could take (and, in 1886, corporations earned legal status as private individuals, granting them even greater leeway to ignore the public interest in their pursuit of profits).[37]

There was more at stake than physical space, in other words, when cities made decisions about public parks and historical monuments like St. Paul's Indian Mounds: "Already, as I am informed, [the Mounds] have been ruthlessly robbed of the archeological treasures they contained, which should on no account be suffered to remain in private hands, but should either be preserved as one of the possessions of the city, and open to the inspection of all; or be deposited in one of the great collections of similar relics, like that of the Smithsonian Institute at Washington." The holding of Indian bones and artifacts as private property was a way of keeping their meaning static, affirming the rightful conquest of white Americans over the continent's indigenous population: these are mine. In the twenty-first century, we might like to see such relics returned to the appropriate native groups, but Cleveland was at least insisting that they be ever subject to public scrutiny and frank discussion. Museums can also become sites of conquest, of course, through their modes of exhibition— just as airy boulevards can facilitate the deployment of state power against public protests. Ultimately, though, as Cleveland suggested, most museums and boulevards are inherently open spaces, physical embodiments of commonality, standing in stark contrast to the enclosures of private property, which are defined (to a large extent) as places where the owner can do whatever he pleases, without concern for public opinion.[38]

By the mid-1880s, Cleveland, who was still residing in Chicago, had started thinking about the reality that his own bones would eventually have to be buried somewhere, and it seems that both public and private concerns drove him toward a final repose in Minneapolis, though he still daydreamed of New England and often claimed to feel closer to his eastern correspondents than to any local acquaintances. The great solace of the Twin Cities was that his son was there, serving as superintendent of Lakewood Cemetery in Minneapolis, for whose expansion Horace had already contributed some designs. "Ralph writes cheeringly of his work on the Cemetery," Cleveland noted in 1885, and then, the following spring, he and Maryann finally decided to become reunited with their son, for good, for the sake of their granddaughters: "A great object with me in going there is that my little girls may become familiar with Ralph's family, who will be their only relatives when we go,—and it is therefore important to be within easy access of him."[39] After Maryann passed away in 1893 and Horace finished his work in the Twin Cities in 1895, the family wound up moving back to Illinois, so that Ralph could pursue other career opportunities, but all the surviving relatives remained together until Horace finally let go of his life in early December 1900.

Cleveland faced mortality with a strong sense of both his contributions and his limitations. "I have left my mark," he felt, "in the form of parks, cemeteries, and public and private grounds from Nova Scotia to Kansas, and from Minnesota to Virginia. For their merit I have received sufficient commendation, and no one is so conscious of their defects as myself."[40] Remarkably, despite some bouts with depression and self-doubt, he even managed to retain his sense of humor: once, writing to Olmsted at great length, he concluded his epistle by begging "pardon for my garrulity. Walter Scott says somewhere in his journal, 'A man of 80 ought to be allowed to talk long, for in the nature of things he can't have long to talk.'"[41] When Cleveland finally ran out of words, he was buried next to Maryann at Lakewood, in a humble grave, with a small stone, flat in the ground—like Benjamin's, I couldn't help thinking, when I finally found it—like Ian's. It had been covered, completely, by fallen oak leaves. And though the workers at the cemetery office had been happy to look up his plot number for me on their computer, they admitted that they had never heard of him; in fact, despite great pride among local people in the Twin Cities' park system, I couldn't find a single resident who recognized Cleveland's name (admittedly, the sample size was small).[42] There is no plaque, no statue; his grave is not one of the forty-nine stops on Lakewood's self-guided tour; neither his nor Ralph's name comes up in the brochure's explanation of the cemetery's history. Yet there he lies, with his wife, to whom he was devoted—and Ralph is there, too—and I can't help but think that he would have wanted it this way—except, perhaps, for the fact that his two granddaughters, little

Sofia and Julia, are nowhere to be found. I wonder: Did they go west, and grow up with the country, or turn back east, and fulfill their grandfather's longing? (Figure 49.)

Figure 49. Grave of H. W. S. Cleveland, Lakewood Cemetery, Minneapolis, MN, 2010.

The last bit of writing Cleveland published was an article called "The Influence of Parks on the Character of Children," in July 1898, in a Chicago-based journal called *Park and Cemetery* (originally named *The Modern Cemetery* when it was founded in 1891): on the middle border, with its obvious need for landscape design, the Arcadian movement was clearly not dead. "If my words fall upon your ears like a 'voice from the tomb,'" Cleveland wrote, "I can only promise it shall not utter a 'doleful cry,' but rather [an expression] of glad thankfulness." He was near death, but he had lived to see the dawn of a new era of reform, when some urban Americans, at least, acknowledged "the inequality of the advantages of the different classes in the opportunities afforded them." Could the Gilded Age's ideal meritocracy truly persist at a time when some children were being raised in mansions and exclusive suburbs and others were trying to survive in teeming, filthy tenements and factories? Every American child had an equal right to the public culture of "our free schools"; didn't every child also have a right to fresh air, trees, flowers? Consider an innocent boy born "amid the scenes of squalor and vice. . . . Much depends upon the impressions he receives in the years of his childhood, and is it not a peremptory duty devolving upon us to let him see that life has something better to offer him than such misery as is his daily lot?"[43] The smallest park, even an imagined one, invoked in a brief essay by an eighty-three-year-old man, if it provides a whiff of something green and growing, can connect us to the larger world around us—and, in its role as public space, where all kinds of people are free to congregate, where the haves sometimes encounter the have-nots, where invaders sometimes encounter natives, it can also help restore our sense of responsibility to each other.

––––––––––––

Leaving California for New England—going home—turned out to be somewhat more challenging than I had expected, but it still felt right: I still felt lucky that my career path had turned out to be compatible with my sense of familial responsibility. That summer marked some sort of watershed in my relationship to my parents. Maybe the key changes were in them: maybe they had been chastened by illness; maybe they were just happy that I seemed to have settled down and gotten over my interest in earthquake zones. Or maybe I truly did grow up in some way; maybe I had established the necessary distance. In any case, that August, while Christine and I were staying with my parents, waiting to move into our New Haven apartment—which, in fact, was two blocks from East Rock Park—I managed to ask my father about leaving Toronto, and he managed to answer. I still assumed, even after our conversation at the National Zoo, that the break had come as a relief, that it had helped him own his differentness: while his parents and sisters and cousins and aunts and uncles all pursued financial security, he would pursue ideas. But now he told me that his departure had actually caused him a great deal of pain. When he graduated from the University of Toronto and was offered admission to Columbia to pursue his Ph.D. in French literature, he felt he was choosing between his professional development and his family.

Despite the difficulty of my father's confession, I was exhilarated at his new willingness to share his thoughts about his past. My evolving understanding of his inner turmoil stabilized our common ground—from my perspective, at least. I was also ecstatic about living in New Haven, and, by the beginning of September, about my new daily ritual of hiking to the top of East Rock and gazing out at the coastal floodplain, which seemed impossibly green in comparison to the view of Silicon Valley I used to get from San Jose's Alum Rock Park—the view of dusty, sprawling brownfields. Within about three minutes of leaving the apartment—the entire second floor of an airy, south-facing Victorian house, with hardwood floors and plenty of windows—I was on a trail beside the Mill River, enveloped by trees. I could walk downtown, or to campus, in about twenty-three minutes; by bike it was eight minutes. The drive to my parents' house took two hours, and it was an hour and twenty minutes to where my sister lived, in Amherst, with her newborn son and four-year-old twins. I felt relatively connected.

But I also had to start a Ph.D. program, and Christine and I had to plan our wedding. From the moment we left San Jose, in early July, Christine had begun to express reservations about living in the east, and of course I couldn't blame her. She was moving to New Haven with no immediate job prospects, no friends to look up, and no engagement ring (it had been stolen when our car was burglarized at a trailhead, while we were on a week-long backpacking trip, during which Christine came down with a severe case of poison oak). Astoundingly, overall, she remained hopeful and excited, but once we arrived, we had only a week or so to explore and get our bearings before I was suddenly overwhelmed and miserable and desperate for her support. I couldn't handle the workload; I couldn't speak the language; too many of my colleagues seemed aggressive, competitive, pretentious. Both Christine and I probably wanted to move back to California, but neither of us was humble enough to admit it, so we just snarled at each other for a few weeks, or maybe a few months, until we calmed down, adjusted, and figured out that we could hold our wedding in a state park, for a rental fee of fifteen dollars. Christine also found a good position as academic director at an ESL program, and I went from wanting to drop out in December, to feeling like I might have found a niche in January, to deciding that actually I admired most of my professors and fellow students and loved the American Studies Program by June—the month we got married.

What I remember most vividly about our first month in New Haven, though, was the time I spent with my friend Stephen. Back in the late spring or early summer, when we'd told him we were moving to New Haven, he'd immediately said that he was giving up on California, too, and heading home (his house had come out beautifully, and it sold within hours of going on the market, earning him a few hundred thousand dollars). Was there a woman involved? Yes, there was. But he also said that, like me, he missed his family and old friends, and he missed the trees that we'd taken for granted while growing up in one of the greenest suburbs in the country. In fact, he was going to look for a house to fix up right in Newton. He also offered to transport some of our things across the country for us, since he was going to rent a small truck, anyway. Of course, once we had brought a couple of carloads to his storage unit, he told us we'd better be prepared to shell out for a vehicle with a bigger capacity (he was especially annoyed by one of my file cabinets, which I'd packed full of books). Then he pushed his moving date back a few times, which meant we'd be arriving at least a month before him and might have to do without some "necessities" for a while. Still, we appreciated the favor, and were glad we'd have access to his irreverence and nonchalance once we were ensconced in New England. Christine and I had often met up with him at one of the megaplexes between San Jose and Palo Alto to see a movie, and so we wound up saying goodbye in a sprawling parking lot. We had both just hugged him when, almost as an afterthought, he said he wanted to show us something strange, and he held out one of his huge, powerful hands. There was a small hollow at the base of his right thumb, as if a lump of flesh had been removed. He flexed his hand in what I thought was a particularly grotesque way. "My thumb muscle seems to be atrophying," he said, shrugging, smiling. He had already seen a couple of doctors, who had run a few tests; he wasn't worried.

We checked in with him repeatedly over the summer, and eventually he had a diagnosis: it was a rare neurological disorder (a form of peripheral neuropathy) that would probably progress for up to a year and then stop—the same thing, he supposed, that had given our twelfth-grade English teacher, Mr. Harris, a couple of permanently bent, paralyzed fingers on one of his hands. Was it treatable? Possibly. Would he be able to build? He wasn't sure. But he cared more about drawing up the plans than holding the nail gun, anyway, and much architectural design work could already be done on a computer, and he was already getting pretty good at doing things with his left hand. Stephen—like Christine, I suddenly realized—had an amazing talent for remaining unconcerned. Or maybe he was just legitimately relieved, since he'd learned that another possible diagnosis was amyotrophic lateral sclerosis— ALS—Lou Gehrig's disease—which generally killed people within three years of the time they experienced their first symptoms.

We were a little bit annoyed when he bypassed New Haven in early September to drive straight to his parents' house in Newton, but he immediately offered to help me build a couple of bookcases if I could come hang out for a day (and pick up some of the boxes he had unloaded for us in the garage). Bookcases: he had said the magic word. They're surely the hottest commodities on the academic black market—they can make or break relationships, since, if you're not careful, your books can take over any apartment or house—and Stephen was providing me with the chance to custom-make two of them, big ones, which, he assured me, would last forever. Did he realize what a gift this was? I told him I would bring the beer, trying not to sound too giddy on the phone.

It was a perfect late-summer day, with the sun filtering through the trees in a perfect Newton backyard, and I felt grateful for my childhood, and grateful for this break from my endless reading, and grateful for this friend who had made a journey parallel to my own, who knew what it was like out west, who appreciated the splendors of California, who had also decided to come home. Then I saw him walk: it was as if all the weight of his body had become concentrated in his right leg. I was devastated. But he claimed to be fine: he could do everything he needed to do, just a little more slowly.

We drove to the lumberyard, and in the car I asked him about sustainable forestry, about where this wood might have come from. He shot me a look that was both amused and reproving. I understood that I needed to let him do the talking: builders surely got better deals than environmentalists. We eyed the cherry, but came away with some oak, and then spent the rest of the day working, drinking, talking, listening to music. It didn't matter to Stephen that my carpentry skills were about as well developed as my gardening skills; it didn't matter to me that he had a few laughs at my expense and almost shot a nail into the flesh between my thumb and index finger. I was never going to be able to talk to him about the most important things, about my parents' health, or tensions with Christine, or the alienation I felt in my seminars—and I noted that distance occasionally, but it didn't seem to bother either of us. We just had a good time, and I focused on learning from him, shaking my head at his obsessions with pop stars and video games and the Internet. By the time twilight finally arrived, and we finished our work, I was deeply in love with those two sturdy bookcases; I figured they would be fixtures in my household for the rest of my life. Stephen said he would drive them down to New Haven the following weekend in his pickup truck, along with the leftover boxes I hadn't been able to fit in my car.

In New Haven, after we did the unloading, I reminded Stephen of when he had told me about the trails in the Stanford foothills, and asked him, looking down at his leg, if he'd be game to hike up East Rock. He said he couldn't stay long—he was on his way to D.C. to visit our old friend Josh, whose father had been killed in the car accident back in 1992—but yes, he'd love to, and then maybe we could get some pizza or subs, and he'd get back on the road. It was a long, slow walk, and I annoyed him a couple of times by asking if he was OK. My memories of that humid afternoon are strangely vivid: the poison ivy in the cracks of the Giant Steps; the weighted, drooping branches overhanging the trail; his denim shorts and brown work boots; the drops of sweat he wiped from his red forehead. But we joked and laughed almost the whole time, and I felt the lightness of his spirit in those heavy bookcases.

All that autumn, as he got closer and closer to the woman he would eventually marry and have a child with, he visited doctors at Boston's most famous hospitals, and underwent test after test. In December, he was diagnosed with ALS. He had come home to die.[44]

---

Henry George did not move back home to the east coast until the late summer of 1880, a few months after he published *Progress and Poverty*. He was middle-aged, about to turn forty-one, and ill with "biliousness," "bladder trouble," and "nervous strain."[45] It seems he did not quite know what to do with himself. How to proceed after one completes a magnum opus? In letters to friends, George wrote of "the intellectual poverty" of the west coast and noted that one of "the many projects which I have been vaguely meditating is that of lecturing through the East." But so far there was no indication that anyone would be interested in listening, as his book had sent barely a ripple through the ocean of the public sphere. One supporter, certain that "San Francisco did not appreciate him," because the city was "ruled by strenuous men too busy with mines and wheat and empire building to listen to prophecy," sent George some traveling money and told him of a promising opportunity to write for the *New York Herald*. That was the immediate spur that put him on an eastbound train, yet, with his father entering his ninth decade and his mother her eighth, he may simply have wanted to renew family ties and show his parents that he had made something of himself. "I am grateful," he had written to his father, enclosing one of the very first copies of *Progress and Poverty*, "that I have been enabled to live to write it, and that you have been enabled to live to see it. It represents a great deal of work and a good deal of sacrifice, but now it is done. It will not be recognized at first—maybe not for some time—but it will ultimately be considered a great book, will be published in both hemispheres, and be translated into different languages."[46] Remarkably, George's prophecy of his international success would be borne out in just a few years; in the meantime, though, his failure to catch on with the *Herald* did not prevent him from settling in New York, which would be his base of operations for the rest of his life. Continuing to ponder the land question, George had moved to the most intensely urban spot in the entire country, where "open land" was little more than a fantasy. Central Park itself, to most New Yorkers, seemed smaller and more remote with every passing year, as adjacent property values crept upward and development extended the city's reach. Every day, George would be confronted with hard evidence that civilization's greatest accomplishments were built on wretchedly unjust foundations, but there would be no long, loping rides into the countryside to clear his mind.

George claimed that "the opportunity to write this book came to me out of crushing disaster"[47]—a seeming reference to the violence that met the railroad strikes of

1877, during which he started drafting his manuscript. Yet what actually gave him the privilege of spending long days thinking and writing was the greater financial stability he had attained in the mid-70s, through his work as a newspaper editor and as the official State Inspector of Gas Meters, a plum position to which he was appointed by an admiring Democratic governor on the first day of 1876. By the spring of 1878, he was ready to stand for election again, this time to be an official delegate to the convention that California was holding to amend its constitution (again, he lost), and at the end of March he gave a lecture in San Francisco, called "Why Work is Scarce, Wages Low, and Labor Restless," in which he hoped to bring together some of the key arguments of his manuscript.

Much of George's message had remained constant: *Progress and Poverty*, as his son suggested, would turn out to be "the oak that grew out of the acorn of 'Our Land and Land Policy.'"[48] Yet his thinking had taken some new turns (it was in *Progress and Poverty* that he proposed the Single Tax as his ultimate solution),[49] and his rhetoric had developed some new resonances. George still insisted that it all came down to the use we made of the gifts of nature: "Look around this hall," he entreated his audience, in San Francisco's Metropolitan Temple. "All that you see is the product of land—aye, even that with which you see. Truly, the earth is our mother. This very flesh and blood is but borrowed from the soil." And he still insisted that, since all of civilization depended on land, everyone should have free and equal access to it: "Can anything be more absurd than if I, who have no house, want to build myself one out here on land that has never been put to use by human being since the creation of the world, I must first pay someone, two or three thousand dollars . . . ? Why, with as much justice I might be asked to pay him for the light of the sun or for the air from heaven!"[50] The emphasis on borrowing, though, and the comparison of soil to sunlight and air, might themselves have been borrowed from the protests lodged by Native Americans throughout the nineteenth century against the legal property regime—which, more often than not, amounted to a justification of theft—imposed on them by white American invaders.[51] Urban workers, George thought, were in some ways the new slaves, but they were also the new Indians—"impoverished, misunderstood, cheated, and abused," deprived of their fair share of what they had formerly taken for granted (hunting grounds, wood supplies, soil, water, light, air), because they were now "looked upon as belonging to an inferior race."[52] Indeed, one of the most radical new thrusts in George's argument was his assault on racial thinking in general, designed to help him establish that "the poverty which in the midst of abundance pinches and embrutes men, and all the manifold evils which flow from it, spring from a denial of justice," from social structures, from "traditions, beliefs, customs, laws, habits," and not from any "innate" or "hereditary" differences in ability between distinguishable groups. And though he was primarily interested in defending the rights of white laborers who had been drawn off the land by rampant industrialization and the promise of factory jobs, he incidentally posited the basic worthiness, the "natural capacity," of every "race," even (quite explicitly) the Chinese, and even the Indians, who, it was true, sometimes stood in the way of his horticultural utopia, but who, in their "primitive social organization," embodied the recognition of "the common right of men to the use of the earth."[53]

Moreover, while George still idealized agrarian smallholders, he now upheld the commons, rather than private property, as being the key to the ideal social contract, and he sought to cordon off as much land as possible to be maintained as publicly owned open space. In 1878, he led the struggle to establish a free public library system in San Francisco and throughout the state of California, which can be seen as meeting many of the same goals as Cleveland's park systems, and which George seems to have associated most powerfully with the example of America's free public school systems. Libraries and schools: what better models for society in general, suggesting the advantages of sharing resources and coming together in a public place to confront the challenges of getting along with one another? At the Metropolitan Temple, in a passage that he then transferred almost verbatim to *Progress and Poverty*, George pointed out that "all sorts of things, from a wheelbarrow up to a railway, are owned in common, without the recognition of common rights interfering with their proper use. So with land. There is a lot on the corner of Fifth and Market streets in this city, to which the common right of the people of San Francisco is yet legally recognized. That lot is not cut up into infinitesimal particles, nor yet is it unused. . . . The only difference between it and adjoining property is that the rent of the land goes into the Common School Fund instead of into private pockets." And then, in the book version, came the kicker: "What is to prevent the land of a whole country being held by the people of a country in this way?"[54]

George wanted to revert to Jefferson's original principle that republican virtue came not of owning land but of working it, that in fact all land should be understood as a public trust. Consider "the little islets of St. Peter and St. Paul," George proposed, "in the Aleutian Archipelago . . . , the breeding places of the fur seal. . . . To throw such a fishery as this open to whoever chose to go and kill—which would make it to the interest of each party to kill as many as they could at the time without reference to the future—would be utterly to destroy it in a few seasons, as similar fisheries in other oceans have been destroyed." Either you get the tragedy of the commons, in other words, or you get a private owner who turns as much of a profit as possible and then moves on—unless you keep the islands as "the common property of the people of the United States," and lease them to a company at a very high rate, and place a strict limit on the annual take—a compromise that in George's time seemed to be keeping the seal population stable and also adding more than $300,000 a year to the national treasury.[55]

As George well knew, private companies exist to make profits—and the enforcement of government regulations has never been easy anywhere, let alone on the Alaskan frontier. Trying his best to remain hopeful about public land and public culture, he ended his 1878 lecture in San Francisco with an image of firm belief in a horticultural commonality: "The ground is plowed; the seed is set; the good tree will grow! So little now, only the eye of faith can see it. So little now; so tender and so weak. But sometime, the birds of heaven shall sing in its branches; sometime, the weary shall find rest beneath its shade!"[56] In *Progress and Poverty,* he tried to imagine a huge increase in "public revenues made to foster efforts for the public benefit," resulting in "public baths, museums, libraries, gardens, lecture rooms, music and dancing halls, theaters, universities, technical schools, shooting galleries, play grounds, gymnasiums," not to mention streets "lined with fruit trees."[57] Yet both his lecture and his book were marked more powerfully by a sense of coming disaster, perhaps the most important new element in his work. "Do you imagine that the gifts of the Creator can thus be misappropriated with impunity . . . ?" he asked his San Francisco audience. "Do you say, 'After us the Deluge?' Nay the pillars of the State are trembling even now; the very foundations of Society are quivering with the pent up forces that glow underneath."[58]

Despite George's success in establishing libraries, and despite the popularity of places like San Francisco's Golden Gate Park, established in 1870, and despite improvements in schools throughout the nation, the overall trend continued to favor privatization of land in all its forms, and, to George, it was precisely this trend that was pushing the country to the brink of catastrophic conflicts. "The public domain is almost gone," he wrote, anticipating Frederick Jackson Turner's Frontier Thesis by more than a decade, and because "our national character" owed all its best qualities—"the power of adaptation and assimilation, the free, independent spirit, the energy and hopefulness"—to this "enormous common" of "unfenced land," there would now be an inevitable decline, as "the dweller in crowded cities," deprived of any "wellspring of hope" and faced with "the increasing necessity for straining every nerve to prevent being thrown down and trodden under foot in the scramble for wealth," began to experience, understandably, a "general feeling of disappointment," followed by "an increased bitterness," until entire cities were filled with "unrest and brooding revolution."

There was simply no stability in injustice and inequality, as world history suggested. "The earth is the tomb of the dead empires," George noted, "no less than dead men," and all past civilizations had been destroyed from within, because the benefits of progress had always been unfairly distributed. The Civil War had ended, but George now wondered if that had been merely a first tremor, a hint of the great cataclysm to come. He thought that "industry everywhere tends to assume a form in which one is master and many serve," and when single masters could "control thousands of miles of railroad, millions of acres of land, the means of livelihood of great numbers of men," then the servants would start to consider revolt, "as sure as the turning tide must soon run full ebb, as sure as the declining sun must bring darkness," and eventually no dam would be able to "pen up the swelling waters." George imagined the apocalypse over and over again in *Progress and Poverty,* in terms that would be recapitulated in American culture for the following twenty years, until the turn of the century, and he even went so far as to suggest that all of his nation's so-called modern improvements would probably fare quite poorly against the test of time: "It is startling to think how slight the traces that would be left of our civilization did it pass through the throes which have accompanied the decline of every previous civilization. Paper will not last like parchment, nor are our most massive buildings and monuments to be compared in solidity with the rock-hewn temples and titanic edifices of the old civilizations." Indeed, perhaps thinking of the mysterious Indian Mounds that so fascinated men of his generation, he also noted "how inadequate and utterly misleading would be the idea of our civilization which could be gained from the religious and funereal monuments of our time, which are all we have from which to gain our ideas of the buried civilizations."[59]

The morbid undertones of George's book, in other words, reflected his middle-aged mood, and as he wandered around New York in 1880, he could only pray that he would eventually find some direct outlet for his "earnest, burning desire to do what I might to relieve human misery and make life brighter."[60] The opportunity came quickly, over the next few months and years, through his cherished public sphere, as favorable reviews of *Progress and Poverty* suddenly poured in, and he started getting constant invitations to lecture all along the east coast and in Ireland and England, and his publisher issued cheaper and cheaper editions of his book, and translations appeared, and a Free Soil Society arose in New York, and he started getting drafted by labor unions and alternative political parties to run for office. George would spend the remainder of his life in a rush of writing, speaking, organizing, and campaigning, finding himself at the center of a remarkable coalition of the urban and rural poor, giving himself more and more to the cause, even as, all the while, his health slipped away from him. Over these final two decades of the century, he seemed to waver between faith in the dawning of a new Arcadia and the conviction that Arcadia would not reappear until the "austral seas, sweeping northward, bury the seats of present civilization under ocean wastes."[61]

In the fall of 1883, his parents died, in quick succession, a week apart, and though he was grief-stricken, and though he worried that his father, in his old age, "did not give enough heed to the pressing, struggling world about him to see the full purpose and strength" of *Progress and Poverty*, Henry nevertheless knew that both of his parents went to their grave respecting his commitment to "justice and equality" and appreciating his importance to a broad social movement. "Yes," he said to himself, "I could die now," too, since he had fulfilled his familial obligations and had finally taken the kind of action he had always meant to take: "I could die now and the work would go on. It no longer depends upon one man."[62] Meanwhile, though, he spread his social gospel, most widely, perhaps, in his almost successful bid to become mayor of New York in 1886, during which he became famous for speaking at seemingly impromptu but huge gatherings on street corners, carving out public space wherever possible, since his campaign couldn't afford to rent the city's grand halls, and since Central Park had already become a symbol of privilege (his crowds of supporters probably would have been kicked out, anyway). The children of New York, he said, in his speech accepting the nomination of the United Labor Party, "thousands and thousands, have no place to play. It is a crime for them to play ball in the only place in which they can play ball. It is an offence for them to fly their kites. The children of the rich can go up to Central Park, or out into the country in the summer time; but the children of the poor, for them there is no playground in the city but the streets; it is only some charity excursion which takes them out for a day, only to return them again to the same sweltering condition."[63]

About eleven years later, in May 1897, George, for the first time, suffered the death of one of his own children, a daughter, Jennie, named for his favorite sister, twenty-nine years old, married, mother of a seven-month-old boy. Until that point, George felt, he had been living something of a charmed life: he and his wife were secure in their ever-increasing love for each other; all four of their children had been healthy, and successful in any number of endeavors, from sculpture to newspaper work; and George's own labors had met with stunning public approbation (*Progress and Poverty* became one of the best-selling books of the nineteenth century). Though the corruption of the Gilded Age was still rampant, and the industrial depression of 1893 proved to be the worst yet (with some 400 banks and 150 railroads failing, and 20 percent of workers losing their jobs),[64] and the gap between rich and poor just seemed to widen, and the repression of labor got even more violent, and corporate power increased—nevertheless, George had been delighted to witness the rise of the Populists, and the launching of powerful attacks on laissez-faire economics and politics, and the galvanizing efforts of other reformers like Edward Bellamy, Robert Ingersoll, and Jacob Riis, author of *How the Other Half Lives* (1890). When Jennie passed away, though, from what had seemed to be a minor case of the flu, he admitted that he "had for some time felt a disaster impending . . . ; that it was not in the order of things for men to have unbroken prosperity; that evil comes mixed with good; that life is a strife."[65] Shortly afterward, he had an attack of weakness, which "the family physician admonished him would be the close forerunner of an apoplectic stroke if he proceeded" with the strenuous writing regime he had been pursuing. So he paused, drew up a last will and testament, and, apparently, over the following months, he "more freely than ever before in his life talked of his personal history, and in the household and to immediate friends, in a casual way told of past scenes with a candor and unaffectedness that left lasting impressions on the listeners' ears." When, early that fall, several political organizations joined together to ask him to run for mayor of New York again, this time as an Independent, and he admitted to being inclined toward accepting the nomination, his doctor told him that the effort of the campaign "will probably prove fatal." "But I have got to die," was George's response. "How can I die better than serving humanity! Besides, so dying will do more for the cause than anything I am likely to be able to do in the rest of my life."[66]

Five days before the election, as one of his friends later reported, George gave a series of talks on Long Island, and on the train "he looked to me as if he was almost exhausted. Every now and then, however, he would arouse himself, brighten up and ask some member of the party some question. The extreme gentleness of his manner is what particularly impressed me." The predicted stroke came the next morning, and he died right away. Out in the streets, over the next couple of days, there was an "outpouring of unrestrained human feeling in recognition of a noble life and a noble death." "No one can describe the chaos into which our city was thrown by the shock of Mr. George's sudden death," claimed one eyewitness. "The people seemed to be panic stricken." One of his eulogists pointed to his coffin and said, "There lie the remains of Thomas Jefferson, reincarnate." Another would later claim that "no death since that of Abraham Lincoln has so stirred the world." According to several newspaper accounts, about 100,000 people, many of them sobbing, filed past George's body as it lay in state at the Grand Central Palace, while some 50,000 more stood outside and then followed the cortège all the way to the George family home in Brooklyn. Mothers and fathers held their children high in the air to catch a glimpse of the catafalque, "heavily draped with black, drawn by sixteen black horses," and there were hundreds of other unaccompanied children, "children of the tenements, whose faces showed that they had early learned the sterner lessons of life."

That evening, "the casket was placed in the front parlor, and watching by it during the night were some of Mr. George's dearest friends," among them Hamlin Garland. At ten o'clock in the morning, on Monday, November 1, the day before the election, there was a private service at the house, and then the body was carried over to Brooklyn's sixty-year-old Greenwood Cemetery, where George was buried next to his daughter, on a ridge called Ocean Hill, overlooking the Atlantic. The following summer, a monument was erected in his honor at the gravesite. And that November, among the many memorial celebrations marking the first anniversary of his death, was one at which Hamlin Garland's brother, Franklin, read excerpts from *Progress and Poverty* to the crowd, and at which the playwright and activist James Herne made a lively speech very much in George's spirit, looking ahead to the day when everyone would have "equality before the law . . . , regardless of sex, race, creed, or color," when "women [would] have a voice in the government under which they live," and when "not another acre of our mother, the earth, shall ever again be bought and sold." "We of the single tax philosophy," Herne explained, "know exactly what we need and want, and we are asking for it intelligently, persistently, fearlessly. We want the earth."[67]

———————

What do the dying want? Distraction? Help in confronting the inevitable? Both, simultaneously? If Henry George, at the age of fifty-eight, truly did spend the last months of his life reminiscing with his family and friends as well as running for mayor, it is a testament to his calm generosity—and perhaps also to his culture. Once my parents' age started catching up with them in 1998, there was nothing I wanted more than to hear their stories. I wanted to sit down at the kitchen table, roll the tape, and interview them. But, despite my initial breakthrough with my father, they quickly reverted to their characteristic discretion and taciturnity. Especially once they got over their most serious health problems, it seemed that they wanted to be moved out of the "dying" category and back into the "still very much alive, with plenty of time to go" category. Occasionally, my mother would say, "We're going to be dead eventually, and then you and Debbie are going to be stuck with all the stuff in this house, so you may as well start taking it now." And so, occasionally, I elicited some memories by pointing to a particular book, or bookcase, or photograph, or oil lamp, or spice box, or ring. In general, though, they deflected my questions, and I grew more and more hesitant to ask any.

Stephen and his family certainly didn't want to talk about mortality. Immediately after the diagnosis, his brother Jamie had started a nonprofit medical research institute whose immediate goal was to save Stephen's life. He was young and strong, and a very small percentage of ALS patients—the scientist Stephen Hawking is the most famous example—do survive much longer than the typical two to five years. As the months passed, Stephen tried all kinds of experimental therapies, and his family lobbied hard for even more to be made available, but clearly nothing could stop his rapid decline, which I couldn't help but connect to my parents' slower, more subtle decline. Since he and his new wife did buy a house in Newton—he designed and oversaw the renovations—I often visited him when I came up from New Haven to spend time with my parents. I saw him gradually lose the ability to walk, and feed himself, and hold his son, and talk, and breathe. Various devices helped him cope with these losses, though, and it was especially amazing to see how long and determinedly he communicated his sense of hope and humor. "Some parts are still working," he had said, after his wife Wendy got pregnant. Even when the voice simulator started to fail, his eyebrow could convey the old mischief. "When are *you* going to have a kid?" he always managed to ask me. Did I really think I could get a job? Would anybody read my book? Had I heard about the chip they were thinking of implanting in his brain that might be capable of reading his thoughts? I had to steel myself, sometimes, to go over to his house, but I went—I thought of Ian, and I went. By the summer of 2004, when Christine and I and our own young son moved to Ithaca so that I could start my first job as a professor, Stephen was frightfully diminished, wispy, wraithlike, but hanging on, and who was to say that he would die anytime soon? He had his wheelchair, his respirator, his computer, his family. It had already been six years.

My parents, meanwhile, stopped traveling, stopped writing letters, stopped seeing most of their friends. But I think Stephen helped me focus on what they *could* do. Perhaps the simplest and most wonderful blessing was that they could take care of themselves, in their own home. They could go shopping, prepare meals, pay bills, drive to doctors' appointments. We eased into a comfortable new relationship: I had proved my independence from them, and now they were proving their independence from my sister and me. Every week or two I'd call, and they'd tell me what they'd accomplished. Even when certain holiday traditions broke down—when we had to cancel Rosh Hashanah dinner with our friends the Schmidts, or postpone the Chanukah party for two weeks—we always seemed to adjust, determined to maintain some sense of continuity. My mother still made the most perfectly sweet-tart cranberry sauce at Thanksgiving and delivered small batches to all the neighbors.

She still made latkes, even if, in difficult years, they came from a mix, and she still sent everyone she knew a dishtowel calendar from the Massachusetts Audubon Society as a Chanukah present, and she still made *charoset* at Passover, and my father still led the seder when my uncle the rabbi wasn't with us (he increasingly wasn't). I even managed to take both of my parents to a couple of Red Sox games.

Their eyesight was failing, their hearing was failing, they breathed heavily, they moved slowly. Yet their lives also bore brand-new fruit, and I felt intensely grateful for the gift of these extra years after cancer and cardiac arrhythmia, for the chance they had to start fresh, the chance I had to get beyond some of my youthful self-involvement and see them with different eyes. My mother, whom I had always thought of as stubbornly practical, suddenly started taking art classes, and the house filled up with paintings. The colors were much richer and brighter than I would have expected, deep reds and shining blues; what had become of her brown-and-gray world-view? With the paintings multiplying, I started noticing other things: the dozens of plants, which she had always complained about but which she always kept alive, freshening the air, livening up all the downstairs rooms; the prisms she hung in windows; the birdfeeders she hung outside, surely recalling her bird-fanatic parents, with all the latest, cleverest squirrel baffles, which never came close to baffling any squirrels. But I was baffled by the paintings, and dazzled, as this quiet, self-contained woman, whom I had never before seen with a brush or canvas (she hadn't painted, in fact, since she was a child), who blushed more easily than anyone I had ever known, who shunned attention, started having exhibitions, contributing to art shows around town, sending out invitations to everyone she knew. She did a still life now and then, and a portrait or two of a grandchild, but mostly she painted landscapes, which she copied, skillfully, from magazines, or books, or her old postcard collection: mountains and meadows in Switzerland, barns and fields in Vermont, missions in California, row houses in Holland, wildflowers blooming by streams in Wyoming, lighthouses on jumbles of rocks in Maine. Her parents had dragged her all over the world, and she clearly had some vivid, romantic memories of certain places, but she did not actually want to go back, did not want to succumb again to that loss of control. I grew up thinking that she hated to travel: as soon as she had established her own household, where she could comfortably grumble about her houseplants, she had clung to it, nurturing her new roots, agreeing to leave only for quick trips to see family or an obligatory summer vacation to hide out in some slightly cooler patch of New England. Now, though, she was revisiting old haunts, and imagining new ones, traveling back to her childhood of travel without having to leave home, getting outside, beneath trees and open skies, even during the gray, paralyzing winter—and I realized that my needful connection to the outdoors had not in fact skipped a generation, but had been there all along, inside my mother.

My father, meanwhile, for the first time in forty years, was writing a book. Before his retirement, he had focused on teaching, and when he had turned to scholarship he tended to take on small projects that were essentially done as favors to colleagues and friends: encyclopedia entries, conference papers, review essays. In a profession obsessed with production, with inflated lists of publications, my father spent much of his time commenting on manuscripts for students and editors and acquaintances, often anonymously, graciously agreeing to do whatever he was asked, never expecting any credit for helping to prop up the structures that allowed him to get paid to read and think and have conversations. My impression was that he was often content but sometimes felt like a bit of a martyr, and as I entered the academy I planned to aspire to his generosity, but not reflexively, not in a way that would prevent me from writing my own books. I constantly pondered the differences between my father and me: maybe I had more book-length ideas; maybe I was just more selfish and more ambitious; maybe I was more skeptical about the profession, more hesitant to support structures that in my view sometimes fostered arrogance, elitism, cut-throat competition, and territorialism (as well as, occasionally, ideal forms of intellectual community, a culture of caring). In any case, I was delighted when my father launched a major project of his own devising, after those first two or three years of struggling with retirement—though at first I was surprised that he was proposing to write what sounded like a work of history. Rather than pursue his long-standing interest in Flaubert, or Balzac, or Daudet, he planned to produce a reinterpretation of the Dreyfus Affair, the infamous scandal of turn-of-the-century France in which an obscure Jewish soldier had been wrongly convicted of treason to cover up the army's incompetence, and had then become so polarizing a public figure that French politicians had to start identifying themselves not, primarily, as republicans or monarchists, nor as left-leaning or right-leaning, but as pro- or anti-Dreyfus. Of course, many literary figures played key roles in the Affair—most prominently, Émile Zola, whose public letter, known by the title *J'Accuse*, essentially asserted that the army was trying to make all Jewish immigrants into scapegoats, who might take the blame for the nation's political and economic difficulties and thus distract the populace from rampant corruption at the highest levels of government. And here was my father's angle: he would offer a literary reading of French anti-Semitism, depending on nuanced psychological portraits of key individuals and on a deep understanding of the cultural traditions that helped make the Dreyfus case so contentious. In other words—words he never

used himself—he was hoping to use his professional background in French literature to explore his personal background as a Jew, to ponder what his parents experienced as they fled the anti-Semitism of Polish and Lithuanian shtetls to confront the
milder but still palpable anti-Semitism of Toronto.

It's not such a stretch to think of my father's book project in these terms, because
shortly after he started the research for it he also started serving as a translator of old
documents for the National Yiddish Book Center. Every now and then, people around
the country would contact the center to ask for help with letters, diaries, even published books—anything in their family collections that they couldn't read. Then the
center would send these materials to volunteers who had registered as potential transla-
tors, like my father. He had last spoken and studied Yiddish in high school, in the late
1930s and early 40s, but he did the work passionately, quickly, artistically, and always
for free, despite getting several offers of payment from grateful families. As more and
more of his translations went out into the world, he developed a reputation for both
eloquence and "*Sprachgefuehl* (native feeling for the language)," as one admirer put it,
and soon his Yiddish commissions threatened to overwhelm his Dreyfus research. But
he somehow managed to keep working on everything at once, and he seemed truly
happy. Living the life of the mind had clearly done him some good, had kept him
fresh, sharp, sensitive. After a couple of glasses of wine, during this period of his life, he
would typically start talking animatedly about Dreyfus and then eventually switch
gears and offer up a glowing character sketch of the Yiddish teacher he'd had back
when he was a teenager: this was a man, he'd say, who took such delight in the sound
and meaning of words, who was so committed to hearing the nuances and resonances
of every sentence, that you couldn't help, in his classroom, but feel called to study
literature. My father had gotten to French through Yiddish; now he was going home.

When I left New England again, to start teaching at Cornell, I was thirty-four, my
mother seventy-four, and my father eighty. I was somewhat sorry to go—Ithaca was
six hours away from Newton, instead of just two—but not particularly worried about
my parents. They seemed to be thriving. During my job search, I had even fantasized
about landing an open history position at a college in San Diego: we could live on
the beach and soak up the sun for a few years, before thinking about going back east
again. I suppose I was focusing my energies and anxieties on myself: I had ruptured
a disc the previous fall, and so was learning how to cope with chronic pain while
also becoming a first-time parent, first-time professor, and first-time homeowner. I
felt incredibly lucky (the Cornell job had seemed like such a long shot that I almost
didn't apply), but also overwhelmed. The emphasis was on day-to-day survival. I still
shuddered at late-night phone calls, still knew that anything could happen, still

thought of my parents, and Stephen, as being relatively close to death. But I never had Henry George's sense of foreboding.

———————

The back-trailing Hamlin Garland, twenty-four years old, was at first deeply relieved to be away from his parents. This time, he told himself, as he arrived in Boston in October of 1884, having sold his claim in Dakota, he was going to stay in the east and become a teacher, an intellectual, an urbanite. With no prospects and no connections, he haunted the city's public spaces, renting a tiny apartment close to the Common and becoming a regular at the nearby Boston Public Library, where he embarked on a self-designed course of reading, focusing first on the science of evolution and then on the historical development of literature. By subsisting largely on coffee and bread, he was able to spend just five dollars a week for room and board, and when he wasn't reading he attended free lectures, honed his own oratorical skills (a focus of his studies back at Cedar Valley Seminary in Iowa), and even wrote a little bit, until spring finally came and he managed to catch on at the Boston School of Oratory, whose director Garland had approached after hearing him give a talk at the Young Men's Christian Union. Moses True Brown first asked Garland to provide him with some translations of French documents relating to a particular system of rhetorical aesthetics, and then, pleased with the results, he made a more permanent offer of employment, and for the next five years Garland received a steady income at the school as a teacher and lecturer. Gradually, Garland learned how to navigate Boston's cultural landscape, and acquired a number of advisers and supporters, including William Dean Howells, whom Garland visited in Newton and whose commitment to realism would guide the aspiring writer's entry into the realm of fiction. On Sabbath mornings he often took to the suburbs, walking "along winding lanes under great overarching elm trees, past apple-orchards in bursting bloom"; at other times he stayed downtown and "roamed the parks, or took excursions down the bay"; occasionally, he would just spread himself out "on the grass of the park in West Roxbury, watching the wild birds come and go, hearing the sound of the scythe-stone in the meadow." When he sat down at his desk to write, though, he realized that the picturesque, shady byways of New England had already had their poets, and his thoughts always drifted back to the middle border. He started sketching scenes of men husking corn and pitching hay, trying to convey the "grim" and "bitter" aspects of the work as well as its satisfactions, "the painful as well as the pleasant truth . . . , the mud and cold of the landscape as well as its bloom and charm." When he received his first paycheck for a piece of magazine writing, he "hastened to purchase some silk for my mother, and the *Memoirs of General Grant* for my father," and, in the summer of 1887, made arrangements to take a trip west.[68]

He wound up visiting his parents in both 1887 and 1888, and it was during this period of urgent bouncing between east and west that he most fully seized on his life's central tension. For the moment, he could not imagine living anywhere other than Boston, the cultural capital of the nation—yet he also knew that his politics and aesthetics would forever be grounded in his experiences of the frontier. If he needed a city to support his desired life of the mind, that city, in turn, depended on the support of the countryside to supply it with food, fuel, and labor, and Garland felt an increasing sense of responsibility to acknowledge that relationship, and especially to recognize the cost borne by the people who stayed on farms. In "Up the Coolly," one of his earliest stories, he staged a confrontation between one brother, named Howard, who has moved to the east and become a successful actor, and another, named Grant, who has stuck it out in Wisconsin and become hardened, resentful, unwilling to abide his brother's surprise that the family has gotten poorer despite decent land and a solid work ethic: after all, Grant points out, "We fellers on the farm have to earn a livin' for ourselves *and* [for] you fellers that don't work." (Grant, of course, is explicitly the namesake of the general, and in the story he's the one who receives the gift of the *Memoirs*—though, in his bitterness, he refuses to accept the "handsome volumes" from his brother.)[69]

During his 1887 trip, Garland repeatedly noted the contrast between the glorious natural scenery and the desolation of middle-border civilization, "the sordid quality of the mechanical daily routine of these lives." As he cast about for explanations, for the reasons that development in the west might have gone so awry, he came back to the theories of Henry George about the social impact of speculation. "I now perceived," he wrote, "that these plowmen, these wives and daughters, had been pushed out into these lonely ugly shacks by the force of landlordism behind."[70] At some point, Garland actually heard George give a lecture at Boston's Faneuil Hall and found his style "vivid, burning with inward fire," surely comparable, Garland thought, to that of the famous Boston activist Wendell Phillips, who had often taken the same stage, and who had not only insisted that African Americans deserved full social and economic equality with whites but had also defended the land claims of the Sioux even after they humiliated Custer in 1876. Now, "another voice" was ringing out to raise up "those whom the law oppressed"—the nation was witnessing "the beginning of a new abolition movement"—and Garland wanted to join his voice to George's, hoping to achieve a similarly "graceful lucidity of utterance." George's "altruism," Garland wrote, "his sincere pity, and his hatred of injustice sent me away in the mood of a disciple." So, in the fall of 1887, after returning to Boston from Dakota, he started spending his Sunday evenings at "the old Horticultural Hall on Tremont Street," attending meetings of the local Anti-Poverty Society, whose parent organization had been founded in New York a few months before, in the wake of George's first mayoral campaign. By November, "Professor Hamlin Garland" was being announced as a featured speaker, and on the twenty-seventh he gave an address called "The Social Aspect of the Land Tax" to an audience of six hundred, lamenting that "the tillable land is almost gone, and unless we rob the Indian again in the course of a few years the last of our government farming lands will be but a memory. Aye! I will go further and say that for nearly a century free land has been a myth. Every foot of it was bought with blood and sweat and tears." The system of monopolization and speculation, Garland explained, had not only dispossessed Native Americans and made the rich richer but had also created rural communities that were too dispersed—each isolated sod house appeared "on the side of a mighty wave of the waste like a tiny ship adrift on the boundless ocean"—and urban communities that were too crowded, where children had to play "on the stones among piles of tin cans, old boots, and broken bottles." The only remedy, for both country and city, was to adjust taxation so that land had to be "held for use, not for sale."[71]

By March 1888, Garland had given at least two more public speeches, including one on the Boston Common in the midst of winter, and had ultimately been elected as vice president of the Boston Anti-Poverty Society, after having offered his services directly to George, who wrote an encouraging reply and helped bolster Garland's reputation via his New York newspaper, the *Standard*. At the same time, though, Garland was feeling guilty, yearning to go back to his parents' lonely farm on the plains; his mother, Isabelle, wrote letters that spring complaining of drought and dizziness. So, after spending the season giving lectures more widely in New England, Garland arranged a western speaking tour for the summer, advertising dates in Chicago and Minneapolis and offering to stop elsewhere if local activists could secure a small honorarium for him, to help pay his way to Dakota. Alas, when he arrived at the homestead, which his father, in desperation, had expanded to five hundred acres, Garland immediately saw that "another dry year was upon the land," and the trees and grass had "withered in the heat," leaving everyone hopeless and resentful, with no hint of relief: "No green thing was in sight, and no shade offered save that made by the little cabin." Every time he looked at his mother, he "bled, inwardly," and he worried that his little sister, Jessie, was bound to inherit the same life of drudgery if he couldn't find a way to remove her from "this sterile environment."

One day, as he harangued his sister in the house, trying to convince her that she ought to get an education rather than stay on the frontier waiting for a husband, a shriek came from the front yard, and Hamlin went outside to find his mother paralyzed from the waist down, having suffered a stroke. She ultimately recovered, but this was one of the worst moments of Garland's life, as he explained in language seemingly haunted by the legacy of the Civil War: "My heart filled with bitterness and rebellion, bitterness against the pioneering madness which had scattered our family, and rebellion toward my father who had kept my mother always on the border, working like a slave long after the time when she should have been taking her ease. Above all, I resented my own failure, my own inability to help in the case."[72] In "Up the Coolly," the returned brother, Howard, berates himself for ever having left: "This was his mother—the woman who bore him, the being who had taken her life in her hand for him; and he, in his excited and pleasurable life, had neglected her!" And, in the story's final scene, he comes to realize that his offer of financial help has come far too late, as he stares at Grant's "long, rugged, Scotch face, bronzed with sun and scarred with wrinkles that had histories, like sabre-cuts on a veteran, the record of his battles."[73]

Howard, and Hamlin too, like so many other members of the postwar generation, struggled constantly with the question of how to lead a responsible life amid "the ceaseless change and shift" of modern society. What did he owe his family? What did he owe the land, now that many of the best opportunities clearly lay in the city? The model of the yeoman farmer, so long an ideal type in European and American culture, no longer carried much weight; Arcadia seemed impossible. "Labor," Garland decided, "when so prolonged and severe" as it often had to be in the fields of the middle border, ". . . is warfare."[74] Meanwhile, despite the burgeoning cultural scene in the nation's largest cities, urban landscapes were also characterized more by strife than by repose: "We have settled, with a tremendous war, the question of Negro slavery,—a danger that threatened our very life at one time. . . . But *are* we at peace?. . . . Is there not a feverish stir, a distrust of social conditions? Why have we hundreds of strikes, those terrific and fratricidal wars of Capital and Labor?"[75]

Garland stayed on "the shadeless farmstead" until the start of the school year, "to share in the work of harvesting" and to help care for his mother. But his life lay in Boston. Still trying to persuade his sister to get more education, he insisted that she come along with him at least as far as "the great city of Minneapolis," where H. W. S. Cleveland was working away at his park system. Jessie, though, couldn't wait to get home. On the way to New England, Garland stopped off in New Jersey to visit Walt Whitman, "whose work I had been lecturing about," and found that the sixty-nine-year-old poet "was quite lame but could move without a crutch" and came across as "gentler and sweeter than I had expected him to be."[76] Two months later, Garland reviewed Whitman's new book, *November Boughs,* an eclectic collection of prose pieces that reminded him of *Specimen Days,* especially since it contained a number of additional "war memoranda," again demonstrating the extent of the poet's "self-sacrifice" in tending to wounded soldiers, a labor of love that had surely "[laid] the foundations for the sickness which chained him to his chair before he was sixty years of age." In the end, Garland thought, the book was "a most remarkable outpouring of exalted passion, prophecy, landscape painting, songs of the sea and, above all, calls for deeper love for Nature and for men."[77] And in this same spirit, Garland continued his political lecturing, now emphasizing the need for economic reformers to take up sexual equality as well: "The single tax men have made a mistake in not getting the women interested," he argued, in a speech urging Georgists all over the country to follow the example of the Grange and establish meeting places where families could "get together in an informal way," perhaps occasionally to organize protests but mostly to relax and support each other.[78] Meanwhile, women ought to be given reasonable choices in both the public and the private sphere, at work and at home, which meant that the fight for suffrage was necessary but not sufficient: "The sufferings of the women of America are not unknown to me," he wrote, in a letter to the editor of the *Boston Woman's Journal,* "especially the life and toil of the farmer's wife, and my criticism of the JOURNAL, which I feel is just, is that it does not deal with the deeper problems concerning women's work and wages. It is not 'radical' enough, to use a good old word. It concerns itself too largely with the mere question of voting, and not enough with the wide-spread poverty and resultant despair of the home."[79]

The despair of home—the loss of the very idea of home, the possibility of home—is at the heart of most of the fiction Garland wrote during this period. "Can any other country on earth surpass the United States in the ruthless broadcast dispersion of its families?" he would later ask.[80] He knew that the life of a farmer's wife had never been easy, but he remained convinced that his mother's health and happiness would have been significantly bolstered if only his father had been willing to stay in Wisconsin amidst both of his parents' extended families.

Garland's first book, *Main-Travelled Roads* (1891), perhaps the most remarkable of his career, collected six stories, including "The Return of a Private" and "Up the Coolly," which drew on his own life to combine raw, moving characterizations with pleas for social reform. Even "Under the Lion's Paw," which Garland wrote explicitly to illustrate the arguments of *Progress and Poverty* and which he often read aloud at Single Tax rallies, manages to inspire real empathy, because the hero is flawed and confused, and because the authorial viewpoint comes across not as doctrinaire but as ambivalent, searching: the characters come to understand that rootedness has become virtually impossible in the late nineteenth century, but they cannot stop looking for roots. The story's "lion" is of course a landlord, a speculator and monopolist, who loans some Iowa land to a poor farmer named Haskins, on the run from the grasshoppers of Kansas. After three years of pitiless labor (his own and his young son's), Haskins has made a go of it and is ready to buy—but the owner, seeing the quality of Haskins's improvements, smugly doubles his original asking price. Haskins seizes a pitchfork—he himself seems to have been seized by the devil—and is about to kill his tormentor, when he thinks of his family and decides simply to purchase the farm, taking on the kind of mortgage that will keep him both poor and harnessed to the plow for the rest of his life. It seems a tragic but reasonable choice, given the options—one foreshadowed by the dedication on the very first page of *Main-Travelled Roads*: "To My Father and Mother, whose half-century pilgrimage on the main-travelled road of life has brought them only toil and deprivation, this book of stories is dedicated by a son to whom every day brings a deepening sense of his parents' silent heroism."[81]

Garland clung to hope, continued searching for potential solutions to the social and economic ills confronting both his family and his nation. But the landscape looked grimmer than ever. His sister Jessie had died suddenly, from a seemingly minor skin infection, in October 1890, a year after getting married, "leaving my father and mother alone on the bleak plain. . . . Hopelessly crippled, my mother now mourned the loss of her 'baby,' and the soldier's keen eyes grew dim, for he loved this little daughter above anything else in the world. The flag of his sunset march was drooping in its staff."[82] Many other westerners, meanwhile, felt desperately marginalized in a political culture still dominated by the North-South divide and increasingly controlled by the corporate industrialists and bankers who seemed to dictate policy to the long line of postbellum Republican presidents (Grant, Hayes, Garfield, Arthur, Harrison).[83] Some frontier farmers and urban workers had followed Henry George into the Democratic Party, despite its continued association with the Confederacy, but their internal power was negligible compared to that of the New South's entrepreneurial class. And all along, during the two and a half decades after the war, more and more small farmers found themselves unable to pay their mortgages, succumbing to foreclosure and compelled either to move to the city or become tenants on their old land. While the railroad companies and mining companies and manufacturing companies, aided by the federal government, continued to break strikes and successfully stigmatize strikers, the agriculturists who did persist in frontier regions were forced to pay whatever transportation costs the railroads demanded, and, often, in the face of low grain prices (which fell steadily from 1865 to 1900), they had to expand their holdings and invest in expensive machinery that might make their labor more efficient. They were now operating in a system of international commerce capable of magical triumphs (the selling of unspoiled farm products thousands of miles from where they were grown) but unduly influenced by abstract markets and manipulative financiers, as inscrutable and unpredictable as the weather.[84]

By 1892, Garland's father was attempting to work a thousand acres, essentially on his own. But he had also joined the brand new People's Party, or Populists, the political organ of the National Farmers' Alliance, a true mass movement for democracy that had swept across the country in 1889 and put at least fifty sympathetic representatives into Congress in 1890. Ultimately, Garland suggested, using Georgist logic, the Populists were so successful in stirring things up and earning the allegiance of farmers, because "in the years between 1865 and 1892 the nation had swiftly passed through the buoyant era of free land settlement, and now the day of reckoning had come." Perhaps, through representative politics, those who still cared about agrarianism could carve out the space for a modern, sustainable version of a cooperative commonwealth, in which entities like telegraph systems and railroads might be publicly owned, and the federal government, rather than commercial middlemen, might regulate the supply, warehousing, and pricing of farm commodities.[85]

In the fall of 1891, Garland left his job at the Boston School of Oratory and traveled along the middle border, especially old, familiar Iowa, where he got to know many of the Farmers' Alliance activists; then, deciding that they were sufficiently receptive to his Single Tax sermonizing, he agreed to join the Alliance's network of some forty thousand lecturers, who traveled the country drumming up support for candidates and initiatives. With a presidential campaign on the horizon, Garland became convinced that the nation was going to see a "popular upheaval similar to that of '61." The dedication of a novel he published early in 1892, called *Jason Edwards, An Average Man*, revealed the extent of his new faith: "To the Farmers' Alliance, whose mission it is to unite the farmer and the artisan, the north and the south, the blue and the gray under one banner, marching in a continent-wide battle-line against the denial of equal rights, I dedicate this story, with its implied hatred of all special privileges." Of course, despite the passionate conviction with which he delivered his message, the actual words he used reveal his deeper confusion. Did the so-called "farmer's revolt" represent the start of a new civil war, or the ultimate resolution of the old one? Did the west really want to join with the north (still dominated by the Republican business class) or the south (still dominated by the white supremacist, Democratic planter class)? What remained clear about Garland's framing of the agrarians' clamorous activism was that it could be understood only in terms of the Civil War.

In any case, Garland was there, as a featured speaker, in Omaha, Nebraska (this was another time he could have run into H. W. S. Cleveland, who just then was laying out the city's most famous boulevard), on Independence Day, 1892, when the Populists held their national convention and offered their official platform to the public. He read "Under the Lion's Paw" to the masses, among whom stood his amazed father, who had not realized just how involved Hamlin had gotten in the movement. As the crowd cheered for his son, old Dick Garland "dropped his head on his arms and his body shook with sobs."[86] Hamlin was pleased that his father had witnessed his performance, but dismayed to see "the old soldier" displaying such "deference," "irresolution," and "timidity": this wrinkled "pioneer had always been so patriotic, so confident, so sanguine of his country's future," but now, like so many of his fellow farmers, he had sunk into a "slough of discouragement." The son, too, lost some of his enthusiasm after the Populist candidate for president, a Civil War general named James Weaver, managed to win only twenty-two electoral votes in November (the states of Kansas, Idaho, Colorado, and Nevada). By 1893, Garland was starting to think less about national reforms and more about the problem of how he might fulfill his obligations to his parents, and especially about how he might save his mother from his father's latest scheme, to sell off the Dakota acreage "and try irrigation in Montana." Hamlin's counterproposal, which he had been discussing with his mother ever since her stroke, was that they should all move back to the old coolly in Wisconsin, where his parents had gotten married, where he had been born, where several of his aunts and uncles still made their homes, "sheltered by the hills and trees." "The time has come," said the son to the father, "for a 'bout face. *You must take the back trail.*"

It took a few months to convince Dick Garland. And, meanwhile, Hamlin had to tear himself away from the urbane east. "How can I best serve my mother?" he asked himself, on the one hand—but it was only through his Boston connections that he had been able to sustain himself thus far and attain a position (he published four novels in 1892) where he could even dream of helping his parents purchase a new homestead. "Shall I give up my career at this point?" It tortured him to contemplate saying "goodbye to the artists and writers and musicians" who had made up his stimulating and supportive community; moreover, "to leave the Common, the parks, the Library, and the lovely walks and drives of Roxbury, was sorrowful business."[87] He had also taken to spending a good deal of time in New York, often visiting Henry George, and he felt a keen regret at having to abandon his evening tradition of walking "over to the East Side, to the unpretentious brick house in which The Prophet and his delightful family lived."[88] But Garland consoled himself with the thought that he could spend more time in Chicago, which, he thought, was about to transform itself from the nation's commercial hub to a true cultural capital.

As he noted in an 1893 essay called "The Literary Emancipation of the West," Chicago was in the midst of hosting a fabulous World's Fair; the Art Institute of Chicago, the Newberry Library, and the University of Chicago had all been founded in the previous decade; and the city was fast becoming a gathering place for practitioners of a new national literature, which "draws its inspiration from original contact with men and with nature," the common experience of common people.[89] Garland was surely trying to convince himself as well as his readers, but ultimately he and his father both warmed to the idea of the relocation, helped along by Isabelle, who now freely admitted that she longed to end her days back in the La Crosse Valley, yearned "for the repose of the country, the solace of familiar scenes." During the summer, Hamlin took great pleasure in showing his parents around the World's Columbian Exposition—yet another place where he might have encountered H. W. S. Cleveland, who attended the fair specifically to see the parts of the landscape that had been designed by Frederick Law Olmsted—and then he brought them to the familiar town of West Salem, Wisconsin, where he had already selected a cottage to be the new Garland homestead, on four acres of "rich, level ground" that featured "enormous maples" and "a double row of New England elms" and expansive gardens, which, "rich in grape vines, asparagus beds, plums, raspberries and other fruiting shrubs, appealed with especial power to my mother who had lived so long on the sun-baked plains that the sight of green things growing was very precious in her eyes." Dick Garland insisted on going back to South Dakota (an official state since 1889) for one last harvest, but agreed to put his land up for sale immediately after getting his grain to market; he promised he would get to West Salem in time for Thanksgiving.

*A Son of the Middle Border* ends in November 1893, with "a homecoming and a housewarming," giving the book a perfect feeling of circularity and closure. Garland was now thirty-three, and he finally "acknowledged the peace of the old, the settled," finally "acknowledged myself at home and for all time. Beneath my feet lay the rugged country rock of my nativity. It pleased me to discover my mental characteristics striking so deep into this typically American soil." The new homestead represented an ideal middle landscape, a compromise between town and country, a solution to the problem of modern development, allowing Garland to indulge his "love of the wilderness" while at the same time retaining access to "roads and bridges and neighbors." And the land seemed fertile, resources abundant: they were "back where cranberries and turkeys and fat squashes grew." Moreover, Garland noted, the nearby farmhouses and lanes and streams and fields and hills and patches of woodland "all had delightful associations in my mind." The previous year, when Hamlin had brought his mother to West Salem to look for property, they had both found the "atmosphere" to be "profoundly restful and satisfying"—"no one seemed in a hurry and no one seemed to fear either the wind or the sun"—and as they sat on Isabelle's brother's porch, "talking of war times . . . , a sweet and solemn mood came over us," and for a while "it seemed as if the spirits of the pioneers . . . had been called back and were all about us." Now, at Thanksgiving, with aunts and uncles and cousins seated around the table, Garland felt again that "note of sadness which is inevitable in such a gathering, and the shadow deepened as we gathered about the fire a little later. The dead claimed their places."[90] It seemed a true Arcadia.

The problem was that Garland didn't actually want to live there. Who can say exactly why not? Some of the reasons were surely personal, and some historical—if the two categories can be disentangled. He needed to be around other artists and activists (he was a tireless joiner—and founder—of clubs and associations of all kinds). He was looking for a wife, and was attracted to the larger pool of candidates to be found in a city. He thought that cities represented the future of civilization, were home to everything exciting, innovative, stimulating. He found it easier, in certain neighborhoods of certain cities, to distract himself from the tragedies and injustices of American Progress. In any case, for the next several years, he mostly left his parents to their own devices in Wisconsin, and spent most months of each year living in Chicago or New York, or traveling through the far west, exploring wilderness areas and visiting Indian reservations.

Earlier Arcadians (like Margaret Fuller and Henry Thoreau) had been able to look to the frontier with a sense of hopefulness: the west was the land of potential, where true compromises might be reached between city and country, even whites and Indians. But by the 1890s, even if in reality a great deal of land remained to be opened (mostly the arid high plains of places like Montana, so intriguing to Dick Garland), many Americans had begun to think of the frontier as having passed away: it seemed clear now that the United States would be predominantly an urban, industrial society. As for the Indians—well, after a few decades of relative peace in the middle of the nineteenth century, the nation had been explicitly at war with various tribes throughout the 1870s and 80s, until the massacre at Wounded Knee in 1890 (when Sitting Bull was killed) seemed to mark an end to the fighting; now the survivors were mostly squeezed onto tiny plots of land far from where their ancestors were buried. Moreover, after the passage of the General Allotment Act in 1887, Indians were required to renounce common ownership, as each "family unit" (according to the white Christian model) got assigned to a small, private homestead, thus reducing the total acreage available to each tribe even further. The era of the Wild West had settled the question of America's dishonor: every bit of the land was tainted. In the aftermath of the Civil War, the newly unified nation had displaced much of its violent racism onto Native Americans.[91]

In writing *A Son of the Middle Border* during World War I, Garland had tried to re-capture his feeling for the frontier, but, for all the book's beauty and effectiveness, it could not heal his wound of disillusionment. In 1923, having long since married an artist and settled in New York City (with a summer home in the Catskills, near the town of Tannersville—a nod to a slightly earlier version of Arcadia, perhaps), he took a trip through Wisconsin and recorded in his journal a sense of relief that "my wife and daughter are not confined to even the best of these towns." Instead of experiencing a sense of rosy nostalgia, he found his mind wracked with "torturing memories. . . . I had no desire to enter the homestead or the farm."[92] Even back in 1900, when he had gone to West Salem to speak at an Old Settlers' Reunion, he found himself at odds with the crowd, most of whom wished simply to celebrate the heroic securing of northwestern Illinois and southern Wisconsin in the Black Hawk War of the early 1830s, by bands of intrepid pioneers and of course the U.S. Army, whose ranks in-cluded a young Abraham Lincoln. Apparently, according to a newspaper account of the event, Garland had "declared the Indians in the Black Hawk war entirely right and the whites entirely wrong. He said the name of Black Hawk should ever be re-vered and remembered."[93] Though Garland, in line with Henry George, always placed the ultimate blame on the "speculative holders of land" who made condi-tions more difficult for the common pioneer family, he nevertheless insisted that the yeoman settlers had to accept some responsibility for continually "moving on, dis-persing to the north and west, robbing and destroying the Indian."[94]

It's easy to see Garland as becoming more selfish, vain, conservative, and escapist as he grew older (this is the received wisdom about his life and career).[95] After the early 1890s, he rarely wrote about the land question again; he even made a fairly large speculative investment in some Oklahoma (formerly Indian Territory) real estate. He became increasingly suspicious of immigrants, especially those who came from south-ern and eastern Europe. In middle age, concerned about supporting his family, he mostly churned out conventional romance novels set amidst the sublime scenery of the mountain west. He failed to be present when his mother passed away at the Wis-consin homestead in 1900, even though for several weeks his father had been writing to him, urging him to come, telling him how poorly Isabelle was faring and how desperately she wanted to see him. And, despite all his works of autobiography (*A Son of the Middle Border* was followed immediately by the Pulitzer Prize–winning *A Daughter of the Middle Border*, not to mention additional volumes such as *Back-Trailers from the Middle Border* and *Trail-Makers of the Middle Border*), he never wrote a public word about the pain it caused him when his father remarried just a year after his mother's death. Nor did he ever acknowledge the grief he felt when his first child was stillborn. A true commitment to Arcadia would seem to demand a more direct confrontation with darkness, a frank acknowledgment of limits.

Yet there were times in the second half of his life when Garland did maintain this kind of commitment—when his reformist inclinations led him to uphold the possibility of an American Arcadia predicated on the recognition of wrongs inflicted on both nature and Natives. Between 1895 and 1905, Garland traveled to several Indian reservations, developing a better understanding of various tribal cultures, enlarging his sympathies, and gradually coming to scorn the propaganda that, in his view, "helped to make the English-speaking peoples the most ruthless conquerors the world has ever seen, ruthless in the sense that they displace and destroy with large-hearted, joyous self-sufficiency, blotting out all manners, customs, religions, and governments which happen to differ from their own." Garland's goal was to observe the details of Native American life and write about them with a respectful realism, depicting what he saw as their nobility and their weaknesses, and emphasizing the Indians' "common humanity. We spring from the same good brown earth, and return thereto with an equal awe of 'the great mystery.'" Often, Garland conducted extensive interviews, sometimes using them to write articles and stories that attempted to capture Native perspectives, as in the scathing "General Custer's Last Fight as Seen by Two Moon," and "The Silent Eaters," which portrays mid-century Sioux civilization as an Arcadia ruined by the violent greed of white invaders hungry for gold and land. Like most turn-of-the-century Indian advocates, Garland held to a fundamental assumption that, overall, white American civilization was probably more developed than, say, Southern Ute civilization, but he nevertheless insisted that the rituals of the Southern Utes—their "mysterious and somber" burial practices, for instance, or their "unutterably sad" way of playing the flute—were filled with as much meaning and resonance as white rituals and deserved to be sustained. And if Indians ever acted in ways that Garland's white readership might find offensive, he was quick to supply reminders that the Natives had every reason to despise white people and every right to defend their land: "It is the self-interest and local barbarism of the whites which keep the Indian continually alarmed, suspicious, and revengeful." The federal government owed it to these tribes—so often forced onto a particular patch of land "because it was supposed at the time to be unhabitable by any other human being"—to put fences up around the reservations, to "keep whites off the Indian's land," to make it "perfectly plain that this land is the Indians' and that no scheming of greedy ranchmen and pliant politicians can ever take it from them."[96]

Some day, Garland hoped, a new class of Americans would arise who might understand how to cultivate respect and empathy, who might learn "to civilize in a new and reverent way the land we must possess." Meanwhile, he said, in a convocation address at the University of Chicago in 1905, "my heart aches to see the forests destroyed, the flowery meadows burned black by the plow, the mountain streams despoiled, while the wild sheep are harried from peak to peak, and the red hunter dies in squalor. In my veins runs the blood of the pioneer, the hunter, the trailer. I cry out against every act of wanton desecration of the wild. . . . I deny the right of a careless, insensate few to mar and lay waste this glorious land, on which future generations have a most authentic claim." Perhaps there was some way to salvage the culture and history of the middle border, some common ground to be found between settlers and Indians: back in the early days, after all, the two groups had sometimes managed to share resources, as the pioneers developed rural lifeways modeled on Native adaptations to local conditions. "I believe in civilization," Garland asserted, "a true civilization; but not in our tin-can, barbed-wire civilization, which is indeed only a temporary stage of progress. The crude, fierce, destructive epoch of the mine, the railway, the saw-mill, will soon be over. It came like a blight; it will pass swiftly, and those who love beauty and sanity and good-will among men will hasten to bind up Nature's wounds. Of this I am very certain. Between the trailer and this gentle man of the future there will be a vital chord of sympathy—a bond woven of reverence for Nature and desire to preserve her sanctuaries. The tepee, the log cabin, many of the signs and symbols of the trail, can be carried forward to the future, bearing with them a reminder of the best of that which is now vanishing in the sunset glow."[97]

In his early days, caught up in the idealism of his friend Henry George, Garland worked endlessly "to help hasten the golden age."[98] In mid-life, though, he was often "filled with doubt of my ability," often felt "restless and dissatisfied. . . . How it will all end I do not know."[99] It had gotten harder for everyone to face death, in part because social and familial roles had become so fluid that people no longer knew whether or not, when they reached the end, they would feel that they had lived a Good Life. Once, shortly after part of Garland's house had burned to the ground, when his sense of homelessness became a fact, he thought everything was "dwindling into futility. I was in physical pain much of the time and tortured by a fear of the future."[100] He had no idea how anyone might manage to swim against the tides of modernity, how the old Arcadian ethic of limitation, of humble engagement with the land, of kinship and care, might be renewed and reinstituted, especially considering that the common person could not even conceptualize his or her relationship to the economy anymore: "how can this ever-increasing complex web of human life here in America flow on peacefully?"[101] Perhaps, like George, Garland suspected that no true civilization could rise again until the current one had been swept away in some sort of apocalypse.

# 7

# ATLANTIS:
# ARCADIA AND ARMAGEDDON

The island lay, as through the ages past, fair and imperial in the Atlantic. Though now
was it becoming wanton, even to its undoing. Else would not this be written.
—Elizabeth G. Birkmaier, *Poseidon's Paradise: The Romance of Atlantis* (1892)

The great American apocalypse, according to many observers, seemed to arrive in
1893, with the most devastating economic collapse the country had ever experienced. But it had been sighted many times before. In the previous year, for instance:
when the Populists gathered in Omaha to choose their presidential candidate and
articulate their political vision, they characterized America as being "on the verge of
moral, political, and material ruin." "A vast conspiracy against mankind has been
organized on two continents," they asserted, in the famous preamble to their official
platform, "and it is rapidly taking possession of the world. If not met and overthrown
at once it forebodes terrible social convulsions, the destruction of civilization." Of
course, the very overthrowing of the "corporations, national banks, rings, trusts," an
act of revolution meant to forestall the apocalypse, might itself become apocalyptic,
especially since the "plundered" farmers and workers, deprived of the fruits of their
labor, clearly had nature on their side.[1] It seemed possible that, as the people rose, so
too would the world's water.

The man behind the Populists' preamble was a Minnesota politician, lawyer, and
literary celebrity named Ignatius Donnelly, who just two years earlier had sold tens
of thousands of copies of a dystopian novel, *Caesar's Column: A Story of the Twentieth Century* (1890), and eight years before that had published an even more popular

nonfiction work called *Atlantis: The Antediluvian World* (1882). Both books drama-
tize the cosmic risk taken by societies whose leaders overreach, pushing expansion
with too much confidence and certainty, refusing to recognize limits. The "arrogance and oppressions" of such societies cannot go unpunished.[2] Donnelly's politics
indicate a thinker who was deeply invested in the hope that the downtrodden majority
would be able to construct some new form of Arcadia. His writing, though, suggests
someone who suspected that, whatever might happen in the long term, the immediate future of American civilization would be characterized by violent upheaval. In
*Caesar's Column*, which is set in 1988, New York City has been transformed into a
dazzling high-tech metropolis, with a clean, noiseless transit system, ample and deli-
cious food from around the world, geothermal heating, and a network of pipes to and
from the stratosphere to provide cooling air whenever necessary—but all these marvels, all the luxuries and conveniences of urban life, are built on the brutal exploitation of the productive classes by devious plutocrats. Eventually, the workers, receiving
aid from international terrorists, revolt, and the ensuing battle reduces the entire society to rubble. A few survivors, having commandeered an "air-ship," float above the
planet and look down on all the "blackened and smoking masses of ruin."[3]

Atlantis also tells a story of deserved destruction, but it dwells for a much longer
time on apocalypse's prehistory, evoking an ideal society that lasted for centuries
before finally becoming corrupt and bringing about its own downfall. The book's
mood is somewhat less alarmist or vengeful—though it does strike certain caution-
ary notes—and more rueful or nostalgic. Like Henry George, whose *Progress and
Poverty* came out three years before *Atlantis*, Donnelly was born in 1830s Philadelphia (home of the relatively expansive Fairmount Gardens and Laurel Hill Cemetery, modeled on the Boston Common and Mount Auburn) but fled westward in the
1850s, as his home town became more crowded and cramped: he hoped to find a
new balance between city and country on the middle border. By the harvest season
of 1880, when he turned forty-nine and started working up his Atlantis materials, he
had realized that Arcadia's time had probably passed, that, on the frontier as well as
back home on the east coast, Americans were embracing urban industrialism once
and for all. His book project, then, represented a long look back.

Donnelly's argument was that Atlantis had actually existed and was the source for
every paradise in Western mythology[4] (it was "the true Antediluvian world; the Garden of Eden; the Gardens of the Hesperides; the Elysian Fields"), and the book takes
readers on a sweeping tour of the textual, linguistic, folkloric, architectural, archaeo-
logical, geographical, and anthropological evidence. Most likely, though, the basic
premise held so much appeal in postbellum America because it rested on people's

rosy memory of what antebellum life had been like. Quoting Plato—two of whose dialogues, the *Timaeus* and the *Critias*, provide the origin of the myth of Atlantis— Donnelly explained that the Atlanteans "were furnished with everything which they could have, both in city and country" and that "the cultivated fruit of the earth, both the dry edible fruit and other species of food, which we call by the general name of legumes . . . [were] brought forth fair and wondrous in infinite abundance." Atlantis, much like the state of New York in the 1830s and 40s, was apparently dominated by an extensive canal system, allowing inhabitants to live simply "by agriculture and commerce," sending their ample produce (especially apples) to numerous towns and cities, which were decorated with elegant fountains and cisterns and which boasted "all manner of trees of wonderful height and beauty, owing to the excellence of the soil."[5] Though there were clearly elements of pure fantasy in this Atlantis—its inhabitants, the ultimate natives, did not have to deal with the guilt of displacing anyone— the book's overarching tone marks it as an act of mourning for the lapsed Arcadia of Donnelly's childhood. And many of his compatriots clearly shared his feelings: the book launched a veritable Atlantis craze in American culture, which lasted into the twentieth century.

Labors of loss and retrospection, like the celebration of twilight, represent classic Arcadian impulses, and they can couch trenchant social criticisms.[6] But they can also point to a kind of fatalism that goes beyond the basic acceptance of limits. While Donnelly clearly did have a political program, his engagement with the Arcadian tradition was ultimately less constructive than it might have been. Henry George and H. W. S. Cleveland and even Hamlin Garland all coped with the disenchantment of modernity by envisioning and starting to build a reenchanted society, which would blend urban and rural elements in new ways. Donnelly, though, whose despair exceeded even Cleveland's and sometimes canceled out his inclination toward protest, often fell in with the general postbellum trend toward tired acquiescence to corporate capitalism: most Americans were going to have to live as wage-earning consumers, not self-sufficient producers, in dark, polluted cities, whose contours would be shaped by railroad and mining and manufacturing magnates—so the most important thing was being able to afford an occasional escape. Donnelly's Atlantis was the temporal equivalent of a western wilderness area, a roped-off historical monument, a national park of the imagination.

To be sure, Donnelly could be radical, especially in the context of 1890s Populism, and throughout his career he maintained a strong sense of egalitarianism that led him to speak out in defense of minorities and the poor, despite his own weakness for get-rich-quick schemes. But his proposed solutions to social problems usually had more to do with tariffs and greenbacks than community agriculture or green spaces: his political thinking tended to be financial, not spatial. He had read and appreciated *Progress and Poverty*, but he could not support the Single Tax, because he thought Georgism too similar to communism, and because he thought it was simply too late for most people to go back to an agrarian way of life: "A human being on 80 acres of unimproved land is as helpless as if he were on 80 acres of water."[7] The most overtly political moment in *Atlantis* is not an invocation of horticultural utopianism but a rant against national monetary policy: just as the Atlanteans worshipped gold in by-gone ages, so too did the American bankers and lawmakers of the aptly named Gilded Age, hewing to the gold standard instead of printing more paper money (greenbacks), which could have wrested some control over prices away from gold-rich corporations and helped farmers pay their debts.[8] While Donnelly did share George's antimonop-oly sentiments (in 1873 he was elected to the Minnesota state senate as the candidate of the Anti-Monopoly party), he was not about to break up and redistribute the rail-roads' land holdings (he was also a railroad lobbyist for part of his career), because his conception of "commonwealth" held private property to be sacred; he simply wanted the government to promote inflation, so that the price of farm commodities would rise and the agriculturists of the middle border—the ones who already owned land, anyway—could get back on their feet.

Donnelly himself owned quite a bit of land: just like Hamlin Garland, he bounced back and forth between speculative real estate ventures and righteous condemna-tions of speculation. Back in 1856, when he first went to Minnesota, he had immedi-ately joined with the land mogul John Nininger to found Nininger City, a classic "paper" town, laid out on a grid, about fifteen miles south of St. Paul on the Missis-sippi River. To his credit, Donnelly offered lots with the stipulation that buyers had to spend at least $250 on improvements within two years: they could not simply wait for real estate values to rise and then sell off to new migrants, pocketing the unearned increment. Indeed, Donnelly was thoroughly committed to Nininger City, immedi-ately helping to organize lyceum lectures, an Athenaeum Association, and a public school. Even when the Panic of 1857 struck, extinguishing plans to put a rail line through town and causing the entire development scheme to go bust, as banks failed and money simply disappeared from the middle border (where everyone's wealth had been based on speculation), Donnelly nevertheless kept his Nininger residence, converted some of his town lots to agricultural fields (though he had no idea how to be a farmer), and settled into a frontier life with his wife and young son, who was joined by a sister in 1858. And though Nininger never really became a city—by 1889 it did not even merit a post office any longer—Donnelly helped shape it into a pleasant patch of rurality.[9] "Beautiful nature!" Donnelly once wrote. "Each year as I grow in age I grow in the knowledge and the love of thee. Thou art our noblest study." A man, weighed down with the particular responsibilities of modern life, might carry his cares with him into a nearby wood or meadow, and nature would remain "beautiful calm unworried—meeting him with the same bright flowers in youth, in middle years, in age, and blossoming above his tomb."[10]

In the summer of 1881, when a reporter from the *St. Paul Globe* heard that Donnelly had been working on a quirky book project about Atlantis, she sought him out at his home and wound up publishing a long article about the local landscape, dwelling on how strangely "cheerful" and "impressive" the "decayed" town seemed, with "a cemetery as a suburb," located just down the road from Donnelly's estate and "kept in admirable order by affectionate remembrance": "A broad view of the river gives a fine stimulus of the pure air in this region, and the scene lays hold of one with a forgetfulness of all else save the endless expressions of earth's face, and a pensive thought of the human dust beyond all glories of this material universe."[11]

By the time of the journalist's visit, Donnelly was in good spirits, as his manuscript had been accepted by Harper & Brothers, one of the biggest New York presses, and writing it had been, well, an immersive experience.[12] His personal landscape had seemed utterly bleak the previous November, though: "Alas and Alas! This is my 49th birthday, and a sad day it is. . . . The future settles down upon me dark and gloomy indeed. . . . My life has been a failure and a mistake. My hopes have so often come to naught that I cease to hope. . . . Well, well. All I can do is to face the music and take my damnable fortune as it comes."[13] Earlier in 1880, he had gone deep into debt, struggled with farming (he never became an adept or enthusiastic agriculturist), and lost a prolonged legal battle in Washington over the congressional election of 1878, in which he had been defeated under suspicious circumstances (he had already served three terms in the U.S. House of Representatives and also spent some time as Minnesota's lieutenant governor as well as a state senator). Getting ready to leave the nation's capital and head back home to attend to his crops, he had felt "weary" and "sick" and "ready to jump into the Potomac."[14] Nininger was at least reposeful, and once the harvest had come in and he'd survived his birthday, he turned eagerly to his research and writing. Ultimately, Donnelly wanted to be a politician, but after a couple of decades of switching parties and shifting positions on everything from railroads to Indians, he seemed pleased to pause for a while, to work out some of his ideas and opinions in the context of a scientific inquiry, to escape into the deep Atlantean past, to embrace the complexity and contradictions of literary creation.

Even nostalgic escapism can help keep a tradition alive, and Donnelly's imagining of an Arcadian Atlantis was powerfully compelling for many Americans because a significant number of those millions who accepted the new industrial order nevertheless experienced a keen sense of loss. *Atlantis* came out in February 1882, and by March all the newspapers were reporting that "the first edition has been exhausted."[15] That year, it went through seven full print runs—unheard of for a work of nonfiction— and by the end of the decade there had been twenty-three American editions and twenty-six in England.[16] The book's popularity rested on countless factors—not least, the author's passionate prose style ("Can all these precise coincidences be the result of accident?")[17]—but one of the keys was clearly its successful evocation of a place that readers could easily visit in their minds: "Whether we are as yet fully prepared to believe it or not," one reviewer wrote of Donnelly's creation, "we shall delight to gaze into it, and reflect upon it, and dream over it. It opens up a magnificent vista of speculation and vision-seeing and palace-building. It leads us to the gates of a new wonder-world, and bids us enter and wander at our will."

Wonder-world, Underworld: Donnelly was guiding readers into the land of the dead, and explaining how it was still connected to the land of the living, how everything leads back to Atlantis, how all cultures have a common origin, how traditions of burial and memorialization, planting and harvesting, bind us together through time and space. The book is full of Indian Mounds and stone monuments and orchards and gardens, and Donnelly suggested that these immediately recognizable elements of antebellum culture lent the United States an unfathomable antiquity and geographical reach, because they represented forms of thought that were echoed all over the world, preserved by the scattered survivors of Atlantis. "The burden of his argument," said another reviewer, "rests always upon the astonishing similarities that exist in regions the most remote."[18] In a splintered postbellum society that was busy annihilating space and time, Donnelly proposed the ultimate theory of unification. *Atlantis* was, in a sense, his own answer to the righteous, wrathful speech he had made on the floor of Congress back in May 1864, on the eve of the Battle of the Wilderness, when he insisted that slavery had to be wiped out completely, that the white and black races had to understand and accept their kinship with each other, or else all would suffer the consequences of "the rising flood which the breath of God is swelling and lifting over all the wrongs and iniquities of the world."[19]

The global, comparative approach that Donnelly used to construct his argument about Atlantis, while objectionable in all kinds of ways—most problematic, surely, was the conflation of his basic assumptions with the propositions he was supposedly trying to prove—carried a great deal of weight in the nineteenth century and reflected a serious engagement with contemporary science. When he pointed out, for instance, that very similar pyramidal structures "were used as places of sepulture" in Asia, Africa, and the Americas, and that a "system of earthworks and mounds, kindred to the pyramids, is found even in England," he could back up his claim by citing one of the most important authorities of the century, Alexander von Humboldt, who pioneered this relational method in his efforts to recognize and understand "unity in diversity."[20] The anti-Humboldtian leap that Donnelly took was to explain this kind of parallelism monistically: clearly, he posited, it must derive from the broad diffusion of Atlantean burial practices. But along the pathway to this unwarranted conclusion (which was really an assumption), he delineated a number of possible patterns in human-nature relations that are remarkable for their radical empathy and inclusiveness.[21]

In an era stained by its forest-destroying tendencies, Donnelly—who had tried, unsuccessfully, to sponsor a national tree-planting bill in 1866 and who in 1874 had launched a sweeping investigation of Minnesota lumber companies thought to be illegally cutting trees on state-owned lands and Indian reservations—argued that virtually every successful civilization in history had engaged in a kind of tree worship, had respected trees as perfect converters of the sun's energy, bearers of fruit, sources of knowledge, long-lived witnesses to history.[22] Moreover, at a time when scientific racism was on the rise and many Americans justified the Indian Wars by characterizing all Natives as inherently savage,[23] Donnelly made a point of defining "civilization" very liberally (historically, he thought, "the dark races were the more civilized"), and, like Henry George, he insisted not only that Indians were fully capable of developing complex cultures but that many of them already had, as demonstrated especially by the elaborate rituals and stories that guided their understanding of death and the natural world. Like the French "at the cemetery of Père-la-Chaise," who "still put cakes and sweetmeats on the graves," the "American Indian leaves food with the dead." Like the ancient Romans, the typical Indian felt he owed everything to those who came before him, and constantly prayed "to the spirits of his forefathers." And like all good Christians, many Indian groups believed that it made sense to bow before whatever divine force controlled the elements, because in ancient times there had been a great, punishing deluge from which only a few people and animals had escaped.[24]

Donnelly had followed the explosion of scholarly work on Indian Mounds quite closely—he had lectured about the St. Paul Mounds as early as 1858,[25] perhaps after having read the very first publication of the Smithsonian Institution, *Ancient Monu-*

*ments of the Mississippi Valley* (1848)—and though the majority opinion in 1882 held that the Mound Builders must have been chased southward by the more primitive "nomadic tribes who succeeded them and preceded us" (as one author put it in 1879),[26] Donnelly's firmly stated position was that at least some of the tribes of the nineteenth century were direct descendants of the Mound Builders, and, in any case, all Indians were human beings and therefore kin to all other human beings. Like most of his countrymen, Donnelly was of course inclined to rank his own civilization higher than most others, and he believed that some races were irremediably "savage,"[27] but when he looked at particular peoples he almost always saw their common humanity and even advocated for their rights. He consistently argued for African American suffrage and access to education in the 1860s, and even though he tacitly approved of the displacement of Indians from areas like Minnesota—"What a beautiful land has the red man lost and the white man won," he wrote, in 1857—he also recognized the injustice of this theft of the earth, and as an elected official he actively defended the state's remaining tribes from depredations by settlers, corporations, and other government agents.[28] By the time he wrote *Atlantis*, he was ready to suggest that Adam, the Bible's first human being—whose name shares its root with the Hebrew word for the ruddy earth, "Adamah"—was "a red man," that Indians showed just as much diversity as white people, and that all of humanity was "a mongrel race" characterized by millennia of "intermingling" and "crossing of stocks," all of which derived from the original diverse groups that had populated the ancient lost continent between Europe and the Americas, of which "Atlantis was but the stump."[29]

What, in the end, can we say about all of humanity? We are born; we die; in life, we depend on sunlight, air, water, soil, and the rooted things that soil nurtures. Other thinkers (usually seeking to prove the legitimacy of the Bible) had already pointed out how many different cultures owned legends of the Flood: we all start off enwombed, surrounded by lapping water, but soon we crawl out onto the shore and cling to mother earth, and then water, the universal solvent, with its power of erasure, comes to embody our fear of death. When the deluge comes, it wipes out any hint that you ever lived. Donnelly's brilliance lay in giving our shared dependence, our shared fear, our shared humanity, a specific name and place: Atlantis belonged to everyone. It was the ultimate commons.

---

In August 2005, a year after Christine and I and our first child, Sam, moved to Ithaca, we sat in our living room staring at a small screen that showed the water rising on the edges of New Orleans: Hurricane Katrina. The next year, after our second son,

Abe, was born, I sat in a darkened theater staring at a much larger screen that showed the water rising on the edges of Manhattan: *An Inconvenient Truth*. In the era of global warming and extreme weather, of perfect storms, of melting polar ice, the seas of American culture seemed to be welling up again. And the nature of this catastrophism was markedly different from that of my Cold War childhood, when it was nuclear bombs that loomed largest as potential causes of the apocalypse. As I started laying the groundwork for this book, started thinking through our obligations to the dead and the unborn, to the past and the future, to nature, to the earth, to each other, I thought I could discern some capillary fractures in the edifice of American denial: the dam was cracking, and a few drops of water were seeping through. The national political campaigns of 2006 and 2008 bespoke an anxious and even angry electorate; the mass media finally started treating climate change as an established fact; and some American citizens, often spurred by their own children, began to express a desire to change the system through which they had unwittingly contributed to a threatening rise in planetary instability. And then came another one of the worst economic downturns in modern history, and another period of what can only be described as general environmental apathy. The threat of Armageddon can still sometimes capture our national imagination, but we now have few positive visions with which to counter our premonitions of doom. We've gradually begun to accept that we can't live in a virtual world: the free-floating future society depicted in the movie *Wall-E* (2008), where thoroughly sated Americans whiz around space stations on lounge chairs enjoying every convenience, is the perfect science-fiction nightmare for the twenty-first century. And meanwhile Arcadia seems a dimmer and dimmer memory, a hopelessly outdated concept, one of those wild, utopian schemes that usually failed even at the village level and could never possibly work on a national scale.[30]

I remember feeling desperate, in 2006, to cultivate some sense of Arcadia for myself, some sense of being at home in central New York. In early May, at the end of my second year of teaching, I tried to pause and collect my thoughts and feelings. I loved my students, loved being so fully engaged with them, but I also recognized that my experience of Ithaca did not extend very far beyond the path I had worn between my house and office, mostly on the trail through Cascadilla Gorge. Abe was just three months old; Sam was two and a half; Christine and I felt as though we hadn't slept since moving to Ithaca. I wasn't about to lead my environmental history students in a march on Washington to demand a carbon tax (though I sometimes wanted to), or become a farmer, or shrug off my New England roots and my ties to other far-off places. But it seemed reasonable to carve out some time for exploring local landscapes and histories. Perhaps, later in the summer, we could visit some of the other gorges, lakes, orchards, and wineries that the area was known for; meanwhile, I thought, I wanted to learn about how this culture of the Finger Lakes had developed. I wanted what I always want: a good book. So, preparing for a trip to Christine's home town in southern California—a suburb of Los Angeles called (I'm serious) Arcadia—where I had to give a talk and Christine was hoping to reconnect with some childhood haunts (and friends), I stopped by our neighborhood bookstore, The Bookery, and found a meditation on Ithaca and its surroundings called *From Where We Stand: Recovering a Sense of Place* (1993), by the poet Deborah Tall, who apparently lived just a few blocks away. There were blurbs by one of my favorite essayists, Phillip Lopate, and one of my favorite geographers, Yi-Fu Tuan. So I paid my money, slipped the book into my backpack, and prayed that the kids would sleep on the plane. Unsurprisingly, they didn't. As it happened, though, my ruptured disc acted up a couple of days after I fulfilled my professional obligation at the Huntington Library, and I found myself flat on my back on a couch, with nothing to do but read. Back pain was a defining force in this period of my life: when I was free of it, I felt light, almost giddy, expedition-ready; when it struck me, every few weeks, and I could no longer pick up my tiny children, I questioned everything, wallowing in bitter self-disgust. I was useless to my employer, my students, my family; I couldn't recognize myself. How had Stephen managed to adapt so matter-of-factly to his wheelchair? Thankfully, in this case, I was consoled—again—by the sense of kinship I found in a book.

Sometimes you have to go away before you can learn how to belong somewhere. Though I relished being back out west, a part of me, as I read *From Where We Stand*, became desperate to get home, to meet Deborah Tall, to make a pilgrimage to every place she had described, the Indian sites, the state parks, the wildflower preserves. It was her skepticism about her own project that inspired my empathy: "What danger has there been, I have to ask, in my own form of wandering? What land would I defend? Will I ever be 'a local'? Do I even want to be, with the term's implication of provinciality?" Indeed, I can rarely support place-making unless it is balanced by a fluid, open-minded cosmopolitanism, because space in the world is limited, and those who proclaim firm attachments to particular patches of land too often do so in order to exclude others. Most people in the world don't have a garden to cultivate. While the defense of a home or even a nation might make sense for historically oppressed peoples, like Native Americans or Jews, the ethics of living in Zion can get complicated very quickly. Moreover, like Hamlin Garland, Henry George, H. W. S. Cleveland, and Ignatius Donnelly, I'm attracted to mobility because of its liberating hopefulness, because sometimes you need to escape the "influences and expectations that a home place holds." Only after acknowledging that localism can be stifling—it is still difficult simply to be gay or black, for instance, in most small towns in America— am I able to agree with Tall that, "thought of another way . . . , the local defines a circle of obligation, a territory of responsibility," even, potentially, a realm of deep caring. When, in her thirties, Tall decided to "settle down" with her husband, when she gave up living on an Irish island and moved to the shore of an inland lake, planning to have children and work a steady job at a college, she felt she was "giving up [her] youthful grasping at the infinity of ocean and accepting limitation, a boundary on aspiration." She was ready for such constraint: "The arena has necessarily shrunk, but thereby intensified. I rely on the lake as imaginative hearth. The horizon of middle age knows how much we can really take in at a time: a good four-mile stretch."

The horizon of middle age: yes, it seemed appropriate to stay put and get to know a particular landscape and community, to give my kids a chance to feel as though they were *from* somewhere. But how to be sure that Ithaca was the right place? Maybe it was too small, too isolated; maybe Christine and I would never be accepted, never break into the preexisting social circles, which seemed so rigidly defined. At times, I fantasized about quitting my job and moving back to New England: even though I would never want to revert to the days when it was unthinkable to leave one's home town, what was wrong with going back of one's own free will, after having seen a few other parts of the world? I needed a job, though, and I had a particularly good one in Ithaca; and New England wasn't home for Christine; and I felt a responsibility to try harder to put down roots here in central New York, to adapt to this environment. It was at least comforting that Tall, too, was confused and ambivalent, "oddly unbalanced, not yet settled, even after two years."

Ultimately, though, what she helped me appreciate was that Ithaca could feel like "a place where the natural world still informs human life," even if you lived downtown and did not participate in any back-to-the-land movement. Children could grow up picking their own fruit all summer long, visiting the farms where some of their other food came from, sampling antique-variety apples with bright pink flesh, swimming in creeks, getting to know hawks and herons and deer and woodchucks, exploring both gorges and cemeteries. I admired Tall's commitment to see historically, to spend days "hunting down stories so that the land rings for me," picking out "evidence of the past left visible in the present." She found old Indian trails and old lines of trees and even old burial mounds, like the one at Kanadesaga, which the Seneca used to visit once a year in the nineteenth century, and in her book she gradually wove together her deep soundings of herself and her landscape into a narrative of continual seeking and witnessing. "The abyss between us and the past of the land," she wrote, "seems impossible to bridge sometimes," but through her writing, "an act of deliberate adoption," she managed to make contact with a new set of ancestors, people who inspired her in their "willing accommodation" to their environment. She felt uncomfortable claiming them as hers, and I understand the problem—what right do I have to see H. W. S. Cleveland as my spiritual and intellectual ancestor, when he has his own legitimate descendants?—but she felt she had to acknowledge her developing sense of attachment. And "when people are attached to their forebears, they want to remain close to where they lived, continue their traditions, tend their graves, embody their hopes." In this impulse to linger lies the seed of stewardship, "because the lived-in land then becomes an extension of the self, the family and group; to endanger the land is to wound one's collective body."[31]

Like Ignatius Donnelly, Tall cultivated her gift for seeing the traces of ancient civilizations in the landscape, and pondered the different ways in which human beings have connected themselves to the earth and the cosmos. Staring out at the "large rolled carpets of hay" that are mainstays on many local farms, "like big jelly-roll mounds erected in a field, a haphazard pattern of circular straw sculptures," Tall found herself remembering a visit to "Carnac in Brittany—that field of granite monuments, eleven long avenues of more than three thousand standing stones, huge to tombstone-sized, unexplained, of an age with Stonehenge." Both Carnac and Stonehenge are now thought to be not only sophisticated markers of astronomical alignments (local pagans congregate every year at both sites to celebrate the summer solstice) but also cemeteries that gathered together the bodies of people from all over Europe, places where space and time converged. As Tall walked and drove along the pathways and roads of the Finger Lakes, she came to realize that the main upstate thoroughfare, the New York Thruway (itself modeled on the Erie Canal), was a precise mirror of the old Iroquois longhouse line, that Euro-American settlement echoed Native American settlement, and that these kinds of lines on the land often reflected either deeper patterns in the earth or cosmic patterns in the atmosphere. The longhouse line, for instance, marks a division between weather zones: "while lake-effect snow routinely pummels the area just south of Lake Ontario, snowfall invariably diminishes right around the New York Thruway, making it more reliably passable, as the Iroquois no doubt observed." When I took my family to see the Great Serpent Mound in southern Ohio, on our way to visit my grandparents' grave in Cincinnati, the weather was clear and sunny until we got within a few yards of the snake's hilltop home—over which hovered an intense, punishing thunderstorm, and under which, apparently, there is a highly unusual fault line, known today for its tectonic activity.[32]

The mysterious connections between nature and culture, once you start to look for them, provoke endless questions. When I lived in California and toured the local wineries, I was told that grape-growing there, as in France, depended on a reliable dry season, long months of full sunshine and absolutely no rain; so how is it that viticulture has thrived on the gray and humid shores of the Finger Lakes? How to explain the cultural geography of the upstate "Burned-Over District," so incredibly productive of prophets, utopians, spiritualists, millenialists, psychics, abolitionists, feminists, environmentalists? Tall eventually started to wonder about theories of the earth as a living organism, with its own pulsing veins and arteries, its own nervous system, and she noted the resonant parallelism of the Chinese practices of acupuncture and geomancy, both of which were designed to guide the flow of *ch'i*, the ultimate energy or life force: in traditional Chinese culture, "Site selection for temples and even houses depends on the recognition of and alignment with the channels of *ch'i*, for human health is seen as intimately related to terrestrial health. The idea is applied even to the dead. Chinese graveyards were for centuries laid out by a geomancer, an adept using the elaborate science of *feng-shui*—literally 'wind and water.' The geomancer sees in the lay of the land—the arrangement of hills, valleys, rivers, and a sensation of what lies between and beneath them—the presence of benevolence or danger." Leaving aside the question of what might actually be there for a geomancer to see, Tall emphasized the caring caution with which some cultures have interacted with nature, and lamented the lack of attention to environmental design in the modern Western world, not to mention the apocalyptic power we now possess to obliterate places that might otherwise serve to connect us with rich traditions of mutual cultivation and accommodation: "Given our technology, whole landscapes can be cleared in a day. A familiar stretch of land can readily disappear beneath a parking lot or reservoir. . . . To belong to the land again in a vital way, we have to preserve enough to walk out into and recognize."[33] Tall seemed to have predicted Cornell's destruction of Redbud Woods.

I came back from California humbled and determined. For the first time in my life, I went to see a therapist, finally acknowledging how rattled I was by the unpredictability and severity of my back pain (I have been seeing her regularly ever since). I tried acupuncture for the first time, and a full summer of treatments actually seemed to help: perhaps I was finally starting to align myself with Ithaca. I started spending more mornings with my kids, even when I couldn't lift them, and I learned to say quiet prayers of thanks for their smiles and hugs and raw joy. And, more and more, we took field trips together, and I watched their eyes widen as they recognized the sound of the waterfall that was just around the next bend, watched them smell flowers and hug trees, watched them taste juneberries, watched them freeze as we stumbled upon rabbits. Eventually, I started taking them on what we called the Two Cemetery Walk, Abe in the stroller and Sam on foot, and Sam came up with a comedy routine about how it was really a death march: "I can't go any further! Just bury me right here!"

In September, I heard that Deborah Tall was giving a reading from her new memoir, *A Family of Strangers* (2006), at The Bookery. Given my time constraints, I almost never went to cultural events during my first few years in Ithaca, but I made an exception in this case, and I was deeply moved by Tall's gentle voice and presence. I sat perfectly still in my chair, wanting to speak with her, wanting to thank her for her wisdom and honesty, worrying that her head scarf might be a sign of serious illness. In the end, my shyness, and the swarming of the crowd, and a vague sense of mournfulness in the air, all got the better of me: I resolved to write her a letter, but instead of introducing myself to her I shuffled out the door and set off to wander around town for a little while, stopping at two places that I knew were important to her, that were becoming important to me—the Mulholland Wildflower Preserve, and the confluence of Indian paths at the base of Cascadilla Gorge, where the air always feels just a little bit cooler. That night, I read the first seventy pages or so of *A Family of Strangers*, a lyric essay broken up into page-long fragments of elegiac questioning, and I was utterly swept up in Tall's story of the secrets that her parents had guarded from her, captured by the clipped evocations of her sense of exclusion: "I understood it would be cruel of me to ask my father anything more." But then, in the rush of work-related obligations, I set the book aside, telling myself I would save it for a quieter time of year, when I could truly savor it, when I could fully absorb its complex tonal structure. In the years since then, I have often asked myself how this could have happened—no matter how busy I am, I almost never stop reading a book that I want to be reading—but I suppose the answer is simple: I was in denial. If I had read to the end, I would have learned, on the penultimate page, that, while working on the last section of the book, Tall had developed a "rare, aggressive form" of breast cancer.[34]

Throughout the fall, I planned to write her that letter, but in a way her new book—the part I had read, anyway—turned my attention away from Ithaca and back to my own parents. I wondered: Was my father a stranger to me? He was eighty-two now, and had completed his manuscript about the Dreyfus Affair the year before, but couldn't find a publisher for it. From the start, he had tried to protect himself by telling us that he was writing this book for his own sustenance, that it was a labor of love, that it didn't matter if it ever appeared between two covers: it had been decades since he had published a book, and he knew that standards and procedures had changed drastically. But we all understood that he wanted to offer these pages to the world. I had tried to help, without being intrusive, by reading and commenting on a few chapters. It was a delicate business, and I had the ulterior motive of simply getting closer to him, of opening up some space in which he might feel comfortable enough to confide in me a little more about his relationship to *his* parents. I was still learning to stop deferring to his moods and assumptions, still learning to approach him openly and ask direct questions. His opinion about the book was that it should come out with a university press and thus reflect his scholarly identity, so he got in touch with some old editorial contacts at Harvard, Yale, and Oxford, people who had supported his work in the past, and they all summarily rejected the manuscript, which left him baffled and demoralized. The problem, I told him, might be that the book fell in between disciplines—it was a literary approach to a historical subject—and so the university presses didn't know how to evaluate its "contribution to the field." I asked around and did some research and ultimately proposed a couple of small trade publishers that specialized in serious nonfiction. But my father turned instead to a few other scholarly presses, and in the summer of 2006 he reported that an editor at the University of Delaware had responded enthusiastically to his solicitation and was sending the manuscript out for review: this was the first time it had gotten to this stage. He seemed sure that it would work out, and I was delighted to imagine this final validation of my father's book arriving in the centennial year of Dreyfus's exoneration.

It took until just before Thanksgiving for the rejection letter to arrive. As usual, we celebrated the holiday at my sister's house in Amherst, in central Massachusetts. But my father was not in a festive mood. His morose deflation was familiar to me; what I didn't expect, as we sat down to discuss what the reviewer had written, was the bitter rage that suddenly possessed him. "He didn't even read the book!" he screamed. "This makes no sense!" On the one hand, I sympathized completely: the reviewer, hiding behind his anonymity (I'm guessing he was male), dismissed my father's efforts as worthless, ridiculing him for having done no archival research, expressing disbelief at the number of "important" historical studies he failed to cite (including, surely, those written by the reviewer himself), and ultimately positing that my father simply did not understand what it took to produce a scholarly work of history in the twenty-first century. Just like my father, I despised the reviewer for his territorialism, his condescension, his contempt, his nastiness. Far too often, the academy seems to cultivate precisely this kind of behavior. And it was wrong, unjust even, for the editor to accept such a report so uncritically. Clearly, the reviewer did not even try to understand the book's framing or evaluate it on its own terms. On the other hand, though, I was utterly unsettled by my father's willingness to let the judgment of this anonymous scholar unnerve him so completely. I can remember exactly one other time when I heard my father raise his voice in anger: I was about seven and had locked him out of our hotel room in Maine or New Hampshire. Moreover, he had always been adamant about being guided only by his own conscience and by the opinions of those few people in his life whom he loved and trusted. Even though I knew how much was at stake—his self-definition as a writer, a thinker, a Jew—I still felt that this episode might be the final proof that I had never really understood him. I did my best to deflect attention from his manuscript and put all the blame on the profession, on the narrow-mindedness of the historical discipline. But it was hard to figure out what he should do next. He wanted to rewrite the introduction, wanted to declare explicitly that the book was not intended as a new empirical study of the Dreyfus case but rather as a meditation, an interpretive essay in the manner of Montaigne. I told him that would be fine, but, regardless, maybe he should steer clear of the tyranny of scholarly review. "But I'm a scholar," he said, reverting to deflation. "It's a scholarly book."

We drove home on Saturday, and on Sunday morning my back went out again, and then, two days later, the phone rang, and I learned that Stephen had died over the weekend. There was no warning: I had seen him a couple of months before, and he seemed stable, though he could no longer speak or even make a sound. It had been eight and a half years since the onset of his symptoms; we all assumed he was going to be as long-lived as Stephen Hawking, if perhaps not quite so cerebral. At first, no one I talked to could tell me what exactly had happened: the obituary in the *Boston Globe* didn't explain the cause of death. But then I found out from Stephen's brother Jamie that the problem had been technological: his respirator had somehow gotten disconnected in the middle of the night, and no one was awake to notice. He must have died silently gasping for air.

It's not easy to admit this, but I didn't go to the funeral. Was it my back that felt too unstable, or my psyche? The year before, I had noted that Hurricane Katrina struck New Orleans on August 29, the seventeenth anniversary of Ian's death. Now another friend was gone. At times, I felt as though I had grown up and learned something about facing tragedy; at other times, I still felt like a terrified, inundated, eighteen-year-old kid.

What I did, instead of traveling back to Massachusetts to see Stephen buried, was sit down to write a long letter to Deborah Tall. I told her that I found her to be an acute, sensitive guide, to Ithaca, to the Finger Lakes, to the practice and understanding of history, to living. I told her that I was Jewish, too, that I shared her simultaneous desire both to keep wandering and to overcome restlessness, that it resonated for me when she wrote about what it meant "to not belong, to imagine constantly an elsewhere."[35] I told her that I had never sent an admiring letter to an author before, but that my first book had just come out in August, and now I understood more clearly how moving it might be to hear that one's work had touched a particular reader in an important way. I asked her questions: To what extent did she think that Chinese geomancy had an impact on landscape design in Britain and America in the nineteenth century? When had she first learned about Indian Mounds, and in what context? What other writers of creative nonfiction, perhaps people who combined history and memoir, had she found inspiring? How did her experience with poetry inform her prose? Did she ultimately feel settled in Ithaca? Did she yearn for wilder experiences, or maybe the rush of the city? Would she consider having coffee with me sometime?

I got the news about Stephen on Tuesday, November 28. I sent the letter to Deborah Tall that Saturday, December 2. On Pearl Harbor Day, December 7—all these dates are noted in my journal—I received a somewhat somber email from my friend Amy, the only other person I knew who had read *From Where We Stand* (she and I had been in graduate school together in New Haven, but before that she had lived in Ithaca and had just recently moved back to the area; I was overjoyed to have her as a neighbor again). She said that she had recently stopped in at The Bookery and taken a look at the store's quarterly newsletter. Had I heard? Deborah Tall had passed away in October.

I wilted in my chair, bereft, embarrassed, imagining the pain her husband and daughters must have been feeling. Had they read my letter? I pulled out a card, wrote them a note of apology and condolence, put it in the mail right away. And then I spent the rest of the day completely immobilized. "I waited too long," I kept muttering to myself. I'd poured out my gratitude and appreciation to a ghost.

---

*From Where We Stand* begins with an anticipatory invocation of the Finger Lakes— "two of them are so deep they're below sea level"—and an expression of relief that though Tall was moving far upstate and far inland, she would not have to cease identifying herself as "a walker of shorelines," a connoisseur of the coast, "that edge from which new continents can be journeyed to, a precipice, the avant-garde."[36] Margins, I think, lead to both new continents and lost continents: wrinkles in space lead to wrinkles in time.

Hints of the deluge have been around forever, but it was specifically the discovery of the so-called New World that resuscitated Plato's legend of Atlantis in the Western imagination. And it was the Indian Mounds on the far edge of the newly united

States, in the late eighteenth century, that brought Atlantis into American culture and spurred American thinkers to consider the possible relationship between the Bible's flood and Plato's flood. (It's a good bet, too, that it was the Indian Mounds of the Minnesota frontier that initially inspired Donnelly's Atlantean research.)[37]

By the late 1790s, when the well-known natural historian Benjamin Smith Barton (mentor to Jacob Bigelow, the founder of Mount Auburn) published his *Papers Relative to Certain American Antiquities* and *New Views of the Origin of the Tribes and Nations of America*, it was common to propose that "the countries of America derived their inhabitants from Asia, from Europe, from Africa, or from the unknown Atlantis." When Barton went into the field to try to interview friendly Indians, he always made a point of asking, first, whether they "pay any kind of adoration to any of the extraordinary works of nature on this globe, such as large Mountains, the Cataracts of Rivers, extraordinary Animals." Then came the follow-up: "Have they any idea of a Deluge?—If they have, do they believe this Deluge was *universal*, or only *partial*?—Do they speak of anything like a destruction of mankind, in this Deluge?—Was this destruction universal, or were a few, of many, preserved from the general destruction?" Barton was a careful scientist, putting more emphasis on his "Queries" than on any potential conclusions, but in general he seemed to find the myth of Atlantis useful because it echoed the Bible's positing of humankind's common origin—"differences between nations are but inconsiderable," he suggested—and thus conformed to his suspicion that all races, cultures, and faiths might somehow be interconnected. Moreover, the memory of apocalypse provides a good check against hubris. A thorough study of Indian Mounds, he thought—those startling monuments that few American schoolchildren ever learn about (I did not encounter them until graduate school)—"teaches us, a mortifying truth, that nations may relapse into rudeness again. . . . It may be our lot to fall into rudeness once more. There are good reasons for conjecturing, that the ancestors of many of the savage tribes of America are the descendants of nations who had attained to a much higher degree of polish than themselves."[38]

In the course of the nineteenth century, many more thinkers and theorists invoked Atlantis in their generous, if sometimes quirky, attempts to demonstrate that a kind of Humboldtian unity was the law of the universe.[39] Other writers, though, used the legend of Atlantis to emphasize division: like most mythical stories, including those found in the Bible, this one could be manipulated to produce a number of different morals. In 1832, William Gilmore Simms—the poet who later consecrated Magnolia Cemetery in Charleston, South Carolina, and eventually became widely known as an apologist for slavery—published a reputation-making play, in verse, called *Atalantis:*

*A Story of the Sea,* which pits a powerful "monster" called Onesimarchus against the kind, queen-like Atalantis. Onesimarchus rules over the ocean's depths, with the help of his slaves, while Atalantis abides in the higher realms of the atmosphere, where "the elements do her bidding." With the hope of making a strategic alliance, Onesimarchus lures Atalantis to him by raising up a beautiful island in the middle of the sea, but once she arrives she takes grave offense at the monster's cruel practice of punishing his slaves by chaining them to rocks that are regularly lashed by fierce waves. Onesimarchus can't believe her naïveté: " 'Twere a poor state, and brief the pow'r, if thus,/O'er-zealous though it be, each slave should leap/His bond unchastened." Meanwhile, some foolish mortals crash their ship into the rocks of the uncharted island, leaving only one survivor, a Spanish sailor named Leon, who immediately falls in love with Atalantis, prompting a Shell Spirit to identify love as in fact the truest form of slavery. (Simms's readers probably would have understood the sailor as a stand-in for Juan Ponce de León, the conquistador known for his expeditions to Florida and his interest in finding the mythical Fountain of Youth.) The outcome of the clash between Onesimarchus and Atalantis seems a foregone conclusion: the monster simply stirs up the ocean and causes his island to sink back down into the depths, forcing the two lovers to retreat to Atalantis's celestial empire. Leon hopes that it will be a kind of heaven on earth, a version of the Hesperides, "girt with all/Of natural wealth and splendor—jewell'd isles— /Boundless in unimaginable spoils," and Atalantis tries to assure him that, indeed, he will be "free from the jar,/The heat, the noise, the dust of human soil." But it's clear that, from the human perspective, Atalantis's realm is just an ethereal fantasy, not a place that can sustain life in all its messiness, with all its basic needs: Leon will exist there only as a spirit, will quickly learn "the mighty difference/'Twixt those two worlds—the one, where nature toils, / The other she but dreams of."[40] The Arcadia of the antislavery North, in other words, was a mere myth; it was only in the grounded, realistic South that Americans were creating a sustainable society. Especially after Nat Turner's infamous slave rebellion of 1831—the year before Simms wrote his book—it was common for Northerners to argue that the inherently unnatural system of Southern slavery would eventually go up in millennial, apocalyptic flames.[41] Simms's counterargument asked where the North would be if the South simply withdrew its labor and natural resources from the national economy: how would the Lowell mills produce textiles with no one willing to do the back-breaking labor of growing cotton?

Still other nineteenth-century Americans simply excised the disagreeable aspects of the Atlantis legend—tidal waves can be inconvenient, after all—and focused on imagining their country, especially in its frontier territories, as a "New Atlantis"—a possibility first suggested by Francis Bacon back in 1624.[42] "Atlantis is still in the West," exclaimed an anonymous American more than two hundred years later, in 1855, in *Putnam's Monthly Magazine of American Literature, Science, and Art.* This was the period before the dominance of the railroad, when numerous development projects bore the stamp of Andrew Jackson Downing, when city plans sometimes looked like they were based on Mount Auburn, when downtown water supplies were being secured by means of elaborate systems of reservoirs and aqueducts, as in New York—when it was inspiring to glance at the "town-plots and diagrams of cities, with copious Croton refreshing them, and parks and cemeteries adjacent." The *Putnam's* author imagined a new kind of "spacious, airy" metropolis, surrounded by fertile fields and rich orchards full of "all the grains and fruits of the earth," as well as "ancient woods" and "old groves," while "cottages, like those in Arcadia, peep out from the forest's edge." Yet this writer, whose identity I have not been able to discover (I would not be surprised if it was someone like Robert Morris Copeland or H. W. S. Cleveland, or even Frederick Law Olmsted, who had recently started working as an editor at *Putnam's*), was no mere booster, but a skeptic and a realist. He realized that western cities and towns could just as easily be dominated by special commercial interests, by certain kinds of "politicians and speculators," who, "like old monsters, come to drink at the water-courses, fill the air with clamor, fire the citizens with the fever of business, and (in the confusion) steal away the beauty of the landscape." Indeed, there are even hints here of what a pioneer like Hamlin Garland might eventually experience in the arid regions beyond the Mississippi: "I shall wonder if the rude and boisterous frontier life . . . on the burning plain, can quite fill the need of his soul, and he will not turn again and again to the refinement he has left behind, and will not long for the green fields and woods of home." In the end, this perceptive, imaginative writer expressed gratitude for his culture's passing down of the Arcadian ideal— "I am glad that none of the old triremes and galleys ever touched at Plato's Atlantis, and that the sailors, from the high sterns, never discerned its green and perfect shore"—but also warned that anything close to a realization of that ideal would require much "toil and trial." "That new Atlantis," he wrote, "promising such wonderful land, such riches, such a new life without labor, such an Elysium in estate and religion and morals—let us not be too confident of it. I fear we can none of us buy Elysium, on this earth, at one dollar and a quarter per acre."[43]

As late as 1891, when Mrs. Frances Fuller Victor published *Atlantis Arisen; or, Talks of a Tourist about Oregon and Washington,* an occasional writer might still celebrate the American west as a potential new Atlantis, where hardy pioneers were laboring "to restore to earth on this favored soil the glories of the buried continent."[44] But, generally speaking, by Ignatius Donnelly's time, the meaning of Atlantis had drifted away from the realm of the future and back toward a yearning nostalgia. Between the Civil War and the publication of *Progress and Poverty* in 1879, Americans not only started traveling farther, faster, and more frequently than ever before, thanks to the transcontinental railroad, but also saw their first electric streetcars, refrigerated rail cars, submarines, cigarette-making machines, telephones, typewriters, phonographs, gas engines, and incandescent bulbs. The very act of perception was shifting drastically, as more and more people transcended the rhythms and cycles of nature, outpacing river currents, using light when they would otherwise have been enveloped in darkness, communicating with each other instantaneously over unfathomable distances. It was a head-spinning, overwhelming time—in my opinion, the most transformative era of American history.[45] A twenty-first-century American would probably find Jefferson's agrarian world quite foreign, but Theodore Roosevelt's society might seem recognizable. Though Roosevelt himself craved wildness as an antidote to modernity, many others found comfort in the image of Arcadia, in a calm, if increasingly outdated, rurality. In early 1881, when a southerner named William Walton Hoskins published a book called *Atlantis, and Other Poems*, which Donnelly might have read while pursuing his own Atlantean studies, the immediate goal was clearly to re-create antebellum rhythms:

> Come, reader, go with me unto the sea's dark caves,
> And let us solve the secrets of its hidden graves. . . .
> The same tall trees shall lift their heads again,
> The same rich fruits shall bloom on hill and plain.
> The same bright streams shall irrigate the soil,
> And the same harvests bless attentive toil.
> The same wild birds shall thrill the list'ning air,
> And the same flowers shed their fragrance there!

Yet even in this poem of longing for a supposedly simpler time, which also managed to express longing for national reconciliation, Hoskins retained some of the edginess of the Arcadian tradition:

> The pulseless dead shall wake again to life,
> And know the old contentment—and the strife!
> The man, who, in his golden pride and prime,
> Seemed lost to earth before the needful time;
> The woman, who, with matron-face, sedate,
> Bowed her meek head and yielded to her fate;

The boy, who, in his thoughtless, careless glee,
Smiled a sweet smile, and smiling, ceased to be;
The girl, who, in her radiant summer years,
Took flight amid fair Nature's sighs and tears;
The infant, which, scarce welcomed to the earth,
Was nursed by Death the moment of its birth.[46]

Of course, all the pre-Donnelly Atlantean references in American culture constitute a mere trickle in comparison with the veritable deluge of poems, novels, articles,
and scientific treatises that swept the nation between 1882 and the end of the century.
It's difficult to generalize about the ways in which these texts dealt with the legend:
some envisioned potential utopias; some were straightforward idylls, evocations of
an ideal past; some focused on Indian Mounds and recently excavated artifacts, on
questions of origin, descent, evolution, differentiation, degeneration; some were exploration romances. More and more of them, though, tended to invoke the possibility
of a new Armageddon, triggered by society's denial of nature. Modernity, in its swamp-
ing, upending power, was both exhilaratingly attractive—we can light the darkness!—
and utterly horrifying: What business do we have lighting the darkness?[47] Many
Americans still assumed that certain aspects of nature could never be entirely conquered, and even attempting to harness their power might result in catastrophe. In
1876, the economist David Wells, pondering the shift from the immediate physical
labor of the farm to the deferred, mechanized labor of the factory, understood the
great promise of mass manufacturing but also worried about its implications: "Like
one of our mighty rivers, its movement is beyond control."[48] Sixteen years later, Elizabeth G. Birkmaier published a novel called *Poseidon's Paradise: The Romance of
Atlantis*, in which she lingered for several chapters on the earthquakes, eruptions,
tempests, tidal waves, and swirling vortices, the untamable natural forces, that finally
caused Atlantis to sink into the depths—as punishment, it turns out, for the ultimate
sin: the island's king and its high priest had secretly begun draining young maidens
of their blood, in an effort to create an elixir of life, a potion that would keep them
forever young, that would deny the limit of mortality.[49]

---

In late summer 2007, a brain surgeon told me I might not survive until the end of
the year. Thankfully, his suspicion of an arterial hemorrhage turned out to be mis-
guided. But that didn't become clear for another three weeks; meanwhile, I had a
new limit to adjust to, since it's hard, in our society, not to take the word of a brain
surgeon pretty seriously. I tried to invoke the spirit of my cousins, the ones who had

constantly cracked jokes at our grandfather's funeral: maybe I would get a second opinion, from a rocket scientist. And at least it wasn't a brain tumor! Such feeble attempts at lightness actually helped, as did regular doses of walking and swimming. Jews have always been pretty good at staring into the abyss, at finding the redeeming qualities in eternal nothingness. Still, this was the most direct confrontation with death I'd ever had. I was thirty-seven.

The anxiety had started on Sunday, August 19, at about three o'clock in the afternoon, when I had almost fallen over in the shower, afflicted, suddenly, with a violent throbbing at my temple, a burst of consciousness-obliterating pain that I later learned to call a "thunderclap headache." My awareness of a world beyond agony started to come back after about twenty seconds, but I was left with a hangover that seemed like it might persist forever. I couldn't think about anything else. On the other hand, it seemed pointless to go to the emergency room, especially on a Sunday (yes: denial). So I spent most of the rest of the day doing some crude medical research, and ultimately I came to the conclusion that it had probably just been an especially severe headache, but that it could have been a small brain hemorrhage. I went to bed nauseous, exhausted.

First thing in the morning, I called my doctor, and that led to a series of tests over the course of the following ten days. On Tuesday the twenty-first I had a CT scan, and the results came back in just a few hours: "normal." Of course, the blood from a hemorrhage could already have been reabsorbed by the time of the test. This kind of bleeding, I later found out, typically doesn't show up unless you get a scan within a few hours of the headache (yes: I should have gone to the ER on Sunday). On Thursday, I had an MRI, to check for tumors, as well as an MRA, designed to show the flow of blood through veins and arteries. But these results would take much longer to interpret: I was told to distract myself as well as I could, and wait a few days.

At least I now had license to embrace denial. Of course, it was hard not to scrutinize myself: Was I exerting myself too much, going on too many hikes? Was I becoming more forgetful? Why couldn't I come up with that word? But I made a point of watching more movies, and taking Sam and Abe to the gorges, and picking lots of blueberries. Fortunately, my shadow headache started to lift over the weekend, and on Tuesday the twenty-eighth, after doing some writing in the morning—I was working on the very beginning of this book—I took the afternoon off (I had no immediate teaching responsibilities) and drove half an hour to Watkins Glen State Park, a place I'd been eager to explore for months. Though my preference for cemeteries over gorges had been developing in earnest that year, I recognized that it was the ubiquitous gorges, in part, that defined this region's unusual topography, and Watkins

Glen was known for its dramatic cliffs and cascades. Frankly, I needed to get away from my usual haunts. One reason I love hiking is that it provides such a powerful feeling of engagement: the world opens up all my senses, and the swirling images, sounds, smells, start to connect in unexpected ways. But I figured that a too-familiar landscape, on this particular day, might leave me too free to remain inside my head. As it turned out, I had a hard time warming up to the dark, narrow base of the Glen, where you're forced to creep through tunnels and edge along rock faces, but once the trail opened out to the sunshine, and I was strolling along the glistening creek, I experienced a strange sense of peace, as if I could just slide down into the water and close my eyes and not worry anymore. Then, on the way back, I took a path up out of the gorge, and got myself lost, and stumbled upon the town cemetery, Glenwood, which reminded me a great deal of Sleepy Hollow in Concord. It was a calming, resonant afternoon.

The next day, Wednesday the twenty-ninth, was the nineteenth anniversary of Ian's death, and my doctor called at 9 A.M.: the MRA had picked up a slight bulge, showing "unusual flow activity." The most likely explanation was that a couple of blood vessels were simply lying on top of each other—but it could also be an aneurysm, a ballooning weak spot in the wall of an artery. I would have to undergo another test on Friday, a CT-scan angiogram: they would inject me with a dye so that they could see the blood vessels more clearly.

These results came back quickly, at 6 P.M., just a few hours after the test: I had a two-millimeter aneurysm. It would have to be monitored for the rest of my life. The best-case scenario was that it had already been there for years and would remain stable; the worst-case scenario was that it was brand new and growing larger every day. If it was new, then my thunderclap headache had probably signaled a hemorrhage, and I would probably need surgery to prevent further bleeding. So: how to tell? I had to see a specialist, and he would probably order some more tests. The appointment was a week later, on Friday, September 7. And that was when the brain surgeon gave me his considered opinion: the likelihood was that I'd already had one hemorrhage, which meant I was at very high risk of having another in the next two to three months, and the next one would be worse; in such cases, he explained, the second hemorrhage had a mortality rate of about 50 percent. He wanted to check me into the hospital right away, for an indefinite stay.

I had spent the previous week just trying to contain my panic and desperation, cursing my luck, wishing I could get back to focusing on normal, everyday problems. But now I found myself smiling and shaking my head. The whole thing seemed so abstract. All this drama, based on one headache, a few computer-generated images, and some statistics? I have two small children, I told him. We were leaving that after-noon for my cousin's wedding in New York City. It was true that I was on a partial leave that semester from Cornell—designed to give junior faculty time to pursue the kind of extended research and writing that were necessary to earn tenure—but I couldn't imagine withdrawing from my family. At the same time, though, it was hard to envision simply going about my business after receiving that kind of warning—and I said as much. What did he actually expect me to do? Well, he said, if you won't check into the hospital, then you at least need to go see a *vascular* neurosurgeon right away, someone at a teaching hospital in a large city (Cornell's medical school is in Manhattan, not Ithaca), someone who was familiar with all the latest research on this particular problem; and you need to have a traditional angiogram, which would pro-vide much clearer images of all the relevant blood vessels. He could call a colleague in Rochester and get me in right away. I agreed; the appointment was set for Tuesday, the sixth anniversary of 9/11.

The Rochester specialist provided some immediate relief: his guess, based on all the previous images, was that I didn't have an aneurysm at all, but merely a bit of "asymmetry in the anterior communicating arteries," which was fairly common, and probably benign. He didn't see any more thunderclap headaches in my future. But I did need to sign up for an angiogram, because he still wasn't sure, and if I *did* have an aneurysm, then he wanted to do surgery right away, to reinforce the wall of the weakened artery. The thing about angiograms—the reason they hadn't done one in Ithaca—was that they were painfully invasive and carried a small risk of stroke: the odds were about 1 in 200. I'd have to schedule another office visit for the following week, and then he could do the angiogram at the end of the month. It at least sounded better than sitting in a hospital room, wearing monitors, waiting to hemor-rhage. I thanked him, shook his hand, and told him I would talk it over with Chris-tine and then give him a call. By Friday, which was my parents' forty-sixth wedding anniversary, both appointments were on the calendar: with luck, I'd have some reso-lution two weeks later, on September 28.

Meanwhile, there was plenty of time to think about death. To tell the truth, my obsession with mortality did not begin with Ian; it has been with me ever since I was introduced to the concept as a small child. Starting at about age five, and lasting through most of high school, I was haunted by a recurring nightmare: somehow I had been buried alive, in a cramped, dusty coffin, and I was aware of everything happening just above me, in the cemetery, and the scene was always the same, with dry, brown leaves rustling on a dirt path in an autumn wind, and a man wearing an old-fashioned brown hat, folding up his newspaper as he walked by and then letting it slide directly onto my flat gravestone, its headlines just outside my angle of vision. Death was exclusion, was being the youngest in my family, was listening at the top of the stairs to a conversation far below that I could never quite make out. But the nightmare had faded once I started to make some good friends, and now, entering middle age, I had Christine and Sam and Abe, and I had a sense of history, and I had my cemeteries. During my twenties and thirties, though the old panic sometimes welled up in my chest, and kept me awake for hours, I usually managed to shift my focus away from the future obliteration of my own consciousness and instead concentrate on my responsibilities as a provisional survivor—and I learned to draw inspiration from the efforts of various adopted ancestors, Arcadians who had inscribed their bittersweet caring on the physical and cultural landscape. So as I pondered aneurysms and angiograms, as I tried to imagine my death in the most immediate terms I could conjure, I did feel afraid of the void, and I did worry about my children, and I did wonder what kind of world they were inheriting, but I also found myself able to see death as the constraint that gave life its urgency. For the first time, I understood, viscerally, the potential satisfaction, however grim, of stepping aside to make room for others. I caught a glimpse of repose. Meanwhile, though, the more I considered this evolution in myself, and the more gratitude I felt to past Arcadians, the more desperately I wanted to keep living—to make a contribution, to write this book, to teach, to remake my relationship with my parents, to grow old with Christine, to see our kids become loving, caring adults, to share the world's beauty with them.

After driving home from Rochester, I stopped by the Ithaca City Cemetery to visit the old firemen's memorial, and I found that someone had decorated it with fresh flags in honor of 9/11. And I went back to the cemetery the next day, which was Erev Rosh Hashannah, New Year's Eve for Jews, to spend some time with the oldest Jewish graves, to trace their weathered inscriptions. At work, I had decided to split my time between drafting this book's prologue and revising a short memoir about my grandparents. On the seventeenth, I celebrated my grandfather's birthday (also the day my grandmother died), by pulling one of his books off the shelf, *Understanding the Prophets* (published the month I was born), and rereading what Grandaddy had written on the first page when he gave it to me, a year before he died: "For Aaron, with love from his grandfather—yes, add these guys to the great men of the past among your models." I also, finally, put up our mezuzah on the doorpost of our house—something I'd been meaning to do for three full years. On the twentieth, I had my follow-up appointment in Rochester, and on the twenty-second I fasted, in honor of Yom Kippur, as I always do, though in most respects I am far from religious. I refrain from eating once a year not to honor any God, but to encourage a sense of gratitude for the bounty I enjoy on every other day of the year. And, indeed, on the very next day, I spent the afternoon hiking farther up a local gorge than I'd ever been before, then straying into the surrounding countryside, getting lost for a couple of hours, and eventually finding my way to the Six Mile Creek winery, where I tasted every single wine they had on offer, and bought a bottle to bring home for dinner. Then, on the evening of the twenty-seventh, I made my way back up to Rochester, this time with Christine and the kids, and I had my angiogram the next morning, and the surgeon confirmed that there was no aneurysm, that I had simply been born with some vascular asymmetry—that I was, as it were, mentally unbalanced. He did think that my thunderclap headache might have signaled some bleeding, but from a less-pressurized vein, not an artery, and he was sure it had been a one-time occurrence, a fluke, rather than the result of any systemic weakness. I limped home in a fair amount of pain, but with a clear head. I could wander again in my thoughts, roam freely through the past and even look forward into the future with calm hopefulness rather than desperation. Maybe it was my lack of mental balance, but suddenly anything seemed possible. Maybe my generation would even solve the problem of global climate change.

———————

The most famous utopian novel of the late nineteenth century, Edward Bellamy's *Looking Backward* (1888), opens in Boston, in late May 1887, on the annual holiday that had been "set apart under the name of Decoration Day, for doing honor to the memory of the soldiers of the North who took part in the war for the preservation of the union of the states." The narrator, Julian West, and his fiancée, Edith Bartlett, are preparing to accompany Boston's veterans on their mission "to visit the cemeteries and lay wreaths of flowers upon the graves of their dead comrades." Edith's brother "had fallen in the war, and on Decoration Day the family was in the habit of making a visit to Mount Auburn, where he lay."[50]

On that very night, though, after paying tribute to America's Arcadian tradition, West is magically catapulted into the future, into modernity—into the Boston of the year 2000 and an ideal, egalitarian, consumer-oriented society that functions with perfect order and regularity. There are a few decorative trees here and there, but otherwise hardly a hint of rural culture, and it isn't missed.[51] The key innovation of the modern world is the "nationalization" of the economy: all the means of production are held in common, and every able-bodied citizen between the ages of twenty-one and forty-five is a member of the super-efficient "industrial army," supplying everyone's needs through labor in factories and fields that are far enough removed from living spaces to be, in effect, invisible. When you want to buy something, you go to a generic distribution center, take a look at samples of all the goods available (they're the same everywhere), and place an order; your commodity gets sent to your home through a system of pneumatic tubes.

Workers are generally enabled to find a job in the corps that suits their talents and inclinations, and they maintain control over their leisure activities, but, overall, everyone has to submit to a kind of cult of impersonality, sacrificing certain elements of individualistic development for the sake of a disciplined solidarity and the common good. It's a true army, then, ruled by officers who have already been through the system (workers are unable to vote; only "alumni" over the age of forty-five have a role in the government). If you don't cooperate, you get thrown in jail, so all children "are taught habits of obedience, subordination, and devotion to duty." Personalities come out rather bland and puritanical, and there's not much epicurean spontaneity, but everyone seems content and well educated, and there is no wealth, no poverty, and no discrimination. This is a society that runs like a well-designed and diligently maintained machine. And, according to West's host in the future world, "thanks to the better conditions of existence nowadays, and above all the freedom of everyone from care, old age approaches many years later and has an aspect far more benign than in past times. . . . It is a strange reflection that at forty-five, when we are just entering upon the most enjoyable period of life, you already began to think of growing old and to look backward."

Bellamy's book, despite its unabashed socialism, was fabulously popular among moderate, middle-class Americans—who immediately bought hundreds of thousands of copies, created dozens of Bellamy Clubs, and even organized a Nationalist political party—largely because it condemned the most egregious outrages of winner-take-all capitalism without condemning consumerism, corporate industrialism, or modernization. Though Bellamy felt anxious about the rash of strikes that had wracked the nation since the early 70s, and fully acknowledged that "the relationship between the workingman and the employer, between labor and capital, appeared in some unaccountable manner to have become dislocated," he was not one of those strident critics who went "so far as to predict an impending social cataclysm."[52] His radicalism addressed itself to the question of unequal distribution, but when it came to production, Bellamy endorsed the existing definition of Progress, touting the incredible growth in output that would be possible if all the different corporations were made to work together rather than compete against each other. The only sense of limitation in his utopia was on cultural and psychological development; with regard to material concerns, the goal was to have a perpetual surplus, to extract and process as

many resources as possible, while the populace was encouraged to remain blithely
ignorant of any spatial or ecological consequences of this "maximum yield" approach.
It's true that, in a magazine called *The New Nation*, which Bellamy founded in January 1891, he did publish articles lamenting "the reckless cutting of timber" and
promising that, under Nationalism, forests would be "guarded more zealously than a
gold mine." And in *Equality* (1897), his sequel to *Looking Backward*, which extends
Julian West's knowledge of the future, he made a point of celebrating wilderness: "It
was found after the Revolution that one of the things most urgent to be done was to
reforest the country," and that sense of urgency resulted in a park that stretched for
thousands of miles.[53] Yet Bellamy's original, basic version of utopia—the one that
helped *Looking Backward* to sell, ultimately, in the millions, the one that emphasized
the mutual dependence of all humanity—clearly allowed Americans to embrace the
modern conveniences that removed them further and further from their dependence
on nature.

When Ignatius Donnelly published *Caesar's Column* in 1890 and announced the
political radicalism that would define his final decade, he was, in part, responding
directly to *Looking Backward*.[54] Though he agreed with Bellamy about certain social
ills—and there was some overlap between the Nationalist movement and the Farmers' Alliance, of which Donnelly was a leader[55]—he generally had a much darker view
of modern trends, and a much sharper desire to pillory the violent greed and egregious injustice and thoughtless rush of his society, which made life so unstable. To
Donnelly, "the rise of the industrial middle class," which Bellamy saw as a means of
bridging the gap between rich and poor, was part of the problem: it wasn't a matter of
dividing up "material prosperity" more equally but of questioning the very valuation
of "material prosperity." Most likely, America had already passed some kind of tipping point, but if any solution were possible, it would have to be cultural, not economic, would have to overturn the assumption that work was just a series of motions
to go through in order to procure commodities—would have to address the fact that
"we have ceased to be men—we are machines." At bottom, Donnelly was an Arcadian:
he suspected that the only way for human beings to live harmoniously with each
other was for them to slow down and once more connect directly (and harmoniously)
with nature. But he recognized that, by the 1880s, too many Americans had already
become alienated from their environment, having either moved to the tenements
or suffered in silence as their farms were drained of value "by railroad companies
and money-lenders." Arcadia had become inaccessible to them, psychologically; so,
in the New York City of *Caesar's Column*, Donnelly cuts off physical access: Central Park still exists in 1988, with its "century-old trees, of great size and artistically

grouped," but its gates are "guarded by sentinels to exclude the ragged and wretched multitude."

The faint hope of a new Arcadia does hang in the air throughout *Caesar's Column*, because the narrator, Gabriel Weltstein—the angel Gabriel blowing his trumpet of doom—is a visitor to New York from a rustic colony in Uganda that was settled by emigrants from Switzerland, and every now and then he finds that the dazzling metropolis "fades away, and I see the leaning hills, the trickling streams, the deep gorges where our wooly thousands graze; and I hear once more the echoing Swiss horns of our herdsmen reverberating from the snow-tipped mountains."[56] The bulk of the book, though, is dedicated to countless, protracted evocations of the apocalypse that Americans have set themselves up for. Gabriel is a sturdy witness to the final conflict between two equally revolting legions: the merciless plutocrats, holding the higher ground, and the degraded laborers, rising from below. "How thin a crust," Gabriel says to himself, while visiting the palace of a prince, "separated all this splendor from the burning hell of misery beneath it. And if the molten mass of horror should break its limitations and overflow the earth! Already it seemed to me the planet trembled; I could hear the volcanic explosions; I could see the sordid flood of wrath and hunger pouring through these halls; cataracts of misery bursting through every door and window, and sweeping away all this splendor into never-ending blackness and ruin." Of course, the oligarchs bear more responsibility for bringing on the current state of affairs, but this is a dystopia, so the desperate masses seem just as ruthless, and just as unlikely to overcome their resentment or their appetites. No one is innocent: all the "men of the world have eaten away the walls of society in a thousand places, to the thinness of tissue-paper, and the great ocean is about to pour in at every aperture. And still they hoot and laugh their insolent laugh of safety and triumph above the roar of the greedy and boundless waters, just ready to overwhelm them forever."[57]

To Gabriel, "the ignorant and brutal Plutocracy . . . are like the slave-owners of 1860; they blindly and imperiously insist on their own destruction." And this observation suggests a compounding reason for Donnelly's pessimism: like Hamlin Garland, he saw all too clearly that the nation was still in shock, even two and a half decades after war's end—still desperate for escapist fantasies of unification and fulfillment—still in denial. It was denial that had allowed slavery in the first place: "our ancestors were blind, indifferent, heartless. . . . We are the inheritors of the hurricane which they invoked."[58] By the 1880s, the Social Darwinists had swooped in and reassured the ruling classes that they belonged at the top of the heap, and the beggar had no one to blame but himself. In the New York of 1988, then, preachers actually urge the plutocrats to forget about the poor and downtrodden, to let nature take its course, to hold more dances and feasts, to flaunt their wealth and pleasure and luxury, to reinforce social distinctions, to abandon naïve notions of solidarity based on things that seem to unite humanity, like death: "The ancient Egyptians brought into their banquets the mummied bodies of the dead, to remind them of mortality. It was a foolish custom." Indeed, the robber barons of the future, entirely untroubled by guilt or empathy, take no notice of death, especially when it strikes the laboring hordes, who are not even provided with "a pauper's grave," in which "they might have claimed, perhaps, some sort of ownership over the earth which enfolded them, which touched them and mingled with their dust." No: instead, they are "whisked off, as soon as dead, a score or two at a time, and swept on iron tram-cars into furnaces heated to such intense white heat that they dissolved, crackling, even as they entered the chamber, and rose in nameless gases through the high chimney. That towering structure was the sole memorial monument of millions of them. Their graveyard was the air." Because there is no commemoration, there is also no accountability, no sense of obligation, and no sense of dependence on the earth: humanity and nature have been decoupled, Arcadia obliterated.

Predictably, there is also no hint in Donnelly's New York that the earth is necessary for food production, though we do learn that Caesar, who turns out to be the leader of the revolutionaries, started out as a farmer. In fact, he could have fit perfectly into one of Hamlin Garland's early short stories, several of which were written within months of the publication of *Caesar's Column:* "a quiet, peaceable, industrious man," he winds up losing everything after taking out one small loan, because "the money-lender demanded large interest on the loan and an exorbitant bonus besides; and as the 'bankers,' as they called themselves, had an organization, he could not get the money at a lower rate anywhere in the vicinity." A Garland character would have put his head down and simply labored for the rest of his days, but Caesar casts himself as an avenging angel, and eventually takes responsibility for the book's climactic uprising, in which about a quarter of a million people are killed—leading to a serious corpse disposal problem. At first, Caesar just wants to incinerate them, but then he hits upon the perverse plan that gives the novel its name: "By G-d, I have it! Make a pyramid of them, and pour cement over them. . . . We'll have a monument that shall last while the earth stands." And his troops immediately execute the order, though the artificial megalith turns out to be more of an obelisk than a pyramid.

A few days later, Caesar's head is impaled on a pole, mobs are running through the streets setting fire to the city, food supplies have run out, and it's clear that it will be a long time before anyone reads the grim inscription on the column's base: "This great monument is erected by Caesar Lomellini, Commanding General of The

Brotherhood of Destruction, in Commemoration of the Death and Burial of Modern Civilization." As Gabriel makes his escape, in his ark-like airship, bound for Uganda, he stares mournfully at the massive memorial, wondering if at least some aspects of modern civilization might have been worth saving. To his American companion, though, who seems to be Donnelly's mouthpiece, it's an irrelevant question. There was just too much to handle—"the breaking-strain on humanity was too great"—as people tried to cope with global migration flows, the mingling of every race and religion, the alienation of industrial labor, the combination of irrepressible resentment with massive destructive power. "The crash was inevitable. It may be God's way of wiping off the blackboard. It may be that the ancient legends of the destruction of our race by flood and fire are but dim remembrances of events like that which is now happening."

In Uganda, in the book's denouement, we get a glimpse of Donnelly's Arcadian utopia—worlds apart from Bellamy's ideal, and far more backward-looking—for Gabriel has brought along a number of hand-picked Americans, with the goal of expanding his Swiss colony into a realization of his social vision. The colonists' new constitution is keenly sensitive to the ways in which politics, economics, and spatial issues overlap: "We decree a limitation upon the amount of land or money any one man can possess. All above that must be used, either by the owner or the government, in works of public usefulness. . . . We shut out all speculators." And the new village— called Lincoln!—is a picture of calm unity, with "wide streets" that are lined with "fruit trees, the abundance of which is free to all. Around each modest house there is a garden, blooming with flowers and growing food for the household." The people also make their own clothes, enjoying all the fruits of their labor, and in a world without textile mills or any other factories, there can be no captains of industry. In fact, the adjective "industrial" fades from the language, and "industry" reverts to its former meaning: "There are no lordly palaces to cast a chill shadow over humble industry; and no resplendent vehicles to arouse envy and jealousy in the hearts of the beholders. Instead of these shallow vanities a sentiment of brotherly love dwells in all hearts. The poor man is not worked to death, driven to an early grave by hopeless and incessant toil. No; he sings while he works, and his heart is merry."

Needless to say, the village is surrounded by thick woodlands and rolling meadows, which are filled with ample sheep: it is paradise on earth. Yet it is a paradise whose perfect union is founded on homogeneity, isolation, and exclusion. Gabriel's country is high in the mountains, accessible only by a single wagon road that "winds upward through a vast defile," and "at one point the precipitous walls of this gorge approach so closely together" that Gabriel and his fellow citizens found it possible to block the road with a high, straight, dam-like barrier, which "completely cut off communication with the external world . . . , so thick and strong that it would be impossible for any force that was likely to come against us to batter it down." And of course there is always a guard posted "at a high point near the wall, and commanding a view of its approaches for many miles," watching over Lincoln in the same way that the sentinels of the plutocrats had monitored Central Park.[59]

Donnelly's readers, if the scores of reviews are any indication, barely registered his portrait of utopia; what resonated was his vivid prophecy of Armageddon.[60] I think Donnelly himself found some solace in the proposition that, no matter what form of apocalypse might strike society, life would nevertheless continue. His own research indicated that at least a few Atlanteans must have survived, after all. "While God permits man to wreck himself," Gabriel muses, "he denies him the power to destroy the world. The grass covers the graves; the flowers grow in the furrows of the cannon balls; the graceful foliage festoons with blossoms the ruins of the prison and the torture-chamber; and the corn springs alike under the foot of the helot or the yeoman. And I said to myself that, even though civilization should commit suicide, the earth would still remain—and with it some remnant of mankind." What Donnelly felt the need to lament was humanity's increasing inability to draw inspiration from the earth's wondrous capacity to produce life from death, which should have been obvious even in times of peace. In a pained but loving tribute to Walt Whitman's *Leaves of Grass*, Gabriel rails against Americans' modern blindness to the gifts of nature: "The humblest blade of grass preaches an incontrovertible sermon. What force is it that brings it up, green and beautiful, out of the black, dead earth?"[61] Perhaps Donnelly was thinking of Whitman's famous poem, "This Compost," which was first published under the title, "Poem of Wonder at the Resurrection of the Wheat":[62]

O how can it be that the ground itself does not sicken?
How can you be alive you growths of spring?
How can you furnish health you blood of herbs, roots, orchards, grain?
Are they not continually putting distemper'd corpses within you?
Is not every continent work'd over and over with sour dead?

. . . Behold this compost! behold it well!
Perhaps every mite has once form'd part of a sick person—yet behold!
The grass of spring bursts noiselessly through the mould in the garden,
The delicate spear of the onion pierces upward,
The apple-buds cluster together on the apple-branches,
The resurrection of the wheat appears with pale visage out of its graves.

Whitman died in 1892, two years after *Caesar's Column* appeared. Hamlin Garland had paid tribute to him at his seventieth birthday celebration, in 1889, but he was unable to attend the poet's funeral. The eulogy fell to Whitman's friend Robert Ingersoll, known as a radical agnostic and as one of the era's most dynamic orators. "He was the poet of Life," Ingersoll said, a man who always "enjoyed the breath of morning, the twilight, the wind, the winding streams. . . . He loved the fields, the hills; he was acquainted with the trees, with birds, with all the beautiful objects of the earth." And, at the same time, "He was the poet of Death. . . . He had the courage to meet all, and was great enough and splendid enough to harmonize all and to accept all there is of life as a divine melody." As it turned out, Whitman had survived a good two decades after his postwar paralytic stroke, and Ingersoll suspected that those golden years of simple living, of walking and writing and revising, constituted the old poet's greatest accomplishment: "For many years he and death were near neighbors . . . , and for many months he sat in the deepening twilight waiting for the night, waiting for the light." Yet, consistently, "from the frontier of life, from the western wave-kissed shore, he sent us messages of content and hope." Whitman faced mortality as he had faced the trauma of war, in a spirit of acknowledgment, determination, and caring, and Ingersoll, appropriately, treated him as a veteran, decorating his grave with flowers, embracing the power of that resonant postbellum gesture, with its blending echoes of both stalwart masculine commitment and graceful feminine gentleness: "And so I lay this little wreath upon this great man's tomb. I loved him living, and I love him still."[63]

Despite the challenge posed by the lingering shadow of war, Whitman had clearly managed to succeed William Cullen Bryant as America's poet of Arcadia. But no new heir had stepped forward in Whitman's old age.

Throughout the 1890s, Ignatius Donnelly did his best to harness all his remaining powers in an assault against American wealth and privilege and industrial consumerism. He was joined by many other radicals: historians generally point to this decade as the period when the Gilded Age was supplanted by the Progressive Era, known for its crucial, long-standing social reforms, its reining in of American excess. But another way of seeing this transitional moment is as the last gasp of the reform tradition that had already galvanized so many struggling workers and adamant Single Taxers and antirailroad activists in postwar America[64]—and as the last gasp of the older Arcadian tradition. Generally speaking, Progressivism struck a modern, urban pose, often relying on rational management, an orderly efficiency, utilitarianism, statistics-driven maximization, a grid-like regularity: it conformed much more closely to Bellamy's vision than to Donnelly's. Many exceptions immediately leap to mind, but I think that the undercurrent of antimodernism in this period tended to suffer from its lack of a program for fundamental change. Populists tried to defend the interests of farmers against those of industrialists, but they were often led by people like Donnelly and Garland, who felt ambivalent, at best, about American farming. And, by the end of the century, Populism had sputtered out: clinging to its embrace of an inflationary monetary policy (and its attack on the gold standard), unable to appeal to most urban workers, and torn apart by various prejudices, especially against African Americans and the recent immigrants from southern and eastern Europe, the movement simply couldn't counter the business community's mono-poly on Progress, based on the provision of mass-produced shirts, hats, hams, candies, cameras, coffins.[65]

One of Donnelly's pet projects of the mid-90s was a renewal of his crusade against the destruction and abuse perpetrated by private lumber companies on the middle border, and his activism on this front flowed together with enough other initiatives to make the Progressive Era into one of the best-known periods of environmental re-form in American history.[66] But most Progressive environmentalists had abandoned the premise that trees and other elements of nature ought to play a crucial spiritual role in the average citizen's daily life. Donnelly's basic goal with his so-called Pine Land investigation was merely to provide better regulation of tree-cutting, to ensure that the public was receiving the full value of its lumber. Meanwhile, he seems to have taken little notice of the trees that H. W. S. Cleveland planted along the boule-vards of Minneapolis and St. Paul, and though the efforts of landscape architects like Cleveland and Olmsted eventually helped spawn the urban planning profession, in the immediate term most municipal governments gave up on creating park systems and instead embraced the so-called City Beautiful Movement, which focused less on green spaces and more on grand monumentalism, modeled on the gigantic, sym-metrical, neoclassical, museum-like buildings of the "White City" at the 1893 World's Fair in Chicago—buildings that reassured Americans of the power of their econ-omy.[67] The year before, John Muir, America's greatest popularizer of the wilderness ethic, had founded the Sierra Club, and he certainly tried to inject Progressive reform with a little more soul and spontaneity: he truly worshiped trees and mountains and meadows and rocks and birds and squirrels and bears. But ultimately he thought of nature as a place modern Americans might visit on vacation or the weekend, as the scenic backdrop for their escapism.

Meanwhile, the strand of environmental thinking that would become dominant by the turn of the century fit perfectly in the Progressive mold: Theodore Roosevelt's Conservation philosophy sought, primarily, to use natural resources more efficiently—

to impose scientific management on forests, to extract every last seam of coal from each mine. It was an environmentalism of tree farms and fish hatcheries and massive dams—all potentially worthy interventions, but hardly Arcadian. Certainly, this period produced a great variety of environmental thinking, some of which was much more retrospective in spirit, ranging from the enthusiasm for nature study in science education, to the push for more urban playgrounds, to the rise of the Boy Scouts and summer camps, to the "prairie style" of environmental design pioneered by Jens Jensen, to New York's Fresh Air Fund, a loose conglomeration of organizations dedicated to taking the city's least privileged children on excursions to the countryside.[68] At least superficially, the idea of Arcadia retained some hold on the American imagination, and many histories remain to be written tracing this continuity. Still, though, the best-entrenched environmental mode of this era, the style of thought that became institutionalized—perhaps most famously in the symbol of the National Forest, "Land of Many Uses," established in 1891—was based on the strictly utilitarian principles of George Perkins Marsh's 1864 book, *Man and Nature*, which emphasized again and again that when nations, or empires, failed to ensure that they would be able to use their resources sustainably over the long term, they doomed themselves to collapse.

Though Marsh's argument was remarkably eloquent and perceptive, it failed to dwell on the history of constructive human interactions with the landscape; it always returned to its portrayal of humanity as "everywhere a disturbing agent."[69] In the late nineteenth century, when Conservationists defended trees, it was in terms that were usually pragmatic, and often alarmist, and sometimes apocalyptic. "Our forests are still of immense value for their marketable products," wrote the historian and horticulturist Francis Parkman, in an 1885 essay, "for the good effects they produce, and for the evils they avert; but it is clear that if the present wasteful ways of dealing with them are not changed, a time must soon come when the nation will have cause to repent its reckless improvidence." And then Parkman referred to a recent government-sponsored report written by a friend of his, the botanist Charles Sprague Sargent, who frequently collaborated with Frederick Law Olmsted, during these years, to expand the legacy of the Massachusetts Horticultural Society and make Boston the greenest city in the world. Sargent, it seems, was worried: "The great mountain forests of the country still exist, often almost in their original condition. Their inaccessibility has preserved them. It cannot preserve them, however, much longer. Inroads have already been made into these forests; the axe, fire, and the destructive agency of browsing animals are now everywhere invading them. Their destruction does not mean a loss of material alone . . . ; it means the ruin of great rivers for navigation and irrigation, the destruction of cities located along their banks, and the spoliation of broad areas of the richest agricultural land."[70] Trees, after all, regulate the flow of water in their immediate environment: once they're cut, the soil erodes and loses much of its absorptive power, and water runs off the land instead of soaking into it. Especially given the "vast quantities of timber" being used by the rapidly expanding railroads, Sargent foresaw "widespread calamity" unless conservation measures were instituted right away (and recent studies have revealed that the rate of deforestation in the 1870s and 80s was higher than in any other period of American history).[71] He and Parkman, ensconced in Arcadian Boston, were sure that the floods were coming.[72]

---

Almost as soon as Ignatius Donnelly died, on New Year's Day, 1901, having suffered a heart attack at the age of sixty-nine, his reputation started to sink. He was a crank, a demagogue, a failed political leader, an anti-Semite, a charlatan, a fool. History had proven his irrelevance: modern America was not going to look anything like his Ugandan utopia. Yet, even though the majority of Populists had joined with the Democrats as of the election of 1896, it seems worth noting that the People's Party did run a campaign in 1900, and that Donnelly was their nominee for vice president. Even as he grew more cynical and despairing, he retained his faith in the political process, in direct democracy, in the right and responsibility of the people to speak out and question the direction of Progress. "I tremble for the future," he said in 1896,[73] but, having been elected to the Minnesota state legislature, he quickly launched his usual series of protests and public service investigations, one of which proved that several corrupt politicians had accepted payoffs from the Rockefellers in exchange for access to some rich mining lands: apparently, the Mountain Iron Mining Company had stolen about ten million dollars' worth of ore from the people of Minnesota. In March of 1897, Donnelly's fellow radical, Henry Demarest Lloyd, author of *Wealth and Commonwealth* (1894), wrote to him to say that this exposure of corruption and resource exploitation might have been the most important crusade of his long career.[74] I think Donnelly truly assumed that he would die watching the great American Republic spiral down toward a calamitous collapse, and occasionally he asked himself, "is it fit to be saved?"[75] But despite his visceral pessimism, he continued to act like an idealist until the very end of his life.

Before my father's mind started to deteriorate, I imagine that he would have identified the balance between doubt and hope as being at the core of his approach to the world as well. During the seventh-inning stretch of almost every Red Sox game we watched together, no matter the score, he'd say the same thing: "It doesn't look good." But he always kept watching. He surely would have enjoyed chatting about Ignatius Donnelly's contradictions. Most likely, he had certain assumptions about how Populists characterized Jews: since the platform of the People's Party had always been built on an attack against American plutocracy, and since so many bankers and financiers were assumed to be Jewish, some Populist rhetoric infamously wound up invoking ethnic stereotypes.[76] Donnelly's case is particularly complex, though—and this would have fascinated my father—because it was almost exclusively in his fiction that he fell back on caricatures of Jews. Even the archetypal fictional Jew, Shylock, still perplexes scholars who seek to interpret Shakespeare's general perspective on Jewish moneylenders. While Shylock's features are harsh and hawkish and his bargains vicious, helping to make him one of the stage's most notorious villains, Shakespeare also asks his audience to sympathize with the Jew's deeply human pain: "Hath not a Jew eyes? Hath not a Jew hands, organs, dimensions, senses, affections, passions?" In *Caesar's Column*, which is not quite so nuanced as *The Merchant of Venice*, Donnelly cast most of the plutocrats as Jews, and they brutalize the masses without any hint of guilt or empathy—but, especially given the parallel brutality of the masses, some of the actions of the ruling class come across as potentially justifiable. "Christianity," a character explains, "fell upon the Jews, originally a race of agriculturalists and shepherds, and forced them, for many centuries, through the most terrible ordeal of persecution the history of mankind bears any record of. . . . Now the Christian world is paying, in tears and blood, for the sufferings inflicted by their bigoted and ignorant ancestors upon a noble race."[77] It's a story of the Fall, of the demise of Arcadia, and of power struggles, more than a story about racial characteristics. Virtually none of the reviews of *Caesar's Column* even mentioned the Jewish angle,[78] so it's hard to sustain the charge that Donnelly's writing fomented prejudice, whatever his own feelings may have been.

When people did actually accuse Donnelly of anti-Semitism, he was quick to respond in the press with sweeping attacks against all forms of bias and discrimination: "We are fighting Plutocracy not because it is Jewish or Christian, but because it is Plutocracy. . . . We have lots of Christian money sharks in western Minnesota who would drive Shylock to hang himself out of shame." The last thing he would ever want to do, he insisted, was "pander to prejudice against any man because of his race, religion, nationality or color." At the outbreak of the Spanish-American War in the spring of 1898, Donnelly noted that the conflict might well be a boon to the economy, and especially to farmers and workers, but he considered it "a crying shame that we can only loosen the grip of the money-power, on the throats of the people, by murdering tens of thousands of innocent producers." And I know my father would have been intrigued to discover that when the Dreyfus Affair spurred anti-Jewish rioting in much of Europe in 1899, Donnelly came out as a staunch supporter of Dreyfus and condemned the rioters. "The Jews are not all plutocrats," he reminded the readers of the newspaper that he was then editing; "a large majority of them are the poorest people in the world. The half-starved workers of the sweatshops of London, Berlin and New York are mostly Hebrews." When it came to religion, Donnelly preached the gospel of acceptance: "Live and let live should be the motto of the world."[79] Only when he saw injustice did he believe in intervention.

My father didn't know whether to accept it or fight it when he received the rejection letter from the University of Delaware Press in the fall of 2006, telling him just how far removed his Dreyfus manuscript seemed to be from scholarly norms. He was suddenly, dramatically, out of balance. It was as if, a few years earlier, he had subconsciously decided that he could die in peace once the book was published—the prospect of scholarly accomplishment had perhaps allowed a healthy acknowledgment of mortality—and now the mellow twilight glow of the horizon had been replaced by a brightness so intense that he had to look away. But I didn't realize just how dramatic the swing had been until two years later, in late December 2008, when my mother, quite uncharacteristically, sat me down and said that she needed to tell me something about my father.

It makes little sense to speak of a "trigger" for Alzheimer's Disease, but I'm now sure that my father's slide into depression and denial, in the aftermath of the Delaware rejection, quickly edged into dementia. Sometime in the intervening two years, my mother told me—she didn't know exactly when—my father had become obsessed with those junk mail "sweepstakes" letters that so many Americans receive every few days, some of which are straightforward scams designed explicitly to drain money from the accounts of vulnerable senior citizens. And, she said, he was becoming more irritable, less reliable, and possibly less competent: she was worried that he was ignoring not only his Dreyfus book and his Yiddish translations but also his basic bill-paying chores. There had recently been a disquieting phone call from the electric company. She tried to ask him about it, but he just wanted to be left alone and told her not to be concerned—he had everything under control. Mostly she went about her business: they had always adhered to a fairly traditional division of household labor. When she did look in on him, though, he always seemed to be filling out another sweepstakes form, each of which took several hours of work, with a magnifying glass, because his eyesight had become so poor. For several weeks she had planned to tell Debbie or me about what was going on, but she just hadn't found the right moment. Maybe she was exaggerating the seriousness of the problem, she said;

maybe she was just annoyed with him. But her tone, her entire manner, suggested to me that this was the most unsettling thing that had happened to them since my mother's breast cancer and my father's heart failure.

I can only imagine my look of shocked incomprehension—or was it denial?—during our conversation. I knew my father to be utterly meticulous about all his responsibilities, utterly skeptical of things like sweepstakes, and utterly uninterested in accumulating wealth. How had he become an entirely different person without my realizing it? As my mother was speaking, I was going back over the last several times I had seen him, castigating myself for not having paid attention to various signs of trouble, for not being engaged enough in his life. I put some of the blame on myself—I was just too wrapped up in other things—but I was also trying to think more broadly: here, perhaps, was one of the awful costs of the scattering of families, one of the drawbacks to the modern American expectation that children should head off into the world to pursue various kinds of opportunities and leave their parents to fend for themselves in old age. Maybe Christine and the kids and I ought to be living in Newton, getting together with my parents for Shabbat dinners, surrounding them with grandchildren eager to hear their stories, giving my father something better to concentrate on than sweepstakes. After the Civil War, when so many young men had left home to fulfill an abstract duty and then never come back, the old ideal image of multiple generations inhabiting one hearth, of white-haired patriarchs and matriarchs dying in the bosom of their families, came to seem almost bitterly farcical.[80] But why couldn't that tradition be reinvigorated?

Hamlin Garland missed his mother's death, but when his father's time came, the whole family was in the habit of spending at least the summer months together in Wisconsin, and so Richard's "last days were spent in calm content with his granddaughters to delight and comfort him."[81] Then, when Garland himself approached the ripe old age of seventy, he made the difficult decision to abandon his professional life in the east and move to Los Angeles, where both his daughters had settled, where he could enjoy his grandson, where he could tend his roses and embrace California's "brightness and newness and freedom from winter." And, until he died ten years later of a cerebral hemorrhage, he considered himself a "fortunate exile"—despite his wistful acknowledgment that "I suffer when I think of abandoning all that New England has meant to me. I remember its hills and storms and deep snows as I remember poetry or song."[82] The choice, in modern times, frequently comes down to attachment to people *or* attachment to place. Only rarely can you have both. Often you have neither. In my parents' kitchen in Newton on December 29, 2008, I asked myself: how is it that, at 39, I feel so disconnected?

The talks I had with my father over the next few days and weeks were among the most painful of my life. He seemed to shift in and out of denial: one minute he would express embarrassment and shame and shake his head, saying he didn't understand how this obsession had come about, and he knew it would be best for him to cut off his involvement with sweepstakes right away; the next minute he would get defensive, explaining that it was all perfectly rational, that filling out the sweepstakes forms often involved solving little puzzles and playing word games, which he enjoyed, that he had lost hardly any money, and the potential payoff was enormous, and that in some cases it wasn't about getting rich at all but about offering financial assistance to people who were in dire need, and he owed it to these people to continue doing what he had been doing. This was what my mother had been living with, what we would all come to expect in the following months and years; this was the shape of his dementia. It was impossible to guess, from moment to moment, whether you'd get clear-eyed coherence, acuity, sensitivity, or deluded rambling, aggression, confabulation. And I had to confront him, repeatedly—had to ask him hard questions about bank accounts and credit card numbers—had to break the news to him that he had been duped, victimized—had to watch him tremble and cry. My father, my articulate, eloquent father, who had taught me grammar and diction and countless puns, now fumbled for words, groped for some sort of rationale, refused to meet my desperate gaze.

The month of January was consumed by meetings with doctors and lawyers and bankers, plus long strategy sessions with my sister. Debbie took on most of the work: she's the older sibling, she lives in Massachusetts, and Christine was eight months pregnant with our third child. But, together, we determined that Dad had given out crucial financial information to several scammers, some of whom were withdrawing money directly from his checking account on a daily basis; others were racking up charges on one of his credit cards. The total loss was a few thousand dollars, up to that point; even more troubling was the problem of putting a permanent end to the withdrawals and charges—not a straightforward process, given that Dad had (in a sense, anyway) offered the account numbers of his own free will. We also figured out, within a few days, that he no longer knew his birth date or phone number— that, in fact, he could no longer work with numbers of any kind in any reliable way. Though he insisted on spending several hours putting his check book in order, and claimed to have succeeded, he was not able to convince us that his current balance was actually sixty-seven million dollars. So, over the course of the month, we hired a bookkeeper, tied up as many loose ends as possible, and arranged for Dad to get some neurological testing. And I tried to adjust to the unpredictability of my conver-

sations with my father, to the idea that his identity had become fundamentally unstable, to the possibility that his dementia would forever color the way I remembered
him. What would I say when my children asked me to describe his character? What
kind of eulogy would I be able to write for him? Sometimes it wasn't sufficient to tell
myself that dementia makes people do inexplicable things. I wanted to understand
what it *meant* that my father had become obsessed with sweepstakes. Had he gotten
greedy in his old age? Had he always been greedy? Looking through his tax documents from previous years, I was happy to find long lists of his charitable donations,
lists that went on for pages and pages of narrow-ruled yellow paper filled with his
tiny, careful, cursive notations, hard evidence of his generosity, his commitment to
organizations that fought poverty and disease and pollution and discrimination, that
promoted the arts and education and public-mindedness. Each gift was just a few
dollars: he clearly believed that every little bit might help. So, for a while, I managed
to convince myself that his sweepstakes entries represented nothing more than deluded attempts to extend his giving. Yet there was also evidence suggesting that they
were nothing more than deluded attempts to get rich as quickly as possible.

Since it was so often excruciating to speak with my father during this time, I
tended to avoid it when it wasn't absolutely necessary, sometimes calling my mother
and asking her explicitly not to tell Dad I was on the line. And I clung to old memories of him: I didn't want to hear him sound crazy or spiteful or embarrassed. As
February approached, though, and my thoughts turned from death to birth, I started
to realize the danger of allowing myself to lose contact with my father. Even as his
awareness of the wider world started to fade, he seemed to cling to his immediate
family, seemed always to know who we were and what we were doing, seemed to want
to remain the person we had always known him to be: the argument that finally convinced him to give up his sweepstakes, I think, was that they ultimately had nothing
to do with what we understood as his core values. It was precisely our full engagement with him that could keep him alive. When I tried to empathize with him, I
was able to recognize that, most of all, he wanted our love and respect, wanted us to
go back to seeing him as kind, gentle, good-natured, generous. After our baby was
born, Dad would want to be introduced right away, would eventually want to be
trusted to hold him and read him a story. So, when the time came, though I was
tempted just to tell my mother and have her relay the news, I instead made sure they
were both on the phone, and then gave the joyful particulars: a healthy boy, ten
pounds and two ounces, twenty-one and a half inches long, at 7:05 A.M.—named
Oscar. There was no hesitation. "Oscar!" my father said. "That's Wilde!" I started to
laugh and cry at the same time. There he was: my father, quick as ever, enamored of

innocent pleasures, humbly literary—but now a little more excitable. There were times when he screamed at my mother in anger and frustration, in the winter of 2009—something I cannot even imagine very clearly—because she couldn't see the little imp-like figures that he thought were scampering across the top of his dresser. But in the minutes after my third child was born, my father expressed a thrilled exuberance—an emotion that was satisfyingly different from the calm contentment I perceived in his voice when he reacted to the arrival of Sam and Abe in our lives.

Dementia, then, does have its benefits. I'm convinced that, at times, its loosening of my father's inhibitions has given him access to a kind of surprised giddiness that he probably hadn't felt since he was a child. Often, now, when we walk through the back door of my parents' house, he seems overjoyed to see us, as if he'd had no idea we were coming for a visit. I think Alzheimer's disease has even helped him forget to be depressed, forget to worry about dying, forget to feel constrained by old age, disease, frailty—by all the limitations that seem, from the outside, to define his existence. In the late winter of 2011, he fell down the stairs, at home, in Newton, and for about three weeks, at the hospital and the rehabilitation center, he was unable to walk at all, not because of any physical problem but because of the psychological scarring. Then he forgot that he couldn't trust his sense of balance. And he's even forgotten about his obsession with sweepstakes.

Even when denial is seemingly adaptive, though, and even when it is abetted by dementia, it is never complete; despair has a way of creeping back in. My father sometimes forgets about his Dreyfus manuscript; sometimes claims still to be rewriting the introduction; and sometimes seems to see the whole project as confirming the ultimate inadequacy of his life. I have been yearning, recently, to have his manuscript privately printed, so that he can at least hold it in his hands as a book. But I have no idea how he would respond to that: probably, on some days, he would be profoundly grateful and even happy; and on other days, he would resent me bitterly for depriving him of his opportunity for redemption, since I think he still believes that eventually he'll get around to completing his revisions, and then some editor at a legitimate press will see the light and go forward with publication.

My father's new tendency toward denial also makes it hard for him to accept help, or acknowledge how burdensome he has become to my mother. "People keep telling me I have this disease," he sometimes says to me, "but I don't see any signs of it." Debbie and I have tried, on many occasions, to speak with him openly about the future, to get him interested in moving to an assisted living facility in Amherst or Ithaca, to solicit his opinion about how he wants to die while he still has occasional access to coherence. He won't respond. His focus on the present is perhaps what sustains him now, in his familiar routine: Yiddish translations, at his desk, in the study, during the day; news shows and old movies, in the room we call the library, in the evening; toast for breakfast, fruit for lunch, chicken for dinner. More people are coming to the house to help with various chores and activities, to provide support and companionship, and I've had to get more involved with my father's translation clients, letting them know the limitations on what he can accomplish these days. But he's getting by. And my mother is still taking her art classes, and seeing a therapist, and gradually finding ways of caring for herself and my father simultaneously, which sometimes means simply steering clear of him. I'm grateful for what they have; I just wish things were a little different, wish we could be closer, wish, at certain moments, that we lived in an earlier time, when families stayed together and elders died at home, before, as the novelist Julian Barnes recently put it, we became invested in the "process—from doctor to hospital to undertaker to crematorium—in which professionals and bureaucrats tell us what to do, up to the point where we are left to ourselves, survivors standing with a glass in our hands, amateurs learning how to mourn."

Shortly after celebrating his sixtieth birthday, Barnes set out to write a book about dying, but in the end *Nothing to Be Frightened Of* (2008), which I read with a fair amount of urgency in the summer of 2009, turned into a meditation on the death of his parents, which led to the suggestion that, in the modern world, the truly frightening thing might not be mortality itself, or nothingness, but the deathbed. His father, Barnes explained, had "died a modern death, in hospital, without his family, attended in his final minutes by a nurse, months—indeed, years—after medical science had prolonged his life to a point where the terms on which it was being offered were unimpressive."[83] Over the last few years, I have found some measure of peace in visiting cemeteries—I even got the chance to find Dreyfus's grave in Paris, and I brought back a photograph, which my father keeps on his desk—but when I think of my father's imminent passing, my imagination stumbles on the likelihood that it will be lonely, sterile, detached, with everyone rushing to follow certain procedures, rather than a calm slipping away, among those who have always cared for him, followed by a humble but dignified trip, a couple of days later, to a familiar family plot. Many years ago, my parents did purchase a gravesite in a Jewish cemetery, somewhere in Greater Boston, but I don't know exactly where, and even they have never visited it. It's at least a few miles away from where Benjamin is buried. My mother answers vaguely when I ask the obvious questions: she thinks it's in Dedham; she doesn't remember why; she thinks they were just following the advice of friends and lawyers.

I wish I could talk to my father about his death and burial, but I also wish he could tell me his thoughts on the more distant future. What's his opinion about the immediacy of global warming? I miss his Donnellian ability to look back into the past and see both plenty of evidence of hubristic blundering and also occasional grounds for hope. What does he think it means that so many people have predicted the apocalypse so many times before? Has old age made him more fatalistic? What wisdom does he want his grandchildren to inherit? Does he think we'll be able to break through our cultural denial of environmental damage and limits?

I suppose I've become slightly more pessimistic over the last couple of years, though I can't tell if that's due more to the stalling of environmental politics or more to the experience of watching helplessly, from a distance, as my father's mind decays. When I saw Werner Herzog's documentary about Antarctica, *Encounters at the End of the World,* in 2007, I was annoyed by the film's shrugging acceptance of global warming and imminent human extinction. The melting of polar ice ought to spur us toward greater attempts at scaling back our society's ecological footprint! I hope I never lose that idealism, but I have to admit that modernity seems more and more catastrophic to me,[84] that I am now sometimes tempted to join Herzog in wondering whether it might be time for our species to fade from the scene. I'm focused on endings right now, wishing the final years of my father's life weren't looking so bleak.

If I grow old before I die, I might witness shocking floods of environmental refugees, might witness Miami and New Orleans abandoned, might witness brutal conflicts over a narrowing pool of crucial resources. Of course, that prospect shouldn't distract us from the horrors of poverty, oppression, violence, and despair that are already haunting so many of the world's people. And such horrors have always been with us: studying history should give us pause, should remind us that, despite the radical discontinuities of modernity, every new alarm is an echo. Arcadia and Armageddon, like humanity and nature, have always been intertwined; global warming represents not planetary revenge but the ultimate inextricability of social and environmental forces.

Back in the 1820s and 30s, Thomas Cole, one of America's consummate Arcadians, not only reminded his compatriots that "The Course of Empire" usually ended in "Desolation," but also invoked the legend of the Flood to re-pose the question of how we might rebuild a good society after bringing cataclysm down on our heads yet again. *Subsiding of the Waters of the Deluge* (1829) shows a dark, desolate, rocky landscape, with a prominent skull in the foreground. (Figure 50.) Yet in the center of the image viewers could barely make out the ark, floating on calm waters, and the dove, bound for land, and, as one contemporary critic noted, "the glow of the returning sun is spread like a promise of hope in the midst of so great desolation."[85] Trees lie splintered against the rocks, all is in upheaval, the lines and curves of the painting

Figure 50. Thomas Cole, *Subsiding of the Waters of the Deluge*, 1829, oil on canvas.

are harsh, ragged—but a concerted effort might yield some flat ground to stand on, on the edge between shadow and light.

Six years later, Cole put a similar uncertainty about civilization at the center of perhaps his most famous work, *The Oxbow* (1836), showing a river in the shape of a question mark and a forested mountain in the background with the Hebrew name "Noah" carved into its flank, presumably by loggers or farmers. (Figure 51.) The right side of the canvas suggests a pastoral paradise of well-watered fields dotted with trees and bathed in sun, while the left side captures a punishing storm over a tangled wilderness of rocky pinelands, with a couple of leaning, blasted trees in the foreground and a tiny artist figure looking out from among the boulders in the middle distance. Apparently, the people of Massachusetts were carving out a viable civilization in the welcoming Connecticut River valley, despite occasional tempests. But the picture also suggests that the wild and the calm are never in perfect balance: the river is threatening to overflow its banks, and no one knows what the next storm might bring. The artist waits, watches.

Figure 51. Thomas Cole, *View from Mount Holyoke, Northampton, Massachusetts,
after a Thunderstorm—The Oxbow,* 1836, oil on canvas.

The apocalypse usually arrives in trickles rather than a flood. History suggests that the nightmare scenarios proposed by twenty-first-century environmentalists are unlikely to be borne out anytime soon. On the other hand, history also suggests that the unlikeliest events sometimes occur, and I do happen to think that the industrial-scale violence of modernity has raised the stakes, that Ignatius Donnelly's apocalypse represents a graver threat than Thomas Cole's apocalypse. The record of the last 150 years, since the Civil War, is riddled with destructiveness, if also laced with a few traditions emphasizing commonality and kinship. No individual knows exactly when or how he or she is going to die, which is probably a blessing; similarly, we remain in the dark about how long our society and species are going to last, and that ignorance at least makes it seem rational to retain some small amount of faith in the future. Some of our letters will always arrive too late, but that doesn't mean we should stop writing them. Maybe my father will pass away tomorrow; maybe the world will end tonight; or maybe we'll all muddle through for a while longer, and in thirty or forty years one of my sons will take a road trip to Boston and visit his grandparents' grave.

*Epilogue*

# American Gothic; or, Death by Landscape

In the course of the nineteenth century bourgeois society has, by means of hygienic and social, private and public institutions, realized a secondary effect which may have been its subconscious main purpose: to make it possible for people to avoid the sight of the dying. Dying was once a public process in the life of the individual, and a most exemplary one; think of the medieval pictures in which the deathbed has turned into a throne toward which the people press through the wide-open doors of the death house. In the course of modern time dying has been pushed further and further out of the perceptual world of the living. There used to be no house, hardly a room, in which someone had not died. . . . Today people live in rooms that have never been touched by death, dry dwellers of eternity, and when their end approaches they are stowed away in sanatoria or hospitals by their heirs. It is, however, characteristic that not only a man's knowledge or wisdom, but above all his real life—and this is the stuff that stories are made of—first assumes transmissible form at the moment of his death. . . . Death is the sanction of everything that the storyteller can tell. He has borrowed his authority from death. In other words, it is natural history to which his stories refer back.
—Walter Benjamin, "The Storyteller" (1936)

Graves tend to be important to children and grandchildren; by the time we are three generations removed from the dead, their burial sites begin to look abandoned. Individual stones soften and crumble at the edges, sometimes start to lean; inscriptions fade. But cemeteries, as public spaces, as landscapes of both mourning and hope, cared for by municipalities or nonprofit organizations, have demonstrated some staying power. They can serve as connections to our common past, and reminders of where we are all headed.

347

Environmentalists, of necessity, are future-oriented: the whole point is to cultivate modes of interaction with nature that can be sustained over time. It's not that we necessarily ignore the present (though sometimes we do); often enough, it's the perceived crises of today that compel us to consider the likely crises of tomorrow. But this anxious focus tends to preclude any deep attentiveness to the past. When we do cast a backward glance, too frequently we take note of little more than our history of destructive behavior. And, unfortunately, I've come to believe that a narrow attitude toward the past may close off certain approaches to the present and future. We've quite possibly trapped ourselves in a narrative that casts our ancestors as villains and ourselves as formerly passive bystanders who must now rise to the level of heroes if we wish to save future generations. It's an all too American story of ultimate redemption and progress, a last chance at true salvation, the realization of a special, private, exceptional destiny.[1]

It's also a story of radical discontinuity: "We're not, in other words," writes Bill McKibben, "going to get back the planet we used to have."[2] That antiromantic pose, that embrace of a kind of ultrarealism, is supposed to lead to action, but I worry that it might lead to an immobilizing fatalism. Its confidence deprives us of the uncertainty that is the basis of hope. As the essayist Rebecca Solnit has commented, with her usual combination of perspicacity and eloquence, we too often "transform the future's unknowability into something certain, the fulfillment of all our dread, the place beyond which there is no way forward. But again and again, far stranger things happen than the end of the world."[3]

For decades now, environmentalists have suggested that we'll probably need a major catastrophe to spur any fundamental changes in our behavior, that only the deep, visceral fear of nature's indifference, and of its power to wipe out our children and grandchildren, might cause Americans, in particular, to give up their addiction to the pursuit of consumerist satisfaction. But what if modernity—the modernity created by new forms of human-nature interaction—is itself catastrophic, even traumatic?[4] In the past, fear might have brought certain communities together in solidarity; in modern times, though, it more often seems to breed further denial, or resignation, or a fierce, individualistic competition for survival. For at least fifty years, since Rachel Carson published *Silent Spring* (1962), environmental thinkers have been forecasting doom; today, we are probably more fearful, and more aware of ecological limits and dangers, but probably not any more willing to make sacrifices, for our children or anyone else.[5]

I guess I see more creative potential in an old-fashioned engagement with history and mortality, in labors of loss and limitation that both cling to the past and acknowledge passing, in the work of mourning that is never complete. "Like love," wrote the French critic Roland Barthes, grieving for his mother, "mourning affects the world—and the worldly—with unreality, with importunity."[6] Mourning relies on memory, on imagination, on the wish that things were different, and as the past comes alive again as something cherished, perhaps the future, in all its uncertainty, with all its potential, will also come alive, as something not to be missed, as something to be witnessed.

I've been struggling, then, to get through the latest environmental treatises, which more and more frequently adopt a prophetic pose and insist that their readers simply shake off their doldrums and help their children and grandchildren cope with the coming storms and heat waves.[7] What I've been able to focus on more readily is the recent flurry of books dedicated to bringing death and mourning back into the mainstream of public discourse.[8] It's mortality (and birth), after all, not parenthood, that human beings ultimately have in common, and I think we may need a true sense of commonality more than anything else right now. Yes, we ought to consider the needs of future generations, as H. W. S. Cleveland did when he laid out his park systems. But, these days, I find myself looking backward as much as forward, pondering ancestors, both genetic and adopted. I find myself encouraging my children not just to note signs of global warming, but to discover evidence in their everyday landscapes that they are connected to history. Look carefully, and you'll be able to see ghosts—the dead, our guides—in books, beneath our feet, demanding our care. And, even closer to home: the bereaved, and the dying. I don't think it's a matter of writing an epitaph for the planet; I think the key is, simultaneously, to accept constant change in the webwork of nature and culture, and to labor persistently to preserve certain continuities. "History and elegy are akin," says Anne Carson in her book *Nox* (2010), which she wrote in response to her brother's death—an observation also at the heart of *The Glen Rock Book of the Dead* (2008), by Marion Winik:[9]

> I got the idea to make a series of portraits of dead people I have known, or whose lives have touched me in some way. . . . This never seemed morbid or depressing to me. I have lost too many people, I think, to make talking and thinking about them an unpleasant thing to do. My life has been shaped as much by people who are no longer living as by people who are, and perhaps this has been particularly true since I moved, in middle age, to Glen Rock, a quiet place. . . . In Mexico, they do something like this on El Día de los Muertos: the Day of the Dead, which is observed on November 1 and 2 every year. On these days, people build altars to their loved ones with pictures and flowers and candles, with the old favorite sodas and books and T-shirts and cigarettes. Then they go to the cemetery and stay all night, praying,

singing, drinking, wailing. They tell the sad stories and the noble ones; they eat cookies shaped like skeletons. They celebrate and mourn at once.

I don't assume that more familiarity with death, or the past, would result in more familiarity with nature, or would even help encourage a keener ethic of care in our culture. Less denial would probably be a good thing, but talking more about limits won't necessarily convince people to respect or accept them. What matters, I suppose, is how you approach the conversation. What matters is that we bear witness, cultivate empathy, insist on kinship.[10]

My hope, for all future generations, is that they will have (in addition to sunshine, fresh air, clean water, and fertile soil) a somewhat slower pace of life, with plenty of time to pause, in quiet places, like Glen Rock, and Mount Auburn, and the Wilderness, and Indian Mounds Park, and Atlantis—haunted places—everyday, accessible places, open to the public—places that are not too radically transformed over time— places susceptible of cultivation, where people can express their caring, and nature can respond—places with tough, gnarled roots and tangled stalks, with digging mammals and noisy birds—places of common remembrance and hopeful guidance— places of unexpected encounters—places that breed solidarity across difference—places where children can walk in the footsteps of those who have gone before—places that are perpetually up for adoption—places that have been humanized but not conquered or commodified—places that foster a kind of connectedness both mournful and celebratory.[11]

———————————

Though much of our retrospection, in recent years, has focused on the voracious American appetite for natural resources, it is also true that we have often looked back wistfully to times when more Americans had a more immediate connection to the land. The Arcadian tradition, though it lost momentum in the last third of the nineteenth century, never died or disappeared, because Americans remained undecided about modernity, and about its tendency to wipe the slate clean and plow under the past and rebuild from the ground up, with its sleek, new buildings always pointing toward heaven. Even at the peak of the early twentieth century's Progressive movement— perhaps especially then—in an era seemingly dominated by the machine and the skyscraper, when most environmental reformers were touting either remote tree farms or remote wilderness areas, the Arcadian imagination continued to flicker, and occasionally, over the following century, its images flashed into the national consciousness. We have never been entirely modern.[12]

It was fairly early in the twentieth century, precisely when urban industrialism moved to the center of the nation's identity, that the region of the middle border started to take on a new, nostalgic resonance as America's true "heartland." If New York, and, a couple of decades later, Los Angeles, symbolized the fast-paced, cutting-edge United States of the future, the states around Iowa came to represent the comforting narrative of nineteenth-century settlement and the continuing cultivation of down-home wholesomeness.[13] In 1913, Willa Cather, living in New York, published her second novel and called it *O Pioneers!*, in direct homage to a patriotic poem by Walt Whitman. The book's action is set in the 1880s and 90s, on the central plains, where a matriarch named Alexandra Bergson attempts, with some success, to adapt to the rhythms of a lonely, arid, windswept environment: "From the Norwegian grave-yard one looks out over a vast checker-board, marked off in squares of wheat and corn; light and dark, dark and light." The brightness and decadence of big cities seemed more palatable when balanced by the calm moderation of hardworking midwestern-ers and their orderly landscapes. Cather's Arcadia, which she continued to develop in popular works like *The Song of the Lark* (1915) and *My Ántonia* (1918), was itself significantly more modern than Whitman's, more regular and commercial, but it still evoked the power of "the land itself," with its "fierce strength, its peculiar, savage kind of beauty, its uninterrupted mournfulness."[14] And it opened the way, thanks to Cather's evocative probing of her experiences as a girl growing up in Nebraska, for Hamlin Garland's series of middle border autobiographies. During the years of the Great War, as Garland stewed over the form of *A Son of the Middle Border*, worrying that a mobilized, outward-looking nation would take little interest in his family's struggles, he tried to draw solace from the fact that his book, like *O Pioneers!*, would be set "in the midst of a charming landscape and during a certain heroic era of western settlement," which clearly continued to hold some appeal for many Americans. He imagined that some readers would find his work "unduly personal," while, "no doubt, others will wish the revelation had been made more complete"—concerns with which I can identify—but he banked on the historical symbolism of the frontier itself, with its blending of town, forest, and field, to capture his readers' attention. In the end, *A Son of the Middle Border* outsold all his other books.[15]

Almost a century later, few Americans know of Garland's middle border books, but many of us still grow up reading Laura Ingalls Wilder, who was born just six years after Garland, and just eighty miles away, and whose first book, *Little House in the Big Woods* (1932), which launched her astoundingly successful late-in-life career, re-capitulates many of the moods and episodes of Wisconsin pioneering that Garland had made famous. The iconic status of the "Little House" books, in turn, opened up space for any number of later writers seeking to invoke the agrarian strand of the Arcadian tradition, from the Wisconsin ethicist and ecologist Aldo Leopold, to Wendell Berry, the Kentucky poet and farmer, to Wes Jackson, founder of the Land Institute in Salina, Kansas.

Meanwhile, perhaps the most prominent Arcadian of the early twentieth century was a scholarly activist whose footsteps I have sometimes traced around Ithaca: the Cornell botanist and horticulturist Liberty Hyde Bailey, leader of the Country-Life movement. Though he had roots on the middle border, in Michigan, Bailey spent most of his long life in central New York, and in much of his work he seemed to invoke the spirit of antebellum reform, perhaps modeling himself on Andrew Jackson Downing. "If it were possible for every person to own a tree and to care for it," he noted, in a book called *The Holy Earth* (1915), "the good results would be beyond estimation."[16] Most often, if Bailey is remembered at all (he and Garland were equally influential and have been equally forgotten), he is identified as a dedicated agrarian who resented the new dominance of the American city. But in his writing he was always careful to distinguish between his engagement with rurality and "the present popular back-to-the-land agitation," explaining that his goal was not to undermine urban life but merely to address "the lack of adjustment between city and country."[17]

Bailey frequently sounded like a modern Henry George, abhorring "the sinfulness of vast private estates that shut up expanses of the surface of the earth from the reach and enjoyment of others that are born similarly to the privileges of the planet."[18] While he sometimes saw the archetypal city as "a parasite, running out its roots into the open country and draining it of its substance," he also recognized that cities could produce the kind of people who might go back "to the country with new and large ideas, active touch with great affairs, keen business and executive ability, generosity, altruism, high culture."[19] Perhaps most of all, Bailey emphasized the necessary kinship between city and country, their "organic relation," the "balance . . . that exists between urban and rural forces," the responsibility of all "city folk and country folk" to think of each other "fraternally" and "work together on all great public questions."[20] How would urban and suburban development shift if it were overseen not exclusively by a city's downtown bankers but also by farmers and villagers from its hinterlands?

Since Bailey perceived the countryside as having declined in the early twentieth century, he put most of his energy into efforts to improve rural education and create incentives for practiced family farmers to stay on their farms. In the end, though, he felt that everyone's mindset would have to change, that we would all have to work harder to recognize our commonality and reliance on one another—that agrarians would have to embrace their "guardianship" of nature more fully, but that urbanites would also have to understand that "the farmer cannot keep the earth for us without an enlightened and very active support from every other person." Bailey didn't want untrained city dwellers to move back to the land but rather to appreciate their connection to the land wherever they lived, perhaps by having a small kitchen garden, or by buying produce directly from growers at a public farmers' market, or by considering the impact of their everyday actions on the wider world, or by expressing gratitude for the environmental gifts without which they could not survive. He constantly directed his readers' attention to what he called "the background spaces," which encompassed not only liminal landscapes—the atmosphere, the ocean, the forests and fields that surround our dwellings—but also the bygone eras that provide a context for the present day: we need to connect ourselves to these "ancestral" and "everlasting backgrounds" so as to grasp our "inescapable responsibilities," the obligations implied by our lack of wholeness and our inevitable dependence, by our limitations. "To feel that one is a useful and co-operating part in nature is to give one kinship," he suggested. ". . . Here arise the fundamental common relations. . . . Here also the responsible practices of life take root."[21]

In practical, spatial terms, Bailey often proposed that, to establish his ideal Arcadia, "what is really needed is a back-to-the-village movement," rather than either a new agrarianism or the expansion of the already sprawling urban and suburban spheres: "We have over-built our cities at the expense of the hamlets and the towns. I look for a great development of the village and small community in the next generation."[22] Ithaca, it seems, was the realization of his dream, and he is buried right here, on a quiet hillside, not in the City Cemetery but over at Lakeview, about a mile north, where my son Sam always used to claim that he was about to keel over from having been forced to hike too far.

Hamlets like Ithaca, though, as livable and lovable as they might be, may always seem just a bit too small and isolated to those Arcadians with stronger urban inclinations, and I've always felt that such places would have to be balanced by slightly larger, more diverse metropoles. My own sympathies, then, lie more with the urbanist and cultural critic Lewis Mumford, who was born in 1895 but who spent his life in the twentieth century casting his gaze back to the turmoil of the post–Civil War era, in the hope of coming to grips with his own time, with the fragmented world of high capitalism and modernism. "The commonest axiom of history," he wrote, "is that every generation revolts against its fathers and makes friends with its grandfathers," and as he came of age in the 1920s he repudiated the industrial materialism that he grew up with and joyfully rediscovered the works of Melville, Whitman, Olmsted, George Perkins Marsh, and Henry George. Indeed, he is one of the few scholars who have ever noticed the career of H. W. S. Cleveland, and Mumford quoted him at length on the question of city planning, because, he explained in 1931, "his criticism could not be improved upon today."[23]

Mumford referred to the Gilded Age as the "Brown Decades," because he thought that "the Civil War shook down the blossoms and blasted the promise of spring," and now "the country *looked* different—darker, sadder, soberer." Buildings were dusted with a sooty veneer from the burning of coal, and Mumford suspected that the same film had coated the "spectacles that every sensitive mind wore," as the war's survivors struggled to overcome their disillusionment and disorientation, often sinking into gloom or indulging frenzies of escapism. "Dead men were everywhere," Mumford imagined. "They were present in memory; their portraits stoically gathered dust in empty parlors; they even retained possession of their bodies and walked about the streets; they spoiled gaiety, or rather, they drove it to fevers of license and distraction." Yet he also insisted that this same era could just as easily be called the "Buried Renaissance." While from some perspectives it seemed as though "the laval flow of industrialism after the war had swept over all the cities of the spirit," nevertheless, "one must not forget the measure of intellectual hope" that arose in American culture thanks to the radical critics and reformers who would not accept the injustice of the railroad grants, and the strike-breaking, and the deforestation, and the sequestering of impoverished immigrants in wretched tenements. And Mumford suspected that the most significant current of resistance in the postbellum years derived from the tradition of expressing a "concern for the soil," an ethic of care regarding Americans' "relation with the land" and their shaping of habitable space.[24]

Mumford expressed great gratitude to Liberty Hyde Bailey for his efforts toward the "re-ruralizing of thought," but his ultimate goal was to canonize thinkers like Olmsted and Cleveland, who were more attuned to the urban scale, who "renewed the city's contact with the land" and made even densely packed populations much more "conscious of air, sunlight, vegetation, growth."[25] Over time, Mumford's ideal pattern of development crystallized into a regionalist vision of interconnected, midsize "garden cities." His inspiration had come, first, from places like Olmsted's Boston and Cleveland's Minneapolis, with their systemic designs, laid down on "excellent social and hygienic grounds"—with their "shade trees to line the street, wider malls and promenades and open squares, and a system of small recreation parks"; and then from the English urban theorist Ebenezer Howard, who, Mumford noted, had been deeply influenced by Henry George, and who "re-introduced into city planning the ancient Greek concept of a natural limit to growth of any organism or organization."[26] In his book *The Culture of Cities* (1938), Mumford explained that "the new type of regional center would combine the hygienic advantages of the open suburbs with the social advantages of the big city, would give an equal place in its scheme to the urban and rural possibilities of modern life: in short, it would be a balanced environment."[27] Mumford celebrated openness, connection, and, perhaps above all, a grave but liberating sense of limitation, based on a tradition of responsibility that was both practical and ethical in its roots. A society with no boundaries may lack restraint; a society with rigid boundaries may lack respect for what lies beyond, for the uncertain and unknown. What Mumford believed in was the constant, democratic labor of discussing boundedness, of establishing more or less porous borders, which would inevitably have to be shifted, like blinds on a window that either block or let in the light, depending on the weather and time of day.

Look at the broad history of city design and redesign in the twentieth century; at experimental garden towns like Radburn, New Jersey, or Greenbelt, Maryland; at planned communities like Reston, Virginia; at the urban growth boundaries famously adopted by Portland, Oregon; at the dynamic "green cities" and urban ecology movements of the twenty-first century—and Mumford's wide-ranging influence is clear, which suggests that, wherever urbanism and environmentalism overlap, the landscape traditions of the nineteenth century are still in play.[28] In recent years, an organization called the Arcadia Center for Sustainable Food and Agriculture established itself on George Washington's old Woodlawn Plantation, just twenty miles south of the nation's capital, and set about linking the metropolitan area's millions of consumers with the practice of producing fresh food, through education and training programs and the provision of fruits, vegetables, and grains to schools, restaurants, nonprofits, neighborhood centers, and markets.[29] Meanwhile, out on the middle border, the notoriously decaying city of Detroit, even during the most recent economic downturn, has fostered a thriving network of urban farms and gardens in formerly empty lots, in the scarred, charred, seemingly ruined spaces of industrial and racial conflict. When Rebecca Solnit published a meditation on the city's seeming reflorescence, noting the economic and racial diversity of the farmers and gardeners and the powerful pull of common green spaces on the entire downtown population, she called her article, with perfect appropriateness, "Detroit Arcadia."[30]

At the same time, though, as was evident in the debate surrounding Ithaca's Redbud Woods, urbanists and environmentalists don't always agree on priorities. In the summer of 2011, one could read a relatively long, erudite article on "the latest debates about city life," in a highly regarded magazine, without being forced to ponder the question of accessible parks or the city's dependence on the countryside for fresh food and clean water.[31] The most committed green-city activists might well invoke the work of Lewis Mumford, but they are unlikely to see urban ecology as a field with deep historical roots and a compelling tradition of espousing limitation, kinship, and empathy. In the manifestos of the "new" environmental urbanism you probably won't see references to the sober opening of Mumford's epic book, *The City in History*, where it becomes clear that "the city of the dead antedates the city of the living," that in fact "the first hints of civic life," as embodied by "the first grave mounds and tombs," by "great stones, sacred groves, monumental trees, holy wells," were all connected to "a ceremonious concern for the dead, manifested in their deliberate burial— with growing evidences of pious apprehension and dread." Mumford was offering a potent reminder that the tradition of city-building was launched not just for the pragmatic purposes of promoting group survival and commerce, but with the goal of establishing a sacred, ritualistic place of communion with nature and history, "a site to which family or clan groups are drawn back, at seasonable intervals, because it concentrates, in addition to any natural advantages it may have, certain 'spiritual' or supernatural powers, powers of higher potency and greater duration, of wider cosmic significance, than the ordinary processes of life."[32] A real garden city would be a place of both perpetual renewal and perpetual care.

The one iconic glimpse of Arcadia—and it is only a glimpse—that most Americans, whatever their political persuasion, might still recognize, can be found in a painting that was completed in 1930, at the dawn of the Great Depression: Grant Wood's *American Gothic.* (Figure 52.) A man and a woman stare back at us, the man meeting our eyes directly, the woman looking slightly askance, either submissively or subversively. They could be husband and wife; they could just as easily be father and daughter (the artist offered mixed messages about his intent). The pitchfork—whose shape is echoed in the man's mass-produced denim overalls, and the lines in his face, and the windows and siding of the house, and the roof of the barn, and one of the plants on the porch—seems to mark the two people as farmers. But their clothes are those of middle-class townsfolk; if not for the overalls, which have perhaps been thrown on because the man is planning to pitch some hay after a day at the office (the gentleman who posed for the painting was an Iowa dentist), they could be dressed for church. Indeed, there is a tiny gothic spire on the left, in the far background, piercing the light blue sky, and there is a somber formality to the man's black jacket and the woman's stiff collar and factory-made calico pinafore, whose texture and pattern connect it to the curtain in the gothic window in the gable. That window helps to identify the church-like house as having been designed in the well-known rural gothic style, a form favored by Andrew Jackson Downing in the 1840s for its combination of picturesque, cathedral-like airiness and straightforward simplicity, afford-

Figure 52. Grant Wood, *American Gothic*, 1930,
oil on beaver board.

ability, and ease of construction (this was a so-called balloon-frame house, whose standardized boards, posts, and rafters could be quickly nailed together). The man's bald pate and elongated head seem to mark him as a Puritan, and the woman's expression is darkly concerned. Yet there is ample sun in the scene, and the man's pressed lips could indicate heroic perseverance rather than grim defeat, and the woman's wheat-gold hair blends harmoniously with the rounded, sun-dappled tree in the background, and one stray lock dangles down along her neck, perhaps suggesting that she might not be quite so prim and trim as we thought (the female model was the artist's sister). Wood has given us two people who recognize the difficulty of life, who are confronting economic uncertainty, who are not entirely sure if they belong to the agrarian past or the industrial future, but who have planted themselves on the border and seem to be living in an uneasy peace with their surroundings, in a house that won't last forever but that, meanwhile, provides a good window onto the world. At the very least, it's a house of their own, a place where they can envision growing old and dying.[33]

Or does the word "gothic" in the picture's title imply something more ominous? Is the pitchfork a symbol of the devil? What might these people be hiding? Are they haunted by the small-town secrets that were the stand-bys of gothic literature in America—seduction, incest, physical and psychological torture, murder, possession? Did Wood dream up this scene back when he was an art student, paying for classes by working the night shift at a mortuary?[34]

Initially, most viewers of the painting saw it, either delightedly or angrily, as satirical, a send-up of a hopelessly middlebrow Middle America, which was mired in repression, provincialism, a sour, stern, suspicious sobriety, an old-fashioned rigidity, a drab thriftiness, a philistine's inclination toward predictability, standardization, conformity, the regularity of the machine-made rickrack ribbon (a much more sensible option than lace) that the woman used for the trim on her apron.

Yet Wood himself decried such readings of the painting, insisting that he had meant to show affection for his subjects, that, even if they had certain faults, they were nevertheless "basically good and solid" citizens: "I hate to be misunderstood," he explained, "as I am a loyal Iowan and love my state."[35] Indeed, though it seems perfectly clear that Wood actually had deeply mixed feelings about his fellow midwesterners, he did paint a number of pictures in the 1930s that effectively romanticized the life and landscape of the heartland. And, from the start, some interpreters of *American Gothic*—their numbers increased as time went on—saw Wood as declaring his allegiance, for better and worse, to the legacy of the stalwart pioneers of the late nineteenth century, who had built an enduring, rooted, self-sufficient society, now overseen by upright, earnest, middle-aged farmers and villagers. They could be narrow-minded and prudish, but you could rely on them.[36]

While the captains of industrial capitalism were driving the nation to ruin and preying on ordinary citizens, who were encouraged to fuel the economy by buying stocks on credit (a practice that made them extremely vulnerable to bank failures), Iowans were focusing on the age-old rhythms of agricultural production, and they were managing to feed much of the nation. Since the turn of the century, the United States had clearly owned the largest and most powerful economy in the world, and in the boom years of the 1920s, some six million farm owners abandoned their land and moved to cities to take advantage of plentiful industrial jobs and an upswing in middle-class purchasing power. The lucky ones lived in electrified buildings and bought radios, vacuum cleaners, cars. At the same time, though, there were lots of unlucky ones: by 1929, while the wealthiest 0.1 percent of Americans (about 24,000 families) held 34 percent of the nation's savings, 80 percent of families had no savings whatsoever.[37] Grant Wood seemed to recognize, then, that the safest strategy might be to stay in the heartland, where most people could probably afford a house and some land, and where, if need be, they could probably raise enough of their own food to weather the worst kind of Depression.

Over the last eighty years, through dozens of parodies and competing interpretations and condemnations leveled by pundits on both the left and right, *American Gothic* has persisted as possibly our nation's most famous painting. The distance that Wood created between his subjects and any potential viewers—we just don't quite know what to make of these two people; we certainly don't empathize with them— suggests to me the inappropriateness of trying to portray them as representative, national figures. Yet it's easy to see how, with the passing decades, they might have come to stand for the quintessential American couple—white, middling, stable, conservative. Compared to the rich Arcadian images of the nineteenth century, this one comes across as somewhat flat in its seeming exclusion, its elision of so much history. There are no hints of Indian Mounds, or the legacy of slavery and war, or the great migratory flows that so shaped the nation; there is no direct confrontation with the alienation and injustices of industrial capitalism. Rather, the picture remains compelling for its aloof ambiguity: surely, part of its popularity lies precisely in its openness to varying interpretations. But I think its ambiguity is of a particular sort, which may well have national implications. Perhaps, in its shiftiness, it captures a broad cultural ambivalence about the waning of Arcadia.

---

I am often overwhelmed with ambivalence. Ithaca is probably as close to Arcadia as I'm going to get, in this century, in this nation. I love it here—love the gorges and the cemeteries, the farmers' market, the public schools, the human scale. But Christine and I regularly find ourselves pondering the possibility of moving to a slightly larger city, closer to family and old friends. We don't know where we want to be buried. I still feel unsettled; maybe I always will.

Every couple of years, I reread an essay by Wallace Stegner called, in an impeccable rhythm, "Letter, Much Too Late." He wrote it at age eighty, to his dead mother, as a way of acknowledging that "age and experience have not made me . . . qualified to tell others about how to live their lives. I feel more like Theodore Dreiser, who confessed that he would depart from life more bewildered than he had arrived in it. Instead of being embittered, or stoical, or calm, or resigned, or any of the standard things that a long life might have made me, I confess that I am often simply lost, as much in need of comfort, understanding, forgiveness, uncritical love—the things you used to give me—as I ever was at five, or ten, or fifteen." Yet Stegner also felt compelled to insist that, over the years, his mother had never ceased to help him find himself when he needed to be present for others, and that he remained grateful for that: "Obviously, you did not die. Death is a convention, a certification to the end of pain, something for the vital-statistics book, not binding upon anyone but the keepers of graveyard records. . . . Your kind of love, once given, is never lost. You are alive and luminous in my head. Except when I fail to listen, you will speak through me when I face some crisis of feeling or sympathy or consideration for others." Maybe Stegner always felt lost, but he never lost track of the voices in his head; they grounded him. (In my junior year of college, whenever I seemed particularly depressed, Lou, my advisor, would always say the same thing: forget the assignment for next week— just go home and read Stegner.)

"You believed in all the beauties and strengths and human associations of place," Stegner wrote, of his mother; "my father believed only in movement."[38] I feel as though I must have grown up with the same opposing influences. When I lived in California, I used to wander through Stegner's old neighborhood in the foothills of the Santa Cruz Mountains, wondering whether he had been happy to settle down, happy to teach at Stanford. Now, I try to imagine dying in Ithaca, but my dreams often take me back to California, Minnesota, Washington, New England; I strain to hear the voices of my parents and grandparents; I yearn for guidance. Some of my environmentalist colleagues, understandably, grow impatient with my equivocation. The whole point, to many of them, is to proclaim an attachment to place, to put down roots, to defend a patch of ground, to demonstrate how modern families can live sustainably.[39] I know what they mean; I realize that my openness to experience, my faith in uncertainty, can be a weakness. I have at least tried to adopt Ithaca, tried to find new ancestors whose paths I can follow through the local landscape.

I also realize how dangerous it is to deny that we need a global approach to environmental challenges. My work tends to focus on Americans, and on what I think of as our common past, but some of my provincial retrospection was initially inspired by *Our Common Future*, the famous 1987 report of the United Nations World Commission on Environment and Development, which first popularized the concept of sustainability. I've hoped, all along, that an extended exploration of American history, rooted in a few local landscapes, might yield something particular that this country could contribute to the international struggle to reshape various human-environmental relationships—something more constructive than the wilderness ethos, more humble, more likely to counteract the American style of frenzied consumption, our most toxic export. (Given Americans' disproportionate responsibility for global environmental problems, ranging from carbon emissions to deforestation to overfishing to hazardous waste, shouldn't we spend some time investigating modes of self-restraint?) From my perspective, anyway, to home in on one national culture, to draw at least a few provisional borders, is to enhance one's opportunities to see an ecology of ideas in action, to serve as a witness to connectedness, to trace the ties of kinship that bind not only people and times but also places—that bind the Minneapolis park system to both Washington Irving's Sleepy Hollow and the Sleepy Hollow Cemetery in Concord, Massachusetts. And, in our era of alienation, there can be a thrill to discovering such connections, an exhilaration of echoes and resonance. The practice of history is often chastening, but sometimes bolstering.

I think, in my cousin Stuart's terms, it has made me more resilient. Stuart studied resilient teenagers, people who were somehow able to cope with "vicious cycles of violence, abandonment, or abuse"; natural scientists, in recent years, have started to lobby for the nurturing of resilient ecosystems, landscapes capable of fluid adjustments to long-standing patterns of mistreatment as well as to catastrophic shocks.[40] That seems a promising approach, especially as compared to "restoration ecology," which always raises the historical question: How do you choose a "baseline" worthy of being restored (and how can you expect it to withstand future change)? Another of my hopes is that history might help to shape a more resilient culture—not, of course, a culture that honors the status quo, but one that can make good use of traditions even while acknowledging the need to adapt them to new circumstances. It seems clear that the twentieth-century American environmental tradition, compared to that of most other nations, has overemphasized "amenities," has often treated nature as a luxury item, but I think that the Arcadians of the nineteenth century intended their landscapes to be at the very heart of their culture, markers of mortality, sources of solidarity.[41] Unfortunately, the antebellum landscape ethos was not quite resilient enough to adapt to the catastrophic trauma of the Civil War. But it had built a powerful foundation, and the Arcadian tradition was kept alive after the war by those who were able to dwell with the violence of American history rather than deny it. Arcadian America had its flaws and blindnesses, but it successfully combined an ethic of care and limitation with an embrace of sensual pleasure and renewal, as its adherents strolled along the enchanting borders of cities, towns, fields, and forests, and looked simultaneously back into the past and forward into the future, while always keeping an eye open to the urgency and delights of the present.[42]

There is sustenance, in such a culture, for many different kinds of people, and bits of it have survived and even evolved in auspicious ways. (Figure 53.)

Figure 53. A playground in a cemetery, Newburgh, NY (Andrew Jackson Downing's home town), 2010.

There's a story I've been telling recently about how death and nature started flowing together in my thoughts. It starts on January 4, 2003, when I found a body in the woods.

A man. Maybe in his late fifties or early sixties. Short, dark hair; dark, plain clothing. Next to him was a black wool hat that had fallen from his head. He was lying on his back in the middle of the trail. I called out a few times as I approached from below; I stared. It seemed as if he could have fallen backwards on his way downhill. I noticed that the snow had soaked the undersides of his polyester pant legs. There was no response, no sign of breath. So I turned and ran, as fast as my hiking boots would take me, in search of a phone.

Christine and I were still living in New Haven, but, during the previous summer, we had been forced to move away from the East Rock neighborhood, because our landlord had sold the house we were living in, and the new owners wanted to move in, and we couldn't find anything else to rent nearby. Fortunately, there's another park and promontory across town, where we had resettled: my daily walk now took me to the top of West Rock. There was even more green space here—it was a state park rather than a city park—and it was slightly wilder. I would sometimes see deer, and turkeys, and I often had the place to myself, though in spring I liked to stop and watch the Little League games at the base of the cliffs, and there were occasionally some roped-up rock climbers.

On this particular winter afternoon, as twilight approached, I figured I'd be unlikely to run into anyone. The body was just five minutes from the field, right in the transition zone between the brambly swampland around the West River and the thicker trees leading up to the steepest, rockiest part of the trail. I was quite near the beginning of my hike. As I raced back into the open air, heedless of icy patches, I actually saw two people walking their dogs; neither one had a phone. About a block away from the field, I pounded on a friend's door, rang the bell repeatedly: no answer. I ran another block to the post office: closed. Of course—it was late on a Saturday afternoon. I decided to run the additional three blocks to my apartment. Christine would be there, and we could call 911 together.

On the phone, I explained where the body was—three different times. I kept getting transferred. The last person said she'd send out the information on the radio, and send an officer over to my house. Christine bundled up and joined me on the porch. We waited. I was still strangely alone; this was an experience I could never fully share, I slowly realized, even with the closest confidante I've ever had. I reached out every few seconds just to feel the warmth of her body.

Finally, an officer arrived, and we drove over to the parking lot next to the baseball field. As we pulled up, I reached for the place where there should have been a door handle, and then realized: you can't get out of the back of a police car unless somebody lets you out. The officer took his time. I strode across the gray, crusty snow of the clearing and saw that a group of firefighters and EMTs were headed up the wrong trail, going west instead of north. Had my directions been that bad? I called to them, pointed, led them into the underbrush at a brisk pace; I read an unhurried skepticism in their body language as they followed. The path, predictably, seemed much longer than it should have. I knew every curve, every step, and I knew what I'd seen, but there was a desperation rising in me, a panic that the body would be gone and I'd be exposed as a liar. All these people, converging on one spot of ground, drawn there solely by my personal testimony, would turn on me, demand an explanation. But there he lay.

One of the EMTs approached and said, "I can tell you right now, he's already dead." The other one explained that the dull skin color was a give-away. Still, they were thorough: checked for vital signs, ripped open the man's three flannel shirts, announced that he was clearly gone but that his trunk was still a bit warm. One of them leaned over him, pressed his hands to the man's chest, started pumping. I watched the bare stomach for a few seconds, the waves of skin looking as if they covered only air, empty space. I felt sick, but I couldn't look away. And then they gave up. There was no blood, one of them said, no sign of foul play. It was probably a heart attack. But there was no wallet, no ID. His description, it turned out, didn't match any missing person reports; an autopsy would be ordered.

Christine and I were there for three more hours, shivering in the dark, as various officers came and went, arguing about jurisdiction: was this a case for city police, state police, or park police? A TV crew arrived, and there were a couple of detectives, with huge flashlights. Eventually, an officer from the Department of Environmental Protection—they have their own police force—took my statement, and we finally got to go home.

On the news at eleven, it was reported that a jogger found a man lying on a trail in West Rock Park at 6 P.M. This raised the question: Who would go for a run in a park on snow and ice about an hour and a half after sunset? (I found him at 3:40; also, I hadn't been a jogger since my freshman year of college.) The man, it seems, was taken to Yale–New Haven Hospital and pronounced dead.

The next morning, a page-two story in the *New Haven Register* explained that the man had been in his mid-forties and that he had been found (by the jogger) with vital signs, but was later pronounced dead on arrival—at the Hospital of Saint Raphael.[43] (So how can I possibly trust all the newspapers that I use for my historical research?)

I had told the police officer who took my statement that I wanted to be contacted if they ever found out who the man was. No one ever called.

For the next few days, the whole episode felt acutely traumatic. I kept waking up at four in the morning and not being able to get back to sleep. I did continue with my West Rock hikes, every day, but instead of taking my usual loop trail I headed west and went up the south slope and then turned around and retraced my steps, avoiding the path to the north altogether, so that I didn't have to relive the moment of discovery.

It seemed a grim, tragic death, at first: he was alone, unknown, cold, removed from his family and friends. After a few weeks, though, I started hiking the loop again, and I found myself reconsidering. Sudden, unexpected deaths are perhaps the most merciful. He had been well enough dressed for the winter weather. Maybe he was calm when he passed away, happy to have taken some time for himself on a Saturday afternoon, to have found a peaceful, picturesque trail in the midst of a city, to get a little exercise, to be out in public, to be among tall, old trees. Maybe he just slipped on the snow and slipped into death, nestled by the earth; maybe he was ready to be absorbed back into the landscape; maybe this was a good way to go.[44] I started to feel a vague kinship with him. I wrote about him, determined to act as a witness. I realized that I would remember this man forever, that we would always be linked, that he was both an utter stranger and my intimate companion. I realized that the place where he died would become a pilgrimage site for me, like a family grave, a patch of woods and dirt that, no matter where I was living, I would always want to revisit.

And then—this is what I've been telling people, anyway—I realized that I needed to understand the pull of such places—that I needed to write this book.

But now, as I approach some kind of ending, the possible beginnings have multiplied in my mind.

Surely the most important spur was walking home from work one day through the Ithaca City Cemetery, along the winding terraces of Mount Repose, past its giant spruces, its woodchucks and woodpeckers.

Or maybe this story started back in the summer after sixth grade, when I walked all over Newton, discovering green spaces, in the Environmental Science Program.

A part of it started when Ian fell ill, and I faltered in my friendship, and then, in despair, followed my friend's memory to the woods of northern Minnesota.

It started when my grandfather died, and I couldn't contain my sobs in a seminar room.

It started when I came back from Minnesota and studied environmental literature with Larry Buell, and Lou Masur told me to read Whitman, and that led to a term paper on Hamlin Garland, and Jan Thaddeus suggested that I write about death and family and nature.

It started when I moved to San Jose and walked all over the city, unable to find the parks, the pockets of public space, that I had come to expect in urban areas.

It started when my mother was diagnosed with breast cancer.

It started when Stephen told me about his runs in Foothill Park, behind Stanford.

It started when I recognized my debt to Henry David Thoreau, and Margaret Fuller, and Andrew Jackson Downing, and Winslow Homer, and H. W. S. Cleveland, and Robert Coles, and Donald Hall, and Deborah Tall.

It started when I was writing about explorers and far frontiers and extreme environments, and I wondered what was happening back in the cities.

It started when I turned to the philosophy of history, in my first few years as a professor, and I read a "Guide" to historical practice by Allan Megill, and stumbled upon his argument that, "in view of the vast, utterly unmanageable body of primary historiography that has been produced," it may be time to push for a "historiography more in the manner of meditation or commentary, which, in a Montaignean spirit and in the essay form, would comment on the significance of that body for us, now."[45]

It started in the year I turned forty, which was also the year my department granted me tenure and my father was diagnosed with Alzheimer's. "When I first began to write," noted Julian Barnes, "I laid down for myself the rule—as part of the head-clearing, the focusing, the psychological primping and tamping—that I should write as if my parents were dead. This was not because I specifically wanted either to use or abuse them; rather, I didn't want to catch myself thinking of what might possibly offend or please them. (And in this, they were not just themselves, they were also standing for friends [and] colleagues.)"[46]

It started, in earnest, when my cousin Stuart died: there was a deep shift in my mental landscape. I had just finished drafting the Mount Auburn chapter, and then, suddenly, Mount Auburn took on a radically different meaning for me. My first-person asides could no longer be quite so casual, because I had gained a deeper understanding of just how much labor it must have taken for my historical subjects, the Arcadians of the nineteenth century, to deal so constructively with death. In a book purporting to address the cultural denial of environmental limits—which is also the denial of mortality—I would have to be more forthcoming, more open to the full range of human emotion, more committed to the painful process of confronting my own denial.

As it turned out, once I got back into the story, it seemed to start writing itself: past and present merged, as I pondered my parents' persistence after Benjamin's death, and the persistence of American Arcadians after the Civil War. And then I found myself reluctant to give the story up, unwilling to face the end—until a few weeks ago, when Christine and I finally planted a pear tree next to our house.

We water it constantly. It took us a few years to commit to it; it took me a few minutes to fall in love with it. It seems small, frail, wispy, and I can't help but wonder how it's going to weather the next couple of decades of climatic change. But it's young; it will get sturdier, as its roots inch out into the soil. I sit in the yard on late summer afternoons and watch the sunlight filtering through its foliage: that luminescent green is my favorite color in the world. The branches are rough, knobby, slightly irregular, unpredictable, picturesque. My kids run their fingers along the bark, hug the skinny trunk, stare upward, expectantly. I imagine the smell of the white blossoms that, I hope, will arrive in the spring. One day, perhaps, it will bear fruit. I've read some nineteenth-century horticultural manuals; I wonder if I've learned enough to be a husbandman. It's the most common commercial variety, Bartlett, but I don't think these pears will taste like the Bartletts we buy at the store. According to Andrew Jackson Downing, writing before fruits were commodified and regularly transported thousands of miles from orchard to market, "this noble pear is, justly, one of the most popular of all the summer varieties. . . . It is an English variety, originated about 1770, in Berkshire. . . . When first introduced to this country its name was lost, and having been cultivated and disseminated by Enoch Bartlett, Esq., of Dorchester, near Boston, it became so universally known as the *Bartlett* pear that it is impossible to dispossess it now. . . . Flesh white, and exceedingly fine-grained and buttery; it is full of juice, sweet, with a highly perfumed, vinous flavour."[47] (Figure 54.)

Figure 54. *Bartlett*, 1850, lithograph.

Well—permit me to dream. "In physical perfectness of form and texture and color," wrote Liberty Hyde Bailey, "there is nothing in all the world that exceeds a well-grown fruit. Let it lie in the palm of your hand. Close your fingers slowly about it. Feel its firm or soft and modeled surface. Put it against your cheek, and inhale its fragrance." I imagine cradling the tree's first pear. It is "not only the product of your labor, but it holds the essence of the year and it is in itself a thing of exquisite beauty. There is no other rondure and no other fragrance like this."[48] I know: I'm romanticizing. Most of the fruit, if there is any, will probably be eaten by birds or squirrels or even deer. But that first pear is vivid in my mind. I think of a French dessert that my father introduced me to: *poire belle Hélène*. Ever since, I have craved the combination of pears and chocolate. I think of the time my father took us to France, when I was eight. We went out to eat and were served a salad composed solely of fresh tomato slices, sprinkled with olive oil, and I said to him: this is the first time I have tasted a tomato. I think of the pear-shaped fruit ripener he has kept in the kitchen since I was a boy. I think of him appreciating every apple, every plum, every grape, and suddenly I know that, one day, I will bring round, ripe fruits to place on his grave. This tree is a tribute to his cultivation. And a memorial to Stuart. And a contribution to the neighborhood's ecology and public culture, since it will both feed and be fertilized by our local pollinators, and since its blossoms will be visible to passersby. And perhaps, eventually, it will be a gift to whoever comes after us in this house. Meanwhile, for all my appreciation of slowness, I hope that this tree will start producing pears right away, in just a year or two—in time for us to share them with my parents.

# ACKNOWLEDGMENTS

From the start, I have thought of this book project as being dedicated to Christine Evans, who graciously enfolded it into the life we have been building together, even when that entailed significant sacrifices on her part. She is more skilled than I at the art of acknowledgment, in all senses. But I at least want to try to express my daily sense of gratitude for who she is and all she does. Most of what I know about pausing, and resisting despair, and settling down, I have learned from her. Without question, the best thing about my life is that I am living it in her close company.

My next book will be for our children, Sam, Abe, and Oscar. Meanwhile, not much could be better than seeing the excitement on their faces as they follow mouse tracks in the snow, or pick mulberries in the cemetery, or catch glimpses of woodpeckers. I also learned a lot about rhythm and sound by reading books out loud to them, written by such linguistic masters as Dr. Seuss, William Steig, Robert Mc-Closkey, Margaret Wise Brown, Sandra Boynton, and Lauren Child.

My last book was for my parents, Murray and Miriam Sachs, and I feel blessed to have enjoyed their continuing support through the writing of this one. Old age closes certain doors, yet also—I have been overjoyed to discover—provides unexpected opportunities for empathy, closeness, connection.

My sister Debbie Sachs Gabor has continued to be a source of many different kinds of support. And I am honored that she would trust me to write about our family and its history in so public a way. My departed grandparents, Sheldon and Amy Blank, are at the heart of this book; I think about them every day—when I pass Grandaddy's canoe paddle in the dining room, when I read poems, when I stop to listen to the birds. Grandma's two-volume Family Chronicle was another key source of inspiration. And thanks, also, to my cousins.

I could not have attempted this project, or even imagined it, without the help and caring of certain teachers. John Demos was the professor whom my cousin Stuart recommended to me when I went to graduate school, and Stuart could not have been more right about how John and I would get along. John's solid, sensitive support has been invaluable to me, and I feel extraordinarily lucky to be collaborating with him on the series in which this book is being published. A mutual friend, Robert Johnston, remains a model of integrity, passion, and thoughtfulness. Robert's incredibly detailed comments and hard questions, scribbled in the margins of my manuscript, were absolutely essential to my revisions; his relentless and generous alertness makes him an ideal reader. I'm fortunate to be able to depend on him. And Lou Masur has been there for me, like a trusted bench coach, for more than twenty years now: "Do your work and I shall know you." It was Lou who first helped me to see the literary possibilities of history, and the life-embracing potential of pondering death. He also keeps me laughing, in part by reminding me that denial can be really fun.

My closest writing colleague over the last few years has been Amy Reading, whose last name is pronounced exactly the way it should be. I am continually amazed at the fullness of her engagement with texts, at the generosity and enthusiasm with which she commits herself as a critic, at the acuity of her comments.

About five years ago, Amy and I started a writing group together, and that quickly became one of my main Ithaca anchors. I've learned a huge amount from Geno Tournour's memoirs, Jennifer Wilder's fiction, and Rachel Dickinson's science and travel writing. Geno, Jennifer, and Rachel have all become great friends, and I'm thankful for their support as well as their always just criticism. Alas, they know exactly how prolix I can be. Thanks, also, to former members Lizabeth Cain, Michael Sharp, and A. K. Summers.

At Cornell, I have been exceedingly lucky to work with a number of graduate students who have become both friends and critics, especially in the friendly confines of the working group known as HAW! (or Historians Are Writers!—the exclamation point is part of the name, as in Earth First!) I will always be grateful to Daegan Miller for many things, but especially for founding HAW! And I expect to be trading manuscripts with him for the next forty years or so. Thanks also to Laura Martin and Amy Kohout for establishing the Nature Reading Discussion Community (NRDC), which bolstered my sense of intellectual community in important ways; both Laura and Amy embody creativity and care. Heather Furnas's sensitivity and consideration saved me from a couple of serious missteps. Josi Ward continually expanded my understanding of landscape. And Sarah Ensor blew me away with her quiet but cogent readings of various kinds of relationships. Daegan, Laura, Amy, Heather, Josi, and Sarah all improved not only my arguments but also my phrasing, pacing, and tone. Every day, they make me grateful that I have this job.

Nobody believes you when you say that you learned more from a given student than she learned from you, but I will stand by that assertion in the case of Rebecca Macmillan. In her creative and nuanced essays and our long discussions about gender categories, modernity, trauma, and everything else, she always pushed my thinking in brand-new directions. And her kindness and thoughtfulness remain an inspiration. Living in Ithaca for a while after she graduated, she wound up doing some research for this book and becoming my kids' favorite babysitter. She's also a phenomenal reader, and her impeccable ear for language has made a huge difference in my prose.

One last reader: it was my good fortune a couple of years ago to discover that Jonathan Holloway was engaged in a similar experiment with history and memoir, and his sympathetic but rigorous suggestions were an unexpected boon, as was the deepening of our friendship.

I'm also grateful to the many people and institutions who supported my research, long before I was able to start writing. Both Conrad Wright and Paul Erickson provided encouragement and resources at a very early stage, through their respective organizations, the Massachusetts Historical Society and the American Antiquarian Society. Meg Winslow welcomed me at the Mount Auburn archives. The Cornell History Department gave me a research account and also granted me tenure. Cornell's Society for the Humanities—thanks especially to Brett de Bary and Tim Murray—allowed me to spend a year immersed in rich interdisciplinary conversations (especially with Monique Allewaert, Sam Baker, Verena Conley, Jenny Gaynor, and Christine Marran) and gave me an extraordinary opportunity to push myself as a teacher.

It was also a pleasure to do archival work at the Library of Congress (especially the Manuscripts Division), the New York Public Library, the Huntington Library, the Special Collections at the University of Southern California, Cornell's Kroch Library, and the Minnesota Historical Society. Sincere thanks to the many archivists and other staff members who helped me all along the way, and also to the folks I corresponded with at the Mead Art Museum, the New Britain Museum of American Art, the Joslyn Art Museum, the New-York Historical Society, the Crystal Bridges Museum of American Art, the Museum of Fine Arts (Boston), Art Resource, A. J. Kollar Fine Paintings, the Denver Art Museum, the Art Institute of Chicago, and the National Gallery of Art.

Countless colleagues at Cornell—faculty, staff, and students—offered friendship, advice, knowledge, logistical assistance, book recommendations, letters of support, and much more. I'm especially indebted to Anurag Agrawal, Lauren Chambliss, Abby Cohn, Stephanie Contino, Duane Corpis, Ray Craib, Chris Davis, Harry DiFrancesco, Frank DiSalvo, Barb Donnell, Maggie Edwards, Paula Euvrard, Sarah Fitzpatrick, Jeremy Foster, Jessica George, Melissa Gniadek, Harry Greene, Mike Gründler, Andrea Hammer, Drew Harvell, TJ Hinrichs, Mike Hoffman, Gail Holst-Warhaft, Carol Kammen, Michael Kammen, Virginia Kennedy, Cliff Kraft, Katie Kristof, Peter Lavelle, Dan Magaziner, Lena Masur, Larry Moore, Paul Nadasdy, Sara Pritchard, Katie Proctor, Shirley Samuels, Elizabeth Sanders, Paul Sawyer, Helene Schember, Phoebe Sengers, Greg Tremblay, Claudia Verhoeven, Ben Wang, Zellman Warhaft, and Dave Wolfe. Special thanks to Eric Cheyfitz for spurring me to think harder about kinship, to Steve Collicelli for early research assistance, and to Jake Seligman for the gentle encouragement to be more experimental in my writing.

Several colleagues and organizations invited me to offer up pieces of this book while they were still in development, and I'm grateful not only for the invitations but for all the thoughtful and challenging responses I got to my work. Thanks especially to Chandra Manning and Adam Rothman of the Georgetown 19th-Century U.S. History Workshop; Henry Cowles of the Princeton Modern America Workshop; the incomparable Steve Berry and Tom Okie at the University of Georgia; and Johnny Faragher and Christine DeLucia at Yale University. And I'm also grateful to all the people who attended my talks and participated in the discussions. Audience members were also a great help to me at sessions of the World Congress on Environmental History and the annual meetings of the American Society for Environmental History, the American Studies Association, and the Nineteenth-Century Studies Association.

Many other scholars and friends offered both direct and indirect assistance with this project. I never would have been able to track down a couple of the paintings that appear in this book without the amazing Betsy Broun. And thanks to Amy Kohout for mentioning that I really had to check out the Hall of Wonders exhibit at the Smithsonian American Art Museum when I was in Washington: that visit led me to Betsy. (Additional thanks to the private collectors who allowed me to use their paintings but who wished to remain anonymous.) Larry Buell got me started in the environmental humanities, more than twenty years ago, and just a few days ago he gave me a crucial Thoreau reference. Johnny Faragher, my dissertation director, continues to be a wonderful intellectual influence: he followed his first book, about western migrants, with a book about people who settled down—"stickers," he called them, in his marvelous *Sugar Creek*—and I have followed a very similar trajectory in writing first about explorers of frontiers and then about dwellers in middle landscapes. Sandy Zipp always kept his wit about him, and made sure I was up to scratch in urban history. I'm also grateful to editor Mark Cioc and two anonymous reviewers for the journal *Environmental History*, which published some of my early work on Mount Auburn. Martha Hodes suggested that I pick up Daniel Mendelsohn's book *The Lost*, and Ann Fabian told me to find Robert Harrison's *The Dominion of the Dead*; both of those reading experiences had a major impact on my writing and thinking.

Other key colleagues include Ben Cohen, Jim Goodman, Karl Jacoby, Peter Mancall, Kathy Morse, Megan Nelson, Kristen Neuschel, Michael Robinson, Paul Sabin, Doug Sackman, Marni Sandweiss, Sam Truett, Laura Walls, and Rob Young. Their support has meant a great deal to me.

And I've long depended on such friends as Adam Arenson, Lila Corwin Berman, Lou Greenberg, Ari Handel, Brian Herrera, Tom Iurino, Kip Kosek, Mark Krasovic, Adriane Lentz-Smith, Roger Levine, Ben Liebman, Mary Lui, Christian McMillen, Bob Morrissey, Barry Muchnick, Devah Pager, Vicki Shepard, Catherine Whalen, Roxanne Willis, and many others. Midori Evans first mentioned the Brook Farm site to me, and thus utterly transformed this project. Stephanie Satz Alden suggested that I might want to take a look at the little hill adjacent to the new Guthrie Theater, in downtown Minneapolis, on the shore of the Mississippi—and, indeed, Gold Medal Park was a revelation.

In Ithaca, I remain grateful to the Beer and History gang: Derek Chang, Jeff Cowie, Michael Smith, Michael Trotti, and Rob Vanderlan. All five of them read the first 100 to 150 pages of this book and provided excellent criticisms; they also helped me exercise my wrist at the Chapter House and the Bowl-O-Drome. (And, speaking of beer: if you ever get the chance, try an Arcadia Ale.) Thanks also to Brian Hall, Mary Lauppe, Eric Miller, Bob Proehl, Sarah Rubenstein-Gillis, Gary Weissbrot, and John Young.

Besides the authors discussed explicitly in these pages, a number of others provided directly relevant inspiration over the last few years. Greg Dening (*Beach Crossings*), Amitav Ghosh (*In an Antique Land*), Saadiya Hartman (*Lose Your Mother*), and Bill McFeely (*Sapelo's People*) all helped me understand the possibilities of combining scholarship with memoir. I often reread works by Lewis Hyde, W. G. Sebald, and Yi-Fu Tuan. Rebecca Solnit continues to dazzle with her prose: we often seem to be thinking along parallel tracks, but she's always several steps ahead of me. And though I've never met Robert Pogue Harrison, his ideas have been absolutely essential to my outlook: together with *The Dominion of the Dead*, his books *Forests* and *Gardens* have combined to form something like a Holy Trilogy for me.

Zoe Pagnamenta has continued to be an effective and thoughtful agent. Her comments on Chapter 2, and especially her encouragement to do more with the first person, were exactly what I needed. Thanks also to Gavin Lewis for some extremely sensitive copyediting. At Yale University Press, Chris Rogers has been staunchly supportive and understanding; this book may not have made it without him, and I will always be grateful for his help. Christina Tucker has been a paragon of friendly competence, as has Margaret Otzel. And many thanks, as well, to the press's two anonymous reviewers, who challenged me in a number of useful and constructive ways.

You can't be an academic for long without recognizing your dependence on the generosity of people whose identities you may never know. Many anonymous students have written letters of support on my behalf; many anonymous professors have done the same; and many anonymous committees have read my work with care and open minds. They have made a huge difference in my life, and I'm grateful. So, one last acknowledgment: to all those thinkers out there committed to cultivating a sense of commonality.

Aaron Sachs
February 2012
Ithaca, NY
Five minutes from the cemetery

# NOTES

## PROLOGUE. WATERFALLS AND CEMETERIES

1. See D. Morris Kurtz, *Ithaca and Its Resources* (Ithaca: Journal Association Book and Job Printing, 1883), 7–8 and 53–55; Spence Spencer, *The Scenery of Ithaca and the Head Waters of the Cayuga Lake* (Ithaca: S. Spencer, 1866); and Solomon Southwick, *Views of Ithaca and Its Environs* (Ithaca: D. D. and A. Spencer, 1835).

2. A friend of mine, Rachel Dickinson, noticed these sculptures in other locations around town and eventually tracked down the artist; see her article (posted in August 2010), at http://www.yourlifeisatrip.com/home/balancing-rocks.html.

3. Though the numbers are in dispute, Cornell and Ithaca seem to have higher than average suicide rates—largely, according to local psychiatrists, because of "the availability of lethal means." As one of my students pointed out to me, if you type "gorge" into the search engine on the website of the *Cornell Daily Sun*, the results are grim.

4. The classic study tracking this environmental tradition is Roderick Frazier Nash, *Wilderness and the American Mind*, now in its 4th edition (New Haven: Yale University Press, 2001). My own work is especially influenced by the group of scholars who in the last fifteen years have increasingly questioned Nash and the legacy his book celebrates. The keynote of this critique was sounded by William Cronon in his crucial essay, "The Trouble with Wilderness; or, Getting Back to the Wrong Nature," in Cronon, ed., *Uncommon Ground: Rethinking the Human Place in Nature* (New York: Norton, 1996), 69–90. Also see: J. Baird Callicott and Michael P. Nelson, eds., *The Great New Wilderness Debate* (Athens: University of Georgia Press, 1998); Nelson, ed., *The Wilderness Debate Rages On: Continuing the Great New Wilderness Debate* (Athens: University of Georgia Press, 2008); and Michael Lewis, ed., *American Wilderness: A New History* (New York: Oxford University Press, 2007).

5. For an extended exploration of this perspective, see Jennifer Price, *Flight Maps: Adventures with Nature in Modern America* (New York: Basic Books, 1999).

6. These landscapes have traditionally been studied much more by cultural geographers than by historians. Just in the past decade, though, environmental historians have begun some productive digging in this soil: see Richard White, "From Wilderness to Hybrid Landscapes: The Cultural Turn in Environmental History," *The Historian* 66 (September 2004), 557–64. On hybridity and boundary-drawing, see Bruno Latour, *We Have Never Been Modern*, trans. Catherine Porter (Cambridge, MA: Harvard University Press, 1993), esp. 10–43.

7. See Aaron Sachs, "American Arcadia: Mount Auburn Cemetery and the Nineteenth-Century Landscape Tradition," *Environmental History* 15 (April 2010), 206–35.

8. J. R. McNeill has to be at least partially correct when he argues, in a not-unrepresentative formulation, that "what people thought specifically about the environment, nature, life, and such mattered only very marginally before 1970." Yet, even if we grant the dominance of other "big ideas"—most notably, the pursuit of perpetual economic growth—it seems potentially misleading to brush aside thoughtful protests against environmental devastation. Indeed, as Stuart Hall has suggested, the "social forces which lose out in any particular historical period do not thereby disappear from the terrain of struggle"—quoted in Michael Denning, *The Cultural Front: The Laboring of American Culture in the Twentieth Century* (New York: Verso, 1997), 464. And see J. R. McNeill, *Something New under the Sun: An Environmental History of the Twentieth-Century World* (New York: Norton, 2000), 326 (and 326–56 for the extended argument). For the deep history of our addiction to growth, see Steven Stoll, *The Great Delusion: A Mad Inventor, Death in the Tropics, and the Utopian Origins of Economic Growth* (New York: Hill and Wang, 2008).

9. For the cider-soaked horticulturists and their creative schemes, see the annual proceedings of the Massachusetts Horticultural Society throughout the early 1830s, especially: Thaddeus William Harris, M.D., *Discourse Delivered before the Massachusetts Horticultural Society, on the Celebration of its Fourth Anniversary, Oct 3, 1832* (Cambridge, MA: E. W. Metcalf and Co., 1832), 56–82.

Despite the brilliance and influence of William Cronon's aforementioned essay, "The Trouble with Wilderness" (above, note 4), it seems driven by a teleological assumption that every force in nineteenth-century American culture was working toward enshrining the frontier mentality and the aesthetics of the Romantic sublime in what became the wilderness mythos. For studies that are more sensitive to the American landscape tradition, see Anne Whitson Spirn, "Constructing Nature: The Legacy of Frederick Law Olmsted," and Kenneth R. Olwig, "Reinventing Common Nature: Yosemite and Mount Rushmore—A Meandering Tale of a Double Nature," in Cronon, *Uncommon Ground*, 91–113 and 379–408; Edward Halsey Foster, *The Civilized Wilderness: Backgrounds to American Romantic Literature, 1817–1860* (New York: Free Press, 1975); Barbara Novak, *Nature and Culture: American Landscape Painting, 1825–1875* (New York: Oxford University Press, 1980); John R. Stilgoe, *Common Landscape of America, 1580 to 1845* (New Haven: Yale University Press, 1982); David Schuyler, *The New Urban Landscape: The Redefinition of City Form in Nineteenth-Century America* (Baltimore: Johns Hopkins University Press, 1986); James L. Machor, *Pastoral Cities: Urban Ideals and the Symbolic Landscape of America* (Madison: University of Wisconsin Press, 1987); Stilgoe, *Borderland: Origins of the American Suburb,*

1820–1939 (New Haven: Yale University Press, 1988); Gunther Barth, *Fleeting Moments: Nature and Culture in American History* (New York: Oxford University Press, 1990); Kent C. Ryden, *Landscape with Figures: Nature and Culture in New England* (Iowa City: University of Iowa Press, 2001); and Andrew McMurry, *Environmental Renaissance: Emerson, Thoreau, and the Systems of Nature* (Athens: University of Georgia Press, 2003). Schuyler is also one of the editors of a book series put out by Johns Hopkins University Press called Creating the North American Landscape; many of the volumes in this series have helped me frame my own work.

10. The key theorist of the picturesque was the eighteenth-century English writer William Gilpin, but he was read in many different ways, and the three main aesthetic categories in play during the nineteenth century—the picturesque, the sublime, and the beautiful—all overlapped with each other to some extent. In American art and culture, though sublimity came to be dominant by the end of the century, the picturesque was more important to the early development of Romanticism and could even be said to have contained the sublime within itself for a number of decades. See the extended discussions in Foster, *The Civilized Wilderness*, esp. 3–22; Marjorie Hope Nicolson, *Mountain Gloom and Mountain Glory: The Development of the Aesthetics of the Infinite* (1959; Seattle: University of Washington Press, 1997), 1–33; Andrew Wilton and Tim Barringer, *American Sublime: Landscape Painting in the United States, 1820–1880* (London: Tate Publishing, 2002); and Blanche M. G. Linden, *Silent City on a Hill: Picturesque Landscapes of Memory and Boston's Mount Auburn Cemetery* (Amherst: University of Massachusetts Press, 2007). Though American Romantics sometimes repudiated their British counterparts for a lack of wildness, they simultaneously developed imaginative ways of inhabiting nature that owed much to Coleridge and Wordsworth. See, for instance, Joel Pace and Matthew Scott, eds., *Wordsworth in American Literary Culture* (Houndmills: Palgrave Macmillan, 2005); James C. McKusick, *Green Writing: Romanticism and Ecology* (New York: St. Martin's Press, 2000); Richard Gravil, *Romantic Dialogues: Anglo-American Continuities, 1776–1862* (New York: St. Martin's Press, 2000); Eric Wilson, *Romantic Turbulence: Chaos, Ecology, and American Space* (Houndmills: Macmillan, 2000); and Michael T. Gilmore, *American Romanticism and the Marketplace* (Chicago: University of Chicago Press, 1985).

11. This basic trajectory has become canonical in part because it was posited so vigorously (and elegantly) in Nash, *Wilderness and the American Mind*, as well as in an even earlier classic, Hans Huth, *Nature and the American: Three Centuries of Changing Attitudes* (1957; Lincoln: University of Nebraska Press, 1990). Even David Nye, who is generally much more careful to point out that ideologies of progress and restraint often evolved simultaneously and interdependently, posits a chronological split "between the confident story of expansion in the first half of the nineteenth century and the widespread acceptance of counternarratives thereafter." See David E. Nye, *America as Second Creation: Technology and Narratives of New Beginnings* (Cambridge, MA: MIT Press, 2003), 148; also 20, 117, and 289.

12. On the postbellum period, see John Brinkerhoff Jackson, *American Space: The Centennial Years, 1865–1876* (New York: Norton, 1972). On the relentless progress of industrialism, still too often seen as inevitable and virtually unopposed, see: John F. Kasson, *Civilizing the Machine: Technology and Republican Values in America, 1776–1900* (1976; New York: Hill &

Wang, 1999); Walter Licht, *Industrializing America: The Nineteenth Century* (Baltimore: Johns Hopkins University Press, 1995); and David R. Meyer, *The Roots of American Industrialization* (Baltimore: Johns Hopkins University Press, 2003).

13. See, for instance, Robert V. Wells, *Facing the "King of Terrors": Death and Society in an American Community, 1750–1990* (New York: Cambridge University Press, 2000), 35–147, and Gary Laderman, *The Sacred Remains: American Attitudes Toward Death, 1799–1883* (New Haven: Yale University Press, 1996).

14. For a relevant meditation on what defines Arcadians (based on their contrast to Utopians, as first suggested by W. H. Auden), see Rebecca Solnit, *Savage Dreams: A Journey into the Landscape Wars of the American West* (1994; Berkeley: University of California Press, 1999), 112–44. The original Auden essay is "Dingley Dell and the Fleet," in Auden, *The Dyer's Hand and Other Essays* (New York: Random House, 1962), 407–428; see esp. 409–15, where Auden explains that Arcadia is in some ways parallel to Eden, while Utopia is closer to the idea of a New Jerusalem.

15. I'm most interested in the scholars who have at least taken these Arcadians seriously as social critics—perhaps Leo Marx most iconically, in his classic book *The Machine in the Garden: Technology and the Pastoral Ideal in America* (New York: Oxford, 1964). Marx sees people like Thoreau as having developed a "complex pastoral" mode that expressed a displeasure with the way American society was evolving. But ultimately he posits this mode as so highbrow as to be almost irrelevant, insisting that "there was not (nor would there be) any effective opposition to industrialization. This is not to deny that there were impulses to resist. But on the whole they were sporadic, ineffectual impulses; they provoked a number of vivid, symbolic gestures (chiefly of a nostalgic cast), but they did not produce an alternative theory of society capable of enlisting effective political support" (180–81). From Marx's perspective, the only "dissidents" from this time period were members of "small, ineffectual groups—socialist, transcendentalist, literary, religious—far from the centers of influence and power." Marx admits that these people filed their protest quite often but also argues (without any real evidence) that "it appears in print with a frequency out of all proportion to its apparent popularity with the public" (219). Henry Nash Smith, Marx's mentor, makes a similar claim in his study of attitudes about the American West and its conquest: "Such a mood of refined hostility to progress affected a surprising number of [Francis] Parkman's contemporaries. Nevertheless, it could hardly strike very deep in a society committed to an expansive manifest destiny. A romantic love of the vanishing Wild West could be no more than a self-indulgent affectation beside the triumphant official cult of progress, which meant the conquest of the wilderness by farms and towns and cities." See Smith, *Virgin Land: The American West as Symbol and Myth* (1950; Cambridge, MA: Harvard University Press, 1978), 52.

In more recent years Marx has altered his position: in a 1997 essay, for instance, he went so far as to say that the antebellum period saw "the rise of an adversary culture that would reject the dominant faith in the advance of the mechanic arts as a self-justifying social goal. Indeed, a direct line of influence is traceable from the intellectual dissidents of the 1840s to the widespread 1960s rebellion against established institutions"; see his "Technology: The Emergence of a Hazardous Concept," *Social Research* 64 (Fall 1997), 965–88, quotation on 972.

In general, my attitude toward the relevant American skeptics is probably most in line with David Schuyler's, David Nye's, Christopher Lasch's, and Lee Clark Mitchell's; all of these scholars see a deep ambivalence as one of the defining elements of nineteenth-century culture. I believe many Arcadians did have legitimate social visions and that their protests and alternatives resonated with a significant sector of the population. Schuyler said it well when he noted, in reference to the founders of the urban parks movement, that, "tempting though it has proven to some historians, to attack these reformers and to dismiss parks as examples of social control ignores the more positive aspects of their creators' motivations" (6); and also see Nye, *America as Second Creation*; Christopher Lasch, *The True and Only Heaven: Progress and Its Critics* (New York: Norton, 1991); and Lee Clark Mitchell, *Witnesses to a Vanishing America: The Nineteenth-Century Response* (Princeton: Princeton University Press, 1981).

16. A. J. Downing, "The New-York Park" (August 1851), in *Rural Essays*, ed. George William Curtis (1853; New York: Geo. A. Leavitt, 1869), 152; this volume is a collection of the writings Downing published in the *Horticulturist*, a magazine he edited from its inception in 1846 until his death in 1852.

17. The insight embodied by Poussin's painting—that a sense of darkness is crucial to our relationship to nature—might actually be considered one of the defining features of the pastoral mode, dating back to the melancholy cast of the original Greek Arcadia, as conceived by writers like Theocritus and Virgil—which, in turn, suggests some overlaps between my argument and the endorsement of "dark ecology" by Timothy Morton in his *Ecology Without Nature: Rethinking Environmental Aesthetics* (Cambridge, MA: Harvard University Press, 2007), 185–97; and see especially Paul Alpers, *What Is Pastoral?* (Chicago: University of Chicago Press, 1996).

18. Back in 1873, the landscape architect H. W. S. Cleveland suggested that "No impression upon the youthful mind exerts a more powerful and lasting influence than that which is made by daily familiar intercourse with scenes of simple natural beauty, and the man whose boyhood was passed amid such scenes will find that he recurs to them in after life with a keener sense of their loveliness, as he contrasts them with the magnificence and ostentatious display which mark a more artificial condition of life." See Cleveland, *Landscape Architecture, as Applied to the Wants of the West; with an Essay on Forest Planting on the Great Plains* (Chicago: Jansen, McClurg & Co., 1873), 88. More recently, Robert Pogue Harrison has made a compelling case that the human response to gardens is almost always positive in part because of "our biophilia, as well as what I would call our chlorophilia." See *Gardens: An Essay on the Human Condition* (Chicago: University of Chicago Press, 2008), 43. And also see: Yi-Fu Tuan, *Topophilia: A Study of Environmental Perception, Attitude, and Values* (1974; New York: Columbia University Press, 1990); Henri Lefebvre, *The Production of Space*, trans. Donald Nicholson-Smith (Oxford: Blackwell, 1991); S. R. Kellert and E. O. Wilson, eds., *The Biophilia Hypothesis* (Washington, DC: Island Press, 1993); Richard Louv, *Last Child in the Woods: Saving Our Children from Nature-Deficit Disorder* (Chapel Hill: Algonquin Books, 2006), esp. 39–111; and Esther M. Sternberg, *Healing Spaces: The Science of Place and Well-Being* (Cambridge, MA: Harvard University Press, 2009).

19. In emphasizing visions, ideas, and belief systems, I am differing with a number of scholars who have insisted both that environmental history is best suited to a materialist approach and that materialist histories of environmental change over time are most relevant to current environmental problems. Without in any way wanting to discount their perspective, I hope to further the argument that environmental perception and thought might matter as much as material transformations. See especially J. R. McNeill, "Observations on the Nature and Culture of Environmental History," *History and Theory* 42 (December 2003), 5–43, esp. 7–8 and 17, and Ellen Stroud, "Does Nature Always Matter? Following Dirt Through History," ibid., 75–81. For perspectives more in line with my own, and, indeed, for work that moves toward blurring the line between the discursive and the material, see Verena Andermatt Conley, *Ecopolitics: The Environment in Poststructuralist Thought* (London: Routledge, 1997); Gregory Bateson, *Steps Toward an Ecology of Mind* (1972; Chicago: University of Chicago Press, 2000), esp. 486–513; Raymond Williams, *Culture and Society: 1780–1950* (New York: Columbia University Press, 1983); Michel Serres, *The Natural Contract*, trans. Elizabeth MacArthur and William Paulson (Ann Arbor: University of Michigan Press, 1995); Arran E. Gare, *Postmodernism and the Environmental Crisis* (London: Routledge, 1995); Robert J. Brulle, *Agency, Democracy, and Nature: The U.S. Environmental Movement from a Critical Theory Perspective* (Cambridge, MA: MIT Press, 2000); and Bruno Latour, *Politics of Nature: How to Bring the Sciences into Democracy*, trans. Catherine Porter (Cambridge, MA: Harvard University Press, 2004), esp. 9–52. One might also cite any number of cultural geographers and landscape theorists, such as Denis Cosgrove, Yi-Fu Tuan, J. B. Jackson, John Stilgoe, Jay Appleton, Arnold Berleant, and Rob Shields. And note Lawrence Buell's assertion that the "environmental crisis is not merely one of economic resources, public health, and political gridlock," but also one of "attitudes, feelings, images, narratives," in *Writing for an Endangered World: Literature, Culture, and Environment in the U.S. and Beyond* (Cambridge, MA: Harvard University Press, 2001), 1.

20. See Michael M'Gonigle and Justine Starke, *Planet U: Sustaining the World, Reinventing the University* (Gabriola Island: New Society Publishers, 2006), 188–95; and Barbara Whitaker, "At Cornell, a Push to End Stalemate over Parking Lot," *New York Times*, July 18, 2005, B7.

21. Section 3 of the 1916 Organic Act quoted in Richard West Sellars, *Preserving Nature in the National Parks: A History* (New Haven: Yale University Press, 1997), 44; also see Stan Jorstad, *America's Best Idea: A Photographic Journey Through Our National Parks* (New York: American Park Network, 2006), as well as the similarly named documentary film by Ken Burns (2009).

22. Daniel B. Botkin, *Discordant Harmonies: A New Ecology for the Twenty-First Century* (New York: Oxford University Press, 1990); M. A. Davis, "Invasion Biology 1958–2005: The Pursuit of Science and Conservation," in M. W. Cadotte, S. M. McMahon, and T. Fukami, eds., *Conceptual Ecology and Invasion Biology: Reciprocal Approaches to Nature* (Dordrecht: Springer, 2006), 35–64.

23. Marcia Lowe, "Shaping Cities," in Lester Brown et al., *State of the World 1992* (New York: Norton, 1992), 131–2.

24. Jane Jacobs, *The Death and Life of Great American Cities* (1961; New York: Modern Library, 1993), 21–2.

25. Ibid., 118, 25, and 31. A helpful corrective, produced by someone working as an urban planner in the 1980s, is Anne Whitson Spirn, *The Granite Garden: Urban Nature and Human
Design* (New York: Basic, 1984).

26. "The New Cemetery," *Ithaca Chronicle*, July 30, 1845, 2. The author of this article suggests
that the "village authorities" have earned "the thanks of all the Living who cherish the
memory of the Departed. The grounds are handsomely laid out, and . . . are daily assuming new beauties. . . . No point in the vicinity of the village presents a more beautiful prospect. At one view we have the waters of the Cayuga, the cultivated fields and woodland
patches far away of the western and the southern hills, the village, spread over the plain
below, and skirting and climbing the elevations around, the gorges of Fall Creek and the
pleasant Cascadilla, while on either hand the hum of the water-fall sends a tranquilizing
influence."

27. See Barbara Ellen Ebert, "The City Cemetery, Ithaca, New York: 1790–1890," (M.A. thesis,
Department of Historic Preservation Planning, Cornell University, 1992), 86–8 and 99.
The cemetery's name was Mount Repose from 1843 to 1871; then for seventeen years it was
called Silvan Hill; and from 1888 onward it has been known as the City Cemetery.
    An article in the *Ithaca Chronicle* from May 4, 1853, 3, attests to "the skillful manage-
ment of J. W. Pickering," thanks to which "our Cemetery looks more like a flower garden,
or a fashionable resort for the living, than the quiet and silent resting place for the dead.
Those of our citizens who like a pleasant walk, and are fond of beautiful scenery, could not
spend an hour more pleasantly than in making a visit to the Cemetery."

28. The popularity of Andrew Jackson Downing's writings on horticulture and landscape architecture is one of the best pieces of evidence for this assertion; see David Schuyler's illuminating study, *Apostle of Taste: Andrew Jackson Downing, 1815–1852* (Baltimore: Johns
Hopkins University Press, 1996).

29. Ebert, "The City Cemetery," 86. An overview of Ithaca's development in the mid-nineteenth
century can be found in Kurtz, *Ithaca and Its Resources*, 54–7. Kurtz also noted (61) that
"The cemetery, covering 16 acres of the hill slope on the north side of the Cascadilla, with
its natural advantages in the variety of its surface, its native growth of trees and commanding views, is an object of admiration to visitors."

30. See David Schuyler, "The Evolution of the Anglo-American Rural Cemetery: Landscape
Architecture as Social and Cultural History," *Journal of Garden History* 4 (July–September
1984), 291–304, esp. 299–302. At the consecration of London's Abney Park Cemetery in
1840, one of the speakers read long quotations from the consecration address delivered nine
years earlier at Mount Auburn.

31. The textbook is Ted Steinberg, *Down to Earth: Nature's Role in American History* (New
York: Oxford, 2002). Some useful analyses of American spatial thinking include: D. W.
Meinig's monumental work, *The Shaping of America: A Geographical Perspective on 500
Years of History*, vols. 2 and 3: *Continental America, 1800–1867* (New Haven: Yale Univer-
sity Press, 1993) and *Transcontinental America, 1850–1915* (New Haven: Yale University
Press, 1998); Schuyler, *The New Urban Landscape*; Thomas Bender, *Toward an Urban Vision:
Ideas and Institutions in Nineteenth Century America* (1975; Baltimore: Johns Hopkins
University Press, 1991); Andro Linklater, *Measuring America: How the United States Was*

*Shaped by the Greatest Land Sale in History* (New York: Plume, 2003); John Brinckerhoff Jackson, *Discovering the Vernacular Landscape* (New Haven: Yale University Press, 1984); and John W. Reps, *The Making of Urban America: A History of City Planning in the United States* (Princeton: Princeton University Press, 1965).

32. There actually seems to have been a Cayuga trail in the eighteenth century that followed Cascadilla Creek upstream, eastward from what is now downtown Ithaca and what was in the mid-eighteenth century an important crossroads, the meeting place of five well-traveled pathways: see W. Glenn Norris, *Old Indian Trails in Tompkins Country* (1944; Ithaca: De-Witt Historical Society of Tompkins County, 1988), vi, 11–12, and 36–9. That junction wound up being the site of the first cabins built by white settlers in the area. On the broader subject of Native American history in the Finger Lakes region and its erasure in the local landscape, and for a powerful meditation on how modern American culture generally obscures awareness of histories and localities, see Deborah Tall, *From Where We Stand: Recovering a Sense of Place* (New York: Knopf, 1993).

33. Part of the project of rethinking humanity's place in the world entails a deep awareness of how we work the land and actually use resources—of course. But I think it's just as important to carve out and consider territories explicitly dedicated to recreation and reflection, where, in our walks and our conversations, we might develop new modes of ecological storytelling, new modes of dwelling, and where we might remember, in Verena Andermatt Conley's words, that the combination of biological and cultural diversity sometimes "produces an aesthetic pleasure that cannot be entirely commodified" (*Ecopolitics*, 44). Indeed, "ecology can and does include the struggle for a (mental or physical) place of seclusion, an *oikos* of thought that is not subject to systemic control by destructive orders or strategic confrontations" (ibid., 7).

    On ecological labor, see Richard White, "'Are You an Environmentalist or Do You Work for a Living?': Work and Nature," in Cronon, *Uncommon Ground*, 171–85; White, *The Organic Machine: The Remaking of the Columbia River* (New York: Hill & Wang, 1995); Gunther Peck, "The Nature of Labor: Fault Lines and Common Ground in Environmental and Labor History," *Environmental History* 11 (April 2006), 212–38; and Chad Montrie, *Making a Living: Work and Environment in the United States* (Chapel Hill: University of North Carolina Press, 2008). On making space for ecological thought, see Conley, *Ecopolitics*, 108–114 and 149–51, and Michel de Certeau, *The Practice of Everyday Life*, trans. Steven Rendall (1980; Berkeley: University of California Press, 1984), 97–130.

34. Walter Benjamin, *The Arcades Project*, trans. Howard Eiland and Kevin McLaughlin (Cambridge, MA: Harvard University Press, 1999), 419 and 416. My favorite section of *Arcades* is "The Flâneur" (416–55). On the pace of life: "In 1839 it was considered elegant to take a tortoise out walking. This gives us an idea of the tempo of flânerie in the arcades" (422). On industrial production: "The idleness of the flâneur is a demonstration against the division of labor" (427); and "the fruits of idleness are more precious than the fruits of labor" (453). On what he calls "the intoxication of empathy felt by the flâneur" (449), he cites Flaubert: "Today, for instance, as man and woman, both lover and mistress, I rode in a forest on an autumn afternoon under the yellow leaves, and I was also the horses, the leaves, the wind, the words my people uttered, even the red sun that almost made them close their love-drowned eyes."

35. My thinking about death, burial, and nature has been profoundly influenced by Robert Pogue Harrison, *The Dominion of the Dead* (Chicago: University of Chicago Press, 2003): "The awareness of death that defines human nature," Harrison writes, "is inseparable from—indeed, it arises from—our awareness that we are not self-authored, that we follow in the footsteps of the dead. . . . Whether we are conscious of it or not we do the will of the ancestors." We build them shrines, acknowledging our debt to them as we reverently lay them in the ground beneath our feet, in the humus that provides the foundation of our cultures: "To be human means above all to bury" (ix and xi).

36. For a useful exploration of the social problems embedded in environments, see Matthew Gandy, *Concrete and Clay: Reworking Nature in New York City* (Cambridge, MA: MIT Press, 2002); and for a helpful case study, also involving New York City but focused more directly on burial, see Ellen Stroud, "Dead Bodies in Harlem: Environmental History and the Geography of Death," in Andrew C. Isenberg, ed., *The Nature of Cities* (Rochester: University of Rochester Press, 2006), 62–76.

## 1. COMMON SHADE

1. Take a moment from your busy life to read Noelle Oxenhandler, "Fall from Grace," *New Yorker*, June 16, 1997, 65–8—a meditation on pausing that is one of the most moving essays I have ever come across. Also see Carl Honoré, *In Praise of Slowness: Challenging the Cult of Speed* (New York: HarperSanFrancisco, 2005), and Paul Virilio, *Speed and Politics*, trans. Marc Polizzotti (1977; Los Angeles: Semiotext(e), 2006). Meanwhile, for a broadly illuminating discussion of human restlessness, exacerbated by modernity, see Robert Pogue Harrison, *Gardens: An Essay on the Human Condition* (Chicago: University of Chicago Press, 2008), esp. 71–82 and 135–71. The phrase "on time" and the very concept of punctuality as a valued trait seem to have arisen in the late nineteenth century, in the context of the standardization of public time (largely driven by the need of railroad companies to regularize schedules and thus avoid collisions); see Stephen Kern, *The Culture of Time and Space, 1880–1918* (Cambridge, MA: Harvard University Press, 1983), 10–35.

2. Wallace Stegner's narrator in the novel *Angle of Repose* (1971; New York: Fawcett Crest, 1989), which is largely about nineteenth-century American history, sees the title phrase as "descriptive of human as well as detrital rest" and suggests that, especially in modern America, a person's angle of repose is rarely reached until the very end of what is typically a "wandering and uneasy life" (19). "Was the quiet I always felt in you really repose?" he asks his grandmother, rhetorically. "I wish I thought so" (20).

3. See especially Mark S. Schantz, *Awaiting the Heavenly Country: The Civil War and America's Culture of Death* (Ithaca: Cornell University Press, 2008), 6–69. Other studies of how Americans dealt with mortality in this period include Drew Gilpin Faust, *This Republic of Suffering: Death and the American Civil War* (New York: Knopf, 2008); Lucy E. Frank, ed., *Representations of Death in Nineteenth-Century U.S. Writing and Culture* (Aldershot: Ashgate, 2007); Robert V. Wells, *Facing the "King of Terrors": Death and Society in an American Community, 1750–1990* (New York: Cambridge University Press, 2000), 35–147; Gary Laderman, *The Sacred Remains: American Attitudes Toward Death, 1799–1883* (New Haven: Yale

University Press, 1996); James J. Farrell, *Inventing the American Way of Death, 1830–1920* (Philadelphia: Temple University Press, 1980); Ann Douglas, *The Feminization of American Culture* (1977; New York: Noonday Press, 1998), 200–26; and Lewis O. Saum, "Death in the Popular Mind of Pre–Civil War America," *American Quarterly* 26 (December 1974), 477–95. For a relevant study of an earlier period, see Erik R. Seeman, *Death in the New World: Cross-Cultural Encounters, 1492–1800* (Philadelphia: University of Pennsylvania Press, 2010).

4. Nineteenth-century Americans benefited from a deep-seated Christian faith in the afterlife; the growth of religious skepticism over the last two hundred years is part of the reason we now have a harder time engaging with mortality. But even those who, in Schantz's words, "believed that a heavenly eternity of transcendent beauty awaited them beyond the grave" (*Awaiting the Heavenly Country*, 2), were also quick to acknowledge the sting of loss when their loved ones passed away. Families were ravaged with grief in the nineteenth century just as they have been at every other moment in history. I can't, in other words, agree with Schantz's argument that the dominance of a mainstream Christian culture made young men eager to kill and be killed in the Civil War. It is worth noting the point, though, that certain religious assumptions were prevalent in every class of society, and that these assumptions went a long way in accommodating Americans to an inevitable passing. For a thoughtful comparison between today's culture of death and that of the nineteenth century, see Sandra M. Gilbert, "Was the Nineteenth Century Different, and Luckier?" in Gilbert, *Death's Door: Modern Dying and the Ways We Grieve* (New York: W. W. Norton, 2006), 332–65, as well as her preface, "A Matter of Life and Death" (xvii–xxiv). And for more perspectives on death and dying, the subjects of a number of books in recent years, see: Allan Kellehar, *A Social History of Dying* (New York: Cambridge University Press, 2007); Douglas J. Davies, *A Brief History of Death* (Malden: Blackwell, 2005); and Robert Pogue Harrison, *The Dominion of the Dead* (Chicago: University of Chicago Press, 2003).

5. See John Bryant, *Melville and Repose: The Rhetoric of Humor in the American Renaissance* (New York: Oxford University Press, 1993), 3–108.

6. Charles H. Brown's solid biography, *William Cullen Bryant* (New York: Charles Scribner's Sons, 1971), and Gilbert H. Muller's new study, *William Cullen Bryant: Author of America* (Albany: SUNY Press, 2008), both do an excellent job of recapturing the extent to which Bryant was at the very heart of numerous cultural movements from about 1820 until his death in 1878 at the age of eighty-three.

7. Lawrence Buell notes that Bryant is "now deemed a minor figure" but rightly celebrates him as "the first Anglo-American poet of the environment to produce a body of enduring work." Given the general postcolonial tenor of much literary scholarship these days, though, it is perhaps not surprising to note that Bryant is often categorized as being merely an apologist for the conquest of the land (and of Native Americans). Matthew Dennis casually posits that "Bryant celebrated American exceptionalism and . . . endorsed American expansionism," and Peter Fritzell goes so far as to argue that "the vast majority of American nature writing has functioned almost solely to settle the country." A more sympathetic and nuanced reassessment of Bryant comes forth in a number of the essays in Stanley Brodwin and Michael D'Innocenzo, eds., *William Cullen Bryant and His America: Centennial Conference Proceedings, 1878–1978* (New York: AMS Press, 1983); see especially David J. Baxter,

"The Dilemma of Progress: Bryant's Continental Vision" (13–25), and Paul A. Newlin, "*The Prairie* and 'The Prairies': Cooper's and Bryant's Views of Manifest Destiny" (27–38). And see Buell, *The Environmental Imagination: Thoreau, Nature Writing, and the Formation of American Culture* (Cambridge, MA: Harvard University Press, 1995), 77; Dennis, "Patriotic Remains: Bones of Contention in the Early Republic," in Nancy Isenberg and Andrew Burstein, eds., *Mortal Remains: Death in Early America* (Philadelphia: University of Pennsylvania Press, 2003), 140; and Fritzell, *Nature Writing and America: Essays upon a Cultural Type* (Ames: Iowa State University Press, 1990), 19.

8. Parke Godwin, ed., *The Poetical Works of William Cullen Bryant*, vol. 1 (New York: D. Appleton, 1883), 193–4.

9. Ibid., 87–90 ("An Indian Story," 1824). For an excellent revision of the received wisdom on white attitudes toward Native Americans in this period, see Laura L. Mielke, *Moving Encounters: Sympathy and the Indian Question in Antebellum Literature* (Amherst: University of Massachusetts Press, 2008). Mielke does not discuss Bryant, but in my opinion a good deal of his poetry (despite his political support of Andrew Jackson and even Indian Removal) fits well with her argument about works on Native themes that are much more than "articulations of imperial desire shot through with guilt" (6–7). Another relevant example is to be found in a popular book called *Rural Cemeteries of America*, by Cornelia W. Walter (New York: R. Martin, 1847), which goes into great detail about the grave of an Indian woman in Green-Wood Cemetery in Brooklyn, over which her father and husband shed many tears—a scene that, from Walter's perspective, "forever disproves the oft-told tale of the Indian's coldness and stoicism" (Section 2, 23).

10. The most substantial work on Mount Auburn is the magisterial book by Blanche M. G. Linden, *Silent City on a Hill: Picturesque Landscapes of Memory and Boston's Mount Auburn Cemetery* (Amherst: University of Massachusetts Press, 2007); note also the earlier edition, Blanche Linden-Ward, *Silent City on a Hill: Landscapes of Memory and Boston's Mount Auburn Cemetery* (Columbus: Ohio State University Press, 1989). Other important works on Mount Auburn and the rural cemetery movement include: Thomas Bender, "The 'Rural' Cemetery Movement: Urban Travail and the Appeal of Nature," in Robert Blair St. George, ed., *Material Life in America, 1600–1860* (Boston: Northeastern University Press, 1988), 505–18; Stanley French, "The Cemetery as Cultural Institution: The Establishment of Mount Auburn and the 'Rural Cemetery' Movement," *American Quarterly* 26 (March 1974), 37–59; Frank Foxcroft, "Mount Auburn," *New England Magazine* 20 (June 1896), 419–38; Barbara Rotundo, "Mount Auburn Cemetery: A Proper Boston Institution," *Harvard Library Bulletin* 22 (July 1974), 268–79; Rotundo, "Mount Auburn: Fortunate Coincidences and an Ideal Solution," *Journal of Garden History* 4 (July–September 1984), 255–67; David Schuyler, "The Evolution of the Anglo-American Rural Cemetery: Landscape Architecture as Social and Cultural History," *Journal of Garden History* 4 (July–September 1984), 291–304; Schuyler, *The New Urban Landscape: The Redefinition of City Form in Nineteenth-Century America* (Baltimore: Johns Hopkins University Press, 1986), 37–56; Frederic A. Sharf, "The Garden Cemetery and American Sculpture: Mount Auburn," *Art Quarterly* 24 (Spring 1961), 80–88; Jules Zanger, "Mount Auburn Cemetery: The Silent Suburb," *Landscape* 24, no. 2 (1980), 23–8; David Charles Sloane, *The Last Great*

*Necessity: Cemeteries in American History* (Baltimore: Johns Hopkins University Press, 1991), 44–96; Schantz, *Awaiting the Heavenly Country*, 70–96; Garry Wills, *Lincoln at Gettysburg: The Words that Remade America* (New York: Touchstone, 1992), 63–89; and Marilyn Yalom, *The American Resting Place: Four Hundred Years of History through Our Cemeteries and Burial Grounds* (Boston: Houghton Mifflin, 2008)), esp. 45–7.

11. See Joseph Story, *An Address Delivered on the Dedication of the Cemetery at Mount Auburn, September 24, 1831* (Boston: Joseph T. & Edwin Buckingham, 1831), Appendix, 26–7.

12. For antebellum America's engagement with classical culture, see Wills, *Lincoln at Gettysburg*, 41–79, and Caroline Winterer, *The Culture of Classicism: Ancient Greece and Rome in American Intellectual Life, 1780–1910* (Baltimore: Johns Hopkins University Press, 2002), 44–98.

13. Story, *An Address*, 8–9.

14. See Sloane, *The Last Great Necessity*, 13–21, and John R. Stilgoe, *Common Landscape of America, 1580 to 1845* (New Haven: Yale University Press, 1982), 219–31.

15. Clearly, antebellum social reform was many-sided, and just as much of it was sponsored by Democrats as by Whigs. But projects like Mount Auburn were clearly Whiggish. Sometimes this kind of reform was self-serving, paternalistic, and complicit in the trend toward commercial development, but just as often, in my opinion, it upheld real alternatives to the "market revolution" and forced Americans to pay attention to issues that the market tended to obscure. Of course, the cultural politics of this entire era are in dispute among historians, who have produced numerous revisionist accounts over the last couple of decades—justifiably so, for, as David S. Reynolds has recently commented, "the years from 1815 through 1848 were arguably the richest in American life, if we view the whole picture of society, politics, and culture." So far, the most influential reassessments of this period seem to be Daniel Walker Howe, *What Hath God Wrought: The Transformation of America, 1815–1848* (New York: Oxford University Press, 2007); Sean Wilentz, *The Rise of American Democracy: Jefferson to Lincoln* (New York: Norton, 2005); and Charles Sellers, *The Market Revolution: Jacksonian America, 1815–1846* (New York: Oxford University Press, 1991). I agree with Sellers that the market revolution was a defining event in modern American history; but I disagree with him and Wilentz that Andrew Jackson and his theory of democracy formed the most effective opposition to the business class. Rather, I think capitalistic expansion was countered most importantly by the Whigs themselves. Meanwhile, I agree with Howe that it is misleading to call this era "Jacksonian," because in fact Jackson was a divisive figure, but I find unconvincing Howe's soft-pedaling of the market revolution and his argument that, overall, it was beneficial. I am much more sympathetic to the portraits of reform and improvement in this period to be found in the works listed below, all of which take cultural contestation more seriously than the three studies cited above. Those aforementioned works adopt a more materialist approach and emphasize a more narrowly defined social realm (Howe), or the political sphere (Wilentz), or the economy (Sellers). For broader views of antebellum culture, then, see David S. Reynolds, *Waking Giant: America in the Age of Jackson* (New York: Harper, 2008), quotation on 1; Louis P. Masur, *1831: Year of Eclipse* (New York: Hill & Wang, 2001); Carol Sheriff, *The Artificial River: The Erie Canal and the Paradox of Progress, 1817–1862* (New York: Hill & Wang, 1996); Lewis Perry, *Boats*

*against the Current: American Culture between Revolution and Modernity, 1820–1860* (Lanham: Rowman & Littlefield, 1993); and Anne Norton, *Alternative Americas: A Reading of Antebellum Political Culture* (Chicago: University of Chicago Press, 1986).

16. From my perspective, then, liberal reform meant in many cases coming to grips with both social and metaphysical problems, rather than avoiding them: cemeteries facilitated real confrontations with death. On the other hand, though, taking a broader view, one could argue that the establishment of cemeteries was part of a long-term trend toward the rigid boundary-drawing characteristic of modernity—in this case, toward the clear separation of the realms of the living and the dead. See, for instance, Dell Upton, *Another City: Urban Life and Urban Spaces in the New American Republic* (New Haven: Yale University Press, 2009), 203–41; Joseph Roach, *Cities of the Dead: Circum-Atlantic Performance* (New York: Columbia University Press, 1996), esp. 47–55; Thomas Laqueur, "The Places of the Dead in Modernity," in Colin Jones and Dror Wahrman, eds., *The Age of Cultural Revolutions: Britain and France, 1750–1820* (Berkeley: University of California Press, 2002), 17–32; and Farrell, *Inventing the American Way of Death*, 99–145.

17. For a helpful, provocative meditation on the relevance of "older, analogical forms of environmental imagination" such as the one I see in operation among the founders of rural cemeteries in antebellum America, see Jeremy Foster, *Washed with Sun: Landscape and the Making of White South Africa* (Pittsburgh: University of Pittsburgh Press, 2008), esp. 6–13 and 80–90, quotation on 12; and also note Bruno Latour, *Politics of Nature: How to Bring the Sciences into Democracy*, trans. Catherine Porter (Cambridge, MA: Harvard University Press, 2004), 32–49.

18. Story, *An Address*, 8. A month later, another Bostonian, Henry Bellows, gave a speech insisting quite explicitly that places like Mount Auburn "are not for the dead. They are for the living." Quoted in Thomas Bender, *Toward an Urban Vision: Ideas and Institutions in Nineteenth Century America* (1975; Baltimore: Johns Hopkins University Press, 1991), 81.

19. See Bender, *Toward an Urban Vision*, 81, for an especially sensitive reading of the conflicts surrounding the urban, industrial development of New England.

20. Story, *An Address*, 12.

21. "A Boston Boy," "IMPROVEMENTS," Miscellany, for *The Palladium*, July 20, 1824, a clipping with no page numbers in Folder One of the Boston Common Papers, Massachusetts Historical Society, Ms. N-1873. On the importance of the Common as a symbol of resistance to the market economy, see Yi-Fu Tuan, *Topophilia: A Study of Environmental Perception, Attitude, and Values* (1974; New York: Columbia University Press, 1990), 200–1; Walter Firey, *Land Use in Central Boston* (1947; New York: Greenwood Press, 1968), 136–69; Mona Domosh, *Invented Cities: The Creation of Landscape in Nineteenth-Century New York and Boston* (New Haven: Yale University Press, 1996), 127–44; and Michael Holleran, *Boston's "Changeful Times": Origins of Preservation and Planning in America* (Baltimore: Johns Hopkins University Press, 1998), 115–22.

22. To take one recent and prominent example, the urban and architectural historian Dell Upton posits that there was a coherent "spatial imagination" in America, and therefore every aspect of the built environment reflected a broad desire for order, for "civilization" and "urbanity"—the two key terms in his study, *Another City*. Upton's book is full of cogent

insights and clearly acknowledges that Americans were often ambivalent about their cities, but it rarely explores the actual cultural contestation that I see swirling around so many questions of urban development.

23. Unsigned letter, "The Common," December 16, 1824, in Folder One, Boston Common Papers; B, "Communication: 'The Common,'" December 14, 1824, ibid.

   Even David Nye, who is much more aware than most historians of the ideological conflict surrounding improvement, falls into the conceptual trap of assuming that, before any debate arose, there first developed a "foundation narrative," an "original formulation" of technological triumphalism, which meant that "most nineteenth-century Americans believed . . . the natural world was incomplete and awaited fulfillment through human intervention." Only afterward did people excluded from the mainstream begin to construct "alternative narratives, or 'counter-narratives.'" I am much more inclined to see the two kinds of narratives operating dialectically, often within the same people. See David E. Nye, *America as Second Creation: Technology and Narratives of New Beginnings* (Cambridge, MA: MIT Press, 2003), 9–20. Moreover, a love of wild nature did not suddenly spring up in nineteenth-century America; rather, it was present from the earliest days of European contact with the New World. Though the impulse to improve and the impulse to appreciate seem opposed, I think they arose interdependently amidst the confusion of colonial engagements with Native Americans and the American landscape, which was coded as both a howling wilderness and an Eden. See, for instance, Annette Kolodny, *The Lay of the Land: Metaphor as Experience and History in American Life and American Letters* (Chapel Hill: University of North Carolina Press, 1975), 3–25. Also note that agriculturists had their own debates in this period over the concept of "improvement": some, emphasizing the importance of soil conservation, celebrated the improvement of local patches of dirt as opposed to the improvement of transportation and commercial infrastructure, which tended to open up new opportunities on the frontier and draw people away from their land, thereby causing it to suffer from lack of care; see Steven Stoll's excellent study, *Larding the Lean Earth: Soil and Society in Nineteenth-Century America* (New York: Hill & Wang, 2002). But perhaps Thoreau should have the last word on this issue: "The nation itself, with all its so called internal improvements, which, by the way, are all external and superficial, is just such an unwieldy and overgrown establishment, cluttered with furniture and tripped up by its own traps, ruined by luxury and heedless expense, by want of calculation and a worthy aim, as the million households in the land. . . . We do not ride on the railroad; it rides upon us." Thoreau, *Walden* (1854; Boston: Beacon Press, 2004), 86–7.

24. Note the direct comparisons in Jacob Bigelow (president of the Corporation), *A History of the Cemetery at Mount Auburn* (Boston and Cambridge: James Munroe and Co., 1860), 120 and 123.

25. See, for instance, Tamara Plakins Thornton, *Cultivating Gentlemen: The Meaning of Country Life among the Boston Elite, 1785–1860* (New Haven: Yale University Press, 1989), esp. 1–12; also Linden, *Silent City on a Hill*, passim.

26. Story, *An Address*, 16–17.

27. Ibid., 17–19.

28. For a useful analysis of how scholars have placed American pastoralism in various ideological frames, see Buell, *The Environmental Imagination*, 36–52.

29. For a relevant case study, analyzing the blending of the urban and rural over time in one particular metropolitan area, see Richard A. Walker, *The Country in the City: The Greening of the San Francisco Bay Area* (Seattle: University of Washington Press, 2007), esp. 5–8. Also see James L. Machor, *Pastoral Cities: Urban Ideals and the Symbolic Landscape of America* (Madison: University of Wisconsin Press, 1987). And note the following, from a letter dated October 25, 1891, to Wm. A. Moore, Esq., President of the Board of Trustees of Elmwood Cemetery, Detroit, Michigan, from Frederick Law Olmsted: "The term rurality, as applied to a burial place, we assume to mean at least this: that its scenery is to be predominantly natural rather than artificial." Frederick Law Olmsted Papers, Library of Congress, Manuscript Division, Washington, DC, Reel 24.

30. "A Friend of Improvement," *The Boston Common, or Rural Walks in Cities* (Boston: George W. Light, 1838), 8. Also see Robert Manning, *History of the Massachusetts Horticultural Society, 1829–1878* (Boston: The Society, 1880).

31. *The Boston Common*, 13 and 11–12.

32. Ibid., 13, 19, 15, and 17.

33. Ibid., 27–8.

34. Dearborn, in Thaddeus William Harris, M.D., *Discourse Delivered before the Massachusetts Horticultural Society, on the Celebration of its Fourth Anniversary, Oct 3, 1832* (Cambridge: E. W. Metcalf & Co.,1832), 78.

    Also note Edward Everett, writing in 1831, on Mount Auburn: "Here it will be in the power of every one, who may wish it, at an expense considerably less than that of a common tomb or a vault beneath a church, to deposit the mortal remains of his friends; and to provide a place of burial for himself"—in *The Picturesque Pocket Companion, and Visitor's Guide, through Mount Auburn* (Boston: Otis, Broaders & Co., 1839), 12–13.

35. "General Dearborn's Report" [of June 18, 1831], in *Picturesque Pocket Companion*, 42. On American horticulture in this period, see Philip J. Pauly, *Fruits and Plains: The Horticultural Transformation of America* (Cambridge, MA: Harvard University Press, 2007), 51–79.

36. The most influential expression of this perspective came in Stanley French's 1974 article, "The Cemetery as Cultural Institution," where French offered the conclusion that "the rural cemetery through its intended capacity as cultivator of the finer emotions was another facet of the conservative cultural uplift movement" (59). This perspective has subsequently been embraced by a number of other historians, most recently Schantz (*Awaiting the Heavenly Country*, 80), Linden (*Silent City on a Hill*, 146–8), and Upton, whose chapter dealing with cemeteries is actually called "Gridding the Graveyard" (*Another City*, 203–41) and posits that the key innovation of places like Mount Auburn lay in their emphasis on "the security of interment and the permanent visibility of family mementos through the institution of private property" (232).

37. Story, *An Address*, 19.

38. See Raymond Williams, *The Country and the City* (New York: Oxford University Press, 1973), 96, and Williams, *Culture and Society: 1780–1950* (New York: Columbia University Press, 1983), 12.

39. Oliver Goldsmith, *The Deserted Village* (Loughcrew: Gallery Press, 2002), n.p.
40. Williams, *Culture and Society*, 260.
41. Lawrence Buell, *New England Literary Culture: From Revolution through Renaissance* (New York: Cambridge University Press, 1986), 285.
42. Goldsmith, *The Deserted Village*.
43. "General Dearborn's Report," in *Picturesque Pocket Companion*, 40 and 48.
44. Bigelow, A *History*, 3–4.
45. Linden, *Silent City on a Hill*, 142. Such mills shared almost nothing in common with the "busy mill" of Goldsmith's idealized rural village; early mills were for processing grain and lumber and had much less of an environmental and social impact than textile and paper mills. See Kent C. Ryden, *Landscape with Figures: Nature and Culture in New England* (Iowa City: University of Iowa Press, 2001), 234–243, and Nye, *America as Second Creation*, 91–146.
46. Harris, *Discourse*, 61. The students were George Sullivan and Charles W. Green. They actually named the area back in 1801, well before the land was owned by George Brimmer. At that point, it was just the undeveloped woodland adjacent to Simon Stone's farm.
47. On the naming, see George E. Ellis, *Memoir of Jacob Bigelow, M.D., LL.D.* (Cambridge, MA: John Wilson & Son, 1880), 65–73; on New England, see Bender, *Toward an Urban Vision*, 29, and David R. Meyer, *The Roots of American Industrialization* (Baltimore: Johns Hopkins University Press, 2003), 189, 195, and 306.
48. Bigelow, A *History*, 1–2.
49. Bigelow's whole career, according to the historian John F. Kasson, was devoted to the faith that "nineteenth-century man had achieved physical power, bodily freedom, and earthly dominion of which the ancients could only dream in fables. History thus emerged as a record of continuous improvement." See Kasson, *Civilizing the Machine: Technology and Republican Values in America, 1776–1900* (New York: Hill & Wang, 1999), 45–6. And for a fuller exploration of Whiggishness, with its undeniable tendency toward self-congratulation, see Daniel Walker Howe, *The Political Culture of the American Whigs* (Chicago: University of Chicago Press, 1979).
50. Bigelow, *Elements of Technology: Taken Chiefly from a Course of Lectures Delivered at Cambridge, on the Application of the Sciences to the Useful Arts* (Boston: Hilliard, Gray, Little, & Wilkins, 1829), 3.
51. From an unattributed newspaper notice of Ellis's *Memoir of Jacob Bigelow*, inserted into the copy owned by the Massachusetts Historical Society.
52. Ellis, *Memoir of Jacob Bigelow*, 75–6 and 85; quotation is from Bigelow, A *History*, 176; also see the lecture, "On Self-Limited Diseases," in Bigelow, *Nature in Disease, Illustrated in Various Discourses and Essays* (Boston: Ticknor & Fields,1854), 1–58. As Andrew Delbanco has noted, partly thanks to the dominant Romanticism of this period, "History was coming to be understood as a story of degeneration rather than progress"; especially in New England's intellectual circles, it seemed that "a new and strongly pejorative meaning of the term 'civilization' . . . was displacing the older, honorific sense of the word." See Delbanco, *Melville: His World and Work* (New York: Vintage, 2005), 54.

53. Bigelow, *A History* (which contains a reprint of the "Discourse"), 176–7. In an important work of ecocriticism, David Mazel makes a similar case for seeing Bigelow's ideas about burial as part of a proto-ecological intellectual tradition (though he mistakenly cites Bigelow's 1831 "Discourse" as being a speech he gave at the 1825 meeting he called to discuss the possibility of founding a new cemetery); see Mazel, *American Literary Environmentalism* (Athens: University of Georgia Press, 2000), 106–7.

54. Bigelow, *A History*, 195, 194, and 192.

55. Larzer Ziff, *Literary Democracy: The Declaration of Cultural Independence in America* (New York: Penguin, 1982), ix; Delbanco, *Melville*, 75.

56. Zebedee Cook, Jr., *An Address, Pronounced before the Massachusetts Horticultural Society, in Commemoration of its Second Annual Festival, the 10th of September, 1830* (Boston: Isaac R. Butts, 1830), 6.

57. Henry A. S. Dearborn, *Address before the Massachusetts Society for Promoting Agriculture* (Boston: N. E. Farmer Office—Geo. C. Barrett, 1835), 18, 27, and 24.

58. See, for instance, Cook, *An Address*, 27; Alexander H. Everett, *An Address, Delivered before the Massachusetts Horticultural Society, at their Fifth Annual Festival, September 18, 1833* (Boston: J. T. Buckingham, 1833), 18; Dearborn's report of September 8, 1832, included in Everett, *An Address*, 34–45; "General Dearborn's Report," in *Picturesque Pocket Companion*, 46.

59. Story, *An Address*, 14 and 7.

60. Quoted in Sharf, "The Garden Cemetery and American Sculpture," 84.

61. *Picturesque Pocket Companion*, 208.

62. Undated report of the Garden and Cemetery Committee of the Massachusetts Horticultural Society (probably Dearborn's words), included in Story, *An Address*, 29.

63. Walter, *Rural Cemeteries of America*, Section 14, 113.

64. For a provocative and nuanced meditation on circularity and the gradual shift in the nineteenth century toward a more linear modernity, see John Demos, *Circles and Lines: The Shape of Life in Early America* (Cambridge, MA: Harvard University Press, 2004).

65. See Upton, *Another City*; John W. Reps, *The Making of Urban America: A History of City Planning in the United States* (Princeton: Princeton University Press, 1965), 294–314, and Schuyler, *The New Urban Landscape*, 17–23.

66. On the interests behind New York's grid, and its powerful influence, see David M. Scobey, *Empire City: The Making and Meaning of the New York City Landscape* (Philadelphia: Temple University Press, 2002), 120–31; but note that not all nineteenth-century cities developed along these same lines, as Mona Domosh argues, especially with reference to Boston: see her *Invented Cities*.

67. See Andro Linklater, *Measuring America: How the United States Was Shaped by the Greatest Land Sale in History* (New York: Plume, 2003), 160–87, and Richard C. Wade, *The Urban Frontier: The Rise of Western Cities, 1790–1830* (1959; Urbana: University of Illinois Press, 1996).

68. Nathaniel Dearborn, *A Concise History of and Guide through Mount Auburn* (Boston: Nathaniel Dearborn, 1843), 5; another writer noted of Mount Auburn that "you are not only lost in astonishment at what you see, but are in danger of losing yourself among its mazes,

through which you might wander for hours without finding escape"; quoted in Linden, *Silent City on a Hill*, 248.

69. On Bryant and the intellectual origins of Central Park, see Brown, *William Cullen Bryant*, 293; Allan Nevins, *The Evening Post: A Century of Journalism* (New York: Boni & Liveright, 1922), 192–201; and Roy Rosenzweig and Elizabeth Blackmar, *The Park and the People: A History of Central Park* (Ithaca: Cornell University Press, 1992), 15–36.

70. Almost always, Bryant's poetical attitude toward death is taken as simple and obvious. A refreshing exception is Lawrence Buell, who notes of "Thanatopsis" that "the poem flirts with a nihilistic view of death subversive of the values of Bryant's audience, a view that we know, from its recurrence and inconsistency of treatment in his poetry, tempted Bryant greatly"; see Buell, *New England Literary Culture*, 108. Also see Albert McLean, *William Cullen Bryant*, updated ed. (Boston: Twayne, 1989), 22–67; Stanley Brodwin, "The 'Denial of Death' in William Cullen Bryant and Walt Whitman," in Brodwin and D'Innocenzo, *William Cullen Bryant and His America*, 113–31; and R. Rio-Jelliffe, "'Thanatopsis' and the Development of American Literature," ibid., 133–53. Brodwin concludes, significantly, that it is a grave mistake (as it were) to see the bulk of Bryant's death-related work as embracing a benevolent nature in order to deny the sting of mortality; rather, "Bryant deserves a fresh and sympathetic rereading for his authentic struggle to come to terms with his death-suffering" (129).

71. *Poetical Works*, vol. 1, 17, 18, 177, 283–4, 282, and 285–6.

72. Irving quoted in Edward Halsey Foster, *The Civilized Wilderness: Backgrounds to American Romantic Literature, 1817–1860* (New York: Free Press, 1975), 39.

73. Irving, *The Sketch Book of Geoffrey Crayon, Gent.*, Vol. 8 of *The Complete Works of Washington Irving* (1819–20; Boston: Twayne, 1978), 110; John Evelyn quoted by Irving in *The Sketch Book*, 111; letter of Irving to Lewis Gaylord Clark, New York, April 27, 1849, reprinted in *Sleepy Hollow Cemetery, at Tarrytown, on the Hudson River* (New York: C. S. Westcott, 1866), 1; and Irving, *The Sketch Book*, 139. Also note Thomas G. Connors, "The Romantic Landscape: Washington Irving, Sleepy Hollow, and the Rural Cemetery Movement," in Isenberg and Burstein, *Mortal Remains* 187–203.

74. Quoted in Foster, *The Civilized Wilderness*, 39.

75. I consulted *The Miscellaneous Works of Oliver Goldsmith, With an Account of His Life and Writings* (Philadelphia: J. Crissy, 1845), which is an exact reprint of the 1825 Paris edition.

76. Mount Auburn of course has a generally Protestant cast to it, and the Catholic Church's local archdiocese prevented its members from being buried there for more than a hundred years (see Linden, *Silent City on a Hill*, 284). But Jews and African Americans were represented from a very early date, and Catholics of many different backgrounds have purchased plots over the last sixty years or so in the newer sections of the cemetery. Mount Auburn does not actually keep records of religion or ethnicity, so I have never been able to determine whether any Native Americans are buried there.

77. As of 1811, with the passage of a Religious Freedoms Act, Massachusetts had at least given its citizens the right to direct their tax payments, some of which went to support religion, toward any spiritual institution or society of their choosing, no matter how unofficial. Meanwhile, of course, the Congregational Church remained dominant, but the religious

culture of Massachusetts gradually loosened up, until the true separation of church and state was completed in 1833 (the state legislature had actually passed a disestablishment measure in 1831, though it took another two years for a constitutional amendment to be ratified by the populace); see John D. Cushing, "Notes on Disestablishment in Massachusetts, 1780–1833," *William and Mary Quarterly* 26 (April 1969), esp. 185–90. On Mount Auburn's Unitarian background, see Linden, *Silent City on a Hill*, 136–9. On the general tenor of religious culture during this period, see Donald C. Swift, *Religion and the American Experience: A Social and Cultural History, 1765–1997* (Armonk: M. E. Sharpe, 1998), 70–105, and R. Laurence Moore, "Religion, Secularization, and the Shaping of the Culture Industry in Antebellum America," *American Quarterly* 41 (June 1989), 216–42.

78. Wilson Flagg, ed., *Mount Auburn: Its Scenes, Its Beauties, and Its Lessons* (Boston and Cambridge: James Munroe and Co., 1861), 57. Also note what Alexander Everett said in 1833, speaking explicitly about the French style that culminated in Versailles: "A better taste soon after grew up in England, and spread itself thence over all parts of Europe. The improvement lay in substituting a more free and direct imitation of nature, for the formal arrangements and fantastic decorations that were in use before" (*An Address*, 15).

79. Schuyler, *The New Urban Landscape*, 4 and 37–56.

80. Jacob Bigelow, *An Account of the Sphinx at Mount Auburn* (Boston: Little, Brown, & Co., 1872), 8 and 4.

81. Linden, *Silent City on a Hill*, 259–88.

82. Rotundo, "Mount Auburn: Fortunate Coincidences and an Ideal Solution," 265.

83. Dearborn's phrase, in Harris, *Discourse*, 61.

84. See Linden, *Silent City on a Hill*, 169–70, and Manning, *History of the Massachusetts Horticultural Society*, esp. 96–110.

85. Linden, *Silent City on a Hill*, 161.

86. See, for instance, Margaret Atwood, *Negotiating with the Dead: A Writer on Writing* (New York: Anchor, 2002), 164.

87. Harrison, *The Dominion of the Dead*, 31.

88. See Harris, *Discourse*, 55–6; on Bartlett, see Pauly, *Fruits and Plains*, 68.

89. Thoreau, "Wild Apples," in Lewis Hyde, ed., *The Essays of Henry D. Thoreau* (New York: North Point Press, 2002), 297 and 304–5.

90. Michael Pollan, "Why Bother?" *New York Times Magazine*, April 20, 2008, 88.

91. Thoreau, "Wild Apples," 305 and 303.

92. The impression I've gotten from various Arlo Guthrie concerts is that he is the composer of the alternative verse, though I have not been able to confirm his authorship. Folk songs belong to the folk, anyway. But in singing the alternative verse Arlo is clearly following a family tradition; it was his own father, Woody Guthrie, who taught him the "extra" verse to "This Land is Your Land": "As I was walking, I saw a sign there, and on that sign, it said 'No Trespassing.' But on the other side, it didn't say nothin'; *that* side was made for you and me." Trespassing is surely a radical act in a society dominated by a capitalist land system.

93. I took this phrasing from Thoreau's musing about apples left on the branch into November ("Wild Apples," 305): "These apples have hung in the wind and frost and rain till they have absorbed the qualities of the weather or season, and thus are highly *seasoned*."

94. See Thornton, *Cultivating Gentlemen*, passim, and Pauly, *Fruits and Plains*, 63.

95. Harris, *Discourse*, 58. Also note the 1830 toast to *"Diffusion of kind and of kindness—Our grapes can never be sour, for they will be within the reach of everybody,"* in Cook, *An Address*, 32.

96. As Yi-Fu Tuan has commented, "Chickens, eggs, and tomatoes are commonplace objects. . . . Yet they seem to have at times the essence of wholesome beauty, and they can console. The contemplation and handling of a jug or a warm but firm tomato can somehow reassure us, in depressed moods, of the ultimate sanity of life." See Tuan, *Space and Place: The Perspective of Experience* (1977; Minneapolis: University of Minnesota Press, 2005), 143.
    On the significance and radicalism of Epicureanism, which the horticulturists clearly practiced, see Harrison, *Gardens*, 71–82.

97. Everett, *An Address*, 31.

98. Malthus A. Ward, *An Address, Pronounced before the Massachusetts Horticultural Society, in Commemoration of its Third Annual Festival, September 21, 1831* (Boston: J. T. and E. Buckingham, 1831), 39.

99. On the development of the theory of the ice age, see Rebecca Bedell, *The Anatomy of Nature: Geology and American Landscape Painting, 1825–1875* (Princeton: Princeton University Press, 2001), 114–21.

100. Bigelow, *A History*, 19.

101. "H. A. S. Dearborn to Doctor Jacob Bigelow, Brinley Place, Roxbury, Oct 25, 1831," responding to a comment in the letter from "Doct. J. Bigelow to Hon. H. A. S. Dearborn, Mount Auburn, Oct 22, 1831." Both letters are in the archives of the Massachusetts Horticultural Society; I consulted transcripts in the Mount Auburn archives.

102. Note Bigelow's previous letter to Dearborn, in which he explained that "on reflection I am persuaded that the public will be better satisfied with names which are simple, rural, and not liable to be rendered inapplicable by future accidental changes,—than by names which are sentimental, and which may strike some ears as far fetched. I should like any of the following: Mountain avenue, Cypress, Cedar, Beech, Willow, Oak, Poplar, Larch, Walnut, Chestnut, Locust, Maple, Magnolia, Sycamore, Myrtle, Hazel, Hawthorn, Woodbine, Jasmine, Ivy, Rose, Rosebay, Iris"; see "Dr. Jacob Bigelow to Henry A. S. Dearborn, Boston, Oct 10, 1831," archives of the Massachusetts Horticultural Society; I consulted a transcript in the Mount Auburn archives. Also note "Mount Auburn Cemetery," pamphlet published by Whitwell, Bond & Co., 1833, available at Massachusetts Historical Society (Box 1833).

103. Manning, *History of the Massachusetts Horticultural Society*, 7.

104. Ibid., 2.

105. See, for instance, Anthony F. C. Wallace, *The Death and Rebirth of the Seneca* (New York: Vintage, 1972), 141–4, and Deborah Tall, *From Where We Stand: Recovering a Sense of Place* (New York: Knopf, 1993), 25–48. The place-name is sometimes rendered as Ganundasaga.

106. Manning, *History of the Massachusetts Horticultural Society*, 31.

107. Quoted in Tall, *From Where We Stand*, 27.

108. Lloyd A. Brown and Howard H. Peckham, eds., *Revolutionary War Journals of Henry Dearborn, 1775–1783* (Chicago: The Caxton Club, 1939), 191, 185, and 182.

109. Mielke, *Moving Encounters*, 195.

110. Quoted in Walter, *Rural Cemeteries of America*, Section 1, 15.

111. On Indian Removal, see Anthony F. C. Wallace, *The Long Bitter Trail: Andrew Jackson and the Indians* (New York: Hill & Wang, 1993), and David S. Heidler and Jeanne T. Heidler, *Indian Removal* (New York: Norton, 2007).

112. Steven Conn, *History's Shadow: Native Americans and Historical Consciousness in the Nineteenth Century* (Chicago: University of Chicago Press, 2004), 2. Linden's *Silent City on a Hill* does an excellent job of illuminating Mount Auburn's roots in European intellectual and cultural history (see esp. 29–79), but it does not address the cemetery's links to Native American traditions. For a relevant discussion of cross-cultural exchanges about mortality in an earlier period, see Erik R. Seeman, *The Huron-Wendat Feast of the Dead: Indian-European Encounters in Early North America* (Baltimore: Johns Hopkins University Press, 2011). I am also indebted to Eric Cheyfitz for his insights into Native conceptions of kinship and land; see, for instance, Cheyfitz, "Balancing the Earth: Native American Philosophies and the Environmental Crisis," *Arizona Quarterly* 65 (Autumn 2009), 139–162, and Cheyfitz, "What Is A Just Society? Native American Philosophies and the Limits of Capitalism's Imagination: A Brief Manifesto," *South Atlantic Quarterly* 110 (Spring 2011), 291–307.

113. See George S. Conover, "Reasons Why the State Should Acquire the Famous Burial Mound of the Seneca Indians Adjacent to the State Agricultural Experiment Station," a pamphlet dated January 14, 1888, Geneva, Ontario County, N.Y., and addressed to the Hon. W. W. Wright (director of the Experiment Station); copy consulted at the Massachusetts Historical Society and included in Justin Winsor, "Mounds and Earthworks," a bound collection of pamphlets and articles, 1847–95 (E61.W57). Also note Tall, *From Where We Stand*, 71–5; and on the Seneca "cult of death," see Wallace, *The Death and Rebirth of the Seneca*, 93–107.

114. Daniel Appleton White, *An Address, Delivered at the Consecration of the Harmony Grove Cemetery, in Salem, June 14, 1840* (Salem: Gazette Press, 1840), 11.

115. Story, *An Address*, 10–11.

116. On the complexity of cultural attitudes toward Native Americans in this period, see Brian Dippie, *The Vanishing American: White Attitudes and U.S. Indian Policy* (Middletown: Wesleyan University Press, 1982), 45–78, and Lucy Maddox, *Removals: Nineteenth-Century American Literature and the Politics of Indian Affairs* (New York: Oxford University Press, 1991), 3–49.

117. Quoted in Masur, *1831: Year of Eclipse*, 124 and 126.

118. Isaac M'Lellan, Jr., *Mount Auburn, and Other Poems* (Boston: William D. Ticknor, 1843), 35–6. Also note Isaac McLellan, Jun., *The Fall of the Indian, with Other Poems* (Boston: Carter & Hendee, 1830), which includes, besides the title poem, the melancholy work "An Autumn Evening among the Hills," with an epigraph from William Cullen Bryant; "New England's Dead"; "The Decayed Chapel"; "The Haunted Wood"; "The Hymn of a Cherokee Indian"; "A Funeral in the Village"; and "The Departed."

119. Historians are still not sure whether it was O'Sullivan himself or one of his writers, Jane McManus Storm, who originally used this phrase, but O'Sullivan generally got the attribution

at the time. See Amy S. Greenberg, *Manifest Manhood and the Antebellum American Empire* (New York: Cambridge University Press, 2005), 20.

120. See Thomas M. Allen, *A Republic in Time: Temporality and Social Imagination in Nineteenth-Century America* (Chapel Hill: University of North Carolina Press, 2008), 17–28. Allen focuses more on white Americans' carving out of the future as their exclusive domain, but I think his point about time-consciousness being as important as space-consciousness in this period is also borne out by the writings and actions of the backward-looking founders of rural cemeteries. In the case of my main characters, though, I think time-consciousness was aligned not with a rationalization of spatial conquest but with a critique of it.

121. See Conn, *History's Shadow*, 116–35; Henry Clyde Shetrone, *The Mound-Builders* (1930; Tuscaloosa: University of Alabama Press, 2004); David J. Meltzer, "Introduction," in Ephraim G. Squier and Edwin H. Davis, *Ancient Monuments of the Mississippi Valley* (1848; Washington, DC: Smithsonian Institution Press, 1998), 1–95; George R. Milner, *The Moundbuilders: Ancient Peoples of Eastern North America* (London: Thames & Hudson, 2004); Bradley T. Lepper, *Ohio Archaeology: An Illustrated Chronicle of Ohio's Ancient American Indian Cultures* (Wilmington, Ohio: Orange Frazer Press, 2005); and Robert Silverberg, *Mound Builders of Ancient America: The Archaeology of a Myth* (Greenwich, Conn.: New York Graphic Society, 1968).

122. Caleb Atwater, "Description of the ANTIQUITIES discovered in the State of Ohio and other Western States," in *Archaeologia Americana: Transactions and Collections of the American Antiquarian Society* 1 (1820), 164. By 1820, the range of knowledge about such antiquities was impressive; as Atwater indicated, explorations had been undertaken of structures all along the Ohio and Mississippi valleys, including the massive city at Cahokia, just outside of St. Louis (ibid., 188). And many Americans had taken notice: see Roger Kennedy, "Jefferson and the Indians," *Winterthur Portfolio* 27 (Summer–Autumn 1992), esp. 107–13. Many antiquarians of this period could not describe the Mounds without recourse to biblical flood imagery or an invocation of Atlantis. When Atwater, for instance, said of the Mounds that they "are fragments of history, as Bacon would say, which have been saved from the deluge of time" ("Description," 195), the reference was to Francis Bacon's classic 1623 work, *The New Atlantis*. Students of the Mounds were obsessed with the power of God or nature to erase history and civilization both in the past and, potentially, in the near future, given what they saw as the United States' decadent and imperial rush toward development and expansion. At least the Mound Builders had constructed a few worthy, timeless works.

123. Harris, *Discourse*, 50–51.

124. Thaddeus Mason Harris, *The Journal of a Tour into the Territory Northwest of the Alleghany Mountains; Made in the Spring of the Year 1803. With a Geographical and Historical Account of the State of Ohio* (Boston: Manning & Loring, 1805). Today, this book is virtually unknown, but it is mentioned briefly in Howard Mumford Jones, *O Strange New World: American Culture: The Formative Years* (New York: Viking, 1964), 366.

125. Harris, *Journal of a Tour*, v and 51–2. On Putnam, see Linklater, 51–88 and 143–8.

126. Harris, *Journal of a Tour*, 22.

127. Ibid., 29. Jacob Bigelow would certainly have taken an interest in this comment; after all he was a professor of materia medica at Harvard and the author of *American Medical Botany*, 3 vols. (Boston: Cummings & Hilliard, 1817–20).

128. Harris, *Journal of a Tour*, 18, vi, and 14.

129. Ibid., 147, 62, 64, and 152.

130. See William F. Romain, *Mysteries of the Hopewell: Astronomers, Geometers, and Magicians of the Eastern Woodlands* (Akron: University of Akron Press, 2000), esp. 142, and Maureen Korp, *The Sacred Geography of the American Mound Builders* (Lewiston: Edwin Mellen, 1990). Also note that Atwater reported on cardinal point alignment and his impression that some structures were arranged in perfect squares and circles ("Description," 144).

131. See Kennedy, "Jefferson and the Indians," 107–13, and John C. Greene, *American Science in the Age of Jefferson* (Ames: Iowa State University Press, 1984), 343–75. Among Barton's important works are *New Views of the Origin of the Tribes and Nations of America* (Philadelphia: John Bioren, 1797), and, in collaboration with Winthrop Sargent, *Papers Relative to Certain American Antiquities* (Philadelphia: Thomas Dobson, 1796).

132. Atwater, "Description," 197 and 202.

133. "Mount Auburn Cemetery," *North American Review* 33 (October 1831), 399–400.

134. See Silverberg, *Mound Builders of Ancient America*, passim, and Conn, *History's Shadow*, 116–35.

135. Isaiah Thomas, "An Account of the American Antiquarian Society" (October 1813), in *Archaeologia Americana* 1 (1820), 30. Also note that Benjamin Smith Barton reminded his fellow citizens of the "mortifying truth, that nations may relapse into rudeness again; all their proud monuments crumbled to dust." Quoted in Conn, *History's Shadow*, 25.

136. See Allen, *A Republic in Time*, 47–53, Conn, *History's Shadow*, 24–30, and Angela Miller, *The Empire of the Eye: Landscape Representation and American Cultural Politics, 1825–1875* (Ithaca: Cornell University Press, 1993), 21–64.

137. Josiah Priest, *American Antiquities and Discoveries in the West* (1833; Albany: Hoffman & White, 1835), 41. Priest, like most other American antiquarians of his day, insisted that the Indian Mounds had survived a—or the—great deluge: "The traits of the *ancient* nations of the world are every where shown by the fragments of dilapidated cities, pyramids of stone, and walls of wondrous length; but here are the wrecks of empire, whose beginnings, it would seem, are older than *any* of these, which are the mounds and works of the west, towering aloft, as if their builders were preparing against another flood" (iii).

138. Flagg, *Mount Auburn*, 272. Also note that Cornelia Walter, in a section of *Rural Cemeteries in America* that is devoted to Mount Auburn, praises Indian-style monuments—"the grassy and elevated mound duly planted with the flowers of the revolving seasons, and watered by the hand of affection"—as "more pleasing" than any others (Section 1, 15).

139. "Mount Auburn," *New-England Magazine* 1 (September 1831), 237.

140. Nathaniel Hawthorne, "The New Adam and Eve," in *Mosses from an Old Manse*, Vol. 10 of *The Centenary Edition of the Works of Nathaniel Hawthorne* (1846; Columbus: Ohio State University Press, 1974), 247–9, 259, 266; note that the story was first published in 1843 in the *United States Magazine and Democratic Review*.

141. In my thinking about the potential of an earthbound Eden and what Robert Pogue Harrison calls "the vocation of care," I have been profoundly influenced by his book, *Gardens* (see esp. 1–13).

142. Everett, *An Address*, 25.

143. Story, *An Address*, 20.

144. Zillah, "Mount Auburn," *Lowell Offering* 1 (Oct 1840), 13. For a useful discussion of the relationship of Lowell mill girls to the natural world, see Chad Montrie, *Making a Living: Work and Environment in the United States* (Chapel Hill: University of North Carolina Press, 2008), 13–34. Also note that one Lowell worker, Lucy Larcom, went on to publish a work of literary criticism called *Landscape in American Poetry* (New York: D. Appleton, 1879).

145. For a few exemplary perspectives on Mount Auburn, see: "Mount Auburn," *New-England Magazine* 1 (September 1831), 236–9; "Mount Auburn Cemetery," *North American Review* 33 (October 1831), 397–406; "Mount Auburn," *American Quarterly Observer* 3 (July 1834), 149–72; G. T. Curtis, "Mount Auburn," *New-England Magazine* 7 (October 1834), 316–20; "Thoughts Connected with Rural Cemeteries," *Christian Review* 13 (March 1848), 9–23; *Picturesque Pocket Companion*; Walter, *Rural Cemeteries of America*; and Flagg, *Mount Auburn*.

146. Circular letter relating to cemetery access, from Charles Curtis, Secretary of Mount Auburn, to all the proprietors of the cemetery; copy consulted was addressed to Dr. George Shattuck, dated 1833, and eventually deposited at the Massachusetts Historical Society (Bdses-Sm 1833).

147. Story, in an 1834 report of the Garden and Cemetery Committee of the Massachusetts Horticultural Society, quoted in Bigelow, *A History*, 197. For discussions of access to the cemetery in these early years, see Rotundo, "Mount Auburn Cemetery: A Proper Boston Institution," 271–2, and "Mount Auburn: Fortunate Coincidences and an Ideal Solution," 260.

148. Quoted in Linden, *Silent City on a Hill*, 248.

149. See ibid., 252.

150. See *Picturesque Pocket Companion*; this was an extremely wild and open-ended guidebook, but as the century wore on, these publications tended to become more prescriptive and also more focused on the tombs of famous people than on the landscape. Later examples include: Nathaniel Dearborn (the already-cited first edition of his guide was published in 1843, but it was a big hit and so was followed by many more editions over the next couple of decades; by 1858, the book was titled *Dearborn's Guide through Mount Auburn* and was in its twelfth edition); Walter, *Rural Cemeteries of America*; Flagg, *Mount Auburn*; Henry Parker, *Stranger's Guide Book to Mount Auburn Cemetery* (Boston: James Munroe & Co., 1849); *A Hand-Book for Passengers over the Cambridge Railroad, with a Description of Mount Auburn Cemetery* (Boston: William V. Spencer, 1858); and *Hand Book for Cambridge and Mount Auburn*, 19th ed. (Boston and Cambridge: Moses King, 1883).

151. A. J. Downing, "Public Cemeteries and Public Gardens" (July 1849), in *Rural Essays* (1853; New York: Geo. A. Leavitt, 1869), 154 and 158.

152. *Picturesque Pocket Companion*, 4.

153. Ibid., 193, 194–5, and 198. Of the rage for rural cemeteries, for "the consecration of gardens," Ralph Waldo Emerson said in 1855 that "A simultaneous movement has in a hundred cities and towns, in this country, selected some convenient piece of undulating ground, with pleasant woods and waters; every family chooses its own clump of trees; and we lay the corpse in these leafy colonnades." See Emerson, "Address to the Inhabitants of Concord, at the Consecration of Sleepy Hollow, 29 September 1855," in Ronald A. Bosco and Joel Myerson, eds., *The Later Lectures of Ralph Waldo Emerson, 1843–1871*, vol. 2 (Athens: University of Georgia Press, 2001), 32.

154. See the thorough listing in Linden, *Silent City on a Hill*, 293–5. On the rural cemetery movement in general, see Sloane, *The Last Great Necessity*, 44–96, and Schantz, *Awaiting the Heavenly Country*, 70–96, and note Gunther Barth, "The Park Cemetery: Its Westward Migration," in Craig Zabel and Susan Scott Munshower, eds., *American Public Architecture: European Roots and Native Expressions* (University Park: Pennsylvania State University Press, 1989), 58–81. Some scholars have argued that a radical shift occurred in cemetery design in the mid-1850s, from the "garden" style to the "lawn" or "park" style (see, for instance, Farrell, *Inventing the American Way of Death*, 99, and Sloane, *The Last Great Necessity*, 97–109); I think the distinction is somewhat overdrawn, though there were certainly gradual shifts in style in both new and old cemeteries, and certain reformers, especially Adolph Strauch, did stress a clearer, cleaner look in the period just before the Civil War.

155. Simms, "City of the Silent," in *Poems: Descriptive, Dramatic, Legendary, and Contemplative*, vol. 1 (Charleston: John Russell, 1853), 328 and 336.

156. Quoted in Schantz, *Awaiting the Heavenly Country*, 76. Indeed, as Schantz has aptly noted, the establishment of Magnolia Cemetery "coincided with furious sectional debate over the Fugitive Slave Law in the U.S. Congress. But on the afternoon of November 19, Charleston civic leaders stood arm-in-arm with their brothers in Boston" (ibid.).

157. Stephen Duncan Walker, *Rural Cemetery and Public Walk* (Baltimore: Sands & Neilson, 1835), i, 5–6, and 20.

158. Walter, *Rural Cemeteries of America*, Section 12, 94.

159. D. B. Douglass, *Exposition of the Plan and Objects of the Green-Wood Cemetery* (New York: Narine & Co., 1839), 4 and 12; emphasis in original.

160. Bryant joined with "several other prominent newspaper editors" to argue for the importance of the New York cemetery; see Sloane, *The Last Great Necessity*, 59.

161. Walter, *Rural Cemeteries of America*, Section 2, 19–23.

162. See Sloane, *The Last Great Necessity*, 57–8.

163. Barnard quoted ibid., 62. Barnard was a typical cemeterian of this period, who would go on to denounce the war with Mexico two years later and generally to develop a cosmopolitan worldview very much in line with that of the proto-ecological thinker Alexander von Humboldt—as I've argued in *The Humboldt Current: Nineteenth-Century Exploration and the Roots of American Environmentalism* (New York: Viking, 2006); Barnard appears on 94–5, 106, and 175. Antebellum cemeterians tended to be Humboldtian intellectuals who explored liminal landscapes without feeling the need to travel to distant frontiers.

164. Hon. John M'Lean, *Address Delivered on the Consecration of the Spring Grove Cemetery, Near Cincinnati, August 20th, 1845* (Cincinnati: Daily Atlas, 1845), 13; the correct date of the consecration is August 24.

165. Thoreau worked on his two books simultaneously during the 1840s; even during his time at Walden Pond, he was going back over his river journals. Then, in the late 1850s, he wrote an essay called "Autumnal Tints," in which he seemed to mock cemeteries as being mere echoes of a larger ecological commons, as attempts to enclose and privatize what should be appreciated universally, without boundaries. But he could not have expressed this admiration for what cemeteries stood for without having learned something from the cemeteries themselves: "When the leaves fall, the whole earth is a cemetery pleasant to walk in. I love to wander and muse over them in their graves. Here are no lying nor vain epitaphs. What though you own no lot at Mount Auburn? Your lot is surely cast somewhere in this vast cemetery, which has been consecrated from of old. You need attend no auction to secure a place. There is room enough here. The loosestrife shall bloom and the huckleberry-bird sing over your bones. The woodsman and hunter shall be your sextons, and the children shall tread upon the borders as much as they will. Let us walk in the cemetery of the leaves; this is your true Greenwood Cemetery." Thoreau, "Autumnal Tints," in Hyde, *The Essays of Henry D. Thoreau*, 231.

166. Downing, "Public Cemeteries and Public Gardens," 154 and 156–7.

167. Downing, "A Talk about Public Parks and Gardens," in *Rural Essays*, 144.

168. For a typical emphasis on the "gentility" of this movement, see Adam Sweeting, *Reading Houses and Building Books: Andrew Jackson Downing and the Architecture of Popular Antebellum Literature, 1835–1855* (Hanover: University Press of New England, 1996).

169. See Emerson, "Address," 30–4, and note the famous section on Concord's Sleepy Hollow (before it was a cemetery) in Leo Marx, *The Machine in the Garden: Technology and the Pastoral Ideal in America* (New York: Oxford, 1964), 3–33. The neighborhood where the cemetery was established was clearly known as Sleepy Hollow by the early 1840s; what is unknown is whether or not that name was meant to invoke Washington Irving's famous "Legend of Sleepy Hollow," but the story was widely enough known, and Concord was enough of a literary hotbed, that the odds seem pretty good to me; see Leslie Perrin Wilson, *In History's Embrace: Past and Present in Concord, Massachusetts* (Hollis, NH: Hollis Publishing, 2007), 88.

170. *Picturesque Pocket Companion*, 230–239; quotations on 230, 231, 235, 237, 236, and 238. Note that this story was first published in January of 1839 in the magazine *Southern Rose* (vol. 7, 161–4) and that a few years later it appeared in Hawthorne's collection of *Twice-Told Tales* (1842); see *The Centenary Edition of the Works of Nathaniel Hawthorne*, vol. 9 (Columbus: Ohio State University Press, 1974), 442–50.

## 2. THE MIDDLE LANDSCAPES OF NEW ENGLAND CULTURE

1. See Stuart T. Hauser, Joseph P. Allen, and Eve Golden, *Out of the Woods: Tales of Resilient Teens* (Cambridge, MA: Harvard University Press, 2006).

2. On Hawthorne's obsession with mortality, see Roberta Weldon, *Hawthorne, Gender, and Death: Christianity and Its Discontents* (New York: Palgrave Macmillan, 2008).

3. Elizabeth P. Peabody, "Plan of the West Roxbury Community" (1842), in Henry W. Sams, ed., *Autobiography of Brook Farm: A Book of Primary Source Materials* (Englewood Cliffs: Prentice-Hall, 1958), 62. On Brook Farm, see Sterling F. Delano, *Brook Farm: The Dark Side of Utopia* (Cambridge, MA: Harvard University Press, 2004); on Hawthorne's thinking about Brook Farm and communitarianism, see Andrew Loman, *"Somewhat on the Community-System": Fourierism in the Works of Nathaniel Hawthorne* (New York: Routledge, 2005), and Lauren Berlant, *The Anatomy of National Fantasy: Hawthorne, Utopia, and Everyday Life* (Chicago: University of Chicago Press, 1991).

   On the proliferation of utopian communities, and their environmental dimensions, see especially Dolores Hayden, *Seven American Utopias: The Architecture of Communitarian Socialism, 1790–1975* (Cambridge, MA: MIT Press, 1976); and also Stanley K. Schultz, *Constructing Urban Culture: American Cities and City Planning, 1800–1920* (Philadelphia: Temple University Press, 1989), 8–14; Ellen Weiss, *City in the Woods: The Life and Design of an American Camp Meeting on Martha's Vineyard* (New York: Oxford University Press, 1987); Christopher Clark, *The Communitarian Moment: The Radical Challenge of the Northampton Association* (Ithaca: Cornell University Press, 1995); Donald E. Pitzer, ed., *America's Communal Utopias* (Chapel Hill: University of North Carolina Press, 1997); Carl J. Guarneri, *The Utopian Alternative: Fourierism in Nineteenth-Century America* (Ithaca: Cornell University Press, 1991); and Mark Holloway, *Heavens on Earth: Utopian Communities in America, 1680–1880* (New York: Dover, 1966).

4. Hawthorne, *The Blithedale Romance* (1852; New York: Penguin, 1986), 21. Note that chapter 8 (58–68) is called "A Modern Arcadia."

5. Fuller, undated journal entry, in Sams, *Autobiography of Brook Farm*, 216. On Fuller's Conversations, see the crucial second volume of Charles Capper's intellectual biography, *Margaret Fuller: An American Romantic Life: The Public Years* (New York: Oxford University Press, 2007), 34–9. On the importance of idealism to Hawthorne, see *Blithedale*, 10–11: "Yet, after all, let us acknowledge it wiser, if not more sagacious, to follow out one's daydream to its natural consummation, although, if the vision have been worth the having, it is certain never to be consummated otherwise than by a failure. And what of that! Its airiest fragments, impalpable as they may be, will possess a value that lurks not in the most ponderous realities of any practicable scheme. They are not the rubbish of the mind. Whatever else I may repent of, therefore, let it be reckoned neither among my sins nor follies, that I once had faith and force enough to form generous hopes of the world's destiny—yes!—and to do what in me lay for their accomplishment."

6. Hawthorne, letter to Louisa Hawthorne, Brook Farm, West Roxbury, May 3, 1841, and letter to Sophia Peabody, Oak Hill, April 13, 1841, both in Sams, *Autobiography of Brook Farm*, 18 and 14.

7. On the "Go Ahead!" principle, see Scott A. Sandage, *Born Losers: A History of Failure in America* (Cambridge, MA: Harvard University Press, 2005), 24–7 and 80–98, quotation on 25; on ambition, see John Demos, *Circles and Lines: The Shape of Life in Early America* (Cambridge, MA: Harvard University Press, 2004), 57–83, esp. 69.

8. Hawthorne, *The Scarlet Letter*, in *Great Short Works of Hawthorne* (New York: Harper & Row, 1967), 7, 32, 35, 24, 6.

9. See Loman, *"Somewhat on the Community-System"*, xvii, where he quotes Patricia Dunlavy Valenti, *Sophia Peabody Hawthorne: A Life*, vol. 1, *1809–1847* (Columbia: University of Missouri Press, 2004), 157. Also note Brenda Wineapple, *Hawthorne: A Life* (New York: Knopf, 2003), 144–55.

10. Hawthorne, letter to Sophia Peabody, Brook Farm, "June 1st, 1841—nearly 6 A.M.," in Sams, *Autobiography of Brook Farm*, 21.

11. Eco-critics generally pass over Hawthorne, finding his work to be too focused on interiority. Eric Wilson is a good example; see his otherwise excellent *Romantic Turbulence: Chaos, Ecology, and American Space* (Houndmills: Macmillan, 2000), xix: "Though Hawthorne is an astute critic of the excesses of modern science, he remains much more interested in the human heart—primarily its Calvinistic struggles with sin—than in relationships between humans and nature." A happy exception is Robert E. Abrams, *Landscape and Ideology in American Renaissance Literature: Topographies of Skepticism* (New York: Cambridge University Press, 2004), 1–40. Almost two decades earlier, James L. Machor, writing in the Leo Marx mold, suggested the possibilities of an extended analysis of Hawthorne's work in the context of American pastoralism; see *Pastoral Cities: Urban Ideals and the Symbolic Landscape of America* (Madison: University of Wisconsin Press, 1987), 188–203. And of course also see Marx himself, *The Machine in the Garden: Technology and the Pastoral Ideal in America* (New York: Oxford, 1964), 3–33 and 265–77. Additionally, the material presented by Edwin Fussell, in his marvelous *Frontier: American Literature and the American West* (Princeton: Princeton University Press, 1965), 69–131, raises key questions about the Arcadian dimensions of Hawthorne's work.

12. Hawthorne, *Blithedale*, 2; *Scarlet Letter*, 31 and 33.

13. Hawthorne, *Scarlet Letter*, 32; *Blithedale*, 11.

14. Hawthorne, *Blithedale*, 117–19, quotations on 119 and 117.

15. Miriam B. Sachs, "Benjamin Tevya Sachs" (unpublished manuscript, March 28, 2006), 1.

16. Hawthorne, letter to Louisa Hawthorne, "Brook Farm, West Roxbury, May 3rd, 1841," and letter to Sophia Peabody, "Brook Farm, Septr 25th, 1841—½ past 7 A.M.," both in Sams, *Autobiography of Brook Farm*, 18 and 37.

17. Hawthorne, entries for September 26, 1841, and September 28, 1841, in *The American Notebooks*, ed. Claude M. Simpson, vol. 8 of *The Centenary Edition of the Works of Nathaniel Hawthorne* (Columbus: Ohio State University Press, 1972), 196–7 and 201.

18. Ibid., October 22, 1841; October 8, 1841; September 26, 1841; October 12, 1841; and October 18, 1841; 220, 206–7, 197, 214, and 219.

19. Ibid., September 28, 1841, and September 26, 1841, 201–3 and 197. Also see *Blithedale*, 207–212, quotation on 209.

20. Hawthorne, entries for October 8, 1841, and September 28, 1841, in *American Notebooks*, 207 and 202. Also see *Blithedale*, 205, where Miles Coverdale, the narrator and Hawthorne's stand-in, says that in their mysterious growth the mushrooms "resembled many of the emotions in my breast." Hawthorne wrote much about mushrooms in his journals, noting the way they came up suddenly, "during the night," and imagining them as "little fairy tables"; see his entries for September 26, 1841; October 8, 1841; and October 22, 1841, in *American Notebooks*, 196, 207, and 221.

21. Hawthorne's *American Notebooks* (236–70 and especially 315–397) provide a good picture of the life he and Sophia led in Concord, but also see: Wineapple, *Hawthorne*, 160–70; Valenti, *Sophia Peabody Hawthorne*, 1:170–81; and Philip McFarland, *Hawthorne in Concord* (New York: Grove Press, 2004), 3–124. Robert Manning basically served as Hawthorne's father; see Edwin Haviland Miller, *Salem is My Dwelling Place: A Life of Nathaniel Hawthorne* (Iowa City: University of Iowa Press, 1991), 29–31, and Margaret B. Moore, *The Salem World of Nathaniel Hawthorne* (Columbia: University of Missouri Press, 1998), 60–2.

22. Hawthorne, entries for August 10, 1842, and August 24, 1842, in *American Notebooks*, 328, 330, and 344.

23. Ibid., entries for August 9, 1842, and September 1, 1842, 326–7 and 353; this seems a perfect example of what William Cronon meant by the need to celebrate "the tree we planted in our own backyard"—see Cronon, "The Trouble with Wilderness; or, Getting Back to the Wrong Nature," in Cronon, ed., *Uncommon Ground: Rethinking the Human Place in Nature* (New York: Norton, 1996), 88.

24. Hawthorne, entry for August 22, 1842, in *American Notebooks*, 341–4. Also see Valenti, *Sophia Peabody Hawthorne*, 1:174–8, and Thomas R. Mitchell, *Hawthorne's Fuller Mystery* (Amherst: University of Massachusetts Press, 1998), esp. 71–7.

25. See Louis P. Masur, ed., "*. . . The Real War Will Never Get in the Books*": *Selections from Writers during the Civil War* (New York: Oxford University Press, 1993), 160–79, esp. 177–9.

26. Quoted in Wineapple, *Hawthorne*, 367.

27. Hawthorne, "Chiefly about War Matters," in Masur, "*. . . The Real War Will Never Get in the Books*", 167–8.

28. Quoted in Wineapple, *Hawthorne*, 367.

29. Cleveland, *Landscape Architecture, as Applied to the Wants of the West; with an Essay on Forest Planting on the Great Plains* (Chicago: Jansen, McClurg & Co., 1873), 45. Copeland also went on to make important contributions to landscape architecture; one particularly intriguing project was a picturesque community on Martha's Vineyard—see Weiss, *City in the Woods*, 78–92. On Sleepy Hollow, and especially Cleveland's guiding role in its design, see Leslie Perrin Wilson, *In History's Embrace: Past and Present in Concord, Massachusetts* (Hollis, NH: Hollis Publishing, 2007), 88–91.

    The story of city parks in the United States has been partially told in a few books, which emphasize landscape design or urban planning or cultural geography, but the topic still awaits a full treatment from the perspective of environmental history. Meanwhile, see Galen Cranz, *The Politics of Park Design: A History of Urban Parks in America* (Cambridge, MA: MIT Press, 1982); Irving D. Fisher, *Frederick Law Olmsted and the City Planning Movement in the United States* (Ann Arbor: UMI Research Press, 1986); Heath Massey Schenker, *Melodramatic Landscapes: Urban Parks in the Nineteenth Century* (Charlottesville: University of Virginia Press, 2009), 117–73; and David Schuyler, *The New Urban Landscape: The Redefinition of City Form in Nineteenth-Century America* (Baltimore: Johns Hopkins University Press, 1986), 59–146.

30. Hawthorne, "Sketches from Memory," in *Mosses from an Old Manse* (1846), Vol. 10 of *The Centenary Edition of the Works of Nathaniel Hawthorne* (Columbus: Ohio State University Press, 1974), 432.

31. Hawthorne, "The Old Apple Dealer," in *Mosses*, 445.

32. Hawthorne, "Sketches from Memory," in *Mosses*, 436.

33. Fuller, *Summer on the Lakes, in 1843* (1844; Urbana: University of Illinois Press, 1991), 107. Fuller consistently referred to it as Mackinaw Island, a common practice at the time, though it was also sometimes called Mackinac Island (the preferred name now).

34. On Fuller, see Capper, *Margaret Fuller*, especially for her intellectual life; Meg McGavran Murray, *Margaret Fuller, Wandering Pilgrim* (Athens: University of Georgia Press, 2008), especially for her psychological life; Joan von Mehren, *Minerva and the Muse: A Life of Margaret Fuller* (Amherst: University of Massachusetts Press, 1994); and Fritz Fleischmann, ed., *Margaret Fuller's Cultural Critique: Her Age and Legacy* (New York: Peter Lang, 2000).

    Also note that Joel Myerson has compiled contemporary "recollections, interviews, and memoirs by family, friends, and associates" in *Fuller in Her Own Time* (Iowa City: University of Iowa Press, 2008); Bell Gale Chevigny juxtaposes Fuller's own writings with those of her contemporaries in *The Woman and the Myth: Margaret Fuller's Life and Writings*, rev. ed. (Boston: Northeastern University Press, 1994).

35. Fuller, letter to George T. Davis, "Cambridge, 17th Decr, 1842," in *The Letters of Margaret Fuller*, vol. 3, *1842–44*, ed. Robert N. Hudspeth (Ithaca: Cornell University Press, 1984), 105.

36. Fuller, journal entry of October 30, 1842, printed in Chevigny, *The Woman and the Myth*, 532.

37. Emerson, "Nature" (1836), in John Elder, ed., *Nature/Walking* (Boston: Beacon Press, 1991), 23.

38. Emerson's letter is quoted in Hudspeth, *Letters of Margaret Fuller*, 124; Fuller's letter is on the same page (and is dated May 9, 1843).

39. Fuller, "The Great Lawsuit. Man *versus* Men. Woman *versus* Women" (1843), reprinted in David A. Hollinger and Charles Capper, eds., *The American Intellectual Tradition: A Sourcebook*, vol. 1, *1630–1865*, 2d ed. (New York: Oxford University Press, 1993), 307, 312–13, and 316.

40. This is how she expressed it after she had left; see Fuller, letter to Emerson, Chicago, August 17, 1843, in Hudspeth, *Letters of Margaret Fuller*, 143.

41. This comes from a letter written a few months earlier, but I think it aptly describes her state of mind at this moment of departure: Fuller, letter to Richard F. Fuller, Cambridge, August 5, 1842, ibid., 81.

42. Fuller, *Summer on the Lakes*, 24.

43. Ibid., 3.

44. Ibid., 30. Capper (*Margaret Fuller*, 154) astutely refers to *Summer on the Lakes* as "an insufficiently appreciated contribution to what Leo Marx in *The Machine in the Garden* has called the canonical American Renaissance authors' search for a 'symbolic middle landscape' dialectically bridging the 'wild' and the 'civilized.'" Also see Michaela Bruckner Cooper, "Textual Wandering and Anxiety in Margaret Fuller's *Summer on the Lakes*," in Fleischmann, *Margaret Fuller's Cultural Critique*, 171–89.

45. Fuller, *Summer on the Lakes*, 12; elsewhere, Fuller tells of meeting "a contented woman, the only one I heard of out there" (72), and posits that "the great drawback upon the lives of

these settlers, at present, is the unfitness of the women for their new lot. It has generally been the choice of the men, and the women follow, as women will, doing their best for affection's sake, but too often in heartsickness and weariness. Beside it frequently not being a choice or conviction of their own minds that it is best to be here, their part is the hardest. . . . The women can rarely find any aid in domestic labor" (38).

46. Ibid., 78; one woman, in particular, impressed Fuller with "how well she performed hard and unaccustomed duties" (76). For more on her complicated perspective on frontier gender dynamics, see Annette Kolodny, *The Land Before Her: Fantasy and Experience of the American Frontiers, 1630–1860* (Chapel Hill: University of North Carolina Press, 1984), 112–30.

47. Fuller, *Summer on the Lakes*, 109; for more on Fuller's depiction of Native Americans, see Laura L. Mielke, *Moving Encounters: Sympathy and the Indian Question in Antebellum Literature* (Amherst: University of Massachusetts Press, 2008), 94–114; Abrams, *Landscape and Ideology in American Renaissance Literature*, 75–102; and Susan Gilmore, "Margaret Fuller 'Receiving' the 'Indians,'" in Fleischmann, *Margaret Fuller's Cultural Critique*, 191–227.

48. Fuller, *Summer on the Lakes*, 18, 50, 71, 76, and 38.

49. Ibid., 5.

50. Ibid., 22 and 38.

51. Ibid., 28–9; and see von Mehren, *Minerva and the Muse*, 175.

52. Fuller, *Summer on the Lakes*, 79.

53. Ibid., 29, 33, and 124. On the question of Native Americans, generally speaking, as developing ways of living more in tune with nature's cycles, see Shepard Krech III, *The Ecological Indian: Myth and History* (New York: Norton, 1999), and Michael E. Harkin and David Rich Lewis, eds., *Native Americans and the Environment: Perspectives on the Ecological Indian* (Lincoln: University of Nebraska Press, 2007).

54. Fuller, *Summer on the Lakes*, 121 and 29.

55. Ibid., 12, 144, and 147.

56. Ibid., 76–7.

57. Ibid., 42–3. On Allston, see Susan Belasco Smith's "Introduction" to *Summer on the Lakes*, x.

58. Ibid., 41, 72, and 150.

59. Fuller, journal entry of Thursday, May 23, 1844, printed in Chevigny, *The Woman and the Myth*, 535.

60. Fuller, letter to William H. Channing, Chicago, August 16, 1843, in Hudspeth, *Letters of Margaret Fuller*, 142.

61. Thoreau quoted in Capper, *Margaret Fuller*, 121; also see ibid., 154, and Robert D. Richardson, Jr., *Henry Thoreau: A Life of the Mind* (Berkeley: University of California Press, 1986), 147 and 156.

62. See Capper, *Margaret Fuller*, 498–512; Murray, *Margaret Fuller*, 397–411; and von Mehren, *Minerva and the Muse*, 327–39.

63. Blanche M. G. Linden, *Silent City on a Hill: Picturesque Landscapes of Memory and Boston's Mount Auburn Cemetery* (Amherst: University of Massachusetts Press, 2007), 196–7.

64. Thoreau, journal entries for July or August, 1850, in *The Writings of Henry D. Thoreau: Journal: Volume 3, 1848–1851*, ed. Robert Sattelmeyer, Mark R. Patterson, and William Rossi (Princeton: Princeton University Press, 1990), 95 and 101. Also see Richardson, *Henry Thoreau*, 210–15, and Walter Harding, *The Days of Henry Thoreau* (New York: Knopf, 1965), 277–9. Besides these worthy guides to Thoreau's life, I have relied especially deeply on Lawrence Buell, *The Environmental Imagination: Thoreau, Nature Writing, and the Formation of American Culture* (Cambridge, MA: Harvard University Press, 1995), and Laura Dassow Walls, *Seeing New Worlds: Henry David Thoreau and Nineteenth-Century Natural Science* (Madison: University of Wisconsin Press, 1995); and also see Robert Pogue Harrison, *Forests: The Shadow of Civilization* (Chicago: University of Chicago Press, 1992), 220–32; Stanley Cavell, *The Senses of Walden*, expanded ed. (Chicago: University of Chicago Press, 1992); Lewis Perry, *Boats against the Current: American Culture between Revolution and Modernity, 1820–1860* (Lanham: Rowman & Littlefield, 1993), 141–51; Andrew McMurry, *Environmental Renaissance: Emerson, Thoreau, and the Systems of Nature* (Athens: University of Georgia Press, 2003), 131–83; Abrams, *Landscape and Ideology in American Renaissance Literature*, 41–55; Marx, *The Machine in the Garden*, 242–65; and Fussell, *Frontier*, 175–231 and 327–50.

65. Thoreau, *Cape Cod* (1865; New York: Penguin, 1987), 13–14.

66. See Richardson, *Henry Thoreau*, 386–7, and Harding, *The Days of Henry Thoreau*, 444–51.

67. Fuller, *Summer on the Lakes*, 116 and 12.

68. Thoreau, *Walden* (1854; Boston: Beacon Press, 2004), 10 and 34.

69. Thoreau, *A Week on the Concord and Merrimack Rivers* (1849; New York: Penguin, 1998), 13.

70. "Patriotic ode" is from Lewis Hyde, who truly is a sensitive and sympathetic reader of Thoreau; see his "Introduction: Prophetic Excursions," in Hyde, ed., *The Essays of Henry D. Thoreau* (New York: North Point Press, 2002), xxi. Thoreau quotations are from "Walking," in Elder, *Nature/Walking*, 95 and 80. Note that this piece started off as one lecture, "Walking; or the Wild," in 1851; then Thoreau split it into two different lectures during most of the 1850s; then, in 1861, he unified the material again into one essay called simply "Walking." Leo Marx, alas, finds the essay to be full of "tedious, homiletic assertion": see Marx, "Henry Thoreau," in *The Pilot and the Passenger: Essays on Literature, Technology, and Culture in the United States* (New York: Oxford University Press, 1988), 82. Rebecca Solnit is much more open-minded in her *Savage Dreams: A Journey into the Landscape Wars of the American West* (1994; Berkeley: University of California Press, 1999), 112–44.

71. Thoreau, "Walking," 86, 87, 90, and 94.

72. Ibid., 71.

73. A number of recent histories of the nineteenth-century United States, influenced by recent trends in postcolonial studies, focus on the complicity of all white, male Americans in structures and discourses of domination. A couple of representative examples are Dana D. Nelson, *National Manhood: Capitalist Citizenship and the Imagined Fraternity of White Men* (Durham: Duke University Press, 1998), and Shelley Streeby, *American Sensations: Class, Empire, and the Production of Popular Culture* (Berkeley: University of California

Press, 2002). On the postcolonial angle, see Aaron Sachs, "The Ultimate 'Other': Post-Colonialism and Alexander von Humboldt's Ecological Relationship with Nature," *History and Theory*, Theme Issue on the Environment, 42 (December 2003), 111–35.

74. Note the line ending the first paragraph of Thoreau's essay, "Civil Disobedience": "Witness the present Mexican war, the work of comparatively a few individuals using the standing government as their tool; for, in the outset, the people would not have consented to this measure"—in Hyde, *The Essays of Henry D. Thoreau*, 125.

75. See ibid., 148 and 337–8.

76. Thoreau, letter from February, 1853, quoted in Richardson, *Henry Thoreau*, 290.

77. Thoreau, "Walking," 94, 86, 93, and 89.

78. Too many histories of this time period fail to capture the contingency of American industrialism and westward expansion; to begin to explore this problem, see David E. Nye, *America as Second Creation: Technology and Narratives of New Beginnings* (Cambridge, MA: MIT Press, 2003); John Opie, *Nature's Nation: An Environmental History of the United States* (Fort Worth: Harcourt Brace, 1998), 84–241; Robert V. Hine and John Mack Faragher, *The American West: A New Interpretive History* (New Haven: Yale University Press, 2000), 159–511; and Walter Licht, *Industrializing America: The Nineteenth Century* (Baltimore: Johns Hopkins University Press, 1995).

79. Thoreau, *Walden*, 23–4.

80. Thoreau, "Walking," 104.

81. Ibid., 81, 107, 110, 115, and 111. Elsewhere, Thoreau noted that he actually appreciated returning home from his travels to "our smooth, but still varied landscape. For permanent residence, it seemed to me that there could be no comparison between this and the wilderness, necessary as the latter is for a resource and a background, the raw material of all our civilization. . . . Perhaps our own woods and fields,—in the best wooded towns, where we need not quarrel about the huckleberries,—with the primitive swamps scattered here and there in their midst, but not prevailing over them, are the perfection of . . . what art and refinement we as a people have,—the common which each village possesses, its true paradise"—Thoreau, *The Maine Woods* (1864; New York: Penguin, 1988), 210–11.

82. Thoreau, "Walking," 88.

83. In Thoreau's day, there was, in fact, a healthy debate about what development in the West might look like: see Machor's chapter "Landscape as Cityscape: Urbanization and the Western Garden," in his *Pastoral Cities*, 121–44.

84. Thoreau, "Walking," 121–2.

85. Thoreau, *Walden*, 85.

86. Harrison, *Forests*, 222. Clearly, withdrawing does not have to mean retreating from the social issues of the day. Elsewhere, Harrison argues that a true garden, "however self-enclosed," can often act as "a counterforce to history's deleterious drives"; it is "never a garden of merely private concerns into which one escapes from the real; it is that plot of soil on the earth, within the self, or amid the social collective, where the cultural, ethical, and civic virtues that save reality from its own worst impulses are cultivated. Those impulses are always *ours*." See Harrison, *Gardens: An Essay on the Human Condition* (Chicago: University of Chicago Press, 2008), x.

87. Thoreau, letter of March 2, 1842, Concord, to Lucy Brown, and letter of March 11, 1842, Concord, to Emerson, in Walter Harding and Carl Bode, eds., *The Correspondence of Henry David Thoreau* (1958; Westport: Greenwood Press, 1974), 63–5.
88. Thoreau quoted in Richardson, *Henry Thoreau*, 207 and 258.
89. Thoreau, *Walden*, 290–1.
90. Ibid., 149.
91. Thoreau, *A Week*, 127.
92. Thoreau, *Walden*, 105–6.
93. As Maura D'Amore has argued, Thoreau "insists that suburban spaces, even literary ones, promise more than escape; they offer opportunities to theorize and practice a new form of domesticity grounded in self-nurture and inner cultivation"; see her extremely useful article, contextualizing Thoreau's writings by pointing out his awareness of the rise of American suburbs: "Thoreau's Unreal Estate: Playing House at Walden Pond," *New England Quarterly* 82 (March 2009), 56–79, quotation on 59. Note also Milette Shamir's chapter, "Thoreau in Suburbia," in her *Inexpressible Privacy: The Interior Life of Antebellum American Literature* (Philadelphia: University of Pennsylvania Press, 2006), 175–208.
94. Robert P. Harrison, "Toward a Philosophy of Nature," in Cronon, *Uncommon Ground*, 436–7.
95. Thoreau, *A Week*, 137 and 284.
96. See ibid., 208–33; quotations on 213, 228, 221, and 229–30.
97. As Robert Harrison has put it, "the surrounding world of nature, which preceded us and will succeed us, offers us the spectacle of a longevity and an endurance that are denied us. This spectacle can be a source of anguish or of reassurance, depending on the relation we maintain within ourselves. A great deal of the destructiveness in our dealings with nature arises, it seems, from a stubborn refusal to come to terms with our finitude, to accept our fundamental limitations." Harrison posits that "the ways we try to deny the facts of life . . . are multiple and historical, forever changing with the transformations of culture." But he also wonders—in a move that may be hard for some historians to swallow—whether some form of such denial may be "original, transhistorical, and unredeemable" (Harrison, "Toward a Philosophy of Nature," 436–7).

      It is perhaps also notable that Harrison's *Forests* is dedicated to his friend, the French philosopher Michel Serres, whose own book, *The Natural Contract*, is dedicated to Harrison. "We must learn our finitude . . . ," Serres writes. "Necessarily we will have to suffer, from illnesses, unforeseeable accidents or lacks; we must set a term to our desires, ambitions, wills, freedoms. We must prepare our solitude, in the face of great decisions, responsibilities, growing numbers of other people; in the face of the world, the fragility of things and of loved ones to protect, in the face of happiness, unhappiness, death"—see *The Natural Contract*, trans. Elizabeth MacArthur and William Paulson (Ann Arbor: University of Michigan Press, 1995; orig. pub. in French, 1990), 95.
98. Thoreau, *A Week*, 7, 269, 282, and 305.
99. Thomas Blanding, "A Last Word from Thoreau," *The Concord Saunterer* 11 (Winter 1976), 16–17.

100. See Harding, *The Days of Henry Thoreau*, 357–8, 460, 199, 464, 462–3, 322–4, and 466; Raymond R. Borst, *The Thoreau Log: A Documentary Life of Henry David Thoreau, 1817–1862* (New York: G. K. Hall, 1992), 603–11; and Thoreau, "Autumnal Tints," in Hyde, *The Essays of Henry D. Thoreau*, 230. Also note Simon Critchley, *The Book of Dead Philosophers* (New York: Vintage, 2009), 180–1.

## 3. SLEEPY HOLLOW

1. Irving recommended the name "Sleepy Hollow" for the cemetery in 1849, but his suggestion was not actually implemented until the mid-1860s; see *Sleepy Hollow Cemetery, at Tarrytown, on the Hudson River* (New York: C. S. Westcott, 1866), 1; also note Thomas G. Connors, "The Romantic Landscape: Washington Irving, Sleepy Hollow, and the Rural Cemetery Movement," in Nancy Isenberg and Andrew Burstein, eds., *Mortal Remains: Death in Early America* (Philadelphia: University of Pennsylvania Press, 2003), 187–203; and for Irving's general influence on his home region see Judith Richardson, *Possessions: The History and Uses of Haunting in the Hudson Valley* (Cambridge, MA: Harvard University Press, 2003), 1–80. On the potential relationship between the two Sleepy Hollows, see Leslie Perrin Wilson, *In History's Embrace: Past and Present in Concord, Massachusetts* (Hollis, NH: Hollis Publishing, 2007), 88.

2. See, for instance, David Schuyler, "The Sanctified Landscape: The Hudson River Valley, 1820 to 1850," in George F. Thompson, ed., *Landscape in America* (Austin: University of Texas Press, 1995), 93–109; Richard H. Gassan, *The Birth of American Tourism: New York, the Hudson Valley, and American Culture, 1790–1830* (Amherst: University of Massachusetts Press, 2008); Tom Lewis, *The Hudson: A History* (New Haven: Yale University Press, 2005), 186–224; David Stradling, *Making Mountains: New York City and the Catskills* (Seattle: University of Washington Press, 2007), 46–75; Nassau County Museum of Fine Art, *William Cullen Bryant and the Hudson River School of Landscape Painting* (Roslyn: Nassau County Museum of Fine Art, 1981); John R. Stilgoe, *Borderland: Origins of the American Suburb, 1820–1939* (New Haven: Yale University Press, 1988), 22–123; Judith K. Major, *To Live in the New World: A. J. Downing and American Landscape Gardening* (Cambridge, MA: MIT Press, 1997), 10–24; and Kenneth Myers, *The Catskills: Painters, Writers, and Tourists in the Mountains, 1820–1895* (Yonkers: Hudson River Museum of Westchester, 1987).

3. James Fenimore Cooper also had a great deal to do with creating the iconic status of upstate New York, but ultimately he was less influential than Washington Irving and less of an Arcadian than his daughter Susan. The real impact of his *Leatherstocking Tales* came in the mid-1820s, after Irving had already established himself with tales like "Rip Van Winkle" and "The Legend of Sleepy Hollow," and most of Cooper's popular books depend for their interest on romantic wilderness adventures more than on the complex challenge of settlement—though one could certainly make an argument for the original Natty Bumppo trilogy of *The Pioneers* (1823), *The Last of the Mohicans* (1826), and *The Prairie* (1827) as important Arcadian texts. For useful readings of Cooper, see Laura L. Mielke, *Moving Encounters: Sympathy and the Indian Question in Antebellum Literature* (Amherst: University of

Massachusetts Press, 2008), 36–50 (and especially note her emphasis on the importance of burial and mourning in the *Leatherstocking* books); Edwin Fussell, *Frontier: American Literature and the American West* (Princeton: Princeton University Press, 1965), 27–68; Annette Kolodny, *The Lay of the Land: Metaphor as Experience and History in American Letters* (Chapel Hill: University of North Carolina Press, 1975), 89–115; Alan Taylor, *William Cooper's Town: Power and Persuasion on the Frontier of the Early American Republic* (New York: Vintage, 1996); and Lee Clark Mitchell, "Still Landscapes and Moral Restraint," in Mitchell, *Westerns: Making the Man in Fiction and Film* (Chicago: University of Chicago Press, 1996), 28–54.

4. Nathaniel W. Coffin, *The Forest Arcadia of Northern New York* (Boston: T. O. H. P. Burnham, 1864), 32–3, 195, 194, and 193.

5. Ibid., 193 and 6. On aesthetics and nostalgia, see Leo Marx, *The Machine in the Garden: Technology and the Pastoral Ideal in America* (New York: Oxford, 1964); John Opie, *Nature's Nation: An Environmental History of the United States* (Fort Worth: Harcourt Brace, 1998); John W. Reps, *The Making of Urban America: A History of City Planning in the United States* (Princeton: Princeton University Press, 1965), 294–314; and Adam Sweeting, *Reading Houses and Building Books: Andrew Jackson Downing and the Architecture of Popular Antebellum Literature, 1835–1855* (Hanover, NH: University Press of New England, 1996). On environmental perspectives as predominantly reactive, see David E. Nye, *America as Second Creation: Technology and Narratives of New Beginnings* (Cambridge, MA: MIT Press, 2003); on environmental perspectives as ultimately complicit, see Matthew Gandy, *Concrete and Clay: Reworking Nature in New York City* (Cambridge, MA: MIT Press, 2002), 77–113, and Dell Upton, *Another City: Urban Life and Urban Spaces in the New American Republic* (New Haven: Yale University Press, 2009).

It should be noted, though, that a new wave of spatially sophisticated history, just in the past decade or so, has been putting a slightly different spin on what, from a materialist ecological perspective, was clearly a time of steadily increasing damage. See, for instance: Anne Baker, *Heartless Immensity: Literature, Culture, and Geography in Antebellum America* (Ann Arbor: University of Michigan Press, 2006); Stephanie LeMenager, *Manifest and Other Destinies: Territorial Fictions of the Nineteenth-Century United States* (Lincoln: University of Nebraska Press, 2004); and Steven Stoll, *Larding the Lean Earth: Soil and Society in Nineteenth-Century America* (New York: Hill & Wang, 2002).

6. A good example of this scholarly perspective is M. K. Heiman, "Production Confronts Consumption: Landscape Perception and Social Conflict in the Hudson Valley," *Environment and Planning D: Society and Space* 7 (June 1989), 165–78.

7. This is just one of many images of tanneries and the tanning process that circulated at the time; they appeared as oil paintings and poster-sized lithographs but also in the era's newspapers and magazines. For several examples, see Alf Evers, *The Catskills: From Wilderness to Woodstock* (Garden City, New York: Doubleday, 1972).

8. The Catskills are the preeminent example from this period; see Stradling, *Making Mountains*, 46–108. Also note that such areas could take on a widely perceived health value, as Gregg Mitman argues in his *Breathing Space: How Allergies Shape Our Lives and Landscapes* (New Haven: Yale University Press, 2007), 10–51.

9. One can still visit Pratt Rocks, on the side of Route 23, and I'd recommend the trip highly. Pratt considered himself something of a tree lover, though of course that didn't prevent him from spending twenty years thoroughly deforesting the area around his company town. More important, it's worth noting just how significant tanning was in the general development of American industrialism: as of 1850, it was among the top six industries in terms of "the number of employees, the value added by manufacture, the capital invested, and the number of establishments." See Lucius F. Ellsworth, *Craft to National Industry in the Nineteenth Century: A Case Study of the Transformation of the New York State Tanning Industry* (New York: Arno Press, 1975), quotation from unpaginated preface; Evers, *The Catskills*, 332–77 (esp. 341–50 on Pratt); Martin Bruegel, *Farm, Shop, Landing: The Rise of a Market Society in the Hudson Valley, 1780–1860* (Durham: Duke University Press, 2002), 81–3, quotations on 82–3; Lewis, *The Hudson*, 217–220, quotation on 220; Heiman, "Production Confronts Consumption," 169; and Stradling, *Making Mountains*, 20–45.

10. See Gunther Peck, "The Nature of Labor: Fault Lines and Common Ground in Environmental and Labor History," *Environmental History* 11 (April 2006) 226–8; Reeve Huston, *Land and Freedom: Rural Society, Popular Protest, and Party Politics in Antebellum New York* (New York: Oxford University Press, 2000); and Jonathan H. Earle, *Jacksonian Antislavery and the Politics of Free Soil, 1825–54* (Chapel Hill: University of North Carolina Press, 2004), 17–47.

11. John Humphrey Noyes, "First Annual Report of the Oneida Association," in Lawrence Foster, ed., *Free Love in Utopia: John Humphrey Noyes and the Origin of the Oneida Community* (Urbana: University of Illinois Press, 2001), 298 and 309. On Oneida, see Lawrence Foster, *Women, Family, and Utopia: Communal Experiments of the Shakers, the Oneida Community, and the Mormons* (Syracuse: Syracuse University Press, 1991), 75–120; Mark Holloway, *Heavens on Earth: Utopian Communities in America, 1680–1880* (New York: Dover, 1966), 179–97; and Dolores Hayden, *Seven American Utopias: The Architecture of Communitarian Socialism, 1790–1975* (Cambridge, MA: MIT Press, 1976), 186–223.

12. Bovay quoted in Robert D. Richardson, Jr., *Henry Thoreau: A Life of the Mind* (Berkeley: University of California Press, 1986), 150.

13. Noyes, "First Annual Report," 332–3.

14. Quotations from "Llewellyn Park," *The Independent*, May 26, 1864, 4 (this article, according to a later advertisement, was written by Theodore Tilton, who apparently owned land at Llewellyn Park but never built on it; see ibid., August 10, 1865, 6); from Henry Winthrop Sargent's 1859 supplement to Downing's *Treatise on the Theory and Practice of Landscape Gardening, Adapted to North America*, 6th ed. (New York: A. O. Moore, 1859), 569; and from Richard Guy Wilson, "Idealism and the Origin of the First American Suburb: Llewellyn Park, New Jersey," *American Art Journal* 11 (October 1979), 85—and also note the reference to Tilton as a landowner on 89. All further quotations from Downing's *Treatise* are to this (posthumous) 1859 edition, edited by Sargent, unless otherwise indicated; the first edition came out in 1841. For a useful analysis of the changes that occurred over the course of the different editions, see Major, *To Live in the New World*.

Also see "Llewellyn Park: Country Homes for City People," *The Independent*, May 11, 1865, 6 (continued on May 18, 1865, 6); Susan Henderson, "Llewellyn Park, Suburban Idyll,"

*Journal of Garden History* 7 (July–September 1987), 221–43; Jane B. Davies, "Llewellyn Park in West Orange, New Jersey," *Antiques* 107 (January 1975), 142–58; Dolores Hayden, *Building Suburbia: Green Fields and Urban Growth, 1820–2000* (New York: Vintage, 2004), 54–61; David Schuyler, *The New Urban Landscape: The Redefinition of City Form in Nineteenth-Century America* (Baltimore: Johns Hopkins University Press, 1986), 157–9; and Stilgoe, *Borderland*, 52–5.

15. William C. Bryant, Esq., *An Oration, Delivered at Stockbridge. July 4th, 1820* (Stockbridge: Charles Webster, 1820), 9.

16. Bryant quoted in Allan Nevins, *The Evening Post: A Century of Journalism* (New York: Boni & Liveright, 1922), 194 and 196.

17. Bryant, *The American Landscape* (New York: Elam Bliss, 1830), 15.

18. N. P. Willis, *American Scenery* (1840; Barre, MA: Imprint Society, 1971).

19. Irving, "The Catskill Mountains," in *The Home Book of the Picturesque: Or American Scenery, Art, and Literature* (New York: G. P. Putnam, 1852), 72–3; and Irving, "Forest Trees," in *Bracebridge Hall* (1822; Boston: Twayne, 1977), 60. To my knowledge, no firm documentation has been found proving the editorship of the *Home Book*, but it seems likely that William Cullen Bryant initiated and directed the project; see Motley F. Deakin, "Introduction" to the facsimile edition of the *Home Book* (Gainesville: Scholars' Facsimiles and Reprints, 1967), n.p. Widely popular, the volume featured essays not only by Irving and Bryant but also James Fenimore Cooper, his daughter Susan Cooper, and N. P. Willis, as well as artwork by such prominent artists as Thomas Cole, Asher B. Durand, Jasper Cropsey, and Frederic Church.

20. Irving, *Wolfert's Roost* (1855; Boston: Twayne, 1979), 4; Cooper, *Rural Hours* (1850; Athens: University of Georgia Press, 1998), 108.

21. Bryant, "Washington Irving," in Parke Godwin, ed., *Prose Writings of William Cullen Bryant*, vol. 1 (New York: D. Appleton, 1889), 332–68, quotations on 363 and 348.

Thomas Cole painted a picture called *Landscape, Sleepy Hollow* (1835), though it is unlocated; see Cole, *Exhibition of the Paintings of the Late Thomas Cole, at the Gallery of the American Art-Union* (New York: Snowden & Prall, 1848), 15, and Elwood C. Parry III, *The Art of Thomas Cole: Ambition and Imagination* (Newark: University of Delaware Press, 1988), 164.

22. Andrew Burstein, *The Original Knickerbocker: The Life of Washington Irving* (New York: Basic Books, 2007), 329–30; quotation on 330.

23. "Irving Park, Tarrytown," *Harper's Weekly* 4 (January 28, 1860), 52; also see *Description of Irving Park, Tarrytown; The Property of Charles H. Lyon* (New York: Wynkoop, Hallenbeck & Thomas, 1859); and Schuyler, *New Urban Landscape*, 160–1. On Croton, see Gerard T. Koeppel, *Water for Gotham: A History* (Princeton: Princeton University Press, 2000).

24. This conclusion, though clear-cut in my opinion, is questioned in Hayden, *Building Suburbia*, 50, and openly disputed in John Archer, "Country and City in the American Romantic Suburb," *Journal of the Society of Architectural Historians* 42 (May 1983), 139.

25. Nathaniel Hawthorne, "The Celestial Rail-road," in *Mosses from an Old Manse* (1846), vol. 10 of *The Centenary Edition of the Works of Nathaniel Hawthorne* (Columbus: Ohio State

University Press, 1974), 187 and 192–4; note that the story was first published in 1843 in the *United States Magazine and Democratic Review.*

26. William Cullen Bryant, ed., *Selections from American Poets,* Harpers' Family Library No. 111 (New York: Harper & Brothers, 1840), 84–5. The vast majority of the poems are on nature themes, with no other topic even close. In fact, the only other subjects covered with any consistency in the collection are Native Americans, death, and religion.

27. See, for instance, Christopher Lasch, *The True and Only Heaven: Progress and Its Critics* (New York: Norton, 1991), esp. 184–282; and Lewis Perry, *Boats against the Current: American Culture between Revolution and Modernity, 1820–1860* (Lanham: Rowman & Littlefield, 1993), 105–51.

28. N. P. Willis, *Out-Doors at Idlewild; or, The Shaping of a Home on the Banks of the Hudson* (New York: Charles Scribner, 1855), 286–8 (Idlewild was the name Willis had given to his estate, perhaps invoking the radicalism of idleness in his perfervidly active society). Also see Stilgoe, *Borderland,* 25–32.

    Willis certainly did have an elitist streak, but he tried to adopt an inclusive approach to his rural advocacy, focusing on modest, middle-class improvements that could be accomplished "by the tasteful farmer, or the tradesman retired on small means. . . . As Nature lets the tree grow and the flower expand for a man, without reference to his account at the bank, they have it in their power to embellish, and, most commonly, they have also the inclination." N. Parker Willis, *Rural Letters* (1849; Auburn and Rochester: Alden & Beardsley, 1856), 175.

    Moreover, Willis made sure to advertise his own private estate as a thoroughly public space, where visitors, even perfect strangers, never needed to ask permission to wander the grounds: he noted in 1855 that approximately fifty strangers a day strolled through Idlewild (*Out-Doors at Idlewild,* 155).

29. Robert Pogue Harrison, *Forests: The Shadow of Civilization* (Chicago: University of Chicago Press, 1992), 222. "Where the afterlife of the dead receives new life," Harrison writes elsewhere, "the earth as a whole receives a new blessing." See his book *The Dominion of the Dead* (Chicago: University of Chicago Press, 2003), the entirety of which is really an elaboration of the several pages in *Forests* that deal with death and dying; quotation on 123.

30. Cooper, *Rural Hours,* 45–6 and 179–80, and "A Dissolving View," in *Home Book of the Picturesque,* 82. Robert Harrison, 150 years later, agreed that we must cultivate the kind of "kinship that makes the earth the caretaker of cultural memory and cultural memory the caretaker of the earth" (*Dominion of the Dead,* 50).

    Also note that "A Dissolving View" is usefully reprinted, along with several other essays, in Rochelle Johnson and Daniel Patterson, eds., *Susan Fenimore Cooper: Essays on Nature and Landscape* (Athens: University of Georgia Press, 2002), 3–16. As Johnson and Patterson note elsewhere, Cooper's style of "subtle lamentation might seem merely the effete ramblings of the privileged elite if not for Cooper's criticism of the capitalistic culture that is responsible for the unsustainable practices she opposes"; see Johnson and Patterson, "Introduction," in Cooper, *Rural Hours,* xx. Johnson and Patterson have also edited a volume of scholarly articles about Cooper: *Susan Fenimore Cooper: New Essays on Rural Hours and Other Works* (Athens: University of Georgia Press, 2001); a particularly relevant contribution to that volume is Duncan Faherty, "The Borderers of Civilization: Susan Fenimore Cooper's View of American Development" (109–126), which pays particular attention to "A Dissolving View" and to the influence of Thomas Cole and Andrew Jackson Downing on Cooper's work; and also see Laura Dassow Walls, *The Passage to Cosmos: Alexander von Humboldt and the Shaping of America* (Chicago: University of Chicago Press, 2009), 284–90.

Cooper, despite her strong identity as an independent writer, was not nearly the feminist that Margaret Fuller was; her rhetoric about blending humanity and nature did not have much corresponding resonance in the realm of gender roles—though it is important to observe that the Arcadian tradition of which she was a part was much less stereotypically male than the wilderness romance tradition that was so crucial to her father. See Vera Norwood, *Made from This Earth: American Women and Nature* (Chapel Hill: University of North Carolina Press, 1993), 25–53, and Jessie Ravage, "In Response to the Women at Seneca Falls: Susan Fenimore Cooper and the Rightful Place of Woman in America," in Johnson and Patterson, *Susan Fenimore Cooper: New Essays*, 249–65.

31. It is also worth noting, though, that when Cooper invited three Oneida women into her home, she found that "there was something startling and very painful in hearing these poor creatures within our own community, and under our own roof, declaring themselves heathens!" She observed that Natives often reacted poorly to contact with whites, but, importantly, she acknowledged that they had a right to be angry, and she expressed not just a sense of guilt but a sense of responsibility, a desire to help Indians both retain their dignity and blend into the American citizenry: "It is easy to wish these poor people well; but surely something more may justly be required of us—of those who have taken their country and their place on earth. . . . They have shown bravery, fortitude, religious feeling, eloquence, imagination, quickness of intellect, with much dignity of manner; and if we are true to our duty, now at the moment when they are making of their own accord a movement in the path of improvement, perhaps the day may not be distant when men of Indian blood may be numbered among the wise and good, laboring in behalf of our common country." See Cooper, *Rural Hours*, 109 and 112.

32. See, for instance, Hayden, *Building Suburbia*, 34. For a more sympathetic reading of Downing's interest in "taste," and for the most useful biographical treatment of Downing, see David Schuyler, *Apostle of Taste: Andrew Jackson Downing, 1815–1852* (Baltimore: Johns Hopkins University Press, 1996).

33. See, for instance, Elizabeth Kolbert, "Turf War: Americans Can't Live Without Their Lawns—But How Long Can They Live with Them?" *New Yorker*, July 21, 2008, 82–6, and Virginia Scott Jenkins, *The Lawn: A History of an American Obsession* (Washington, DC: Smithsonian Institution Press, 1994), 23–7.

34. See Jennifer Price, *Flight Maps: Adventures with Nature in Modern America* (New York: Basic Books, 1999), 119–23; Gandy, *Concrete and Clay*, 82–3 and 91; and Sweeting, *Reading Houses and Building Books*, 75–6; also see Philip J. Pauly, *Fruits and Plains: The Horticultural Transformation of America* (Cambridge, MA: Harvard University Press, 2007), 170–1; Therese O'Malley, "Introduction" to A. J. Downing, *A Treatise on the Theory and Practice of Landscape Gardening, Adapted to North America* (Washington, DC: Dumbarton Oaks,

1991), v–xii; Stilgoe, *Borderland*, 86–7; Tamara Plakins Thornton, *Cultivating Gentlemen: The Meaning of Country Life among the Boston Elite, 1785–1860* (New Haven: Yale University Press, 1989), 164–8; Kenneth T. Jackson, *Crabgrass Frontier: The Suburbanization of the United States* (New York: Oxford University Press, 1985), 63–6 (Jackson calls Downing "a snob and an aloof aesthete," 64); and Hayden, *Building Suburbia*, 26–35.

    Downing is portrayed much more positively in Schuyler's works; and see also Major, *To Live in the New World*; George B. Tatum, ed., *Prophet with Honor: The Career of Andrew Jackson Downing, 1815–1852* (Washington, DC: Dumbarton Oaks, 1989); and Robert Twombly, "Andrew Jackson Downing," *Reviews in American History* 26 (September 1998), 531–40.

35. Downing, *Treatise* (6th ed.), vii and ix–x.
36. A. J. Downing, *The Fruits and Fruit Trees of America* (1845; New York: John Wiley, 1850), vi and v.
37. Downing, "Trees in Towns and Villages," in A. J. Downing, *Rural Essays*, ed. George William Curtis (1853; New York: Geo. A. Leavitt, 1869), 303. Also note the entire section on "Trees" in *Rural Essays* (289–382) and especially "Shade-Trees in Cities," 311–18. And also note Willis in *Rural Letters*, v: "I felt—as a man fond of his grounds might do, who should see his favorite tree judged of by a single view at noon—a wish that it might be seen, also, with the shadows falling earlier and later."
38. Wilson Flagg, ed., *Mount Auburn: Its Scenes, Its Beauties, and Its Lessons* (Boston and Cambridge: James Munroe & Co., 1861), 263–4.
39. Downing, "Trees in Towns and Villages," in *Rural Essays*, 304.
40. Downing, "Influence of Horticulture," in *Rural Essays*, 13–14. Downing shares this perspective with many of the agronomists studied in Stoll, *Larding the Lean Earth*.
41. A. J. Downing, *The Architecture of Country Houses* (1850), ed. George B. Tatum (New York: Da Capo Press, 1968), 144.
42. Downing, "Influence of Horticulture," 16.
43. Downing, *Treatise*, 59.
44. Part of Downing's fundamental approach was to try to retain some rural qualities in America's national culture by defining it through horticulture, which seemed more capable of surviving an intense period of urbanization, instead of through agriculture. This perspective, in part, helps explain why Arcadians expressed such complicated views of agricultural development, sometimes seeing it as far superior to industrialism and sometimes attacking it as being pursued in America with the same expansive overzealousness as manufacturing. Horticulture held just as much rural value as agriculture, as it were, but it was generally pursued under more gentle and calm circumstances. Still, like most Arcadians, Downing did not want to see Jefferson's agrarianism disappear completely: note, for instance, the eight articles organized under the heading "Agriculture," in *Rural Essays*, 385–431. "The agricultural class," he wrote, "perhaps is still wanting in a just appreciation of its importance, its rights, and its duties. It has so long listened to sermons, lectures, and orations from those who live in cities and look upon country life as '*something for dull wits*,' that it still needs apostles who draw their daily breath in green fields, and are untrammeled by the schools of politics and trade" (389).
45. See Harrison, "What Is a House?" in *Dominion of the Dead*, 37–54.

46. Downing, "A Few Hints on Landscape Gardening," in *Rural Essays*, 121.

47. Downing, "Public Cemeteries and Public Gardens," ibid., 155 and 157.

48. Tatum, "Nature's Gardener," in Tatum, *Prophet with Honor*, 56 and 79; and Jane B. Davies, "Davis and Downing: Collaborators in the Picturesque," ibid., 93. Note that Davis also designed Idlewild for N. P. Willis shortly after Downing's death.

49. Quoted in Schuyler, *Apostle of Taste*, 76.

50. See ibid., 204–8.

51. Downing, "Our Country Villages," in *Rural Essays*, 240 and 239. On the laws and policies governing the commodification of land in this time period and immediately beforehand, see Paul W. Gates, *The Jeffersonian Dream: Studies in the History of American Land Policy and Development* (Albuquerque: University of New Mexico Press, 1996); Andro Linklater, *Measuring America: How the United States Was Shaped by the Greatest Land Sale in History* (New York: Plume, 2003); and Malcolm J. Rohrbough, *The Land Office Business: The Settlement and Administration of American Public Lands, 1789–1837* (New York: Oxford University Press, 1968).

52. Downing, "Our Country Villages," in *Rural Essays*, 236–43. Also note that Susan Fenimore Cooper, clearly influenced by Downing, made many of the same points some years later in her essay, "Village Improvement Societies" (1869); see Johnson and Patterson, *Susan Fenimore Cooper: Essays*, 64–77.

53. Schuyler, *New Urban Landscape*, 160. Schuyler captures the contingency of nineteenth-century development, as does Mona Domosh, in *Invented Cities: The Creation of Landscape in Nineteenth-Century New York and Boston* (New Haven: Yale University Press, 1996). Other scholars, like Dell Upton (*Another City*), tend to emphasize what they see as America's inevitably capitalistic form. More broadly, on the significance and possibilities of landscape awareness and urban and suburban planning in mid-nineteenth-century America, also see: James L. Machor, *Pastoral Cities: Urban Ideals and the Symbolic Landscape of America* (Madison: University of Wisconsin Press, 1987), 121–203; Stanley K. Schultz, *Constructing Urban Culture: American Cities and City Planning, 1800–1920* (Philadelphia: Temple University Press, 1989), esp. 153–61; Stilgoe, *Borderland*, 1–161; Thomas Bender, *Toward an Urban Vision: Ideas and Institutions in Nineteenth Century America* (1975; Baltimore: Johns Hopkins University Press, 1991); David M. Scobey, *Empire City: The Making and Meaning of the New York City Landscape* (Philadelphia: Temple University Press, 2002); and Jon A. Peterson, *The Birth of City Planning in the United States, 1840–1917* (Baltimore: Johns Hopkins University Press, 2003), 12–54.

54. See Schuyler, *Apostle of Taste*, 192–202, quotations on 192–3; Mount Auburn quotation from Linden, *Silent City on a Hill*, 12. Note Calvert Vaux's claim, in a letter paraphrased by Schuyler, about Downing's hope that his design for Washington would serve as a positive example for urban communities around the country (*Apostle of Taste*, 202).

55. Downing, "The New-York Park," in *Rural Essays*, 147–53.

56. See George William Curtis, "Memoir," in *Rural Essays*, liii–lviii; "Burning of the Henry Clay," *Knickerbocker* 40 (October 1852), 343; "The Henry Clay Catastrophe," *New-York Daily Times*, July 30, 1852; and Kris A. Hansen, *Death Passage on the Hudson: The Wreck of the Henry Clay* (Fleischmanns: Purple Mountain Press, 2004), 40–81, esp. 41, 69, and 79–80.

57. Curtis, "Memoir," lvii; Wilder quoted in Schuyler, *Apostle of Taste*, 223.

58. Copeland's book is R. Morris Copeland, *Country Life: A Handbook of Agriculture, Horticulture, and Landscape Gardening* (Boston: John P. Jewett, 1859); Cleveland's article is H. W. S. C., "Landscape Gardening," *Christian Examiner and Religious Miscellany* (May 1855), 384–401, quotations on 389 and 386; Cleveland and Copeland quotation, *A Few Words on the Central Park* (Boston: n.p., 1856), 4; on the Central Park competition, see Schuyler, *New Urban Landscape*, 75–83, and Roy Rosenzweig and Elizabeth Blackmar, *The Park and the People: A History of Central Park* (Ithaca: Cornell University Press, 1992), 95–9 and 111–120.

59. Olmsted (and then Olmsted and Vaux) quoted in Schuyler, *The New Urban Landscape*, 91 and 85. On Seneca Village, see Rosenzweig and Blackmar, *The Park and the People*, 64–73.

60. Quoted in Schuyler, *Apostle of Taste*, 210.

61. Downing, "The New-York Park," 152.

62. The engravers featured in *American Scenery* (William H. Bartlett) and *Rural Cemeteries of America* (James Smillie) were two of the most famous in the nation. See Albert F. Moritz, *America the Picturesque in Nineteenth-Century Engraving* (New York: New Trend, 1983); Peter C. Mazio, *The Democratic Art: Pictures for a 19th-Century America: Chromolithography 1840–1900* (Boston: David R. Godine, 1979); Theodore E. Stebbins, Jr., ed., *The Hudson River School: 19th-Century American Landscapes in the Wadsworth Atheneum* (Hartford: Wadsworth Atheneum, 1976); Barbara Novak, *Nature and Culture: American Landscape Painting 1825–1875* (New York: Oxford University Press, 1980); Angela Miller, *The Empire of the Eye: Landscape Representation and American Cultural Politics, 1825–1875* (Ithaca: Cornell University Press, 1993); and Andrew Wilton and Tim Barringer, *American Sublime: Landscape Painting in the United States, 1820–1880* (London: Tate, 2002).

63. See Novak, *Nature and Culture*, Miller, *The Empire of the Eye*, and Wilton and Barringer, *American Sublime*; and on Cole specifically see Parry, *The Art of Thomas Cole*; Louis Legrand Noble, *The Life and Works of Thomas Cole* (1853; Cambridge, MA: Harvard University Press, 1964); Earl A. Powell, *Thomas Cole* (New York: Harry N. Abrams, 1990); and William H. Truettner and Alan Wallach, eds., *Thomas Cole: Landscape into History* (New Haven: Yale University Press, 1994).

64. Note that *The Course of Empire* was sometimes misunderstood by confident Americans as being about Europe rather than about the development of their own country; see Angela Miller's useful discussion, *The Empire of the Eye*, 21–39.

65. Cole, letter to Durand, Catskill, February 12, 1838, printed in Noble, *The Life and Works of Thomas Cole*, 188.

66. Quotation is from Margaret S. Nesbitt, in Stebbins, *The Hudson River School*, 27; Orpheus interpretation is from Parry, *The Art of Thomas Cole*, 294–5.

67. Cole, journal entry for October 7, 1841, printed in Noble, *The Life and Works of Thomas Cole*, 226–7.

68. Cole, journal entries for early October, 1828, ibid., 65–7; "Chocorua's Curse" (1830), in Child, *Hobomok and Other Writings on Indians*, ed. Carolyn L. Harcher (1986; New Brunswick: Rutgers University Press, 1998), 161–7. Cole's original painting is unlocated; Child probably saw the engraving rather than the painting, anyway; see Parry, *The Art of Thomas Cole*, 85–6. On Child, see Mielke, *Moving Encounters*, 15–35.

69. Child, "Chocorua's Curse," 166.

70. Hawthorne, "Sketches from Memory," in *Mosses*, 424.

71. Cole, journal entries for early October 1828, in Noble, *The Life and Works of Thomas Cole*, 66. Hawthorne made a point of noting "the red path-ways of the Slides, those avalanches of earth, stones, and trees, which descend into the hollows, leaving vestiges of their track, hardly to be effaced by the vegetation of ages." He stayed at Ethan Crawford's inn, and chatted with the other guests around the hearth: "The conversation of our party soon became more animated and sincere, and we recounted some traditions of the Indians, who believed that the father and mother of their race were saved from a deluge by ascending the peak of Mount Washington. The children of that pair have been overwhelmed, and found no such refuge. In the mythology of the savage, these mountains were afterwards considered sacred and inaccessible, full of unearthly wonders" (Hawthorne, "Sketches from Memory," in *Mosses*, 422 and 428).

72. Miller, *The Empire of the Eye*, 42. Also note Peter John Brownlee (with contributions by Michael S. Hogue and Angela Miller), *Manifest Destiny/Manifest Responsibility: Environmentalism and the Art of the American Landscape* (Chicago: Terra Foundation for American Art, 2008), which argues that a sense of environmental responsibility was not reflected in American paintings until the end of the nineteenth century.

73. Heiman, "Production Confronts Consumption," 169–70.

74. Cole, *Thomas Cole's Poetry*, ed. Marshall B. Tymn (York, PA: Liberty Cap Books, 1972), 112. The poem was published in *Knickerbocker* 17 (May 1841), 516–19, but was first written in 1838; an earlier version survives as "The Complaint of the Forest," printed in Cole, *Thomas Cole's Poetry*, 100–6. Cole dramatized the moment by describing himself simply sitting by the side of a lake and taking in the scenery, when "over my senses stole a sweet repose," and suddenly he could hear the voices of the trees (108). Also note his poem, "On Seeing that a Favorite Tree of the Author's Had Been Cut Down," dating from 1834 (67–8), in which he carefully distinguished between death by natural causes and death caused by human ruthlessness and greed and by the "unpitying axe": "Death sometimes leaves hope. . . . But here no hope survives—never again shall o'er me spread / Never again, the gentle shade of my beloved tree."

75. Cole, letter to Luman Reed, Catskill, March 26, 1836, in Noble, *The Life and Works of Thomas Cole*, 161.

76. Cole, "Essay on American Scenery," in John Conron, ed., *The American Landscape: A Critical Anthology of Prose and Poetry* (New York: Oxford University Press, 1973), 578; Cole's essay was originally published in January 1836.

77. Cole, journal entry for August 1, 1836, in Noble, *The Life and Works of Thomas Cole*, 164.

78. Note such paintings as *Landscape* from 1825 (see Powell, *Thomas Cole*, 17) and *Catskill Scenery* from 1833 (see Truettner and Wallach, *Thomas Cole*, 54). "When they did address human habitation in the valley," Heiman argues, "Cole and the other artists typically preferred Sunday scenes so as to avoid signs of work and the harsher realities of tenant farming" ("Production Confronts Consumption," 170). But *Landscape* foregrounds a red-shirted settler swinging an axe, and *Catskill Scenery* offers a view of fairly intensive settlement, including a mill, some rough dirt roads, and even a brown, clear-cut hillside.

79. See Aaron Sachs, *The Humboldt Current: Nineteenth-Century Exploration and the Roots of American Environmentalism* (New York: Viking, 2006), 94–101.

80. On this painting, see Parry, *The Art of Thomas Cole*, 313–14.

81. "Mrs. Hemans," as she was usually known in the United States, wrote romantic, pictur-esque verses that were perfectly suited to American taste in the 1830s; her poems appear again and again in guidebooks to Mount Auburn and publications like *Rural Cemeteries of America.* Cole, in attempting to describe what he intended in *The Cross in the Wilderness*, simply quoted two stanzas of Mrs. Hemans's poem of the same name; see Cole, *Exhibition*, 6: "Silent and mournful sat an Indian Chief,/In the red sunset, by a grassy tomb;/His eyes, that might not weep, were dark with grief,/And his arms folded in majestic gloom,/And his bow lay unstrung beneath the mound,/ Which sanctified the gorgeous waste around./For a pale cross above its greensward rose,/Telling the cedars and the pines that there/Man's heart and hope had struggled with his woes,/And lifted from the dust a voice of prayer./Now all was hush'd, and eve's last splendor shone/With a rich sadness on th'attesting stone."

82. See J. A. Scott Kelso and David A. Engstrøm, *The Complementary Nature* (Cambridge, MA: MIT Press, 2006).

83. Cole, *Exhibition*, 9.

84. Amy K. Blank, "Eisegesis," in *"I Know Four" and Other Things* (Cincinnati: privately published, 1981), 23.

85. William Cullen Bryant, *A Funeral Oration, Occasioned by the Death of Thomas Cole, Delivered before the National Academy of Design, New-York, May 4, 1848* (New York: D. Appleton, 1848), 37.

86. Cole's last words from Noble, *The Life and Works of Thomas Cole*, 306; Bryant, *A Funeral Oration*, 35.

87. Keats quoted in Wilton and Barringer, *American Sublime*, 68. On Durand, who started his career as an engraver, also see Barbara Babcock Millhouse, *American Wilderness: The Story of the Hudson River School of Painting* (Hensonville: Black Dome Press, 2007), 8–12, 50–53, and 66–73; Kathryn E. Gamble, *A. B. Durand, 1796–1886* (Montclair: Montclair Art Museum, 1971); and J. Gray Sweeney, "The Advantages of Genius and Virtue: Thomas Cole's Influence, 1848–58," in Truettner and Wallach, *Thomas Cole*, 114–16. Durand also painted a picture in 1850 that was based on Bryant's poem "Thanatopsis."

88. Cole, letter to Luman Reed, Catskill, March 28, 1836, in Noble, *The Life and Works of Thomas Cole*, 161. Also see Sweeney, "The Advantages of Genius and Virtue," 114–15, and Gerald L. Carr, *In Search of the Promised Land: Paintings by Frederic Edwin Church* (New York: Berry-Hill, 2000), 44–9.

   Despite the lack of a nearby tree or bush in Church's painting, Cole apparently wound up reposing right where he wanted to, "Where the free winds forever warble wild/Where yon far mountains steep; would constant look/Upon the grave of one who lov'd to gaze on them"—see his poem, "The Burial Ground at Catskill" (Cole, *Thomas Cole's Poetry*, 180), in which he also expressed a wish to be buried with "No marble pile, no vaunting verse . . . /To mark my resting place," since "pomp/An icier chill gives to the cold clay."

## 4. STUMPS

1. Figure 28 comes from the William Oland Bourne Papers, 1819–1901, Library of Congresss (LOC), Manuscript Division. Bourne was the chaplain at Central Park Hospital during the war. Stiles submitted the photo when he entered a left-handed writing contest, sponsored by Bourne, for soldiers who had lost their right arms in the war. In his handwriting sample, Stiles explained that it was "the first of May 1863 when we broke camp and marched for the *Wilderness* and it was march and fight then in stern reality for nine or ten days." Despite his reference to the Wilderness, his injury actually seems to have occurred at the Battle of Chancellorsville. The two battles took place in the same general location, a year apart (Chancellorsville in May 1863 and the Wilderness in May 1864), though conditions were more confusing in the latter, which was part of the reason it gained somewhat more notoriety and earned its own unique name, when it seemingly could have been called Second Chancellorsville. The photo is in Box 6, Folder 8. Stiles's handwriting entry is in Box 5, Folder 6, and is dated June 28, 1867.

2. See for instance Oliver Wendell Holmes, "The Human Wheel, Its Spokes and Felloes," *Atlantic Monthly* 11 (May 1863), 567–80. To Emily Dickinson, amputees perhaps embodied the nation's crisis of faith in the aftermath of war: "Those—dying then, / Knew where they went— / They went to God's Right Hand— / That Hand is amputated now / And God cannot be found—" (Poem 1551, in Thomas H. Johnson, ed., *Final Harvest: Emily Dickinson's Poems* [Boston: Little, Brown, 1961], 298). Also note the song sheets that have survived from this period, usually with titles like "The One-Legged Soldier"; the lyrics were almost all exactly the same (though the author is unknown, as far as I can tell), and individual veterans would have the sheets printed up with their names at the top, to personalize them. The soldiers would stand at street corners, singing and asking passersby to buy one of the sheets. A typical example, held today by the American Antiquarian Society, bears the heading, "George M. Reed, The One Arm and One Leg Soldier, Wounded at the Battle of Shiloh, Sunday Morning, April 6th, 1862."

3. Herman Melville, *Battle-Pieces and Aspects of the War* (New York: Harper & Brothers, 1866), quotation from "The Armies of the Wilderness," 97; note other poem titles, like: "Inscription for Graves at Pea Ridge, Arkansas"; "An Epitaph"; "The Mound by the Lake"; "On the Slain at Chickamauga"; "An uninscribed Monument on one of the Battle-fields of the Wilderness"; "On the Grave of a young Cavalry Officer killed in the Valley of Virginia"; "A Requiem for Soldiers lost in Ocean Transports"; and "On a natural Monument in a Field of Georgia." On Melville and the Civil War, see Andrew Delbanco, *Melville: His World and Work* (New York: Vintage, 2005), 266–79; Louis P. Masur, ed., ". . . *The Real War Will Never Get in the Books": Selections from Writers During the Civil War* (New York: Oxford University Press, 1993), 197–211; and Timothy Sweet, *Traces of War: Poetry, Photography, and the Crisis of the Union* (Baltimore: Johns Hopkins University Press, 1990), 165–200.

4. Walt Whitman, *Memoranda During the War* (Camden: author's publication, 1875–6), 5–6 and 3; Whitman, "The Wound-Dresser," in Mark Van Doren, ed., *The Portable Walt Whit-*

*man* (New York: Penguin, 1977), 228; note that "Drum-Taps" was the title of Whitman's book of war poems, originally published in 1865.

On Whitman and the Civil War, see Walter Lowenfels, ed., *Walt Whitman's Civil War* (New York: Knopf, 1960); Roy Morris, Jr., *The Better Angel: Walt Whitman in the Civil War* (New York: Oxford University Press, 2000); Robert Roper, *Now the Drum of War: Walt Whitman and His Brothers in the Civil War* (New York: Walker, 2008); Kevin Sharp (with contributions by Adam M. Thomas), *Bold Cautious True: Walt Whitman and American Art of the Civil War* (Memphis: Dixon Gallery and Gardens, 2009); M. Jimmie Killingsworth, *Walt Whitman and the Earth: A Study in Ecopoetics* (Iowa City: University of Iowa Press, 2004), 132–63; David S. Reynolds, *Walt Whitman's America: A Cultural Biography* (New York: Knopf, 1995), 383–494; Paul Zweig, *Walt Whitman: The Making of the Poet* (New York: Basic Books, 1984), 325–46; Sweet, *Traces of War*, 11–77; and Masur, ". . . *The Real War Will Never Get in the Books*", 252–81.

5. Whitman, *Memoranda*, 16, 14, and 57; Whitman, "Song of Myself," in *The Portable Walt Whitman*, 94; Whitman, *Specimen Days*, ibid., 482.

6. Leo Marx, *The Machine in the Garden: Technology and the Pastoral Ideal in America* (New York: Oxford, 1964), 220–2, quotation on 220. On Inness, also see Nicolai Cikovsky, Jr., and Michael Quick, *George Inness* (New York: Harper & Row, 1985), esp. 74–7; Rachael Ziady DeLue, *George Inness and the Science of Landscape* (Chicago: University of Chicago Press, 2004), esp. 106–21; and Michael Quick, *George Inness: A Catalogue Raisonné*, vol. 1 (New Brunswick: Rutgers University Press, 2007), esp. 112–15.

7. Char Miller, *Gifford Pinchot and the Making of Modern Environmentalism* (Washington, DC: Island Press, 2001), esp. 108–10.

8. See David E. Nye, *America as Second Creation: Technology and Narratives of New Beginnings* (Cambridge, MA: MIT Press, 2003), esp. 75–8; Michael Williams, *Americans and Their Forests: A Historical Geography* (New York: Cambridge University Press, 1989), 393–6; and Thomas R. Cox, Robert S. Maxwell, Phillip Drennon Thomas, and Joseph J. Malone, *This Well-Wooded Land: Americans and Their Forests from Colonial Times to the Present* (Lincoln: University of Nebraska Press, 1985), 127–53.

9. Inness owed a huge debt to Thomas Cole; even a casual perusal of his opus suggests a powerfully direct influence and a deep investment in the pastoral mode. Besides the previously cited works on Inness, also see Adrienne Baxter Bell, *George Inness and the Visionary Landscape* (New York: George Braziller, 2003). For the Scranton connection, see Cikovsky and Quick, *George Inness*, 74, and on the iron and coal boom, see Martin V. Melosi, *Coping with Abundance: Energy and Environment in Industrial America* (New York: Knopf, 1985), 22–34.

10. On Gifford, see Kevin J. Avery and Franklin Kelly, eds., *Hudson River School Visions: The Landscapes of Sanford Gifford* (New York: Metropolitan Museum of Art, 2003); Ila Weiss, *Poetic Landscape: The Art and Experience of Sanford R. Gifford* (Newark: University of Delaware Press, 1987); and Andrew Wilton and Timothy Barringer, *American Sublime: Landscape Painting in the United States, 1820–1880* (London: Tate, 2002), esp. 120–1.

11. Note John Brinckerhoff Jackson, *American Space: The Centennial Years: 1865–1876* (New York: Norton, 1972), 35–6: "We sometimes call the postwar generation the one which discovered conservation, but it would be more accurate to call it the one which abandoned ancient attitudes toward the environment and began to transform it and redesign it to suit the needs and conveniences of men."

12. Whitman, *Memoranda*, 14–15.

13. I've been pondering the impact of the Civil War for many years, but it was Louis Menand, through his biographical approach to intellectual history, who really brought it home for me; see his book, *The Metaphysical Club: A Story of Ideas in America* (New York: Farrar, Straus and Giroux, 2001). More recently, Drew Gilpin Faust has made a powerful case for the Civil War as a cultural watershed, in stark disagreement with Mark Schantz's argument in favor of continuity: see Faust, *This Republic of Suffering: Death and the American Civil War* (New York: Knopf, 2008), and Mark S. Schantz, *Awaiting the Heavenly Country: The Civil War and America's Culture of Death* (Ithaca: Cornell University Press, 2008).

14. Whitman, *Memoranda*, 5.

15. See, for instance, Schantz; Chandra Manning, *What This Cruel War Was Over: Soldiers, Slavery, and the Civil War* (New York: Knopf, 2007); Aaron Sheehan-Dean, ed., *The View from the Ground: Experiences of Civil War Soldiers* (Lexington: University Press of Kentucky, 2007); Stephen Berry II, *All That Makes a Man: Love and Ambition in the Civil War South* (New York: Oxford University Press, 2003); and James M. McPherson, *For Cause and Comrades: Why Men Fought in the Civil War* (New York: Oxford University Press, 1997).

16. See *Gardner's Photographic Sketchbook of the Civil War* (New York: Dover, 1959), and Alan Trachtenberg, *Reading American Photographs: Images as History, Mathew Brady to Walker Evans* (New York: Hill & Wang, 1989), 93–102.

17. An engraving based on Waud's drawing was published in *Harper's Weekly*, and Waud himself supplied the caption: "The fires in the woods, caused by the explosion of shells, and the fires made for cooking, spreading around, caused some terrible suffering. It is not supposed that many lives were lost in this horrible manner; but there were some poor fellows, whose wounds had disabled them, who perished in the dreadful flame. Some were carried off by the ambulance corps, others in blankets suspended to four muskets, and more by the aid of sticks, muskets, or even by crawling. The fire advanced on all sides through the tall grass, and, taking the dry pines, raged up to their tops" (*Harper's Weekly* 8 [June 4, 1864]: 358).

    For the quotations in the text, see the indispensable and wonderfully eclectic book by Stephen Cushman, *Bloody Promenade: Reflections on a Civil War Battle* (Charlottesville: University Press of Virginia, 1999), 181. Other sources I've depended on for my understanding of the Wilderness campaign include: Gary W. Gallagher, ed., *The Wilderness Campaign* (Chapel Hill: University of North Carolina Press, 1997); Gordon C. Rhea, *The Battle of the Wilderness, May 5–6, 1864* (Baton Rouge: Louisiana State University Press, 1994); *The Wilderness Campaign, May–June 1864*, Papers of the Military Historical Society of Massachusetts, vol. 4 (Boston: Military Historical Society of Massachusetts, 1905); James M. McPherson, *Battle Cry of Freedom: The Civil War Era* (New York: Ballantine, 1989),

718–43; and Shelby Foote, *The Civil War: A Narrative*, vol. 3, *Red River to Appomattox* (New York: Random House, 1974), 146–91.

18. Henry E. Wing, *When Lincoln Kissed Me* (New York: Eaton & Mains, 1913), 13.

19. Quoted in Cushman, *Bloody Promenade*, 199.

20. Henry W. Elson, *The Civil War through the Camera* (Springfield, MA: Patriot Publishing Co., 1912), part 11 (unpaginated). There are numerous Civil War stories about trees damaged by artillery and musket fire. One of the most famous incidents occurred just a week after the Battle of the Wilderness, on May 12, 1864, at the "Bloody Angle," where an oak with a diameter of 22 inches was felled by a long barrage of bullets. Part of the stump left over from this lead-filled tree was preserved and can now be viewed at the Smithsonian Institution. See Robert F. Krick, "An Insurmountable Barrier between the Army and Ruin: The Confederate Experience at Spotsylvania's Bloody Angle," in Gary W. Gallagher, *The Spotsylvania Campaign* (Chapel Hill: University of North Carolina Press, 1998), esp. 108–110 and 124.

21. Frank S. Walker, Jr., *Remembering: A History of Orange County, Virginia* (Orange, Va.: Orange County Historical Society, 2004), 44–7, 60–62, 71–95, 226–35; T. Lloyd Benson, "The Plain Folk of Orange: Land, Work, and Society on the Eve of the Civil War," in Edward L. Ayers and John C. Willis, eds., *The Edge of the South: Life in Nineteenth-Century Virginia* (Charlottesville: University Press of Virginia, 1991), 56–78; Robert B. Gordon, *American Iron, 1607–1900* (Baltimore: Johns Hopkins University Press, 1996), esp. 1–6, 33–44, and 57–86; and W. H. Adams, "The First Iron Blast Furnaces in America," *Transactions of the American Institute of Mining Engineers* 20 (1891), 196–215.

22. Frederick Law Olmsted, *Journey in the Seaboard Slave States, with Remarks on Their Economy* (1856; New York: Negro Universities Press, 1968), 87 and 65, and also see Dana F. White and Victor A. Kramer, eds., *Olmsted South: Old South Critic/New South Planner* (Westport: Greenwood, 1979), esp. the introduction and part 1. On the hog commons, see Jack Temple Kirby, *Mockingbird Song: Ecological Landscapes of the South* (Chapel Hill: University of North Carolina Press, 2006), 113–55.

23. Quoted in Robert K. Krick, "'Lee to the Rear,' the Texans Cried," in Gallagher, *The Wilderness Campaign*, 170.

24. Andrew A. Humphreys, *The Virginia Campaign, 1864 and 1865* (1883; New York: Da Capo, 1995), 11.

25. Raymond W. Smith, ed., *Out of the Wilderness: The Civil War Memoir of Cpl. Norton C. Shepard, 146th New York Volunteer Infantry* (Hamilton: Edmonston Publishing, 1998), 2.

26. Downing, "A Visit to Montgomery Place," in A. J. Downing, *Rural Essays*, ed. George William Curtis (1853; New York: Geo. A. Leavitt, 1869), 197–8.

27. Morris Schaff, *The Battle of the Wilderness* (Boston: Houghton Mifflin, 1910), 108–9; 340; 59; 119–20; 121; and 257.

28. Whitman, "As Toilsome I Wander'd Virginia's Woods" (from *Drum-Taps*), in *The Portable Walt Whitman*, 225–6.

29. Art historians disagree about whether Homer was actually at the Battle of the Wilderness; I tend to think he was, though there is no hard evidence to support this view. He was distantly related to Major General Francis Channing Barlow, in command of the

First Division of the Second Corps of the Army of the Potomac. Barlow was definitely there. One scholar simply posits that Homer was attached to Barlow's command (again, without documentation). Certainly, there are plenty of visual references to Barlow in Homer's extensive Civil War opus (Barlow himself appears in Homer's painting, *Prisoners from the Front*). In *Skirmish*, note especially the red insignia on the cap of the officer leading in the reinforcements, center right; the First Division had a distinctive red trefoil on their caps.

    For the assumption that Homer was there, with Barlow, see Julian Grossman, *Echo of a Distant Drum: Winslow Homer and the Civil War* (New York: Harry N. Abrams, [1974]), 168. Also note Lloyd Goodrich, *Winslow Homer* (New York: Macmillan, 1944), esp. 17, and Goodrich, *Winslow Homer's America* (New York: Tudor, 1969), 44–83, esp. 49. For the insistence that there is no proof of Homer's presence—indeed, for a strong assertion that, after 1862, all of Homer's Civil War battles "were fought in his New York or Belmont studio"—see Gordon Hendricks, *The Life and Work of Winslow Homer* (New York: Harry N. Abrams, 1979), 54–8. For a more balanced perspective, note Randall C. Griffin, *Winslow Homer: An American Vision* (New York: Phaidon, 2006), 19–41, esp. 21–2, and Nicolai Cikovsky, Jr., *Winslow Homer* (New York: Harry N. Abrams, 1990), 15–27, esp. 16. On *Skirmish*, also see Cushman, *Bloody Promenade*, 14–16.

30. Downing, "How to Choose a Site for a Country Seat," in *Rural Essays*, 164–5.

31. See Cikovsky, *Winslow Homer*, 24–5; Grossman, *Echo of a Distant Drum*, 164; and Hendricks, *The Life and Work of Winslow Homer*, 59.

32. The children's book is *Book of Trees* (New York: Mahlon Day, 1837), 4; the cemetery guide is Wilson Flagg, *Mount Auburn: Its Scenes, Its Beauties, and Its Lessons* (Boston and Cambridge: James Munroe and Co., 1861), 244 and 246–8. Also see Benson J. Lossing, "American Historical Trees," *Harper's New Monthly Magazine* 24 (May 1862), 721–41; Gayle Brandow Samuels, *Enduring Roots: Encounters with Trees, History, and the American Landscape* (New Brunswick: Rutgers University Press, 1999), 127–8; Jeffrey G. Meyer, with Sharon Linnéa, *America's Famous and Historic Trees: From George Washington's Tulip Poplar to Elvis Presley's Pin Oak* (Boston: Houghton Mifflin, 2001); and Thomas J. Campanella, *Republic of Shade: New England and the American Elm* (New Haven: Yale University Press, 2003), esp. 73–98.

33. R. U. Piper, *The Trees of America* (Boston: William White, 1855–8), 5; Downing quoted on 3. "We cannot," Piper noted, "without sin, neglect to provide for those who are to come after us. In order to do our duty to our country, to those who are to succeed us, we should do all in our power to encourage the planting of trees" (6).

34. Nathaniel W. Coffin, *The Forest Arcadia of Northern New York* (Boston: T. O. H. P. Burnham, 1864), 75–7. Daegan Miller taught me most of what I know about witness trees; see his forthcoming Cornell Ph.D. dissertation, "Witness Tree: Dissident Landscape Visions in the Nineteenth-Century United States." On witnessing and trauma, see Dominick LaCapra, *History and Its Limits: Human, Animal, Violence* (Ithaca: Cornell University Press, 2009), 60–89.

35. See Nye, *America as Second Creation*, 44–5.

36. Zachariah Allen, *The Practical Tourist, or, Sketches of the State of the Useful Arts, and of Society, Scenery, &c., in Great Britain, France and Holland*, vol. 1 (Providence: A. S. Beckwith, 1832), 263.

37. George B. Emerson, *Report on the Trees and Shrubs Growing Naturally in the Forests of Massachusetts* (Boston: Dutton and Wentworth, 1846), 2, 13, and 11.

38. Piper, *The Trees of America*, 51.

39. See, for instance, David M. Potter, *The Impending Crisis, 1848–1861*, completed and edited by Don E. Fehrenbacher (New York: Harper and Row, 1976).

40. Rev. Frederick Starr, Jr., *American Forests; Their Destruction and Preservation*, report published by the United States Department of Agriculture in 1865 and bound into a volume of *Memorials* by and about Starr donated to the Cornell University Library (BX 9178 S79) in 1867 by Miss Lucy Starr (pagination is that of the original USDA report), 215.

41. Ibid., 220, emphasis in original. For a stellar overview of Civil War deforestation, see Megan Kate Nelson, "Battle Logs: Ruined Forests," chap. 3 of her book, *Ruin Nation: Destruction and the American Civil War* (Athens: University of Georgia Press, 2012), 103–59.

42. George Perkins Marsh, *Man and Nature* (1864), ed. David Lowenthal (Cambridge, MA: Harvard University Press, 1965), 285. When does an author consider his work to be finished? Awareness of deforestation was extremely high in 1864—just as, say, appreciation of firefighters was unusually high in the United States in 2002. Marsh must have considered the fact that his audience would be primed for his message when he decided to make it public.

43. Ibid., 51 and 280.

44. J. A. Lapham, J. G. Knapp, and H. Crocker, Commissioners, *Report on the Disastrous Effects of the Destruction of Forest Trees Now Going on so Rapidly in the State of Wisconsin* (Madison, WI: Atwood and Rublee, 1867).

45. Marsh, *Man and Nature*, 180 and 184–5; William Cullen Bryant, "The Utility of Trees," in Parke Godwin, ed., *Prose Writings of William Cullen Bryant*, vol. 2 (New York: D. Appleton, 1889), 402–5; also see Parke Godwin, ed., *The Poetical Works of William Cullen Bryant*, vol. 1 (New York: D. Appleton, 1883), 93–6.

46. See Cikovsky, *Winslow Homer*, 27, and Griffin, *Winslow Homer*, 39.

47. Whitman, *Specimen Days*, in *The Portable Walt Whitman*, 482.

48. Recall Morris Schaff's comparison of bodies to sheaves of wheat. On this painting, see Griffin, *Winslow Homer*, 35–9, and Cikovsky, *Winslow Homer*, 22–7.

49. Whitman, *Democratic Vistas*, in *The Portable Walt Whitman*, 376.

50. See Whitman, *Specimen Days*, in *The Portable Walt Whitman*, 526–7; Charles H. Brown, *William Cullen Bryant* (New York: Charles Scribner's Sons, 1971), 521–2; and Gilbert H. Muller, *William Cullen Bryant: Author of America* (Albany: State University of New York Press, 2008), 334–6.

51. Whitman, *Specimen Days*, in *The Portable Walt Whitman*, 527 and 615.

52. Ibid., 388.

53. Ibid., 388, 391, 396, 395, 484, 388, and 484–5. On *Specimen Days*, see, for instance, Killingsworth, *Walt Whitman and the Earth*, 164–84, and Eric Wilson, *Romantic Turbulence: Chaos, Ecology, and American Space* (Houndmills: Macmillan, 2000), 118–40.

54. Whitman, *Specimen Days*, in *The Portable Walt Whitman*, 485. "Nature restores itself even as Whitman writes," notes Timothy Sweet. "It has recovered its pastoral power to marginalize death . . . and evade the explicit representation of suffering" (*Traces of War*, 66).

55. Whitman, *Specimen Days*, in *The Portable Walt Whitman*, 486, 583, 637, 499, 506, 513, and 512. When asked, as an old man, if he ever went back in his imagination to the days of the Civil War, Whitman answered, "I have never left them." Quoted in David W. Blight, *Race and Reunion: The Civil War in American Memory* (Cambridge, MA: Harvard University Press, 2001), 19.

56. Whitman, *Specimen Days*, in *The Portable Walt Whitman*, 514–15 and 496. On identity and kinship, see LaCapra, *History and Its Limits*, 65–7; Jeremy Foster, *Washed with Sun: Landscape and the Making of White South Africa* (Pittsburgh: University of Pittsburgh Press, 2008), esp. 6–13 and 80–90; Bruno Latour, *Politics of Nature: How to Bring the Sciences into Democracy*, trans. Catherine Porter (Cambridge: Harvard University Press, 2004), 32–49; and Gregory Bateson, "Pathologies of Epistemology," in Bateson, *Steps to an Ecology of Mind* (1972; Chicago: University of Chicago Press, 2000).

57. Whitman, *Specimen Days*, in *The Portable Walt Whitman*, 517, 575, 576–7, 625, 631, and 639–40. Much of what I understand about elegy I picked up from Anne Carson, *Nox* (New York: New Directions, 2010), and Christie Hodgen, *Elegies for the Brokenhearted* (New York: Norton, 2010). Good elegies look both backward and forward. Other texts I've found helpful include Sandra M. Gilbert, *Death's Door: Modern Dying and the Ways We Grieve* (New York: W. W. Norton, 2006); Jeffrey Berman, *Companionship in Grief: Love and Loss in the Memoirs of C. S. Lewis, John Bayley, Donald Hall, Joan Didion, and Calvin Trillin* (Amherst: University of Massachusetts Press, 2010); Alfred G. Killilea, *The Politics of Being Mortal* (Lexington: University Press of Kentucky, 1988); R. Clifton Spargo, *The Ethics of Mourning: Grief and Responsibility in Elegiac Literature* (Baltimore: Johns Hopkins University Press, 2004); and Max Cavitch, *American Elegy: The Poetry of Mourning from the Puritans to Whitman* (Minneapolis: University of Minnesota Press, 2007), esp. 233–93.

58. Emerson quoted in Jerome Loving, *Walt Whitman: The Song of Himself* (Berkeley: University of California Press, 1999), 189.

59. Whitman, *Specimen Days*, in *The Portable Walt Whitman*, 627–9 and 635–6. And see Robert McCloskey, *Make Way for Ducklings* (New York: Viking, 1941).

60. John Gunther, *Death Be Not Proud* (1949; New York: HarperCollins, 2007), 79.

61. Robert Coles, *The Call of Stories: Teaching and the Moral Imagination* (Boston: Houghton Mifflin, 1989), 97.

62. Quoted in Julian Barnes, *Nothing to Be Frightened Of* (New York: Knopf, 2008), 25.

63. This is the fundamental argument of Ernest Becker, *The Denial of Death* (1973; New York: Free Press Paperbacks, 1997).

64. Philippe Ariès, trans. Patricia M. Ranum, *Western Attitudes Toward Death: From the Middle Ages to the Present* (Baltimore: Johns Hopkins University Press, 1974), 87; also note Barbara Ehrenreich, *Bright-Sided: How the Relentless Promotion of Positive Thinking Has Undermined America* (New York: Metropolitan Books, 2009).

65. See Aaron Sachs, "Dying for Oil: The War on Eco-Justice," *World Watch* 9 (May/June 1996), 10–21, and Rob Nixon, *Slow Violence and the Environmentalism of the Poor* (Cambridge, MA: Harvard University Press, 2011), 103–27.

66. Coles, *The Call of Stories*, 129. Also see Nancy Berns, *Closure: The Rush to End Grief and What It Costs Us* (Philadelphia: Temple University Press, 2011).

67. Michel de Montaigne, *The Complete Works*, trans. Donald Frame (New York: Knopf, 2003), 67, 72, 77–8.

68. John Clive, *Not by Fact Alone: Essays on the Writing and Reading of History* (Boston: Houghton Mifflin, 1989), 32.

69. The first of Grandma's poems chosen by the editor was called "The Edge of the Wood": "All hope is at the edge of the wood/Where the darkness within froths out in bloom/On small outleaning trees." See George Abbe, ed., *Contemporary Ohio Poetry* (New York: Poets of America, 1959), 18.

70. Though some people prefer a long "i," as Jan did (she was right, according to the dictionary), every birder I've spoken with since then has said the word with a short "i."

71. Janice Thaddeus, *Lot's Wife* (Upper Montclair: Saturday Press, 1986), 46. This book won the Eileen W. Barnes Award for 1985. One of the contest editors was the poet Rachel Hadas, whose father, Moses Hadas, once reviewed one of my grandfather's books: "Eloquent Scholarship: A Review of *Prophetic Faith in Isaiah*, by Sheldon H. Blank," *Commentary* 26 (July 1958), 86–8. Many thanks to Jim Goodman for this family connection.

72. Donald Hall, *Life Work* (1993; Boston: Beacon Press, 2003), 11, and 21–2; also see Donald Hall and Barbara Cooney, *Ox-Cart Man* (New York: Viking, 1979).

73. Hall, *Life Work*, 5, 19–21, 23–5; and see Salman Akhtar, "Freud's *Todesangst* and Ghalib's *Ishrat-e-Qatra*: Two Perspectives on Death," in Akhtar, ed., *The Wound of Mortality: Fear, Denial, and Acceptance of Death* (Lanham: Jason Aronson, 2010), 1–5.

74. Hall, *Life Work*, 66, 93, 103, 104, 87, 86, 79, 124, ix.

75. The origins of the famous "Go West" slogan remain unclear; what is certain is that Greeley popularized it. See Coy F. Cross II, *Go West Young Man! Horace Greeley's Vision for America* (Albuquerque: University of New Mexico Press, 1995); "The Homestead Act" (editorial), *New York Tribune*, July 13, 1865.

76. See Richard W. Etulain, ed., *Lincoln Looks West: From the Mississippi to the Pacific* (Carbondale: Southern Illinois University Press, 2010), esp. 1–67 and 90–112, and Robert V. Hine and John Mack Faragher, *The American West: A New Interpretive History* (New Haven: Yale University Press, 2000), 33–61.

77. See, for instance, Heather Cox Richardson, *West from Appomattox: The Reconstruction of America after the Civil War* (New Haven: Yale University Press, 2007), esp. 31–7 and 113–20.

78. Newton Booth quoted in William Deverell, *Railroad Crossing: Californians and the Railroad, 1850–1910* (Berkeley: University of California Press, 1994), 12.

79. If Thomas Cole was the dominant American painter in the 1820s, 30s, and 40s, and if his disciple Frederic Church captured the most attention in the 50s, then Bierstadt's popularity in the 60s and 70s marked a shift not just toward western grandiosity but also toward American triumphalism. On both Leutze and Bierstadt and the artistic trends they embodied, see Hine and Faragher, *The American West*, 487–93; William H. Goetzmann and William

N. Goetzmann, *The West of the Imagination* (New York: Norton, 1986), 114–21 and 145–57; Wilton and Barringer, *American Sublime*, 31–3 and 57–65; and T. J. Jackson Lears, ed., *American Victorians and Virgin Nature* (Boston: Isabella Stewart Gardner Museum, 2002). Also, on Bierstadt in the 60s, see Lee Clark Mitchell, *Westerns: Making the Man in Fiction and Film* (Chicago: University of Chicago Press, 1996), 56–72 and 83–93.

80. See, for instance, Michael L. Johnson, *Hunger for the Wild: America's Obsession with the Untamed West* (Lawrence: University Press of Kansas, 2007), esp. 111–237, and Louis S. Warren, *Buffalo Bill's America: William Cody and the Wild West Show* (New York: Knopf, 2005).

81. On the art show, see Gordon Hendricks, *Albert Bierstadt: Painter of the American West* (New York: Harry N. Abrams, 1974), 141–54; on the Sanitary Commission, see Charles J. Stillé, *History of the United States Sanitary Commission* (Philadelphia: J. B. Lippincott, 1866).

82. On Bierstadt, see especially Hendricks, *Albert Bierstadt*, quotations on 144 and 147; and also note Matthew Baigell, *Albert Bierstadt* (New York: Watson-Guptill, 1981); Alexander Acevedo, Nancy Condon, and Gerald Carr, *Albert Bierstadt: An Exhibition of Forty Paintings* (New York: Alexander Gallery, 1983); and Diane P. Fischer, *Primal Visions: Albert Bierstadt "Discovers" America* (Montclair: Montclair Art Museum, 2001).

83. Whitman, *Specimen Days*, in *The Portable Walt Whitman*, 562.

84. See Robert M. Utley, *The Indian Frontier of the American West, 1846–1890* (Albuquerque: University of New Mexico Press, 1984), 65–98, and Utley, *Frontiersmen in Blue: The United States Army and the Indian, 1848–1865* (Lincoln: University of Nebraska Press, 1967), 261–80 and 231–49.

85. See, for instance, Robert F. Berkhofer, Jr., *The White Man's Indian: Images of the American Indian from Columbus to the Present* (New York: Vintage, 1979), esp. 96–111.

86. U.S. statute cited in Roderick Frazier Nash, *Wilderness and the American Mind*, 4th ed. (1st ed., 1967; New Haven: Yale University Press, 2001), 106.

87. Olmsted, "Preliminary Report upon the Yosemite and Big Tree Grove" (1865), in Victoria Post Ranney, ed., *The Papers of Frederick Law Olmsted*, vol. 5, *The California Frontier, 1863–1865* (Baltimore: Johns Hopkins University Press, 1990), 489.

88. Olmsted quoted in Jane Turner Censer, "Introduction," in Censer, ed., *The Papers of Frederick Law Olmsted*, vol. 4, *Defending the Union: The Civil War and the U.S. Sanitary Commission, 1861–1863* (Baltimore: Johns Hopkins University Press, 1986), 59. Also see Stillé, *History of the United States Sanitary Commission*, 75–84, and Witold Rybczynski, *A Clearing in the Distance: Frederick Law Olmsted and America in the 19th Century* (New York: Touchstone, 1999), 198–226.

89. Olmsted, "Labors of the Sanitary Commission," in Censer, *The Papers of Frederick Law Olmsted*, 4:327. Also see Laura L. Behling, ed., *Hospital Transports: A Memoir of the Embarkation of the Sick and Wounded from the Peninsula of Virginia in the Summer of 1862* (Albany: State University of New York Press, 2005).

90. See Censer, *The Papers of Frederick Law Olmsted*, 4:56–61, and also note Charles E. Beveridge and Charles Capen McLaughlin, eds., *The Papers of Frederick Law Olmsted*, vol. 2, *Slavery and the South, 1852–1857* (Baltimore: Johns Hopkins University Press, 1981).

91. Olmsted, "Preface to the Plan for Mountain View Cemetery, Oakland, California," in Ranney, *The Papers of Frederick Law Olmsted*, 5:479. He was quite excited about this opportunity; upon being asked to do the job, he wrote to his father: "I should very much like to lay out a good cemetery—have never yet had a chance on what I thought an entirely suitable site." Frederick Law Olmsted Papers, LOC, Manuscript Division, Washington, DC, Reel 24, letter from Olmsted to his father, Bear Valley, October 16, 1864.

92. Olmsted, "Preliminary Report upon the Yosemite and Big Tree Grove," 500 and 502.

93. Ibid., 507 and 491–2. Also see Rebecca Solnit, *Savage Dreams: A Journey into the Landscape Wars of the American West*, expanded ed. (1994; Berkeley: University of California Press, 1999), 228–47, and Ethan Carr, *Wilderness by Design: Landscape Architecture and the National Park Service* (Lincoln: University of Nebraska Press, 1998), 1–53; and note that Carleton Watkins took several widely circulated photographs of the Grizzly Giant in the 1860s.

94. See Blight, *Race and Reunion*, esp. 1–139; Kenneth E. Foote, *Shadowed Ground: America's Landscapes of Violence and Tragedy* (Austin: University of Texas Press, 1997), esp. 1–35 and 293–336; and Nelson, *Ruin Nation*. Also note Cathy Caruth, *Unclaimed Experience: Trauma, Narrative, and History* (Baltimore: Johns Hopkins University Press, 1996), 1–24, and Berns, *Closure*.

    My conception of dwelling, in this context, bears some resemblance to what I think Dominick LaCapra intends with his attempt to develop an alternative concept of "working-through," offering the traumatized some hope without implying "a total transcendence or disavowal of the traumas and losses of the past that continue to haunt or even possess the present" (*History and Its Limits*, 84).

95. See R. Morris Copeland, *Statement of R. Morris Copeland, Asst. Adjutant-General and Major of Volunteers, discharged from service August 6, 1862* (Boston: Prentiss & Deland, 1864); and Copeland published a broadside in Boston, dated November 25, 1870, conveying his official pardon—I saw a copy at the American Antiquarian Society (BDSDS.1870).

96. See for instance Cynthia Zaitzevsky, *Frederick Law Olmsted and the Boston Park System* (Cambridge, MA: Harvard University Press, 1982), 36–47; and note the lively correspondence between Copeland and Olmsted in the Olmsted Papers (there are several letters from Copeland to Olmsted on Reels 10–13, dated from 1867 through 1873). Olmsted warmly recommended Copeland to Andrew Dickson White, president of Cornell University, when White was looking for a landscape gardener to design Cornell's campus in 1873: see Olmsted's letter of September 16, in David Schuyler and Jane Turner Censer, eds., *The Papers of Frederick Law Olmsted*, vol. 6, *The Years of Olmsted, Vaux & Company, 1865–1874* (Baltimore: Johns Hopkins University Press, 1992), 650. Copeland has received scant scholarly attention, but see: Charles A. Birnbaum and Robin Karson, *Pioneers of American Landscape Design* (New York: McGraw-Hill, 2000), 68–70; Ellen Weiss, *City in the Woods: The Life and Design of an American Camp Meeting on Martha's Vineyard* (New York: Oxford University Press, 1987), 78–92; and Anne Whiston Spirn, "Reclaiming Common Ground: Water, Neighborhoods, and Public Places," in Robert Fishman, ed., *The American Planning Tradition: Culture and Policy* (Washington, DC: Woodrow Wilson Center Press, 2000), 297–313, esp. 306 and 311.

97. Copeland, *The Most Beautiful City in America: Essay and Plan for the Improvement of the City of Boston* (Boston: Lee & Shepard, 1872), 27 and 30–2.

98. See Faust, *This Republic of Suffering*, passim; Blight, *Race and Reunion*, esp. 1–170; and John R. Neff, *Honoring the Civil War Dead: Commemoration and the Problem of Reconciliation* (Lawrence: University Press of Kansas, 2005). Neff, in my view quite usefully, stresses that, especially with regard to memorials for the dead, Americans may not have become quite so reconciled to each other as other scholars might suggest.

99. Boston branch (Post 15) of the Grand Army of the Republic, "Floral Decoration of Soldiers' and Sailors' Graves, in Mount Auburn" (Boston, 1869), broadside consulted at the American Antiquarian Society (BDSDS 1869). On the complex origins of Decoration Day, see Blight, *Race and Reunion*, 64–84.

100. Thomas Wentworth Higginson, "Decoration Day Address at Mount Auburn Cemetery, May 30, 1870," in Mayo W. Hazeltine et al., eds., *Masterpieces of Eloquence: Famous Orations of Great World Leaders from Early Greece to the Present Time*, vol. 20 (New York: P. F. Collier & Son, 1905), 8599–8602, quotation 8602.

101. See Blight, *Race and Reunion*, esp. 44–63; George M. Fredrickson, *The Inner Civil War: Northern Intellectuals and the Crisis of the Union* (New York: Harper and Row, 1965), esp. 113–238; and Eric Foner, *Reconstruction: America's Unfinished Revolution, 1863–1877* (New York: Harper and Row, 1988).

102. See Faust, *This Republic of Suffering*, esp. 211–49; Neff, *Honoring the Civil War Dead*, passim; and Steven R. Stotelmyer, *The Bivouacs of the Dead: The Story of Those Who Died at Antietam and South Mountain, with Histories and Rosters of Antietam, Washington, Mt. Olivet and Elmwood Cemeteries* (Baltimore: Toomey Press, 1992).

103. David Charles Sloane has argued that the Civil War did not have a major impact on Americans' thinking about cemeteries; I respectfully disagree. See Sloane, *The Last Great Necessity: Cemeteries in American History* (Baltimore: Johns Hopkins University Press, 1991), 112–13. Also note Munro MacCloskey, *Hallowed Ground: Our National Cemeteries* (New York: Richard Rosen, 1968), 11–45, and Robert M. Poole, *On Hallowed Ground: The Story of Arlington National Cemetery* (New York: Walker, 2009), 1–101.

104. On death and dying, see, for instance, Gary Laderman, *The Sacred Remains: American Attitudes Toward Death, 1799–1883* (New Haven: Yale University Press, 1996), 164–75; Michael J. Steiner, *A Study of the Intellectual and Material Culture of Death in Nineteenth-Century America* (Lewiston, NY: Edwin Mellen, 2003), 111–38; James J. Farrell, *Inventing the American Way of Death, 1830–1920* (Philadelphia: Temple University Press, 1980); and W. Lloyd Warner, *The Living and the Dead: A Study of the Symbolic Life of Americans* (New Haven: Yale University Press, 1959), 248–320.

   On health care and medicine, see, for instance, John Duffy, *The Sanitarians: A History of American Public Health* (Urbana: University of Illinois Press, 1990), 110–25 and 157–74; Charles E. Rosenberg, *The Care of Strangers: The Rise of America's Hospital System* (New York: Basic Books, 1987), 97–121; John S. Haller, *American Medicine in Transition, 1840–1910* (Urbana: University of Illinois Press, 1981); and John Harley Warner, *The Therapeutic Perspective: Medical Practice, Knowledge, and Identity in America, 1820–1885* (Cambridge, MA: Harvard University Press, 1986).

And note that the Civil War also had an impact on the scientific study of race; see Ann Fabian, *The Skull Collectors: Race, Science, and America's Unburied Dead* (Chicago: University of Chicago Press, 2010), esp. 164–203.

105. Lieutenant Stiles, for the left-handed writing contest (see above, note 1), was required only to submit photographic evidence of his amputation; he chose also to send in this photo showing off his prosthetic arm.

On amputation and prosthetics, see Ansley Herring Wegner, *Phantom Pain: North Carolina's Artificial-Limbs Program for Confederate Veterans* (Raleigh: Office of Archives and History, North Carolina Department of Cultural Resources, 2004), 1–35; Jennifer Davis McDaid, "'How a One-Legged Rebel Lives': Confederate Veterans and Artificial Limbs in Virginia," and Stephen Mihm, "'A Limb Which Shall Be Presentable in Polite Society': Prosthetic Technologies in the Nineteenth Century," both in Katherine Ott, David Serlin, and Stephen Mihm, eds., *Artificial Parts, Practical Lives: Modern Histories of Prosthetics,* (New York: New York University Press, 2002), 119–43 and 282–99; and Laurann Figg and Jane Farrell-Beck, "Amputation in the Civil War: Physical and Social Dimensions," *Journal of the History of Medicine and Allied Sciences* 48 (October 1993), 454–75. Also see Nelson's excellent essay, "Empty Sleeves and Government Legs: The Ruins of Men," chap. 4 of her *Ruin Nation*, 160–227. And note the remarkable image of a man wearing a prosthetic leg and demonstrating its functionality by rolling a tree stump along the ground ahead of him, in Douglas Bly, M.D., *A New and Important Invention* (Rochester: Curtis, Butts, & Co., 1862), 10.

106. Holmes, "The Human Wheel," 574 and 579.

107. Frederick Newman Knapp, "'Sanitaria,' or Homes for Discharged, Disabled Soldiers" (Washington, DC, May 5, 1865), broadside consulted at the American Antiquarian Society (BDSDS 1865); also see Maj. Gen. B. F. Butler, President of the Board of Managers, "The National Asylum for Disabled Volunteer Soldiers" (Washington, DC, 1867), broadside consulted at the American Antiquarian Society (BDSDS 1867). Butler emphasized "that the Asylums are neither hospitals nor almshouses."

108. See Patrick J. Kelly, *Creating a National Home: Building the Veterans' Welfare State, 1860–1900* (Cambridge, MA: Harvard University Press, 1997).

109. "A Veteran of the Home" (J. C. Gobrecht), *History of the National Home for Disabled Volunteer Soldiers: with a Complete Guide-Book to the Central Home, at Dayton, Ohio* (Dayton: United Brethren, 1875), 18, 159, and 114.

110. Knapp, "'Sanitaria.'"

111. "A Veteran of the Home," *History*, 93, 92, 87, 89, 97, and 61.

112. Whitman, *Specimen Days*, in *The Portable Walt Whitman*, 625.

113. Blight, *Race and Reunion*, 9. Also see Foote, *Shadowed Ground*, 3; Nelson, *Ruin Nation*; and Shirley Samuels, *Facing America: Iconography and the Civil War* (New York: Oxford University Press, 2004).

114. Of course, some scholars have argued that the violence of the Civil War started getting abstracted and erased before it was even over: see, for instance, Franny Nudelman, *John Brown's Body: Slavery, Violence, and the Culture of War* (Chapel Hill: University of North Carolina Press, 2004).

On battlefields, see: Timothy B. Smith, *The Golden Age of Battlefield Preservation: The Decade of the 1890s and the Establishment of America's First Five Military Parks* (Knoxville: University of Tennessee Press, 2008), and Edward Tabor Linenthal, *Sacred Ground: Americans and Their Battlefields* (Urbana: University of Illinois Press, 1991), esp. 1–7 and 87–126.

115. See Steve Szkotak, "Wal-Mart Drops Orange County Battlefield Store Plans," *Richmond Times-Dispatch*, January 26, 2011: http://www2.timesdispatch.com/news/2011/jan/26/11/start -battlefield-walmart-trial-now-targeted-thurs-ar-799687/

116. James M. McPherson, "Foreword," in Georgie Boge and Margie Holder Boge, *Paving Over the Past: A History and Guide to Civil War Battlefield Preservation* (Washington, DC: Island Press, 1993), xv.

117. It gets even weirder. The Wilderness is in Spotsylvania County, named for Alexander Spotswood. Back in the early 90s, when I worked in Washington, I had a friend and co-author named John Young, who was in a band led by Jonathan Spottiswoode. Eventually, the band moved to New York and hit it big, and Spottiswoode and His Enemies has become one of my favorite musical groups of all time. In fall 2010, John Young moved to Ithaca, and we got reacquainted after not having been in touch for several years. When we got together for the first time, I gave him a copy of my book, *The Humboldt Current*, and, since I already had all of the Enemies records, he gave me a CD of Jonathan Spottiswoode's latest solo album, called *Piano 45*, which I quickly realized was all about being middle-aged. That was the CD I was listening to when I drove down to the Wilderness on December 26, 2010. And there's more: track 6, called "Understand," contains the following line: "Maybe in the wilderness I'll stumble on a sign, away from the distractions cluttering my mind."

### 5. THREE MEN OF THE MIDDLE BORDER (PART ONE)

1. Keith Newlin has reinvigorated scholarship on Garland in the last several years; see especially his thorough and insightful biography, *Hamlin Garland: A Life* (Lincoln: University of Nebraska Press, 2008). A previous surge of literary scholarship on Garland came in the early 1980s; see, for instance, Charles L. P. Silet, Robert E. Welch, and Richard Boudreau, eds., *The Critical Reception of Hamlin Garland, 1891–1978* (Troy, NY: Whitson, 1985), and James Nagel, ed., *Critical Essays on Hamlin Garland* (Boston: G. K. Hall, 1982). And also note Donald Pizer, *Hamlin Garland's Early Work and Career* (Berkeley: University of California Press, 1960); Pizer, ed., *Hamlin Garland's Diaries* (San Marino: Huntington Library, 1968); and Keith Newlin and Joseph B. McCullough, eds., *Selected Letters of Hamlin Garland* (Lincoln: University of Nebraska Press, 1998).

2. Ray Allen Billington, "Foreword," in Gilbert C. Fite, *The Farmers' Frontier, 1865–1900* (New York: Holt, Rinehart and Winston, 1966), vi.

3. While the overall population in the United States doubled between 1865 and 1900, the urban population increased sevenfold. See Alan Brinkley, *American History: A Survey*, vol. 2, 11th ed. (New York: McGraw Hill, 2003), 500–1. Also note Constance McLaughlin Green, *The Rise of Urban America* (New York: Harper & Row, 1965), 57–127, and Sam Bass Warner,

Jr., *The Urban Wilderness: A History of the American City* (1972; Berkeley: University of California Press, 1995), 55–112.

4. Garland, *A Son of the Middle Border* (1917; St. Paul: Minnesota Historical Society Press, 2007), 7.

5. "The Return of a Private," in Garland, *Main-Travelled Roads* (1891; Lincoln: University of Nebraska Press, 1995), 112–14, 117–18, and 120.

6. Garland, *A Son of the Middle Border*, 7–8, 15, 10, 26, 32, and 11.

7. Ibid., 312 and 342; and Garland, in an interview recorded by Joseph Gollomb for his review of *A Son of the Middle Border* in a New York newspaper, a clipping of which I read in one of Garland's scrapbooks, dated 1908–1917, at the Huntington Library, San Marino, California, in the Hamlin Garland Papers, Box 28.

8. Garland, *A Son of the Middle Border*, 66. The Garlands' place in Iowa, combining woodland and good prairie soil, seemed to capture some sort of ideal for the young Hamlin, but he actually found much to admire and even love about each of the family's farms. Indeed, he was mystified by his father's restlessness from the very beginning: writing about their original homestead, in a well-wooded Wisconsin valley, he acknowledged that he would probably never be able to "understand how my father brought himself to leave that lovely farm and those good and noble friends" (48).

9. Ibid., 35 and 240.

10. See, for instance, John Mack Faragher, *Sugar Creek: Life on the Illinois Prairie* (New Haven: Yale University Press, 1986).

11. Garland, *A Daughter of the Middle Border* (1921; St. Paul: Minnesota Historical Society Press, 2007), xxii. For studies of frontier agriculture in the postbellum period, see: Fite, *The Farmers' Frontier*; John Brinckerhoff Jackson, *American Space: The Centennial Years: 1865–1876* (New York: Norton, 1972), 39–55; Fred A. Shannon, *The Farmer's Last Frontier: Agriculture, 1860–1897* (New York: Rinehart, 1945); James M. Marshall, *Land Fever: Dispossession and the Frontier Myth* (Lexington: University Press of Kentucky, 1986); and Paul W. Gates, *Agriculture and the Civil War* (New York: Knopf, 1965), 356–79.

12. Garland, *A Son of the Middle Border*, 5, 85, 107, 72, 71, 103, 82, 137, 111, and 125.

13. Ibid., 132 and 138; and see D. Sven Nordin, *Rich Harvest: A History of the Grange, 1867–1900* (Jackson: University Press of Mississippi, 1974), and Solon Justus Buck, *The Granger Movement: A Study of Agricultural Organization and Its Political, Economic and Social Manifestations, 1870–1880* (1913; Lincoln: University of Nebraska Press, 1963), 3–9, 37–9, 40–69, and 280–312.

14. Garland, *A Son of the Middle Border*, 124.

15. Nathaniel Hawthorne, *The Blithedale Romance* (1852; New York: Penguin, 1986), 66.

16. Garland, *A Son of the Middle Border*, 172–3, 92, 107, 84–5, 137, and 121. The interview is from *The Music World* (March 1931), 9, in Box 29 (Ephemera) of the Garland Papers at the Huntington.

17. Garland, *A Son of the Middle Border*, 128, 136, and 186–7; also see Newlin, *Hamlin Garland*, 26. It isn't easy to keep track of Richard Garland's removals: he had already established two different homesteads in Wisconsin and two in Iowa before moving to Dakota Territory in 1881. Hamlin, meanwhile, in *A Son of the Middle Border*, returned again and again to the

intertwined themes of kinship and death and place and dwelling: "Ye scatter like the leaves of autumn," says his Wisconsin grandfather when Hamlin visits him on his way eastward in 1881 (200), and the whole scene is imbued with a sense of loss and broken connections, calling to mind William Cullen Bryant's poem "The Two Graves," about an elderly couple buried without any of their kin as witnesses, since all had fled west—meaning that their graves might never be visited by any family members, since none even knew of their burial, and now nature had reclaimed the stones: "And the keenest eye might search in vain, / 'Mong the briers, and ferns, and paths of sheep, / For the spot where the aged couple sleep." See Parke Godwin, ed., *The Poetical Works of William Cullen Bryant*, vol. 1 (New York: D. Appleton, 1883), 176–9, quotation on 177.

18. Garland, *A Son of the Middle Border*, 185, 215, and 217–9. There is solid evidence that Garland read *Specimen Days*, but not necessarily right when it came out; see his review of Whitman's *November Boughs*, in the *Boston Evening Transcript*, November 1888, a copy of which can be found in Folder 723 (clippings of Garland's periodical writings) of the Hamlin Garland Papers at the University of Southern California.

19. Garland, *A Son of the Middle Border*, 234, 227, 216, 220, 233, 240–2, 244, 247, 237–8, and 236. Besides Hawthorne and Emerson, Garland also invoked Thoreau as a key incitement to visit Concord (216–17).

20. Aaron Sachs, "Virtual Ecology: A Brief Environmental History of Silicon Valley," *World Watch* 12 (January/February 1999), 12–21.

21. Garland, *A Son of the Middle Border*, 241 and 243–5.

22. Henry George, *Our Land and Land Policy* (1871), in *The Complete Works of Henry George*, vol. 8 (Garden City: Doubleday, Page, and Co., 1911), 119.

23. Henry George, *Progress and Poverty* (1879; New York: Robert Schalkenbach Foundation, 2008). Also see John L. Thomas, *Alternative America: Henry George, Edward Bellamy, Henry Demarest Lloyd, and the Adversary Tradition* (Cambridge, MA: Harvard University Press, 1983); Daniel Aaron, *Men of Good Hope: A Story of American Progressives* (1951; New York: Oxford University Press, 1967), 55–91; and Albert Jay Nock, *Henry George: An Essay* (New York: William Morrow, 1939).

24. George, in Louis F. Post and Fred C. Leubuscher, eds., *Henry George's 1886 Campaign* (New York: Henry George School, 1961), 8.

25. George, *Social Problems* (1883; New York: Robert Schalkenbach Foundation, 1963), 234–40.

26. See, for instance, Thomas's chapter, "The Making of a Reformer," in *Alternative America*, 58–82.

27. George, *Progress*, 5–6.

28. George, letter to his friend B. F. Ely, September 30, 1857, included in Henry George, Jr., *The Life of Henry George* (1900; New York: Robert Schalkenbach Foundation, 1960), 50. And note Anna George de Mille, "Henry George: Childhood and Early Youth," *American Journal of Economics and Sociology* 1 (April 1942), 283–306.

29. George, letter to Jennie, September 15, 1861, in George, Jr., *The Life of Henry George*, 117–18.

30. Undated letter from Jennie to Henry; Jennie to Henry, April 20, 1861; Henry to Jennie, June 5, 1862: ibid., 126–32.

31. George, letter of October 1862 to "My Dear Sisters," Henry George Papers, New York Public Library (NYPL), Reel 1. Many of the documents preserved in the Henry George Papers are printed, in part or in full, in George, Jr., *The Life of Henry George*, making for easier accessibility. My citing of the archival source will be an indication that a particular document is available only there or that Henry George, Jr., did not include the entire document in his biography.

32. George, Jr., *The Life of Henry George*, 135 and 147; and George, letter to Jennie, September 15, 1861, ibid., 116.

33. George, letter to Jennie, June 5, 1862, George Papers, NYPL, Reel 1.

34. George, *Our Land and Land Policy*, 69–70. Note that the floods and drought had a disastrous impact on the cattle industry in 1861–3: see Jackson, *American Space*, 186. Also note Paul W. Gates, *The Jeffersonian Dream: Studies in the History of American Land Policy and Development* (Albuquerque: University of New Mexico Press, 1996), esp. 56–83, and the classic book by Carey McWilliams, *Factories in the Field: The Story of Migratory Farm Labor in California* (1939; Berkeley: University of California Press, 1999), 3–59.

35. See for instance George's article, "The Chinese on the Pacific Coast," published in the *New York Tribune*, May 1, 1869, and quoted at length in George, Jr., *The Life of Henry George*, 193–5; George refers to Chinese immigrants as "utter heathens, treacherous, sensual, cowardly and cruel" (194). Also see Ian Tyrrell, *True Gardens of the Gods: Californian-Australian Environmental Reform, 1860–1930* (Berkeley: University of California Press, 1999), 39.

36. On their political power see George, Jr., *The Life of Henry George*, 182–3.

37. Ibid., 178–9.

38. See Post and Leubuscher, *Henry George's 1886 Campaign*, 8 and 28–9, and George, Jr., *The Life of Henry George*, 191–3. Also note Anna George de Mille, "Henry George: The Formative Years," *American Journal of Economics and Sociology* 2 (October 1942), 97–110.

39. George, Jr., *The Life of Henry George*, 208–210. Though Grant remained a hero to many Americans, by the end of his second term he seemed to George to be "distinguished as the President who had had the worst of all political rings and corruptionists about him" (ibid., 317).

40. Most historians agree with George's basic argument; indeed, much more government land was either sold to speculators or granted to railroads in the late nineteenth century than was given out directly to homesteaders. See Gates, *Jeffersonian Dream*, 40–55; Robert V. Hine and John Mack Faragher, *The American West: A New Interpretive History* (New Haven: Yale University Press, 2000), 330–37; and Richard White, *Railroaded: The Transcontinentals and the Making of Modern America* (New York: Norton, 2011).

41. George, *Our Land and Land Policy*, 48.

42. Ibid., 96–7, 119, 91, 97, and 88.

43. Ibid., 67, 91, and 86. Environmental historians have not yet made much of George's career, but see Tyrrell, *True Gardens of the Gods*, 37–9.

44. George, *Our Land and Land Policy*, 68, 99, and 101.

45. See, for instance, Rhoda Hellman, *Henry George Reconsidered* (New York: Hearthstone, 1987), and Steven Cord, *Henry George: Dreamer or Realist?* (1965; New York: Robert Schalkenbach Foundation, 1984).

46. See Rebecca Edwards, *New Spirits: Americans in the Gilded Age, 1865–1905* (New York: Oxford University Press, 2006), 13, and 60–103; Walter Licht, *Industrializing America: The Nineteenth Century* (Baltimore: Johns Hopkins University Press, 1995); Alan Trachtenberg, *The Incorporation of America: Culture and Society in the Gilded Age* (New York: Hill & Wang, 1982); and Sigmund Diamond, ed., *The Nation Transformed: The Creation of an Industrial Society* (New York: George Braziller, 1963), 3–22.

47. Sachs, "Virtual Ecology," 13: as of 1998, Silicon Valley had twenty-nine Superfund sites.

48. Frederic Hall, *The History of San José and Surroundings* (San Francisco: A. L. Bancroft, 1871), 299–332.

49. John W. Reps, *The Forgotten Frontier: Urban Planning in the American West Before 1890* (Columbia: University of Missouri Press, 1981), 112 and 146–7; Reps, *Cities of the American West: A History of Frontier Urban Planning* (Princeton: Princeton University Press, 1979), 167–75; Stephen J. Pitti, *The Devil in Silicon Valley: Northern California, Race, and Mexican Americans* (Princeton: Princeton University Press, 2003), 30–102; Yvonne Jacobson, *Passing Farms, Enduring Values: California's Santa Clara Valley* (Los Altos: William Kaufmann, 1984), 49–191; and Steven Stoll, *The Fruits of Natural Advantage: Making the Industrial Countryside in California* (Berkeley: University of California Press, 1998), 1–62.

50. See Sachs, "Virtual Ecology"; Jacobson, *Passing Farms, Enduring Values*; and McWilliams, *Factories in the Field*.

51. Sachs, "Virtual Ecology."

52. Of course, the Internet is also a crucial tool for environmental activism; see the important argument in Bill McKibben, *Eaarth: Making a Life on a Tough New Planet* (New York: St. Martin's Griffin, 2011), 195–212.

53. Beckett, *The Unnamable*, in *Three Novels by Samuel Beckett* (New York: Grove, 1965), 414. Now this line makes me think of the heart-wrenching preface to Marshall Berman's wonderful study, *All That Is Solid Melts into Air: The Experience of Modernity* (1982; New York: Penguin, 1988), 14: "Shortly after I finished this book, my dear son Marc, five years old, was taken from me. I dedicate *All That Is Solid Melts into Air* to him. His life and death bring so many of its ideas and themes close to home: the idea that those who are most happily at home in the modern world, as he was, may be most vulnerable to the demons that haunt it; the idea that the daily routine of playgrounds and bicycles, of shopping and eating and cleaning up, of ordinary hugs and kisses, may be not only infinitely joyous and beautiful but also infinitely precarious and fragile; that it may take desperate and heroic struggles to sustain this life, and sometimes we lose. Ivan Karamazov says that, more than anything else, the death of children makes him want to give back his ticket to the universe. But he does not give it back. He keeps on fighting and loving; he keeps on keeping on."

54. *San Jose Mercury News*, Thursday, July 24, 1997, 11B.

55. See Reps, *The Forgotten Frontier* and *Cities of the American West*. There were hardly any professional planners at this time, anyway.

56. There were also new attempts to design picturesque suburbs in the postbellum period; the best known was perhaps Riverside, Illinois, near Chicago, designed by Olmsted and Vaux in 1869, which clearly echoed antebellum spaces like Llewellyn Park and Irving Park. See, for example, Jackson, *American Space*, esp. 30–8; Jon A. Peterson, *The Birth of City Plan-*

*ning in the United States, 1840–1917* (Baltimore: Johns Hopkins University Press, 2003), 1–55; Norman T. Newton, *Design on the Land: The Development of Landscape Architecture* (Cambridge, MA: Harvard University Press, 1971), 267–336; Daniel Schaffer, ed., *Two Centuries of American Planning* (Baltimore: Johns Hopkins University Press, 1988), 61–112 and 139–165; and David Schuyler, *The New Urban Landscape: The Redefinition of City Form in Nineteenth-Century America* (Baltimore: Johns Hopkins University Press, 1986), 101–195.

57. Olmsted occasionally took commissions in the west, but his work was focused on eastern cities.

58. Jackson (*American Space*, 31) was wrong to say that Cleveland "left a flourishing practice" to move to Chicago; he had struggled to get work since the start of the Civil War. On Cleveland, who remains understudied (there are a number of essays, but all quite brief), see: Newton, *Design on the Land*, 308–17; Roy Lubove, "Introduction: H. W. S. Cleveland and the Urban-Rural Continuum in American Landscape Architecture," in Cleveland, *Landscape Architecture, as Applied to the Wants of the West* (1873), ed. Lubove (Pittsburgh: University of Pittsburgh Press, 1965), vii–xxi; Daniel J. Nadenicek and Lance M. Neckar, "Introduction to the Reprint Edition," in Cleveland, *Landscape Architecture, as Applied to the Wants of the West*, ed. Nadenicek and Neckar (Amherst: University of Massachusetts Press, 2002), xi–lxxii; William H. Tishler, "Horace Cleveland: The Chicago Years," in Tishler, ed., *Midwestern Landscape Architecture* (Urbana: University of Illinois Press, 2000), 25–40; Karl Haglund, "Rural Tastes, Rectangular Ideas, and the Skirmishes of H. W. S. Cleveland," *Landscape Architecture* 66 (January 1976), 67–70 and 78; Nancy J. Volkman, "Landscape Architecture on the Prairie: The Work of H. W. S. Cleveland," *Kansas History* 10 (Summer 1987), 89–110; William H. Tishler and Virginia S. Luckhardt, "H. W. S. Cleveland, Pioneer Landscape Architect to the Upper Midwest," *Minnesota History* 49 (Fall 1985), 281–91; Daniel Joseph Nadenicek, "Emerson's Aesthetic and Natural Design: A Theoretical Foundation for the Work of Horace William Shaler Cleveland," in Joachim Wolschke-Bulmahn, ed., *Nature and Ideology: Natural Garden Design in the Twentieth Century* (Washington, DC: Dumbarton Oaks Research Library and Collection, 1997), 59–80; and Nadenicek, "Nature in the City: Horace Cleveland's Aesthetic," *Landscape and Urban Planning* 26 (1993), 5–15.

59. Cleveland to Olmsted, letter of September 7, 1870, Chicago, in the Frederick Law Olmsted Papers (microfilm), Library of Congress (LOC), Manuscript Division, Washington, DC, Reel 12.

60. Cleveland to Olmsted, presumably late 1891, Minneapolis (first page of the letter is missing), Olmsted Papers, Reel 22.

61. H. W. S. Cleveland, *Ancestry and Descendants of H. W. S. Cleveland, in line from Moses Cleveland of Woburn, Mass, 1635* (Chicago, 1882), 87: this is held by the LOC and listed in the catalogue as a published work, but it actually turns out to be one of a kind, a ledger book filled with Cleveland's handwriting; also see the autobiographical entry Cleveland wrote for Edmund Janes Cleveland, *The Genealogy of the Cleveland and Cleaveland Families*, vol. 2 (Hartford: Case, Lockwood, & Brainard, 1899), 1075–6, microfilm copy consulted at LOC. For Oatlands, see: Cleveland, "Notes on the Market Gardening of New Jersey," *Horticulturist* 1 (March 1847), 403–6; Cleveland, "Interesting Experiment in Vineyard

Cultivation," ibid., 3 (September 1848), 113–14; Cleveland, "Paving a Non-Preventive," ibid., 4 (September 1849), 128–9; and Cleveland, "A Note on the Curculio, and on Covering Grape Borders," ibid., 4 (January 1850), 301–2.

Also note that Cleveland grew up in Lancaster, Massachusetts, just a few miles from where Fruitlands would be established in 1841; and see Richard Francis, *Transcendental Utopias: Individual and Community at Brook Farm, Fruitlands, and Walden* (Ithaca: Cornell University Press, 1997), 140–217.

62. Cleveland, *Ancestry and Descendants*, 87–8 and 3.

63. Letter to Olmsted, January 27, 1892, Minneapolis, Olmsted Papers, Reel 22.

64. H. W. S. Cleveland, "The Influence of Parks on the Character of Children," *Park and Cemetery* 8 (July 1898), 95. Yes, there was a periodical called *Park and Cemetery!*

65. Letter to Folwell, January 12, 1884, Chicago, the William Watts Folwell and Family Papers, Minnesota Historical Society, St. Paul, Box 15.

66. Cleveland, *Ancestry and Descendants*, 1 and 13. Curtis, of course, was Andrew Jackson Downing's literary executor, and also a close friend to Frederick Law Olmsted. Montaigne made a point of launching his book by claiming that it was a family affair: "This book was written in good faith, reader. It warns you from the outset that in it I have set myself no goal but a domestic and private one. I have had no thought of serving either you or my own glory. My powers are inadequate for such a purpose. I have dedicated it to the private convenience of my relatives and friends." See Michel de Montaigne, *The Complete Works*, trans. Donald Frame (New York: Knopf, 2003), 2.

67. Letter from Robert Morris Copeland to Olmsted, April 26, 1868, Boston, Olmsted Papers, Reel 10.

68. Cleveland, "Landscape Gardening," *Christian Examiner and Religious Miscellany* 58 (May 1855), 386–8.

69. Cleveland, *Ancestry and Descendants*, 88–9.

70. Cleveland, *Hints to Riflemen* (New York: D. Appleton, 1864), 8.

71. Cleveland, *Ancestry and Descendants*, 89.

72. See Peterson, *The Birth of City Planning*, esp. 1–6.

73. Cleveland, *Landscape Architecture*, ed. Nadenicek and Neckar, 79 and 53.

74. Cleveland, "Forest Planting on the Great Plains," ibid., 97.

75. Cleveland *Landscape Architecture*, ed. Nadenicek and Neckar, 53 and 55.

76. Letter of Cleveland to Olmsted, December 19, 1871, Chicago, Olmsted Papers, Reel 12.

77. Cleveland, *Landscape Architecture*, ed. Nadenicek and Neckar, 47 and 69.

78. Cleveland, *The Public Grounds of Chicago: How to Give Them Character and Expression* (Chicago: Charles D. Lakey, 1869), 7.

79. Cleveland is especially significant, in my view, as the most vocal popularizer of the "park system" idea, though Olmsted is usually the one who gets credit for developing it, given his proposal for Buffalo in 1868. See Peterson, *The Birth of City Planning*, 42–7; Francis R. Kowsky, "Municipal Parks and City Planning: Frederick Law Olmsted's Buffalo Park and Parkway System," *Journal of the Society of Architectural Historians* 46 (March 1987), 49–64; Irving D. Fisher, *Frederick Law Olmsted and the City Planning Movement in the United States* (Ann Arbor: UMI Research Press, 1986); and Cynthia Zaitzevsky, *Frederick Law Olm-*

*sted and the Boston Park System* (Cambridge, MA: Harvard University Press, 1982), esp. 35 on Cleveland and "the germ of the metropolitan park system idea."

80. Cleveland, *Landscape Architecture*, ed. Nadenicek and Neckar, 42.

81. Ibid., 63 and 39. Peterson claims that Copeland's approach was bolder, more radical, and more comprehensive than Cleveland's (*The Birth of City Planning*, 53), though I find them more similar than different.

82. Letter of April 8, 1869, Chicago, Olmsted Papers, Reel 11. Also note Zaitzevsky, *Frederick Law Olmsted and the Boston Park System*, 141–4, on the arboretum angle.

83. Cleveland, *Landscape Architecture*, ed. Nadenicek and Neckar, 37–8.

84. See, for instance, Peterson, *The Birth of City Planning*, 29–39; Martin V. Melosi, *The Sanitary City: Urban Infrastructure in America from Colonial Times to the Present* (Baltimore: Johns Hopkins University Press, 2000), esp. 59–99; John Duffy, *The Sanitarians: A History of American Public Health* (Urbana: University of Illinois Press, 1990), 110–37, 175–92; and Stanley K. Schultz, *Constructing Urban Culture: American Cities and City Planning, 1800–1920* (Philadelphia: Temple University Press, 1989), 109–49.

85. See John H. Rauch, *Public Parks: Their Effects upon the Moral, Physical and Sanitary Condition of the Inhabitants of Large Cities: With Special Reference to the City of Chicago* (Chicago: S. C. Griggs & Co., 1869), 44, and Rauch, *Intramural Interments in Populous Cities, and Their Influence upon Health and Epidemics* (Chicago: Tribune Company, 1866), 30.

86. Cleveland, *Landscape Architecture*, ed. Nadenicek and Neckar, 34.

87. Ibid., 33.

88. Ibid., 78–9.

## 6. THREE MEN OF THE MIDDLE BORDER (PART TWO)

1. Michel de Montaigne, *The Complete Works*, trans. Donald Frame (New York: Knopf, 2003), 294.

2. See especially Sarah Bakewell's recent study of Montaigne, *How We Live; Or, A Life of Montaigne in One Question and Twenty Attempts at an Answer* (New York: Other Press, 2010); it's extraordinary how many different kinds of people have seen themselves in Montaigne.

3. Montaigne, *The Complete Works*, 1042 and 1023. This evolution in a reader's relationship to Montaigne's essays is also a pattern that has been well documented over the last four hundred years; see especially the example of Stefan Zweig in Bakewell, *How We Live*, 216–21. My most recent rereading of Montaigne was spurred by a wonderful visit to Cornell by the essayist Phillip Lopate; see Lopate, ed., *The Art of the Personal Essay: An Anthology from the Classical Era to the Present* (New York: Anchor, 1995), esp. xxiii–xxix, xlii–xlvii, and 43–5.

4. And of course death gives meaning to life. See Montaigne, *The Complete Works*, 1018: "Our life is composed, like the harmony of the world, of contrary things, also of different tones, sweet and harsh, sharp and flat, soft and loud. If a musician liked only one kind, what would he have to say? He must know how to use them together and blend them. And so

must we do with good and evil, which are consubstantial with our life. Our existence is impossible without this mixture, and one element is no less necessary for it than the other."

5. Ibid., 975.

6. See "Of Solitude," ibid., 211–22.

7. Ibid., 385. "Also, in the matter of public calamities, the more universally my sympathy is dispersed, the weaker it is"; and, "since God never sends men evils any more than goods entirely unmixed, my health for that time was unusually good. . . . It gave me the means to rouse all my resources and to put out my hand to ward off the blow that would otherwise easily have made a deeper wound" (975). And note Scott Slovic, *Going Away to Think: Engagement, Retreat, and Ecocritical Responsibility* (Reno: University of Nevada Press, 2008).

8. Montaigne, *The Complete Works*, 877, 726, 740, and 1026–7.

9. Letter of Cleveland to Olmsted, February 12, 1881, Chicago, Frederick Law Olmsted Papers, Reel 18, Library of Congress (LOC), Washington, DC, and Cleveland to Olmsted, January 27, 1892, Minneapolis, Olmsted Papers, Reel 22.

10. See Cleveland, *A Few Words on the Arrangement of Rural Cemeteries* (Chicago: George K. Hazlitt, 1881), 8–9. Cleveland also noted having designed cemeteries in the Massachusetts towns of Waltham, Melrose, and Gloucester.

11. Cleveland, letter to his friend and partner (they had a landscape architecture firm together in Chicago) William M. R. French, quoted in Karl Haglund, "Rural Tastes, Rectangular Ideas, and the Skirmishes of H. W. S. Cleveland," *Landscape Architecture* 66 (January 1976), 69.

12. Cleveland, *A Few Hints on Landscape Gardening in the West*, published with W. M. R. French, *The Relation of Engineering to Landscape Gardening* (Chicago: Hazlitt & Reed, 1871), 8.

13. Cleveland to Folwell, April 21, 1881, Chicago, in the William Watts Folwell and Family Papers, Box 14, Minnesota Historical Society, St. Paul. The pamphlet was *A Few Words on the Arrangement of Rural Cemeteries*, quotation from 5.

14. Cleveland to Folwell, May 25, 1885, Chicago, Folwell Papers, Box 15. Note also that he did some consulting work on tree plantings in Arlington National Cemetery: see Cleveland's letter to Folwell of December 14, 1881, Chicago, Folwell Papers, Box 14.

15. Cleveland to Folwell, December 14, 1881, Chicago, Folwell Papers, Box 14. In this case, the area's repose was clearly threatened, Cleveland thought, by its "extended frontage on a street which must become a thoroughfare," especially because the current campus was also "divided transversely by railroads whose future operations will certainly attain a magnitude beyond all present conception": urbanization and industrialization had to be checked, or at least accounted for.

16. See, for instance, Adam Arenson, *The Great Heart of the Republic: St. Louis and the Cultural Civil War* (Cambridge, MA: Harvard University Press, 2011), 16–18.

17. When I looked through the scrapbook collection at the Minnesota Historical Society, I found very little writing about the parks, but I found a huge number of photographs of both the local Indian Mounds and the various green spaces preserved in Cleveland's park system.

18. As noted in the previous chapter, Olmsted generally gets credit for the park system idea, largely because of his 1868 work in Buffalo, but I am more and more inclined to see it as something that probably developed from intellectual exchanges among Olmsted, Cleveland, and Robert Morris Copeland. Cleveland and Copeland had been partners for many years; Olmsted and Copeland were correspondents in the late 60s; and Olmsted and Cleveland worked together on Prospect Park in Brooklyn in 1868. See the letters from Copeland, dating back to 1867, in the Olmsted Papers, Reels 10, 11, and 13; Jon A. Peterson, *The Birth of City Planning in the United States, 1840–1917* (Baltimore: Johns Hopkins University Press, 2003), 42–7; Witold Rybczynski, *A Clearing in the Distance: Frederick Law Olmsted and America in the 19th Century* (New York: Touchstone, 1999), 285–9; Francis R. Kowsky, "Municipal Parks and City Planning: Frederick Law Olmsted's Buffalo Park and Parkway System," *Journal of the Society of Architectural Historians* 46 (March 1987), 49–64; Irving D. Fisher, *Frederick Law Olmsted and the City Planning Movement in the United States* (Ann Arbor: UMI Research Press, 1986); and Cynthia Zaitzevsky, *Frederick Law Olmsted and the Boston Park System* (Cambridge, MA: Harvard University Press, 1982), 33–53.

19. For the reference to Indian Mounds, see: http://archrecord.construction.com/news/daily/archives/070321guthrie.asp. For the reference to the city fathers and original planners, see: http://www.oaala.com/projects/gold_medal_park/gold_medal.htm.

20. H. W. S. Cleveland, *Public Parks, Radial Avenues, and Boulevards: Outline Plan of a Park System for the City of St. Paul* (St. Paul: Globe Job Office, 1885), 13. This pamphlet comprises two separate lectures: "A Park System for the City of St. Paul: Address of Prof. H. W. S. Cleveland, to the Common Council, June 24th, 1872" (3–16), and "Park Ways and Ornamental Parks: The Best System for St. Paul: An Address, delivered by H. W. S. Cleveland, June 19, 1885, on invitation from the Common Council of the City of Saint Paul" (17–31).

    Also see George H. Herrold, "The Story of Planning St. Paul from the Beginnings to 1953," unpublished manuscript, Minnesota Historical Society (Manuscript Notebooks, P2667): page 10 cites a resolution of 1872 by J. T. Maxfield, president of the City Council of St Paul: "Resolved, That in order that this city may avoid the errors of other large cities, and begin in time to provide for parks, wide avenues, public squares, and other improvements on a scale suitable to our future growth, commensurate with the wants of a crowded city, in a manner best calculated to utilize our natural advantages and promote the health and comfort of the citizens, on a basis which engineering skill and experience will approve, Mr. H. W. S. Cleveland, landscape architect of Chicago, be and is hereby invited to make a general outline plan for such improvements, and report to this Council, and that the proposition to perform this work is hereby accepted."

21. See Theodore Wirth, *Retrospective Sketch of the First Half-Century of Minneapolis Park Development under the Board of Park Commissioners, 1883–1933* (Minneapolis: Board of Park Commissioners, 1933), esp. 7; Wirth, *Minneapolis Park System, 1883–1944: Retrospective Glimpses into the History of the Board of Park Commissioners of Minneapolis, Minnesota and The City's Park, Parkway, and Playground System* (Minneapolis: Board of Park Commissioners 1945), esp. 26; C. A. Nimocks (Park Commissioner), *The Early History of the Minneapolis Parks, from 1857 to 1883* (Minneapolis: n.p., 1910); William H. Tishler and Virginia S. Luckhardt, "H. W. S. Cleveland, Pioneer Landscape Architect to the Upper

Midwest," *Minnesota History* 49 (Fall 1985), 281–91; and David C. Smith, *City of Parks: The Story of Minneapolis Parks* (Minneapolis: Foundation for Minneapolis Parks, 2008), esp. 1–72.

    Wirth was Superintendent of Parks in Minneapolis from January 1, 1906, to November 30, 1935; there is now a large park named for him in northwest Minneapolis.

22. Letter of Cleveland to Folwell, October 22, 1890, Minneapolis, Folwell Papers, Box 18.

23. There was Omaha, of course, another of Cleveland's projects, but he was farther away and not so closely involved as in the Twin Cities. And the city of Savannah, Georgia, also benefited from a very early plan that allowed for much more open space than normal: see John W. Reps, *The Making of Urban America: A History of City Planning in the United States* (Princeton: Princeton University Press, 1965), 186–202 and 330–1.

24. Cleveland, *Public Parks* (1872 lecture), 6 and 14, and Cleveland, *The Aesthetic Development of the United Cities of St. Paul and Minneapolis: An Address, delivered in Dyer's Hall, April 2d, 1888, to the Minneapolis Society of Fine Arts* (Minneapolis: A. C. Bausman, 1888), 8.

25. Cleveland, *Public Parks* (1885 lecture), 29, and also see 30: "The promontory on which these mounds are situated is so peculiar in its character, and comprises such features of interest within itself, and such a magnificent prospect of the river and country below the city, that I have no hesitation in urging in the most impressive terms, that an area of at least twenty-five or thirty acres should be secured with the least possible delay."

26. Fort Snelling is named for Colonel Josiah Snelling, who oversaw its construction in the early 1820s. His son, William Joseph Snelling, lived with the Dakota Indians for a time, and then moved back to Boston and wrote about his experiences on the antebellum frontier. In 1840, one of his poems, called "The Birth of Thunder—A Dacotah Legend," was chosen by William Cullen Bryant for his anthology of American poetry (Bryant, ed., *Selections from American Poets* [New York: Harper & Brothers, 1840], 291): "Look, white man, well on all around,/These hoary oaks, those boundless plains;/Tread lightly; this is holy ground:/Here Thunder, awful spirit! reigns."

27. Cleveland lobbied long and hard for the establishment of a park around Minnehaha Falls, and the land was finally secured in 1889, the year after Cleveland gave a long public address focusing on the potential significance of such a park: see *Aesthetic Development*, 13–20.

28. These were not all designed by Cleveland himself, but he got the greenway started with several of them and arranged it so that more could easily be added: see Smith, *City of Parks*; Wirth, *Retrospective Sketch*; Wirth, *Minneapolis Park System*; and Nimocks, *The Early History of the Minneapolis Parks*. Also note that in addition to the grounds of the Fort Snelling Soldiers' Home Cleveland worked on the grounds of the Leavenworth Soldiers' Home in Kansas: see Nancy J. Volkman, "Landscape Architecture on the Prairie: The Work of H. W. S. Cleveland," *Kansas History* 10 (Summer 1987), 106–110.

29. Cleveland, *Aesthetic Development*, 17.

30. Cleveland, *Suggestions for a System of Parks and Parkways, for the City of Minneapolis* (Minneapolis: Johnson, Smith, & Harrison, 1883), 7; in this quotation, Cleveland was actually referring to the Mississippi River, but he applied the same principle to the lakes.

31. Cleveland, *Aesthetic Development*, 5, and Cleveland, *Park Systems of St. Paul and Minneapolis* (St. Paul: H. M. Smyth, 1887), 10.

32. Cleveland, *Park Systems*, 12. It could be argued that Cleveland shared some of the genteel inclinations of most landscape architects of this time period; his New England stodginess is especially in evidence in his late-in-life reminiscence, *Social Life and Literature Fifty Years Ago* (Boston: Cupples & Hurd, 1888). Also see Daniel Joseph Nadenicek, "Emerson's Aesthetic and Natural Design: A Theoretical Foundation for the Work of Horace William Shaler Cleveland," in Joachim Wolschke-Bulmahn, ed., *Nature and Ideology: Natural Garden Design in the Twentieth Century* (Washington, DC: Dumbarton Oaks Research Library and Collection, 1997), 59–80, and Nadenicek, "Nature in the City: Horace Cleveland's Aesthetic," *Landscape and Urban Planning* 26 (1993), 5–15.

33. See Cleveland, *Aesthetic Development*, 5–8; on the international significance of Baron Haussmann's redesign of Paris in the 1850s and 60s, see Donald J. Olsen, *The City as a Work of Art: London, Paris, Vienna* (New Haven: Yale University Press, 1986), 44–53.

34. Nimocks, *The Early History of the Minneapolis Parks*, 17–18.

35. Cleveland, *Aesthetic Development*, 12–13 and 5–6, and Cleveland, *Park Systems*, 10.

36. My suggestion that Americans were retreating from the public sphere is based not on voting rates, which would dip most seriously after World War I, but on the rise of a new middle-class ideology emphasizing private individual initiative. See, for instance, Heather Cox Richardson, *West from Appomattox: The Reconstruction of America after the Civil War* (New Haven: Yale University Press, 2007), and Scott A. Sandage, *A History of Failure in America* (Cambridge, MA: Harvard University Press, 2005).

37. Unfortunately, those who study the public sphere, especially in the tradition of Jürgen Habermas, too often seem either to take physical space for granted or to dismiss its significance; see, for instance, Nick Crossley and John Michael Roberts, eds., *After Habermas: New Perspectives on the Public Sphere* (Oxford: Blackwell/Sociological Review, 2004), in which there is virtually no discussion of actual public spaces, except in an essay exploring the potential of the Internet's virtual spaces (James Bohman, "Expanding Dialogue: The Internet, the Public Sphere and Prospects for Transnational Democracy," 130–55). But also see: Elizabeth Blackmar, "Appropriating 'the Commons': The Tragedy of Property Rights Discourse," in Setha Low and Neil Smith, eds., *The Politics of Public Space* (New York: Routledge, 2006), 49–80; John Parkinson, "Holistic Democracy and Physical Public Space," in Mark Kingwell and Patrick Turmel, eds., *Rites of Way: The Politics and Poetics of Public Space* (Waterloo, Ontario: Wilfrid Laurier University Press, 2009), 71–84; Carol M. Rose, "The Comedy of the Commons: Custom, Commerce, and Inherently Public Property," in Rose, *Property and Persuasion: Essays on the History, Theory, and Rhetoric of Ownership* (Boulder: Westview Press, 1994), 105–62; and Brian Donahue, *Reclaiming the Commons: Community Farms and Forests in a New England Town* (New Haven: Yale University Press, 1999). On general Gilded Age shifts in definitions of male roles and in ideas about social responsibility, see Gail Bederman, *Manliness and Civilization: A Cultural History of Gender and Race in the United States, 1880–1917* (Chicago: University of Chicago Press, 1995).

38. Cleveland, *Public Parks* (1885 lecture), 29–30. Of course, most museums are not free the way the Smithsonian is, but even private museums commit themselves, by definition, to

public display, and, in so doing, enact the dialectical relationship between physical commons and intellectual commons.

39. Letters of Cleveland to Folwell in the Folwell Papers, both sent from Chicago: May 25, 1885 (Box 15), and April 22, 1886 (Box 16). Also see Haglund, "Rural Tastes, Rectangular Ideas."

40. H. W. S. Cleveland, *Ancestry and Descendants of H. W. S. Cleveland, in Line from Moses Cleveland of Woburn, Mass, 1635* (Chicago, 1882), 90.

41. Cleveland to Olmsted, January 27, 1892, Minneapolis, Olmsted Papers, Reel 22.

42. Local pride in the park system as a distinguishing feature goes back a long way, and so does local forgetfulness about Cleveland's crucial role. In 1930, two members of the Minneapolis Board of Park Commissioners decided to publish a volume explaining the policies that had made their park system such a success. They justified this project by citing a report put out by the U.S. Department of Labor in 1928 that claimed that "the park system of Minneapolis is one of the most outstanding systems in the United States from the standpoint of the number of acres, types of properties, distribution of properties, character of development, and quality of maintenance." The authors also made a point of referring to certain key features of the local landscape, like the creek "flowing down to the Mississippi River and creating the immortal Minnehaha Falls." They also cited the contributions of prominent park advocates like Cleveland's friends William Watts Folwell and Charles Loring—but not Cleveland himself. See Charles E. Doell and Paul J. Thompson, *Public Park Policies* (Minneapolis: Parks and Recreation, 1930), quotations from the unpaginated introduction.

43. H. W. S. Cleveland, "The Influence of Parks on the Character of Children," *Park and Cemetery* 8 (July 1898), 95. Progressive reform in the cities often focused on the plight of children, as in the photographs of Jacob Riis and Lewis Hine.

44. Stephen's life would become intensely public: see the book by Jonathan Weiner, *His Brother's Keeper: A Story from the Edge of Medicine* (New York: Ecco, 2004), and the documentary film, *So Much So Fast* (West City Films, dir. Steven Ascher and Jeanne Jordan, 2006).

45. Henry George, Jr., *The Life of Henry George* (1900; New York: Robert Schalkenbach Foundation, 1960), 332.

46. George, quoted ibid., 328, 331, 321, and George's friend John Russell Young, quoted ibid., 327.

47. Letter of George to Charles Nordhoff, December 21, 1879, San Francisco, Henry George Papers (microfilm), New York Public Library, Reel 2.

48. Henry George, Jr., "Introduction to the Twenty-Fifth Anniversary Edition" (1905), in Henry George, *Progress and Poverty* (1879; New York: Robert Schalkenbach Foundation, 2008), xxii.

49. He didn't actually call it "the single tax"; rather, he said the solution was "to abolish all taxation save that upon land values." See George, *Progress*, 406.

50. George, *Why Work is Scarce, Wages Low, and Labor Restless: A Lecture Delivered in Metropolitan Temple, San Francisco, March 26, 1878* (San Francisco: California Tax Reform League, 1885), 8–10.

51. See, for instance, Michael E. Harkin and David Rich Lewis, eds., *Native Americans and the Environment: Perspectives on the Ecological Indian* (Lincoln: University of Nebraska Press, 2007).

52. George, *Progress*, 501, 490.

53. See especially the chapter called "Differences in Civilization—To What Due" (ibid., 489–505), and see specific quotations on 545, 494, 489, 498, 371, 370. All of book 10 ("The Law of Human Progress," 475–552) adds up to an amazingly thorough critique of Herbert Spencer and the American version of Social Darwinism—on which, see George H. Daniels, *Science in American Society: A Social History* (New York: Knopf, 1971), 248–64; Louis Menand, *The Metaphysical Club: A Story of Ideas in America* (New York: Farrar, Strauss and Giroux, 2001), 121 and 140–44; and Richard Hofstadter, *Social Darwinism in American Thought* (1944), rev. ed. (New York: George Braziller, 1959), esp. 13–50.

54. George, *Why Work is Scarce*, 10, and *Progress*, 400.

55. George, *Progress*, 400–1.

56. George, *Why Work is Scarce*, 14.

57. George, *Progress*, 456.

58. George, *Why Work is Scarce*, 14. Also see *Progress*, 551. And on American apocalypticism, especially in the context of religious history, see Stephen J. Stein, "American Millennial Visions: Towards Construction of a New Architectonic of American Apocalypticism," in Abbas Amanat and Magnus Bernhardsson, eds., *Imagining the End: Visions of Apocalypse from the Ancient Middle East to Modern America* (London: I. B. Tauris, 2002); the essay is on 187–211, but see esp. 203–7.

59. George, *Progress*, 389–91, 541–2, 485, 535, 534, 542, and 538.

60. George quoted in George, Jr., *The Life of Henry George*, 329.

61. George, *Progress*, 563. Also see George's letter to Charles Nordhoff, January 31, 1880, San Francisco, George Papers, Reel 2: "I am anything but sanguine—sometimes this amounts to utter hopelessness—of carrying any real reform. . . . But who can tell; and as you say, 'we are to work away all the same.' We *are*, as you say; we *are*."

62. See George, Jr., *The Life of Henry George*, 417.

63. George, in Louis F. Post and Fred C. Leubuscher, eds., *Henry George's 1886 Campaign* (New York: Henry George School, 1961), 27.

64. See Alan Brinkley, *American History: A Survey*, 11th ed., vol. 2 (New York: McGraw Hill, 2003), 543–4.

65. George, Jr., *The Life of Henry George*, 587.

66. See the clipping from the *Herald* (Seattle), March 18, 1899, in the "Miscellany" file of the George Papers, Reel 15, and George, Jr., *The Life of Henry George*, 590.

67. All these quotations come from the "Miscellany" file of the George Papers, Reel 15: see "Memo by Samuel Seabury," November 6, 1897, New York City; "Henry George Funeral Recalled: Dramatic Last Rites for 'Friend of Man' Set Mark among Ceremonial Events," undated, unidentified newspaper clipping; "Big Audience at George Memorial," clipping from the *Providence Evening Telegram*, November 8, 1898; "Unprecedented Sight. Thousands File Past Henry George's Funeral Bier," clipping from the *Boston Herald* (special dispatch from New York), November 1, 1897 (plus a separate, untitled clipping from the same edition of this paper); and the receipt from Freed and Jewett, Undertakers and Embalmers, November 6, 1897.

68. Hamlin Garland, *A Son of the Middle Border* (1917; St. Paul: Minnesota Historical Society Press, 2007), 263, 266, 272, and 274.

69. Garland, in *Main-Travelled Roads* (1891; Lincoln: University of Nebraska Press, 1995), 56, emphasis mine, and 70. In the late 1890s Garland published a well-researched, mostly celebratory biography of Grant, with a full chapter devoted to the Battle of the Wilderness: "It was in the early days of May, when the South was filled with fragrance of blooming plants and trees. The air was soft and sensuous, and all nature was rebuilding, healing, renewing, and the heart of man should have been turned to the planting of seeds in the earth and the driving forth of cattle to pasture." See Hamlin Garland, *Ulysses S. Grant: His Life and Character* (1898; New York: Macmillan, 1920), 268.

70. Garland, *A Son of the Middle Border*, 284 and 286.

71. There are two items of relevance, cited here, from the Hamlin Garland Papers at the University of Southern California (USC), which are catalogued according to a checklist: see Folder 380, "Early Days in the Henry George Movement," a handwritten speech on stationery from the Hotel Jefferson in New York City, undated, and Folder 25, notebook on "Lectures in Social Reform." Also see *A Son of the Middle Border*, 294–5; Donald Pizer, *Hamlin Garland's Early Work and Career* (Berkeley: University of California Press, 1960), 45–8, quotations on 46–7; and Keith Newlin, *Hamlin Garland: A Life* (Lincoln: University of Nebraska Press, 2008), 102–4 and 127. This is one of several cases where Garland mixed up his dates: he says (in *A Son of the Middle Border*) that he saw George speak when he was launching his campaign for mayor, but puts that in the fall of 1887 instead of the fall of 1886.

72. Garland, *A Son of the Middle Border*, 309–12. Note that here and in the Foreword to *Main-Travelled Roads* (written in 1922, xx), Garland misidentifies the year of his mother's stroke as 1889 (and claims he traveled west in 1887 and 1889 rather than in 1887 and 1888). Many other sources, including a notebook he kept in 1888, indicate that he in fact went to Dakota two straight summers and that the stroke occurred in 1888, in July.

73. Garland, in *Main-Travelled Roads*, 53 and 87.

74. Garland, *A Son of the Middle Border*, 278 and 289.

75. See Garland, notebook on "Lectures in Social Reform," Folder 25, Garland Papers, USC.

76. Garland, *A Son of the Middle Border*, 313, 315, and 317.

77. Garland, Review of Whitman's *November Boughs*, clipping from the *Boston Evening Transcript*, November 1888, in Folder 723 (clippings of Garland's periodical writings), Garland Papers, USC.

78. Quoted in Newlin, *Hamlin Garland*, 118.

79. Garland in Donald Pizer, ed., *Hamlin Garland, Prairie Radical: Writings from the 1890s* (Urbana: University of Illinois Press, 2010), 98. Also note Garland's 1891 essay, "A New Declaration of Rights," quoted in Newlin, *Hamlin Garland*, 212.

80. Garland, *A Son of the Middle Border*, 349.

81. Garland, *Main-Travelled Roads*, v. Garland's stories are less readable today than *A Son of the Middle Border* because they frequently break into middle border dialect.

82. Garland, *A Son of the Middle Border*, 322.

83. Note the lone Democrat in this period, Grover Cleveland, 1885–9.

84. See, for instance: Charles Postel, *The Populist Vision* (New York: Oxford University Press, 2007); William Cronon, *Nature's Metropolis: Chicago and the Great West* (New York: Nor-

ton, 1991); Lawrence Goodwyn, *The Populist Moment: A Short History of the Agrarian Revolt in America* (New York: Oxford University Press, 1978); and Robert V. Hine and John Mack Faragher, *The American West: A New Interpretive History* (New Haven: Yale University Press, 2000), 347.

85. Garland, *A Son of the Middle Border*, 341. Note the influence during this period of Laurence Gronlund's book, *The Cooperative Commonwealth* (1884). On the rise of populism, see Postel, *The Populist Vision*; Goodwyn, *The Populist Moment*; Elizabeth Sanders, *Roots of Reform: Farmers, Workers, and the American State, 1877–1917* (Chicago: University of Chicago Press, 1999); and Jeffrey Ostler, *Prairie Populism: The Fate of Agrarian Radicalism in Kansas, Nebraska, and Iowa, 1880–1892* (Lawrence: University Press of Kansas, 1993).

86. Garland quoted in Newlin, *Hamlin Garland*, 164–5.

87. Garland, *A Son of the Middle Border*, 329–30, 337–9, 313, and 355.

88. Ibid., 335, and also see Garland, "Address: Henry George" (two typed pages), Folder 592, Garland Papers, USC.

89. Garland, in Pizer, *Prairie Radical*, 134.

90. Garland, *A Son of the Middle Border*, 357–9, 340, 362, 342, 360, 335, 345, and 361.

91. See, for instance, Frederick E. Hoxie, *A Final Promise: The Campaign to Assimilate the Indians, 1880–1920* (Lincoln: University of Nebraska Press, 1984), and Robert M. Utley, *The Indian Frontier of the American West, 1846–1890* (Albuquerque: University of New Mexico Press, 1984).

92. Garland, "Notebook, 1923: London, Dakota," Hamlin Garland Papers, Huntington Library, Box 7.

93. Quoted in Newlin, *Hamlin Garland*, 255.

94. Garland, Notebook on "Lectures in Social Reform," Garland Papers, USC.

95. See, for instance, Charles L. P. Silet, Robert E. Welch, and Richard Boudreau, eds., *The Critical Reception of Hamlin Garland, 1891–1978* (Troy, NY: Whitson, 1985); James Nagel, ed., *Critical Essays on Hamlin Garland* (Boston: G. K. Hall, 1982); and Pizer, *Hamlin Garland's Early Work and Career*, esp. vii, 1–3, and 167–9.

96. Garland in Lonnie E. Underhill and Daniel F. Littlefield, eds., *Hamlin Garland's Observations on the American Indian* (Tucson: University of Arizona Press, 1976), 182, 64, 66, 157, and 59, and also see Hamlin Garland, *The Book of the American Indian*, ed. Keith Newlin (Lincoln: University of Nebraska Press, 2005).

97. Garland, "Vanishing Trails" *University Record* 10 (October 1905), Folder 723 (clippings of Garland's periodical writings), Garland Papers, USC.

98. Garland, "Early Days in the Henry George Movement," Folder 380, Garland Papers, USC.

99. Quoted in Newlin, *Hamlin Garland*, 247.

100. Garland, *A Daughter of the Middle Border* (1921; St. Paul: Minnesota Historical Society Press, 2007), 299.

101. Donald Pizer, ed., *Hamlin Garland's Diaries* (San Marino: Huntington Library, 1968), 257.

## 7. ATLANTIS

1. Ignatius Donnelly, "Preamble" to the Populist Platform of 1892, reproduced in Martin Ridge, *Ignatius Donnelly: The Portrait of a Politician* (Chicago: University of Chicago Press, 1962), 295–6. Ridge's excellent book remains the most useful and important study of Donnelly to date; it may be time for a fresh look. Also note David D. Anderson, *Ignatius Donnelly* (Boston: Twayne, 1980).

2. Ignatius Donnelly, *Atlantis: The Antediluvian World* (1882; New York: Dover, 1976), 408.

3. Ignatius Donnelly, *Caesar's Column: A Story of the Twentieth Century*, ed. Nicholas Ruddick (1890; Middletown: Wesleyan University Press, 2003), 228.

4. On the history of thinking about the Atlantis legend, see the classic by L. Sprague de Camp, *Lost Continents: The Atlantis Theme in History, Science, and Literature* (1954; New York: Dover, 1970), and also Richard Ellis, *Imagining Atlantis* (New York: Knopf, 1998), and Henry M. Eichner, *Atlantean Chronicles* (Alhambra, CA: Fantasy Publishing, 1971).

5. Donnelly, *Atlantis*, 1, 14, 22, and 17.

6. See Sumathi Ramaswamy, *The Lost Land of Lemuria: Fabulous Geographies, Catastrophic Histories* (Berkeley: University of California Press, 2004), and Alex Owen, *The Place of Enchantment: British Occultism and the Culture of the Modern* (Chicago: University of Chicago Press, 2004).

7. Donnelly in Ridge, *Ignatius Donnelly*, 344; also see 342–3 and 256. The general trend of course favored rural-urban migration, not urban-rural migration.

8. See Donnelly, *Atlantis*, 347. On the question of monetary policy in this time period, see Gretchen Ritter, *Goldbugs and Greenbacks: The Antimonopoly Tradition and the Politics of Finance in America* (New York: Cambridge University Press, 1997).

9. See Ridge, *Ignatius Donnelly*, 14–27.

10. Ignatius Donnelly Papers (microfilm), Minnesota Historical Society, St. Paul, Reel 133.

11. Donnelly Papers, Reel 144, "A Minnesota Village," St. Paul *Globe*, Aug. 14, 1881, clipping pasted in vol. 41 of Donnelly's diary.

12. Donnelly grew even happier—indeed, his sense of his own worth seems to have shifted drastically—once *Atlantis* was published and selling well and garnering favorable reviews. The book came out on February 17, 1882, and on March 4, when a review came out in the Chicago *Times*, he noted in his journal that "the whole world brightened." On March 9, he admitted that "I have been quite in a state of excitement for two or three weeks past." See Donnelly Papers, Reel 144, vol. 42 of Donnelly's diary.

13. Donnelly Papers, Reel 144, vol. 39 of the diary, entry for November 3, 1880. A year later, though he was coping with a much more symbolic birthday (his fiftieth), he was able to express gratitude for the simple fact of being alive: "It is sad to grow old, and yet one must grow old or die; and, if statistics are correct, one half of all those who started in the race of life with me, in 1831, are today—nothing. . . . And so, while conscious that I am growing old I still look forward hopefully." Donnelly Papers, Reel 144, vol. 41 of the diary, entry for November 3, 1881.

14. Donnelly Papers, Reel 144, vol. 38 of the diary, entry for July 31, 1880.

15. Donnelly Papers, Reel 162 (vol. 127 of Donnelly's literary scrapbook), which has several clippings of reviews of *Atlantis*; quotation from the St. Paul *Dispatch*, March 14, 1882 (though the information is repeated in several other clippings). Also see Donnelly's journal entry for March 14, 1882: "*Hurrah!* Merrill tells me that Harper and Bros. write them that the whole of the first edition of *Atlantis* is exhausted! This is grand. . . . *The clouds are lifting.*" (Donnelly Papers, vol. 42 of the diary, Reel 144.)

16. Ridge, *Ignatius Donnelly*, 202.

17. Donnelly, *Atlantis*, 291.

18. These two quotations come from the collection of reviews Donnelly made in vol. 127 of his literary scrapbook, Donnelly Papers, Reel 162: see the St. Paul *Daily Dispatch*, March 8, 1882, and the *Pioneer Press*, February 26, 1882.

19. Ignatius Donnelly, "Speech of Hon. Ignatius Donnelly of Minnesota, on the Reconstruction of the Union. Delivered in the House of Representatives, May 2, 1864" (Washington, DC, 1864), 7; copy consulted at the Huntington Library, San Marino, California (Rare Books 344377). Also note Donnelly's advocacy for freedmen's right to education: Ridge, *Ignatius Donnelly*, 100–1.

20. Donnelly, *Atlantis*, 341. Humboldt is cited on this page and at least five other times in the book, more than Darwin and more than almost any other scientist; for an exploration of what Humboldt might have meant by "unity in diversity" (I think his emphasis was on the *equal* weight of the phrase's two key words), see Aaron Sachs, *The Humboldt Current: Nineteenth-Century Exploration and the Roots of American Environmentalism* (New York: Viking, 2006), 12–13 and 51–3.

21. This approach to Atlantis has remained a tempting one for many writers: see, for instance, Colin Wilson and Rand Flem-Ath, *The Atlantis Blueprint: Unlocking the Ancient Mysteries of a Long-Lost Civilization* (New York: Delacorte Press, 2001). And the search for a lost Atlantis continues: see Gavin Menzies, *The Lost Empire of Atlantis: History's Greatest Mystery Revealed* (New York: William Morrow, 2011).

22. See Ridge, *Ignatius Donnelly*, 101–2 and 156, and Donnelly, *Atlantis*, 157, 166, 325, and 453, and note that Donnelly had a substantial collection of pamphlets and Congressional reports about tree-planting and aridity on the plains, especially in Minnesota: see the Donnelly Papers, Reel 167 (library pamphlets). In other words, he had a great deal in common with H. W. S. Cleveland when it came to the question of trees on the middle border. This, by the way, was the era of the launching of Arbor Day, a holiday created by Nebraskans in 1872.

23. See, for instance, Louis Menand, *The Metaphysical Club: A Story of Ideas in America* (New York: Farrar, Strauss and Giroux, 2001), 97–148; Stephen Jay Gould, *The Mismeasure of Man* (New York: Norton, 1981), 30–74; and Robert J. Berkhofer, Jr., *The White Man's Indian: Images of the American Indian from Columbus to the Present* (New York: Vintage, 1979), 33–69 and 153–75.

24. Donnelly, *Atlantis*, 473, 154–5, and 109–18.

25. See Ridge, *Ignatius Donnelly*, 30, and "Cabinet of Aboriginal Curiosities," *Emigrant Aid Journal of Minnesota*, January 20, 1858: "Mr. Donnelly proceeded in a very interesting

manner to state some of the main facts in reference to the mounds found over the great West. . . . Mr. Donnelly showed the great antiquity of the mounds by a comparison of the bones found in them with the bones found in the barrows of the ancient Britons two thousand years old, and with bones found among the catacombs of Egypt four thousand years old, showing that the remains in the American mounds were equally ancient."

26. J. E. Stevenson, "The Mound Builders," *The American Antiquarian* 2 (October/November/ December 1879), 89.

27. Donnelly, *Atlantis*, 386 and 133.

28. Donnelly quoted in Ridge, *Ignatius Donnelly*, 16, and also see 86–92 and 156.

29. Donnelly, *Atlantis*, 193–194, 197, 475, and 127.

30. As Robert Pogue Harrison has put it: "When history turns against its own memorializing and self-conserving drive, when it is perceived to have become a force of erasure rather than of inscription, of assault on the earth rather than humanization of the earth, then images of an apocalyptic sea inevitably surge up in the human imagination." Harrison, *The Dominion of the Dead* (Chicago: University of Chicago Press, 2003), 16.

31. Deborah Tall, *From Where We Stand: Recovering a Sense of Place* (New York: Knopf, 1993), 47, 97, 69, 68, 12, 84–6, and 71–4.

32. Ibid., 99–103, 161–2, and 144. On Stonehenge, see Marc Aronson, *If Stones Could Speak: Unlocking the Secrets of Stonehenge* (Washington, DC: National Geographic Society, 2010), and Aubrey Burl, *Great Stone Circles: Fables, Fictions, Facts* (New Haven: Yale University Press, 1999), 101–69. And for more on "megalithic science," see John Michell, *The New View over Atlantis* (New York: HarperCollins, 1983).

33. Tall, *From Where We Stand*, 167–75, 140–1, and 124. At the center of Disney's 2001 film, *Atlantis: The Lost Empire* (2001)—yes, I'm in a phase of life when many of the movies I see are animated—is the so-called "heart of Atlantis," described as the culture's "life force." It is a kind of crystal, emanating light, hovering in mid-air, and surrounded by giant tombstones honoring the realm's past kings. The current king explains, at the climax of the film, that "the crystal thrives on the collective emotions of all who came before us. In return, it provides power, longevity, protection."

34. Deborah Tall, *A Family of Strangers* (Louisville: Sarabande Books, 2006), 70 and 294.

35. Tall, *From Where We Stand*, 105.

36. Ibid., 5–6.

37. See "Cabinet of Aboriginal Curiosities," the newspaper article about Donnelly's engagement with the Mounds as it expressed itself in 1858: "Mr. D. alluded to the mounds in this city, and stated that he had commenced the formation of a cabinet of such curiosities, and would be thankful for contributions from any part of the Territory as he intended to give the subject considerable attention." In addition, as he was working on his Atlantis materials, he wrote a suggestive note to himself: "Corroboration of Atlantis: The Mound Builders." See his "Miscellaneous Undated Notes," Donnelly Papers, Reel 133.

38. See Benjamin Smith Barton, *New Views of the Origin of the Tribes and Nations of America* (Philadelphia: John Bioren, 1797), iv (of the main text), 4 (of the Queries section), and v (of the dedication), and Winthrop Sargent and Benjamin Smith Barton, *Papers Relative to Certain American Antiquities* (Philadelphia: Thomas Dobson, 1796). The first of these is

dedicated to Jefferson, and Barton makes a point of protesting the fate of the Indians: "I regret, with you, Sir, the evanishment of so many of the tribes and nations of America." His perspective is remarkable for the seriousness and respect with which he treats Native traditions. While he of course assumes that their civilizations are "ruder" than his own, he dismisses out of hand the proposition that they might be inherently inferior as the kind of assertion made by "those speculative philosophers who retire to their closets inveloped in a thick atmosphere of prejudices" (dedication of *New Views*, v).

39. A typical example is Dr. John B. Newman, who comes across as a quack but who had read all the most serious scientists of his day: "Darwin in his 'Voyage of a Naturalist' says that the geologist who is fully impressed with the vast oscillations of level which have affected the earth's crust within late periods, will not fear to speculate on the recent submergence of land in the West Indian archipelago, as the cause of the present zoological separation of North and South America." See Newman, *Origin of the Red Men; an Authentic History of the Peopling of America by the Atlantians and Tyrians* (New York: John C. Wells, 1849), 30.

40. William Gilmore Simms, *Atalantis: A Story of the Sea* (New York: J. & J. Harper, 1832), 18, 13, 34, and 77. On Simms, see, for instance, Masahiro Nakamura, *Visions of Order in William Gilmore Simms: Southern Conservatism and the Other American Romance* (Columbia: University of South Carolina Press, 2009).

41. See, for instance, Richard H. Brodhead, "Millennium, Prophecy and the Energies of Social Transformation: The Case of Nat Turner," in Abbas Amanat and Magnus Bernhardsson, eds., *Imagining the End: Visions of Apocalypse from the Ancient Middle East to Modern America* (London: I. B. Tauris, 2002), 212–33.

42. Note, for example, the perspective of the famous Massachusetts orator Edward Everett, who took up Bacon's idea in 1824: "In that high romance, if romance it be, in which the great minds of antiquity sketched the fortunes of the ages to come, they pictured to themselves a favored region beyond the ocean, a land of equal laws and happy men. The primitive poets beheld it in the isles of the blest; the Doric bards surveyed it in the Hyperborean regions; the sage of the Academy placed it in the last Atlantis; and even the sterner spirit of Seneca could discern a fairer abode of humanity, in distant regions then unknown. . . . By us must these fair visions be realized, by us must be fulfilled those high auspices, which burst in trying hours from the hearts of the champions of truth. There are no more continents or worlds to be revealed; Atlantis hath arisen from the ocean." See the "Extract from Professor Everett's Address," *Essex Register* 24 (September 13, 1824), 4.

43. "Our New Atlantis," *Putnam's Monthly Magazine of American Literature, Science and Art* 5 (April 1855), 378–84. Working with Olmsted at *Putnam's* at this time was his friend George William Curtis, who had also been quite close to Andrew Jackson Downing—so Curtis is another possible author of this article.

44. Mrs. Frances Fuller Victor, *Atlantis Arisen; or, Talks of a Tourist about Oregon and Washington* (Philadelphia: J. B. Lippincott, 1891), 412.

45. See, for instance, Stephen Kern, *The Culture of Time and Space, 1880–1918* (Cambridge, MA: Harvard University Press, 1983); Rebecca Solnit, *River of Shadows: Eadweard Muybridge and the Technological Wild West* (New York: Viking, 2003); Alan Trachtenberg, *The Incorporation of America: Culture and Society in the Gilded Age* (New York: Hill & Wang,

1982); Rebecca Edwards, *New Spirits: Americans in the Gilded Age, 1865–1905* (New York: Oxford University Press, 2006); T. J. Jackson Lears, *No Place of Grace: Antimodernism and the Transformation of American Culture, 1880–1920* (New York: Pantheon, 1981); and Jackson Lears, *Rebirth of a Nation: The Making of Modern America, 1877–1920* (New York: HarperCollins, 2009).

46. William Walton Hoskins, *Atlantis, and Other Poems* (Philadelphia: Sherman & Co., 1881), 5–6.

47. Note the helpful discussions of the catastrophic logic of modernity in Kevin Rozario, *The Culture of Calamity: Disaster and the Making of Modern America* (Chicago: University of Chicago Press, 2007), and of the relationship between utopian narratives and modernity in Phillip E. Wegner, *Imaginary Communities: Utopia, the Nation, and the Spatial Histories of Modernity* (Berkeley: University of California Press, 2002).

48. Quoted in Trachtenberg, *The Incorporation of America*, 56.

49. Elizabeth G. Birkmaier, *Poseidon's Paradise: The Romance of Atlantis* (San Francisco: Clemens Publishing, 1892).

50. Edward Bellamy, *Looking Backward: 2000–1887* (1888; New York: New American Library, 2000), 13; also see Wegner, *Imaginary Communities*, xxii–xxiii, 2, and 62–98, and Daphne Patai, ed., *Looking Backward, 1988–1888: Essays on Edward Bellamy* (Amherst: University of Massachusetts Press, 1988). On Bellamy, see John L. Thomas, *Alternative America: Henry George, Edward Bellamy, Henry Demarest Lloyd, and the Adversary Tradition* (Cambridge, MA: Harvard University Press, 1983); Daniel Aaron, *Men of Good Hope: A Story of American Progressives* (1951; New York: Oxford University Press, 1967), 92–132; and Sylvia E. Bowman, *The Year 2000: A Critical Biography of Edward Bellamy* (New York: Bookman Associates, 1958).

51. Note the open squares referred to in Bellamy, *Looking Backward*, 25; virtually no spatial details are given, though.

52. Ibid., 80, 129, and 11–12.

53. Bellamy quoted in Franklin Rosemont, "Bellamy's Radicalism Reclaimed," in Patai, *Looking Backward*, 193 and 195.

54. The majority of the reviews I've looked at framed *Caesar's Column* as a reaction to *Looking Backward*: see those collected by Donnelly in vol. 130 of his literary scrapbook, Donnelly Papers, Reel 163. The review in the New York *World*, for example, bears the headline, "In the Twentieth Century: A Pessimistic View of Bellamy's Picture," and the New York *Tribune* ran a review called "Bellamy Reversed."

55. See vols. 113 and 114 of Donnelly's literary scrapbook, Donnelly Papers, Reel 158, to get a sense of just how deeply he was involved in the Farmer's Alliance in Minnesota in 1889 and 1890.

56. Donnelly, *Caesar's Column*, 74, 134, 74–5, 18–19, and 9.

57. Ibid., 50 and 57, and also note 53: "We are all moving together on the face of the torrent, and whither it will eventually sweep us no one can tell."

58. Ibid., 86 and 136, and also note 201: "Your ancestors, more than two centuries ago, established and permitted Slavery. What was the cry of the bondman to them? What the sobs of the mother torn from her child—the wife from her husband on the auction block? Who among them cared for the lacerated bodies, the shameful and hopeless lives?"

59. Ibid., 144, 33, 99, 211, 217, 224–5, 237, 239, and 231.

60. Again, see the reviews collected in vol. 130 of Donnelly's literary scrapbook, Donnelly Papers, Reel 163. In the same scrapbook, Donnelly also posted an article by Prof. Jos. Rodes Buchanan, M.D., "The Coming Cataclysm of America and Europe," *The Arena* (August 1890), 292–312, which argued that the crash was going to come much sooner than Donnelly had predicted in *Caesar's Column*—not in 1988 but within the next few years: "Calamity and catastrophe are as much a part of the plan of nature as successful progress, and as the portents of the coming storm gather thick and dark in the sky, it would be fatuous to refuse to see them."

61. Donnelly, *Caesar's Column*, 181–2 and 137.

62. Whitman, "This Compost," in Mark Van Doren, ed., *The Portable Walt Whitman* (New York: Penguin, 1977), 147–8. Also see M. Jimmie Killingsworth, *Walt Whitman and the Earth: A Study in Ecopoetics* (Iowa City: University of Iowa Press, 2004), 23.

63. Robert G. Ingersoll, "Address at the Funeral of Walt Whitman," in Ingersoll, *Walt Whitman: An Address* (New York: Truth Seeker, 1892), 81–6.

64. I'm certainly supportive of Rebecca Edwards's notion of a "long Progressive Era" (*New Spirits*, 7). Also see Robert D. Johnston, "The Possibilities of Politics: Democracy in America, 1877 to 1917," in Eric Foner and Lisa McGirr, eds., *American History Now* (Philadelphia: Temple University Press, 2011), 96–124.

65. While placing an emphasis here on the limits of the early versions of Progressivism, I certainly don't mean to dismiss them. Indeed, I agree wholeheartedly with Robert Johnston's insistence that "historians make a great mistake in allowing the era's many kinds of oppressions to override the era's vast democratic potential"; see his important review essay, "Re-Democratizing the Progressive Era: The Politics of Progressive Era Political Historiography," *Journal of the Gilded Age and Progressive Era* 1 (January 2002), 71.

66. See especially two classic works, which, some might argue, were responsible for the birth of the field of environmental history: Samuel P. Hays, *Conservation and the Gospel of Efficiency: The Progressive Conservation Movement, 1890–1920* (Cambridge, MA: Harvard University Press, 1959), and Roderick Frazier Nash, *Wilderness and the American Mind* (1967), 4th ed. (New Haven: Yale University Press, 2001), esp. 96–237.

67. Though I'm sympathetic to William H. Wilson's reading of the movement's radical potential (see his book, *The City Beautiful Movement* [Baltimore: Johns Hopkins University Press, 1989]), I still think that many elements of the City Beautiful approach represented a kind of capitulation to the structures of consumer capitalism. See also Wilson, "The Seattle Park System and the Ideal of the City Beautiful," in Daniel Schaffer, ed., *Two Centuries of American Planning* (Baltimore: Johns Hopkins University Press, 1988), 113–37; Norman T. Newton, *Design on the Land: The Development of Landscape Architecture* (Cambridge, MA: Harvard University Press, 1971), 413–26; Jon A. Peterson, "The City Beautiful Movement: Forgotten Origins and Lost Meanings," in Donald A. Krueckeberg, ed., *Introduction to Planning History in the United States* (New Brunswick: Center for Urban Policy Research, 1983), 40–57; and Peterson, *The Birth of City Planning in the United States, 1840–1917* (Baltimore: Johns Hopkins University Press, 2003), 98–122.

68. See, for instance, Kevin C. Armitage, *The Nature Study Movement: The Forgotten Popularizer of America's Conservation Ethic* (Lawrence: University Press of Kansas, 2009); Michael

B. Smith, "'The Ego Ideal of the Good Camper' and the Nature of Summer Camp," *Environmental History* 11 (January 2006), 70–101; Peter J. Schmitt, *Back to Nature: The Arcadian Myth in Urban America* (1969; Baltimore: Johns Hopkins University Press, 1990); Newton, *Design on the Land*, 433–7; and Barry Ross Harrison Muchnick, "Nature's Republic: Fresh Air Reform and the Moral Ecology of Citizenship in Turn of the Century America" (Ph.D. diss., Yale University, 2010).

69. George Perkins Marsh, *Man and Nature* (1864), ed. David Lowenthal (Cambridge, MA: Harvard University Press, 1965), 36.

70. See Francis Parkman, "The Forests and the Census," *Atlantic Monthly* 55 (June 1885), 835 and 838, and Charles S. Sargent, *Report on the Forests of North America (Exclusive of Mexico)* (Washington, DC: Government Printing Office, 1884), 493. For more on Sargent (and Olmsted and Boston's "emerald necklace" of greenways), see Philip J. Pauly, *Fruits and Plains: The Horticultural Transformation of America* (Cambridge, MA: Harvard University Press, 2007), 179–85, and Cynthia Zaitzevsky, *Frederick Law Olmsted and the Boston Park System* (Cambridge, MA: Harvard University Press, 1982), esp. 58–64.

71. Sargent, *Report on the Forests*, and see Michael Williams, *Deforesting the Earth: From Prehistory to Global Crisis* (Chicago: University of Chicago Press, 2003), 303–5.

72. The rhetoric Parkman and Sargent used calls to mind the warnings of environmentalists in the twenty-first century. It makes sense for us to be checking deforestation rates and constantly watching the weather these days, and I do believe that global warming is ushering in a new era of more frequent and more intense storms. But it is also instructive to remember that such eras have occurred before, if perhaps not at exactly the same scale. In November of 1881, as Donnelly was gathering Atlantis materials, he pasted a clipping in vol. 41 of his diary (Donnelly Papers, Reel 144) that highlighted the "Present Astonishing Weather," recalling the "many destructive cyclones of the summer, and the floods of water in early autumn" of that year: "As ascertained at government stations near us, the rain-fall during this period of forty days has been . . . one-half the ordinary *annual* fall for this locality. It is said by the oldest inhabitants that such a fall of rain has not occurred in 25 years at this time of the year."

73. Donnelly, diary, vol. 64, November 6, 1896, Donnelly Papers, Reel 149.

74. Quoted in Ridge, *Ignatius Donnelly*, 373; but note Donnelly's somewhat surprising opposition to the new Conservation movement, which he seems to have associated with wealthy landowners who, he thought, just wanted to set aside forested estates for themselves (see ibid., 396–7).

75. Donnelly, diary, vol. 64, November 1, 1896, Donnelly Papers, Reel 149.

76. See, for instance, Richard Hofstadter, *The Age of Reform* (New York: Vintage, 1955), 70–82; Joe Creech, *Righteous Indignation: Religion and the Populist Revolution* (Urbana: University of Illinois Press, 2006); and Jeffrey Ostler, "The Rhetoric of Conspiracy and the Formation of Kansas Populism," *Agricultural History* 69 (Winter 1995), 1–27.

77. Donnelly, *Caesar's Column*, 27–8. Also see 78: "The real government is now a coterie of bankers, mostly Israelites. . . . The nomadic children of Abraham have fought and schemed their way, through infinite depths of persecution, from their tents on the plains of Palestine, to a power higher than the thrones of Europe. The world is to-day Semitized."

78. See Ruddick, "Introduction" to *Caesar's Column*, esp. xli–xliii, and, again, see the reviews collected in vol. 130 of Donnelly's literary scrapbook, Donnelly Papers, Reel 163.

79. Quoted in Ridge, *Ignatius Donnelly*, 337, 381, and 395.

80. Lewis Mumford is particularly good on the abstraction of the Civil War and its disillusioning aftermath: see Mumford, *The Brown Decades: A Study of the Arts in America, 1865–1895* (1931; New York: Dover, 1971), esp. 5: "All the hopes that had underlain the gallantry and heroism of the war had been suddenly punctured, partly by their fulfillment and partly by their denial. No abstract ideal can be translated into an actual condition or institution without seeming to undergo a blight. . . . The slaves were freed; the union was preserved—what of it?"

81. Hamlin Garland, *A Daughter of the Middle Border* (1921; St. Paul: Minnesota Historical Society Press, 2007), 323. Garland's father's death is the book's concluding episode.

82. Quoted in Keith Newlin, *Hamlin Garland: A Life* (Lincoln: University of Nebraska Press, 2008), 376 and 390.

83. Julian Barnes, *Nothing to Be Frightened Of* (New York: Knopf, 2008), 131 and 10.

84. See Rozario, *The Culture of Calamity*, esp. 10.

85. Quoted in Elwood C. Parry III, *The Art of Thomas Cole: Ambition and Imagination* (Newark: University of Delaware Press, 1988), 89.

EPILOGUE. AMERICAN GOTHIC; OR, DEATH BY LANDSCAPE

1. On the importance of the redemption narrative in American history and culture, see, for instance, Jackson Lears, *Rebirth of a Nation: The Making of Modern America, 1877–1920* (New York: HarperCollins, 2009).

2. McKibben, *Eaarth: Making a Life on a Tough New Planet* (New York: St. Martin's Griffin, 2011), 16.

3. Solnit, *Hope in the Dark: Untold Histories, Wild Possibilities* (New York: Nation Books, 2006), 1.

4. See, for instance, Kevin Rozario, *The Culture of Calamity: Disaster and the Making of Modern America* (Chicago: University of Chicago Press, 2007).

5. Carson was the most important popularizer of the ethos of doom, but you can trace this tradition back to George Perkins Marsh. And note the prominent neo-Malthusian thinkers of the 1940s (such as Fairfield Osborn and William Vogt), as analyzed in Thomas Robertson, "'This is American Earth': American Empire, American Environmentalism," *Diplomatic History* 32 (September 2008), 561–84.

6. Or, as R. Clifton Spargo put it, "insofar as mourning serves ethics, it necessarily depends upon the less-than-realistic hypothesis whereby one treats the dead other as though she were still living." See Barthes, *Mourning Diary*, trans. Richard Howard (New York: Hill & Wang, 2010), 126, and Spargo, *The Ethics of Mourning: Grief and Responsibility in Elegiac Literature* (Baltimore: Johns Hopkins University Press, 2004), 4; and also note Jacques Derrida, *The Work of Mourning* (Chicago: University of Chicago Press, 2001), especially the helpful introduction by the editors, Pascale-Anne Brault and Michael Naas, "To Reckon with the Dead: Jacques Derrida's Politics of Mourning," 1–30.

7. I'm thinking, in particular, of: Sandra Steingraber, *Raising Elijah: Protecting Our Children in an Age of Environmental Crisis* (New York: Da Capo, 2011); Mark Hertsgaard, *Hot: Living Through the Next Fifty Years on Earth* (Boston: Houghton Mifflin Harcourt, 2011); and James Hansen, *Storms of My Grandchildren: The Truth about the Coming Climate Catastrophe and Our Last Chance to Save Humanity* (New York: Bloomsbury, 2009)—all of which, like McKibben's recent book, *Eaarth*, I admire and appreciate, but find overly certain.

8. In the spring of 2011, Cristina Nehring wrote an article about the "recent wave of memoirs about the end of life," and suggested that "the emergence, at this moment in history, of a small but significant cadre of end-of-life thinkers signals a sea change, a return to essentials, a cause for hope." Well, I hope she's right. See Nehring, "The End-of-Life Memoir: Why Thinking about Death Isn't Morbid at All," *New York Magazine*, May 9, 2011, 104–6. Two of the memoirs I most appreciated are Meghan O'Rourke, *The Long Goodbye* (New York: Riverhead, 2011), which is at the heart of Nehring's article, and Joan Didion, *The Year of Magical Thinking* (New York: Knopf, 2005), which Nehring says was the book that seems to have launched the trend.

9. Carson, *Nox* (New York: New Directions, 2010), section 1.1; Winik, *The Glen Rock Book of the Dead* (Berkeley: Counterpoint, 2008), xv–xvi.

10. I find some hope in the growing hospice movement. And, in addition to all the memoirs about the end of life, there have been more and more books appearing on the broader social question of how we die—another encouraging sign. See, for instance, Benjamin Noys, *The Culture of Death* (Oxford: Berg, 2005); Sandra M. Gilbert, *Death's Door: Modern Dying and the Ways We Grieve* (New York: Norton, 2006); Julian Barnes, *Nothing to Be Frightened Of* (New York: Knopf, 2008); James W. Green, *Beyond the Good Death: The Anthropology of Modern Dying* (Philadelphia: University of Pennsylvania Press, 2008); and Sherwin B. Nuland, *How We Die: Reflections on Life's Final Chapter*, expanded ed. (New York: Vintage, 2010).

11. One hears a lot, these days, about the "green cemetery" movement. I certainly appreciate its forswearing of embalming chemicals, but I have mixed feelings about the design rhetoric, which sometimes edges toward the erasure of the human. My preference, I guess, is for cemeteries that come across as humble, harmonious blendings of nature and culture, expressions of both unity and diversity.

12. See Bruno Latour, *We Have Never Been Modern*, trans. Catherine Porter (Cambridge, MA: Harvard University Press, 1993).

13. See James R. Shortridge, *The Middle West: Its Meaning in American Culture* (Lawrence: University Press of Kansas, 1989).

14. Willa Cather, *O Pioneers!* (1913; New York: New American Library, 2004), 57 and 11.

15. Hamlin Garland, *A Son of the Middle Border* (1917; St. Paul: Minnesota Historical Society Press, 2007), 5, and Garland, quoted in Keith Newlin, *Hamlin Garland: A Life* (Lincoln: University of Nebraska Press, 2008), 353. I've attempted to address the infamous "audience question," with an emphasis on the challenges of combining scholarly and literary approaches to writing, in Aaron Sachs, "Letters to a Tenured Historian: Imagining History as Creative Nonfiction—or Maybe even Poetry," *Rethinking History* 14 (March 2010), 5–38.

16. L. H. Bailey, *The Holy Earth* (1915; New York: Christian Rural Fellowship, 1943), 36.

17. L. H. Bailey, *The Country-Life Movement in the United States* (New York: Macmillan, 1911), 1–3. Also note Zachary Michael Jack, ed., *Liberty Hyde Bailey: Essential Agrarian and Environmental Writings* (Ithaca: Cornell University Press, 2008); Kevin C. Armitage, *The Nature Study Movement: The Forgotten Popularizer of America's Conservation Ethic* (Lawrence: University Press of Kansas, 2009), esp. 170–94; Ben A. Minteer, *The Landscape of Reform: Civic Pragmatism and Environmental Thought in America* (Cambridge, MA: MIT Press, 2006), esp. 1–50; and William L. Bowers, *The Country Life Movement in America, 1900–1920* (Port Washington: Kennikat Press, 1974).

18. Bailey, *Holy Earth*, 32.

19. Bailey, *Country-Life Movement*, 20, and L. H. Bailey, *The Outlook to Nature* (1905), rev. ed. (New York: Macmillan, 1911), 73.

20. Bailey, *Country-Life Movement*, 20–1.

21. Bailey, *Holy Earth*, 24, 26, 104–17, x, and 2–3.

22. Bailey, *Country-Life Movement*, 26–7.

23. Lewis Mumford, *The Brown Decades: A Study of the Arts in America, 1865–1895* (1931; New York: Dover, 1971), 1 and 36. Also see Shuxue Li, *Lewis Mumford: Critic of Culture and Civilization* (Bern: Peter Lang, 2009); Mark Luccarelli, *Lewis Mumford and the Ecological Region: The Politics of Planning* (New York: Guilford Press, 1995); Ramachandra Guha, "The Historical Social Ecology of Lewis Mumford," in Guha, *How Much Should a Person Consume? Environmentalism in India and the United States* (Berkeley: University of California Press, 2006), 152–74; and Minteer, *The Landscape of Reform*, 51–80.

24. Mumford, *Brown Decades*, 2–3, 23, 22, 29, and 26.

25. Mumford, *The Culture of Cities* (1938; San Diego: Harcourt Brace Jovanovich, 1970), 360, and *Brown Decades*, 43.

26. Mumford, *Brown Decades*, 40, and Mumford, *The City in History: Its Origins, Its Transformations, and Its Prospects* (1961; San Diego: Harcourt Brace, 1989), 515. On George also see Mumford, *Culture of Cities*, 394; Mumford, *Brown Decades*, 20–1; and John L. Thomas, *Alternative America: Henry George, Edward Bellamy, Henry Demarest Lloyd and the Adversary Tradition* (Cambridge, MA: Harvard University Press, 1983), 360–1.

27. Mumford, *Culture of Cities*, 396.

28. See, for instance, Luccarelli, *Lewis Mumford and the Ecological Region*; Norman T. Newton, *Design on the Land: The Development of Landscape Architecture* (Cambridge, MA: Harvard University Press, 1971), 464–516; Mel Scott, *American City Planning since 1890* (Berkeley: University of California Press, 1969); Daniel Schaffer, *Garden Cities for America: The Radburn Experience* (Philadelphia: Temple University Press, 1982); Eugenie L. Birch and Susan M. Wachter, eds., *Growing Greener Cities: Urban Sustainability in the Twenty-first Century* (Philadelphia: University of Pennsylvania Press, 2008); and Matthew I. Slavin, ed., *Sustainability in America's Cities: Creating the Green Metropolis* (Washington, DC: Island Press, 2011).

29. See http://arcadiafood.org.

30. Rebecca Solnit, "Detroit Arcadia: Exploring the Post-American Landscape," *Harper's*, July 2007, 65–73.

31. Nicholas Lemann, "The Latest Debates about City Life," *New Yorker*, June 27, 2011, 76–80.

32. Mumford, *City in History*, 6–10.

33. My favorite reading of this painting is in Guy Davenport's breathtaking essay, "The Geography of the Imagination," in Davenport, *The Geography of the Imagination* (New York: Pantheon, 1992), 12–15; and also see Steven Biel's excellent book, *American Gothic: A Life of America's Most Famous Painting* (New York: Norton, 2005).

34. See Biel, *American Gothic*, 37, and also note that one of Wood's friends, the undertaker David Turner, offered Wood an old mortuary building for use as a school, studio, and community center for artists (67): this became Wood's Studio House. On the history of the gothic in American literature and culture, see Donald A. Ringe, *American Gothic: Imagination and Reason in Nineteenth-Century American Fiction* (Lexington: University Press of Kentucky, 1982); Teresa A. Goddu, *Gothic America: Narrative, History, and Nation* (New York: Columbia University Press, 1997); and Robert K. Martin and Eric Savoy, *American Gothic: New Interventions in a National Narrative* (Iowa City: University of Iowa Press, 1998).

35. Quoted in Biel, *American Gothic*, 61 and 51.

36. See ibid., passim; Lea Rosson DeLong, *Grant Wood's Main Street: Art, Literature and the American Midwest* (Ames: University Museums, Iowa State University, 2004); and R. Tripp Evans, *Grant Wood: A Life* (New York: Knopf, 2010).

37. Mary Beth Norton et al., *A People and a Nation*, 7th ed., vol. 2 (Boston: Houghton Mifflin, 2005), 659, and John Mack Faragher et al., *Out of Many: A History of the American People*, Brief 3d ed. (Upper Saddle River, NJ: Prentice Hall, 2001), 446.

38. Wallace Stegner, "Letter, Much Too Late," in Stegner, *Where the Bluebird Sings to the Lemonade Springs: Living and Writing in the West* (New York: Penguin, 1992), 22–3 and 33.

39. For Ithaca, see, for instance, Steingraber, *Raising Elijah*, and Liz Walker, *Choosing a Sustainable Future: Ideas and Inspiration from Ithaca, NY* (Gabriola Island: New Society, 2010).

40. Stuart T. Hauser, Joseph P. Allen, and Eve Golden, *Out of the Woods: Tales of Resilient Teens* (Cambridge, MA: Harvard University Press, 2006), 1; and see http://www.resalliance .org/index.php/resilience; but also note the critique of the resilience approach in Paul Nadasdy, "Adaptive Co-Management and the Gospel of Resilience," in D. Armitage, F. Berkes, and N. Doubleday, eds., *Adaptive Co-Management: Collaboration, Learning, and Multilevel Governance* (Vancouver: University of British Columbia Press, 2007), 208–227.

41. See Guha, *How Much Should a Person Consume?* 1–34, and Guha, *Environmentalism: A Global History* (New York: Longman, 2000), 63–145.

42. See Frank Cunningham, "Public Spaces and Subversion," in Mark Kingwell and Patrick Turmel, eds., *Rites of Way: The Politics and Poetics of Public Space* (Waterloo, Ontario: Wilfrid Laurier University Press, 2009), 85–99, esp. 89–92 on the possibility of designing and utilizing public spaces that cater to the image of a human being as "a seeker of creativity, pleasure, fun, and play—*Homo ludens*" (89). Also note Phillip E. Wegner, *Imaginary Communities: Utopia, the Nation, and the Spatial Histories of Modernity* (Berkeley: University of California Press, 2002), passim, on the potentially liberatory, radical qualities of utopian narratives that look simultaneously forward and backward.

43. "Police Blotter: Man Found in Park Dies; Cops Probing," *New Haven Register*, January 5, 2003, A2.

44. Part of this epilogue is inspired by Margaret Atwood's haunting story, "Death by Landscape," which, in turn, was partly inspired by the Australian film, *Picnic at Hanging Rock* (1975). See Atwood, *Wilderness Tips* (1991; New York: Anchor, 1998), 97–118. Also note, on Atwood and Arcadia, Jonathan Bordo, "Picture and Witness at the Site of the Wilderness," in W. J. T. Mitchell, ed., *Landscape and Power*, 2d ed. (Chicago: University of Chicago Press, 2002), esp. 295–309.

45. Allan Megill, *Historical Knowledge, Historical Error: A Contemporary Guide to Practice* (Chicago: University of Chicago Press, 2007), 186–7.

46. Barnes, *Nothing to Be Frightened Of*, 108.

47. A. J. Downing, *The Fruits and Fruit Trees of America* (1845; New York: John Wiley, 1850), 334–5.

48. Bailey, *Holy Earth*, 73.

# ILLUSTRATION CREDITS

1. W. H. Bartlett, *Cemetery of Mount Auburn*, 1839, hand-colored engraving. Author's collection.
2. Nicolas Poussin, *The Shepherds of Arcadia (Et in Arcadia Ego)*, 1640, oil on canvas, 85 × 121 cm. Photograph by René-Gabriel Ojéda, used by permission of Réunion des Musées Nationaux/ Art Resource, NY.
3. J. M. Wilgus, *Map of the City of Ithaca, N.Y., Engraved Expressly for Norton and Hanford's Ithaca City Directory*, 1896. Courtesy of Cornell University Library, Ithaca, NY.
4. Alexander Wadsworth, *Plan of Mount Auburn*, 1831. Courtesy of Mount Auburn Cemetery Historical Collections, Cambridge and Watertown, MA.
5. *Yellow Belle-Fleur*, lithograph. Illustration from A. J. Downing, *The Fruits and Fruit Trees of America* (1845; New York: John Wiley, 1850), facing page 100. Courtesy of the Division of Rare and Manuscript Collections, Cornell University Library, Ithaca, NY.
6. The Kanadesaga monument, Geneva, NY, 2010. Photograph by the author.
7. Charles Sullivan, *Great Mound at Marietta, Ohio*, lithograph. Illustration from E. G. Squier and E. H. Davis, *Ancient Monuments of the Mississippi Valley* (Washington, DC: Smithsonian Institution, 1848), Plate 45, facing page 138. Courtesy of the Division of Rare and Manuscript Collections, Cornell University Library, Ithaca, NY.
8. Thomas Cole, *The Course of Empire: Desolation*, 1836, oil on canvas, 39¼ × 63¼ in.; Accession #1858.5. Collection of the New-York Historical Society.
9. John Bachmann, *Bird's Eye View of Greenwood Cemetery, near New York*, 1852, lithograph. Courtesy of the American Antiquarian Society, Worcester, MA.
10. Mount Repose Cemetery, Haverstraw, NY, 2010. Photograph by the author.
11. B. G. Stone, *View of Samsonville Tannery, Olive Township, Ulster County, New York*, c. 1855, lithograph. Courtesy of the American Antiquarian Society, Worcester, MA.
12. W. Endicott, *Prattsville, Greene Co., N.Y.*, 1850, lithograph. Courtesy of the American Antiquarian Society, Worcester, MA.

13. E. Baumann, *North Western Part of Llewellyn Park*, 1853, lithograph. Illustration from A. J. Downing, *A Treatise on the Theory and Practice of Landscape Gardening, Adapted to North America*, 8th ed. (New York: O. Judd, 1859), Figure 106, following page 570. Courtesy of the Division of Rare and Manuscript Collections, Cornell University Library, Ithaca, NY.

14. W. H. Bartlett, *View of Hudson City, and the Catskill Mountains*, 1840, engraving. Illustration from N. P. Willis, *American Scenery; or, Land, Lake, and River: Illustrations of Transatlantic Nature*, vol. 2 (London: George Virtue, 1840), Plate 35, page 67. Courtesy of the Division of Rare and Manuscript Collections, Cornell University Library, Ithaca, NY.

15. *Dearborn's Seedling*, lithograph. Illustration from A. J. Downing, *The Fruits and Fruit Trees of America* (1845; New York: John Wiley, 1850), facing page 336. Courtesy of the Division of Rare and Manuscript Collections, Cornell University Library, Ithaca, NY.

16. B. F. Smith, *Washington, D.C., with Projected Improvements*, 1852 lithograph. Courtesy of the Library of Congress, Prints and Photographs Division, Washington, DC.

17. Thomas Cole, *The Course of Empire: The Arcadian or Pastoral State*, 1836, oil on canvas, 39¼ × 63¼ in.; Accession #1858.2. Collection of the New-York Historical Society.

18. Thomas Cole, *Dream of Arcadia*, c. 1838, oil on canvas. Denver Art Museum Collection: Gift of Mrs. Lindsey Gentry, 1954.71. Photograph provided by the Denver Art Museum.

19. Thomas Cole, *Evening in Arcady*, 1843, oil on canvas, 32 5/8 × 48 5/16 in. Wadsworth Atheneum Museum of Art, Hartford, CT, bequest of Clara Hinton Gould, 1948.190. Photograph used by permission of Wadsworth Atheneum Museum of Art/Art Resource, NY.

20. Thomas Cole, *A View of the Mountain Pass Called the Notch of the White Mountains (Crawford Notch)*, 1839, oil on canvas, 102 × 155.8 cm. Andrew W. Mellon Fund, National Gallery of Art, Washington, DC, 1967.8.1. Image courtesy of National Gallery of Art, Washington, DC.

21. Thomas Cole, *Daniel Boone at His Cabin at Great Osage Lake*, c. 1826, oil on canvas, 38¼ × 42 5/8 in. Mead Art Museum, Amherst College, Amherst, MA, Museum Purchase, AC P.1939.7.

22. Thomas Cole, *The Voyage of Life: Manhood*, 1840, oil on canvas, 52 × 78 in. Munson-Williams-Proctor Arts Institute, Utica, NY, Museum Purchase, 55.107. Photograph used by permission of Munson-Williams-Proctor Arts Institute/Art Resource, NY.

23. Thomas Cole, *The Cross in the Wilderness*, after a poem by Felicia Hemans, 1845, oil on canvas, 61 × 61 cm. Louvre, Paris. Photograph by Jean-Gilles Berizzi, used by permission of Réunion des Musées Nationaux/Art Resource, NY.

24. Thomas Cole's grave, Catskill, NY, 2010. Photograph by the author.

25. Asher Brown Durand, *Kindred Spirits*, 1849, oil on canvas, 44 × 36 in. Courtesy Crystal Bridges Museum of American Art, Bentonville, AR. Photograph by The Metropolitan Museum of Art.

26. Frederic Edwin Church, *To the Memory of Cole*, 1848, oil on canvas, 32 × 49 in. Private collection. Image courtesy of A. J. Kollar Fine Paintings, LLC, Seattle, WA.

27. John Quidor, *The Headless Horseman Pursuing Ichabod Crane*, 1858, oil on canvas, 26 7/8 × 33 7/8 in. Smithsonian American Art Museum, Washington, DC. Museum purchase made possible in part by the Catherine Walden Myer Endowment, the Julia D. Strong En-

dowment, and the Director's Discretionary Fund. Photograph used by permission of Smithsonian American Art Museum, Washington, DC/Art Resource, NY.

28. Civil War amputee Lieutenant Burritt Stiles, Co. A, 14th Connecticut Volunteers, 1867, photograph. Courtesy of the Library of Congress, Manuscripts Division, Washington, DC.

29. "Ft. Sanders, Knoxville, Tenn.," 1863, stereoscopic photograph. Courtesy of the Library of Congress, Prints and Photographs Division, Washington, DC.

30. George Inness, *The Lackawanna Valley*, c. 1856, oil on canvas, 86×127.5 cm. Gift of Mrs. Huttleston Rogers, National Gallery of Art, Washington, DC., 1945.4.1. Image courtesy of the National Gallery of Art, Washington, DC.

31. Sanford Robinson Gifford, *Hunter Mountain, Twilight*, 1866, oil on canvas, 30 5/8×54⅛ in. Terra Foundation for American Art, Chicago, Daniel J. Terra Collection, 1999.57. Photograph used by permission of Terra Foundation for American Art, Chicago/Art Resource, NY.

32. Timothy H. O'Sullivan, *A Harvest of Death*, 1863, photograph. Courtesy of the Library of Congress, Prints and Photographs Division, Washington, DC.

33. Alfred Waud, "Wounded Escaping from the Burning Woods of the Wilderness," 1864, pencil and "Chinese white" on brown paper. Courtesy of the Library of Congress, Prints and Photographs Division, Washington, DC.

34. Winslow Homer, *Skirmish in the Wilderness*, 1864, oil on canvas mounted on masonite, 18×26¼ in. New Britain Museum of American Art, Harriet Russell Stanley Fund, 1944.05.

35. Winslow Homer, *The Initials*, 1864, oil on canvas, 21×17 in. Courtesy of a private collection.

36. Timothy H. O'Sullivan, *Quarters of Men in Fort Sedgwick*, 1865, photograph. Courtesy of the Library of Congress, Prints and Photographs Division, Washington, DC.

37. Winslow Homer, *Trooper Meditating beside a Grave*, c. 1865, oil on canvas. Joslyn Art Museum, Omaha, Nebraska, gift of Dr. Harold Gifford and Ann Gifford Forbes, 1960.298.

38. Winslow Homer, *The Veteran in a New Field*, 1865, oil on canvas, 24⅛×38⅛ in. The Metropolitan Museum of Art, New York, NY, bequest of Miss Adelaide Milton de Groot (1876–1967), 1967 (67.187.131). Photograph used by permission of The Metropolitan Museum of Art/Art Resource, NY.

39. Pileated woodpecker, near Finland, MN, 1989. Photograph by the author.

40. Albert Bierstadt, *The Rocky Mountains, Lander's Peak*, 1863, oil on canvas, 73½×120¾ in. The Metropolitan Museum of Art, New York, NY, Rogers Fund, 1907 (07.123). Photograph used by permission of The Metropolitan Museum of Art/Art Resource, NY.

41. Albert Bierstadt, *Valley of the Yosemite*, 1864, oil on paperboard, 30.16×48.89 cm. Museum of Fine Arts, Boston, gift of Martha C. Karolik and M. Karolik Collection of American Paintings, 1815–1865, 47.1236. Photograph used by permission of Museum of Fine Arts, Boston.

42. Dayton National Cemetery, 2011. Photograph by the author.

43. Civil War amputee Lieutenant Burritt Stiles, Co. A, 14th Connecticut Volunteers, 1867, photograph. Courtesy of the Library of Congress, Manuscripts Division, Washington, DC.

44. Louis Kurz, *National Soldiers' Home near Milwaukee, Wis., North-Western Branch*, between 1872 and 1878, lithograph. Courtesy of the American Antiquarian Society, Worcester, MA.

45. Grave of Benjamin Tevya Sachs. Photograph by the author.

46. Farview Park, Minneapolis, 2010. Photograph by the author.

47. Indian Mounds Park, St. Paul, MN, c. 1900, photograph. Minnesota Historical Society.

48. Gold Medal Park, Minneapolis, MN, 2010. Photograph by the author.

49. Grave of H. W. S. Cleveland, Lakewood Cemetery, Minneapolis, MN, 2010. Photograph by the author.

50. Thomas Cole, *Subsiding of the Waters of the Deluge,* 1829, oil on canvas, 35¾×47 5/8 in. Smithsonian American Art Museum, Washington, DC. Photograph used by permission of Smithsonian American Art Museum, Washington, DC/Art Resource, NY.

51. Thomas Cole, *View from Mount Holyoke, Northampton, Massachusetts, after a Thunderstorm— The Oxbow,* 1836, oil on canvas, 51½×76 in. The Metropolitan Museum of Art, New York, NY, gift of Mrs. Russell Sage, 1908 (08.228). Photograph used by permission of The Metropolitan Museum of Art/Art Resource, NY.

52. Grant Wood, *American Gothic,* 1930, oil on beaver board, 78×65.3 cm. The Art Institute of Chicago, Friends of American Art Collection, 1930.934.

53. A playground in a cemetery, Newburgh, NY, 2010. Photograph by the author.

54. *Bartlett,* lithograph. Illustration from A. J. Downing, *The Fruits and Fruit Trees of America* (1845; New York: John Wiley, 1850), facing page 334. Courtesy of the Division of Rare and Manuscript Collections, Cornell University Library, Ithaca, NY.

# INDEX

Page numbers in *italics* refer to illustrations.